ALSO BY JAMES DAVIDSON

Courtesans and Fishcakes:
The Consuming Passions of Classical Athens

THE GREEKS AND GREEK LOVE

· THE GREEKS ·
AND GREEK LOVE

A BOLD NEW EXPLORATION OF
THE ANCIENT WORLD

· JAMES DAVIDSON ·

RANDOM HOUSE

NEW YORK

293/014

Published in the United States by Random House, an imprint of
The Random House Publishing Group, a division of Random
House, Inc., New York.

RANDOM HOUSE and colophon are registered trademarks of
Random House, Inc.

Originally published in hardcover in the United Kingdom by
Weidenfeld & Nicolson, a member of
The Orion Publishing Group, London, in 2007.

LIBRARY OF CONGRESS CATALOGING-IN-PUBLICATION DATA
Davidson, James N.
The Greeks and Greek love : a bold new exploration of the ancient
world / James Davidson.—
p. cm.
ISBN 978-0-375-50516-4 (alk. paper)
1. Homosexuality—Greece—History. 2. Greece—Civilization—
To 146 B.C. I. Title.
HQ76.3.G8D38 2009
306.76'60938—dc22   2008040540

Printed in the United States of America on acid-free paper

www.atrandom.com

2 4 6 8 9 7 5 3 1

FIRST U.S. EDITION

Book design by Simon M. Sullivan

For Alberto

With much love

CONTENTS

PART IV

MEN OF WAR

PART V

EROS OFF DUTY

LIST OF ILLUSTRATIONS

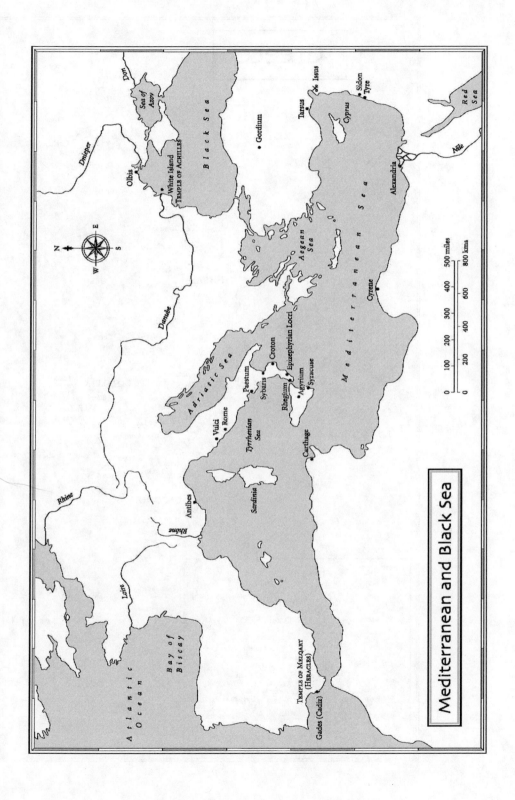

Mediterranean and Black Sea

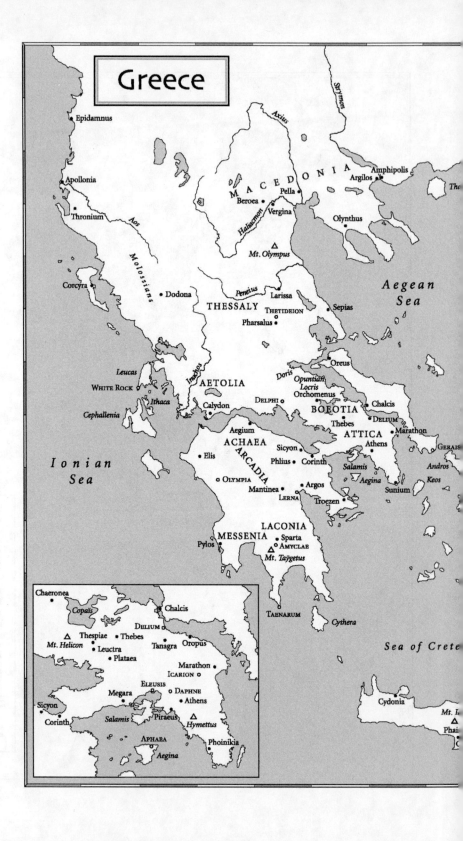

Greece

Epidamnus

Apollonia

Thronium

Corcyra

Molossians

Dodona

Aos

MACEDONIA

Beroea
Pella
Vergina
Haliacmon

Olynthus

Argilos
Amphipolis
Strymon

Axius

△
Mt. Olympus

Peneius
Larissa
THETIDEION
Sepias

THESSALY

Pharsalus

Aegean Sea

Leucas
WHITE ROCK
Inachus

Ithaca

Cephallenia

Ionian Sea

AETOLIA
Calydon

Doris
Opuntian Locris
Orchomenus
DELPHI
Oreus

BOEOTIA
Thebes
DELIUM
Chalcis

Aegium
ACHAEA
Sicyon
ATTICA
Athens
Marathon

Elis
ARCADIA
Phlius
Corinth
Salamis
Aegina
GERAIS

OLYMPIA
Mantinea
Argos
LERNA
Troezen
Sunium
Andros
Keos

LACONIA
MESSENIA
Sparta
Pylos
AMYCLAE
△
Mt. Taÿgetus

TAENARUM

Cythera

Sea of Crete

Inset map

Chaeronea
Copais
Chalcis

DELIUM
△ Thespiae
Mt. Helicon
Thebes
Leuctra
Plataea
Tanagra
Oropus

Marathon
ICARION

ELEUSIS
Megara
DAPHNE
Athens

Sicyon
Salamis
Piraeus
△ Hymettus

Corinth
APHABA
Phoinikia

Aegina

Cydonia
Phai

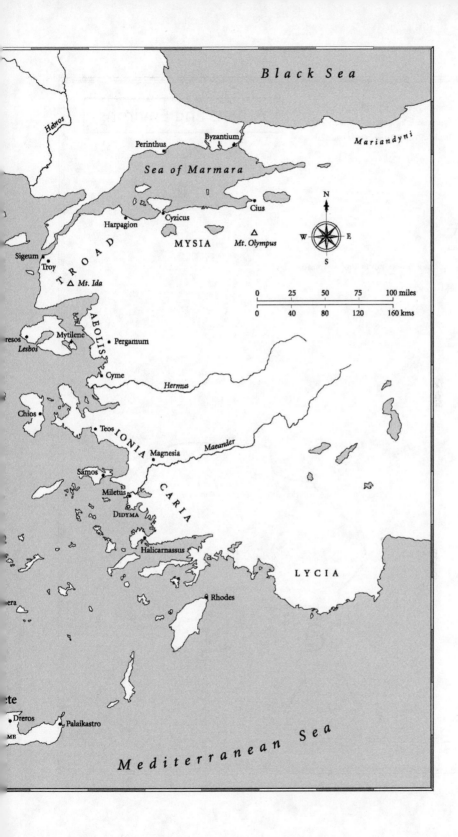

Black Sea

Hebros

Perinthus
Byzantium
Mariandyni

Sea of Marmara

Cius

Harpagion
Cyzicus

T R O A D

MYSIA
Mt. Olympus △

Sigeum
Troy
△ *Mt. Ida*

N
W E
S

0   25   50   75   100 miles
0   40   80   120   160 kms

A E O L I S

resos
Mytilene
Lesbos
Pergamum

Chios

Cyme

Hermus

Teos
I O N I A
Magnesia
Maeander

Samos
Miletus
C A R I A
DIDYMA

Halicarnassus

L Y C I A

era
Rhodes

te
Dreros
Palaikastro
ME

M e d i t e r r a n e a n   S e a

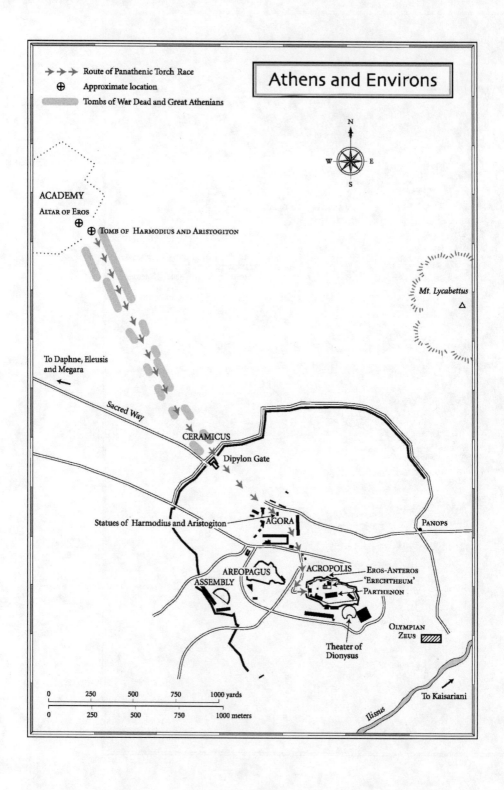

Athens and Environs

→ → → Route of Panathenic Torch Race
⊕ Approximate location
▬ Tombs of War Dead and Great Athenians

ACADEMY
ALTAR OF EROS
⊕ ⊕ TOMB OF HARMODIUS AND ARISTOGITON

Mt. Lycabettus
△

To Daphne, Eleusis
and Megara

Sacred Way

CERAMICUS

Dipylon Gate

PANOPS

Statues of Harmodius and Aristogiton

AGORA

AREOPAGUS

ACROPOLIS

EROS-ANTEROS
'ERECHTHEUM'
PARTHENON

ASSEMBLY

OLYMPIAN
ZEUS

Theater of
Dionysus

0   250   500   750   1000 yards
0   250   500   750   1000 meters

To Kaisariani

Ilissus

NOTE ON TRANSCRIPTION
AND PRONUNCIATION

I have preferred the more familiar Latinized forms of names (Pisistratus not Peisistratos, Conon not Konon), unless—a fine judgment—these are rarely used (Leagros, Peithinos). The conventional pronunciations of these are, e.g., Plato (PLAY-toe), Achilles (a-KILL-ease), Euripides (your-RIP-id-ease), Hyacinthus (higher-SYNTH-uss), Aristophanes (arry-STOF-an-ease), Aeschines (EE-skin-ease), Pylades (PILE-uh-dease), Aeschylus (EE-skill-uss), Elis (EEL-iss), Didyma (DID-i-ma), Cyzicus (SIDZ-i-cuss), Iphigeneia (aye-FIDGE-uh-nigher), Clytemnestra (cligh-tum-NEST-ra), Pisistratus (pie-SIS-stratus), Miletus (mile-EAT-uss), Thespiae (THESS-pea-eye), Xenophon (ZEN-uh-fon), Zephyrus (ZEF-uh-russ), Hebe (HEE-bee), Niobe (nigh-OWE-bee) but, for some reason, Thebes is conventionally pronounced as one syllable (THEEBZ) and ephebes as two (EFF-eebz).

Where quoting from the original, I have followed the conventional transcription of the standard "East Ionic" alphabet (officially adopted by most ancient cities by *c.*370 BC and by all modern editors) into Roman letters: ō = ōmega (Ω), ē = ēta (H), ch = chi (X). Anxious readers may be comforted by the fact that pronouncing ancient Greek properly is *extremely* difficult, so nobody *ever* bothers. There are, however, some conventional approximations. Ancient Greek letters generally represented sounds in a straightforward and transparent wysiwyg fashion: what-you-see-is-what-you-get. There were five basic vowel sounds—the a-e-i-o-u sounds of (roughly) sad, set, siege, sob, sue. Combinations of vowels are combinations of those sounds, Leagros = Le-AG-ross. So "ai" combines the "a" of "sad" with the "i" of "siege" (*aischros* = ICE-cross, *kinaidos* = kin-EYE-doss) and "ei" combines the "e" of set with the "i" of "siege" as in "Taipei," so Peithinos = pay-THIN-os. Likewise "au" is pronounced as in "Bauhaus," so *tauta* = TAO-ta. *Eu* is generally pronounced as "yew" (*euruprōktoi* "wide-arses": your-oo-PROKE-toy).

The main problems in pronunciation derive from the fact that the spoken language had three features not found in English or most other modern European languages, features that will have made classical Greek sound very foreign, rather more like Thai, Tamil or Chinese than French, German or English: (1) three pitch accents—a perfect fifth above, one below, and one up and down, helpfully written in for us by ancient commentators; very occasionally scholars may try to (mis)articulate the first of these pitch accents as a stress accent—*philosophía:* filoso-FEE-ya; (2) vowels differentiated by duration alone, e.g., "o" (o-micron) vs "o-o" (ō-mega), "e" (epsilon) vs "e-e" (ēta). So "e" and "o" as in "help" and "bomb," but "ē" and "ō" as in "He-e-elp! Bo-o-omb!" . . . approximately. These double-length vowels are conventionally pronounced as single-length "eh" and "owe" respectively, so that *hērōs* ("hero") = HAIR-oze; (3) In contrast to English, most consonants (at least the unvoiced or whispered consonantal sounds of "p," "t" and "k") were unaspirated, i.e., you would not feel a breath on your hand close to the mouth of someone speaking; such sounds are only familiar to us in baby talk. But ancient Greek did have three (at least) aspirated consonants, which are conventionally transliterated as *ph, th* and *ch,* although, since English-speakers always aspirate these consonants, the added aspiration is redundant and misleading. So a word transliterated as *thophich* should really be pronounced as "topic"—not, e.g., "thofich" or "thh-hophhhikhhh." The problem is the original unaspirated Greek *topikon,* very hard to pronounce, although whispering "dobigon" might get you halfway there . . . approximately.

ACKNOWLEDGMENTS

The study of Greek Homosexuality is a marginal field in Classics, under-funded, unconferenced and unseminared. No thanks are due, therefore, to some "Center for the Study of Greek Love," nor to research assistants, nor to "all those who contributed to the seminar series on Same-Sex Eros in ancient Greece, London 1999," for if there has ever been such a gathering on this side of the Atlantic, no one told me about it. Which is certainly remarkable, but not necessarily a bad thing; it will quickly become obvious that I have enjoyed having had such an enormous playground largely to myself. On the other hand, it does peculiarize my acknowledgments.

In the first place it means that writing this book has been an unusually solitary exercise, conducted as a series of forays over a long period. A couple of terms of study-leave from Warwick helped to get the project off the ground and to keep the show on the road and a matching Research Leave award from the Arts & Humanities Research Council in spring 2006 allowed me to reach a conclusion. But by far the greatest portion of research was done in snatches of time between doing other things: teaching, spending time with family and friends. At times even birthdays, marriages and deaths seemed like rude impositions on my important minutes of reading and writing. First of all therefore I thank my family, my current and former colleagues at Warwick and Birkbeck and my friends, for putting up with a permanently distracted version of myself over the last ten years. For the same reasons, the book is dedicated to my partner, Alberto Perez Cedillo, who has had more to put up with, in me being thus engaged, than anyone else.

Such a solitary and revisionist endeavor drew, unusually deeply, on my basic training, not just my first encounter with the subject of ancient gender and sexuality in William Harris's graduate class at Columbia in the 1980s, and my first researches on it under Oswyn Murray's always encouraging supervision in the 1990s, but the men who taught me Latin and Greek at the Manchester Grammar School in the 1970s and my undergraduate tutors in Oxford. From teachers and tutors I learned one lesson in particular over and over again: look at the evidence in the original, think about it, and then, time allowing, see what other people have thought about it. My tutor at Wadham, the much-missed Peter Derow, was especially important in this regard, so that each tutorial seemed like a conversation about some newly discovered text—Solon, Herodotus, Thucydides—that no one had ever said anything about before.

That does not mean I have not benefited a great deal from the labors of other scholars, especially those who have done the spadework of editing and commenting on texts, compiling dictionaries, cataloguing vases and inscriptions (and, more recently, making the results of their researches as widely available as possible), through decades-long feats of individual data collection or ancient ongoing projects of international cooperation, such as the *Inscriptiones Graecae* inaugurated in 1815, the *Corpus Vasorum Antiquorum* inaugurated in 1919, and, more recently, the *LIMC,* the Beazley Archive, *CAVI* etc. For access to books I was wholly dependent on the staff and resources of the Joint Library in the Institute of Classical Studies in London; a precariously stuck-together institution, it has recently threatened to come unstuck, which would be a bit of a disaster for me and many others.

And in default of a community of like-minded researchers, I have benefited from innumerable one-to-one conversations with a wide range of scholars on a wide range of subjects. Among others, Daniel Ogden, Stefan Radt, Bruce Knauft, Peter Wilson, Eva Stehle, Paul Cartledge and Nick Fisher made available not-(then-)published or hard-to-get-hold-of work. The late Keith DeVries gave me his catalogues of homo-*erōtikos* vase-images, *kalos* inscriptions and notes for a book on Homosexuality and Athenian Democracy; it is his response to this book I would have feared the most, despite his reassurances. Probably the most decisive of such exchanges was the briefest and most perfunctory one, with Alan Bray, just before he died, but that nevertheless managed with one little off-print to demolish my resistance to the idea of same-sex weddings in antiquity, by asking what I thought a "wedding" was and introducing me to the Cottonian Chronicle and Gerald of Wales.

Probably the most one-sided was with Robert Hannah of Otago, as knowledgeable about the ancient night skies in their northern hemispherical landscapes as I am ignorant, so that each immediate response to my innumerable questions had to include an elementary tutorial on astronomy. The longest, by far, was with Julia Annas, who tried to educate me about what students of ancient philosophy do and that it was not necessarily rude to fail to respond to an email.

Over the years preliminary conclusions have been presented to audiences of scholars and the general public in, among other places, Berlin, Potsdam, Heidelberg, Paris, Hamburg, Princeton, Bristol, Exeter, Berkeley, Boston, New York, Newcastle, Philadelphia, Oxford, Amsterdam, Manchester, Cambridge, London, Sydney, Los Angeles, and to my students at Warwick and Birkbeck, who became overly familiar with the experience of a mismatch between what they were told in class and what they read in books. On all those occasions, the call for "any questions" kept me in touch with prevailing assumptions and some unexpected connections and helped me keep track of which of my novel theses was likely to encounter most stubborn resistance. Occasionally I listened and changed my mind and sometimes someone told me something I didn't know or had "forgotten."

A couple of people have been decisive in their support for—or perhaps "faith in"—the project over such a long period, Michael Whitby and Robin Osborne, neither of whom should be considered my uncritical admirers. The latter especially has seen snapshots of my progress since my very first paper on the subject in the early 1990s and in particular forced me to think harder and work harder on the subject of age-classes through his brilliant impression of someone who still needed to be convinced.

Probably the fact that the book exists at all owes less to the Academy and more to the book trade. Always aware of what a big job it was and how often it had failed to be done, I would probably have put off starting it for several years longer had not Ravi Mirchandani and Philip Gwyn Jones provoked me and Rebecca Wilson pinned me down. That it can now be said to have been finished is largely thanks to the team at Weidenfeld, Alan Samson, Steve Cox, Francine Brody and Tom Graves. The one constant over those years of gestation has been my friend Peter Robinson, who midwifed the project from conception to parturition and whose faith in me and my book never ceased to sustain me.

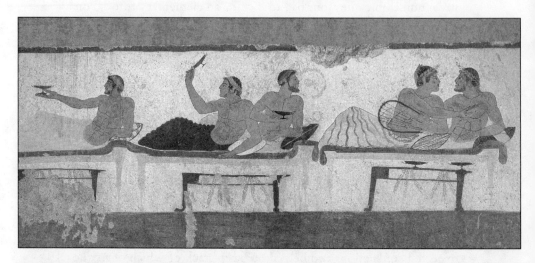

Ghostly niches in the sanctuary of Eros-Anteros directly below the
Erechtheum on the Acropolis. Here the disdainful *erōmenos* Timagoras
leapt to his death on top of the corpse of his disdained *erastēs* Meletus.
An inscription cut into the rock above the square niche at bottom left
records a festival of Eros, 'on the fourth of the lunar month Mounichion.'
This was traditionally the oldest of Love's cults in Athens.

INTRODUCTION

For centuries, Greek Homosexuality or Greek Love—what the Romans referred to as "the Greek custom" (*mos Graeciae, mos Graecorum*)—has been one of the knottiest problems in all of Western history.[1] For Christians, it was a moral knot: how could the ancient Greeks, who had so many good things to say about virtue, be so thoroughly addicted to this vice? But John Addington Symonds, writing in 1873, observed that it was already a problem for the Greeks themselves—"A Problem in Greek Ethics." The Greeks themselves, he showed, worried about it and expressed strongly divergent views about it.[2]

So here was another knot: What was the Greeks' attitude to their own Greek Homosexuality? For sometimes they seemed to approve, and approve wholeheartedly, even to celebrate and praise same-sex loving, but at other times they seemed very anxious about it and might even express the strongest disapproval. But what was this "it" anyway? Sometimes the Greeks seemed to assume it was very definitely centered on the physical attractions of members of the same sex, sometimes that it was properly focused on the personality, the "soul" (*psychē*). Sometimes they seemed to imply that it included sex, sometimes that it did not or need not or had better not or must not include any sexual consummation. Yet another knot seemed to present itself: What was this "Greek Love" in the first place? What did Greek Loving involve? What did one have to do to qualify as a Greek Lover?

Contradictions were apparent even when the sources discussed very particular cases. Some ancient authors insisted that in Sparta and Crete above all Greek Love was about sex and sexual pleasure, others that in those same places above all Greek Love was chaste. Even those who came from the same community might present contradictory testimony about their own local version of Greek Love. Some Athenian writers insisted that any kind of sexual intimacy with underage boys should be punished, even with death, the punishment meted out to adulterers, and they noted that in their city special slaves (the *paidagōgoi*) were employed precisely to prevent this kind of thing (whatever it was) from happening, but there were a few scenes on Athenian cups that seemed to show Athenians molesting and abusing underage boys with impunity. And here is yet another knotty subject: What do the authors mean by "boy" (*pais*), and how do you recognize a "boy" in paintings?

The knottiness and the contradictions extended even to the realm of mythical figures. Sometimes it seemed that mighty Heracles and Iolaus, his constant companion, were just the very best of friends, engaged in a brotherly kind of love. But others noted that Theban same-sex couples took Heracles and Iolaus as models for their own relationships, which were anything but "brotherly." As for the great hero Achilles and his love for Patroclus—not to mention his love for charming Antilochus, or his more murderous love for the Trojan Troilus—well, there was debate in the first place about whether Achilles was more loved against than loving, and about what exactly this love of Achilles might entail, either way. Homer had mentioned no nights of passion with Patroclus in the *Iliad,* but the tragedian Aeschylus certainly thought "thighs" and "frequent kisses" had featured in their relationship, and Homer himself had seemed to drop some pretty straightforward hints that Patroclus was to be considered not merely Achilles' friend and companion, but the same-sex equivalent of his wife.

Not even the gods were consistent. What was the story behind Sparta's great hero Hyacinthus? Was his relationship with Apollo pure or not so pure? And where did Zephyrus, the West Wind, fit into the relationship? Was he merely watching enviously from the sidelines, or was he the lover of Hyacinthus too? Some images seemed to offer clear-cut evidence that Hyacinthus was having a sexual relationship with Zephyr, but, then again, on one image, though Zephyr seemed definitely to be having sex with Hyacinthus, it also seemed, no less definitely, that Hyacinthus was fully clothed. And then there was Pelops, hero of the sanctuary of Olympian Zeus, home of the original Olympic Games. He seemed to have a very important relationship with Zeus, and served for a while as Zeus's attendant on Olympus, pouring out nectar and ambrosia. But in that case why did the poet Pindar claim Pelops had a love affair not with Zeus himself, in whose sanctuary Pelops was resident after all, but with Zeus's elder brother Poseidon, god of the sea? The sea is a long way from Olympia.

There are various ways of dealing with complicated knots. Alexander the Great, who is also a part of this story, dealt with them in a straightforward fashion:

> Alexander, when he reached Gordium, was seized by an aching desire to go up to the citadel, where the palaces of Gordius and his son Midas were, and to see Gordius's ox-wagon and the knot of the wagon's yoke . . . There was a story about this wagon, that whoever untied the knot of the wagon's yoke would rule Asia. The knot was made from the smooth bark of the cornel tree, and neither its end nor its beginning was visible. Alexander was quite baffled about how to untie the knot, but he didn't want to leave it untied, in case it provoked a disturbance in the ranks, so, according to some, he struck it with his sword and cut it right through, declaring the knot unfastened; but Aristobulus says that he removed the pin from the wagon pole (a wooden peg had been driven into the pole and it was this that kept the knot together), and so separated the yoke from the wagon pole. I cannot say for sure how Alexander dealt with the knot. But he and his group went away from the wagon as if the prophecy about the loosing of the knot had been fulfilled. And in fact, that night, thunder and lightning added to the impression; so, next day, Alexander made sacrifice to the gods who had made manifest both the signs and the loosing of the knot. Next day he went to Ankara . . .[3]

Many of those in recent times who have turned to face the problem of Greek Homosexuality have followed Alexander's example and tried to undo the knot with a single blow. These Slicers we might usefully group together as the "All-About" School. They fall into two main groups: those who think Greek Love is all about initiation through insemination, and those, far more numerous nowadays, who think Greek Love is all about domination through penetration.

In this book I have tried a different approach. Faced with such a magnificent knot, I checked my immediate desire to hack through it and discover what it was "all about"; that would be jumping the gun. First I thought it would be interesting to take the knot itself as my subject, to look at it from every angle, to try to identify some of the strands of which the knot was composed and then to follow, so far as I could, where each strand led. And I found that they led in many different directions.

One strand led to the center of the cult of Eros, the god of love on Mount Helicon, and to the nearby garden of Narcissus that the emperor Hadrian mentioned in a poem he wrote on a piece of stone, dedicating to Eros the head of a she-bear he had hunted down and killed. Another led to the sanctuary of Eros-Anteros, Love and Anti-Love, at the foot of the Acropolis in Athens below the Erechtheum. Here, it was said, a thwarted lover committed suicide, closely followed by his disdainful beloved, suddenly gripped by an urge to join his rejected suitor in death, who managed to land right on top of his corpse. Another strand led to the idea of grace and sexual favors, and, via the Hail Mary, to the Girl from Ipanema.

Then there was the age problem. Some insisted that Greek Love was a form of organized pedophilia, others demurred or did not talk about it. But behind this knot was an even bigger one: How did the Greeks understand age in the first place? If they celebrated no birthdays, how did they know how old anyone was? This was not just a problem for students of Greek Love; it was a problem for students of Greek civilization, no matter what their field of study. Before it was possible to say anything about the prevalence of *paiderastia,* it was necessary first to find out what a *pais*—a "boy"—was. And following this particular strand took me a long way from Greece, to the Shavante and Kayapo Indians of Brazil, some of whom seemed, despite first impressions, to have rather a lot in common with the Greeks, suddenly making vivid for me some curious Spartan marriage practices that might otherwise beggar belief.

But having come this far, and having discovered a rather courtly and romantic world of passionate same-sex love that seemed to resemble nothing so much as the slightly preposterous heterosexual loves depicted by the medieval troubadors or by French eighteenth-century painters, I began to wonder why those who had gone before me seemed to have come up with such a different picture, one that more closely resembled a sadomasochistic sex club in 1970s San Francisco, all domination and humiliation, role playing and sex acts. In particular, how had sodomy come to assume the conspicuous position it currently enjoys in

Hellenic studies, whether the scholar is examining a poetic account of a sea battle or Pericles' Funeral Speech, delivered at the beginning of the Peloponnesian War? And somehow or other this obsession with sexual acts was tied up with a modern theory that was widely accepted in the academy, and had begun to spread far outside it: that the Greeks did not have sexualities in the way that we understand them, homosexuality/ heterosexuality. In fact, it was argued, the ancient Greeks did not have sexual orientations at all, from which it followed that sexual orientation per se was not an inherent, hardwired human trait, but instead was constructed from scratch on each occasion by each different culture. This was hard to believe. But in that case how had so many people, including, it would appear, Colin Farrell, who played Alexander in Oliver Stone's film about him, and the artists Gilbert and George, come to believe it?

So here there was a whole set of problems. Why was there so much emphasis on sodomy in the modern scholarship of Greek Homosexuality? How had people come to the conclusion that something that seemed so natural and innate as sexual orientation was in fact a product of a powerful, superstrong "superculture"? And what did these two things, sodomy and the theory that sexuality was culturally determined, have to do with each other? Finally, another question needed to be added to these two. How had these theories been affected by modern attitudes toward homosexuality, by gay liberation on the one hand and by homophobia on the other? I got there in the end, but the journey was a long one, and took me through the history of the discipline of History and modern debates about the importance of culture and the contingency of truth. It began in the nineteenth century with Leopold von Ranke, often called the father of modern history, and his insistence on an amoral, nonjudgmental history, which emphasized the most original primary documents. It ended with the French philosopher Michel Foucault, and his "knowledge-regimes."

What I didn't expect was that language would play so important a part in the story, in particular the celebrated "Eskimo Words for Snow," made even more famous by Peter Hoeg's novel *Miss Smilla's Feeling for Snow,* and that I would even be taken back to the Indo-Europeans, the Aryans, who are believed to have spoken the language from which so many modern languages are descended, from Hindi and Iranian to Norwegian and Welsh, and who are believed to have lived somewhere north of the Black Sea perhaps around four thousand years BC. Nor did I expect to find that modern theories about ancient Greek sexuality would have been influenced so greatly by the work of the anthropologist Margaret Mead in Samoa, or that Hitler's Third Reich had also had an impact on how we viewed ancient Love.

That was enough of the nightmares of the modern world. I returned to the world of antiquity and ancient Eros. First, a study of the loves of the gods Zeus, Poseidon and Apollo for Ganymede, Pelops and Hyacinthus, respectively, which took me unexpectedly to the myths about the origins of constellations of stars, and a look at what Plato did with myths of divine abductions in his mystically soaring *Phaedrus,* one of the most influential of all his dialogues. After so much heaven gazing, something more down to earth: the loves of battle-scarred warriors and their beloved companions, the legendary heroes Achilles and Heracles, the real-life brutes of Sparta, Crete and Macedonia, and the famous Army of Lovers, the Sacred Band, who had a permanent encampment on the citadel of Thebes. And then as a kind of respite from all the clanking armor, a softer version of Greek Love, the world of the love poets, Lesbian Sappho and the gentle Ionians, and finally back to the Athenians, who produced so much of the discourse we started out with, their discussions of Eros and Grace and Favoring. Athenians were notoriously garrulous, but another explanation was needed for the fact that some particular Athenians—Plato, Xenophon and Aeschines, all contemporaries, as it happens, and probably known to one another, if not acquaintances—seemed to have had so much to say about this subject in particular, at this particular moment in time, which we could narrow further to *c.*380–*c.*345 BC. All of a sudden they seemed to be worried. All of a sudden they seemed to have a problem with a practice that seemed to have gone unquestioned for hundreds of years.

My intention was to look at Greek Love as a *Greek* phenomenon. By which I meant a number of things. On the one hand, I meant "not just Athenian." Because so much of our information comes from Athens, and because the city became so culturally dominant after the classical period, when we talk of "Greek" history, "Greek" language, "Greek" religion, "Greek" homosexuality, we often end up talking merely of the

Athenian varieties. But Athens was only one of hundreds of autonomous city-states (*poleis*), each with its own traditions, cults, calendar, coinage, food-ways, drink-ways . . . and Love-ways. The garrulous Athenians were unavoidable, but I would try to keep them in their place.

This phenomenal cultural diversity of ancient Greece is one reason why Greek history is so complicated—and why books for general readers on the Hellenic world are so much rarer than books about Rome. Rome is at least a single political entity. To study "Greece" is to study a cultural confederation of microstates. Any conclusions you may draw about one city may well not apply in another. But with the topic of Greek Love there was material from an unusually large number of places, not just from the usual pair of Athens and Sparta. There was material from Thespiae and the city of Thera, which perches on the rim of the great volcanic crater, which is all that remains of the island of Santorini. The important city of Elis in the northwestern Peloponnese, the city that ran the Olympic Games, could enter the picture, and even the cities of Apollonia on the Adriatic coast of Albania, Aegion on the Corinthian Gulf, Samos in the Aegean, Pharsalus in Thessaly, Paestum in Italy, Lyctus and Gortyn on Crete. Each city may have provided only a few tiny tesserae for the mosaic I was trying to piece together, and it may sometimes have been difficult to see where they might fit, but Greek Love provided a rare opportunity to resurrect and introduce a much bigger and more various Hellenic world than the version presented in many ancient history books.

If that diversity makes ancient Greece a difficult era to write narrative histories about, it makes it quite fascinating to explore. The Greek world reaches out in all directions. You never know what lies around the corner. And you never know what strange artifact, what surprising new image, what unfathomable custom or cryptic text will emerge from an excavation or from a piece of papyrus painstakingly unwrapped from an Egyptian mummy. It might be an unknown poem by Sappho of Lesbos, or one of the earliest of all Greek poets, crude Archilochus of Paros, telling us in his own voice how he seduced a woman and—at the climax of the narrative—"let loose my *menos*." We had known that *menos* meant spunk in the sense of "manly energy." Now we knew that it could also mean spunk in the sense of "sperm"; some old translations of ancient texts might need to be revised. A new version of Strabo might be discovered lurking underneath an old manuscript of Christian homilies and revealing a long-lost "embrace" between a Cretan man and his abducted beloved, or we might discover forty-two Athenian "year-heroes," each hero attached to a year's cohort of citizens, previously unknown.

There was another aspect to my emphasis on the "Greekness" of Greek Love. Too often information—the texts and images—had been cut from context, as if Greek Homosexuality was a phenomenon that could be separated from the world it so signally belonged to, as if it were something marginal, private, possessing little or no relevance to politics and religion, something the Greeks did, as it were, in their spare time, as if, when they retired to the bedroom, they retired for a while from the business of being ancient Greeks. This was especially true when the subject was Macedonian Homosexuality. Few scholars doubted the rather plentiful evidence that Alexander liked boys, and that there was plenty of same-sex passion at the court of the Macedonian kings, but only a few scholars had thought about the role played by such relationships in court politics. The same applied to Cretan Homosexuality, of which we have a very vivid account from the fourth-century historian Ephorus. Modern historians had not neglected the subject, but they had ignored the considerable political ramifications. Even in Athens, where sources sometimes seem to imply that the entire democracy was run by a mercenary mafia of men who had sex with men, scholars had tended to play down the broader significance of same-sex relationships, as if they were necessarily transitional and superficial, or merely the product of comic invectives about a politician's misspent youth. There are not many references to homosexual relationships in modern textbooks on the Athenian democracy, but the ancient sources on the politics of the Athenian democracy are full of them.

Instead of constantly zooming in on Greek Homosexuality, on the precise nature of the relationship, what was *really* going on between these same-sex Lovers, peering into the bedroom, into the bed, into the rarely specified details of the sexual acts its occupants may or may not have performed, I wanted to zoom out somewhat and scan the surrounding landscape. Instead of asking whether or not Achilles and Patroclus had a sexual relationship and who did what to whom, I wanted to ask what it meant for Homer to place this passionate relationship be-

tween two men at the center of the plot of the *Iliad,* what the relationship meant for those Greeks who saw the image on the Sosias Cup on
which a wide-eyed Achilles gently bandages Patroclus's wound with
brilliantly white bandages, while Patroclus grits his brilliantly white
teeth, what the relationship meant for the Thessalians who came to Troy
to sacrifice to Achilles and to offer something to dead Patroclus too, because they thought the ferocious warrior would like that, what it meant
for Alexander and Hephaestion when they came there to honor the two
heroes at the start of the campaign to conquer Persia, or to the man from
Croton who claimed to have seen the two heroes together in the sixth
century BC, seen them as ghosts on the White Island that lies off the
coast of Ukraine where the Danube debouches into the Black Sea, an island of white limestone and white birds and white poplars, a tree that,
in spring, produces masses of fluffy white seeds, which must, I surmised,
have covered the island in a solider version of dry ice.

Which leads me to another important element of reconstituting
"Greekness": it also means stepping back from modern ways of thinking. By restoring the context for these decontextualized images and ex-
cerpted quotes—even if that meant no more than turning a cup over to
see what was painted on the other side—one was drawn a little further
into the ancient world as it actually existed, in all its four dimensions. It
was not always obvious what the connection was between, say, an image
of underage boys being molested by their seniors in a gymnasium, and
the image on the interior of the same cup, which showed Achilles'
mother, Thetis, transforming herself into a series of savage and dangerous creatures to escape the iron grip of Achilles' father, Peleus, but there
it was. That is the scene the painter painted, that is the scene the ancient
viewer saw. And when we turn over the Sosias Cup, with Achilles ban-
daging Patroclus's arm, we find a grand procession of gods running all
the way around, with Heracles at one end calling out to his father Zeus
at the other: "Zeus, friend." These juxtapositions may seem baffling to
us, but they are juxtapositions that really exist; indeed it is only in photographs and books that the scenes can be separated. And as soon as we
turn the cup over, we are vividly reminded of the rest of the Greek
world in which all this Greek Loving takes place.

The Achilles who features as a fierce lover of his own sex in the *Iliad*
and elsewhere is also the Achilles whose mother was honored at the

sanctuary called Thetideion in his hometown of Pharsalus in Thessaly. Here Euripides set his play *Andromache,* which flattered the royal family of the Molossians, who claimed to be descended from Achilles, and who controlled the oracle at Dodona, which advised the Thessalians to make sacrifice to Achilles at Troy. It was a Molossian who was said, though bearded, to have been the beloved of Meno of Pharsalus, who also stars in Plato's dialogue of that name as one of the handsomest men in the world, and who commanded Xenophon on the march of the Ten Thousand on their unsuccessful expedition to seize the throne of Persia for Cyrus the Younger. When Meno was murdered, Xenophon wrote one of the bitterest of all Greek obituaries. Those same Molossians provided a wife for Philip of Macedon, Olympias, mother of Alexander, who offered special honors to Achilles at Troy on his more successful expedition to seize the throne of Persia . . .

The knot was made from the smooth bark of the cornel tree, and neither its end nor its beginning was visible.

So a book about *The Greeks and Greek Love* is a book about Greek Love in its Greek context, but also a book about the extraordinary world of the Greeks as a whole, explored by means of their most idiosyncratic custom. It is a sketch of the kinds of things we students of the Greeks could have been doing with Greek Love over the past thirty years, had we not been so strangely preoccupied with sodomitical penetration, the kinds of things I hope we will do more of in the future.

PART I

THE GREEKS HAD WORDS FOR IT

EROS IN LOVE

Before we start looking at how the ancient Greeks talked of affairs of the heart, we need to remind ourselves how we moderns do it. Even when you know a language inside out, it can be difficult to pin words down, and words of love are especially slippery. Here are a few fragments of conversations overheard. See if you can work out the nature of the affections and guess which ones are talking about sex, which are going to end in tragedy and which will live most happily ever after.

1 "I love you." "I love you too, mate."
2 "I'm not in love." "No you're not. You're in lust."
3 "I love you." "Look, I really like you."
4 "I'm really sorry. You know how much I love you. But I like boys."
5 "She's nice." "Yeah. She's a really lovely person. I'm terribly fond of her."
6 "He's nice." "He's to die for."

Try explaining to a foreigner what the words "like" and "love," "lovely," "in love" and "nice" mean in English. It doesn't help to look them up in the *Oxford English Dictionary,* where there are pages and pages that try to explain. These are words that belong to our own very peculiar and socially promiscuous environment. They have evolved a high degree of ambivalence and diplomatic sensitivity, and have a lot of work to do in getting us through a minefield of possible misunderstandings and embarrassments with the fewest accidental detonations. The Greeks too had a number of words for love, quite apart from the two that most concern us: *philia,* "intimate love," and *erōs,* "the love drive." As to whether the Greeks made a better job of delimiting the field, here is my schematic guide to a few ancient loves the Greeks had words for . . .

AGAPĒ

Let's start at the shallow end. If you go to Greece today you will hear countless songs about love on the radio. You may be able to make out the words *s'agapo*—"I love you"—and *m'agapeis*—"do you love me?" In ancient Greek the word *agapē* and its verb(s) are used above all for the feelings of proud and indulgent parents slaughtering a fatted calf for an eldest son, or the tail-wagging pleasure of old retainers when the master of the house comes home at last. It can certainly be used in the context of sexual relationships, but it has little sexual heat, a "fondness" or "affection" expressed as a "fussing over" of someone who "pleases you," expressing neither intimacy nor an impassioned desire, but something closer to "proud regard."

Agapē and its relatives are used by Xenophon to describe the chaste-ish feelings of Spartan men for boys they have relationships with, the affection of the soldiers in the Theban "Army of Lovers" for their younger partners, or that of Zeus for Ganymede.[1] Although most modern scholars discount claims of chasteness in Greek "homosexuality," since they think that "homosexuality" is desire for sex, and though *agapē* certainly doesn't rule out a sexual relationship, it seems clear that these authors were using a word that need not entail sexual passion. Greek Christians certainly thought so. *Agapētos* is all over the New Testament, the word normally translated "beloved," as in "Dearly beloved, we are gathered here today . . ." Christ is God's "beloved son," John the "beloved disciple," etc., setting up an opposition to *erōs,* which thereby took the first steps toward sex.

POTHOS

Now we come to the masculine "loves" often represented as little male Cupids. *Pothos* and its relatives are usually translated as "longing." It seems to refer to a kind of missing of, or yearning for, something or someone who may be far out of reach. It first appears (as *pothē/pothos*) in Homer's *Iliad* as a simple "need for someone you have come to rely on," as when Achilles goes missing from the ranks of the Greek army while he sulks in his tent, a feeling that someone isn't there whom it would help to have around. In slightly later writers it seems to assume a more sentimental intensity—Demeter yearning for her abducted daughter, people longing for Odysseus who has been away so long. Much later it appears as something inside Alexander the Great that sends him halfway across the world, a kind of "restless questing." In affairs of the heart however it is less energetic, and is best described as a *manque langoureux,* a "languorous missing" or "pining."[2]

Pothos often seems barely distinguishable from other words for *erōtikos* desire, but there is something odd about the syntax of its verb *pothein.* Whereas other "desiring" verbs take an indirect object, implying "striving after," *pothein* takes a straightforward direct object, like verbs of "asking" or "begging," and inanimate objects can experience this *pothos,* although they cannot feel desire—e.g., "but that just begs [*pothei*] the question . . ." It seems therefore to retain something of its old Homeric inertness. Indeed originally it probably meant simply "seek." One recent scholar suggests that *pothos,* therefore, is originally "desire for that which is not easily obtained by the subject's actions alone."* This sense of yearning without active targeting can be conveyed in the English "crying out for," as in "That table is crying out for a great big vase of flowers," "That outfit is crying out for a string of pearls," "Ithaca is crying out for its king." It is the abandoned dog returning to the side of the motorway to the place it last saw its master, someone running down each morning as soon as the postman delivers to see if that letter with the familiar writing has finally arrived, waiting for a phone call from the daughter given up for adoption in the 1950s, "watching this space," "crossing your fingers." A man in love can hope that the youth he "pines for" will "pine for him in return," *pothōn antipotheisthai.*[3] *Pothos* is perhaps best described as "a person-shaped hole in your heart."[4]

---

* A subject in this sense is a grammatical subject, which in those languages that have "cases," notably German, Latin and Greek, would appear in the nominative case, e.g., *servus, homo.* This subject is the active I, She, He, We or They who *experience* smells, tastes, loves etc., the "Person Doing" as my teachers used to say. Above all, this is the Interior I or megalomaniac Ego of Descartes—the thinking subject, the Cogito, the "Cartesian subject"—the very same subject who might feel able to imagine that the entire world is nothing more than the product of Her (or His) own active imaginings, His (or Her) own imposition. This (grammatical) subject is conceptually opposed to a (grammatical) object that appears in the accusative case, e.g., *servum, hominem,* that is, the Me, Him, Her, Us, Them this subject acts upon, the "person done," "done-to," "done-upon."

HIMEROS

Another of these little Cupids is sometimes labeled Himeros; you often
see him with Dionysus and Ariadne who, soon forgetful of Theseus
who had sneaked off and abandoned her there, fell in love with Dionysus on Naxos and vanished with him into heaven. On one vase Himeros
puts a sandal on Dionysus's outstretched foot. On another he drenches
Ariadne with love poured from a sacred bowl.[5] *Pothos* is when the object
of love is absent, *himeros* when it is present, says Socrates in *Cratylus,*
Plato's dialogue on words. Plato often defines words as what he thinks
they should mean rather than as what they normally do, but here I am
inclined, provisionally, to trust him. Some have suggested that *himeros*
properly refers to a desire generated from outside oneself—"a sudden
urge [*himeros*] came over me to get out of the house . . ."—which may
suddenly depart of its own accord. It often tends to prompt immediate
action on the part of the stricken subject, or to focus on something or
someone imminent. In the field of amorousness it seems to describe a
warm feeling you get, which may seem like a kind of emanation from
the object, when the object is in range, something that "streams" over
you or "radiates" from someone.[6] Later Greeks were somewhat amused
to find that among the songs attributed to Solon, the revered founder of
the Athenian Constitution, were some lines about "spending fond hours
in the company of a boy [*paidophilein*]"—hours that seemed to include
"desire for imminent [*himeirōn*] thighs and sweet-tasting mouth."[7]

Himeros is "captivation," in the manner of that Girl from Ipanema
who leaves a wake of sighs as she passes obliviously along the *caminho do
mar;* her obliviousness of charm is part of the charm—it mustn't be con-
trived. *Himeros* has the effect of turning a passive object of desire into an
innocent agent, and a subject of desire into an assault victim, attacked,
penetrated through his eyes. Modern advertisements invoke *himeros*
when they suggest that wearing a certain kind of perfume or aftershave
will have a dramatic effect on passersby—cars crash into lampposts, men
fall off ladders, pneumatic drills puncture water pipes.

In Plato's *Phaedrus, himeros* is a kind of current that streams unwittingly from the *erōmenos,* the young man who is the object of interest,
and drenches the *erastēs,* the man who is in love with him, when they
touch for the first time and get socially intimate, a feeling that manifests

itself long after the suitor has fallen in love, i.e., been put under the spell
of Eros, and been accepted into the boy's company, and a little time before sex is in the cards. The love-stream is so copious that having soaked
the enamored it flows back into the soul of the boy and gets him too all
aflutter. This streaming surge was first identified by Zeus himself, says
Plato, when *himeros* was pouring out over him from Ganymede. It seems
clear that he is allegorizing the shining nectar and ambrosia that
Ganymede poured out into the king of the gods' cup, a stream later authors identified with the shimmering liquid of stars that seems to pour
out from the constellation Aquarius.[8] Himeros is perhaps best described
as a "love attack."

ERŌS

Now we reach the kernel of this book. Eros is Greek Love himself. He is
the original of these fairy Cupids. He smells divine, carries flowers, especially roses, sometimes with petals clinging to his feet, where he has
been walking. He wears a mischievous smile, is sometimes armed with
bow and arrow and sometimes a whip or a cattle prod. And though
never a "god of homosexual love" and certainly no stranger to love between males and females, yet when set alongside his mother Aphrodite
he does seem to complement rather than reinforce her, a god of Love in
general, but with a special purview over one Love in particular, the em-
bodiment of the object of Love for Boys, as beautiful Aphrodite embodies the object of desire for women.[9]

Eros is sometimes brother, sometimes father of Pothos and Himeros,
and he seems to combine elements of both: the energy of imminent
himeros, the distance and longing of pathetic *pothos.* One key aspect of
Eros, however, is that he possesses the person in love. He is the demon
that puts your life offtrack, robs you of all your common sense, and of
sleep at night. He is very much an interior force, supersubjective, something you nurse inside you, getting your blood up, pushing and pester-
ing, goading you with his whip, driving you mad.

In the fourth century BC, the sculptor Scopas, revered for his ability
to inject a miraculous life into marble, made a group of all three of these
Cupids, Himeros, Eros and Pothos, for the temple of Aphrodite Action
(Praxis) in the town center of Megara.[10] How Scopas differentiated

1. The Judgment of Paris. Eros works on a fishily attired Paris
("ALEXAND[ROS]"); Pothos confers with Aphrodite. Himeros sits on a
rock reserving himself for the moment when Helen first meets her
arranged lover. Water jar (*hydria*) by the Kadmos Painter (*c*.420).

them is now lost to us, but on a vase of the fifth century we can see all
three together in the famous episode from myth in which the Trojan
prince called Paris or Alexander has to choose the most beautiful of
three beautiful goddesses. Athena and Hera never stood a chance;
Aphrodite had brought her whole gang with her. Aphrodite wins the
contest by bribing the judge with the offer of Helen, the most beautiful
woman in the world. The artist has painted Pothos close to the goddess,
evoking longing for some distant object in her gift: beautiful Helen.
Himeros is off duty, lounging around. He won't have anything to do
until Helen is within Paris's imminent reach. As for Eros he is concentrating on the judge himself, clouding his judgment, whispering "go for
it," and making his heart race.[11]

We should remember that these Cupids, these aspects of loving, are not
necessarily to do with amorousness unless they are used in an amorous context. It is perfectly proper to talk of a *himeros,* a "sudden urge," to ask a
question or of Alexander's "longing," *pothos,* to visit Gordium and untie
the Gordian knot. This is especially important to remember when we are
talking of Eros, for his field is more than that of the heart. Homer talks
readily of *erōs* for food, dancing, sleep, war. And much later Thucydides

talks of how the Athenians were filled with *erōs* to mount a naval expedition to conquer Sicily, a desire more targeted than Alexander's *pothos* to conquer the world, as if he had a world-shaped hole in his heart.[12] *Erōs* is a particular kind of targeting energy, not just a romantic love or sexual desire. A more scientific investigation into his origins concludes that *erōs* must have lost two throaty consonants; among the prehistoric Indo-Europeans "*erōs*" sounded something like "khherrrgghh . . . ," an appropriate vocalization for a primordial lump of rock and not unrecognizable perhaps for those who have been in love and have had a hard time of it. But the point is that this original "*erōs*" meant, it has been tentatively deduced, something like "wanting the pleasure of a piece of it."[13]

It is hard to say when this now familiar figure first appears in the record, since gods don't always have labels in Greek art, although often they do. Possibly the image of the Cupid was born in Sparta, for on one cup from Sparta of the sixth century BC we see pictures of men and women lying on couches enjoying a feast, while above them flutter little winged figures, sometimes naked, sometimes dressed, sometimes bearded, sometimes not, carrying wreaths, i.e., leafy tiaras, to crown the feasters, and stylized flowers.[14] There are many of these winged spirits in early Spartan art, and we don't always know their significance, but here the wreaths and the flowers and the drinking party give the game

2. Spartan Symposium with Sirens and Erotes. Cup by
the Naukratis Painter (*c.*565).

away. On one vase in particular, these little winged men alternate with little bird-women, seductive female Sirens, and one must, I think, consider them proper Cupids, Erotes. And there's also an Eros on a mirror, symbol of beauty and vanity, next to a naked goddess who must be Aphrodite.[15]

WORSHIP OF EROS

Eros is unusually prominent in Athens. He is depicted with his mother on the Parthenon frieze looking out over the assembled processional Athenians, and he received sacrifices and other honors at a number of places, notably in the gymnasium of "Academy," just outside the city walls, where Plato chose to site his School, thus partially accounting for Plato's preoccupation with Love. The great philosopher's complaints about the lack of honor paid to Eros are not unlike the complaints of a medieval academic from Oxford lamenting the lack of honor paid to St. Frideswide. Certainly we should learn to look at his great dialogues on Love, notably the *Symposium* and *Phaedrus,* as acts of piety honoring the locally presiding deity . . . among other things.[16]

Here at Love's altar in the Academy naked eighteen-year-olds lit their torches for the great nocturnal relay runs that finished at another altar in the city center.[17] Eros also had a cult alongside his mother Aphrodite on the north cliff of the Acropolis under the Erechtheum; like his mother, Eros has an affinity with undressed stone; he is nothing if not natural.[18] An inscription cut into the rock above a man-made niche informs us that he had his own festival in Athens on the fourth day of the late spring month Mounichion, when roses bloom. More niches were carved into the rock, over twenty of them, made to hold painted plaques and other offerings, now as ghostly as the permanent shadows on the walls of a former gallery.[19]

One of these dedications, we are told, showed a beautiful naked boy running headlong with two cocks in the crooks of his arms, a same-sex pair (cf. Fig. 55). This image, which sounds like a description of an archaic painting, marked the spot where the supercilious youth Timagoras had leapt from the Acropolis on top of the smashed body of his suitor Meletus. Poor Meletus had been sent on all kinds of difficult and dangerous quests by the "arrestingly" handsome but "cold and indifferent"

3A. Ghostly niches in the sanctuary of Eros-Anteros directly below the
Erechtheum on the Acropolis. Here the disdainful *erōmenos* Timagoras leapt
to his death on top of the corpse of his disdained *erastēs* Meletus.

———

3B. An inscription cut into the rock above the square niche at bottom left
records a festival of Eros, "on the fourth of the lunar month Mounichion."
This was traditionally the oldest of Love's cults in Athens.

Turandot-ish youth, tasks that were "leading him to the very brink of
death." For instance, he was sent to "get hunting dogs from some foreign country," to steal "a fiery stallion from one of Athens's enemies,"
"and finally" to steal a pair of "already-reared domestic fowl of amazing
pedigree."[20] Having got everything he was asked to get, he brought
these gifts to the boy, but the boy was ungrateful and even spurned the
birds. So Meletus, "on fire with *erōs*," ran up to the Acropolis, "fast as his
legs could carry him," and hurled himself down onto the rocks below.
That was not the end of the story; for then, taking the cocks in his arms,

Timagoras found himself running up to the Acropolis, treading in
Meletus's very footsteps, as if dragged along against his will. The followed now turned into a follower of his *erastēs*. When he reached the
same spot he threw himself onto Meletus's body, smitten too late with a
"love in return" (*anterastheis*), a "slow love." On that same site the community of aliens resident in Athens dedicated an altar where they worshipped "Anteros, Timagoras's Nemesis."[21]

You do not have to be overly subtle to see that this tale of Meletus
running "on fire with *erōs*" as fast as his feet can carry him, and his
beloved following in his footsteps with a "slow love," resonates somewhat with the races with torches lit from the altar of Eros in the Academy. The legend transforms the relay race into an "erotik" pursuit, each
runner, so to speak, carrying a torch for another.[22]

There were other notable cults of this great god. The Spartans sacrificed to Love before going on campaign and the Cretans before battle;
such similar practices imply, almost certainly, a common origin in a time
before Crete was colonized, at least as early as the early first millennium
BC.[23] The people of Samos celebrated Love in a great "Freedom" festival; the many stories of love-pairs assassinating tyrants mean that the
connection between Eros and liberation is unlikely to have been merely
abstract in Samos. He also had his own temple in a sacred wood deep in

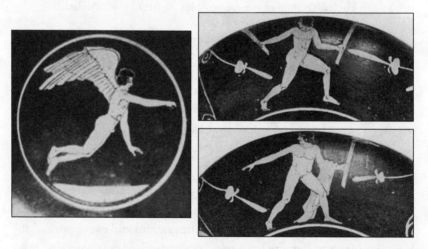

4. Eros in the center of the cup presides over the ephebes' torch race
from his altar in the Academy to the altar in the city.
Cup by the Hasselmann Painter (*c*.430).

fallen leaves with a river running through it, in a town on Spartan territory.[24] But the great center of Love's cult in classical Greece was in the
city of the Thespians.

The cult, which was thought to be very ancient, centered on the worship of Eros in the form of a rock, any information about the nature or
the whereabouts of this rock remaining most mysterious.[25] There was a
story told about the origins of the cult similar to the story of Meletus, a
story we know only from the Patriarch of Constantinople, Photius,
whom Roman Catholics blame for the "Great Schism."[26] In his spare
time he wrote reading notes on hundreds of books that no longer exist,
an example of the Byzantine specialty of "abridgements as might amuse
the curiosity, without oppressing the indolence, of the public."[27] On
this occasion, Photius (c. AD 810–893) is giving the gist of a chapter he
read in a work written 900 years previously by one Conon, a contemporary of Augustus:

> In Thespia in Boeotia (a town near Mount Helicon) there was a boy
> Narcissus, very beautiful and indifferent to Eros and admirers [erastai].
> Although the majority of his admirers gave up making love to him
> [erōntes], Ameinias would not desist from his demands. But Narcissus
> not only did not admit him, but sent him a sword, which Ameinias
> used to kill himself, in front of Narcissus's door, making many prayers
> of supplication to the god to be his avenger. And Narcissus caught
> sight of himself, the beauty of his form, reflected in the water of a
> spring and became his own first and only bizarre erastēs of himself. In
> the end finding himself at a loss and realizing that he was getting his
> just deserts for disdaining Ameinias's love, he killed himself. And
> from that day forth the Thespians resolved to honor Eros exceedingly
> both in public celebrations and in private sacrifices. And the locals
> think the narcissus flower first sprang up on that piece of ground on
> which the blood of Narcissus was poured.[28]

The site was near the peak of Mount Helicon. Narcissuses flourish in the
fields round about (Sir George Wheler saw them in the seventeenth century, at least) and mists make the mountain a magical place.[29]

Conon's seems to be the oldest extant version, anticipating Ovid's by
a whisker, of the myth of Narcissus, and probably the most original and
authentic, since the same basic plot—Narcissus's rejection of manly in-

tercourses (*coetus . . . viriles*), the punishment arising from the curse of one of his admirers, the gradual realization that it is his own reflection he is in love with—can be seen, without too much effort, to provide the core for Ovid's more celebrated version. But Ovid, famously, has an ingenious interlude, starring the once-too-chatty nymph—her name is Echo—who now can only answer back using the words that have just been spoken to her. Crucially, however, she can modify the text by abridging it, so that it may mean something rather different from what it was meant to. And so before he sees himself in the pool Narcissus, hot and bothered from hunting, is already propositioning himself in a hollered dialogue amid the mountain peaks where he has gone to hunt wildlife, an exchange that grows more ruttish by the minute, even though it is his own chaste self he is talking to, unwittingly acceding to that virile coitus he had previously rejected: *Huc comeamus,* "Let's meet at this spot," he says. *Comeamus,* "Let's fuck," is his own echoing reply; though Ovid triangulizes this intimate homosexual relationship between a beautiful boy and his nymphomaniac other self by interposing an actual lascivious nymph, the semi-personage Echo.[30] Narcissus is not seduced by his own perfect image but by an imperfect, foreshortened version. And it is the removal of words that provides the come-on. If you want to be more Freudian about it, his echo reveals the repressed desire latent in his superficially unexciting speech, and the desire is revealed not by adding something, but by Echo's omissions.

In fact, as in Athens, there seem to have been at least two distinct cults of Eros in Thespiae (and probably several more). The one most talked about was in the city center. Here the courtesan Phryne dedicated a marble statue of Eros sculpted by her lover Praxiteles, "from the very mold of his love for her."[31] This city temple seems to have been the focus for private worship and has a very strong feminine flavor. Here Plutarch came during Eros's quadrennial festival of sport and music, called the *Erotika* or *Erotidia,* with a whole group of friends and his bride shortly after their marriage so that she could sacrifice and pray to Love.[32] Nothing to do with their own relationship; both sets of parents were engaged in a violent dispute and the newlyweds needed the god's help to reconcile them. No sooner had they arrived than they had to flee the city along with all the other tourists, because of a violent dispute that had broken out between rival groups of fans of competing lyre-singers:

hooliganism is by no means a modern invention. They spent the night on the mountain and next morning made their descent to the town, falling into conversation with two locals about the local god. For a wealthy young widow had proposed marriage to a Thespian ephebe and he had asked his friends to help him decide whether or not to accept the offer. In the course of the conversation news arrives that the widow, impatient for an answer, has had said boy kidnapped as he was leaving the gymnasium and quickly had him stripped and dressed in a shining white wedding cloak.

There is an untidiness about the tale, full of intractable particulars, that gives it the smack of authenticity, and one is encouraged to believe that Plutarch did indeed visit Thespiae not long after his wedding to honor the great god of the city in the hope that he might use his influence to bring his and his wife's families together, that they thought it wise to retreat from the city for a night due to high spirits among various fan clubs of lyre-singers, and that they learned of a local dispute concerning a wealthy young widow and a boy she intended to marry. On that question, quite possibly, various locals expressed various opinions, but as to what they said and how they said it, here my credulity goes outside to smoke a cigarette.

Anyway, as Plutarch tells it, one of these locals was one of the boy's admirers. Hence the dispute turned into an argument about the relative merits of love of men for boys versus love for women as wives. Members of Plutarch's party divided along similar lines, with newly married Plutarch defending marriage. The dialogue finishes when they all reach the city once more to hear news that the kidnapped boy has seemingly accepted the proposal. Indeed the now happy couple are even now making their way to the temple of the god of Love for sacrifice.

Inside the temple there was a statue of the courtesan Phryne herself, alongside another of Aphrodite. But Praxiteles' original Eros had been replaced by a copy. The Romans managed to keep their hands off this most celebrated work of art for two hundred years, although they removed everything else from Thespiae, "because the statue was consecrated."[33] The emperor Caligula, however, not famous for his self-restraint, had had no such qualms and brought it to Rome. The next emperor, Claudius, had given it back, but his successor, Nero, had it removed once more to Rome, where it was soon lost forever in the Great

Fire, the one allegedly ignited by the newfangled cult of "Devotees of the Anointed One" otherwise known as "Christians."

Greeks seem to have been outraged by this series of sacrileges. It was in the aftermath of this disaster that Plutarch chose to recall his own earlier visit to the shrine, and a few decades later Pausanias the traveler told an, in context, very pointed anecdote about the original gift to Phryne half a millennium before. Her admirer the great Praxiteles had promised to his beloved his most beautiful work, but refused to tell her which that was. So she had a servant rush in with the news that his workshop was on fire. "I have worked for nothing if my Eros and the Satyr are consumed in the flames," he shouted, and so Phryne's choice was narrowed down to two.[34] Pausanias even thought he could see the hand of vengeful Eros in the sticky ends to which Caligula and Nero had recently come. For Caligula was killed by a member of the Praetorian Guard, Chaerea, whom he had provoked by insisting on amorous passwords that Chaerea then had to pass on to the night watch, to their persistent amusement and his more and more dangerous embarrassment; in the Greek version the provocative passwords were "Aphrodite" and "Pothos."[35] And had not Eros also involved Nero in scandalous and disgusting practices with his wives?[36]

In this context, the emperor Hadrian's visit to Thespiae in AD 124 takes on a new urgency. Mindful of the amatory problems of his predecessors caused by their sacrilege against the great god of Love at his holiest shrine, he begged Eros to take pity on him, writing his own prayer in eight lines of Greek verse, each exactly eleven syllables long:

> O Boy, Archer, son of the clear-voiced Cyprian goddess, you who dwell in Heliconian Thespiae beside Narcissus's flowering garden, be merciful. Receive the head of this she-bear which Hadrian is giving you, the bear he himself killed hitting it from horseback. May you, chaste Eros, breathe on him, in return for this, the grace [charis] which comes from Heavenly Aphrodite.[37]

This little piece of imperial poetry was discovered on a piece of stone not far from Thespiae. No one doubts that it is Hadrian's own, more than passable, composition. But Eros was not so easily propitiated. On his next tour of the east he made Hadrian, Greekest of emperors, fall in love with one Antinous of Bithynia, the province that lies opposite Istanbul, and then in the autumn of 130 Antinous drowned in the Nile. The emperor's response was to encourage the most extraordinary honors for the lovely young man: games, cults, divine honors, a city named after him, and innumerable statues of his splendid form, giving many a modern visitor to a provincial museum an eerie sense of déjà vu. This extraordinary blip in the database of ancient art must also, I think, be viewed as an act of piety on Hadrian's part, an act of obeisance toward the vengeful Love who dwells in Thespiae, so furious a defender of his own prerogatives.[38]

For all that they are revealing about Hadrian, the emperor's verses also reveal an important fact about Thespian Eros; apart from the famous city sanctuary visited by brides and courtesans he had another cult high on Helicon, next to the "blooming garden" of Narcissus, a place used for trysts it would appear, for Ovid has the poor youth ask the surrounding trees if they have ever seen a lover as sorry as he is, given their great experience of lovers: "you who have provided cover for many men."[39] Perhaps this was (also) the sanctuary for the "Heavenly" Uranian Eros that Hadrian seems to specify.[40] Moreover, not at all far from here lay Ascra, hometown of the poet Hesiod, who, in his genealogy of the gods, the *Theogony,* was inspired by the Muses of Helicon to give a namecheck to the great divinity with whom they shared the mountain, an older primordial Eros, not the son of Aphrodite but one of the very earliest of the primitive entities to emerge at the dawn of creation, following (1) Chaos, (2) Earth and (3) Tartarus—One, Two, Three, Four: Eros.[41]

Despite Hesiod's evidence, some have been skeptical both about the antiquity of the cult of Eros—even suggesting that the whole thing was started by the courtesan Phryne and her famous statue—and about Eros's association with Narcissus: "probably pure story-telling, connecting two well-known Thespian names," as if there could ever be a version of the tragedy of Narcissus in which the great local god played no part.[42]

But a tiny detail on the city's coins (Figs. 5a and 5b) provides, once you catch it, unmistakable proof of the connection between these two most famous sons of Thespiae. A city's coins often carry a symbol of the city's most important cult—e.g., in Athens, of Athena and an owl—and Eros was to Thespiae what Athena was to Athens,[43] but the coins of Thespiae

5A.   5B.

5A. Thespian Aphrodite with crescent of the fourth day of the moon,
sacred to the goddess and to Eros, the city's patron deity. Its mirror image is
at right. Silver didrachm from Thespiae (fourth century).

5B. Mirrored crescent moon. Silver obol from Thespiae (c.387–c.383).

use the device of a crescent moon. This is not a reference to the Moon
goddess Selene, nor to the "Black Aphrodite" who also had a cult in
Thespiae, but a symbol of Eros, since this is what the Moon looks like on
the fourth day of the month, his sacred day, the day of his festival in
Athens, for instance, his birthday. For, as the Muses of Helicon subtly
pointed out to Hesiod, Love is . . . the "fourth-born" god—One, Two,
Three, Four: Eros.[44]

But this crescent is sometimes shown as if lying on the baseline underneath the name of the city, like a big grin, and sometimes there are
two crescents, one above, one below, and sometimes they are back to
back like mirror images of each other. This of course is exactly what the
Moon would have looked like to anyone who happened to make a nocturnal pilgrimage to the spring of Narcissus on the fourth day of the
Moon for a spell of "virile coitus" in the knowing woods, to celebrate
Eros's birthday. The crescent is fourth-born Love and Love's Reflection,
Eros and Anteros, or, indeed it is the Loved-Loving youth himself.[45] For
according to an otherwise unexpected late tradition, Narcissus was no
Thespian but the son of Endymion and the Crescent Moon. And it was
his mother he took after: "You have the form of a heavenly body, the
image of the Crescent Moon, the perfect likeness of gracious Narcissus."[46] Looking for Narcissus's vanished body, shouting for him in the
mountains above Thespiae, and hearing only our own voices back, looking into his pool and seeing nothing but the reflection of the sky, we
didn't realize that he was that reflection; all this time he was staring us in
the face.

Narcissus's tragedy represents not the essence of same-sex *erōs,* as some have thought, but its dangerous obstruction. It can be said that Narcissus rediscovers not just any old Love, but Hesiod's most ancient Love of Mount Helicon, the fourth thing to come into existence, the Love that precedes individuation, distinction and separation, the lumpen rock of a Subject with no Object, the primeval swamp of Self. Narcissus has been sent back to a time when he is the only boy in the world and he is the only boy. Elsewhere, Ovid, as pithy as in the *Metamorphoses* he is prolix, puts his finger on it: "Poor boy, you were your only alternative."[47] One, One, One, Narcissus.[48]

ERŌS AS A ONE-WAY STREET

Erōs is, with only a few exceptions, utterly one-sided. You can be longed for, loved (*philein*), desired "in return" (*anti-*) with no problem, but for the Greeks there can be no mutual *erōs,* not concurrently.[49] Eros doesn't work like that. He is a vector, a one-way ticket from A to B. It is only when Meletus has killed himself that Timagoras is consumed with an equally hopeless and catastrophic "love in return" (*anterastheis*), and the story of Narcissus only serves to point out the paradoxical nature of a perfectly matched Eros—two young men, the same age, carrying a torch for each other. In fact Anteros more often means not "love in return" but a "contrary Eros"; it implies a contest or conflict, or simply Meletus's vengeful god of spurned lovers, occasionally invoked on curse-tablets, the dread demon that Queen Dido, for instance, was believed to have called upon when Aeneas rejected her.[50]

Following Constantine's Christian conversion, the stubbornly pagan Themistius told a story about this pair. Aphrodite was worried about her son Eros: he seemed stunted. She was advised that he needed a brother and so she gave birth to Anteros. Eros soon started to grow, now that he had a rival on the scene, and each competed with the other to see who could grow the most.[51] The same pair was shown wrestling in the *palaestra* (the training ground in a gymnasium) of Elis, home of the Olympic Games. If Eros was the son of the archetypal happy couple, Hermes and Aphrodite, Anteros should be the son of Ares, god of war.[52] He is Eros Thwarted.

Plato, exceptionally, claims that the beloved boy does indeed feel *erōs* in return, a mirror image anti-*erōs* of the love felt by his admirer, which is going to set him off on his own journey into love, but it's not in fact an *erōs* for his *erastēs*. He doesn't know what it is he is in love with; like Narcissus he is "at a loss," and anyway he misreads it and calls it *philia*. But this is a very peculiar passage, and Plato's insistence on Eros-sparked *erōs* is critical for his own peculiar argument, as we will see. Even in the great myth of Aristophanes in the *Symposium,* which claims that lovers are halves of a once-single entity seeking to reunite with their other half, *erōs* seems one-sided. One of the halves of the homosexual original is an *erastēs* and does all the work, the other is *philerastēs,* "one who loves [*philein*] the one in love."[53]

Before we try to solve this puzzle let's have a look at this *erastēs,* plural *erastai:* "lover," "admirer," "an adherent of," "eager for," "fond," suggests my dictionary. The first thing to observe is that originally the word appears to have been a specifically Athenian ("Attic") term; other Greeks had other words for perhaps rather different roles, but since the Attic dialect predominates in so much Greek literature (which is why we refer to Poseidon not Potidas, Potoidan or Pohoidan, Zeus not Zas, Zan or Tan, Dionysus not Zonnyssus) we find these Athenian terms *erastēs* and *erōmenos* cropping up in accounts of same-sex *erōs* in, say, Thespiae and Sparta, words that may well have fitted local roles and practices imperfectly.

The second thing is that, whatever the terminology, there are two quite distinct types of *erastai* and two quite distinct kinds of Greek Loving:

1 The Wolf-Pack *erastai,* who are represented as Multiple Groupies or Fans or Pests or Suitors competing in their devotions displayed to a boy—the most absurdly flattering songs, the most extravagant promises, the biggest bunches of flowers; and
2 The Chosen One, the Winner, the Special or Super-*erastēs,* who gets to accompany the boy to athletics meetings—his Sponsor, his publicly recognized Other Half.

The former type, Type 1, Fans or Admirers, is by far the most numerous and appears soonest in the literature, albeit quite late, in the fifth century BC. But just as Eros is not necessarily amorous, so even among these *erastai* "admirers of boys in particular" are at first in a minority. One of the earliest examples of the word in literature came, supposedly, from the mouth of Athens's greatest statesman, Pericles, in 430 BC, when he delivered an oration for those who had died in the first full year of Athens's exhausting war with Sparta. In this speech, says Thucydides, Pericles invited her citizens to be *erastai* of Athens, i.e. "filled with love" for their city.[54]

After Pericles' "Athens-lovers" we get "war-lovers," and a couple of ambitious "lovers of tyranny." An "*erastēs* of children," in Euripides, is no pedophile but someone "eager for" sons,[55] while an *erastēs* of "things people are up to" in Aristophanes is another word for an informer or a "busybody."[56] Pericles' use of the word in the Funeral Speech gives us some idea of what it means to be an *erastēs*. It seems he was asking the surviving soldiers to demonstrate *uncalculating* devotion and heroic self-sacrifice on Athens's behalf. This is a central motif in the literature of *erōs*. Achilles in the *Iliad,* throwing himself back into battle and certain death for his beloved Patroclus's sake, was the example that sprang most readily to mind, and in Athens they would also find their thoughts turning to one Aristogiton, who gave his life to avenge an insult against his boyfriend's family during the dark years of the sixth-century dictatorship. The loving pair received heroic honors in the very town center. At Thespiae in Eros's hometown, they might rather think of Menestratus, whose *erōmenos,* an ephebe, was about to be offered to a giant snake which was terrorizing the city. He offered to go in his place but first covered himself in fishhooks so that the monster when he swallowed him would also die. He saved the city through his sacrifice, and his strange armor, was, it seems, commemorated in the cult statue of Zeus Savior.[57]

If the admirer gazes on a youth with passionate devotion, the loved one, in this case the city of Athens, is watching him from a distance and expects him to display no signs of unmanly cowardice such as a wound in the back as he flees, though even the bravest *erastēs* might trip and fall and end up, horror of horrors, lying facedown on the ground: "Do not inflict a shameful and cowardly wound, but strike me in front on the chest, lest my beloved [*erōmenos*] convict me of cowardice and be wary of laying out my corpse."[58] What Thucydides' "Pericles" is trying to say by urging citizens to fight like *erastai,* like *men hopelessly in love with* their city, is not terribly difficult to understand.

That does not mean it is not a striking metaphor. It implies a strange—for the Greeks a very strange—distance between citizens and their own community, as if she is a remote object of fantasy. Pericles is asking for that servile-looking but honorable and competitive devotion typical of *erastai*. "Serve your country," says Pericles, in the nicest possible way, beginning to look a little like Lord Kitchener or Uncle Sam staring and pointing on a recruitment poster, though in this case the poster would show an image not of Pericles but of Pericles' brand-new Acropolis in all her white and gold splendor with little Cupids fluttering around the columns and pediments. Before citizens sharing in a community became subjects of an abstract nation-state, they first, it seems, became subjects of love for "her."

The object of a passionate admirer's love is called an *erōmenos* or, if the object is female *erōmenē*, a passive participle of the verb *eran*, "to be in love with," i.e., "hopelessly loved one," "someone someone is enamored of," or according to Suda, a Byzantine encyclopedia, "the one doted on [*agopōmenos*] by *erastai*," usually translated by modern authors as "beloved," though that perhaps implies too proprietorial a relationship. It is significant I think that neither of these words, *erastēs/erōmenos*, used by the Athenians for those entangled in Love's nets sounds terribly technical or specialized. For it seems there were indeed specialized terms in other cities, notably in Sparta, Crete and Thessaly.

Since an *erastēs* is nothing more than someone in love with someone, it is perfectly possible that the one he is in love with, the *erōmenos*, would be completely unaware of his devotion. So Plato has no problem with the concept of a "secret admirer," a crypto-*erastēs* who tries to seduce a boy by pretending not to be an *erastēs*, although he really is![59] In another dialogue Plato describes a young *erastēs* who watches his beloved talking to Socrates, from the back of the crowd. He may be thoroughly passionate but he is clearly a very distant admirer. Indeed it is not at all sure that the Boy really knows what his admirer is going through. For although he has bored his friends to distraction, the *erastēs* tries to conceal the nature of his obsession from the Boy himself, lest he take offense. When it looks as if Socrates is on the verge of giving the game away—"my friend fancies you and has been writing songs about you"—and bringing him into the conversation, the *erastēs* is contorted with anguish. Socrates realizes just in time that it would have been a big mistake and passes on.[60] Sometimes, then, it seems the relationship between an *erōmenos* and his admirers is rather like that between a sports star and fans, an image plastered over the bedroom walls of the soul. Being an admirer in these cases involves a certain amount of conspicuous action, performing a particular social role. So Narcissus's admirers could cease "making love" (*erōntes*), not of course cease "having sex with" the chaste youth, nor even cease "being in love with him," but "cease their amatory practices." And the Athenians could pass a law forbidding slaves "being in love" (*eran*) with free boys, which sounds nonsensical until you realize that what was being forbidden was certain kinds of visible behavior.[61] Likewise when Xenophon spits venom at the gorgeously handsome Meno of Thessaly who had the audacity to be *erastēs* of someone with a beard, he means that Meno "performed the role of an *erastēs*," i.e., pursued and courted him and bought him presents.[62]

Hopefully, however, one of the admirers will defeat his rivals and be offered the chance to develop a one-to-one relationship with the boy, sometimes clearly establishing a publicly recognized partnership. In Crete the titles *philetor* and *kleinos* ("famed") were formally awarded on conclusion of a wedding ceremony to the admirer and the admired, respectively. In Sparta and Thessaly, home of Achilles and Patroclus, the respective terms were *eispnelas*, "inhaler" (?), and *aïtas*, "breeze" (?).[63] But it isn't clear what words in Athens might distinguish this new stage in the relationship—"boyfriends," "partners"—from more distant admirings. When Thucydides wants to emphasize that the relationship between the so-called tyrant-slayers Harmodius and Aristogiton went further than mere pursuit he says: "Aristogiton was Harmodius's *erastēs* and had him."[64] What does he mean? The dictionary suggests it's the same use of "have" that you find when Greeks talk of married couples: "have to wife or as husband." So when the tyrant's brother "made a pass" at the boy, Aristogiton was "enraged in the manner of one passionately in love [*erōtikōs*]."

In other versions of the tale, Harmodius is a kind of acolyte of Aristogiton, and is called his *paidika*.[65] *Paidika*, "favorite" or "darling," can be used of males or females (it is in fact a neuter plural, cf. "babes"!) and seems almost synonymous with *erōmenos/ē*, although it may be more specific, identifying a more intimate kind of relationship. Plato describes Agathon, "barely Eighteen," as Pausanias's *paidika*, at the start of a relationship that will last decades. The orator Lysias, a very mature man, is described as Phaedrus's *paidika,* while the orator Isocrates, who was probably in his twenties, is described as the *paidika* of Socrates. I don't think we should imagine there is any particular sexual relationship implied in either case. Socrates and Phaedrus are "passionate fans" of each writer, as the Byzantine encyclopedia points out.[66]

Possibly one term used for those in a relationship was *hetairos,* "comrade," "companion," although it is a very common word and can mean merely "associate." Patroclus is Achilles's "dear companion" and the early poet Theognis complains about the deceitfulness of a boy "whom I thought out of all men I would make my faithful companion" (*hetairos pistos*); now the very sight of him should put men off the love of boys (*paidophilein*). A woman, on the other hand, can never have a "faithful companion"; instead she is destined "ever to love [*philein*] the man who is around."[67] Socrates summarizes his lifetime hobby of " 'erotik' acquisition of friends" by calling himself "lover of companions," *philetairos.* Aeschines describes the whorish collusion between Timarchus and his boyfriend as "in the manner of loving companions" (*philetairōs*). Although in most cases there is no obvious sexual or even amorous connotation to the word *hetairos,* nevertheless it is the masculine form of *hetaira,* "courtesan," and the verb formed from it, *hetaireō,* almost always implies not just a sexual relationship but mercenary sex, "work as a (hired) escort."[68] There may be a hint at this mercenariness when Jesus calls Judas *hetairos* (normally translated "Friend") when he kisses him and betrays him for money.[69]

Understanding the connotations of *hetairos* becomes important if we are looking at the longevity of same-sex relationships ("boyfriends" may often be hiding behind neutral-sounding terms like "friends" and "companions"), or indeed the antiquity of the phenomenon itself. For *hetairos* has a much longer pedigree than terms such as *erastēs:* "Don't treat your companion as equal to your brother," Hesiod advises his less than brotherly brother Perses in *Works and Days.* "And if you do . . ." This *hetairos* sounds already very much like a one-and-only: "Status as *hetairos* appears to be a rather formal matter and one that can approach the intimacy and commitment expected of kin."[70] Already, then, around 680 BC, we have a formal same-sex relationship on Helicon, and it would not be surprising to learn that the local god, Eros, was already playing an important part in making it happen.

CUPID'S BOW

But why did the Greeks feel so strongly that *erōs* was only for the *erastēs*? First, we need to bear in mind that *erōs* involves some kind of a distance *from* an object of love, an impulse to move *toward* it. His wings are emblematic. The figures who have wings in Greek art are often messengers or movers: the winds, swift Hermes, god of travel, Iris the rainbow, messenger between heaven and earth, the randy goddess Dawn who sweeps across the sky and swoops down on unwitting huntsmen. The wings of Eros put him in the same class of movers and shakers. We are not talking about the kind of permanent, stable, intimate love you have for your mother or your husband or your pet cat; this is not the love of "I love you"; it's a love that sweeps you off your feet.

Greek conveys this sense of distance by putting a genitive ending on the object in question, *-ēs, -ou, -idos, -atos,* making it an "indirect object," the same genitive ending that is used for verbs of, e.g., tasting, smelling, hearing.[71] English, which long ago pushed nearly all of these accusatives and indirect genitives into retirement, can convey that sense of distance by means of fussy prepositions, longing *for,* attraction *toward,* enamored *of.* But we retain a trace of these indirect objects in the case of personal pronouns, so a brutal translation of Greek expressions of such verbs would be not "I love him," "She loves me," "I smelled him," "She heard me," but "I smelled of him," "She heard of me," "I love of him," "She loves of me."

Since antiquity, linguists have been puzzled by this linguistic peculiarity and wondered what it said about the nature of *erōs.* In 1905, Basil Lanneau Gildersleeve, who had fought on horseback for the Confederates in the American Civil War, and lost his horse and his pocket Homer in the course of it, wondered if something as dry as syntax might not provide insights into psychology. He drew attention to an interesting passage in an ancient treatise "On Syntax" by the little-read ancient philologist known as Bad-Tempered Apollonius (Dyscolus). "To see" took a direct object ("an accusative"), whereas other verbs of sensing took an indirect object, he observed. It was because seeing was vigorously active. You could shut out the affecting object by closing your eyes; you could, if you wanted, refuse to see. The subject was not such a master of his other senses—the noises that filled his ears, the smells that encroached upon his nostrils; in these cases he was (kind of) passive.[72] Apollonius then went on to consider the verb "to be in love," *eran;* it was more like smelling than seeing, putting the admirer in a quasi-passive role: "Everyone knows that being in love means being affected [*to prosdiatithesthai*] by the *erōmenos.*"[73] You cannot simply refuse to be in love, close your heart. Love is like a deafening noise that keeps you awake, or an overwhelming smell. It is not like a brilliant spectacle you might nevertheless fall asleep in front of.

This notion that the *erastēs* is essentially a passive victim who "just can't help himself" is central to the understanding of how Greek Love functions and how it was understood by contemporaries: the *erastēs* is "in a state of dependency," "hung up" on someone.[74] Indeed, following his discussion of *himeros* as an emanation that "pours forth" from the object, like a sound or a perfume, Socrates offers an etymology of *erōs* from *esrei* because it " 'flows in' [*es*, "into," *rei*, "flows"] from without." The *erastēs* is "penetrated," if you like, by Eros's arrows, breath and streams.[75]

But as regards the grammar, modern linguists tend to take a different tack and refer rather to the concept of targeting rather than passivity, observing that an indirect object is also used for verbs of aiming at, hitting upon, thirsting for, starving after. They put the indirect senses in the same category: hearing (catching the sound of), smelling (catching the scent of). Most often *eran,* "being in love with," is included with other verbs of "aiming at" or "throwing a spear at" someone, like Hadrian "hitting his she-bear from horseback," a "genitive of the end desired," and sometimes these are all grouped alongside verbs of "reaching" and "attaining," as an example of the "genitive of the goal," whether desired or attained. There is a difference between "I love you" and "I am in love *with* you," and the difference is a degree of separation.[76]

It is not true of the very earliest Greek literature, Homer's *Iliad,* but certainly true thereafter, that Eros must have plenty of space to fly in. And so begins the endless saga of love's long relationship with frustration, the object of love two steps ahead of his admirers, who follow impatiently behind. This element of tantalizing distance in *erōs,* ever on the verge, is reflected in countless poems and speeches and texts, which have hardly gone unnoticed by readers. In her essay on *Eros: The Bittersweet,* Anne Carson introduces the idea in a chapter called "The Reach" with a song in which, it seems, Sappho compared a girl, a bride, possibly, to an apple . . .

> As a sweet apple turns red on a high branch,
> high on the highest branch and the applepickers forgot—
> well, no they didn't forget—were not able to reach . . .

. . . (her translation). She analyzes the form of the song: "Desiring hands close on empty air in the final infinitive, while the apple of their eye dangles perpetually inviolate two lines above." "Eros has no pleasure in what's ready to hand," says Xenophon, "but in what is hoped for."[77]

Distance is a theme of more than one of the speeches about Love, made on that cold February night of 416 BC in the playwright Agathon's house, which Plato describes in the *Symposium*. There are even suggestions that distance from the object *defines erōs;* he is therefore the very opposite of intimacy. Most famous is the speech of Aristophanes describing how Eros was invented through an act of separation, by splitting four-legged humans into two sections, each half then roaming the world in search of its lost other half, a love that even sexual intercourse cannot quite satisfy, that will only be perfectly satisfied when a god stands over the bed and merges them into one body again, erasing distance completely. In Hesiod's *Theogony* fourth-born Eros's role in creation is not to bring together for reproduction but to separate in the first place the primordial undifferentiated entities of the universe, like a butterfly making room to spread its wings.[78] *Erōs* often seems most spectacular in the context of bereavement.

Absence is also a theme of Socrates' speech in the *Symposium,* which emphasizes the gulf between Eros and what he desires, his lack of ownership; indeed he is the child not of Aphrodite, but of Poverty, says Socrates, for you can only desire things you do not already possess; you cannot want your cake and have it. Apart from anything else Eros needs space to be able to use his equipment, the bow and arrow that he shoots *from afar,* and the goad that gets someone *on the road to somewhere.* That *erōs* is defined by separation from the object of love is illustrated most succinctly perhaps by the goddess Athena at the end of Aeschylus's *Oresteia.* The vengeful Furies, the dread goddesses, who have been harrying Orestes all over Greece are offered a stark choice by Athens's patron deity: either they can behave and settle down in Athens as friends, or they can leave and go elsewhere and "be this here country's lovelorn admirers," "*tēs gēs tēsd'erasthēsesthe*."[79] *Erōs* is a kind of purgatory.

We can differentiate among the three passions, therefore, in terms of space and time. If *himeros* is a sprinter over short distances, a hummingbird, and *pothos* is an emperor penguin waiting in Antarctica for the return of his mate, *erōs* occupies the middle distance, a hawk. It is much more focused than *pothos,* much more sustained than *himeros*. This is the real knot at the heart of Cupid's bow. This is the big perplexity. On the one hand the *himeros*-aspect, the mouth-watering palpitating chest-compressing reason-confounding excitement you get at the prospect of something within reach, and on the other hand the *pothos*-aspect, the gaze across miles of space and memory and social gap toward a handsome athlete or the beautiful powerful city of Athens and its temple-topped hill.

The best way to reconcile these two elements of intensity and distance, a lover's *violent* admiration of his love object, is to think of a powerful magnet, separated from a hunk of metal. When they are stuck together you cannot see the magnetic force between them, nor can you see it if they are held at a great distance apart, but you can see it if you bring the magnet close enough to feel a certain pull, and then watch the metal move across the table. Now just before the metal meets the magnet, move the magnet away, keeping just enough distance between them. That's the best way, turn down the lights, to see little Eros in three dimensions. For Cupid is not consummation, the thwack of an arrow in a target, genital acts. He thrives on distances. He's the arrow's trajectory, the climber straining for the summit. He is forever swooping over the highest mountains, the lowest valleys, and rivers not quite wide enough. He's the force you can feel in a piece of elastic. He's essentially an intermediary, says Socrates. He's like an angel between loving heaven and beloved earth. He's the force that shrinks the distance in between.

That's one reason why it sounds odd in classical Greek for an object of love to reciprocate *erōs,* even for the two halves of Aristophanes' made-for-each-other couples. In Greek Love one member of the future couple, the *erastēs,* has to do all the running. The other stays at home, completely motionless, rooted to the spot, erotically quite passive, waiting for the knock at the door, although of course it wasn't unknown for some

young men to behave coquettishly, to bow their heads modestly while
batting their eyelashes, which might jeopardize their reputation.

The other reason Eros is so one-sided is that he is always represented
as a High Drama, an "Oh No! Here we go again. Saddle up. Gird your
loins" kind of passion, hammers and anvils, a heat hot enough to melt
metals, and then a sudden chill as the hot metal is plunged in water, and
the water hisses and seethes. This is especially striking in Athenian court
cases, where we sometimes find a defendant or a plaintiff standing up
and talking of passion for a boy in open court. You don't have to be too
much of a homoskeptic to observe that it is often very convenient for
the speaker to have been robbed of his senses by Love at this particular
juncture, for this is why he didn't examine the contract very carefully. It
seems as if the speaker expects the audience of citizens to nod in agreement: "Oh he didn't really want to buy the shop, he just wanted to get
his hands on the shop assistant. That explains everything."[80] It is in this
context that we find one of my favorite Greek verbs, *katapepaiderastēke-
nai,* "to have squandered an estate through hopeless devotion to boys."[81]
Erōs and sound finances do not mix. In that respect it has something in
common with the ruinous competitive generosity of what anthropologists call potlatch. An *erastēs* with a calculator and good sense is not the
real McCoy.

Erōs is always represented as a Great Big Deal, therefore. It implies an
energy-consuming project, an enterprising journey of the soul, and that
trip won't be made on a donkey's back, but in a racing-chariot down a
highway. Thucydides describes the Athenians as filled with *erōs* as they
set out to conquer Sicily. It is perfectly appropriate that the Cretans and
Spartans sacrificed to Eros before they went into battle or into war.[82] He
is an expeditionary force, a Ferrari inside you.

It would be comical rather than romantic if, once you had completed
the journey and arrived at the door of the loved, he immediately started
revving up his own Ferrari with the same insane and energetic passion
for you. Where is his highway? Where is he to go? *Erōs* reciprocated
would conjure up images of two people carrying a torch for each other,
returning obsessions in kind; they camp out on each other's doorstep,
wait outside the changing rooms for each other to emerge, beg each
other for a kiss. One may as well expect a star to return a fan's adoration,
a rabbit to turn on a fox and chase it to its lair, a crystal-clear jug of water

to match the thirst of the mouth that drinks from it—the comedy of Narcissus. *Erōs* can indeed be reciprocated; it is just that when that happens, by the very fact of reciprocation, *erōs* becomes something else.

PHILIA

When an *erōmenos* gets friendly we are in the territory that belongs to *philia,* intimacy, mates. Indeed French scholars often refer to "Greek Homosexuality" as "Homophilia." *Philia* is often translated as "friendship" and it does entail much of the niceness and mildness that we associate with friendliness, but it is not "friendship" in our sense of "just good friends"; that doesn't seem to be a category the Greeks cared very much about defining. *Philia* includes all close relationships, family members, business partners, coevals, dear ones and lovers, as well as friends, although as we might have come to expect, English "friends" used to cover the same range. *Philotēs* in Homer is how he indicates "loving," i.e., sexual intercourse, but all these different types of closeness make it very difficult to tell whether or not sex is involved in any particular relationship of *philia.* The problem is apparent in its English derivatives. Philadelphia is the city of "brotherly love," not incestuous sex; neither a "necrophiliac" nor a "pedophile" is supposed to be interested in mere friendship; yet a philatelist doesn't want to make love to his stamps, nor a philologist to words. There again, though, a philanderer seeks something more than just holding hands.

So in Crete the *erastēs* is entitled *philētor,* "lover," after he has succeeded in abducting an admired youth and the youth has publicly agreed to the association; no modern scholar thinks this is an asexual relationship. *Philia* is what the two slices of Aristophanes' couple have when they physically connect;[83] Aphrodite "loves" (*philei*) her adulterous lover Ares, thus dishonoring her husband Hephaestus, and the courtesan Theodote describes the men we might think of as her "clients" as *philoi*—"friendlies." The same word *philia* is used of the devoted love of a wife for her husband. Occasionally writers make it a bit easier for us by qualifying *philia* with *erōtikē,* to specify a love-derived relationship.[84]

Of course, as Bad-Tempered Apollonius observed, unlike *erōs, philia* takes a direct object, like looking, because it is reasonable, rational and self-possessed, and indicates not a crazed involuntary dependency on a loved object but an active direct engagement with the beloved, e.g., in "teaching" him. *Philein* is the word you use if you want to say "I love you"—*philō se*. As in English, a child can use it of a parent and a parent of a child. *Philein* can also refer not just to love but to loving, being friendly with someone, being fond with someone, "making love" in the old-fashioned sense, performing deeds of intimate acquaintanceship, as in Elvis Presley's "more often than I should." "I am sure you know how *to be a lover* [*philein*]," says Socrates to the courtesan Theodote, "with both softness and sincerity."[85] So Solon's *paidophilein* does not mean "being just good friends with a boy," nor does it mean "falling in love with a boy and writing songs about him . . ." but "*making love to* a boy," "spending intimate moments with a boy" and that includes, we recall, "*being attacked with desire for* [*himeirōn*] thighs and sweet-tasting mouth."[86]

There is nothing intrinsically "pure" or unerotic, therefore, about "*philia.*" *Erōs* indeed can be called "hunting for intimates [*philoi*]," and a history of "*philia*" that excludes *erōs* is a waste of time. The "official school definition" of *erōs* among the Stoics was "friends-making impulse" (*epibolē philopoiias*), and Roman Cicero calls "Greek Homosexuality" *amor amicitiae,* not "love of friendship" but an "*erōs* for *philia,*" "a drive to establish intimate relationships."[87] Again, classicists often forget this, so that translations are littered with misleading "friendships" that are in context "intimacies" or even "loving relationships," and "friends" who are in fact "lovers."[88]

Loving someone does not give you the same drama, the sleepless nights, the obsession, the energy etc., that you can anticipate from being *in love* with someone. But although *erōs* is more dangerously violent than *philia,* it is a mistake to think, as some do, that *philia* is halfhearted, or, worse, that one of these is hot lust and the other is cold sexless friendship. They are two completely different things. *Erōs* is an ambition, *philia* is a relationship. *Erōs* is driving force, *philia* is where you are driving to. *Philia* is what you feel for your own dear husband, *erōs* is what you feel for that man who just moved in across the road. We can see the difference being maintained, even much later, in love spells from Egypt. "*Erōs*" spells are designed to provoke movement, to get someone on the road to a new relationship, often to give a woman such burning passion and insomnia that she leaves her home, even her husband and children, and finds her way to the house of the spell-caster. Note that even here the one-way principle persists. One person, the spell's victim, the woman, does all the running, the other, the hexer, simply waits for a knock on the door. They are nasty tormenting spells designed to burn and goad the victim, close to the spells that are used to curse enemies, sometimes making use of voodoo dolls. "*Philia*" spells are much nicer and are designed to stop a partner, usually a man, a husband, lover or boss, from being angry with you, or to restore the quality of loving affection to a relationship already in existence. They resemble spells for healing or warding off evil.[89]

We can see this difference of tone in a line of Plato. The secret admirer, the crypto-*erastēs,* has hatched a cunning plan to steal a march on a posse of rival *erastai* by denigrating their *erōs,* which is really, he claims, just a kind of mindless hunger or lust, and does not include kindliness (*eunoia*) toward the boy: "*Erastai* getting friendly with [*philousin*] a boy is like wolves doting on [*agapōsin*] lambs."[90] We can also see the difference when authors talk of love for different types of action. "I love playing tennis" is *philein,* which means you are *fond of* doing something or just *tend* to do something, something habitual. You would never use *erōs* in this way. An *erōs* for *doing* something involves a much more enterprising and ambitious venture, a grand project.

Contrary to what Plato's crypto-*erastēs* cynically claims when he compares *erastai* to wolves, there is supposed to be no stronger relationship than the *philia* of an *erastēs* and an *erōmenos* once the *erōmenos* has decided to engage. Men who pursue a Boy under Eighteen should be punished by law, says Pausanias in the *Symposium,* for they cannot be interested in his personality since it hasn't formed properly, just his passing youthful attractions. Men who wait (as he did for Agathon, just) until a Boy is fully grown, i.e., Eighteen, show instead that they are planning to "share a life together," joined "all life long" (as indeed he was with Agathon). It is this adamantine *philia* of mutual affection, this "solidarity" (*koinōnia*) "which *erōs* above all implants," that terrifies tyrants and makes the Theban Army of Lovers as solid as a rock.[91]

LUSTING AFTER *EPITHUMIA*

If you are "in love with" a woman or a man it can be safely assumed, normally, that you want intimacy with them, physical intimacy. But although we all know that "to be in love with" is not the same as "to desire sex with," it can be hard to tell if someone who claims to be in love with another just wants sex. It can even be hard to tell the difference when you are talking about yourself—"I thought I was in love with him, but I now realize it was only lust." The word "lust" in the King James Version of the Bible never corresponds to Greek *erōs,* but to *epithumia,* "desire," and its relatives.

The Greeks were generally no more consistent than we are in distinguishing love from desire, but occasionally some of them felt a need to look more closely. Aristotle came up with a couple of ways to tell the two apart. Point one: You can be "in love with someone," *eran,* to a greater or lesser degree, i.e., you can be insanely in love with someone, or just passionately in love. Also you can have *epithumia,* "lust" to a greater or lesser degree—anything from wildly randy to mildly interested. Moreover, continues the great philosopher, being in love and desiring sex can often go together. However, someone who is more madly in love does not necessarily have an increased desire for sex, and someone with an increased desire for sex is not necessarily more in love. Since lust and love can increase or decrease independently of one another, they cannot be one and the same.

Elsewhere he uses *erōs* to demonstrate a piece of logic. This example depends on the assumption that an *erastēs* really wants a "favorable response" from his adored youth, rather than sex itself. Every single man in love (*pas erōn*), he says, in accord with his *erōs,* would always prefer to meet with a disposition "to favor" (*charizesthai*) that is not realized, rather than a reluctance "to favor," that nevertheless is. Therefore in affairs of *erōs* a "disposition to favor" is preferred to "favoring" per se.

To put some flesh on this abstract piece of logic, what Aristotle seems to be saying is that an *erastēs* would always prefer it if (a) a young man responds to all his wooing and moves his lips closer, opening up the possibility of months or years of amorousness, even if nothing happens (maybe at just that point his father walks in), rather than if (b) the young man is clearly not at all enthusiastic but nevertheless consents. Aristotle simply assumes that this would always be the case, because of the nature of *erōs.* Therefore, he concludes, in the case of *erōs,* being loved (*phileisthai*) is preferable to intercourse (*sunousia*). *Erōs* therefore has more to do with *philia,* "intimate love," than "having intercourse" (*suneinai*), which means that *philia* is the "objective" (*telos*) of *erōs,* while *suneinai* has nothing to do with the objectives of *erōs,* or rather it is only an objective inasmuch as it is a part of "being loved."[92] In other words, when it comes to sex between true lovers, it is the thought that counts.

We didn't really need Aristotle to tell us that there is a difference between being in love and desiring sex, although we also know that they might be hard to distinguish in practice. Nevertheless it is important to keep in mind the very specific and peculiar character of the phenomenon of Greek Love. We can safely assume, I think, that there was plenty of gay sex in antiquity that did not involve all the song and dance associated with *erōs.* We can even assume there was plenty of homo-love and homo-besottedness that was less formal and conspicuous. Was every gay relationship in Crete announced by means of negotiations, a two-month-long ritual abduction, the exchange of extravagant presents and the sacrifice of an ox? Was there never an occasion when someone fell in love and got it on with someone in his own year-group, especially if they were all living and sleeping together? For that reason alone, as a cultural phenomenon, a historical Thing, Greek Love is not the same as Ancient Greek Homo Sexual Behavior, or Ancient Greek Homo Sexual Desire. It doesn't even cover all Ancient Greek Homosexual Passions or Attachments, just the noisy ones and/or those that follow the rules.

On the other hand, on rare occasions an ancient author feels the need to present us with a Greek Love that has *nothing* to do with sexual lust. Xenophon, for instance, seems to claim that young Spartan men pursued "doting," fatherlike, strictly "hands-off" loves for boys, but nevertheless these relationships seem very much a part of Greek Love, and indeed Xenophon makes the claim as part of a discussion of what he calls *paidikoi erōtes,* "loves for boys."[93] Few believe him about the lustlessness, exactly as Xenophon anticipated, but the point is not whether or not his claim is true. What is striking is that Xenophon not only talks of an *erōs* that does not include penetration—there are lots of cases of *erastai* who, like Narcissus's admirers, aren't getting any—and even of "lovers" who somehow manage to restrain themselves, given an opportunity—for there are some famous cases of that also, the Platonic Love of Socrates lying chastely alongside the gorgeous and clearly up-for-it Alcibiades— the point is that a Greek of the classical period can talk of an *erōs* in which there is not only no sex and no attempt at sex, but no physical interest, a passionate yet chaste admiration for a young man's beautiful personality, and errr . . . impressive muscular development . . .

Xenophon's *paidikos erōs,* as pure as a family relationship, is not without its paradoxical elements—an *erōs* for, a "passionate love for," your brother or your son would set anybody's alarm bells ringing, and elsewhere he implies that you cannot have *erōs* within a family: you can stop yourself falling in love with your own daughter; therefore you can stop yourself falling in love.[94] But the point is not that when ancient authors claim that *erōs* for boys is perfectly chaste they are being false or hypocritical; what matters is that such a claim is possible in the first place; it is not a contradiction in terms. In these limit cases it is impossible to translate *erōs* as "exclusive and obsessive lust" as some would like, for that is no way for a father to feel toward his son, or a brother toward a brother, not even in ancient Greece.[95]

This is why, following John Addington Symonds, I have chosen to call the subject of this book "Greek Love." For the phenomenon we are talking about is first and foremost what belongs to the realm of Cupid, Greek Eros, i.e., *falling* in love with a member of the same sex, and, one might add, making a great big song and dance about it; for whatever "it" is, it belongs in the first place to public spaces, not to the bedroom or behind the bushes.[96] One should never confuse Eros with his mother, Aphrodite, who is so closely connected to sex that sex is called "the things of Aphrodite," *ta aphrodisia.* "The work of Aphrodite can be bought for a drachma," but money can't buy you love.[97] "Greek Homobesottedness" would give a more accurate impression of how the phenomenon manifests itself, though it would fit less neatly on a title page.

In fact there is a major problem with the sexual connotations that "erotic" or "erotica" have acquired in English over the last hundred and fifty years, due to the influence of the *érotiques* French; it used to be perfectly proper in English to entitle a collection of sweet little love poems "Erotica"; "erotic" just meant "to do with love." Since the shift in meaning occurred, however, the Greek words *erōtikos* and *erōtika* have become "false friends"; they sound as if they are all about sex, sex, sex, and we have to make a real effort to remember that they are in fact all about love, love, love. A work of literature called *erōtikos* or *erōtika* is a disquisition about Love, and Socrates is the archetype of the *erōtikos* man because he is permanently besotted (with knowledge, with handsome young men) and never manages to achieve a finality, not because he was "an erotic philosopher" in the modern sense of the term—someone who converses about sex, or who gives lectures wearing fishnet stockings and a red silk basque. It sounds obvious, but you'd be surprised how many classicists make that mistake.

What has drawn attention to the Greeks down the ages is the demonstrations, sometimes very noisy and theatrical, of "can't help myself, want you and nobody else"—devotion toward a particular youth or young man and the attachments, *philias,* that arise, hopefully, from such humiliating endeavors. Now, such a performance might well end up in the bedroom, though sex could never, looking at the record, be something you could confidently book into your diary. Moreover, despite the halfhearted protestations of later fourth-century authors—Plato, Xenophon, Ephorus—the "beauty" (*kallos*) of the boy or girl was almost always mentioned as the major factor in the contracting of a homolovesickness. But sex itself belonged to quite a different field from published Love. It belonged to the area of life that Xenophon calls the *aphanē,* the realm of the "invisible."[98]

GRACE, SEX AND FAVORS

THE MYSTERIES OF *CHARIS*—GRACE[1]

The word normally used to denote a boy giving a positive response to all the importuning is *charizesthai,* normally translated "to favor." It is formed from a word—*charis*—which has a long and very extensive career in Greek literature, especially the literature of Piety, Sport, Politics and Love; a proper understanding of all that *charis* implies will take you a long way in understanding many of the mysteries of Greek Love, its ethics and its exalted position in Greek society. It is a word we can still recognize in charisma and Eucharist and, for those who have visited modern Greece, *efcharistō*: "much obliged." *Charis* was in turn formed from the verb *chairō,* "rejoice," "hello." It is the *charis* of the "Hail Mary, blessed art thou," *Chaire kecharitōmenē.*[2] The Romans translated *charis* as *gratia*—*"Ave Maria gratia plena,"* cf. *gracias, grazie, gratis*—and in English versions of the Bible it is often translated as "grace." *Charis* is the stuff and nonsense of protocols and politesse, or the nice gesture that costs you nothing and makes someone happy; it is ingratiation or karma, humbug or what makes the world go round. Of the ancient Greek version a recent study concludes: "*Charis* is, then, an adornment of social relationships or moral qualities—gold on silver, as Homer said, or the icing on the cake, as we might say. But as adornment it is functional, not superfluous and merely decorative. The pleasure of *charis* is the spur to social activity, the engine of morality, the reward of altruism."[3]

By grace of the Greeks, *charis* is an essential element in any understanding of Christianity. But Greek *charis* is alien to a hierarchical, institutionalized, rules-and-regulations religion like Christianity, which imported this fundamentally here-and-now-oriented entity, essentially a lubricant in ongoing relations between gods and men, into a fundamentally hereafter-oriented cult. Greek *charis* bounces around in multiple exchanges over time of gifts, gifts of sacrifice, statues, plays, dances, hymns etc. It looks both ways, both *in return for* and *in anticipation of* divine favors, thus establishing a meaningful and consequential relationship with gods *in the present,* which is simply a metaphysical version of the whole interplay of relationships of kindness and faith that you establish with other people.[4] The Christian architecture of time that leaves the present as a humble zone between two grand precipices, an original Fall from *Charis* and a Final Settling of Accounts, finds no room for a meaningful ongoing relationship of faith in God in the here and now, inasmuch as it believes in the omniscience of a totalizing God who knows both past and future in every detail, and insists on the supreme importance of the final tally of debits and credits, thereby undermining the "logic of practice," i.e., the way things actually work from day to day, rather as if a friend were on his deathbed to present you with a comprehensive list of everything he had done for you and everything you had done for him, the prices of all the presents he had given you and those he had received, and then to suggest that if he wrote you a check for such and such a sum, he could call it quits. It would misconstrue the whole relationship, the basis on which you had done those acts of kindness and chosen those presents. Although the ledger might be accurate, it would be a false accounting nevertheless, simply by the fact of accounting. It is precisely because there is no possibility of any great checkout at the end of time, because ancient *charis* is never finally to be accounted for, that it is done for no *specific* return, and because no one knows what will happen in the future, that it can be described as "the engine of morality," i.e., the foundation of free ethical responsibility. Christians may consider the heathen amoral inasmuch as they fear no payback in Purgatory; the Greeks would consider Christians amoral precisely because they do.

True, there is an essential ambivalence or mystery at the heart of the Greek concept of grace, but it is a useful and limited ambivalence, dependent on and productive of a localized faith, faith that the gods will respond eventually, that your kindnesses to other people will be returned somewhere along the line. But such an evanescent concept is ill-suited to dogmatic religions: there can be no "doctrine of *charis*." Meanwhile, in the poem he wrote to accompany his dedication at Thespiae, *charis* is the stuff that Hadrian wants his god, chaste Eros, who dwells by the garden of Narcissus, to be breathing over him in return for the head of the she-bear, "the *charis* that comes from Celestial Aphrodite."

The goddesses who presided over the domain of *charis* in antiquity were the *Charites,* who enjoyed a very ancient cult with an important festival in the polity of Orchomenus, not far from Thespiae on the other side of the marshy Copaic lake. During George Wheler's visit in the seventeenth century the lake was whirring with all kinds of waterfowl, in antiquity it was famous for its eels, but now the lake has drained away and you would be lucky to see a duck.[5] The *Charites* are none other than the Three Graces, but at Orchomenus they were worshipped in the form, not of the three fine ladies made famous by Canova and others, but (like their associate, Heliconian Eros) as lumps of rock, rocks that once had fallen like meteorites out of a cloudless sky and landed right at the king of Orchomenus's feet.[6]

Three lumps might seem a very precise way to think of qualities that seem extremely difficult to pin down, and the *Oxford English Dictionary* groups its innumerable definitions of "grace" under three main headings. Which one of these three graces did Hadrian want Eros to breathe over him?

Lump One is the grace you say before a meal, "thankfulness," "gratitude," so someone who receives a present and tosses it to one side may be considered to have received it gracelessly.[7] So perhaps Hadrian is asking Eros to make him truly thankful for something he is about to receive or has already received. Lump Two is the grace of "favor." Perhaps it is a favor that Hadrian wants from gracious Eros? We should note that both these kinds of grace belong to those exchanges between gods and people or people and people, whether givers or receivers, which are characterized by kindness not contract. *Charis* "hates unbearable Necessity."[8]

But there is a contradiction at the very heart of this grace of exchanges, or, if you like, a functional hypocrisy: These graces are either altruistic and spontaneous, acts of unlooked-for kindness, or else they are due and proportionate responses to something that someone has done for you. We can see this contradiction in two very different definitions provided by Aristotle.

Definition 1:

> The community [*polis*] is brought together through reciprocating in proper proportion. Men seek to repay a bad deed with bad deeds— otherwise it would look like slavery. And to repay good with good— otherwise there is no exchange and it is through exchange that men are brought together. This is why they set up a shrine of the Graces in a public place, so that there might be reciprocity; for this is the unique quality of *charis;* the recipient of favors must repay the service, but another time must himself take the initiative in doing favors.[9]

Definition 2:

> *Charis* . . . is a service to someone in need, *for no return,* performed for the benefit of the one in need and him alone . . . But there is no *charis* if a service is in one's own interest, if it is unintended or performed under compulsion or involves giving back rather than giving, whether consciously or not. For either way it is a favor in return *for something* and therefore there would be no *charis.*[10]

We could resolve, or partly resolve, this contradiction by saying that *charis* always implies freedom from necessity, freedom to give, freedom to return a favor, or not, in a manner of your own choosing. Altruistic *charis* is simply a more extreme version of the reciprocal *charis,* the most charitable, the furthest from necessity, the freest kind of giving.

There is a third grace apart from "thanks" and "think nothing of it": Hadrian could be asking Eros to make him more attractive. This third grace, the grace of "grace-notes" and Tuesday's child "full of grace," comes first in the *OED*'s definitions and is perhaps the hardest of all to grasp: "The quality of producing favorable impressions; attractiveness, charm. Now usually with more restricted application: The attractiveness or charm belonging to elegance of proportions, or (especially) ease and refinement of movement, action, or expression." My Greek dictionary (under "*charis*") is pithier: "outward grace." But I will stick with the *OED*'s "charm" as the more efficient translation of this third grace, although it is missing one vital element, represented by Prince Charming, which is "class." *Grace* is also that ineffable quality a "person of quality" has that distinguishes her or him from a "person of quantity," an industrialist, a successful chain-store owner, or any other nouveau riche no matter how superior in wealth or assumed demeanor. This is no less true of Greek *charis:* the "gracious," the *charientes,* are "the classy ones," "posh people." Don't have dealings with vulgar people, says Theognis; they have no *charis.*[11]

This outward grace is the *charis* we often find inscribed on ancient protective amulets and magic rings. An advertisement for one such ring survives, with instructions on how to make one at home: "The world has nothing better than this. For when you have it with you, you will always get whatever you ask from anybody. Besides, it stops the furious rages of kings and masters. Wearing it, whatever you may say to anyone, you will be believed, and you will seem *charming* to everybody."[12]

This is the *charisma* showered on a victor at the moment of victory in the Olympic Games.[13] It is what allows a footballer in a crucial national game miraculously to bend a ball into a goal, or an emperor to throw a charmed spear from horseback and with it to strike and kill a she-bear. For Hadrian has already been the beneficiary of "arrow-shooting" Eros's *charm* on Mount Helicon, which is why, presumably, it occurred to him in the first place to offer his trophy to the god: "May you *continue* to breathe *charis* on Hadrian."

The early classical poet Pindar thought you could see this *charm* on the island of Tenedos, "dwelling in the son of Hagesilas." Indeed the prime of youth is preeminently "full of *charm,*" and when Odysseus is on his way to the house of the witch Circe in search of his missing, now piggy, companions, he sees it in an epiphany of the god Hermes, who offers him an antidote, "looking like a young man at the very peak of youthful *charm,* just beginning to grow a beard." Sappho, in an uncharacteristically sarcastic mood, would like the antique Zoolander whose good looks are too much appreciated to show her his "look of charm": "Stand in front of me and roll out for me, my friend, the *charm* that crowns your gaze."[14]

Jowett saw it in the elegant proportions of Plato's early dialogues, but lacking in the later. In Hogarth's "Analysis of Beauty," published in London in 1753, it is the serpentine line that appears last in his ascending scale of forms, after (1) those composed of straight lines only, like squares, (2) those composed of straight lines with a curve, like the top of a column or a vase, (3) those composed of all the above plus a waving line, like flowers—this is the "Line of Beauty"—and:

Fourthly, those composed of all the former together with the serpentine line, as the human form, which line hath the power of superadding grace to beauty. Note, forms of most grace have least of the straight line in them . . . And that the serpentine line, by its waving and winding at the same time different ways, leads the eye in a pleasing manner along the continuity of its variety, if I may be allowed the expression; and which by its twisting so many different ways, may be said to inclose (tho' but a single line) varied contents; and therefore all its variety cannot be express'd on paper by one continued line, without the assistance of the imagination, or the help of a figure . . . that sort of proportion'd, winding line, which will hereafter be call'd the precise serpentine line, or *line of grace,* is represented by a fine wire, properly twisted round the elegant and varied figure of a cone. (38–39)

CHARIS—*LE* JE NE SAIS QUOI

So somehow or other we have gone from "thanks" to "favor" to "altruism" to an ever-receding spiral in three dimensions, a spiral *en abîme.* The Three Graces are interweaving sisters. They dance in a circle, and if we can get them to dance really fast we will see that somehow or other *charis* manages to retain its continuity along its variety of meanings.

Sometimes, especially in fantasies of a metaphysical bestower of benevolence, a link between generosity and beauty is banal, the outward expression of an unlooked-for favor from above. It is only appropriate that Hermes, about to bestow a saving grace on Odysseus, something that will protect him from Circe's evil spell, appears in the form of a "most gracious" youth. Here is an archaic elegist, writing about six centuries before Christ: "Boy, since the goddess, the Lady of Cyprus, gave you love-streaming *charm* [*charis himeroessa*], and all the young men are obsessed with [the loveliness of] your form, listen to these lines, and don't forget *my charm,* knowing as you do that Eros is a hard thing for a man to bear."[15] The gist seems straightforward: This is a good-looking boy in whom lots of young men are interested, not least because they have heard our poet's songs about the boy and have been heard singing them all over town, but now the poet (neither young nor good-looking, we might surmise) is feeling at a disadvantage. Passively aggressive, he asks the boy to be generous toward him. On first inspection this is a poem about outward grace. The boy has it and so does the poet's song. But it is also about exchange. The boy's *grace* is grace of Aphrodite, but the poet has superadded to this *charm* by celebrating him in his songs, advertising his beauty to all the young men who sing his songs about the boy in symposia. So the boy now owes him *thanks* for that favor, it is implied—"*Don't forget,*" as if the poet were some goblin having once granted a favor to a king, now come to collect his dues—which finally allows the boy, hitherto a mere recipient of *grace,* from Aphrodite, from the poet, to view himself as the poet's potential benefactor. The *charis* of the Annunciation likewise refers first to Mary being favored, second to the je ne sais quoi in her that both provoked the blessing and that the blessing amplified, and finally to her humble gratitude as she receives this unlooked-for blessing out of the blue: Hail, *graceful* Mary, *gratefully* receiving *grace*.

Outward grace retains something of the ineffability, the mystery of properly gracious exchanges. It is like a blessing or an unlooked-for act of generosity, a beauty that is simply there, a given, a *datum* (Latin *dare,* to give). This is why English "grace" seems so often to be happily stumbled upon, in the rhythm of a sentence, the movement of a body, the proportions of a building: a something extra you cannot quite put your finger on. In Spanish *graciosa* refers to someone who may not be pretty or witty, but is nevertheless, for some indefinable reason, "really nice." It is a present, a present to the one filled with grace, a present from her to the world, but in the first place simply present.

This is dizzy stuff, so to illustrate perhaps we might be allowed to call again on the Girl from Ipanema, who captures in moments the ineffable connection between outward grace and the grace of exchanges. The first verse of Norman Gimbel's English version of the song— "Tall and tanned and young and lovely, the girl from Ipanema goes walking, and when she passes, each one she passes goes 'Ah' . . ."— somehow manages to evoke inexplicitly but vividly a sense of that *certain something* that in the original Portuguese version, with its slightly moving tune and soft guitar, so thoroughly Greek it could almost have been written by Sappho and quoted by Plato, is less vivid and more explicit:

Look, the loveliest thing,
Imbued with peerless *grace* [*mais cheia de graça*];[16]
It's her the girl
Who comes and passes
With sweet deportment
Along the promenade [*do maaar*],

The girl with a body goldened
By the sun of Ipanema,
The way she moves,
More than a poem,
Is the loveliest thing
I have ever seen go past [*passaaar*].

Ah why am I so lonely?
Ah why is everything so sad?
Ah the beauty that there is,
Beauty which is not only mine,
Which passes just as lonely.

Ah if she could know
That when she passes,
The smiling world
Is filled with *grace* [*o mundo sorrindo se encha de graça*]
And becomes lovelier,
Thanks to love.[17]

The girl obliviously delights the world with her grace, which is simply *there,* a datum in the first line, "Look . . . it's her," "Tall and tanned and . . ." And she spreads some of what she has over the world, an act of unwitting kindness. But her grace is itself a gift, a gift in part of the sun superadding to her beauty with gold. And of course, like the *grace* that lies in the elegist's lines of poetry about the charming boy, the ineffable *grace* of her walking is ineffably embodied in the rhythm of the song, just as the sighs of the narrator are redoubled on the saxophone or clarinet, taking her *grace* out of Ipanema and sharing it with the rest of us in the smiling world through concert halls, radios and CD players: "But on you the sweet-speaking lyre and melodious oboe sprinkle *grace*."[18] This *grace* of performance is especially the prerogative of the singer, who enters into a further exchange, an exchange with the song, with the tune, with the band. Like Billie Holliday bending a line or a flamenco singer under the influence of spirit, *duende,* ornamenting a tune with vocal grace notes, João Gilberto does not just sing the song, he has a relationship with it, sometimes complying with the beat, sometimes playing with it, ever so gracefully: "If you start to pay attention at the technical level you feel your mind being pulled apart as you try to follow these two different times simultaneously."[19] The isolation of the lonely narrator, of the girl's lonely beauty, the distant sun, the enormous world, listening in, creates a sense of gigantic space. And it is above all in that space, rather than in any particular corner of it, that grace is to be found, in the spaghetti junction of *gracious* exchanges, as *charm* bounces around off bodies as far-traveling light waves, heat waves, air waves, and something altogether less tangible, love.

Even when it seems to reside in someone or something, *charis* never loses its sense of circulation. If it appears in a song, it is because the Muses or the Graces have momentarily *graced* the composer with their presence. *Charis* therefore is never, properly, something you can vaunt. It is not yours to be proud of. It is always *reflected* glory, even though the *fons et origo* of all this munificence may not be readily definable. The metaphysical powers who sprinkle it or pour it or fill people with it are invoked primarily to dispossess the one they sprinkle with it of agency—you should not be able to "turn on the charm," though I have known a few who do—and of ultimate ownership, to remind one, especially the one *graced* with *charm,* that it is but a gift, a loan without interest. This is how *charis* can be so closely associated with humility or "a sense of shame" (*aidōs*), and how *grace* for ancient Greeks is so potent a word of piety.

The Girl from Ipanema also helps us to see why *charm* can be seen as a prerogative especially of youth. *Charis* is fleeting not only because you cannot quite pinpoint exactly what it is, or who has it, but because whatever it is tends to magically appear and then to be gone again, as evanescent in fact as it is to comprehension. The key conceit of this song is that the girl's loveliness, her beauty, is passing her, as she passes, as if, like a hummingbird, *charm* has temporarily nested on her, graced her with its presence. But of course it is precisely in its passingness that her charm lies; the narrator loves the way she passes, that is, he loves the way she passes him by, her beauty passing.

Like Hogarth's spiraling line of grace it is forever receding, as hard for her to take permanent hold of as it is for the world she walks through, or for the poet who puts pen to paper and still—because it's "more than a poem"—misses it, or for the listener as she passes through the song. However, the song with all its charm will also grace her fleeting *charis* with memory for future generations. For by now, whoever she was, that girl must be in her sixties. This is another very Greek notion: Others, despite their beautiful accomplishments, are forgotten in Hades unsung, but not you, since "on you the sweet-speaking lyre and melodious oboe sprinkle *grace*." By grace of Sappho, the loveliest things on Lesbos *c.*600 BC, no less well endowed in the art of walking, are still gracing us today.

GRACELESS WIVES AND GRACIOUS BOYFRIENDS

Like *erōs, charis* is not intrinsically homosexual. The Graces are regular attenders of weddings between men and women. Nevertheless, inasmuch as Greek males are more autonomous, out and about in the world and not just confined to the house, and there are more exchanges between them over longer distances and over a longer period, more wooing and longing, in other words, *charis* is spoken of much more in a homosexual context. For *charis* belongs to the world of courting, and decent women should neither court nor allow themselves to be courted. The same applies to slaves and under-Eighteens, relationships with whom are also devoid of *charis,* it is said, and "only to do with sex," because gracious exchanges reveal the *psychē,* the personality, because gracious exchanges actually *produce* personality by allowing it an occasion to perform, to exercise its discretion, and space and time to grow. And without the fully grown personality to be attracted to, there is only the body to be interested in, mere lust.[20] People are people only when they engage with you. That's the only way you get to know *what they are like*. Inasmuch as proper women (other men's women) don't engage (with you), they have no personality. As far as you are concerned women aren't really people at all, and Love, after all, is necessarily a relationship between people.

The elegists imply that *charis* is characteristic of relations with boys

precisely because, as autonomous subjects, they are free to favor or to return generosity, and cannot be pinned down. When they repay a favor,
they are also repaying one's freely given faith in them. Here *charis* is best
translated "credit." Hence the not infrequent invectives directed at the
graceless, thankless, faithless boy do not undermine but rather help to
sustain the system of exchanges that constitutes Greek Love: "Boy, you
pay your benefactor back a shoddy [*kakēn*] return, there's not a trace of
gratitude in you [*oude tis . . . charis para soi*] for the goods you have ac-
crued. As yet, you've done nothing for me; while I, despite my mounting benefactions, get nothing from you but bare-faced cheek."[21] For
such invectives serve not only to encourage gratitude by attacking in-
grates, but to remind all boys that, unlike common prostitutes, they do
in fact have options, that obligation is not forced, that there is a choice,
the possibility of doing precisely nothing in return, of taking the offered inducements and nevertheless avoiding corruption by calling the
"freely giving" giver's bluff—No strings attached? Very well, then:
nothing obliged.

A Greek woman, unless she is a courtesan, lacks that autonomy
(however compromised) in matters of love, and that choice (however
compromised) of keeping faith with an admirer. She is constrained by
law and contract. Such a situation produces paradoxes and ironies,
fully intended. The faithful wife is not really faithful at all, she just
loves the one she's with: "A boy's got credit [*charis*], but a woman can
never have a companion of trust, instead she is destined to love
[*philein*] the man who is around."[22] There is no faith in relations with
a respectable woman precisely because she has no option but to "be
faithful."

It is here in the difference between Greek men and respectable Greek
women as subjects and objects of *charis,* either autonomous in interpersonal exchanges or legally constrained, either free or not free to repay a
favor you choose to confer, to repay your faith in them, that we should
look for the "social" explanation for Greek Love. It did not prevail because Greek men were starved of women or found them not very interesting to talk to, but because respectable Greek women were severely
limited in their gracious exchanges with men, though not, of course,
with other members of their sex. A Greek man could not be *gallant* with
the ladies, but he could certainly be *gallant* with the boys.

CHARIZESTHAI—TO FAVOR; CHARISASTHAI—TO PUT OUT

It is impossible, even for an ancient Greek, to sustain this ineffableness forever: "Someone asked Simonides to write an encomium, saying he would get *charis,* but he wasn't giving him any money. 'I have two chests,' said Simonides, 'one for all the *charis* I receive, one for money; and in time of need, the chest with my *charises* I discover to be empty, the other is the only one of any use.' "[23] At some point there must be some actual favors or acts of generosity, and some of those favors will be sexual favors, some of those acts sexual acts. Indeed occasionally *charites* seems to mean specifically "sexual favors." Hadrian may, as some believe, have been asking Eros to help him get a boy into bed: "It's the garden of Narcissus, so handsome a young man. The emperor turned his thoughts readily to a young favorite in his entourage . . ."[24] This is perhaps the kind of "grace" referred to on an extraordinary black phallus found in the Greek colony of Antibes in the south of France. The phalloid pebble speaks: "I am Enjoy [*Terpōn*], servant of the awesome goddess Aphrodite. May the Lady of Cyprus give *charis* in return to those who put me up."[25]

When does the general and ineffable become the specific and unspeakable? It happens in the shift from *ze* to *sa.* When Aristotle turns to logic to prove that a man in love just wants to be loved rather than to get a boy into bed, the word he uses for the willing response of a boy to an admirer is *charizesthai:* "disposed to favor." But when he comes to the bit about the loved one who was "ill-disposed to favor," but who favored nevertheless, some manuscripts have a different form of the verb: *charisasthai,* a "past" tense, "to sexually oblige," "to put out."

It may seem a minor shift, *ze-sa,* but it makes a major difference. The Greeks divided activity into two types: ongoing situations and simple occurrences. The "past tense" (aorist) in Greek indicates not just whether an action happened yesterday—"I did"—rather than one that is happening now—"I do"—or one that will happen tomorrow— "I will do"—but the *potential* "pastness" in any action, even in the present, or future, i.e., whether it is the *type* of one-time action that could theoretically be over with, put into the past at some point once completed, like killing, kissing, having sex, or if it is rather something that continues, like having a sexual relationship, loving someone, being amenable: The latter are ongoing actions, the former simple occurrences. So in Greek you can distinguish different types of action that aren't distinguished in English, but which, if translated into English brutally, might sound a bit like this:

> Ongoing: "I really think you need to do more exercise for your own good. *Be doing it,* please, for me!"
>
> Simple occurrence: "One bullet and all our problems are over. Just *did it!*"
>
> Ongoing: "*Will you be doing that* for me, going to the gym?"
>
> Simple occurrence: "*Will you did it,* shoot him, as soon as he arrives?"
>
> Ongoing: "*He tried to be doing it,* but after a while he just couldn't face another exercise bike."
>
> Simple occurrence: "As soon as he arrived and started fumbling for his keys, she stepped out from behind the rhododendron; but though *she tried to did it,* she couldn't, and stepped back."

This is useful when you take a normally ongoing kind of action, like love, and use the past tense to make it a simple occurrence. So *philein* in the past tense, "to loved," means to perform an act of love: "As soon as he walked in the door he tried to loved me [*philēsai*]" means "he tried to give me a kiss (or a hug)"—a simple occurrence. So when Luke 7:21 says of Jesus that "unto many that were blind he gave sight," the Greek says "he graced [*echarisato*] many with seeing." He was not just gracious to them, he performed a single act of grace; it was an occurrence. And Aristotle (or some of his copyists) thought that while it was OK to talk of a boy "disposed to favoring—*charizesthai,* ongoing situation—it was more appropriate to use the past tense *charisasthai* when he was talking of the *act* of gratifying or when Aristotle concluded that the main focus of love was not in fact "getting the beloved to *perform an act of grace,*" i.e., "getting into his pants."

In fact whenever the Greeks are clearly talking about the substance of favors—tangible occurrences, rather than a vaguer "favoring"—they will use the past tense, *charisasthai.* "Many make passes at Comedy," says Aristophanes, "but she pulls her knickers down [*charisasthai*] for only a few."[26] The Athenian princess Procris had been entrapped by her husband Cephalus; he approached her dressed as a stranger and offered her money for sex. She decided to get her own back. She dressed up as a man and became his hunting companion. Cephalus coveted his new friend's magic javelin. He could have it, (s)he said, if he agreed "to put out [charisasthai]. He accepted the proposal, but when they lay down, she revealed herself and rebuked him . . ."[27] It is only after all his trials and tribulations, having been possessed by driving erōs, having been thoroughly soaked with streaming himeros, having somehow or other got the boy, now "of age," into bed, that Plato's patient erastēs looks at last as if he will see some action, since as they lie in each other's arms there is something in the boy that is perfectly happy "to perform acts of graciousness," charisasthai . . .[28]

So we know that charisasthai, as a simple occurrence, means "put out," "sexually oblige," but what about the ongoing situation implied by charizesthai? What does it mean "to favor an admirer" for a length of time? Is highfalutin Pindar talking about buggery when he prays: "May it be mine in time to be in love and another's love in time to gratify"?[29] Certainly it is clear, as we have seen, that in Athens, provided you were over Eighteen, to favor an admirer might involve a good fumble and more, under the city walls or behind a bush on the deserted hills of Lycabettus or Pnyx. On the other hand, not to favor an admirer, what older English writers referred to as "love lost," meant totally ignoring him, neither to speak nor to look, or, like Narcissus, not even opening the door. So there was space for a very wide range of "favors"—a look, a word, an assignation, a kiss. And it seems absolutely clear that a wide range of responses is signified under the heading "graciously favor," when it is used in the ongoing "present" tense.

Indeed, sometimes when Greek authors talk of wooers, even of sex-obsessed adulterers or courtesans, "graciously favoring" their admirers or their prey, they cannot be talking of sex. In those cases, "smiling upon" seems to be a question of tea and sympathy, paying visits, making sure that your guests are well looked after. In what is sometimes called the first European novel, The Education of Cyrus, Xenophon describes how Araspas pays visits to the lovely Panthea, a married woman. He starts to pay court to her (therapeuein), thinks that he charms her (charizesthai), and sees that she is not ungracious (acharistos), indeed she takes care that when he comes calling he finds what he requires, and if ever he is ill, that he lacks nothing.[30] Before long he is in love and is compelled to address words to her on the subject of "getting it on to-gether" (*sunousia*). She refuses. She is faithful to her husband though he is far away. She loved her husband very strongly (*ephilei . . . ischurōs*), notes Xenophon.[31]

A parallel scenario is Xenophon's account of Socrates' visit to the house of Theodote, even though she is what we would call a courtesan. Socrates is sure both that Theodote has learned how to charm (*charizesthai*) her "friends" "with a certain eye-contact" (*emblepousa*) and also "that you need to make sure someone who pays you lots of attention has been assiduously charmed" (*kecharisthai*)—the jolt of "assiduous" and "charm" is fully intended I think. Again, this may involve particular attentions such as congratulations on a success, or visits full of concern if he falls sick, a prominent motif in all premodern relationships of affection.

Theodote must gradually build up the gracious exchanges, asking her boyfriends for small things and paying them back by graciously favoring (*charizomenēn*) in the same manner. She must not be too lavish with her courtesies, however, for she will most graciously delight them (*charizoio*) if she gives what she has when they are feeling the lack of it. She should keep them keen "by being manifestly reluctant to favor them [*charizesthai*], by running away until they are really begging for it." Even for a courtesan, it seems, there is rather more to "putting out" than snogs, gropes, kisses and sex.[32]

I suspect that Athenian youths followed a code not far removed from that of the courtly courtesan, although I doubt very much if even the most cunning anthropologist sent back in time two and a half thousand years would be able to get a young man to admit to anything concrete. Indeed, the curious observer who subjected a young citizen to the kind of examination that Socrates inflicts on the courtesan would probably risk something rather more serious than Theodote's feeble retort: "In the name of Zeus, I employ no such devices."

Thus a fundamental conflict divides us students of the Greeks from the Greeks whom we would study. They deliberately resist spelling out what we want specified, and by specifying—guessing—we are likely to traduce their relationships, which depend, precisely, on a margin of discretion and misdirection: By attempting to extract a particular kind of "truth," a set of rules, we end up with a completely false idea of what is going on. They are not merely being prudish and trying to conceal from future historians, speaking newer languages, the shameful goings-on beneath the walls. Being vague is what allows relationships to prosper. Humbug makes the world go round.

Pausanias in Plato's *Symposium* paraphrases homosexual "favoring" as "becoming fond intimates [*philoi*]." But the kinds of favor that might be performed by a muscular young Athenian citizen are very different from those a foreign woman like Theodote can perform. Pausanias describes the "favors" of an *erōmenos* if performed for the wrong motives as "toadying" (*kolakeia*), alluding to the flatterers, parasites and hangers-on who surrounded any important figure.[33] Such services might well include the sexual, but let's not forget the other substantial favors that a powerful man might require of those he has corrupted—strong-arm services, bearing false witness, acting as a malicious prosecutor, a secret envoy to take treacherous letters to the enemy, or even a future client-king or client-satrap; someone, even, to do away with one of his enemies, a handsome assassin.

Still, the use of gracious *charizesthai* puts amorous intimacies in a particular perspective. Even *charisasthai,* "putting out," has a different coloring from other words that could be used for sex; it might suggest an attempt to view the boy's behavior in a certain light, as a delightful concession in an ongoing series of *galanteries*. All that other host of uses of *charis* in religion, politics and not remotely amorous relationships rescue the word from losing its charm. Luke had no need to worry that, when he referred to Jesus "performing an act of graciousness" by making the blind to see, his readers would giggle and smirk. Indeed, during their heated debate about the relative virtues of love for women and love for boys, on their way down to Thespiae from their refuge on Mount Helicon, one of Plutarch's friends defends marriage by noting that *charis* is occasionally used to refer even to heterosexual sex, as if there were a kind of courtliness within marriage, i.e., in the marriage bed. A woman engages in gracious exchanges by being sexually amenable, and it is through sexual concessions that "love," *philia,* is built up between husband and wife. He spoils his point somewhat, however, by citing an example of sexual *charis* between Heracles and a girl, which includes the possibility of "favors" coerced, i.e., rape.[34]

Strange though it may seem to us, the amorous and sexual exchanges between members of the same sex might be seen as the very epitome of the *noblest* form of *charis*. When Aristotle is trying to define the greatest, most altruistic, least self-interested form of *grace,* the example he thinks of first is *erōs,* i.e., the favor an *erōmenos* might do for an *erastēs,* precisely because the boy is doing a tremendous favor ("most difficult," *chalepos*) for someone who is desperately and urgently in need, a favor in which he has supposedly no self-interest.[35] This is what underpins the *ideology* of "the frigid *erōmenos*": the more a boy actually enjoys having sex the less the offer of sex is an act of supreme charity. It is not in fact sexual asymmetry at all, but an asymmetry of *kindness,* as if the *erastēs* were a beggar being given a generous check by someone who can ill afford it. Sexual *charis* stands for a particular construction of sex as part of a gracious exchange; it is never merely a euphemism for buggery or frottage, though sometimes, of course, that is exactly what *charity* meant in practice.

All this courtliness, all this rhetorical behavior, flatters the motives of both the admirer and the boy, each of them seeking nothing in return, supposedly: "Oh how sweet of you to offer to get jiggy with me, without a thought for yourself." Two hours later: "Oh how sweet of you to buy me that horse." The hypocrisy lies not in pretending that a relationship centers on romantic love when really its purpose is sodomy. It lies in pretending that an interested relationship is disinterested. Consistently, throughout the archaic and classical literature of Greek Love, the problem in Greek ethics, the impudent question, is not "What exactly did you do?" but "For what exactly did you do it?"

CAPYS GETS STUFFED

Such hyperbolic romanticism makes Greek boys seem like eighteenth-century ladies, like Madame de Tourvel desperately resisting Valmont's advances then graciously conceding, only to be thoroughly disabused. And reading about Greek Love one sometimes feels as if one has been beamed down into a painting by Watteau, *The Pilgrimage to Cythera,* for instance. But just as an eighteenth-century lady, not to speak of a courtesan like Theodote, might in fact be assumed to enjoy sex, despite playing hard to get, just as she might even, once seduced, turn seducer, so with a Greek youth. Although he wasn't supposed to be making any moves, the Greeks were well aware that he might be quite keen to put out, and might in some cases even use the *erastēs* to gratify his own desires:

> It is the only kind of steel that Capys cherishes. If it's not an upstanding penis sinking into the hidden corridors of his glutes [*gloutōn*], it is, for him, no sword worth talking about. He is happy to see a lover [*erastēs*] only so long as he is getting enjoyably prodded. Soon as it stops, his current friend's lost, and he finds more sinewy mounters. Therefore, may Zeus let genocide reduce the love-lacking race of those who get bounced for pleasure [*kinoumenōn*].[36]

That was a late item, possibly very late, from a manuscript in the library of the Holy Father, the Vatican, pretending to be by the seventh-century BC poet Archilochus. A more famous example comes from the first century AD, from Petronius's *Satyrica*. Eumolpus describes a visit to the city of Pergamum in northwestern Turkey, where he had managed to get lodgings with a family. The host's son was extremely handsome. In order to avert suspicion Eumolpus pretended to be utterly disgusted whenever the dinner conversation turned to "intercourse with beautiful boys." The mother thought he must be some kind of philosopher and entrusted the boy to his care. He gave the boy lessons, and took him to the gymnasium. Eumolpus took advantage of his position and warned the young man (an ephebe, i.e., eighteen to nineteen years old) to make sure that no sexual predator (*praedator corporis*) was allowed in the house.

One night they were lying in the dining room, too tired to go to bed. Around midnight, realizing that the boy was awake, Eumolpus pretended to pray to Venus. If she would let him kiss the boy without his noticing, he would give him a pair of doves. The boy fell to snoring. Eumolpus stole his kisses, the boy got his doves. In next night's prayers, Eumolpus made a higher bid, two fighting cocks for a grope. The ephebe shoved up of his own accord, Eumolpus had his way, the boy got his cocks. On the third night, Eumolpus whispered in his ear a prayer to the immortal gods to let him get away with "his dream, full intercourse" (*coitum plenum et optabilem*). For this he would give the boy a Macedonian thoroughbred, but only on condition that he "should feel nothing." Never did an ephebe sleep so deeply. Eumolpus does a rerun through the pleasures of previous nights. First he squeezes his juicy pecs (*implevi lactentibus papillis manus*), then a long lingering kiss, "and finally, all my wishes in one . . . I conjoined." But next day, there was a snag. It was hard to get hold of a Macedonian thoroughbred, and such a conspicuous gift would arouse suspicions. He returned home empty-handed and gave the boy nothing but a kiss. The boy put his arms around his neck. "Excuse me, good sir," he said, "where is my horse?"

Relations take a bad turn. When the next opportunity arises, with the boy's father snoring nearby, Eumolpus tries to make it up to him. The boy is unimpressed. "If you don't go back to bed, I'll tell my father," he protests. But even as he is saying "I will wake my father. I will. I will wake my father," Eumolpus takes his pleasure, meeting only half-hearted resistance. The boy seems not to mind these iniquities, although he does complain about how he has been cheated, and has become a laughingstock among the other trainees at the gymnasium, to whom he had boasted of Eumolpus's riches. "However," says the young man, "you will find I am not going to be like you. If there's something you want, do it again." Glad to be back in the boy's good graces, Eumolpus takes advantage of the offer, then falls asleep. But the young man is at his peak, at an age that is gagging for it (*plenae maturitatis et annis ad patiendum gestientibus*). Twice wasn't enough. He wakes Eumolpus up. "Don't you want it?" he says.

Obviously this was still a chore (*munus*) Eumolpus didn't mind doing, so somehow or other, amid a great deal of commotion, the boy got the grinding (*tritus*) he wanted and Eumolpus, exhausted, fell asleep once more. Less than an hour later the boy was digging him in the ribs. "Why aren't we at it?" At that point Eumolpus had had enough: "If you don't go back to bed, I'll tell your father."[37]

Such extended jokes at the expense of the code of Greek Love are, thus far, only to be found in later literature. The classical Greeks were hardly unaware that Pergamene boys might exist among the ranks of citizens, but they took such code infringements much more seriously. Of the tens of thousands of images on Greek vases, a small percentage depict sex acts, but scenes showing homosexual sex are rare. Only one or two of those seem to show a boy being enthusiastic, like our Pergamene friend.

SUNDRY DEVIANTS

Insults can be among the most nuanced and difficult features of a culture's discourse to interpret accurately. Take "cunt" and *coño,* which are cognate words. "Cunt" is so strong in British English that you would use it face-to-face only to lash out at someone dangerous or threatening, someone you were ready to fight. Spanish *coño* is much milder, more like "flipping heck," a word that even your mother might use, like "bugger" in British English. One should by no means suppose that insults are translatable between communities, that there will be any equivalent at all in another idiom. It is not just that what is considered insulting varies between cultures. Each culture has its own great structures of discourse, in which hostile terms must find their place.

One might think, to take one instance, that the Greeks were mostly rather earthy, but outside the festival license of Aristophanes and the graffiti artists, even a word like "buttocks" (*pugai*) seems to be carefully avoided. When scientists and philosophers are forced to discuss such a part of the anatomy, they may well use a term like *hedra,* "seat," while genitals are regularly referred to as "the shamefuls" or "discreets," *aidoia.* Greek literature was split into two opposed camps, one could infer: a very proper highfalutin literature of the tragedians and epic and lyric poets, and a very improper speech of comedians and iambic poets like Archilochus or Hipponax. Shakespeare can seem terribly vulgar compared with Sophocles, rather prudish compared with Aristophanes. It is just that literature was structured differently in Elizabethan England and in classical Greece.

But the same considerations apply to everyday speech. One reason why insults are so vicious, obscene, explicit and commonplace in much of Western culture is that we don't really take them to heart: We don't believe that words can hurt us very much. Few of us, certainly, believe in a dark world of malignant powers, in witchcraft, the evil eye, or a "damn you to hell," that might give teeth to the malignancy voiced, or that someone who calls across the street at us "batty-boy" or "-woman" might have the power literally to spirit away our masculinity by scratching a word of power on the bottom of a cup.

By which I mean to say no more than that insults are a complicated business. Forewarned, we may proceed. Now, according to an almost universal consensus, certain Greek insults—*eurupróktos,* "wide-arse," *kinaidos, katapugón*—all mean the same thing: First and foremost they pour scorn over boys believed to welcome being penetrated, thus reflecting a fundamentally bipolar sexual morality in which one group, mature men, tries to score as many women or boys as possible to loud universal applause, while the other group, women and boys, but especially boys, tries at all costs to avoid becoming notches on the bedpost, inasmuch as it means being humiliated and defeated; sex is viewed as a "zero-sum game." But most of those so insulted are not boys by any definition, but mature men, sometimes very mature. If we gave any credence to the invective we would have to assume a vast array of sexual encounters in which young advocates in their Twenties, tragedians in their Thirties, politicians in their Forties, generals in their Fifties, regularly bent over to be pleasured by . . . by whom? In fact when you read a little more carefully, and less imaginatively, rather different, more straightforward and sometimes quite surprising meanings, as if by magic, appear.

Item 1: the "wide-arse," *eurupróktos.* What might provoke you, sitting there in the twenty-first century, to call someone "a wide-arse"? It took me ten years to get it, but the joke now seems completely obvious.[38] A clue: Put aside, if you can, for a while, all thoughts of buggery.

As insults go, "wide-arse" has an extremely short career, and in context it is used especially to refer to sophistry, especially that of young "assistant state prosecutors" (*sunégoroi*), trained by the likes of logic-choppers like Socrates and Protagoras, who used their newfound skills to run rings around elder statesmen accused of corruption. One such was Euathlus, who scored a lucky hit, like "a vile archer" (shooting from the sidelines), against one of the most venerable statesmen of his time, Thucydides, son of Melesias, a relative, very probably, of the famous historian. The trial and Euathlus's dazzling performance caused a sensation, and it reverberates throughout contemporary comedies. In his prime, said Aristophanes, old Thucydides could have thrown "ten Euathluses" in a wrestling match. The phrase "ten Euathluses" became proverbial for an old trooper worth ten of the man who finally beat him in his dotage. Euathlus went down in history as "an orator, vile . . . a blabbering *wide-arse.*"[39] Another was Alcibiades, handsome, clever, rich and well connected, who seemed, in addition, to have monopolized all the charm that was reserved for his generation, until it was thoroughly undermined by treachery and betrayal. Before all that, however, Alcibiades too made an impression, it seems, as an assistant state prosecutor. Still going on about the trial of Thucydides, the chorus of "Old Men of Acharnae," in Aristophanes' *Acharnians,* insists that it's just not right for men of their generation, however corrupt, to be prosecuted by someone in his twenties, like that "blabbering *wide-arse*" Alcibiades; he should only be allowed to take on someone his own age.[40]

Now, what particular quality might provoke someone to call a young barrister, (unjustly) successful in prosecuting a venerable politician, a "blabbering wide-arse"? More hints: There are variants without the "wide" and without the "arse." Hence we have a merely "blabbering prosecutor" and also a merely "blabbering arse," in fact more than one, and an "arse with a sophistic trick." The most obvious clue lies in an example of the insult that has to be adjusted so that it does indeed refer to someone who has been buggered rather a lot, the effeminate tragedian Agathon, "a wide-arse *not through words* but practices."[41] This could not make it clearer that the primary meaning of "wide-arse" refers to blabbering speech; *euruprōktos* is simply a vulgar form of the word "wide-mouth," *eurustomos*. For hollow rhetoric was often referred to as windy or gusting. It refers to people who talk out of their arses, farting on about something or other, windbags, barristers, politicians.

The idea provides the centerpiece to Aristophanes' play about sophists, *Clouds*. Showing off his talent for turning abstract ideas into crude images, the poet introduces two characters who turn out to be personifications of two kinds of speech. The one represents the way people used to talk in the past, the old kind of speech used by men like poor old Thucydides; this Speech is called by the commentators "Just," or "Fair" or "Superior." His opponent is the newfangled way of talking, the speech of young men trained in rhetoric and argumentation by sophists; this Speech is called "Unjust," "Unfair" or "Inferior." They engage in a formal public debate, which reaches a climax with newfangled Speech showing off his skills in sophistry by proving that there is nothing wrong with being a "wide-arse," i.e., nothing wrong with sophistry: "Out of what do they make speeches of prosecution?" "Out of wide-arses." "Out of what do they sing tragedies?" "Out of wide-

arses." "Out of what do they make speeches of national importance?"
"Out of wide-arses."[42]

Item 2: *Kinaidos* is much more obscure—"lewd fellow," "sexual degenerate," "man-woman"—but, the general consensus about the word is
similar, that it specifically denotes "boys who take the passive role."
Again that does not seem to be how it is used in classical literature. It is
never used, for instance, much to the disappointment (or indeed disbelief) of many, in the long speech attacking the "male whore" Timarchus, the prime pathic supposedly, although he is called every other
name under the sun. It is, however, used in the same speech and elsewhere to attack Demosthenes, a politician at the height of his powers.
This is not a random distribution of insults or an error. Timarchus is not
accused of the crimes associated with the *kinaidos*. Demosthenes here
and elsewhere is.

It is rare in classical Greek literature, but it seems in its earliest career
to be a reasonably proper word, used by Plato, for instance, and
Aeschines, neither of whom would allow the other vulgar obscenities
into their vocabulary lists.[43] By the same token, comic poets, at least the
surviving ones, seem to have avoided it. In context, *kinaidos* is associated
first and foremost with effeminacy, seduction and, not unrelated, general lewdness, not least in speech, "talking dirty." The bird attached to a
wheel used in magic to draw beloveds (*agapōmenoi*) toward you, the so-
called *iunx,* was therefore also called a "little *kinaidos* bird"—*kinaidion*.[44]
In the period after Alexander, in the "Hellenistic world," the *kinaidos*
becomes increasingly popular and increasingly monstrous, until by
Roman times he is almost an obsession, a bogeyman, especially among
astrologers and their fellows who specialized in physiognomy, the science of reading character from mannerisms and appearance.

There is moreover a whole genre of literature called cinaedic,
founded in the third century BC by Sotades, "inventor" of the palindrome. *Kinaidoi* even seem to have their own Sotadean meter. It has
proven almost irresistible to view Sotades as the first fully developed
"radical queer writer," a sexual outlaw, like Genet, perhaps writing as a
self-confessed *kinaidos* and using dirty talk to attack the regime of the
Ptolemies, a true political-cultural rebel, inverting words and parodying
the *Iliad,* the great manly classic, rewriting it to his own flexible effemi-

nate skippier beat.[45] In Hellenistic Egypt you could hire a *kinaidos* for parties, a "lewd entertainer"; one such was accused of adultery.[46]

The ancient dictionaries suggest that a *kinaidos* is "an effeminate man-woman," "soft, degenerate" (*malakos*), "licentious" (*aselgēs*), "depraved" (*exōlēs*) or "lascivious" (*eklutos*). The opposite of a *kinaidos* is the chaste man (*sōphrōn*).[47] If a fondness for taking it up the bottom is a defining characteristic, it is certainly not the first thing that sprang to the lexicographer's mind, nor the second, nor the third, nor the fourth . . . Perhaps that just got lost in all the lewdness.

Although the representation of *kinaidoi* stresses their appearance—their ladylike clothes, their hair, their ornaments, their perfumes—these seem to be mere outward expressions of an interior *nature,* a nature they might try to disguise, but that would nevertheless be revealed in an unguarded moment:

> You see him really flashing and rolling his eyes looking around with a brazen liquid gaze; with a furrowed brow and cheeks; he moves his cheeks and eyebrows too much, with his head tilted to the side. His pelvis moves, he often moves his back and limbs, all his parts, as if they were loose, and he trips along with little jumping steps; his knees touching, his palms are turned upward, he looks around him, and his voice is thin, mournful, high-pitched and languorous.[48]

> There is a story that Cleanthes claimed that, according to Zeno [founder of Stoicism], a man's character could be grasped from his appearance. So some facetious young men brought him a *kinaidos,* hardened by work in the fields, and suggested he expound upon the man's character. Cleanthes was perplexed and dismissed the creature. But he, as he was leaving, sneezed. "I've got him," said Cleanthes. "He is a soft man [*malakos*]."[49]

People born under a particular astrological conjunction, in fact lots of different conjunctions, for there seem to have been many such characters to be spotted on the streets of the Roman Empire, would inevitably become *kinaidoi,* although some particular astral conjunctions would enable the *kinaidos* better to disguise the fact, or to reduce the metaphorical goatish stench that he got from Capricorn. Such men could be rich and famous and even achieve high positions at court.[50] The notion that *kinaidoi* are born that way lies behind one of the first explicit debates about whether homosexuality is a product of nature or culture. Young Celtic men were very prone to having sex with other men, noted Bishop Eusebius in the fourth century AD, even marrying each other, and since "it is not possible that all the men in Gaul who make godless assaults on each other do it because they happened to be born under the same astrological configurations" it must be their law or custom (*nomos*) which was at fault.[51]

But it was also possible to transform someone into a *kinaidos* using magic. All you had to do to make a man more like a woman was to scratch on a piece of obsidian the image of a castrated man staring at the ground where his manhood lay at his feet and then put it in a golden box with the "stone" of a *kinaidos* fish, possibly a wrasse. The stone having been thus activated you could unman someone a little by touching him with it. If you could get him to carry it unwittingly on his person the effect would be to make him even more effeminate. But if you wanted to turn him into a "complete *kinaidos*," you would have to get him actually to ingest the stone.[52] Because of this innate effeminacy, some have suggested that the *kinaidos* is the closest thing in the ancient world to a "poofter," a "gay," a "fag," a "homosexual," and the term is still sometimes translated like that.[53] Sir Richard Burton indeed called the geographical belt around the world, somewhat narrow in the European longitudes, i.e., the Mediterranean, and in the Middle East, i.e., Pakistan and Afghanistan, but expanding dramatically in the Far East to encompass the Pacific Islands, China and Japan, "the Sotadic zone" after the inventor of cinaedic poetry and the palindrome. For these were the lands where homosexualness prospered, the lands of "sexual inversion."

There was nothing remotely passive or inactive about these *kinaidoi*. And apart from the eunuch priests of the Great Mother Cybele, it was a merely symbolic castration they suffered. Their "manhood" may have been lying at their feet, but their actual virile member was more often not only intact but usually very substantial and ready for action. They were dangerous characters, very busy with their lewd activities. Already at the start of their long and colorful career, Plato uses them as an example of the effortfulness of the dissolute life.[54] They are insatiable, spending their whole lives trying to satisfy their pleasures however unsuccessfully.

We need to fast-forward a few hundred years to actually meet one in vivid sexual action, even demonstrating for us a song in the loose cinaedic rhythm. Petronius, once more, will have to be our host, though at this part of the narrative, "the Quartilla episode," the text has been savagely cut, whether because of damp or monkish priggishness it is always hard to tell.

The antiheroes of the *Satyrica,* the devious, well-hung Ascyltus and the impotent narrator, his soon-to-be-ex-boyfriend Encolpius, are beginning to relax. They think they could easily take on Quartilla and the two other women who seem to have taken them prisoner, whatever their sinister plan, but something goes wrong, they end up being overpowered, their legs and arms tied up with straps. And then "finally a *cinaedus* joined us, dressed in myrtle-green hitched up with a belt . . . one minute he launched himself at us wrenching our buttocks apart. Next minute he was abusing us with foul-smelling kisses" . . . (CUT) . . . Their hostess has them released . . . (CUT) . . . "we both swore the solemnest oath that we would take our horrifying secret to our graves" . . . (CUT) . . . They are treated to a rubdown and a feast with fine wine. They begin to relax and to doze off, but they are not out of the woods yet. For once more:

Enters the *cinaedus,* the most disgusting creature on earth, but without a doubt quite up to the standards of that household. Limp-wristedly clicking his fingers, he poured out a wail-song that went something like this:

> "O come all cinaedi,
> Rampant and licentious,
> O come ye with ready thighs
> And buttocks agile!
> Fly ye, wing-footed,
> Fingers at the ready!
> No matter if you're fresh meat,
> No matter if you're old meat,
> No matter if your man-meat
> Has been sacrificed."[55]

Having done his turn, he turned to me and slobbered me with kisses of the most monstrous kind. Without more ado he climbed on my couch and ripped my clothes off. Upon my groin he went to work, for ages, most energetically, but to no purpose. Rivulets of sweaty pomade, acacia, poured from his brow and there was so much slap collecting in the furrows of his cheeks you would have thought he was a wall flaking after a heavy downpour. I could hold back my tears no longer . . . Then, worried lest my boyfriend, Ascyltus, might be getting the better of the bargain, I said; "Your ladyship, is Ascyltus the only one in this dining-room on a break?" "Good point," said Quartilla, "Ascyltus must not be deprived of our acrobat." On command, the *cinaedus* changed horses, and having transferred to my comrade, ground him to bits with buttocks and kisses.[56]

As many have noticed, Petronius's *kinaidos* is a "stage-*kinaidos*" transported into the real world, as formal a stereotype as the queens in seventies sitcoms, or a pantomime dame, even singing in a cinaedic rhythm, but the episode also reveals the truth of the saying quoted twice by Plutarch: "It makes no difference if you are a *kinaidos* with your front parts or your rear."[57]

The remark was said to have been directed at a group of adulterers—*moichoi,* "women-burglars"—the young effeminate dandies who attempted to seduce the females under your protection, your wife or daughters, sisters, mother or aunties. And the two notorious types are often found together. One particular vase, formerly in Munich, shows a randy man tied to a pillar awaiting punishment with the title "*kinaidos* adulterer."[58] Adulterers used to sport a particular haircut "in the fashion of *kinaidoi.*"[59] But there is some kind of difference between these cousins in crime. In the great city of Syracuse in Sicily there was a "law forbidding a man from beautifying himself wearing excessive or distinctive raiment, unless he agreed that he was out woman-burglaring [*moicheuein*] or was a *kinaidos.*"[60] This kind of law—"agreed that he was"—implies having one's name written on a public list (plus a heavy fine). But if so, it seems there were two lists, one for adulterers, one for *kinaidoi.* What was the difference? There seems little doubt. Both were seducers, but the one was interested in other men's women, the other in members of the same sex. It was a difference in preference, in the probable object of seduction, a difference in gender orientation.

The two main elements in the profile of the *kinaidos,* his effeminacy and his aggressive lewdness, reflect two apparent etymologies or perhaps folk-etymologies; for the true origin of the word remains obscure. In the first place it *sounds* like a version of a much older word, *kinados* (neuter), "cunning fox," "devious beast," "villain," as if it had been first feminized, *kinaida,* and then masculinized, *kinaidos*—"he-vixen," "he-bitch."[61] This may account for the insistence on gender bending, and why decent writers such as Plato and Aeschines felt able to use it, because if you lingered on the "i" in *kiiinaidos* another etymology, the one given us by ancient experts, is much more sexually explicit, a compound of "*kineō*" (*kiiinēo*), "agitate" (as in *cinema,* "the movies"), and *aidōs/ aidoia,* "genitals," i.e., a "jig-willy."

But whose genitals did these word analysts think he was jigging: his own, a "willy-waggler," or someone else's, a "willy-fiddler?"[62] The answer seems to lie in an extraordinary scene from a cinaedic mime preserved on a vase, which shows a whole group of "*KINAIDOI*" making a raid on a flour mill, perhaps to rescue one of their number who has been tied to a pillar. In the riot that ensues, the millworkers look up from their work in alarm, while one is stripped and grabbed from behind. Stage left, the supervisor rushes in. One of these lewd figures, however, sports a prominent erection and reveals his gender orientation by doing something very strange—"his deed, so typical for a cinaed, requires no description"—well, it may not *warrant* putting down in words, but it is hardly something you might otherwise surmise: The *kinaidos* is reaching out to fiddle with the willy of a donkey, the donkey being not unresponsive.[63] This strange gesture is precisely what a Greek might describe as *kin-aidō.*[64] It is a "talking picture," a "willy-fiddler," "willy-fiddling," and placed alongside the dictionary derivations, pretty conclusive evidence that in this period a *kinaidos* could be popularly interpreted as a "sexual abuser of other males."

This is important, since "willy-fiddling" was exactly the kind of attention that Athenians tried to protect their under-Eighteen-year-olds from. The exiled pederast in Aristophanes' fantasy *Birds* fantasizes about a utopian anti-Athens "where the father of a handsome boy meets me on the street to complain of my wrongful treatment: 'A nice way to treat my son, Stilbonides, you caught him coming out of the gymnasium all nice and clean and you did not kiss him, you did not speak to him, you didn't hug him, you didn't go for his balls, and you a family friend' "— precisely the kind of conversation that could never occur in classical

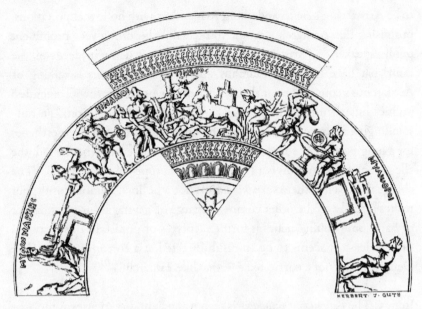

6. *Kinaidoi* raid a mill. Scene from a mime?
Mold-made "Megarian Bowl" (Hellenistic period).

Athens, of course.[65] And there are occasional scenes on Athenian vases that show men doing to boys exactly what the *kinaidos* on the vase is doing to the donkey. One in particular, much reproduced, shows a mature man with a beard and an erection apparently having come right into the gymnasium off the street, and putting his hand to the genitals of a young boy. This is normally interpreted as an everyday illustration of Greek Homosexuality, but the gymnasium was strictly off-limits to over-Twenties when the under-Eighteens were exercising, unless they were elderly and past it like the slave chaperons, the *paidagogoi,* or Socrates. It should be viewed instead as a cautionary scene, another talking picture: a villainous *kin-aidos* at work, "willy-fiddling."

This also explains why Aeschines accuses Demosthenes but not the much-abused Timarchus of being a *kinaidos*.[66] Timarchus may have sold his body to other men, but he is never accused of seducing boys; other men's wives, yes, but not their sons. Demosthenes, on the other hand, a man in his Forties, who, according to Aeschines, secretly wears soft seductive underwear that belongs to a woman's wardrobe, not a man's, was accused of seducing a rich fatherless boy called Aristarchus, "pretending to be Aristarchus's *erastēs* and filling Aristarchus with hollow expectations, promising that Aristarchus would immediately become a very prominent public speaker . . . Aristarchus's initiator and instructor in deeds of the kind that have forced Aristarchus into exile." Aeschines is talking of Aristarchus's conviction for the murder of one of Demosthenes' enemies; politics in Athens could be rough.[67] Then there was Aristion, "an outstandingly handsome young man, who once cohabited with Demosthenes for a long period. As to what was done to him there and what he did, the allegations vary, and this is a subject quite improper to talk about."[68] The charge that Demosthenes is a *kinaidos* is not a hollow, random insult, but relates directly to the other common charge of having seduced a number of handsome young men, his former acolytes or pupils. In this early period, at least, it seems to be an insult directed at a corrupting *erastēs* like Demosthenes, not a corrupted *erōmenos* like Timarchus.[69]

Item 3: The *katapugōn/katapugos* is seen by ancient dictionaries as more or less synonymous with *kinaidos* and seems in context to have a similar range of meanings: lewdness, lack of sexual restraint, general degeneracy.[70] Aristophanes' very first play, *Banqueters,* opposed a "virtuous" (*sōphrōn*) son to his *katapugōn* brother who, it seems, indulged in all kinds of luxury and decadence. And in *Lysistrata* the heroine is worried that her sex strike will fall apart because of the "unrivaled lecherousness" ("nothing more *katapugōn*") of her sex. The tribe of women, indeed, is *pankatapugōn,* "totally lecherous," says Lysistrata.[71] One can even refer to fancy food as *katapugosunē:* "All that stuff is *lechery* compared to a big piece of meat."[72] One can almost watch *katapugōn* being replaced by *kinaidos* over time, dying out around 400 BC, just as the *kinaidos* takes off. Indeed, later in the Roman Empire, when the fashion for speaking in precisely the way that classical Greeks had spoken five hundred years earlier was at its height, you could use the word to show off your knowledge of obsolete expressions, rather like someone nowadays referring to someone as a "scurvy blackguard."[73]

But there is a difference between the two insults that reflects the differences in the kinds of literature that survive from different periods and the evolution of notions of an interior sexuality and of "personality types," not least because of the rise of "human sciences" like astrology and physiognomics, which turned the *kinaidos* into such a star. Hence *katapugōn* puts less emphasis on a perverse effeminized *nature,* "faggot," and more emphasis on behavior lacking in self-control, "debauched." Unlike *kinaidos,* it never graces the speech of philosophers (with one predictable exception) or public speakers, and seems to have been a much more obviously rude word, beloved of the old-fashioned obscene comic poets like Aristophanes and writers of graffiti, some of which are very old indeed. But, like "shoot" for "shit," *katapugōn/pankatapugōn* may also have served as a more humorous form of some other malign insults beginning with *ka-, kakourgos/pankakourgos*—"evil-doer," "felon"—or *kataratos/pankataratos*—"accursed"—use of which might get you into trouble in a culture where cursing and slander were taken more seriously. One of the latest examples was written on a lamp from Sicily: "I belong to Pausanias an utter *katapugōn.*" We cannot rule out the possibility that Pausanias wrote it himself.[74]

It also functions as an inversion of the ubiquitous positive acclamation celebrating members of the elite, "So-and-so is *kalos,*" which is a short way of saying: "I'm a big fan of so-and-so, admirable young fellow, fine, beautiful, noble, good." Here *katapugōn* functions to denigrate the acclaimed, a denial or contradiction of actual or anticipated worthiness: "I'm no fan of so-and-so, a no-good, thoroughly debauched." "Alcaeus is *kalos* according to Melis," "Alcaeus is *katapugōn*"; "Aristomenes is *kalos,*" "Aristomenes is *katapugōn*"; "Sosias is *katapugōn.* So says the one who wrote this"; and, among the very earliest, "Titas the Olympic victor is *katapugōn.*"[75] The implicit politicking going on behind all this becomes more obvious when we come to ballots, or *ostraka,* used in the process of ostracism, which allowed the most unpopular politician to be voted into exile for ten years. Most were mass-produced to hand out to illiterate supporters, but a few could not resist adding insult to injury in their own hand. Thus we find an allegation of incest against the founder of the Athenian Empire, son of the victor at Marathon: "Cimon, son of Miltiades. Marry [your sister] Elpinice and go"; an accusation of seducing other men's women: "Megacles, son of Hippocrates. Adulterer"; and one directed at a man responsible for spreading rumors of such a kind: "Leagros, son of Glaucon. Slanderer." We will come back to this Leagros, but later. We also find one directed at the architect of victory in the Persian wars—"Themistocles, son of Neocles. *Katapugōn.*"[76]

That by the time of Aristophanes *katapugōn* is "a very general word of abuse and contempt" has long been acknowledged. But just like *kinaidos* the word invites more precise analysis: It contains an element "*pugai,*" "buttocks" (callipygean = "bootylicious"), plus *kata,* "downward," "oriented toward" or "right into" (catarrh is "what runs down," a catalyst "what breaks something right down," a catastrophe "a turning right over"). In fact *katapugōn/katapugos* sounds exactly like "right-up-buttocks," "buttocks-oriented," "buttocks-bound," but although there has been debate about when it lost its "true original meaning" and became a generic term of abuse, there has been no debate about whose buttocks were being "gone up" in the postulated "true original meaning": it was the subject's own. The recently discovered graffito, therefore, provides evidence for a previously unknown slur on the reputation of Themistocles, by all accounts an exceptionally family-oriented and unusually uxorious Greek: that he was a passive homosexual.[77]

But, although Themistocles made many enemies and we are not short of scandalous anecdotes about him, a predilection for bending over has not hitherto been among them. There is, however, one scandalous sexual misdemeanor attached to his name that may be more relevant. For he was said to have introduced courtesans to Athens, driving into the city through the red-light district, the Ceramicus, early one morning when the streets were packed, in a chariot drawn by four courtesans. We are even given their names: Lamia, Scione, Satyra and Nannio.[78] This is precisely the kind of debauchery that would have led someone like Aristophanes, fifty years later, to call Themistocles a *katapugōn*.

Already, therefore, at the very start of the classical period, in the time of Themistocles, the word denoted general lecherousness, or licentiousness. Well, not necessarily. As with *kinaidos* the point is not, in fact, what *katapugōn* truly originally meant way back in the seventh century, for in fact its origins are obscure, and as with other such insults, perhaps rather complicated and surprising—a *katapōgōn* for instance is someone with a very long beard (*pōgōn*). What counts for us is what a classical Athenian would *deduce* the word referred to, and he or she might just as easily deduce someone with a predilection for going up other people's buttocks, an "arse-bandit," as for having his (or hers) gone up, just as the -er ending on the word "bugger" might mislead someone into thinking he was properly a "doer," a "buggerer."

So an Athenian could read the insult "up-buttocks" either way. If anything, there might be a slight preference for the "active" meaning, for the closest parallel *katakardios* ("heart-directed"—*kardia,* "heart") refers, of course, to blows "striking the heart," not to a man "struck heart-wise."[79] If one imagines an image of Themistocles, therefore, in a chariot with a team of courtesans bent over in front of him on all fours, bottoms up, one does not need much more provocation to label him an "up-buttocks" or "buttocks-oriented."

The same logic applies to an episode in Aristophanes' *Knights.* Some Athenians, appalled at the way the vulgar demagogue Cleon has managed to seduce the people of Athens, have decided to create their own demagogue to prize the people from his grip. They find the perfect candidate, a former male prostitute now selling sausages in the Ceramicus, and launch him on his new career. About to make his maiden speech to the Council, he receives a lucky omen when an "up-buttocks statesman" (*katapugōn anēr*) thunders ("farts") on his right. He knows what to do: "I bent over; then thrusting with my arsehole . . ."[80] Why would your response to the presence of an "up-buttocks statesman" be to bend over and start thrusting with your arse? Unless . . . The joke seems completely straightforward. But classicists have come up with all kinds of ingenious rationalizations to prevent the "up-buttocks statesman" from performing exactly the role his name suggests and to turn him into a pathic who has nothing to do with the Sausage-Seller bending over and thrusting with his buttocks, and takes no part in the subsequent action, beyond bystanding.

One final example returns us to poor old Demosthenes. Some visitors were asking after the notorious *kinaidos* and seducer of vulnerable, handsome, useful, young men. The cynic philosopher Diogenes "extended his middle finger and said, 'Here he is the statesman of Athens.' "[81] This finger was known in antiquity, we learn, as the *katapugōn* finger, up-buttocks finger.[82] It is impossible for scholars, especially American scholars, not to experience a sudden lightning bolt of recognition when they read this, a shared set of prejudices connecting our own culture in the twenty-first century with what had hitherto seemed an alarmingly alien system of sexual mores in the fourth century BC. Diogenes is "giving Demosthenes the finger," saying, "Up yours, Demosthenes," or "Sit on this," implying he might like it. In fact if you think about it for a couple of seconds the shock of recognition evaporates. The finger is a "false friend"; it means more or less exactly the opposite of what it would mean in America today. For Diogenes is not making the gesture to Demosthenes, he is saying to people inquiring after him: "*This is* Demosthenes." The finger represents not his own but Demosthenes' member, his "up-buttocks, buttocks-oriented member," i.e., if we are looking for a modern translation, "Backs to the wall."

To conclude this lengthy promenade, none of these words is the prerogative of boys who put out, and none is used specifically to stigmatize homosexual passivity. Up until the age of Alexander, at least, they are used overwhelmingly in the context of politics, not private life, and it is men not boys who had most to fear from it. "Wide-arse" is a short-lived insult. It refers first and foremost to "talking out of your arse," and only by extension to other modes of anal dilation, whether through buggery or adultery, for adulterers were believed sometimes to be punished by the husbands and fathers they "cuckolded" with a "radish up the arse," the radish then being grown to a much larger size than the modest one that we are accustomed to.

Katapugōn is an old word with origins in the mists of time that seems to die out suddenly and dramatically around 400 BC, between the age of Aristophanes and the age of Plato. It is used above all to attack men of power, a kind of inverse acclamation, alluding to general bad morals and in particular to sexual degeneracy and untrammeled sexuality: "The famous X? No, the infamous X"; "The glorious X? No the notorious X." If there is any implication of a particular gender orientation this is not obvious, and it can be used to insult members of either sex. It sounds like "up-buttocks," and although it might well imply that a man or a woman was prone to bend over to be pleasured, a knee-trembler, quickie fashion, it could equally imply a man with a predilection for other people's, other men's or prostitutes' buttocks, and on a few occasions seems fairly definitely to mean precisely that.

Finally *kinaidos* is a more up-to-date version of the same, but he is a type of person, someone "born that way," with or without the help of certain astrological configurations, who might even try to disguise that true nature with false signs of masculinity. *Kinaidos* is also much more stereotyped in literature, thanks in the first place to the growth of the genre of cinaedic poetry, and to cinaedic performances you could book for parties. He is a "man-woman," a lewd seducer, and differs from his close cousin, the adulterous *moichos,* because of his male orientation (though not even he is *exclusively* homosexual): an effeminate sexual seducer of males (mainly). His name may originally have been a variant of *kinados,* "fox, cunning beast," and *kinaidos* was a word Plato could use in a philosophical dialogue, or Aeschines in public speeches, not obviously obscene. But for those careless of etymology it *looked* like a compound of two words, "jig-willy," and it was this derivation that ancient scholars preferred. Although "jig-willy" could conceivably be interpreted as "willy-waggler," e.g., a lewd dancer, a more straightforward interpretation is "willy-fiddler," a male molester of males, which means that images of men fiddling with the undercarriage of masculine specimens, human or asinine, are probably to be interpreted as "talking pictures," images that encode the word in just the same way as a cartoon of someone thumping a holy book with his fist says "Bible-basher" or the figure of a man with his arms around the trunk of a large ligneous plant says "New-Age environmentalist." The vividest scene of a *cinaedus* at work comes from the Quartilla episode in Petronius's *Satyrica,* in which a *cinaedus* molests two adult males in every conceivable way, indeed rapes them.

A PROBLEM WITH *PORNEIA*

It was men in power who had most to fear from such insults. The slur that a young man at the start of his career, an *erōmenos,* must be sure to avoid was the charge of *porneia,* "whorishness": being too eager to put out in whatever position and for all the wrong reasons. Here, for example, is an account of the early years of the dictator Agathocles, who took the Sicilian city of Taormina toward the end of the fourth century BC, sending one of its most prominent citizens, Timaeus, into half a century of exile. Unfortunately for Agathocles' reputation, Timaeus spent his exile writing history, a history in which he included the following notorious squib about the tyrant who had taken everything away: "In his first youth he was a common prostitute [*pornos*] available to the most dissolute, a jackdaw, a buzzard, putting his rear parts in front of anyone who wanted."[83] For in fact, there is no great mystery about ancient Greek sexual morality: Don't be a whore.

All the courtly graciousness of Greek Love, all the talk of *charis* and charitable altruism, was essential for guarding against the charge of mercenary sex, not excluding nepotism and corruption. A zeal for establishing a firm, though not always realistic, distinction between gracious favorers and "whores" is explicit in a wide range of authors on the subject of intermale relationships. Pausanias's analysis of Athenian sexual mores in Plato's *Symposium* is focused on precisely this question of motives: that it is not what you do, but what you do it *for,* that matters: the crucial distinction is not sex but profit, whether you seek "improvement" or some political or financial advantage. In the words of Kenneth Dover: "The difference between good and bad *erōs* lies in the whole context of the ultimate physical act, not in the presence or absence of the act itself."[84]

The same emphasis is found in several other philosophical treatises, in speeches made in the Assembly and the courts, in law, and on the comic stage. A nice example of this morality and its ironies is provided by Aristophanes: "They do say those Corinthian tarts pay no attention whatsoever when a poor man tries it on, but if a rich man comes along they bend over and present themselves forthwith." "Yes and they do say that boys do the same, not for the sake of [*charis*] their *erastai,* but for money." "Only the whores among them, not the decent ones [*chrēstous*]; decent boys aren't after money." "For what then?" "A fine horse, some hunting dogs." "That's because they're ashamed to be looking for cash, and are perhaps covering up their depravity with words" (*Wealth,* 149–59). In other words, decent boys may bend over for their admirers, but only if they do so, like the mythical hero Cephalus, "graciously." What would be indecent would be charging a fee.

One gymnasium was emphatic that it wanted no such people hanging around: "BANNED: . . . MALE COURTESANS . . ." (*hētai[r]eukōs*) reads a clause in the long list of regulations (a measure that, if enforced today, might put some gyms out of business).[85] Moreover, in democratic Athens it was an offense for a male prostitute even to make a speech. If it could be demonstrated that someone who had made a speech was a male prostitute, or had been in the past, he could be permanently excluded from the city's institutions. This law seems to have been used very rarely, but in 346 BC it proved to be just what Aeschines needed.

Aeschines, formerly a tragic actor, had been sent out as an envoy to try to come to terms with the threatening power of Alexander the Great's father, the no less remarkable Philip of Macedon. Aeschines and his fellow ambassadors managed to (temporarily) avert war, but he got on a bit too well with his host, and found himself, on his return, accused of taking bribes (probably he was one of the few who had not done so). To sell yourself like that, betray your own city, was an extremely serious offense: A conviction could easily destroy him. Aeschines had to do something. He remembered that clause in the law that banned prostitutes from civic life and thought it might be just the thing to scupper the prosecution. For his accuser was one Timarchus. He, it appears, had been a prominent beauty in his youth, and even now in his late Forties was not above exposing a bit of extra flesh when he stood on the speaker's platform, denouncing Aeschines and his peace. Too much flesh, perhaps. Aeschines claimed it had not been a pretty sight, and that people looked away in disgust from the body of a man who had once been so beautiful. If the story is true, Timarchus may have made a fatal miscalculation when he failed to tuck in his toga.

Since his heyday as a young heartthrob, Timarchus seems to have made a moderately successful career for himself as a small-time politician, a hired hand; so claims Aeschines, plausibly. In other words he was a political whore, a "*sykophant*," a "*parasite*" doing the dirty work of more important figures like Demosthenes, Aeschines' bitter rival. Twice appointed to the Council, proposer, it is said, of over a hundred laws, one-time governor, probably, of one of the islands in Athens's imperial league, Timarchus had reaped the rewards of *homoerōtikos* networking, and no one had ever thought fit to accuse him of immoral earnings.[86] Aeschines did. And by invoking gossip and the goddess of rumor (*Phēmē*), by reminding the jury of the times they had seen Timarchus in the company of that rich man who always surrounded himself with handsome young musicians, the sort who are hired out for parties (enough said), the time Timarchus shared a house as "apprentice" to a doctor (and we all know about "apprentices"), the time he was found, shockingly, at breakfast with a group of men he didn't know, and helped no doubt by a jury who hadn't liked Timarchus parading in the Assembly and making trouble in the middle of peace negotiations, Aeschines won the case. Some years would pass before anyone dared to accuse Aeschines of being a perverted ambassador again.

Unfortunately for Timarchus, Aeschines was also a master of prose, a great and celebrated writer, so the witty speech he delivered in court raking over Timarchus's "scandalous" career was preserved for posterity, forever labeling this middle-ranking politician and onetime pinup "Timarchus the male whore" and providing students of ancient sexuality with one of their prime texts—one that we will visit on more than one occasion. But there is something odd about Aeschines' brilliant indictment. We might imagine that Timarchus would defend himself by simply denying these relationships, or claiming there was nothing in them. It is not as if any soiled sheets were going to be produced as Exhibit A; no DNA left on cloaks, or receipts signed for services rendered. But Aeschines anticipates a different line of defense from Timarchus and his supporters, led by great Demosthenes and some unnamed general. Timarchus, it seems, would not be claiming that these relationships didn't exist, but rather that they had been maliciously misclassified by Aeschines. They really belonged to the field of disinterested *erōs* and altruism—Achilles and Patroclus, Harmodius and Aristogiton and all the rest. It's a shame that these speeches in Timarchus's defense do not survive. An address by a general glorifying homosexual *erōs* in front of a jury of ordinary citizens in the mid-fourth century BC would have made fascinating reading.

Porneia then is whorishness in every possible sense of the term: doing it for money, doing it readily, doing it to further your career. It was a terrible thing for a free Athenian citizen to be accused of, a charge that could destroy his life, but it's not always clear what tips the scales, which is of course the whole point. *Porneia* is the dark and threatening cloud that is the necessary obverse of all the extravagant can't-help-myself courtliness of Greek Love and its oh-so-gracious responses. It is all that Greek Love insists that it is not.

CONCLUSION

Agapē therefore is "fondness." *Pothos* is "longing." *Himeros* is a "love attack." *Philia* is "intimate love." *Erōs* is "driving love." An *erastēs* is "one possessed by such love," an *erōmenos* "the object of such love." And neither of these has anything whatsoever to do with *porneia,* "selling oneself cheap." And yet if the gifts of an *erastēs* delight the *erōmenos,* the *erōmenos* may "graciously grant," *charizesthai,* a few moments alone, or even one evening around midnight, "put out," *charisasthai,* that is lie down with him where no one can see and share with him the delights of Aphrodite.

It will be obvious by now that Greek Love amounts to more than a list of words. These terms are the key fragments of an integrated structure, an amatory universe, and though none of them, I hope, is beyond our ken, yet each item in that system can only really be understood in relationship to all the others. *Erōs* can be defined, therefore, entirely in terms of difference, complement, affinity and opposition, more outgoing than *intimate love,* more internal than *a love attack,* more energetic than *longing,* more passionate than *fondness,* less sexual than *lust,* and it is answered by *gracious favoring,* armed with which *erōs* stands out starkly against the dark encroaching field of *mercenary promiscuity.*

We can imagine these Love Actions as thick swaths of color in a Rothko painting, each color field a different amatory demesne, each color affecting the others by contrast or resonance—it is darker or lighter, richer or redder—and slowly changing over hours or centuries, as the light changes, as the colors fade or darken, as the greener or the bluer hues come through, or begin to bleed one into the other, a system of feelings and energies that itself interlaces with a grand cultural system, a room, a wall, a gallery, a Greek world of words, art and songs, social structures, moral values, criminal penalties and patterned practices.

AGE≈CLASSES, LOVE≈RULES AND
CORRUPTING THE YOUNG

I have been trying to understand Greek Love—not how it functioned or why it was so central, but just what it was—for about fifteen years now. Three questions have proved especially important: "What is love?" "What is gracious favoring?" "What is a boy?" The first section of this book presents my answers, and the last question, "What is a boy?" was the most demanding. Apart from the Greek word *pais* itself, which I knew was a slippery character and long acknowledged as such, two other crucial words were in common use to describe the objects of courting and admiration: *meirakion* and *neaniskos*. Both are normally considered diminutives of two other words, the very rare *meirax,* "lad," and *neanias,* "young man," so, as a rivulet is smaller than a river, and a baronet less than a baron, the diminutive versions are often (if only subliminally) believed to be smaller versions of "lad" and "young man." But translations varied wildly, and when authors were tempted into putting an age to the subject referred to, the ages assigned would vary wildly too, thus vividly displaying one of the vexing problems with Greek Homosexuality, and one of the most misunderstood: the question as to whether it was all about "young boys."

THE PEDOPHILE MYTH

Of all the many misconceptions about Greek Love, perhaps the most unwarranted is the idea that it was essentially "pedophile" in character, that its key feature was sex between "old men" and "young boys." It is unwarranted for various reasons. First, because sex with those in their earlier teens, even supposing that it was a feature, would hardly count as a *distinctive* feature of ancient Greek homosexual relations. Very few premodern societies offered young teenagers protection from sexual predators. In medieval Europe, following a pattern laid down by the Romans, marriageable age was twelve for girls and fourteen for boys, and it was only in the Victorian period that the age of consent began gradually to be raised. The Greeks were more or less in line with this pattern in disposing of their daughters, and if you seek repellent relationships between fifty-year-old men and fourteen-year-old children, or even younger, you will find plenty in the Greek marriage bed, and indeed in any number of premodern heterosexual relationships, married or otherwise; Juliet was underage, fourteen years old, when Romeo came calling.

But as regards their sons, the Greeks were unusually protective, even in comparison with many modern societies, a double standard which, curiously, has received little attention from feminist historians. In Athens, the city we know best, wealthy families had slaves, the *paidagōgoi* (as in "pedagogue") whose only job it was to chaperon Boys under Eighteen. Those whose families could not afford to maintain a *paidagōgos* were no doubt less vigorously protected, but even when someone talks of being in intimate love with a slave-boy, he is often at pains to point out that the boy is in his late teens, Eighteen or Nineteen, a group I will call Striplings. Laws forbade anyone of Twenty or over from entering the gymnasium when under-Eighteens were exercising: The strictest penalties, not excluding the death penalty, were imposed on those who transgressed. Striplings, however, were allowed into the gymnasium when Boys were exercising, as were old men it seems, like Socrates and, of course, the slave chaperons, considered too old to present a threat, but even Eighteen-year-olds were forbidden from "mingling" or "chatting" to under-Eighteens except on special holidays, notably the festival of Hermes, a kind of holy sports day it seems.

Under-Eighteens and the Eighteen-to-Nineteen-year-olds seem in fact to have been placed at opposite ends of the training ground, which might help to preserve the Boys' purity, but not necessarily their lives, especially when the Striplings were practicing the javelin, thus giving one of the earliest ambulance chasers, Antiphon (c.480–411), a useful test case for his students in the art of apportioning blame. The victim's father begins: "In the gymnasium my Boy was killed instantly when he was struck in the side by a javelin thrown by this Stripling here." The defendant's father replies: "My Stripling . . . was practicing the javelin with his classmates and though he did indeed make the throw, he didn't exactly 'kill someone,' not strictly speaking . . . The Boy ran into the path of the javelin and put his body in its way . . . My son is not the perpetrator of an accident but the victim of one, inasmuch as he was prevented from hitting the target."[1]

In fact in Athens Eighteen seems to have been considered the effective age of consent for boys, since anyone over that age accused of prostitution could himself be prosecuted; under that age, and it was his legal guardian, his father, who was penalized. Moreover the most likely transgressors of these rules were not dirty old men, it was believed, but those under Forty. Hence sometime around 400 BC, it seems, a new law was passed to make sure that the rich man who sponsored the "Boy bands," the circular choruses of under-Eighteens trained to sing and dance in festival competition, was at least Forty: "to make sure he has already reached the age of greatest self-restraint when he comes into contact with your sons."[2] One defendant feels a need to excuse himself to the jury for losing his head over a Stripling in a way unsuited to his maturity.[3] Most men under Forty would have been still unmarried: Plato thought men should not think of getting married until past Thirty, and Aristotle thought Thirty-seven the optimum age, so that you would produce your first child no sooner than twenty years after becoming a citizen. There seems in other words to have been much *less* of an age gap between couples in a same-sex relationship in ancient Greece than between heterosexual couples. It was certainly not "intergenerational" sex, and often involved a difference of just a few years.

So how, one may ask, did the fable of pedophile Greeks ever gain such currency? In large part it is the usual culprits: pictures, prejudice and poor philology. The pictures we will look at later. Suffice it to say, at this point, that images of sexual encounters with under-Eighteens, usually gropings, are not plentiful, though often reproduced, nor are they necessarily either reflections of what went on, or models of how to behave; sometimes pictures may show people behaving rather badly. Then there is the mistranslation of *erastēs* as "lover" of a boy, rather than "admirer." For, as we have seen, *erōs* for a boy need mean no more than being a noisy fan, courting and wooing, possibly writing poems and scrawling graffiti celebrating his virtues; and there was certainly no problem with that, even if the celebrated one were underage. This may seem odd to us, and it did seem odd to some Athenians that it was a good thing to have your son chased after, his virtues and beauty praised on walls and in songs, even to have him followed at a distance by a whole pack of competing men, whereas it was unthinkable, at the same time, for a Boy to be so much as alone with anyone over Eighteen without a chaperon present: Boy fans, yes, the more the better, Boy lovers, out of the question. Here is Aeschines trying to explain the rules:

> The lawgiver did not prevent a free man from being in love, from as-
> sociating with [*homilein*] or following a Boy, nor did he think it
> brought harm to the Boy; rather he thought it might bring evidence
> of the Boy's chasteness. However, I think that so long as the Boy is a
> minor [*akuros*] and as yet incapable of distinguishing kindness which
> is genuine from kindness that is not, the lawgiver *forces chasteness* on
> the one in love and postpones words of intimate love [*philia*] until the
> age of sensibleness and greater maturity; whereas he thought the
> practice of following after a Boy and watching him provided him
> with the best possible garrison and guard of his honor.[4]

The message is clear: An *erastēs* may woo his favorite all he wants, even before he is Eighteen, so long as he keeps his distance and trots along behind him with respect—it is even something to be encouraged. But anything more intimate is banned by the lawgiver, who "forces chasteness on" (*sōphronizei*) the enamored (an allusion, probably, to the official called *sophronistēs* who kept elder teenagers in line) and who "postpones words of intimate love" until the Boy has reached a certain age, implying some kind of law that prohibits intimate conversation with Boys underage. If this ban on conversation with under-Eighteens in Athens seems hard to swallow, we actually have the text of the regulations of a Macedonian gymnasium dating from *c.*175–170 BC, which explicitly include such a ban. One section begins: "Concerning the Boys: none of the Cadets [*neaniskoi*] may enter among the Boys, nor chat [*laleitō*] to the Boys, otherwise the gymnasiarch [an important public official] shall fine and prevent anyone who does any of these things."[5]

I

COMING OF AGE IN ANCIENT GREECE

The subject of this chapter is the question of age itself, how in the first place we know how old someone in a same-sex relationship was supposed to be, how big the age gap between same-sex couples was, how that age gap determined roles, why there was an age gap at all.[6] For the problem of age in ancient Greece is not confined to the area of Greek Love, it is a big black hole in our understanding of Greek civilization. Classicists don't really know what the words for different age-groups mean. Art historians don't know what age any particular image is supposed to represent. Here for instance are some attempts by a variety of esteemed scholars to specify the age designated by the extremely common term *meirakion*, the one I have translated "Stripling": "a young boy" (Guthrie, i.e., about seven years old?), "about eighteen" (Dover), "from about thirteen or fourteen to about twenty-one" (Strauss), "in his late teens" (Todd), "someone about or just under 20 years old" (Podlecki), "between the ages of fourteen and eighteen" (Hammond), "perhaps until shortly before the age of twenty" (Heckel).[7] It will already be clear that I agree with Dover, Todd and Waldemar Heckel on this question, but there is no need for hesitancy or vagueness. A *meirakion* in classical Athens is Eighteen or Nineteen, it would seem, and that is official, but there is a reason why I have felt a need to capitalize these ages, as well as the designation "Boy."

There are good reasons and bad reasons for the confusion, but certainly there is something fishy going on in the sources, as the following bizarre-sounding statements testify:

1 "Which of you two is the older?" "That is a matter of dispute between us."[8]
2 "He would have been still young in another polis."[9]
3 "The Eros of Heavenly Aphrodite . . . ; this is *erōs* for boys . . . In fact there should be a law against falling in love with boys . . ."[10]
4 "Death's deadly tally took down Sarapion, twenty-two, both young and with his first beard, to Hades . . ."[11]
5 "Artists show Apollo as a boy always."[12]

So we are not too surprised to discover that already in antiquity the scholar Aristophanes of Byzantium felt there was a need to clear things up by writing a treatise "On the vocabulary of age." How much easier everything might be if more than just its title survived.

We can go on without him however, and we can start by breaking the problem down into three parts: 1—The Greeks, like most premodern or non-Western societies, thought about age in a very different way from the way we do ourselves; they were either not very interested or completely uninterested in dates of birth, and did not celebrate annual birthdays. 2—Each individual community or polis had its own slightly or very different way of designating age. 3—People in the past, especially before about AD 1800, reached puberty four or five years later than we do now.

The first problem is that although one might think that getting older was one of those completely universal things, as universal as sexual desire and hunger, in fact it turns out to be rather different in different times and places. Although, obviously, age has quite a lot to do with human biology and the amount of time you have spent on the planet, nevertheless it is also a "cultural" process, a natural set of variable facts that each culture molds and shapes for itself into something more lucid and coherent. In fact it is modern societies that are anomalous in the energy they put into precise pinpointing of date of birth, remembering to celebrate it, and to add a year to it every 365 days, considering it a rather grievous crime to "lie about one's age," as if it were one of the most telling facts about you.

Most people throughout history have not been bothered with registrars and birthday parties and have had only a rough idea of how old they were at any given time, which is one reason why when a remote community in the Third World claims that someone in their village is 130 years old, *Guinness World Records* tends not to acknowledge the claim, unless some certificate from a former Colonial Office can be produced. This has long been acknowledged as a problem in antiquity. Tombstones from the Roman period reveal far more round numbers than one would expect: "100," C, was so much cheaper to have carved than "88," LXXXVIII.[13] Greeks seem not to have remembered birth dates, didn't celebrate their anniversaries and were vague about when they were born.

Partly this is God's fault. He managed to get the stars and seasons (the solar cycle, the solstices and equinoxes) nearly perfectly aligned, so that the stars at midnight on midsummer's night will be 99.99 percent identical to the stars at the same time last year. But the lunar cycles do not dovetail with a yearly rhythm. So when stars near and far, Betelgeuse, Sirius and Aldebaran, are doing exactly what they were doing last midsummer, the moon may be anywhere at all in its cycle: invisible, full, crescent, half.

If the calendar you use is a lunar calendar therefore, of twelve moons, there will be an extra ten days or so left over every solar year, which is why the Muslim holy month of Ramadan, which sticks religiously to moons, wanders all over the year. The Greeks too followed moons, which meant they had to skip the "twenty-ninth day" every other month or so, to keep "Day 1" aligned with the new moon, but each community had its own system for deciding when a new moon had appeared and when a day needed to be lost, so that treaties between cities sometimes show that different communities are on slightly different days of the moon-month. Moreover they started their new years at different times: first new moon after midsummer (Athens, Delphi), first after winter solstice (Thebes), second moon after spring equinox etc., and had different names for their moons, so that Athens's month 1, Hecatombaeon (falling sometime from the end of June to the first weeks of August), was (normally) Hecatombeus in Sparta, Clareon in Ephesus, and Panemos in Priene. Moreover, unlike the Muslims centuries later, the Greeks tried to keep their moon-months roughly in line with the solar year, so that a festival in Hecatombaeon would always be in high summer. Given the shortness of a twelve-moon year, they could only achieve this by inserting an extra moon every few years. So if "December" felt a bit too autumny or not wintry enough, they might repeat it so that it was more suitably cold; if "July" felt too much like June and wasn't sweltering enough, do "July" again so that it was. Moreover each community was vaguely aware of what was happening elsewhere. So if, to take a hypothetical example, Americans knew that Thanksgiving was autumny and followed the British Guy Fawkes Night, they might think about having another November if they discovered that the British had not yet celebrated Guy Fawkes when they themselves were about to kill turkeys.[14]

Through such haphazard adjustments therefore Greek calendars kept roughly in line with each other and with the solar year for centuries, but any particular day of any particular moon-month would fall on a different day of our year, wandering back and forth over weeks. In fact if a month was repeated, the same date would fall twice in one year, and anyone who organized a hypothetical birthday party for the first day of the following month would suddenly find themselves having to postpone it for thirty days. The Greeks were fully aware of the rough-and-readiness of their calendars with all their ad hoc adjustments, knowing that its days of the moon were not attached to any very precise time of year but floated loose above the true year of seasons. (If they wanted to specify a particular time of year they would normally talk of the first reappearance of a particular star just before dawn, a far more precise and consistent method for identifying a particular time of year. The sweltering "dog days" of high summer for instance are those days that follow the reappearance of Sirius the Dog Star in the fourth week of July.) In short, if the Greeks did not celebrate annual birthdays it was because there were no birth dates in our own sense to be had.

Years were identified in an even more complicated way. In Athens each year was known by the name of that year's archon, the chief magistrate, in the classical period a mostly symbolic office filled annually by a man selected at random. In order to know how long ago you had been born, you would have to memorize the entire list, which modern historians have painstakingly reconstructed, and count backward. This is why a historian like Thucydides has so few dates, simply counting years and seasons, "the following spring, etc." Look at the effort he has to invest in specifying for a pan-Greek readership the date of the opening of hostilities in the Peloponnesian War: "The Thirty Years Peace, which was entered into after the conquest of Euboea, lasted fourteen years. In the fifteenth year, the forty-eighth year of the priesthood of the priestess Chrysis at Argos, the year when Aenesias was ephor at Sparta, and two months before the end of the archonship of Pythodorus at Athens, six months after the battle at Potidaea . . ."[15] This is why the Boys in Plato's *Lysis* can argue about which one of them is older. The information was simply not available to them.

AGE:CLASSES, AGE:SETS AND AGE:GRADES

But if they were not terribly concerned about their date of birth, the Greeks were nevertheless obsessed with precise distinctions of age. Indeed for many Athenian citizens it was a matter of public information: the elite, at least, had their age-class written on boards in the town center, and later inscribed on bronze. And age was a major element in the structure of Greek society, warfare and politics, as well as of Greek Love. How is this possible? How could a society that didn't know how old people actually were be obsessed with how old people were? To solve this conundrum we have to turn to anthropology, for there is a whole group of societies in exactly the same situation, obsessed with age and yet largely oblivious as to when people were actually born. Anthropologists call them "age-class societies," and it is clear that ancient Greece provided elaborate examples of just such a mode of organization. If this has been acknowledged only rarely, it is because such societies are often viewed as standing at an exceptionally "early stage" on the ladder of societal progress, frankly primitive savages several stages behind the sophisticated Greeks, and scholars have shown themselves predictably reluctant to put the complex and highly organized state that is Aristotle's Athens, with all its treatises on government and its still-standing public buildings, in the same league as an apparently chaotic or even anarchic East African tribe or a community of Brazilian Indians, who paint themselves and live in flimsy villages. But that is the proper yardstick, and their failure to use it, despite all the evidence, is one of the main reasons why understanding Greek age has proved so difficult.

The chief diagnostic of an age-class society is that members of the tribe are only assigned an age when they leave childhood and become official members of the tribe. At that point they are all put into an *age-set* of coevals, i.e., of boys who look roughly the right age, and they will remain in the designated age-set for most or all of their lives. If no one knows or cares about the "actual" age of the members of the set, they certainly know what order they come in, which set is at level 1, which at level 3, which at level 5, and so on—your first, third and fifth year as a member of your set in communities that form new sets annually. Moreover, when they reach a certain level an age-set may be assigned a certain *grade* and have the right to participate in certain ceremonies or councils.

Among the Shavante, for instance, quite famous in Brazil, the youngest grade are Bachelors and are obliged to live together in a big hut, which quickly becomes as squalid as any boy's bedroom when a boy is left to himself. The next grade up is composed of cocky young warriors, who do a lot of dancing and singing and running races. Only at the next grade, however, are they allowed to participate in the tribal Council of "Elders," mid-Twenties plus.

That is a simplification of what can be an extremely elaborate system, and anthropologists often express awe and amazement at the complexity of such organization (especially considering the supposed backwardness of such societies in so many other respects). The basics, however, are familiar to all of us who have been through education. An age-set is exactly the same as the U.S. "Class of 1968," say. Age-grades are exactly the same as our, e.g., "first-former," "sixth-former," and so on. In fact we all become a member of an age-set when we start public education around age five in September of a particular year. If you reflect back on it you will see that one can have a very sharply defined sense of age without reference to how old someone actually is, i.e., "two years above you." Someone born on, say, August 31, 2000, may be forever senior to someone born just hours later, on say, September 1, 2000, and yet in no sense junior to someone born 365 days earlier on September 1, 1999. The former, only a few hours younger, will forever be "in the year below."

Now imagine that you have only a rough idea of your "actual age"— no twenty-first-birthday parties, no birth date to set against the year you were assigned at age five. Children are all simply designated age five when they start school. The start of the school year is also the start of the common year, and on the first day of school way back then, your set was actually given a name, the same name for all those in the country enrolled on that day in that year, a name drawn maybe from some heroic or legendary figure, something like "the year of Arthur," "the year of Galahad"—a name you will always be known by until you leave the system.

That is more or less how the age-class system worked in Athens. The procedure is described in the treatise on the Athenian Constitution—affectionately known as *Ath.(enaiōn) Pol.(iteia)*—discovered at the very end of the nineteenth century and thought to have been written by a pupil of Aristotle:

Citizenship belongs to persons of citizen parentage on both sides, and they are registered on parish [*deme*] lists when they are Eighteen. At the time of their registration the members of the parish, having first sworn an oath, take a vote on them, first whether they *seem* to have reached the age set down in law; if not, they go away *back to Boys* [*palin eis Paidas*] . . . After this the Council [of 500 randomly selected men aged Thirty or over] scrutinizes the list of those registered, and if anyone *seems* younger than Eighteen, it fines the parish that registered him . . .

Persons Fifty-Nine years of age serve as Dispute-Settlers, as appears from the regulations for the archons and eponymous heroes . . . for there are forty-two year-eponymous-heroes; and in former times the ephebes [new citizens] when enrolled used to be listed on whitened tablets, under the name of the archon in whose term of office they were enrolled and of the year-hero of those that had been Dispute-Settlers the year before [i.e., those just turning Sixty], but now they are inscribed on a bronze plaque and this is set up in front of the Council-chamber . . . They also use the year-heroes for military expeditions; when they send out the levy [*hēlikia*], they write up beforehand from which archon and year-hero to which they must march. (42,1–2; 53,4 and 7).[16]

Once a year, then, probably at New Year, following the sighting of the first new moon after the summer solstice, a new set of those *assigned* the age Eighteen after two votes, one at local level, one at national level, would be enrolled in the citizen-body and given the name of one of forty-two heroes, the name surrendered by the set that was leaving the system having reached Sixty and retirement from civic and military responsibilities: *The Year of Panops,* for instance, one of only two year-heroes so far known (or suggested). We can assume that all the heroes had sites of worship at their tombs—that is almost a definition of what a hero (*hērōs*) is in Greek religion: a powerful ghost—and probably those tomb-cults would be somewhere in Attica, so that the forty-two-year cycle would have a topographical dimension; one could go on a tour and visit all the forty-two year-heroes in sequence. Now the hero Panops, "All-Eyes," had a shrine, rediscovered some decades ago, with a fountain near a gate on the northeastern perimeter of the city between Plato's Academy and Aristotle's Lyceum. We know nothing more about him.

The only other possible year-hero so far suggested is a hero called Mounichos, for a dedication to him by newly enrolled ephebes was discovered on the other side of the city, also just outside the wall. Mounichos is more interesting, because we know he was one of the heroes who were supposed to have fought against the Amazons when they invaded Athens in the dim and distant mythical past, a legendary victory the Athenians were inordinately proud of, able to point out to visitors exactly how the battle lines had been drawn up and the course of the action, as well as the places where the Athenian heroes died. In fact scenes from the battle were used to decorate the shield of the great gold and ivory statue of Athena that stood gigantesque in the Parthenon, a temple that was dedicated in 438 BC, to coincide with the start of the first new cycle since the burning of the Acropolis by the Persians exactly forty-two years earlier in 480.[17]

The year-heroes remain extremely shadowy. The bronze tablets recording their names will have been melted down for recycling long ago. But adding one possibility to another possibility, putting two and two together to make twenty-two, as it were, we may offer a remarkable conjecture: that the forty-two year-heroes were in fact the legendary heroes who had defended Athens from the Amazons, forming a *shield* for the goddess Athena, around the perimeter of her city, possibly even in sequence, so that in religious terms each forty-two-year cycle corresponded to a circuit of the city's walls. This is a theory, at least, in a field that conspicuously lacks them, for although it is disconcerting that forty or more year-heroes have gone missing from Athens, the city we know best, it is also true that no one has been looking for them. In fact I have never spoken to an archaeologist who knew that they might exist. Until a few years ago I confess that I had never heard of them, despite decades spent studying Athens. By the same token, we can by no means assume that classical Athens was the only city to have year-heroes. Were it not for the rediscovery of the *Ath. Pol.* at the beginning of the last century, we would not even know about the Athenian heroes, although now that we know, it is clear there are hints in some late antiquarian sources that an especially attentive reader could have picked up on.[18]

As soon as the last year-set of the old year of Fifty-nine-year-olds turning Sixty had passed on its year-hero's name to the new batch of citizens, all now deemed Eighteen, all the other forty-one years would move up a level; set Twenty-nine (twelve years since being assigned the age Eighteen) would now turn Thirty and enter the grade eligible for generalships, juries, magistracies and the Council. We know this is true because the author of the treatise talks of the oldest of the forty-two sets as "those in their sixtieth year," i.e., they are all Fifty-nine together, not those who have passed their indeterminate fifty-ninth birthdays. Likewise, when Aeschines introduces Misgolas, one of whorish Timarchus's supposed boyfriends and paymasters, a man notorious for his fondness for "cithara-boys," he knows exactly how old he is, even though he looks younger and has suspiciously dark hair, because he and Misgolas "matriculated together" (*synephēbos*), they are "contemporaries" (*hēlikiōtēs*), more specifically, they "have the forty-fifth year [*etos*]," which means they are both "Forty-five" (or in their forty-fifth year since matriculation, i.e., they are Sixty-two").[19]

This system, of course, could be very useful for those writing about the past. All Plato's dialogues, for instance, are set in a prior era. Written after 400 BC, they evoke real historical figures who flourished before that date, notably the people around Socrates, who was executed at Seventy in 399. It would be relatively straightforward therefore for Plato to know how old any of his characters were at any time, and how old relative to one another; all he had to do was find out their year-hero, and then go down to the town center and calculate that when someone in year "This Hero" was a Stripling at Eighteen, then someone in year "That Hero" was Twenty-eight, someone in year "The Other Hero" had just become a Senior, and so on. Sometimes, of course, his characters were still alive, and well-known to his audience, thus giving extra vividness to a previous epoch. Readers might know Lysis as a mature man, or even a venerable old man, Seventy to their Fifty. So when Plato introduces him in *Lysis* as a Boy not yet Eighteen, you would have a vivid sense of how long ago the dialogue was set. It was like having a human date-chart set out in front of you.

This then is why I have capitalized ages: to reflect the fact that these are "conventional" or "official" ages. That does not mean that they are false or artificial ages, for there were no true ages to measure against (and why is it truer to say that someone is "five" 364 days after their last birthday and "six" a day later?). Doubtless some Eighteen-year-olds may have been nearly nineteen in our terms, or even older if they looked young for their age, while some may have been seventeen or younger if they looked old for their years. Such calculations would be largely meaningless. And it is not impossible that in problematic cases—for it might be a matter of critical importance when a Boy was to come into his inheritance or be sent to fight in an imminent war—witnesses were called to testify, say, that Olorus's son was born "during the festival of the cleaning of Athena's statue in the twentieth year after the Persian Sack ten months into the archonship of X eighteen years ago," but we never hear of such disputes at matriculation, and consideration both of the numbers of candidates who had to be processed each year and of parallels with other such "scrutinies" of eligibility lead to the conclusion that no evidence of age beyond the physiological was presented and no appeals against the boards' decisions sanctioned: Candidates were accepted or rejected on the nod. Better luck next year: "Back to Boys."

We can elaborate a bit on the "physiological" because there are references to Seniors "viewing the genitals" of boys during the Athenian age-scrutiny.[20] (Similarly, medieval law codes from Germany decided age of maturity by searching for "hair in his beard, down below and under both arms.")[21] Those who supervised the great Pan-Greek games, such as the Olympics, had their own criteria for sorting out age-categories; some, at least, used "bigness," i.e., "height," to assist in assessments.

WHAT IS A "YOUNG MAN"? WHAT IS A "BOY"?

Now alongside all these set-names are names for grades, i.e., the particular status a set achieves when it reaches a certain age. This double system of titles, according to both set and grade reached, threw Western observers into confusion when they first came across age-class societies in Africa, for sets might take their titles not from heroes, Arthurians, Panopticians, etc., but from animals, say, or something more picturesque—"those who ignore their fathers," "impervious to hexes," etc.[22] It might seem something of a relief therefore that Athenian grades that we can reconstruct with a reasonable, if not total, amount of certainty are so transparent seeming:

A Under-Eighteen: Boys (*paides*)
B Eighteen and Nineteen: Striplings (*meirakia* [or *neaniskoi* = Striplings-in-the-Gymnasium/Officer Cadets?])
C Twenty+: Men (*andres*)
  i Twenty to Twenty-nine: Young Men (*neoi*)
  ii Thirty+: Seniors (*presbutai*—as in Presbyterian, a church ruled by its seniors)

But in fact "normal-sounding" words for civic grades create lots of problems. For instance, we are told by some technical writers who had probably read Aristophanes of Byzantium's lost treatise on age-terms that in Sparta teenagers were given a different grade name for every year, corresponding roughly to UK "fourth-former, fifth-former . . ." up to ". . . finalist." Most of these are unique, odd-sounding or archaic terms—*mikkizomenos* ("littl'un?"), *rhobidas* (?), *meleiren* ("about to be *eirēn*" = "about to be a Twenty-something"). One year grade, however, the rough equivalent of "freshman," was called simply "Boys": in Sparta boys are called Boys when they are Eighteen. How do you know if a Spartan "boy" referred to by an Athenian writer like Xenophon is an Eighteen-year-old Spartan Boy, an Athenian under-Eighteen Boy, or just a generic boy? Thucydides is clearly using the Athenian age-class term when he pointedly observes that Alcibiades in his early Thirties would have been "still young in another polis." What he means is "he would still have been in the grade of Young Man in another polis" and therefore ineligible to become a general and to lead the disastrous Sicilian expedition. But elsewhere the same term might just mean "young person." Here is Socrates, executed for, among other things, "corrupting the youth" (literally "destroying the *neoi*," the "Young Men"), disingenuously asking what grade he is not allowed to corrupt: "Until what age are people young [*neoi*]?" "So long as they are ineligible to sit on the Council" is the reply. "Don't even have a conversation with anyone under Thirty."[23]

Moreover, as we can see, different communities had completely different age-assignment machinery. Probably never in the whole history of mankind have so many rigorously different systems rubbed up so close against one another. An Athenian Stripling might get on his horse one morning on the borders of Attica and go for a gallop around some neighboring states and find he had changed his age five times before bed-time: "Look, it's a Stripling, it's a Man, it's a *meleiren,* its a *kouros,* it's a Boy."

Eventually, by fits and starts, Athenian terms took over, though not necessarily meaning precisely what they had meant in classical Athens. Before that, however, we can just about discern what we might call a "general" Greek system of nontechnical terms—i.e., if you were not a boy you must be a man and vice versa. In conclusion we can say with some certainty that "Boy" in Athens meant two very different things: either (1) someone still in the technical local Athenian grade of Boys—i.e., under-Eighteen, not a Stripling yet, or (2) nontechnical, nonlocal, general Greek boy—i.e., under-Twenty, not a Man yet. So an Athenian Stripling who is *by definition* someone who is no longer a Boy, who has passed the age-scrutiny and was *not* sent "back to Boys," can nevertheless casually be called "boy," just as we might call someone a boy—"you boys are all the same"—moments after observing that he used to do something "when he was a boy." When a historian of Alexander wishes to emphasize that the young Macedonians who formed the king's body-guard of "Royal Boys" (*Basilikoi Paides*), usually referred to as "the Royal Pages," were not in fact prepubescent children but in their late teens, he says the boys "were those who had come of age as Striplings," *hosoi es hēlikian emeirakieuonto.*[24] In fact Greek writers might use boy, *pais,* in these two different senses in the same paragraph or even in the same sen-tence. Plutarch would wonder why modern scholars have made so much fuss about a superficially nonsensical but in fact perfectly transparent sentence such as the following: "Spartans call those who have been two years out of Boys '*eirenes*' [20+], and the oldest of the boys are '*about-to-be-eirenes*' [19]."[25] In context it is not that difficult.

In the pan-Hellenic world of same-sex Love, nine times out of ten the "boy" in question is the general apolitical non-institutionalized boy who is not yet a Man, i.e., under Twenty. Here is Socrates, for instance, trying to outdo a speech by Lysias in Plato's *Phaedrus:* "There was this *boy,* or rather this sweet little Stripling [*meirakiskos*] . . . and one of his admirers pretended to the *boy* that he was not in love with him . . . and he made the following speech: 'Look, *boy,* the first thing to do for any-one who puts himself in the position of an adviser is to . . .' "[26] The in-numerable formulaic inscriptions "The boy is beautiful" normally refer to this broader general sense of boy, for the boy depicted is often clearly Eighteen-plus, though there are some exceptions.

A *paiderastēs* therefore, "an admirer of boys," is someone afflicted with *erōs* for someone who might be any age under Twenty. But there is no iron rule and you have to keep your wits about you. See if you can make sense of what the character Pausanias is saying in Plato's *Symposium,* when he tries to explain the distinction in practice between the exalted, "Heavenly" or "Uranian," personality-focused Aphrodite, and her evil twin (according to Plato), the base, sex-obsessed, "Vulgar" Aphrodite Pandemos:

> The *erōs* of Heavenly Aphrodite has, in the first place, nothing to do with the female but only the male; this is *erōs* for boys . . . But even in this context of boy-admiring [*paiderastia*] one may recognize those who are genuinely provoked by this [exalted] *erōs:* for they don't fall in love with boys, unless with boys who are already at the point of beginning to get some sense, that is, around the time they start to grow a beard. I think those who first fall in love with them at this time [i.e., at beard-growth] are ready to be with them their whole life, to share their life with them . . . In fact there should be a law against falling in love with Boys . . . You never know how Boys will turn out, bad or good, personalitywise and bodywise.[27]

THE GREAT PUBERTY SHIFT

Of all the reasons for confusion about the age of bygone boys, however, perhaps the most confusing has been "the Great Puberty Shift." For all these Striplings, officially Eighteen or Nineteen, are regularly described as "Beardless" (*ageneioi*), or rather, since Boys too are beardless, "not *properly* bearded," "not quite yet bearded," "off-of-a-beard," ". . . a Stripling, the first down of youth on his cheeks, etc." For instance, Striplings featured in a great many comedies, raping virgins and falling expensively in love with courtesans, but when we read accounts of the masks the actors wore when playing Striplings we find they are all at various stages of beardlessness, from the "smooth-cheeked Stripling" to the "fluffy-faced Stripling." Completely in harmony with this is the epitaph for poor young Sarapion, which notes not only his age—"22"—and his age-grade—"Young

Man"—but also that he was "recently bearded" (*artigeneios*). Now I was a late developer, one of the last in my class to be thrown out of the altos, but even I had a beard at eighteen—not Karl Marx, but needing attention: "recently bearded" four years before Sarapion, *c.* AD 200.

In fact there is plenty of evidence, from the autobiographies of men like Casanova, to studies of the age of boy-trebles in German choirs, to Rembrandt's dated self-portraits, which demonstrates that people in the past, especially before *c.* AD 1800, hit puberty much later than they do now; indeed the age of puberty has continued to fall in the last sixty years. The reason is not absolutely clear, but diet is almost certainly the main factor, i.e., puberty requires a certain body weight to be reached before it can kick off. The diet of pregnant mothers may also be a factor. One surprise is that wealth does not seem to have made much difference. The emperor Augustus is supposed to have celebrated his first shave when he was twenty-three.[28] Nor, for boys, does the amount of body fat seem to make much difference—exercise is not a factor. Judging from the evidence of skeletons, when man stopped hunting and gathering and turned to eating grass seeds, population levels soared and nutrition levels plummeted. For several thousand years he became a shorter species and puberty came later; thus facial hair would have started to appear roughly around 18.5, not 14.5 years, a "shaveable" beard around 20.5, not 16.5 years.[29] So to say that a Stripling, "not younger than Eighteen," was unbearded, while a Man, "not younger than Twenty," would be just getting his beard might not be too far from the truth. The key point perhaps is the two-year period from first signs of fuzz to shaving; age-inspectors were looking for the first signs of puberty at Eighteen, which would result, two years later, in a face with enough growth on it to look beyond doubt like a Man's.[30]

IMAGES

Now, unlike the Romans, classical Greeks did not shave. A Greek image of a male without a beard, therefore, is an image of a man not yet able to grow one. All those famous nude statues of muscled Apollo or Hermes are therefore images of Striplings. The "Greek god" of popular fantasy is in fact not a fully fledged clean-shaven adult but a croaky-voiced teenager surging with hormones. This is why Lucian can say that artists always show Apollo as a boy, meaning under Twenty; like Achilles, and Apollo's boyfriend Hyacinthus, he was shown as a Stripling.[31] In fact, when we come to look at images of males on Athenian vases, it is easy to make out three different age-groups using just two diagnostics, height and facial hair.[32] Full height with beard is a Man, full height and beardless is the "ephebic" Stripling, or if he is at the gym, riding a horse, or looks a bit swanky, a *Neaniskos,* a Cadet. Finally, beardless and under height is a Boy, under-Eighteen, like the short beardless hero worshipped at a shrine outside Thebes and known simply as Boy (*pais*).[33] Older grades might also be distinguished in art. They seem to have longer, and/or shaggier, beards, as if beards grew year by year, like antlers, and their pectoral muscles have dropped, from a quarter of the way down the chest to halfway down.

One particular vase in Boston by the Telephos Painter from the years following the Persian invasion usefully illustrates an entire age-class cycle for us, from a big Boy just on the brink of matriculating, but still accompanied by his *paidagōgos,* through beardless Stripling to decrepit white-bearded old man.[34] In fact the artist has given adjacent pairs of them identical headgear, bandannas or yarmulkes etc., rather as if they are the same person in an older and a younger version, an Athenian aging, Before and After, right in front of your eyes.

It should be obvious that these images are by no means photographically realistic. People the same age are not all the same height. Boys don't suddenly gain full height and then begin to grow beards. When facial hair does appear, it tends to do so first on the top lip and on the chin, not gracefully to descend from the ears in the form of sideburns, as it so often is said to do in literature and shown to do in art. You see no imperfections in Greek art, no fuzz, no acne—well, almost none, for there are a few images of realistic fluffy-chinned teenagers, with normal-sized genitals, from the start of the classical period when artists seem briefly to have experimented with greater realism. Even men's genitals are neat and tiny and body hair is much less in evidence than you would expect from looking at the Greeks' modern descendants.

So these images point to real facts about physiological changes—that men grow beards, that they increase in height—but these facts have been sorted into a more lucid and coherent pattern. For all its seeming naturalism, ancient art is written in a formal visual language, not realistic but indicative: It refers to things in the real world but does not mirror reality. Greek images have to be read and interpreted as if they were written in code. Greek art did not present "idealized images of Man," it produced "idealized images of age-grades."

The word for "age," "of age," "age-grade," "age-set" and so on is the same word, *hēlikia,* as the word for "height." Showing Striplings as at a particular height, exactly the same height as each other and the same as maturer men, is simply code for "same age," "of age," "same height," "of height." The under-Eighteens, however, who have not yet been

7. Kouros. Such statues were produced in enormous numbers in the archaic period in Attica and neighboring states. The hair is drawn back behind the ear to show where the sideburns—first sign of manhood—will grow, and the left foot is forward, the first foot to move from a starting position; thus, the kouros represents coming-of-age and a New (Human) Year. This example discovered in 1936 is associated with an inscribed base: "Stand by the memorial of dead Croesus and feel pity. He was slain in the midst of the front-line champions by sudden Ares" *IG* I3 1240. Attica, marble (*c.*530), from the ancient cemetery at Phoinikia near Kalyvia beach.

placed in a set, who haven't yet passed inspection, are not only under-height but all different heights, still in a state of undifferentiation, "underage," "not of age," "underheight," "not of height." Sometimes artists even show a little peak on the pubic hair of Striplings. This could easily be decoded by a Greek as *akmē hēbēs,* "the peak of youthful bloom," "as plants first bloom and then seed."[35] Likewise the ubiquitous statues of full-grown beardless males that art historians call *kouroi* often have the hair drawn back behind the ears as if to show the absence of sideburns, or perhaps to show the first trace of sideburns painted on but now long since flaked off. And they put the left foot forward. This is the first foot to advance from a starting position, forward, away from being Boys. Thus these images can be used to indicate the very "moment of coming of age," the new year-set, the New Year.[36] These images with their discrepant physical features *say* "in his late teens," "between Man and Boy," they don't *show* someone in his late teens. It is a little bit like a picture that *says* "middle-class" with an image of a man wearing a top hat and work boots.

II

AGE AND ERŌS

GUARDING THE BOYS

It should be clear then that there is a big problem awaiting anyone who seeks to understand Greek homosexual ethics: In Athens the same word *pais* could be used for someone Eighteen–Nineteen and therefore "legal," and also for someone under Eighteen and therefore untouch-able. Now it is one thing not to be specific about the precise age of a boy of whom you are acclaiming: "Beautiful is the boy," either because it is some anonymous Stripling you have drawn on a pot and whose age-status can be easily decoded, or because it is some named "boy"—"Beautiful is Leagros"—who actually exists in the city, whose current age will be known to everyone, but above all, because acclaiming a boy's beauty/virtue is considered quite innocuous no matter how old he is. However, when there are intimations of intimacy, of *philia,* or merely of "words of love," with a boy or Boy, such ambiguity becomes much more dangerous.

So there is nothing casual about Socrates' little clarification in *Phaedrus*—"this boy, or rather, a sweet little Stripling"—for he is introducing the speech of a man out to sexually seduce a "boy" and needs to make it clear that he is not talking of someone under Eighteen. In fact authors often prove almost comically concerned quickly to inform their readers that the boys in question are Eighteen-plus. In another of Plato's dialogues, for instance, *Protagoras,* we meet for the first time Agathon and Pausanias, who will be his partner till his death over twenty years later. This Pausanias is the same one who in the *Symposium* rails against *erōs* for under-Eighteens, and suggests "there should be a law against falling in love with Boys" that includes the kind of harsh penalties— death on the spot—meted out to adulterers. In *Protagoras,* datified (i.e., its date deliberately flagged by the author) about fifteen years earlier than the *Symposium,* the couple seem to be at the very start of their relationship, and Plato describes Agathon's age here. This is what the Penguin translator renders as "young boy," thereby presenting Pausanias as an astonishing hypocrite, having an amatory relationship with someone under age, exactly what he said should be made illegal. Plato is not beyond such irony, but in fact the phrase he uses is "new-ish Stripling"— *neon ti meirakion.* Plato was trying, for all the good it did him, to underline precisely the opposite: that Agathon was legal at the time, albeit only just.

Another example. When Xenophon, an apologist for Spartan mores, comes to tell of the love of Prince Archidamus for Cleonymus, one of the soppiest and most incongruous episodes in any Greek history, he quickly notes in a parenthesis that Cleonymus "had the age-grade [*hēlikia*] just out of Boys [*ek paidōn*]."[37] Twenty years or so earlier, the plaintiff who delivered the speech "Against Simon," written for him by the great Lysias, refers to the boy he lusts after not as "the boy," but as "the Stripling" (sixteen times), occasionally even as "the Cadet [*neaniskos*]" (three times), and this in the course of what is a very short speech. Moreover, it seems very likely that said boy was not only not an Athenian citizen, but very probably a slave, albeit possibly quite a high-class one. There are even indications that for fourth-century writers (but not for fifth-century vase painters) the very subject of sex with Boys under Eighteen was taboo. For Aeschines is quite happy to describe Timarchus in his late teens as a "common whore," and to name his supposed clientele, but any detailed insinuations about his career as a Seventeen-year-old prostitute before he became a citizen seem to be quite off-limits: "Look how moderate I am going to be, Men of Athens, in my dealings with Timarchus. For I am passing over all those sins he committed against his own body when he was a Boy. Let there be an amnesty for these things . . . But as for what he got up to when he was a Stripling, when he was by now a responsible person [*phronōn*] with knowledge of the laws of the city . . ."[38] Well that, as he demonstrates at some length, will be another story.

Love poets on the other hand eschewed technical terms like Stripling or Cadet, perhaps because they sounded much too legalistic or because the category did not exist in their societies. But if the archaic poet Ibycus wrote lots of love songs about "boys," over a thousand years later Suda, the Byzantine encyclopedia, feels sure these were in fact songs about Striplings.[39] Cicero, a contemporary of Caesar and Cleopatra, writing five hundred years after Ibycus, thinks these early Greek love poems are evidence of sexual lust, *lubidinosos . . . amores,* but lust, he adduces, for "young men," not boys: "What things Alcaeus wrote about love of young men [*iuvenes*]."[40] He is equally disdainful of Spartan homosexual hypocrisy. But here too he assumes that the Spartan boys who are the target of love (and other things) are in their late teens, the equivalent of Roman *iuvenes,* though present-day students of Sparta don't believe it.[41] Likewise, Maximus of Tyre, writing in the reign of Commodus (a contemporary, therefore, like Sarapion, of Russell Crowe in *Gladiator*), is full of praise for the way the Cretans conduct homosexual affairs, and these are relationships, he assumes, between Striplings and Cadets. Presumably he means between Striplings and elite Striplings or Eighteen- and Nineteen-year-olds.[42]

Plato, of course, must be especially careful with Socrates, since it was his relationships with young people that had got him into so much trouble. So when Socrates converses with sexy Charmides, Plato's uncle, the author is at pains to point out that he was by then at least Eighteen (*meirakion, neaniskos, neanias*). Nevertheless Plato makes sure that Socrates makes sure that Charmides' chaperon, his guardian Critias, is at hand: "Even if he happened to be younger it would not be shameful for us to converse with him in front of you."[43] In Plato's *Lysis* Socrates is allowed to be introduced to the eponymous under-Eighteen by young men the same age as Charmides (*neaniskoi*), because it is the festival of Hermes,

Hermaia, "when Boys and Cadets" are, quite exceptionally, permitted "to mingle."[44] Still, there is much caution, and the conversation is arranged only through the mediation of Lysis's best friend, the Boy Menexenus, and Menexenus's elder cousin, the Cadet Ctesippus, best friend of the Cadet Hippothales, Lysis's bashful admirer. The conversation, appropriately about friendship, affinity and amatory objectification, is terminated by thick-accented slave *paidagōgoi* before it reaches any conclusion, for the true subject of the dialogue is dialogue itself, and how much superior it is to an admirer's preposterous acclaiming.

Xenophon is equally careful to make sure that when he places the under-Eighteen all-in wrestling champion Autolycus at his fictionalized symposium, his father is present; and the Boy doesn't recline, but sits at his father's feet, barely joining in the conversation, and leaving before the dancing girls and boy come on. By the same logic the author of a first-century AD scandal sheet discovered in Egypt and now in Oxford would expect his readers to be outraged to discover that the former governor Gaius Vibius Maximus had started a relationship with a handsome young man when he was only Seventeen. There were witnesses, for they dined and drank together quite openly: "Every one of these men would see the Boy at your symposium, sometimes with his father present, sometimes unchaperoned [*monos*]."[45] Any hypothetical sister of this Boy would be expected to have been married by that age, and possibly a mother.

MIND THE GAPS

Now the *neaniskos* Hippothales may be only a few years older than his *erōmenos* the Boy Lysis, or even just one year older, i.e., when Lysis passed out of Boys, his new age-set might have ended up just one year below that of Hippothales, for both are real people. In fact a group of images shows amatory, and amorous, transactions between beardless Cadets and under-height Boys. Moreover the gymnasium regulations that forbid the two age-grades mingling and chatting (*lalein*) clearly reveal an anxiety about relations between these two groups in particular, if only because Cadets shared the same gym space. In fact one of several founding myths of the practices of Greek Love concerns the abduction of Pelops's son Chrysippus, a Boy, by the Stripling Laius, prince of Thebes. The myth (of course) made of the rape a terrible crime, "illegal erōs [para-nomos]," "banned erōs [athemitos]," which resonated down the ages, lead-ing to the tragedy of Oedipus, Laius's son.[46] But the kind of thing Hippothales was spending his time on—the practices of distant besot-tedness, love songs for the benefit of his friends—seems not to have been a problem. It is perfectly possible that Lysis's father would have been dis-appointed if his son did not attract at least one voluble admirer, prefer-ably from a good family, before he left Boys. (Bear in mind again that Greek Love comes in two distinct forms, the wolf pack of erastai with all their noisy protestations, and the special intimate relationship between two members of the same sex.)

Whatever distinction Maximus thinks he is making between Cretan "Striplings" and their restrained, admiring "Cadets"—groups that six hundred years earlier in classical Athens were identical in age—he can-not be thinking of any substantial gap. As for Spartan Cleonymus "in the grade just out of Boys," the date of this little episode is c. 378 and Prince Archidamus was born "about 400," so he would be about Twenty-two, just four years older than his erōmenos. One cannot simply count images to demonstrate facts about life at that time, but it is cer-tainly worthwhile to point out that a number of scholars, notably the Dutch scholar Charles Hupperts, have in recent years drawn attention to a quite substantial number of images, especially in the fifth century, which seem to show members of the same age-group, mostly Striplings, courting or wooing or having sex with coevals—images which have been often overlooked. Hupperts even claims that "one-third of all courtship scenes bear upon this category [coevals] of lovers."[47]

In texts there are some specific references to sex and love and sexual attraction between age-set-mates. A contemporary of Aristophanes put onstage a personification of Mount Lycabettus, a high deserted hill on the edge of ancient Athens to the northeast, and still apparently a site for assignations. "Chez moi," says the mountain, "Striplings, utter Striplings, gratify their age-mates."[48] There has been much de-bate about this unique phrase "utter Striplings."[49] What does seem clear, however, is that they are indeed Striplings gallivanting with their classmates on Lycabettus. But to whom will this be headline-making news?

The most famous amatory coevals in the Socratic discourses are the love triangle of Ctesippus, Clinias and Critobulus. Ctesippus, a Cadet, who in *Lysis* chaffs his best friend Hippothales for his tedious songs about the Boy Lysis, seems to have been the oldest. In another dialogue, still a "Cadet," he is himself *erastēs* not of a Boy but of another Stripling/Cadet (*meirakion/neaniskos*), Clinias, "son of Axiochus, son of Alcibiades" (some older relative of the famous one), although since Clinias is described as "young," he may be in the year below Ctesippus. In the same dialogue we also meet Critobulus, son of one of Socrates' friends. We are told he is "of age" and in the same "age-class" (*hēlikia*) as Clinias, another Stripling/Cadet, though not, his father reckons, so advanced (*propherēs*) as Clinias.[50] His father notes that he needs a good philosophical teacher: Socrates, perhaps.

Xenophon plays with these characters of Plato, but he makes young Critobulus, the fuzz (*ioulos*) "creeping down in front of his ears," dreamily besotted with his more mature classmate Clinias "[the fuzz] already going up behind" (whatever that means), who already, we recall, has a boyfriend in Ctesippus. Critobulus's passion for handsome Clinias had started earlier, we are told, "when they used to go together to the same school." Socrates fears he may even have kissed Clinias, a terribly dangerous thing to do. For this reason his father took Critobulus away and made Socrates his teacher. But absence made the heart grow fonder and Critobulus's obsessive *erōs* for his maturer classmate continued.[51] Elsewhere Xenophon says that, in front of Critobulus, Socrates pointedly warned him, "Xenophon," about the dangers of kissing handsome boys, instancing Critobulus's kissing of Clinias.[52]

This is a nice example of how an Athenian can represent a same-age passion, clearly a cause for comment and likely to worry a father. We can see that it is really only by separating Critobulus from the object of his obsession that his "*erōs*" for his former classmate can be manifested:

"Don't you know" says Critobulus, "that I have so clear an image of him in my soul that if I were a sculptor or a painter I could produce a likeness of him from that image no less than seeing him in person." "Well if you possess an image so like him, why do you waste my time taking me to places you can see him?" "Because, Socrates, the sight of him has the power to make me happy, but the image of him gives me no joy, but simply implants longing [*pothos*]."[53]

The key point is that classmates like Hippothales and Ctesippus, Lysis and Menexenus are already intimate, already friends, allowed to spend time in each other's naked company, allowed even to live together without raising eyebrows, unlike poor Timarchus, who "showed no compunction about leaving his ancestral home and moving in with Misgolas, neither a friend of the family nor an age-mate [hēlikiōtēs], but a stranger and his senior . . ."[54] Love between age-mates simply didn't register; it wasn't noticeable. You cannot have a distance-crossing erōs for someone if there is no distance to cross. You cannot wait outside the classroom for a classmate. People "who matriculated together," sunepheboi, are already "intimates," philoi.

LOVE AMONG THE LEVELS

We can assume therefore, I think, that the noisy kind of erōs might involve anyone from Eighteen to Eighty proclaiming the virtues of anyone from Nine to Nineteen. Indeed one could be seen to proclaim the virtues of someone much older than a Stripling. Some of the figures acclaimed as beautiful on vases, a prime diagnostic of a relationship of erōs, are no youngsters. Socrates and Phaedrus name Isocrates and Lysias as their respective "favorites," paidika, although Isocrates was probably by that time well into his Twenties, "still a Young Man," and Lysias probably much older than that. Intimate philia on the other hand was normally assumed to prevail between people much closer in age, ideally a Young Man in his Twenties and a Stripling certificated as Eighteen, who had perhaps first caught his eye at the gym when he was himself a Stripling and the Stripling a Boy whom he might have tried chatting up once when mingling was permitted at the festival of Hermes. All the stories about noble admirers performing heroic actions to make their boyfriends proud assume that the admirers are at the age of young warriors. Indeed Socrates seems to generalize about this tendency for erastai to be younger, when he wishes someone would write a speech advising boys to graciously favor older men rather than younger men, and poor men rather than the rich.[55]

The question, however, is why erōs is not only one-sided, one man pursuing another, but almost always unidirectional from the older to the younger. There are a number of answers to this, but the key point is to remind ourselves yet again that we are dealing with who makes a song and dance about it, not who shafts whom or who loves whom. Of course there were younger males who fancied older males, like fourth-formers at a public school fancying the captain of rugby. When the handsome Stripling Charmides enters, for instance, it is not only the older men who turn their heads: "The reaction of the Men was not surprising, but it was the Boys who caught my attention, for none of them had eyes for anything else, not even the littlest of them; on the contrary, all were gazing at him as if he were a statue."[56] The point is that no younger male is supposed to *perform the role of love-struck suitor,* besottedly courting someone in a year above. Of course it would strike us as incongruous, even today, for a fourth-former to send a signed Valentine's Day card filled with lovesick doggerel to the Head Boy, or for an undergraduate to wait outside the classroom for a junior lecturer with a bunch of flowers and an invitation to dinner. It subverts the hierarchy. It's unnatural.

In one of the most vicious obituaries in ancient literature, Xenophon spits venom at his former commander Meno, the impossibly handsome Thessalian who had somehow managed to be assigned the doomed leadership of a battalion of mercenaries marching against the emperor of Persia to install a pretender on the Persian throne. After insinuating that he had used his looks to get his command and that there was more to his relationship with one particular Persian, who surrounded himself with handsome Striplings, than mere friendship, he adds the appalling charge that even when he was beardless, Meno had been the *erastēs* of a man with a beard, not that he had buggered him—though Xenophon might well have wished to imply that also, or even that he had fallen in love with him—but that he had *performed the role of his besotted admirer.* This is a passage much cited in accounts of the rules and roles of Greek Homosexuality, but the lesson drawn—that you could not be buggered when you had a beard—is not Xenophon's lesson. He is not attacking the bearded beloved but his beardless admirer. It is Meno who is out of line, a Stripling doing a Senior's job commanding an army, wooing grown Men, turning the world upside down.

Not dissimilarly, Alcibiades the Younger, son of the famous Alcibiades, was accused of "keeping a courtesan before he came of age [*anēbos*]," yet another example of his immorality. And Socrates warns off Critobulus, who seems to have a penchant for (slightly) older men. He playfully accuses him of brushing his naked shoulder against his own, most provocatively: "I formally warn you in front of all these witnesses not to touch me until your beard is as hairy as your head."[57]

The second role-determining factor is the whole obsession with the "beauty of youth," which insists that Boys when they grow their first beard are at the peak of graceful *charis,* "in bloom," *eph'ēbē.* Suddenly at New Year all these off-limits Boys became Striplings, free of their *paidagōgoi,* out and about. In fact they seem to have "come out" in a rather spectacular fashion in Athens, running a nude torch race during the night before the great summer festival of Athena's birthday, the Panathenaea, at the end of Hecatombaeon, from the altar of Love in the gymnasium of the Academy outside the city walls to an altar in the city. Of course the spectacle attracted an audience. Comic authors describe people waiting at the city gate in the Ceramic parish to welcome these new graduates of the gymnasium with "slaps of the Ceramicus"— smacked bottoms for the laggards who didn't run fast enough and so let their tribal team down—and for those men who didn't yet have boyfriends it must have been a bit like an express cattle market, first chance to catch a glimpse of young Charmides in all his famous splendor, the one old Socrates couldn't stop talking about, and maybe to catch his eye.[58] Of course if all the attention was on these new citizens coming out, their admirers would all be older, a matter of demographic economics: "Suddenly, if he happens to be *kalos* [beautiful], he finds himself in possession of an asset in short supply and high demand . . ."[59]

So it is not strictly true that older males courted younger males, any more than it is true that in modern business men with cheaper cars importune men with more expensive cars for jobs and promotion. Nor is it true that *erastēs* was the name given to the older one in a relationship, while the younger one was called *erōmenos,* any more than it is true that in a modern university older people are called Readers and Professors and younger people Lecturers. What is true is that the more beautiful males were the objects of amatory obsession and the younger ones were considered automatically the more beautiful. This is clearly the logic Phaedrus uses in Plato's *Symposium* when he objects most strongly to Aeschylus's error because in one of his tragedies he seemed to imply that Achilles was the *erastēs* of Patroclus and not the other way around:

"Aeschylus talks crap [*phluarei*] when he alleges Achilles was in love with Patroclus [*Patroklou eran*], Achilles who was not merely more beautiful than Patroclus but than all the other heroes, not even with a beard even, younger, much younger, according to Homer."[60]

AGE-CLASS WARS

But in order to understand these age rules properly we have to set them in their very peculiar cultural context. For you don't have to be Miss Marple to deduce that the preoccupation with age difference in amatory relationships in an age-class society may have something to do with the fact that an age-class society revolves around age. If it subverts the hierarchy in our own society for a female lecturer to be courted by one of her undergraduates, how much more must it do so in an age-class society where seniority is the very foundation of hierarchy?

For although such societies believe that power in their societies is organized in perfect harmony with nature—"Nature has provided the distinction when she took something which is the same in terms of species and made it in part younger and in part older, the former fit to be ruled, the latter fit to rule: and no one objects when he is ruled in accordance with age"[61]—there are always tensions, rivalries, resentments, struggles between senior and junior grades. Occasionally there are even full-scale age-class civil wars. In Crete around 220 BC, for instance, the ancient city of Cnossus was trying to recapture the glory days of a millennium earlier, in the reign of mythical Minos, putting itself at the head of a grand alliance and coercing or destroying cities, such as Lyctus, that refused to join, and which consequently saw the rest of the island ganging gradually up on it. In Gortyn the Seniors had decided to join the alliance, but the Young Men who would do most of the fighting opposed them, and indeed took over Gortyn and threw the Seniors out. Around this time, a peculiar body, the Neotas, Council of Young Men, starts turning up in inscriptions with powers that go way beyond what one might normally expect of such a body, not just organizing sports days, honoring victors and thanking sponsors, but issuing edicts about coinage and punishing offenders. The Neotocracy didn't last. The Seniors with the help of Cnossus took back the city and "exiled or put to death the Younger Men."[62] Naturally these events terrified the Seniors in other cities, and a

long inscription from around this time turned up in Dreros containing
an elaborate oath that the Striplings—*agelaoi,* "herdsters"—had been
forced to swear, in the name of every god imaginable, before entering
the ranks of Young Men: that they would never "have kind thoughts
about the people of Lyctus in any way or fashion neither at night nor by
day" but would always be friendly to Cnossus, never betray any of the
border forts, and not only shun conspiracies and revolutions but report
what they knew about any such revolution to the relevant authorities.
The Seniors' foreign policy was now written in stone.[63]

Relations between the grades never reached quite such extremes in
Athens, but age-class conflict is a constant element in the discourse of
the last decades before 400 BC. Antiphon the ambulance chaser included
among his exercises for students not only the accidental killing of a Boy
by a Stripling, but a drunken fight between a Young Man and a Senior
who later dies from his bruises. There was debate about who started it,
and who, drunkenly, lost it first:

> In the first place, let me tell you that younger men, the arrogance of
> their race [*sic,* "*genos*"], their peaking strength, their inexperience of
> inebriation all inspiring them to gratify [*charizesthai*] their fury, are
> more likely to start things and to lose control under the influence than
> their seniors, made temperate by their experience of drunken ex-
> cesses, by the feebleness of age, by their fear of the strength of Young
> Men.

Faced with such an onslaught and knowing that he will be judged by
Seniors, the fictional Young Man flees into exile, leaving his friends to
respond:

> If it were as obvious as seeing with your own two eyes and hearing
> with your own two ears, that Young Men are violent and Seniors
> temperate, there would be no need for a trial. Their very age would
> condemn Young Men; but, as it is, there are many Young Men who
> are temperate, and many Seniors who can't hold their liquor.[64]

Aristophanes' comedies of the 420s and the 410s are obsessed with rivalry between the younger and the older, and often include set-piece de-

bates that the younger normally win. His first extant play, *Acharnians,* is named after the chorus of old warriors of the giant parish of Acharnae complaining about the way the city is headed and in particular about uppity Young Men like Alcibiades. *Wasps* is named after a chorus of Senior Jurymen and inverts the relationship between an immature Senior father addicted to jury service and his responsible Stripling son. They compete in a debate on whether the Seniors really rule. Much hangs on the outcome: if the Senior loses, Seniors will become laughingstocks (540–45). The Senior claims his age-grade is Zeus-like in its royal power, the Stripling proves him quite mistaken, even to the satisfaction of the Senior jurors reluctantly adjudicating against the "fellow-celebrant of the same age-grade as us." *Knights* is named after a chorus of Cadets, the posh young Striplings-on-horseback, recently the butts of attacks by the demagogue Cleon. *Clouds* centers on the famous set-piece debate between personifications of the "just speech" of the old and the "unjust speech" of the young. *Birds* concerns two Seniors in exile from Athens convincing the Birds that they deserve top place in the cosmic hierarchy because they are senior to the gods, on the grounds that Eros is older than the Olympians, and Eros has wings, an honorary bird. It ends with one of the Seniors finally marrying the personification of Royal Power.

What provoked all this anxiety—and fragments from his contemporaries show that Aristophanes was by no means alone—was what we might call the birth of the art of putting words together effectively, the birth of prose. More particularly it was the success of "wide-arsed" Young Men, notably Euathlus and Alcibiades, or even, according to Aristophanes, of mere Striplings, in prosecuting Seniors for magisterial corruption, Young Men who had recently been learning new tricks from "sophists" such as Socrates and Protagoras, who were suddenly seen to be outclassing their elders in the elders' art of talking, leading to the pathetic whining of the Seniors in *Acharnians:* a Young Man should be allowed to prosecute only members of his own grade.[65]

All this culminated famously in the trial and execution of Socrates precisely for "corrupting the youth," for "destroying the Young Men," for although the verb *diaphtheirein* is mostly covered by "corrupting," i.e., sexually corrupting or bribing a jury, it is stronger—a normal word for "devastating a city" or even "killing" someone.[66] Now there has, perhaps, been more ink spilled on this particular trial than on any other in history "except that of Jesus."[67] Can it be true that there was a law in Athens against "corrupting men under Thirty?" The difficulty arises from the fact that Socrates was also accused of "not believing in the gods the city believes in but in other divinities, brand-new ones." But few believe that it was illegal in Athens to disbelieve in traditional gods, nor to introduce new gods, per se. The Athenians were always introducing new gods, "a standard practice"; "Most probably, the practices in the charge were not formally forbidden by a specific law, but were cited as evidence that Socrates was guilty of the broad and undefined offense of 'impiety.' " But this would mean that the specific offense Socrates was charged with, impiety (*asebeia*), appeared nowhere on the charge-sheet, an extraordinary fact, if true, and a principal source of spilled ink.[68]

The question, then, is which was the main charge and which the subsidiary. Was Socrates charged with "believing in brand-new gods rather than the traditional ones in particular by corrupting those under Thirty," or with "corrupting those under Thirty in particular by believing in brand-new gods rather than the traditional ones?" Had he "substituted new gods for old ones by corrupting the young," or had he "corrupted the young by substituting new gods for old ones?" Express it in those terms, and it seems obvious that the latter must be the case—the former proposition makes no sense—but the sources are a little inconsistent, and most experts dismiss this "obvious" interpretation out of hand, discarding the rules of historical methodology and preferring a late source, Favorinus of Arles, to the only extant eyewitness.[69] Perhaps it is simply too hard to believe that the Athenians could have a law both as vague and as precise as "corrupting men up to the age of Twenty-nine," and you will hunt in vain through textbooks on Athenian Law for any reference to such a crime.

Well, to begin with, defining the "substance" of a law, "what regulations forbid," is not necessarily straightforward. Our sources, for instance, often seem to imply that under the very ancient laws of Draco, "the Draconian legislation," the penalty for being caught in the act of adultery was death on the spot. In fact, thanks to the lucky survival of some quotes from the law, we know that this was not the case. Rather, there was a law that absolved those who killed a man in battle, in athletic competition—throwing the discus, say, or hurling a javelin—or a man found "on top of" one of their women, from a murder charge. What had seemed like a law against adultery was in fact a law defining justifiable homicide. Similarly Timarchus was not "punished with deprivation of civic rights for being a prostitute" but rather for the crime of "addressing the people when he was disqualified from doing so." "Having been a prostitute" was one of four grounds for disqualification; the others were being "someone who has squandered his estate," who "deserted," or who "maltreated his parents."

Moreover Aeschines clearly states that there were laws relating to different grades—"First they laid down laws concerning the modesty of our Boys . . . then secondly concerning the Striplings, and thirdly concerning the other age-grades [hēlikiai] in turn"—and that he will go over them grade by grade. "First I will go over with you the laws laid down concerning the propriety of our Boys, then secondly those concerning Striplings, and thirdly, those concerning the other age-grades in turn."[70] Moreover he does indeed allude to the charge of corrupting the youth at the end of his speech: "You put Socrates the sophist to death because he was shown to have educated Critias, one of the Thirty who had overthrown the democracy," a perfect parallel, claims Aeschines, to the way Demosthenes has corrupted his own disciples, "young people [neous] rich and fatherless."[71] In fact one could perfectly well imagine a law headed "Concerning the Young Men" or "If anyone destroys the Young Men" which then went on to inculpate means that included "introducing novel divinities." Aeschines says that a nearly identical charge of "destroying a free Stripling" was laid against the foreigners who had breakfast with Timarchus.[72]

We are also told a little anecdote about the wit of the courtesan Glycera. The Socratic philosopher Stilpo, a contemporary of Aeschines, accused her over a drink of "corrupting the Young Men." "We both fall under the same charge [aitia]," she replied. "They say you corrupt all who come into contact with you, by teaching them useless disputatious [eristika] sophistries, just as they accuse me of corrupting them with erōtika. So to the wrecked and ruined it's the same, whether they live with a philosopher or a courtesan."[73] Likewise a provider of private entertainment complains that some men are plotting to "destroy" his star performer, a handsome Boy. "My god, what on earth do they think he has done to them that they wish to kill him?" asks Socrates disingenuously. "No, not to kill him but to seduce him into bed."[74] The Byzantine encyclopedia Suda claims that another sophist, Prodicus, was condemned on the same charge as Socrates—"Philosopher of nature and a sophist . . . a disciple of Protagoras of Abdera. He died in Athens of drinking hemlock, on the grounds that he had corrupted the young"—although this information has been ruled out of court precisely because it is the same charge as the one with which Socrates was condemned.[75]

But apart from all this, there is one massive impediment in the way of those who would dismiss as secondary the charge of "corrupting the Young Men": the best source insists upon its primacy. Plato, the only extant author who was also in Athens at the time, lists it first in the only version of the indictment that sounds like a real indictment, and has Socrates emphasize its priority on more than one occasion, noting that the man who brought the accusation was himself a Young Man, a (potential) victim: "First the indictment says that I am guilty of corrupting the young men." "The charge? By no means an ignoble one. Indeed for a Young Man to have recognized its supreme importance is no mean matter. He says he knows the way in which the Young Men are corrupted and knows who they are who corrupt them . . . noticing that I was corrupting his age-mates in my ignorance . . . after that, no doubt, he will turn his scrupulous attentions to those more senior . . ."[76] Trying to explain why Plato would have deliberately inverted the charges when there were still plenty of people around who knew the facts has also drawn deeply on the inkwell.

Xenophon, on the other hand, in his version of the indictment puts the religious charge first, and then the charge of corrupting, but as if it were a quite separate charge: "And he is also guilty of corrupting the Young Men."[77] It would anyway be strange to subordinate Plato's testimony to that of Xenophon, who was miles away at the time of the events, thinking dark thoughts about the nighttime frolics of Meno and his bearded boyfriend. Moreover, he frequently shows himself quite uninterested in historical accuracy as regards Socrates, claiming to have witnessed things he couldn't have witnessed. But here we don't need to run down Xenophon, for he does not really disagree with Plato. When he discusses the indictment in detail it is clear not only that the two charges were related but that Socrates' "impiety" was merely an aspect of his "corrupting the Young Men." So if he starts by refuting the charge of impiety it is only in order to argue that if Socrates was himself so pious "how could he have *led others* into impiety?"[78] In his version of Socrates' defense, after disproving the charge of disbelieving in traditional gods and introducing new ones, Socrates continues: "But, Meletus, do you still say that I corrupt the Young Men by doing such things? Yet we know full well, I should think, the things that corrupt the young. So you tell me if you know of someone who under my influence has turned from pious to impious . . ." "By Zeus," said Meletus, "I know of those men you have seduced into believing you rather than their parents."[79] "So . . . I am being prosecuted on a capital charge because I am adjudged by some people best in the business of education."[80] This all seems consistent and straightforward.

It seems clear moreover that further subsidiary charges were introduced into the case reflecting other aspects of Socrates' corrupting influence on the Young Men, not other aspects of his impiety; that he taught them to treat their fathers and relatives with contempt, that he had mocked democratic institutions: "By saying such things, Meletus argued, Socrates inspired the Young Men to despise the established constitution and made them violent."[81] Meletus seems to have drawn particular attention to his pupils Critias and Alcibiades, who together brought such ruin to the democracy. Xenophon argues that they were actually well behaved when they were Young Men and it was only when they left Socrates' care that they went to the bad. He lists a number of his other associates who were always good men "both when younger and more senior."[82] In fact Xenophon finally draws a contrast between the two charges: "On the one hand not believing in the gods . . . on the other hand, corrupting the Young Men." The latter he describes as "in fact the charge formally laid against him," using the technical term *aitiaomai,* the former merely something "he had written on the charge-sheet."[83] Socrates' prime crime was not impiety but corrupting the young. I am with Plato on this one.

To be sure, the "real reason" Socrates was accused was, as Aeschines assumed, because he had been the teacher of Critias and Charmides, two prominent members of the short-lived and murderous oligarchic regime of the "Thirty Tyrants" put in place by the Spartans at the end of the Peloponnesian War and removed not long before. An amnesty had been proclaimed for all crimes committed during those lethal months, so that the community could move on. Naturally, however, when so many brothers, sons and friends had been killed so unjustly—one of Socrates' accusers, Lycon, had lost his son Autolycus, the bashful Boy of Xenophon's *Symposium*—moving on was hard. The amnesty did nothing to quench desire for some requital. Forbidden to rake up the recent past, but reluctant to beat their rakes into plowshares so soon, the families of the victims were forced to make especially creative uses of the law. Around this time, we find some obscure charges being brought against those who seemed in retrospect if not necessarily enemies of the democracy, then at least "collaborators," charges such as "removing a sacred olive stump," while strange objections were raised at scrutinies for eligibility for office that had never been raised in the past nor would be again in the future—"you should not take against a person because he wears his hair long"—in order to get at the foe by other means, while sticking to the letter of the amnesty.[84]

The trial of Socrates must be seen in this context, his accusers perhaps invoking some ancient obsolescent law, or one that had never been used in this way before, to get at the evil bastard who walked the streets of Athens on his bumbling scot-free way, as if none of the terrible recent personal tragedies had had anything to do with him. But in this case the charges they came up with were not trivial or beside the pettifogging point. We don't have to choose between the formal charge and the real political charge. For all his irony, Socrates was quite right to concede that "corrupting the Young Men," the backbone of the army and a group that had not always been and would not always be at one with the Seniors who gave them their marching orders, was a charge to be taken very seriously. One would hardly be surprised to discover such a law being invoked in Gortyn on Crete after the time of the age-class civil war. And how subversive it would have been in the city of Dreros if some sophist were to come along claiming not to believe in all those many gods in whose name the ephebes had sworn their oaths of loyalty with all their dire imprecations: "and if I do not stick to what I have sworn, may all the gods and goddesses by whom I swore be wroth against me, and may I be destroyed with terrible destruction, me and all my property, and may the earth not bear fruit for me nor women bear children for me according to nature . . ."

Indeed, one thing Athenians might have been able to agree on—people on the left and on the right, democrats and oligarchs, revolutionaries and counterrevolutionaries—was that the kernel of Athens's problems over the last few decades resided in the "corruption of the Young Men." The oligarchs had themselves issued a law forbidding the teaching of speaking, a law aimed, says Xenophon, straight at Socrates himself.[85] They had been through not a religious crisis but an age-class crisis, a crisis in the "order of the generations," which had first been brought to the attention of the community in the 420s when a whole new kind of Young Man, not least among them Alcibiades and Euathlus, trained by sophists like Socrates and Protagoras, made their spectacular debut onto the political stage, outwitting their slow-tongued seniors in trials for corruption.

The central text in this sense of crisis was Aristophanes' *Clouds,* which Plato himself has Socrates cite as the source of prejudice against him. For already decades before Socrates' trial Aristophanes had introduced the personification of Unjust Speech who was "ravaging the Striplings" with all his wide-arsed sophistry, as the star lecturer in Socrates' "Thought Factory."

PRETTY YOUNG THINGS

But what does Love have to do with this age-class war? Two things in particular: harmony and objectification, or *philia* and *erōs*. First, intimate one-to-one loves help to draw rival sets and grades together, a vertical bond to weave across the horizontal bonds of coevals, as among the Didinga of southeastern Sudan:

> As soon as an age-set is admitted to the status of junior warrior, each one of its members has to find a best friend among the ranks of the senior warriors. The relationship then instituted is of life-long duration, but the fact that it takes an institutionalized form then, when the juniors are approximately eighteen years of age and the seniors twenty-three, does not mean that the two had not been close friends before . . .
>
> Leaving the personal aspect of the institution, we also find it a strong socializing force: for it is the one link between the different sets in the age-grade system and converts the system from a discrete concatenation of units to a closely knit, homogeneous organization. The link is forged as between each member of the two warrior sets

and their friendships unite the two sets in a way that nothing else could. Not only this, but as the senior warrior set has contracted similar friendships, when it was itself in the status of junior warrior, and the junior warriors will in their turn be linked in this way to their successors, it becomes obvious that the whole system is closely integrated from top to bottom by the institution of the best friend, which thus tends to counteract the exclusive classification of age.[86]

The Shavante of Brazil have a similar type of ceremonial friend, *da-amo*. The friendship and its direction is marked by the older friend giving one of his names to the younger—names that he previously acquired from his own seniors: "They effectively . . . promote continuity between men in and through time."[87] One can see a similar kind of amatory descent in Athens, for Timarchus was *erōmenos* of Hegesander, who had previously been *erōmenos* of Leodamas, a great orator of the past, thus forming a neat lineage over several decades for a group of politicians close to Thebes and hostile to Macedonia, or, as someone else put it, rather less politely, and in the middle of a packed public meeting: "A man and his woman are stealing money from you men of Athens, a thousand drachmas . . . The man is Hegesander over there, though he used to be Leodamas's woman; and his woman is Timarchus."[88]

What then of admiration? What about all the fuss made of the physical beauty of the Young? That too has many parallels in age-class societies. The ethnographer David Maybury-Lewis could hardly disguise his amazement at the primping of the Shavante:

> Members of the young men's age-grade . . . spend much of the day preparing themselves for their evening council. They oil their bodies and faces with a mixture of saliva and *babassú* or coconut juice. They trim their fringes, keep their eyebrows and eyelashes plucked and anoint and smarm their hair . . . When they have completed their toilet they can hardly wait for the sun to be low enough for them to go out to their meeting . . . The young men are careful of their appearance at all times but they take particular care to look their best before they go out to sing and dance by day . . . they know they are being watched and admired . . . All this is very flattering and it is therefore hardly surprising that the members of this age-grade are exceedingly vain . . . They are supposed to be warlike and handsome . . . The whole community takes a pride in them when they dance and sing.[89]

Spartan Young Men provoked similar reactions. Before their brave suicidal stand at Thermopylae, Xerxes sent a spy to the Greek camp. "He carefully observed the warriors stationed outside the wall. As it happened they were Spartans. Some of the Men were exercising naked, while others were combing their hair. Seeing such things the spy was astonished . . . He told Xerxes what he had seen. Xerxes couldn't make head or tail of it . . . what they were doing seemed daft."[90]

But admiration, as any beautiful woman will tell you, is a double-edged sword. The fact that Love flows down the age-levels, from the more senior to the more junior, and the fact that Love flows down the beauty levels, from the less to the more beautiful, are connected, i.e., attractiveness in a *presbyterian* society such as ancient Greece is inversely proportionate to power. Those without power are highly appreciated by those who have more, but appreciated for their bodies, their looks. Passionate admiration for someone's physical attributes may well involve lavish condescension toward their other attributes: eyes wide, ears shut. If to be passively aggressive is to be a quiet little, manipulative little, immovable little pebble in someone's shoe, then perhaps we should call this hopeless devotion of Seniors for their juniors "aggressive admiration": noisily celebrating someone's utter wonderfulness in order to put them in their place.

· PART II ·

SODOMANIA

SEXING UP THE GREEKS

Goading Eros, the love-crazed *erastēs,* the pedestalized favorite graciously granting delightful intimacy or not, the rock-solid relationship of "erotik" *philia,* the pathetic stalking, the lovesick songs, the acclamations, the tears: These are what we find in descriptions of Greek Love over a long period: "all the obsessive longing, despair, self-abasement and devoted self-sacrifice which our most romantic literature associates with heterosexual love."[1] What the Greeks don't enlarge on is sexual acts, Xenophon's "invisibles," the *aphanē.* "A great deal is written about homosexual *erōs* from which the innocent reader would not easily gather that any physical contact at all was involved." So says Sir Kenneth Dover. Likewise, Michel Foucault refers to "the reticences with regard to sodomy and passive fellation in homosexual relations." "It is not possible to infer from this text the acts and gestures that honor would compel one to refuse . . . the acts are never designated." "There was a reluctance to evoke directly and in so many words the role of the boy in sexual intercourse."[2]

However, despite all this reticence, modern work on ancient Greek culture is remarkably obsessed with the ins and outs of homosexual sex acts performed two and a half thousand years ago. It is hard to convey to general readers the pervasiveness of anal sex in the work of classicists today, most of them happily married men whose knowledge of sodomy tends to be the kind you get from books or dim rememberings of reckless nights at boarding school. For the present consensus, an *erastēs* is not a lovesick admirer, but "the aggressive male who pursues and penetrates boys."[3] This modern obsession has had particularly unfortunate results for the bottoms of the boys of Sparta and ancient Crete. We are poorly informed about the Spartans, but Xenophon, who lived among them, is normally considered by far the best source. You will not be able to find a single modern scholar, however, who gives him the slightest credit when he claims that they didn't touch the bodies of under-Eighteens and treated them like brothers. As for Crete, in 1831 a German editor of the text of Strabo that describes the peculiar Cretan abduction ritual that concludes with a formal public association decided that a few words had been missed by one of the copyists. When the mock tug-of-war reached the men's club of the suitor, he suggested, there should be a phrase like "Then, the *erastēs* wished the boy welcome," or as Italian translators reasonably prefer, "embraced him." Many years later, a new manuscript of the text, written *c.* AD 500, was discovered, underneath some Christian homilies. Much is barely legible even with the most sophisticated modern technology, but there is enough to show that the German scholar had guessed almost word for word what had dropped out.

These "words of welcome," however, or this "warm embrace," are the only things in the whole text that refer to any kind of fond intimacy between the suitor and the boy during the wedding ceremony, up to two months long. The couple are never left alone, and in Crete, moreover, "forced sex" with male or female merits one of the severest penalties in the law code, an advanced piece of sexually non-discriminatory rape legislation that was only achieved in Britain in the 1990s. This has not deterred scholars, however, from indulging in a little homosexual fantasy. One of them thinks he has evidence (don't bother to look it up) of anal sex at the heart of the ritual; another insists that "sexual intercourse" was certainly included. Others go further, so that you might well read that on Crete boys were "abducted and raped" or "sexually forced."[4] Why on earth do meticulous scholars who normally cling to the facts to the point of boredom suddenly start to fantasize as soon as the topic of homosexuality comes up, insisting without so much as a "probably" or a "perhaps" that Cretan boys were forcibly sodomized on a regular basis? "Rump-presentation as an invitation to mate is a gesture of submission inhibiting an aggressive response from the stronger partner. It is astounding how corresponding behavior recurs in human ritual."[5]

In fact this is only one aspect of a widespread movement to sex up Greek texts. Other examples are more insidious, quietly digging themselves into student editions, commentaries and translations. To take a small but typical example, Aristotle in his *Politics* notes that a king of

Macedon was assassinated by his former boyfriend when the king revealed by his later actions that their relationship had been "an abusive
one," based on *hubris* ("bad attitude," "contempt") rather than on
"*erōtikos* desire," the kind inspired by "passionate, hopeless devotion."
What gave the assassin cause seems straightforward: He thought the
king had loved him, and then realized that he had been used merely for
sex. The Penguin translation of 1962 thought the fatally missing element
had been "passionate love." Benjamin Jowett in 1885 thought it was "affection" that had been felt to be lacking. Jowett, however, left a legacy
to be used to improve and correct his translations, and so in the 1990s his
"affection" was changed: Now the ex-boyfriend was upset because the
king's actions showed that their relationship had been based on contempt instead of "sexual desire." Modern readers of *Politics* will now
come away thinking that the king of Macedon was assassinated because
his boyfriend later discovered that the king had not truly lusted after
him.[6]

It may seem bizarre that modern classicists use money left by revered
scholars of earlier times to corrupt their translations, but reverence is
part of the problem. What contribution could the sixties generation
make to the work of their great predecessors? Well, the Oldies may have
been unassailable in their knowledge of ancient languages, but it is no
secret that our Victorian ancestors had one deep moral flaw: They were
bashful and repressed; they thought even a piano leg was an incitement
to lust. Therefore this is one area in which modern scholars can demonstrate a clear advance over the work of their predecessors: Nowadays we
can be much more grown-up and explicit. This extraordinary modern
crusade against the supposed follies of Victorian scholars, this insistence
on bravely uncovering all the sexual details that had been veiled by earlier generations of silly old fools, was brilliantly satirized as long ago as
1976 by Michel Foucault, as if it were itself a religious movement: "A
great sexual sermon—which has had its subtle theologians and its popular voices—has swept through our societies over the last decades; it has
chastised the old order, denounced hypocrisy, and praised the rights of
the immediate and the real." The insistence that sexuality has been in
chains "is coupled with the grandiloquence of a discourse purporting to
reveal the truth about sex," "one goes about telling, with the greatest
precision whatever is most difficult to tell."[7]

But there are numerous cases we have looked at in which *erōs, erastēs* and so on cannot possibly refer to sex, so how can the sexual interpretation deal with an *erastēs* of tyranny, hard to get a sexual grip on, or an *erōs* to go on an expedition, or the Furies in the *Oresteia* threatened with the awful prospect of being sent into exile by the goddess Athena and becoming Athens's "lovelorn admirers?" Did Athena really mean to threaten the Dread Goddesses with an exile where they would nurse a desire sexually to penetrate Athens?

A number of strategies have been used to explain these local difficulties. Although, the commentators claim, *erōs* can sometimes be translated as "love," its *core meaning* is "sexual desire." Although in the earliest occurrences *erastēs* seems to mean "eager for" or "a fan of," nevertheless the *primary meaning* is "the older, active male partner in the relationship of pederasty," except that he may not be older, or male, or in any relationship, let alone a "pederastic" one, nor, therefore, taking the "active" role in it.[8] You can see how easy it is in practice to discuss all the evidence to the contrary as an extended use that has strayed from the true narrow meaning established by academic doctrine. Thus the sex interpretation becomes formally incontrovertible.

One of the commonest shifts is to say that when it can't be sexual, *erōs* is being used *metaphorically.* Take Pericles' Funeral Speech, for instance. By asking them to become Athens's *erastai,* the great statesman was not, it now seems, asking for hopeless devotion, but inviting her citizens to shaft their beloved Athens. The perfectly good translations of earlier scholars, who thought that Pericles was inviting Athenians to "fall in love with" their city, to be "filled with the love of her," were now seen as completely sentimental, too innocent of the concrete realities that Pericles "clearly" intended. Hence one scholar felt inspired to write an article on Sex with the City for a distinguished journal of political thought. "The term 'lovers' (*erastai*) has very clear sexual connotations," she observed. "It alludes to the physical act of penetrating," she continued. And went on: "The term *erastes* clearly denotes the assertive, superior partner in sexual activity between either same-sex or different-sex partners. Pericles' use of the term unquestionably evokes an image of the erect, penetrating phallus and asserts the manliness of Athenian citizens." Unquestionably, for "Athens *arouses* them." But there was a problem: "The metaphor seems implicitly to cast the target of citizens' erotic attention—the city—in the role of the sexual object, that is, the passive partner in a sexual relation. In so doing it might appear to cast the city in a potentially shameful, instead of valorized, position."[9] To be fair, the author eventually manages to rescue Athens from the mess she had *seemed* to have gotten (her) into, for Athens, like a vigilant boy, had various strategies—frottage, for instance—that she could deploy to rescue herself from sexual submission, establish a more reciprocal and chivalrous relationship with her citizens and live happily ever after. But all the same . . .

The act of metaphorical buggery has now assumed a rich life of its own. The ingenuity and imagination invested in recent years in the topic has developed into something that can only be described as a poetics of sodomy, the inflation of a great speculative bubble that makes the dot-com shares of the 1990s seem like sound investments. Some years ago, to give one random example, I went to a conference on Aristophanes. One speaker was reconstructing the stagecraft of Aristophanes, brilliantly and sensibly for the most part, until he came to the comedy called *Knights*. In this play, of course, the frequent entries and exits of the *erastai* through the door of the house symbolize their sodomizing of an old man called Demos, who personifies the People of Athens. One of the favorite examples of the devotees of "homosexual submission" is a vase that shows a man bending over and another running toward him holding his penis in his hand. "I am Eurymedon," he says. He represents, they insist, the river Eurymedon in Turkey, site of a famous battle, about to homosexually "triumph" over a Persian, a triumphant colonic irrigation, although some think it shows a Greek about to sodomize said river. It has proven rather difficult to find parallels for this extraordinary metaphor. Now, finally, another example has turned up: a previously unnoticed description of sodomy in the work of the poet Timotheus. At first sight, it seems to describe a man in the process of swallowing seawater after a shipwreck, but in fact, claims the scholar, it is another homosexual triumph: "Most obvious is the openness of his body to 'foam' . . . a word that can mean 'semen,' which pours into his *angōn*, 'vessel' . . . the barbarian is 'sated' [i.e., full of seawater] at the moment he is (figuratively) raped by the sea." Timotheus, it seems, was describing a rare case of a man drowning through his arse.[10]

This may seem amusing, but it raises serious questions. Our understanding of the Greeks is deteriorating. Old translations are better than new ones. Knowledge is regressing. How can you follow the arguments of Plato's *Phaedrus, Symposium* and *Lysis* if you think *erōs* and *philia* are "sexual desire" and "friendship"? Plato will stop making sense. How can you understand Greek citizenship if you think that by calling them *erastai* Pericles is inviting his fellow citizens to "sodomize the city"?

It perplexes me to witness this pandemic of perversity among colleagues I may otherwise admire, so I have thought about it a lot. The problem, as I see it, is not at all a tendency toward shoddiness in scholarship but, paradoxically, an obsession with facts and telling the truth. But to understand how we came to be in this bizarre position we need to scamper through the whole recent history of the human sciences. It happens that the study of *the truth about ancient Greek Homosexuality* is central to the study of modernity, culture, history and truth itself. Such a claim requires substantiation.

SEX AS IMMEDIATE AND REAL

That Greek Love often focused on the physical attributes of the boy or girl in question, and might well include sex, was only ever a secret from those who refused to inquire. The hands-off type of homosexuality is called "Platonic" or "Socratic love" precisely because Socrates, according to Plato, was so unusual in this regard. But because sex with other men had become a criminal act that might, if you were unlucky, lead to prison, torture, and burning at the stake, the question "Did they or didn't they?" became a very urgent and important one: *pothos,* "never sexual in Homer," *agapē,* "rarely sexual," *erōs,* "often sexual." It is rather like zealous vegetarians trying to differentiate between words for hunger in terms of whether or not meat is going to be involved: "peckish"—rarely carnivorous, "hungry"—often carnivorous, "starving"—almost always infers desire for meat. Was there sex in this text? Was it dangerous? Who should be allowed to read it? Is it suitable for schoolboys? What love exactly does this word "*erōs*" refer to? What designs does it have, wicked or pure? Here is a pair of "lovers." Are they or aren't they about to commit vicious criminal and unnatural acts?

In the seventeenth century, the classical scholar Richard Bentley had no doubts. He was scrutinizing a strange text that purported to be the let-

ters of the notorious ancient tyrant Phalaris. Bentley thought it was a for-
gery and that he had caught the forger out. For the author had written
the phrase "*paidōn . . . erastai*" as if it meant "fond of their children,"
whereas in classical Greek, he claimed, it could only have meant a "flagitious love of Boys." "Flagitious"—felonious, criminal, punishable—was
no idle term, for Bentley's London was on the verge of an antigay
pogrom. Two years after he wrote his dissertation in 1699, and then again
in 1707 and 1726–27, there were raids on Holborn's Molly Houses, a kind
of early modern gay bar with added camp pageantry. Arrests, executions
and suicides followed. Scores of gay people died.[11]

As we have seen, it is perfectly good classical Greek to talk of "*erōs* for
children" without implying either sodomitical or incestuous intent.
Bentley was wrong about that; the forger may even have been showing
off, for all the good it did him. But Bentley was right that the letters
were indeed ancient forgeries (rhetorical exercises), and his careful
demonstration of this by close scrutiny of the text was celebrated as a
landmark in the history of scholarship. By carefully proving the inauthenticity of long-revered texts and correcting fraudulent readings that
occasionally appeared and then were passed down by copyist monks in
the Middle Ages, revealing thereby the line of transmission, the study of
texts began to look like a science: rigorous and precise. Because of this
rigorousness, hard though it is to believe, philology has had a tremendous impact on the history of the West over the last two centuries.
Philology explains why the Nazis mythologized the "Aryans." Philology is why we talk of the anti-Semite rather than the anti-Arab or the
anti-Jew. Philology helped give birth to feminism, antiracism, postmod-
ernism and even gay liberation. Some philologists claimed they had been
the first to discover, long before Darwin, the principle of evolution
through small changes over time. She is not being ridiculous when one
recent scholar says: "In the beginning, there was philology."[12] Philology is the mother of the human sciences.

A century after Bentley, a German Classics teacher decided to extend
his field of study into more recent periods, and brought some of this
philological rigor with him. He was Leopold von Ranke, "father of
modern history." In a famous preface Ranke set out what he would and
would not be doing in his book about the Holy Roman Empire. The
statement became a kind of manifesto: "To History has been assigned

the office of judging the past and instructing the present for the benefit of the future: the current *essay* has no pretensions to so exalted a position: it wants merely to show how things were."[13] There were two sides to Ranke's approach. On the positive side was what we might call empiricism, using your own eyes and ears. Of course you couldn't use them to observe past events, but instead of relying on secondhand or thirdhand accounts, historians could follow the classicists into the Renaissance libraries of Italy, not to the collections of manuscripts but into the archives, and cleanse the historical record of all the errors that had accumulated over the centuries. They could delve into government records and find original documents, accounts of trials, letters from ambassadors, bills, the most primary witnesses, as close as possible to the sights and sounds of the events themselves. The negative side, so beautifully expressed in Ranke's preface, was what we might call amoralism. The historian should put aside any pretensions to improving the human race or judging the past. These two elements of modern scientific historical ideology might be neatly combined in the idea of "letting the facts speak for themselves."

In 1837, just thirteen years after von Ranke's famous declaration of history without judgment, a philologist, Moritz Hermann Eduard Meier, published forty pages on Greek *"Päderastie,"* love of boys, for a giant Encyclopedia of Sciences (*Wissenschaften*) and Arts.[14] It would concentrate only on authentic nonpartisan documents, he declared. He was not interested in incriminating the Greeks, nor in whitewashing them— that was a way of obscuring truths that were perfectly obvious. Rather he would study the subject exclusively from a historical point of view. "What we want is the truth, and nothing but."[15] Meier's clear scientific exposition of Greek Love, however, came in a form that was itself most obscure. When Pogey-Castries—an assumed name—prepared a French version in 1930 he had more or less to reconstitute it, clarifying the logic of Meier's elegant classicizing sentences, and complaining that sometimes he found only four or five lines of main text with 150 lines of tiny footnote. It didn't help that the Encyclopedia was typeset in Gothic letters. The author, moreover, had disdained any scandalous reports and all *"détails pittoresques,"* which M. "Pogey-Castries" (re-)inserted in a series of appendices.

Meier's achievement was nevertheless quite remarkable, and some think his forty pages surpass anything written since. The question of flagitious sensuality was still to the fore:

> One should not believe that, even in its noblest forms, the love that the Greeks had for boys was something exclusively spiritual, a completely aesthetic satisfaction in the presence of beauty, a straightforward communion of the spirit and the heart, an exchange of tender courtesies offered and accepted. The spiritual elements of this affection were always mixed with a powerfully sensual element, the pleasure which had its origin in the physical beauty of the loved one; and those in love never appreciated it otherwise than do those who judge feminine beauty today. Physical beauty always played a very important role, even in the purest loves, even when the admirer demanded no other enjoyment than that of looking.[16]

SIR KENNETH PLEASURES HIMSELF

Sir Kenneth Dover is very much part of the great philological tradition going back to Meier and Bentley. He has written a study of the speeches that have come down to us under the name of Lysias, Plato's rival for the title of "master of Greek prose," sorting out the wheat from the chaff, the spurious from the true works, and has done a great deal to further restore ancient texts of Aristophanes and Plato, by carefully tracing the accumulation of errors in manuscripts, in order to reach a version as close as possible to what the ancient audiences of Aristophanes and Plato actually heard with their own ears in the decades around 400 BC. He is one of the most muscular champions of truth in the whole field of the humanities, and it is to his authority and in particular to his 1978 book *Greek Homosexuality* that modern scholars have deferred when they have changed the translations of *erōs* from "in love" to "sexual desire." If the liberation of sex from the perceived trammels of Victorian prudishness really was a kind of religious movement as Foucault claimed, Kenneth Dover is its Grand Ayatollah.

If his name rings any bells it is because in the 1990s this obsession with truth got him into a certain amount of trouble, when he published a confessional autobiography. The trouble started when an article in the London *Evening Standard* claimed that the book would contain an account of this most distinguished British academic masturbating over a view of the snowcapped Matese massif in Italy. His inclusion of the episode was not gratuitous, he told *The Times,* "because it has a bearing on a passage in Plato's *Phaedrus.*" "It is not thoughtless reductionism on our part, but Plato's own (sometimes startling) choice of words, which identifies the first intimations of Beauty with the sensation in the genitals which heralds arousal." The implication seemed to be that if you could get sexually turned on by a beautiful figureless landscape, it was not too hard to see how a Greek could get sexually turned on (*erōs*) by a beautiful boy: "The explanation of such events is scientific rather than philosophical." Of course to equate a critical moment in one of the most important and influential works a Greek ever produced with a wank on a mountaintop is spectacular reductionism, but it is not "thoughtless."

EDITING *CLOUDS*

I first became aware of Dover's work in about 1980, when I was still at school. We were reading Aristophanes' *Clouds,* with its satirical attack on Socrates, using the edition Dover had produced for schools and colleges in 1967. Dover devoted 26 pages to an analysis of the 67 different medieval manuscripts of *Clouds* he had taken into account, each referred to by an abbreviation that disguises some of the grandest libraries in a selection of Europe's grandest Renaissance cities: P(aris)17, P19, P8; V(enice)—"Koster argues that V must be dated late in XII, on the grounds that its reading at *Pl.* 162 (*hēmōn*) is a conjecture of Ioannes Tzetzes for *autōn.* It must, however, be recognized that the scholion as we have it may be using language appropriate to the description of a conjecture when Tzetzes actually expressed a preference for an existing variant"—V3, V4; Vv(Vatican); 2, Vv5; R(avenna)—"parchment, *c.*1000. Text in minuscule hand similar to that of Laurentianus 32.9."

Building on the work of earlier students Dover tried to deduce the date of the manuscripts, their history and the relationships between them, which versions had a common ancestor, which had been cross-fertilized by others: "Md1 and Vb3 are akin not only in extensive dislocations throughout the middle part of the play . . . but also in numerous errors, many of which are shared with V." At the foot of each page of text in accordance with traditional scholarly practice there were about ten lines that included the most significant alternatives to the text he had printed, and some corrections by earlier scholars, notably Bentley: "Modern study of the play may be regarded as beginning in 1708, when Richard Bentley communicated to Kuster his brief but remarkable observations, including many emendations which are now supported by good manuscript evidence not known to him."

The kind of comprehensive expertise you need to edit a Greek text is not to be despised. Greek is an intricate and elaborately structured language. I started to learn it when I was thirteen. Given plenty of time and resources I can probably give you a new English translation of an old piece of Greek that equals or surpasses any translation hitherto produced, but please don't ever ask me out of the blue what the Greek for "You two stand up!" is. I don't "speak" ancient Greek; I piece it together with the help of dictionaries, grammars, earlier translations, databases and books. Knowing ancient Greek is a grand collective enterprise. We pygmies of the twenty-first century have giants to stand on, giants standing on giants standing on pygmies standing on giants. A text editor, however, needs to keep a good range of the possibilities for emendation, a large part of the vast intricate structure, on call in his head.

The vastly intricate grammar is all child's play: the basic materials, the kind of nerdy knowledge that teenagers, especially male teenagers, and trainspotters and football commentators are famous for—a burden now largely lifted by computers. But after the nouns, the adjectives, the verbs, the conjugations, the declensions, the irregulars, there's the syntax, how it fits together, a feel for the latent "pastness" in an aorist verb that is talking of something that will happen in the future, the knowledge that you need a "genitive of the goal" after verbs of ambition, but that you don't need one for "longs for," that if it's a verb of pulling or dragging, the genitive form is used for the thing by which someone is dragged, a cloak, a nose, a foot, but an accusative for the person or thing you're dragging.

There are also the "particles," the little word-bits, sometimes consisting of no more than a single letter "g," "t," "d," that are sprinkled around to indicate how one sentence relates to the previous one: "but," "and," "though," words that tend to get dropped out of manuscripts or attached to other words, altering the meter, for of course when you are editing a poetical text like a Greek comedy your emendations must also fit one of a number of changing meters, the correct pattern of long vowels and short vowels. You also need to know about the errors characteristic of a particular period script—the time when "q" was written "q" and might get mixed up with "p," or the time when it was written "Q" and might get mixed up with "O." Or perhaps if you know that at this time manuscripts were usually dictated, the time when long "e" was pronounced "e-e" and might get mixed up with "e," or the time when long "e" was pronounced "i" and might get mixed up with "i."

For all these reasons, text editors are the "rocket scientists," the "brain surgeons" of Classics, and Dover's reputation as one of the best scholars of the postwar period is not unfounded. Critics were impressed by his new *Clouds:* "a work of unusual excellence," "easily the best edition of a play of Aristophanes yet to appear in this country," "at last we have a major edition and a splendid commentary remarkable both for its learning and its conciseness." But the reverence given by the scholarly community to its cherished rocket scientists can offer a hostage to fortune. The prestige of a brilliant reconstruction of a text, a difficult, rare and highly valued achievement, a large deposit in the academic bank, is what sociologists call "symbolic capital," and it can be cashed as common currency and spent on other things. This can happen in any sphere—"Our lecture on Mozart will be given by Tanya Braithwaite, whose performance as Queen of the Night in *Magic Flute* earned her the highest accolades." But the justly valued authority who can identify Rembrandt's authentic hand from fifty paces may not be able to tell you what a particular Rembrandt painting is about; a brain surgeon may have little to say about the memories of a man, and don't ask a rocket scientist about planets and moons.

At the age of sixteen, it has to be said, the merits of Dover's comparison of manuscripts did not rate high. We judged textbooks differently. Dover's notes might not include enough translations of the difficult bits, but this was more than made up for by their sexual explicitness. Dover explained that he couldn't understand how it could ever have seemed "morally objectionable to foster adolescents' appreciation of the more light-hearted aspects of sex" (ix). We adolescents thoroughly agreed. Two notes in particular grabbed our spotty attention, and we waited to ambush our teacher with a prolonged scholarly discussion of the matter.

At line 518, Aristophanes had stepped out from behind the mask of the chorus and, speaking in his own voice, berated the Athenians for having dared to award this wonderful comedy of his, a comedy he had labored over, a comedy he himself thought excellent, third (and last) place in the festival competition of 423 BC. I am far more skillful than my rivals who steal my ideas and repeat themselves and resort to cheap laughs, Aristophanes tells his audience. Unlike them, he would not sink so low as to introduce a "stitched-up leather penis swinging down, red at the end thick too, to amuse the children" (ll. 538–39).

A marginal comment in one of the manuscripts had drawn Dover's attention, and therefore our own, to a problem with the punctuation in the description of this penis, "red at the end thick too," to which we, in turn, drew the attention of our teacher. What did the phrase "at the end" go with, "red" or "thick" or both? Was the leather penis Aristophanes boasted of not employing for cheap laughs (i) red *and* thick, but only at the end, (ii) thick all along its length with a red bit at the end, or (iii) red all along its length and thick at the end? It was a problem, and Dover devoted half a page of notes to a discussion of the arguments for and against each of the three alternatives.

The question is in some ways unanswerable. Aristophanes didn't use punctuation (it had not been invented), and performers and listeners would have had to interpret the words as they saw fit, based on their own experience of penises and comic plays, but the superficially obvious solution, one that most previous editors had adopted, is (ii) that the stuffed leather willy that Aristophanes' rival(s) had been using to provoke childish sniggers was "red at the end and thick," following the natural order of the words and the experience of even the most unworldly of teenage boys. Some comedian, in other words, had recently substituted the normal elephantine but flaccid cock and balls traditionally worn by comic actors for something more obviously erectile, thick and red at the end, in order to get a cheap laugh—potentially a scandalous break with tradition. But Dover saw a difficulty. The offending penis is described as "hanging down," erect penises do not dangle, so this penis cannot have been erect. If the penis was indeed "red at the end," the joke must have been at the expense of people with "an inflamed foreskin," "not particularly humorous" even to children, or—and this seems to be Dover's favored interpretation—a joke at the expense of Egyptians and

Jews, who, as the Greeks were well aware—Dover supplies a couple of supporting passages—practiced circumcision.[17] But there is a further problem. If it's just a cheap joke at the expense of the "chopped-off Jews," why is the penis described as "thick"? Nevertheless, that circumcised penises were a conventional joke on the comic stage in classical Athens has now become a factoid of student editions.[18]

Twenty years later, I realize that Dover's autobiography casts some light on this curious note:

> I was born at a time when the craze for circumcision, which infected England in the latter part of the nineteenth century, was reaching its peak, and I was one of its millions of victims . . . One night . . . just before I went to sleep, a message which seemed to come from outside myself told me, with magisterial finality, that foreskins are good and circumcision bad. This message was not articulated in words, but invaded me in two shock-waves about a second apart: whoof! . . . whoof! . . . This was the first of three occasions in my life on which a "voice" has communicated with me . . . My dislike of circumcision did nothing to make me anti-Jewish . . . partly because I knew from my reading in anthropology and ancient history that it wasn't the fault of the Jews; it began independently in ancient Egypt, from which it has spread into central and eastern Africa and over the whole Islamic world, and in some areas of the south-western Pacific. I am pretty sure, however, that it turned me off Semitic languages . . . and reinforced my loyalty to the Greeks and Romans, who rejected and ridiculed circumcision.[19]

The clinical language of the note about the thick red phallus—option (i), option (ii), option (iii)—was a kind of rhetoric in the service of a burning sense of moral outrage. But if Dover had been more honest about what he really thought, if he had said that he thought this was a joke at the expense of the "*abominable* practice of circumcision," would as many people have been as convinced that his argument was right?

We had to wait a couple of weeks before we reached the second prurient crux. It came in one of Aristophanes' most celebrated theatrical coups, the scene where he dramatizes the problems of "Socratic" sophistry with a debate between personifications of "Just Speech" and "Unjust Speech." "Just," who stands for the good old ways, complains about contemporary mores. "Unjust" is clever and fashionable and ties him in logical knots. It is possible they were represented on stage as two fighting cocks, battling with words.[20]

According to Just Speech, who, as the dialogue progresses, comes to seem more and more like a dirty old man rather than a spokesman for old-time virtues, boys used to be trained in a vigorous and masculine style with lots of physical exercise and plenty of nudity no matter how cold outside: "No boy in those days rubbed himself with oil below the navel, so that a dew [*drosos*] and downy fur blossomed on his shamefuls, as if on quinces" (977–78). Again, the meaning seemed clear: Whereas, by implication, modern boys pour oil even on their genitals, in the olden days they didn't, so that their genitals were decorated with nothing more than sweat, the "dew" or *drosos* that provokes the imagination of Just.

But Dover was galloping off in a different direction:

Drosos [dew] would at first suggest "semen" to Ar.'s audience, but a more realistic picture is obtained if we take it as referring to Cowper's secretion, which in some individuals is emitted when the penis is fully erect. What stimulates "Just"'s aesthetic imagination is the visual and tactile contrast between the matt surface of the penis as a whole and the secretion revealed by pushing back the foreskin; the same kind of contrast as is obtained by taking a small bite at a peach.[21]

(NB "a *small* bite.")

But there was a problem, surely. Just Speech's modest, decent, old-fashioned boys were now, thanks to Dover's elaborations, walking around with erections and playing with themselves, if not actually ejaculating all over the gym. In his keenness not to leave the ruder bits of Aristophanes shrouded in the veils of euphemism and embarrassment, Dover spied sexual details that did not exist.

Cowper's secretion seems especially bizarre, for Dover does not seem to be arguing that this is what an Athenian audience would think of when they heard the word "dew"—they, to his mind, would mistakenly identify it as semen. Rather he seems to treat this picture conjured up by a fictional character as a window onto a reality, the sights and sounds of ancient Greece, an actual fact on which he can bring to bear his own considerable learning in order to make Just Speech's vague description more scientific, "more realistic"—what was going on back there *really*, what was the objective scientific truth that lies behind the "dew" that

Just imagines. It is a kind of scientific empiricism, a reliance on your own eyes and ears, but an empiricism that has spectacularly overreached itself.

You would think that interpretations this wayward would long ago have put the scholarly community on guard, but that didn't happen, for reasons I will try to explain. A decade later, Jeffrey Henderson, then a young scholar, now highly esteemed, pointed out that Dover's sexual interpretation was surely wrong: "Dew" referred to sweat. His book was reviewed by Professor Sir Hugh Lloyd-Jones, who succeeded to the royal professorship of Greek at Oxford after Dover, according to his autobiography, turned it down. Lloyd-Jones had to concede that Henderson's interpretation of "dew" as "sweat" was indeed superior to Dover's secretion, but he nevertheless exacted vengeance on Henderson for daring to point it out: "H. is not quite so good a grammarian as one who would patronize Dover needs to be." A short list of Henderson's grammatical mistakes followed; "other errors will be mentioned presently . . . *trōthein* comes from *titrōskō*."[22]

Even the cocky classicists of Cambridge have been known to suffer anxiety, ill disguised with bravado, when confronting an audience of Oxford dons armed with texts that may be thought to demolish their argument. Someone might stand up and say: "Yes, but your whole paper is based on an obsolete reading that Grünewald proved was metrically impossible as long ago as 1895, and how do you square it with Euripides' *I. T.* 546, eh?" Such nerdish rivalry and terror of error can be excellent spurs, prompting meticulousness and perfection, but they become disastrous when pride becomes pretension, when fear of slipping up discourages challenges, and daftnesses are allowed to pass into common parlance because no one wants to risk an error of grammar. But Dover didn't steal academic capital, he was given it. If our understanding of the terminology of Greek Homosexuality makes a nonsense out of Plato, it is in part because of a failure to be facetious. A lot of the time Dover knocks spots off his expert rivals, but often too he reaches conclusions that defy common sense. The same scientific rigor and logical tenacity are evident in both the brilliance and the blindnesses: Is it so hard to understand that the same quality is sometimes a tremendous virtue and sometimes a vice?

How far an obsession with sex can blind people to the most obvious truths can be illustrated by the climax of that debate between the two logoses, the two types of speech, "just" and "unjust," which centers on the topic of "wide-arsedness." As we have seen, this is a farty metaphor for windbag speech itself: "Out of what do advocates advocate?" "Out of wide arses." "I couldn't agree more. What next? Out of what does the work of tragedians come?" "Out of wide arses." "How right you are. Out of what do they make public speeches?" "Out of wide arses." Aristophanes' dilation on the subject of wide arse is therefore a neat and clever climax to a debate between types of speech. Trendy Unjust Speech, the presiding spirit of the fashionable young wide-arse advocates, demonstrates the sophistic art of the Wide Arse, by discoursing sophistically about the topic of wide arses—pure genius, Aristophanes at his vulgar, brilliant best. This is no coded metaphor, nothing could be simpler, and yet countless lexicographers and commentators, even modern, scientific, objective philologists, fail to see it.

Obsessed with flagitious anal penetration we had oblivionized the fact that arseholes are famous for quite a few other things apart from occasionally getting shafted. One piece of commentary illustrates the blind spot. Immediately after noting Aristophanes' fondness for fusing rhetoric and farts—"the authority of a politician's voice depends on the width of his *prōktos* [arsehole]"—the scholar moves on to a discussion of wide arse: "used *only* with reference to those whose *prōktoi* have been widened by constant buggery and who are on that account depraved or evil" (emphasis added). But there is another casualty of sodomania apart from missing the point of Aristophanes' jokes: politics. For why all this fuss about the speeches of arseholes like Callistratus and Demosthenes? Why this ridiculing of the farty clever-clever Unjust way of arguing that young advocates like Alcibiades and Euathlus had learned from professional "sophists" such as Protagoras and Socrates? Which sophistry, when, arguing what, against whom? Speeches to make policy of course, sophistry designed to destroy the power and prestige of distinguished elder statesmen: hot air with solid consequences, words that change things, potentially deadly words that need to be disarmed.[23]

DOVER'S *GREEK HOMOSEXUALITY*

Riding high on the acclaim for his edition of Aristophanes' *Clouds,* when Dover's *Greek Homosexuality* came out in 1978 it quickly took its place as the most authoritative account of the subject. It has been the basis for all further research, and not just in the English-speaking world: "without doubt one of the most influential of post-war classical studies"; Michel Foucault called it an instant classic.[24] The unflinching gaze Dover turned on himself in his autobiography was in this book directed onto the topic of Greek homosexual behavior, and the same brutal frankness, the duty to tell it as it is, the preference for "nasty truths" over "silly lies," is manifest on every page.

In the preface he outlined his prime qualification for the job: "I am fortunate in not experiencing moral shock or disgust at any genital act whatsoever." In his memoirs he quotes one reader who thought this was "an extreme, perhaps the ultimate, expression of scholarly amoralism." That seemed to imply a posture, however. Dover was having none of that. Without a hint of irony he dismisses the charge: "I was . . . telling the plain truth . . ." But perhaps some clarification was in order: He didn't mean to say that he didn't find certain genital acts "*aesthetically repulsive,*" although the prospect of buggery was not as aesthetically repulsive as putting "melted mutton fat into my mouth."[25]

Like Ranke, father of modern history, a century and a half earlier, Dover announced that he wanted to rid the subject of "moral evaluation," quoting another German student of ancient Greek Homosex for the view that this was "the deadly enemy of science." Like Ranke's, his book had "a modest and limited aim: to describe those phenomena of homosexual behavior and sentiment which are to be found in Greek art and literature between the eighth and second centuries BC . . ." This was to be an empirical study: "My primary object is to describe what is most easily and clearly observed."

Reviewers celebrated this "matter-of-fact, methodical description" as a great advance in the human sciences, a landmark, shining the light of day onto a subject till now "prettily sentimentalized, dismissed as peripheral or blandly ignored": "the love that in Victorian England dared not speak its name is examined with a clinical eye, its Greek terminology defined with philological exactness, its physical manifestations unblushingly described . . ."[26] While most readers got carried away on the tide of this triumph of science, one reviewer, Nancy Demand, held her ground. There was, she thought, something fundamentally wrong: "It is unfortunate that a book on such a popular subject should put forward a characterization of Greek attitudes which is so poorly founded."[27] Meier's early-nineteenth-century account was still superior, she advised.

In the preface, Dover seemed to be steeling himself for some very explicit "phenomena," "easily and clearly observed" in the sources—lots of "genital acts" and "homosexual behavior"—but this was a realm of behavior that even a Greek had described as "invisible," so what was he referring to? He couldn't be talking about images; a flick through the pictures revealed very little gay porn. Though tens of thousands of images have been discovered on Greek vases, decorated with scenes of Greek myth and daily life, scenes of consummated homosexual copulation are exceedingly rare, although there are some scenes of imminent frottage and touching up. For want of explicit homosexual acts, Dover filled up the plates with scenes of heterosexual copulation—the supposedly buggered women acting, he suggested, as stand-ins for images of buggered boys—and even with some abstract designs that he found "suggestive of anus or nipple."[28]

Maybe, then, the explicit phenomena he was bracing his readers for were texts? But these too turned out to be disappointing. The Greeks were generally reticent about such things, as Dover freely admitted on several occasions. And yet, despite the reticence of the sources, Dover's book was very graphic indeed. For he had decided to "translate" what he saw as Greek euphemism into something rather more explicit, immediate and real, what he called "concrete realities."

Even Aristophanes proved once again to be not quite explicit enough. In *Knights* the vulgar Sausage-Seller describes starting out on a political career. Just before he makes his first speech he hears thunder, a lucky omen, a sign that he will be a great success. It is coming from his right, a propitious direction. But, this being a comedy, it is not thunder, a sign from Zeus, but a fart, produced by a degenerate *katapugōn*. Farty speeches; we have been here before. It is not one of Aristophanes' funniest jokes, but at least it is direct. However, just as he once perceived Cowper's secretion glistening on the penises of boys in the ancient gymnasium, Dover (p. 142) now hears the sound of this particular fart, whose timbre and tone *Knights* does not, of course, describe. What he hears turns out to be comprehensively revealing about the sexual history of this anonymous man in the crowd: "The anatomy of the anus is altered by habitual buggery [a footnote provides further reading], and there are modern jokes which imply (rightly or wrongly) that the sound of farts is affected by these changes." A more recent writer on Greek sexuality, Bruce Thornton, trumped even this, hearing a particularly positive cosmic sonority erupting from the degenerate's bottom and producing one of my favorite quotes from the annals of sodomania: "Presumably the anus . . . widened and loosened by buggery, produced propitious tones."[29]

If Dover's tendency to zoom in on "concrete realities" amused us when we read *Clouds* at school, and gave journalists something to write about when the memoirs were published, here, in an attempt to get to the heart of Greek Love, it had more serious consequences, reducing a complex public phenomenon, essential to understanding Greek politics and philosophy, warfare, art and society, to a series of unseen and unspoken-of genital acts.

In that famous speech, a central text for students of Athenian Homosexuality, Pausanias, one of the guests at Plato's *Symposium* (185b), talking of the response of a youth to a "passionate admirer," concludes that "any kind of gracious favoring [*charizesthai*] is admirable if offered for the sake of improvement [*aretē*]." This is the main basis for the popular notion that Greek Love was all about education, the lovers acting like adult volunteers in a youth club, helping teenagers to develop useful skills and knowledge of the world. Pausanias's suggestion is interesting, perhaps a little provocative, shifting graciousness from the how to the why, but not exactly hard porn—well, not yet. Because what Plato means, according to Dover, is something altogether racier: "acceptance of the teacher's thrusting penis between his thighs or in his anus is the fee which the pupil pays for good teaching . . ."[30] I am quite sure that Plato would have been utterly horrified at such a translation: *charizesthai,* "paying a fee"?

Dover ought to have known what he was talking about because he was in the middle of preparing another new text, an acclaimed new edition of Plato's *Symposium,* getting a little bit closer to Plato's actual words by scraping off the accumulated typos of thousands of years, but now he seemed to think that Plato's text itself was just another layer to be scraped away to get at a truer text, a subtext of hard facts, buried beneath the author's evasions. Dover reads Plato's *Symposium* therefore as if it were full of sexual innuendo and double entendre, like an episode of *Are You Being Served?* (*charizesthai*). Whatever else you call it, this is far from what readers of *Greek Homosexuality* were promised, the empirical, objective study of phenomena "easily and clearly observed."

Translating "graciously gratifying behavior" as if it just meant "homosex" causes problems, since Pausanias, the speaker in Plato's *Symposium,* had earlier distinguished "admirable" (*kalōs*) and "base" (*ponērōs*) ways of "graciously favoring" (*charizesthai*) an admirer (183d). This has been a critical passage for those who want to argue that "Plato" advocated only "purely Platonic" relationships—that "admirable" responses are nonsexual, "base" responses sexual—a reasonable inference in the narrow, but not in the wider, context. Dover has a different problem: For him it's *all* sex. He draws his sword and cuts through the Gordian knot with a single blow. There are two different kinds of sex, it turns out: "between the thighs or in the anus," respectively honorable and base.

This idea that the Greeks thought homosex was fine so long as the youth didn't bend over, but faced his lover, standing bolt upright, head held high, while his lover bent his knees and got on with it, is one of Dover's most celebrated—it introduced the word "intercrural" ("'twixt the thighs") into classical studies and the *New York Review of Books*—and precarious inventions. The Athenians do seem to have practiced what a Princetonian once described to me as the Princeton rub—"Give me a between-the-thighs in return," it says on one cheeky vase (BA 306425)—and it is the position seen most frequently, in fact nearly exclusively, in early scenes of homosexual copulation (*c.*550–525 BC; cf. Figs. 45, 53, 54, 56b, 58).

Moreover it seems reasonable to assume that the Greeks thought different sexual positions had different significances. Some difference of nuance between homosexual positions may well turn up in the future, but from the texts currently available to us the main attention seems overwhelmingly to focus on *the fact* of getting sexually intimate and the care taken to make sure that you didn't get a reputation as a whore. No one ever says: "Yes, I did put out, but it's OK, I kept my chin held high and I didn't bend over." It was the whole context of the relationship that was important, not specific sexual positions. Indeed intercrural was practiced it seems even by Aristophanes' "Sausage-Seller," a low-life former prostitute and no example to anybody. At any rate he is said to have stuck a piece of "meat in his perineum."[31] But Dover's distinction between homosexual positions has a much wider significance.

TIMARCHUS TAKES THE STAND

For in his discussion of Athenian attitudes in Plato's *Symposium,* our speaker, Pausanias, had described the situation in Athens as "complicated" in comparison with other places: "not easy to understand." Admirers put themselves in some very humiliating situations, camping outside closed doors, petitioning, and so on. They behaved toward the boys they admired like beggars or like men toadying up to a rich, powerful man in the hope of a sum of money or a job, yet while venal men like that were despised for their servile behavior, boy admirers, on the other hand, were encouraged to abase themselves. So you might think that we approved, Pausanias continues. Yet, paradoxically, despite all the apparent sympathy for the admirer's plight, if the boy stopped avoiding him the boy would be condemned, even if he so much as exchanged a few words. Pausanias resolves the paradox as a kind of contest or game, an ideal way to test the admirer, his sincerity and his seriousness of purpose, making sure that a boy has time enough to tell. But Dover is unimpressed. It doesn't add up. Something else is going on.

The centerpiece of Dover's book, its starting point and fulcrum, is Aeschines' now notorious indictment of the politician Timarchus for homosexual prostitution and other vices. This clever speech may have been, in the words of a Roman fan of Aeschines, "savage, criminal and poisonous," but it nevertheless counted as a document in von Ranke's terms, a very primary witness, close to the sights and sounds of ancient Greece, the very words (more or less) heard in a popular court of the Athenian democracy in the winter of 346 BC.[32] In the nineteenth century, Meier had used the speech to introduce the topic of homosexuality in Athens, despite his misgivings about its viciousness, and Dover made it the "mainstay" of his work on Greek Homosexuality, organizing the whole of the first part of his book around the speech. Dover acknowledges the political context of debates about the threat of Macedon, and does not fail to observe that the law and the speech are superficially concerned with prostitution, nor that the Greeks considered prostitution a dreadful offense, but that is not enough. Dover wants to dig deeper.

For he had made a discovery that left him "in no doubt that practically everything said during the last few centuries about the psychology,

ethics and sociology of Greek homosexuality was confused and misleading." It is a dramatic moment. His sexual emphasis will be seen to
pay off, because it is only here in the nitty-gritty, in the realm of the invisible, in the precise details of sex acts the Greeks didn't speak about,
only here that all that pursuing and graciously gratifying finally starts to
make sense: "The root of the confusion was the failure to understand
how quite different attitudes to the 'active' and the 'passive' role coex-
ist . . ."[33]

Though the sources harped on about it, therefore, whorishness per se
was not the *real* concern of Aeschines and the law and the population
of Athens, for if today a girl is labeled a "whore," it means, according
to Dover, only that she has not preserved her virginity. Although
Aeschines' speech seemed to deal with prostitution, payments and being
mercenary and promiscuous, deep down it was about the ins and outs of
anal penetration, and in particular about men who took "the woman's
part" and let others penetrate their bodies, something the Greeks abhorred, argues Dover, although you could emerge with your honor intact if you kept it "intercrural."

Of course, if you read Aeschines' speech, you will find no discussion
of sexual acts, whether anal, intercrural, or hanging from a trapeze;
once more, according to Dover, it's all in the subtext. For Dover's long
discussion of the Timarchus case climaxes after a hundred pages in a ten-
page section headed "Dominant and Subordinate Roles." It is to this
section that readers are referred for enlightenment concerning "the
terms in which the important distinction between prostitution and 'legitimate eros' was conventionally drawn" and "the reasons for making
[the law]" in the first place: It claims to make the grounds for hostility
toward the choice made by male prostitutes "sufficiently obvious."[34] In
this section, Dover examines pictures showing women being penetrated
anally—"the vulva, carefully depicted, is nowhere near the point of
penetration"; "the point of entry is so high . . ."; "the painter cannot
have been unaware of the distance he has put between the woman's
pubic hair and the point of entry of . . ." An art historian, another "Professor, Sir," wondered if Dover was seeing things again: "I do not believe it possible to determine from a painting . . . (approaches which are
at any rate in life closely adjacent and parallel)."[35] Dover contrasts these
poor women with scenes of boys being penetrated between the thighs,

standing up, heads held high: The women look subjugated, the boys strangely dignified, for these boys aren't really being penetrated at all, just rubbed up against. But the missing boys—those who, in life, would have been placed in the same position as the women, i.e. bent over, buggered—must of necessity have been placed, like the women, in a subordinate role. We can see now why the intercrural position is so crucial for Dover. How else can you have lots of sex between men without constant problematic humiliation?

To prove his theory about the nature of sex, Dover cites a whole range of evidence, from Viking sagas to the film *Deliverance,* which shows that throughout history and all over the world, even in the animal kingdom, being penetrated is humiliating, although Dover notes that animals, unlike humans, don't always have the capacity to follow the gesture through: "Karlen . . . observes that humans, unlike many animal species, which have ritualised homosexual 'submission,' *can complete* a genital act 'in expressing a power relationship' " (104–105 and nn. 91 and 96)—it is not hard here to detect the influence of Desmond Morris, whose *The Naked Ape,* published in 1967, and its sequels had an enormous impact at the time: "The original, straightforward pattern of copulation is, for the male . . . a fundamentally assertive and aggressive act of penetration."[36] All in all it is clear, a fundamental fact of nature, that to be bodily penetrated by a male is universally a sign of submission and defeat. How on earth do women cope with this nightly humiliation?

> I do not countenance the strange notion that women "really want" to be raped, but I am aware of a case in which, according to her own private testimony, a woman violently resisting rape suddenly became aware that her immediate desire for sexual intercourse had suddenly become much more powerful than her hatred of her attacker . . . The Greeks may have thought that such an occurrence was common; they did not expect the passive partner in a homosexual relationship to derive physical pleasure from it [i.e., pleasure of submission].[37]

Dover is right, of course, to say that in some modern cultures sex is used as a metaphor for dominance and aggression. We live amid a daily chorus of "Up yours," "Get stuffed," "Screw you." At an examiners' meeting I attended the chairman managed to make five references to anal sex in the first five minutes: three "sods," a "bugger" and a "pain in the arse." In the early 1990s I thought it might be a good idea to collect some of the more salient examples of this phenomenon. I soon gave up after watching an episode of an American sitcom that threatened to overwhelm the database.

If the power-penetration metaphor is ubiquitous in modern society, we have to be careful, when we look at other periods and places and species, to make sure that we aren't simply projecting our own dismal images onto them. In fact so far as I can tell from the *Oxford English Dictionary,* the ubiquitous everyday use of the language of sex to indicate aggression or humiliation is a recent phenomenon, going as far back as 1700, perhaps, in one or two cases, but above all a phenomenon of the second half of the twentieth century.[38] People did not go around telling each other to fuck off in the Middle Ages. Proper cursing—damning and blinding—and oaths were far more important. And if verbal sexual aggression is indeed, in Dover's words, a feature of "vulgar idiom in many languages," such usages are conspicuously absent from ancient Greek. The Greeks commonly referred to sex in lots of ways—as taking pleasure, wrestling, blending, a "mixing" (*mixis*), "associating" (*homilia*), "being close" (*plēsiazō*), "being with" (*sunousia*), "marrying" (*gamō*), "agitating" (*kineō*)—and, like people in many other cultures, including not so long ago our own, they worried about an exchange of vital fluids that might involve a dangerous drying out or loss of substance for the man, but never as "fucking someone" in the modern sense with its modern connotations. There is no report of anyone emerging from the marketplace muttering "I've been screwed." Timarchus did not accuse Aeschines of "shafting" the city.

Dover imagined he had found a word, *"laikazō,"* which was used in the modern sense of "fuck," and he translates it accordingly: "Well I'll be f . . . ," "I'm f . . . if I'll . . . ," "Get f . . . !," "F . . . you!" Two years later a learned article demonstrated that it must refer to oral sex, which means that my summary of Greek sexual morality is not quite adequate; there was another important principle, "Honor thy mouth," since "going down on" a man was considered absolutely vile, as indeed was going down on a woman. This has nothing to do with penetration, but rather with the concept of pollution. As Robert Parker concludes in his study of *miasma:* "The most honorable part of the body, and the purest is the head, and of the head the purest part should be the mouth, which receives food, utters prayer, and implants chaste kisses; it is thus in particular danger of contamination by contact with dirty and shameful organs."[39]

ERASTĒS AND ERŌMENOS: ACTIVE AND PASSIVE

By dismissing what the Greeks actually said on the subject as the product of euphemism and embarrassment, by scraping away the supposedly decorous surface of the text to expose the invisible—hence all the more authentic—sex acts "underneath," by invoking universal and natural facts about the meaning of those sexual acts, by reducing the often plural admirers to one, shutting him in the bedroom with his loved one, locking the door and imagining the view through the keyhole, Dover finally emerged with a truth that had been hidden for centuries: Greek homosexual relationships, far from being in any sense "Platonic," revolved around sex. They were obsessed with penetration—why else avoid talking about it, unless it was a matter of the utmost significance?—keen to dominate other males sexually, and fearful of the social and political consequences if they themselves should yield to an act of what Dover calls "homosexual submission."

Dover's erastēs was no forlorn admirer, sighing outside the changing rooms with all the boy's other admirers, but a dangerous would-be penetrator; the erōmenos was no swaggering star of the exercise ground, surrounded by adoring fans whose feelings for him he might in some cases be only dimly aware of, but a victim locked in an abusive relationship, trying to cling to his dignity, desperately hoping his "lover" might be fobbed off with a bit of frottage. Erōs was no playful hovering Cupid firing arrows of pulse-racing passion, but a raging desire to dominate and penetrate. Dover can never quite bring himself to translate "to be in love with" as "to fuck"—to have erōs for someone means, he says, "have a passionate desire for"—but he sidles toward it: Erōs is "the exclusive and obsessive lust which one feels for a particular person. Most of us are so constituted that we necessarily desire the satisfaction of lust by orgasm." This is how the erōtikos becomes "sexual," identical with "erotic." This is how one's erastēs becomes one's "lover." Any instances, and there are very many, in which a "desire to screw someone" seems impossible in context—*erōs* for the motherland, for war, for power, for sailing, for ugly old Socrates, for dinner, or meat, or sleep, or for parenthood—"can fairly be regarded as sexual metaphor."

Well might the Greeks have distinguished two different roles in relationships between males, therefore, for of course they were really talking about roles not in love but in the sexual act. *Erastēs* and *erōmenos* are now, according to Dover's definition, "the 'active' (or 'assertive,' or 'dominant') and 'passive' (or 'receptive,' or 'subordinate') partners in a homosexual relationship." Oh how the *erastēs* must sometimes have wished it was so.[40]

SEX VERSUS HOMOSEXUALITY

The campaign to sex up Greek Love viewed itself therefore as a bold crusade launched under the banner of modernity and science to face up to brutal truths about relationships between Greek men, truths that had been covered up or prettified not only by the "Victorians" but by the Greeks themselves with all their obfuscations about hopeless devotion, Cupid and lurve. One case in particular, the speech "Against Timarchus" in which Aeschines defends himself from a vicious attack by accusing his attacker of homosexual prostitution, has captured a central place in this modern approach to the subject, both as a primary document, and as one that seems to cut through all the cant, shedding light on one particular relationship that is ruthlessly exposed as brutally interested and politically mercenary.

But there have been bizarre consequences of this unsentimental approach. Sodomania has meant divorcing Greek Homosexuality from supposedly nonsexual relationships, such as that of Achilles and Patroclus in the *Iliad,* and from women-loving women like Sappho, whose appearances right at the heart of the culture of Greek Love are sometimes seen as just the most amazing coincidence. However, a lot of Dover's readers thought, and continue to think, that all this emphasis on sex represents a pro-gay approach to Greek Love, and that people who argue, as I do, that it is not *all about sex* are playing into the hands of those who would deny the sexual element completely. (Here I have to say that I have never met anyone, outside modern Greece at least, who believes that Greek men just held hands.) And yet the feeling that homosex, anal sex, must be energetically insisted upon as the essence of Greek Love persists in many conversations I have had with colleagues and others, as if, three hundred years after Bentley's casual assumption that *erastēs* indicated a "flagitious love of Boys," his assumption is still under threat and the phantom band of "Victorian" sex deniers is plotting an imminent comeback.

But Bentley's use of the word "flagitious" to describe Greek Love on the eve of the London Molly-House pogroms reminds us that this is not a tranquil corner of research. Telling the truth about Greek Homosexuality is not the same as telling the truth about Greek Heterosexuality or the causes of the Peloponnesian War. It also reminds us that the insistence on sex, on "homosexual genital acts," does not necessarily reflect a modern liberal pro-gay attitude.

Is it conceivable that behind the modern festival of sodomania, another kind of repression has been at work? Is there denial in all this truth telling? Is it possible that these nice classicists—not all of them straight, not all of them men—who are so keen on anal rape in Crete, and who imagine poetical descriptions of drowning men being forcibly sodomized by the sea, are not quite the cool, gay-friendly scholars they purport to be? What if it is not Love that has been marginalizing sodomy, but sodomy that has been used to marginalize Love? Let us be careful here. I am not accusing the sodomaniacs of homophobia, and I am fully aware with all this talk of mercenary interests, "song-and-dance" performances and politics, that I could be accused myself of "denying" Greek Love. There is no such thing as a quintessentially pro-gay or homophobic fact, nor a racist, nor an anti-Semitic fact—it just depends; but there is such a thing as homophobia, and anti-Semitism, and racism, and it does have an effect on how a subject is approached.

ONE HUNDRED YEARS AND COUNTING

Oliver Stone had made a film about Alexander the Great. It was to be historically accurate. My former tutor, Robin Lane Fox, had advised the director; in fact he had been dreaming of a film on the subject and starring in it in a minor role for over twenty years, "leading a cavalry charge at Gaugamela." Since he had been my tutor on Alexander the Great, I had some idea of what to expect. It's all about horse riding and buggery, I seem to remember him commenting on at least one occasion, and *Alexander* duly did not shy from the Conqueror's homosexuality, or did it? It was complicated, and Colin Farrell—"Alexander"—tried to explain:

The sexuality is in there, you know he's bisexual. You don't even need to know that, because there was no categorizing it as homosexuality, bisexuality, heterosexuality back then. There was no term for it. It was a time when men and men laid together and they shared knowledge and women had babies primarily. Later, as we got more technologically adept and sociologically inept, we started to put titles on everything. We decided for the few what was right or wrong, or the few decided for the multitude what was right or wrong.[1]

Remarkably, Farrell was offering a version of some rather highfalutin academic work on the history of human sexuality that derives from the work of Michel Foucault. It's not often you get French post-structuralist philosophy from a Hollywood star.

Dover, to be sure, had called his book *Greek Homosexuality*. But was it really "homosexuality" and what, by the way, does that mean? "I think it would be advisable not to speak of it as a sexuality at all, but to describe it, rather, as a more generalized ethos of penetration and domination, a socio-sexual discourse structured by the presence or absence of its central term: the phallus." That quote comes from a book by David M. Halperin that appeared in 1990 under the title *One Hundred Years of Homosexuality*. The influence of Dover is obvious, as Halperin acknowledged—"eminent," "superb philologist," "brilliant," "knighted"—and as Dover himself underlined, after repaying Halperin's fulsome compliments in a review: Halperin's book was "founded upon data which I presented in *Greek Homosexuality* but did not subject to generalization beyond a certain limit."

But in generalizing from Dover's buggery-obsessed Greeks, Halperin had drawn extravagant conclusions: Homosexuality did not exist in nature. That in itself wasn't new, of course. There are still countless people who think homosexuality is unnatural, the product of disease/my mother/degeneracy/Western civilization/living in London/the sixties. But Halperin went further. There was no such thing as homosexuality because there was no such thing as sexuality, which meant there was no such thing as heterosexuality either. Sexual attraction between people of the opposite sex was a product of culture, with no biological basis: The Greeks proved it, though Halperin didn't dwell on it.

The "hundred years" in the title of his book referred to the fact that the earliest occurrence of the term "homosexuality" in the *Oxford English Dictionary* was dated 1892. Homosexuality arrived in Anglophonia in C. G. Chaddock's English translation of Richard Krafft-Ebing's *Psychopathia Sexualis*—by which time the Germans had already enjoyed twenty years of *Homosexualität*. I hope they made the most of those two decades, for Halperin was not arguing about a mere relabeling process like the renaming of a brontosaur as an apatosaur. He thought the very labeling process had somehow called something into existence that had previously not been, as if scientists, like ancient magicians, had invented a new rune of power.

So, just as Oscar Wilde in the summer of 1896 had seized upon the fact that "eminent men of science" had recently given him a starring role in their accounts of mental, social and spiritual sickness—"Professor Nordau in his book on 'Degenerescence' published in 1894 having devoted an entire chapter to the petitioner as a specially typical example of this fatal flaw"—in order to present himself as a sufferer from "erotomania," now Halperin saw himself as a victim of malign forces beyond his control: "Just because my sexuality is an artifact of cultural processes, doesn't mean I'm not stuck with it," he complained (51). But whereas Wilde had been pitiably grateful to find a word to describe a technical condition from which, he now realized, he had long been suffering, Halperin, a century later, was less sanguine. Wilde's solution had become his problem. Halperin seemed to be suffering from the effects of the very science Wilde had invoked to get a remission of his sentence. He was the victim of a word, the homosexual word, and the particular organization of the world the word had catalyzed, for although sexuality had no basis in nature, the sexuality each culture created was experienced as if it were a nature and was therefore as impossible to escape as if it were nature, which is rather convenient.

> Particular cultures are contingent, but the personal identities and forms of erotic life that take shape within the horizons of those cultures are not. To say that sexuality is learned, is not to say that it can be unlearned . . . I can't imagine deacculturating myself any more than I can imagine de-sexualizing myself . . . (51–53)

One could agree perfectly that experiences of the same thing differed somewhat over time, that sex yesterday was not the same as sex today, and sex tomorrow, that our "fuck-sex" was experienced somewhat differently from the Greeks' "mixing-sex," or "gracious putting out," that the ancient Greek experience of homosexuality did not involve tight T-shirts, gay bars and/or shopping for nice furniture on a Saturday afternoon, any more than their heterosexual fantasies featured Benny Hill–style images of half-clad serving girls bending over to pick something up off the floor. One might even agree that the words used to describe and typify people may affect that experience, that having difficulty with writing became a different kind of experience for somebody diagnosed as "dyslexic," that labels and organizing principles affect expectations, which in turn affect practice and experience, but what Halperin was saying seemed to be "considerably more radical than that." It was not simply that experience of the same thing differed over time: there was no same thing.

Moreover, whereas plenty of people would love to believe that homosexuality is unnatural, to say that there is no biological basis for attractions between male and female was rather harder to swallow. It seemed daft, incredible. Halperin agreed: "I don't and couldn't possibly, believe in what I've been saying . . . There's just no other equally sensible way to interpret the evidence I'm familiar with or to understand the gap between the recorded experiences of persons living in ancient and in modern societies."[2]

We should not be unsympathetic. Halperin seemed to find himself thrown between the Clashing Rocks. On the one hand his own sensible straightforward observation of the world as it is, on the other the sensible straightforward observations, the "data," of ancient Greek writers, the "recorded experiences" of the world as it used to be, as if, to adapt someone else's example, he had studied the recorded experiences of ancient apples and discovered they did not fall from trees but rose up into them, thus confounding Newton.

But Halperin did not invent this idea he found so incredible, that homosexuality began in 1892, and a large proportion of clever people working in the human sciences today seem to accept it, in one part of the brain, at least, without demur. But before we get to them I am afraid we need to return to Sir Kenneth pleasuring himself on a hill while the Second World War was coming to a close in Italy.

A TRIP TO THE ZOO

For there was something really odd about all this. Halperin seemed to think that the theory that homosexuals were not real (or heterosexuals either, mind) was in some way a pro-gay position, and he even accuses those who talk of biology and genes of homophobia. That was one part of the book that Dover disliked. For Dover, the author who provided the "data" on which Halperin's conclusions were based, had been worried that the same accusation of homophobia might be leveled at him, and with good reason. People wonder how on earth the Greeks could have "tolerated homosexuality," he says in conclusion; such people are, it seems, taking homosexuality far too seriously. For "religious prohibition" has prevented them from inquiring about "the variety of sexual stimuli which can arouse the same person or about the difference between fundamental orientations of the personality and *episodic behavior at a superficial level*" (emphasis added). This picks up an odd comment in Dover's preface where he objected to the title of his own book on the ground that what is called homosexual is not properly sexual at all— only the heterosexual deserves that title—nor does it belong to the parasexual, to perversion, rather it is a counterfeit, a subdivision of the "quasi-sexual" or "pseudosexual." He anticipates some reaction to this statement: "Anyone who wishes to make an impression on me by ascribing my inclination to prejudice must first persuade me that he has made a serious attempt to distinguish between prejudice and judgment."

And there is another strange statement about homophobia among academic experts in the preface to *Greek Homosexuality,* a quote from Arno Karlen: "Other researchers and clinicians reveal in private a vengeful hatred toward sexual deviants that they would never display in print or in public." "From personal knowledge I endorse" that comment, says Dover. Who on earth is he talking about, and why vengeful?

Dover's central notion of pseudosexuality first appeared in an article he wrote in 1973. For Dover had changed his mind about Greek sexual morality between 1964 and 1978, discarding an empirical approach based on what texts actually said, which had concluded that the problem for Plato and Aeschines was "the whole context" and payment in particular, not acts, and moving toward a secret subtext, backed up by sociobiology, which concluded that it was indeed about acts, and about sodomy in particular. The reason was that in 1964 he came into contact with a man called George Devereux.

Devereux was a Hungarian left stranded in Romania after the First World War until he moved to Paris. Greatly impressed by his intellect, Dover devotes several pages to him in his autobiography. He had worked as an anthropologist in Vietnam and California before practicing as a psychoanalyst. In 1963 he was able to combine his two interests, becoming director of studies in Ethnopsychiatry at the École des Hautes Études in Paris. From there he submitted an article to the *Classical Quarterly*, a journal Dover was editing. They corresponded and became friends. In 1971 Dover sponsored Devereux for a Visiting Fellowship at All Souls in Oxford, to enable him to finish a book on *Dreams in Greek Tragedy*. The college consulted one of France's most distinguished classicists, Jean-Pierre Vernant, who described him as "brilliant but mad," and he was accepted. Dover did not inquire how he got on with the other fellows and Devereux offered only one detail. One of the male dons had propositioned him. George had declined.

Dover himself was not entirely convinced by Devereux's ethno-psychoanalytical approach, but then, shortly before a lecture given by Devereux, he had a dream of a trip to the zoo. He doesn't describe what happened in the dream, but he gives the "punch-line: 'Never walk under a giraffe!' " Every ingredient seemed explicable to him in terms of a Freudian "primal scene," bringing to mind some event that had occurred at the age of twelve. He doesn't spell out the event, but it seems probable it has a bearing on perhaps the most bizarre episode in the whole autobiography. A friend from school called Alec, a boy "with no religious scruples," offered to give Dover a masturbation demonstration, though he would have preferred "a nance," which Dover understood to mean sodomy, sod being "a special word so potent that it had to be communicated in a hushed voice." Dover refused. Alec pleaded— "Oh, come on! I haven't had a decent nance for *ages*!"—in vain. Finding that he could not manage to masturbate under Dover's patient gaze, he shut him out in the kitchen and told him to wait. He called him in at the last minute "just in time for the eruption," then "stuffed away his cock, rubbed the semen into the rug with one stroke of his shoe, and that was that."

Dover's reaction to the incident was extreme and odd. He was at first

furious with Alec for shutting him out of the room and abjured masturbation from that moment on. On the other hand he was furious at himself for refusing to let Alec bugger him. It implied aesthetic disgust, out
of the question (sodomy is not "melted mutton fat"), or conventional
morality, also out of the question. What was immoral, he concluded,
was his refusal to reciprocate a favor of no moral significance with another favor equally neutral.

What is extraordinary about this conclusion is that the amoralism,
the lack of prejudice, which was an absolute necessity for good scientific
scholarship whether you were reconstructing a text from manuscripts
or reconstructing events from texts, was here being applied to sex itself,
the amoral historian transformed into an *amoraliste*. Just as the editor of
an ancient text reconstructed words without anticipating what the text
ought to mean, reading words without interpreting yet, so little Alec,
free of religious scruples, seemed to be more objective about sodomy,
more honest. He seemed closer to the truth about sex, able to see it the
way von Ranke saw history, "as it was in its bare essentials," i.e., simply
as genital acts, *only sex, sex facts speaking for themselves*. He was in a place
before morality, before sexuality, before significance, the world of pure
cheerful sexicity.

What Dover doesn't seem to have considered is that there may have
been something more devious in the casualness of the invitation, that
the playful understatement of a "nance" is what we might call an ideological construction, a defense against the seriousness of a "sod," not
naïve unthinking innocence, but a disclaimer—"I'm innocent." Anthropologists studying sex in other cultures have sometimes made the
same mistake when they return with glowing reports about the natives'
complete lack of sexual hang-ups and later it transpires they have been
well and truly had.

But in that case why did Dover, blessed with an absence of disgust for
genital acts that would later be vaunted as a "qualification" for writing a
book on Greek Homosexuality, and equally disdainful of conventional
morality, he claims, even at that young age, rebuff the proposition?
Dover had had no solution to this dilemma at the time, apart from "primal scene trauma," but he had assumed that in this "nance" he would be
playing the passive role, and many years later he would demonstrate that
always and throughout history among almost every kind of species, the

passive role is seen as subordinate: Perhaps it would not have been a fair exchange after all. It cannot be a coincidence, at any rate, that Dover later invented a theory about Greek Homosexuality that placed the *erōmenos* in exactly the position in which he had found himself in Alec's house, i.e., refusing to turn around despite the favors he had received from his friend, and desperate for a good view.

There is another candidate for this twelve-year-old's trauma, though not really an event so much as a sequence of events. Often at the end of breakfast, Dover's father would cough with increasing violence, then leave the table and spit in the sink. This provoked undoubtedly the strongest emotion he ever felt in his life, a mixture of "rage, hatred and despair." It was his father's hiding away of his expectoration that was so awful. Had he done it in front of everyone, and spat out of the window, "like a Greek village headman by whom I was once entertained," it would have been fine. At fifteen, having read Freud, he concluded that the problem was the resemblance between mucus expectorated and semen ejaculated; it came to him that he must have been suffering from a primal scene trauma, having witnessed his father being masturbated by his mother at a very early age, though that particular text from his early life had been lost and had to be reconstructed. Given that background of trauma, real or imagined, we can see, I think, why it was a matter of utmost importance, a sheer *necessity,* for Dover to confront genital acts without disgust—"It is only when we insist, as we must, on translating such words as 'pursue' and 'accomplish' into concrete realities that the extent of the disguise which convention imposed upon the expression of homosexual eros becomes apparent"—to translate into "plain English" the "thrusting penis between his thighs or in his anus" that lay behind Plato's embarrassed reference to "smiling upon an admirer."[3]

Dover consulted two psychiatrists about this primal scene. They were not very interested. Then he had that dream of a trip to the zoo, and the long-necked giraffe you should never walk under. Clearly the whole thing, "without residue," was explicable in terms of that "primal" scene at age twelve. It seemed that the reading methods of psychoanalysis could indeed provide access to authentic early texts, and so perhaps even to those you could not remember, the "covert" text. The truth of the dream converted him to Devereux's psychoanalytic methods and he recommended Devereux's book, *Dreams in Greek Tragedy,* to the publishers Blackwell. In fact he was perhaps doubly converted to Devereux's theory of pseudohomosexuality, if the dream did indeed call to mind Alec and a vivid image of a playful, episodic, superficial example of the pseudohomosexuality Devereux had identified in ancient Greece, that homosexuality "as it was in its bare essentials," "only sex." Jolly would-be rogerer Alec with his lack of religious scruples was a model reader of *Greek Homosexuality,* if not a model for the Greeks.[4]

Dover was able to add a new modification, however, something he had learned while fighting in Italy during the war, to Devereux's theory of pseudosexuality. For there was something missing from Alec's religiously uninhibited episodic homosexicity: beauty. There had been no gazing at Kenneth's naked body, no sculptures commissioned, no vases decorated with acclamations, but Dover had concluded that Plato's description of getting turned on, even physically turned on, by beautiful youths was just like a modern metaphysician getting turned on by a Beethoven symphony or a Highland sunrise: an *aesthetic* experience. This was why his wartime experience of masturbating over the sight of the Matese massif south of Mignano gave him such insight, he imagined, into Plato's contemplation of the beautiful boy in the *Symposium* and *Phaedrus.* That was why, when the first rumors emerged about his memoirs, he told journalists the episode was "important." I do not think Dover would count his wartime experience either as a parasexual perversion, i.e., sexual desire for mountains, orophilia, or as something truly sexual, i.e., heterosexual. Plato's homosexual gaze could be incorporated as another subdivision of Dover's experience of the pseudosexual: boys, mountains, music, victory, all of them potentially a turn-on. Devereux was able to talk of four sexualities: authentic "psychological" homo- and heterosexuality and their merely "behavioral" pseudoversions. Now, following his sexually aesthetic experiences on the mountaintop, Dover could reduce even the so-called authentic, psychological homosexuality to the category of the pseudosexual.

In fact he is rather inconsistent. In particular it is not quite clear what Dover thinks of Plato himself. He is prepared to view his "inclination" as "exclusively homosexual," but then he has said that the homosexual is always pseudo. Has he been careless in the exposition of his thoughts, has he changed his mind, or is he prepared to concede to Plato at least the status of an authentic pervert?[5]

SAPPHO THE MASCULINE LESBIAN

Though never taken very seriously by most classicists, anthropologists are less critical of him, and Dover's beloved Devereux is a major figure in their field. Devereux had a lifelong interest in the study of homosexuality in different cultures, so his "ethnopsychiatry" is worth a closer look. In 1970 he published an article in the *Classical Quarterly* on Sappho's poem (fragment 31) beginning "He seems like a god to me . . . ," which describes her response to watching a man talk to a girl she would love to have talked to but couldn't. Devereux argued that the poem was not, as it appeared to many, a poem about jealousy. Rather it presented a list of clinical symptoms of anxiety, and any emendation of the text should conform to the pathology of such symptoms, in particular that Sappho's mouth would be dry and her tongue must therefore be described as sticking to the palate.

He cites a recent case he had come across of a man whose girlfriend had left him. He was anxious, but not jealous. Devereux concludes that it was because the girlfriend was really a lesbian and that subconsciously her lover knew this, finding proof in the fact that she had "tried to maneuver him into the feminine sexual role." When the analyst explained this to the patient, the anxiety attacks ceased at once. Sappho was suffering from a similar very specific condition, but the prognosis was not so optimistic. She was not jealous of her male rival, but anxious about her own inadequacies as a lover of women. He is described as "like a god" because he could give her girlfriend something, a phallus, that she could not, something "she would give her life to have." She might try to repress her desires and initiate a relationship with a man, but this might provoke strong suicidal impulses, because of the aggressivity inherent in all homosexuality, even the pseudo kind. So there might be a psychological truth underlying the story of her love for a man and consequent suicide: Sappho was an authentic pervert, a parasexual, a masculine lesbian.

Devereux's article on male homosexuality, however, took a quite different tack, attempting to distinguish Greek Homosexuality from modern perversions, with lots of added emphasis to drive the point home. For mere homosexual behavior, i.e., men having sex with men, is less pathological than psychological homosexuality—while "behaviorally real," it is "psychologically spurious." The good doctor can therefore give Greek men, or most of them, a clean bill of health: "The *average* Greek . . . was not *psychiatrically* a pervert." Plato and Sappho, however, were only too authentic, as far as Devereux was concerned. The irony is patent: Whereas in earlier centuries sensuality had condemned the Greeks to sinfulness, now it was their very sexicity, their mere innocent sex acts, that saved them from the charge of perversion.

Devereux's hostility to homosexuality was explicit—"I gladly concede that what *Plato* calls love, is for the clinician quite as much as for the normal, heterosexual man, abnormal in every sense of the word." Even the "psychiatrically less pathological" ancient Greek version of homosexuality is referred to as "the *darker* side" of Greek psychology, an abnormal prolongation of adolescence, ascribed to inadequate fathering. But Dover was impressed by Devereux. Not only did he begin to incorporate Devereux's ideas into his work on sexuality, particularly the notion of pseudohomosexuality, he even invited him to be coauthor of his book.

Unfortunately, one day in mid-discussion Devereux growled: "I hate queers!" but still, Dover saw no reason to cancel their joint project, although it did make him realize, "dejectedly, that our collaboration was not going to be easy."[6] Ultimately Devereux, who according to Dover also hated feminists, eco-freaks, Catholics and the Chinese, dropped out of his own accord, more interested in writing money-spinners. But he was always on hand to provide guidance while Dover wrote the book: "I have invariably profited from discussing with him many of the problems which have arisen in writing it; I have not attempted to do myself what his great experience and learning in anthropology and psychoanalysis qualify him to do." All the same, now that he had discovered that the inventor of Greek "pseudohomosexuality" hated queers, it is no wonder that he was so worried about incurring a charge of prejudice when he himself invoked the term. It had impeccable homophobic credentials.

The irony of all this, I think, is that if Dover's *Greek Homosexuality* had been published as *Greek Pseudohomosexuality* by George Devereux

and Kenneth Dover, Devereux's scholarly overdraft would have can-
celed out Dover's academic credit, the book would have attracted much
more critical appraisal, Foucault might well have ignored it and I, perhaps, would not have had to write such a confrontational book.

THE POLITICS OF "IT'S ONLY SEX"

As a public figure, Kenneth Dover is aligned with enlightenment and
reasonableness, a good man in practice, true to his principles of objective
truth whenever he has been in any position of power and influence, as
several people pointed out in the flood of commentary that followed the
publication of his autobiography. Yet no one should think that by emphasizing sexual acts Dover was giving Greek Love its due. On the contrary, by equating being in love with having sex, by confusing Greek sex
with Greek Love, a courting couple with a couple in a relationship,
Dover not only sexualized passionate *erōs,* but made homosexual relationships look intrinsically impermanent, and by the same token trivial,
as if Greek Love stopped short when the courting was over and *erōs*
achieved *philia.*

The whole point about a pseudosexuality, mere sexual activity, acts,
is its/their insignificance, its/their superficial, episodic nature: "It's only
sex." If the speech about Timarchus was "really" all about mere
buggery—active or passive—then it could not "really" be dealing with
(corrupt) relationships between mature politicians, for instance, despite
the context of the debate on foreign policy that provoked Timarchus's
trial and numerous references to mercenary collusion between
Timarchus and his boyfriend ("husband," "comrade," "client") Hegesander, long after the age of youth had gone by. One might go so far as
to say that politics, even geopolitics, provide the context for a large proportion of all references to love between men in ancient sources, as, one
might add, in many more recent sources, and it is not just a matter of
comic poets teasing statesmen with clichéd invective.

Plato's *Symposium* itself is full of political references. But Dover, who
puts so much effort into inserting sodomy into the text, plays the politics down, arguing that the *politikai dunameis,* "political influence" or
"position of political power," and *diapraxeis politikai,* "the achieving of
political ambitions," offered by a politically powerful *erastēs* to his fa-

vorite cannot refer to "politics" except "in the broadest sense," because the boy or youth is too young (who says? who knows?). Likewise, Aristophanes' reference to the Athenian political class being entirely dominated, apparently, by born homosexuals (i.e., male-oriented woman-rejecting males seeking their original other male half) is reduced to mere "tongue-in-cheek" allusion, to comic "taunts" about sexual acts of statesmen in their youth. There is a little more to it than Dover is prepared to concede, I think, and a failure to grasp that the *Symposium,* no matter how humorously expressed, is also about "serious same-sex relationships" is a serious misunderstanding of the whole dialogue and the phenomenon it describes. The reason these ancient Greeks spend so long talking about Love is not because they are mincing their words about buggery, it's because an adamantine alliance, a "community of interest" (*koinōnia*) between citizens, had important implications for the city-state.[7]

A classic case of the way that the emphasis on sex acts can be used to divert attention from relationships is the famous Cretan abduction ceremony described in the work of the geographer Strabo.[8] In Crete an *erastēs* engages in a mock kidnapping of his chosen boy or youth, and pulls him toward his "men's club," while a group called "the friends" put up a mock resistance. Then they all go hunting for a couple of months, and on the party's return there are large expensive ceremonies, extravagant ritual gifts are exchanged, and the boy formally accepts the relationship (or not), and from then on wears a special costume and is given positions of distinction in the community, while both men are given special titles.

As we have seen, most modern scholars reading the text have focused on something not mentioned in it, a supposed homosexual rape. But while they were concentrating so hard on imaginary rape scenes, they were diverting attention from the extraordinary things that were actually contained in the Strabo text, namely an elaborate series of ceremonies leading to a formally acknowledged relationship between two males, an enduring public relationship. Instead, they had converted the rituals establishing a relationship into the essence of the relationship itself. In their categorical view, the whole procedure was about transition, turning the boy into a man, though, again, the text explicitly states that the abduction does not achieve that. It is only recently that the late John

Boswell and a couple of German scholars have started to restore the relationship to a place in Cretan politics and society, not as dividing men
through a humiliating act, but uniting them in same-sex love.[9] But as
early as 1981 Paul Cartledge had studied "the politics of Spartan pederasty" and found that same-sex relationships had a significance "by no
means confined to the erogenous zones." At the time it seemed a terribly radical claim.[10] By reading between the lines to find sex that was
otherwise invisible, scholars had lost sight of the real and very visible
area of politics and relationships.

THE SOUTH THROUGH NORTHERN EYES:
MEDITERRANEAN PERSPECTIVES

As well as Devereux, another theoretical influence on Dover was D. J.
West's Pelican book *Homosexuality,* originally published by Duckworth
in 1955, to which readers of *Greek Homosexuality* were referred for "the
power of culture and society to determine sexual behavior." According
to the publisher's blurb, "Dr. West concludes that, while there are many
facets to the subject, homosexuality as seen today arises chiefly from
fears and inhibitions about sex. He puts forward suggestions for the
checking of homosexuality and also advises on the treatment of the
confirmed homosexual." West ends his book with a chapter outlining a
program of "prevention" of homosexuality. Modern societies should
adopt the carefree attitude to sex found in Samoa and some parts of the
East, for far from impeding it, repression institutionalizes homosexuality: "Paradoxically, a too repressive attitude and a too narrow view of
what is natural and unnatural in the sexual field aggravates the situation
by instilling at an early age the fears and anxieties that lead to adult neuroses and perversions." A liberal approach to sex will produce a "health-
ier" atmosphere. Homosexuality would be greatly reduced, if not
necessarily eliminated, under this easy regime of "mental hygiene."[11]

It did not take a voyage to Samoa, however, to find sexually uninhibited playful young men devoid of religious scruples. In Catholic Italy,
when one had finished work on the manuscripts of ancient texts in a
Renaissance library, reading without anticipating significance, one
could find a handsome gondolier, one of those "so accustomed to these
demands that they think little of gratifying the caprice of ephemeral

lovers," or when one had had enough of ancient ruins, go and be served an espresso "by a waiter whose classical face reminded one of a profile of Alexander the Great on an ancient coin." If one offered him a tip, or even better, took him to a restaurant, then one might find that "Roman boys would do anything in exchange for food." Such adventures led some to believe that in the Mediterranean there was no such thing as our northern sexuality, until the all-powerful H-word came to spoil things: "The post-1968 generation, by bringing words like homosexuality to formerly unknowing ears, inhibits the one-time innocent distribution of sexual favors: before they wouldn't have known what the word meant." Perhaps this same credo explains the curious statement made to one of my friends by a member of the faculty where I was applying for a job: "You know there are no homosexuals in Spain."

The notion of the extraordinary amenability of Mediterranean men to homosexual genital acts has a long history. It can be found in northerners' Protestant denunciations of Renaissance Italy and Spain for their sodomitical tendencies. Then it was ascribed to Muslim, then to climatical influence: Richard Burton's famous Sotadic zone, named after Sotades the inverted *kinaidos,* a wrap-around-the-world band covering tropical and semitropical regions of Europe, Africa, Asia and Central America, where in ancient times, as today, so the story goes, homosexuality is prevalent. Some northerners saw this amenability as a kind of relaxed casual attitude to sex, deriving from the simplicity, "innocence" or inherent sensuality of the south. Again, I think they were failing to take into account the ideological role of "playfulness," and the strange coincidence that such playfulness tends to be found in the least liberal, especially Catholic and Muslim, countries: "All-important is the alibi— 'I was just passing.' "[12] Perhaps what the visitors to the Mediterranean thought was a playground was more an exclusion zone. Sodomy was so horrendous, so monstrous, that it couldn't possibly have anything to do with a nice boy like me. We will have to come back to the question of what the Greeks were up to, but I will say a priori that it is utterly incredible to me that the impact of the sexual morality of Christendom and Islam—the burying under a brick wall, the stonings and castrations you heard about, sometimes someone you knew, the burnings and torture, ruined reputations, fears of denunciation, Hell, a sense of evil, the sermons and imprisonments and executions that those religions launched into the field of homosex in the Mediterranean from the fourth century AD onward—had no tangible effect on the concept or the experience of desire and sex between men over more than fifty generations, whereas the mere word "homosexual" could dramatically change the sexual world in the space of a decade. To be sure the new religions may not have had the impact they expected or wanted. To be sure "sodomy" was something other people got up to, not you. To be sure human nature will out. To be sure there are important continuities. To be sure sex and sexuality in the ancient world were not identical with what we might think they are now.

And yet there are countless modern scholars who understand Greek Homosexuality on the basis of what they have heard or seen on trips to twentieth-century Italy or Greece, claiming a straightforward continuity from once upon a time in the ancient world until suddenly last summer in the Mediterranean. In the twentieth century there was the great scholar and editor of Latin texts A. E. Housman, who was not without familiarity with at least one Venetian gondolier and may have adventured farther south: In 1931 he wrote in Latin in the German journal *Hermes* that it was "difficult for people accustomed from boyhood to follow the laws of Paul of Tarsus and the *Hebrews* to accept the idea, which seemed as *perfectly natural* to Catullus and Martial as it would to any modern denizen of the slums [*de plebe*] of Sicily or Naples, that fellators and pathics were obscene, but not their active partners" (emphasis added).

But there was more to the One-hundred-years-of-homosexuality, No-sexuality-without-a-word-for-it theory than the readiness with which macho Italians from the slums of Naples and Rome obliged tourists from the north. And there are other reasons, apart from the poverty and loose morals of Venetian gondoliers, why modern scholars can accept with no problem the idea that a culture can dictate a completely different "sexuality." The idea drew its cogency from two great intellectual tsunamis driven by the traumas of the terrible twentieth century, one in the first half, one in the second. In order to understand what happened, we need to engage with some famously difficult ideas, with Michel Foucault, Miss Smilla's feeling for snow, and a little bit of anti-Semitism.

LANGUAGE AS A MIRROR OF THE WORLD

I
SUPERCULTURE

Both of Dover's theoretical inspirations, West and Devereux, were operating in what was once a mainstream current of anthropological and sociological thinking. There are two main interweaving strands in this tradition. One of them is the application of comparative psychiatry or Freudian psychoanalysis in different cultural contexts. Freud himself had tried his hand at anthropology in his essay "Totem and Taboo," and Bronislaw Malinowski, who laid the foundations for modern British anthropological research in practice—i.e., talking to people in their own language, rather than merely measuring their skulls—tried to revise Freud's theories in the light of data from other cultures, notably arguing that the people of the Trobriand Islands had no "Oedipus complex." For Freudians this ought to mean that what Freud had concluded about the production of human desire and sexuality did not apply universally but varied according to the culture and social organization of different communities—different relations to the father, different penis envies, different perversions, different desires. But after its early successes psychoanalysis eventually went out of fashion among anthropologists, and psychoanalysts were not prepared to concede to any non-Western culture any kind of immunity from the universal laws Freud had decreed in Vienna.

The second, and more influential, strand came from the American school of cultural anthropology, and in particular the work of four remarkable people. Edward Sapir, Ruth Benedict and Margaret Mead were students of Franz Boas, a man who may take more credit than anyone else for making the world we live in a better place than it might have been. Germany, capital of culture, gave us Nazism, but she also produced the strongest possible antidote.

Boas, born in 1858, was a Jewish German with a doctorate in Physics and Mathematics based on a thesis entitled "Contributions to the Understanding of the Color of Water." He always belonged very much to the data-gathering empirical school of scientific achievement, and abhorred grand abstractions and reductionism. In 1883 he set out to study geography among the Inuit of Qikiqtaaluk (Baffin Island) in the Canadian Arctic, comparing and contrasting the physical environment with the way the inhabitants perceived it. He found that they did not "know" their environment scientifically as objective fact but rather as it was mediated by culture. Apart from measuring skulls, and collecting skeletons, he also copied down lots of stories and myths. He used this research in his 1911 "Introduction" to *The Handbook of North American Indians,* where he noted that there were four unrelated words for snow in Inuit languages—*aput,* "snow on the ground," *qana,* "falling snow," *piqsirpoq,* "drifting snow," and *qimuqsuq,* "a snowdrift"—a taxonomy of icy precipitations somewhat different from those made by other peoples, and a good example, one might add, of culture mediating the physical environment, like the taxonomy of wetter precipitations—spitting, drizzling, cats and dogs—in English, he observed.

Moreover, Boas had noticed something odd when he was transcribing words in Inuit languages. Going over his records he discovered that he had sometimes spelled the same word in two or three different ways, and could not hear the sounds that previous Danish transcribers had written down. The Inuit were producing sounds that did not exist in his own language, and his transcription assimilated one letter sometimes to a "c" and sometimes to an "s," because he couldn't hear it as it was, a novel sound with elements of "c" and of "s." Sometimes he discovered that he heard two different sounds as if they were the same, and on one occasion he had to listen to someone say the words for "you" and "we" "about twenty times without being able to discover the difference." To indicate "we" you had to insert a very slight hiatus after the "d"—"*d'aléngua.*" The same thing happened when he asked a Tlingit to say English "l." It came out sometimes as "l," sometimes as "y." It was not, as some had believed, that the Inuit could not speak properly or had a vague, unformed language. They could readily distinguish sounds that Boas could not distinguish after hearing them twenty times. He compared it to the way people from cultures without a word for green would call a series of green worsteds sometimes yellow, sometimes blue, and would classify colors "today as yellow, tomorrow as blue. He apperceives green by means of yellow and blue." People from different cultures lived in slightly different learned aural universes and slightly different learned landscapes. It was an important part of Boas's argument, however, that the thing perceived was in fact consistent, the same thing, and that one could indeed tell similar-sounding letters apart, after a lot of practice, learning like a child.[1]

The very language of "primitives" could be seen as a great cultural achievement, a representation full of complexity and precision on a par with more tangible achievements such as literature or cathedrals. In the words of Boas's student Edward Sapir:

> One may argue as to whether a particular tribe engages in activities that are worthy of the name of religion or of art, but we know of no people that is not possessed of a fully developed language . . . Many primitive languages have a formal richness, a latent luxuriance of expression, that eclipses anything known to the languages of modern civilization.[2]

Sapir, who had been born in Prussia to a Lithuanian Jewish family, came to New York, via Liverpool, as a child, and was perhaps the most brilliant, a "genius," and certainly one of the most important of Boas's students, straddling the disciplines of linguistics and anthropology, collecting and recording Amerindian languages just years, in many cases, before these mental cathedrals died in the mouths of the last speaker, and producing numerous articles and books. In 1912 he developed Boas's hints in an article on language and the environment, noting that you could not talk of purely environmental influences on human beings because even the simplest element of the environment was already molded by social factors, both of which were reflected in language. Instead of the Inuit words for snow he compared the numerous words for different wild plants in native languages with the English classification of them all as "weeds," the numbers of names for marine animals among coastal tribes and Basques, the countless terms for different aspects of desert geography—canyon with a creek, dry canyon, canyon wall receiving sunlight, shaded canyon wall, "spot of level ground in mountains surrounded by ridges"—among the Paiute of Nevada and Arizona, distinctions seemingly "almost too precise to be of practical value."

In the same paper, Sapir considered the evidence of grammar:

Can it be . . . that the formal groundwork of a language is no indication whatsoever of the cultural complex that it expresses in its subject-matter? . . . Thus one might infer a different social attitude toward woman in those cases where sex gender is made grammatical use of. It needs but this last potential example to show to what flights of fancy this mode of argumentation would lead one.

Sixteen years later, he let his caution drop a little:

The fact of the matter is that the "real world" is to a large extent unconsciously built up on the language habits of the group. No two languages are ever sufficiently similar to be considered as representing the same social reality. The worlds in which different societies live are distinct worlds, not merely the same worlds with different labels attached . . . We see and hear and otherwise experience very largely as we do because the language habits of our community predispose certain choices of interpretation.[3]

But just what flights of fancy this line of thinking might indeed produce was immediately demonstrated by Sapir's student Benjamin Whorf. In a study of the sentence structure of the Hopi Indians, Whorf noted admiringly: "English compared to Hopi is like a bludgeon compared to a rapier." From his admiration of "primitive" languages, Whorf went on to formulate what has become known as the Sapir–Whorf hypothesis, that languages build quite separate worlds for the people who speak them: "Every language is a vast pattern-system, different from others, in which are culturally ordained the forms and categories by which the personality not only communicates, but also analyzes nature, notices or neglects types of relationship and phenomena, channels his reasoning, and builds the house of his consciousness." This idea of language could lead to an extreme view of the power of culture to construct thoughts and experiences: "We are thus introduced to a new principle of relativity which holds that all observers are not led by the same physical evidence to the same picture of the universe, unless their linguistic backgrounds are similar . . ." And so culture becomes superculture.

The most famous example of the theory concerns "Hopi Time," since, according to Whorf, "the Hopi language is seen to contain no words, grammatical forms, constructions or expressions that refer directly to what we call 'time' or to past, present, or future, or to enduring or lasting . . . Hence, the Hopi language contains no reference to 'time,' either explicit or implicit." "He has no general notion or intuition of TIME as a smooth flowing continuum in which everything in the universe proceeds at an equal rate, out of a future, through a present, into a past."[4] This Whorfian hypothesis found its way into numerous handbooks and textbooks in the 1960s and 1970s. One of the favorite illustrations, first introduced by Whorf himself, was Boas's four Eskimo words for snow, the number of which kept multiplying over the years, until they reached their hundreds. This knowledge became part of popular culture, and Inuit vocabulary even reached the cinema screen in the film adaptation of Peter Hoeg's bestselling novel *Miss Smilla's Feeling for Snow,* which begins: "It is freezing, an extraordinary -18°C, and it's snowing, and in the language which is no longer mine, the snow is *qanik*—big almost weightless crystals falling in stacks and covering the ground with a layer of pulverized white frost." Smilla, thanks to her Inuit-speaking mother, is endowed with a language-derived special power to see snow in more detail than Danes can, and this gives her a better understanding of the clues to a suspicious accident.[5]

This commonplace that language influences or determines experience (even in Whorf it is not always certain if he means that different languages produce an experience of the world "not identical with the way other people experience the world" or "nothing to do with the way that other people experience the world") can be traced further back than Whorf and Boas. It had important outposts in France thanks to the anthropologist Lucien Lévy-Bruhl, a less admiring student of "primitive mentality," and entered history at an early date, most notably in the work of Lucien Febvre, who argued for the impossibility of Unbelief in the time of Rabelais, thanks in part to the deficiency of Rabelais's mental toolbox. The reason for its success is in part due to the fact that elementary linguistic determinism appeals to our sense of the exotic—a tribe with no sense of time, Inuit with special snow perception, people with eyes in the middle of their stomachs, ancient Greeks with no sexuality . . .

For when Michel Foucault explained to a gay readership that the Greeks did not divide up sexuality into homo- and hetero-, just as we do not differentiate between the sunny and the shaded walls of a canyon, he could easily move on to argue that they had no concept and therefore no experience of our homosexuality, just as we have none of the Paiute experience of the sunny wall of a canyon, and still expect to find everyone nodding their heads:

> What seems to me the most important thing in this book [*Greek Homosexuality*] is that Dover shows that our division of sexual behaviors between homo- and hetero-sexuality is absolutely irrelevant for the Greeks and Romans. This means two things: on the one hand, they had no notion of it, no *concept,* and, on the other hand, they had no experience of it. A person who slept with another of the same sex did not *feel* homosexual. That seems to me fundamental.[6]

By a collateral logic, when David Halperin argued that there was no homosexual feeling until the word homosexuality appeared in the *Oxford English Dictionary,* some readers might reasonably be expected to respond, "It's just like an Eskimo's *feeling* for snow."

This linguistic determinism explains why it became quite important to view the ancient Greek *erōmenos* not as "someone that someone is in love with" but as a label or a title, a technical term, even, a term that might construct the youth's passive experience of himself. For it was surely important that this "technical label" was grammatically *passive* (for what it is worth, the *erastēs* too is often described with a passive participle as the *erastheis,* "the love-smitten") or that he was grammatically the *object* of love (in fact usually an indirect object, as we have seen, and that *is* significant) while the *erastēs* was the grammatical *subject,* the one who acts, of an *active* verb *eran,* "to be in love," hence also lust . . . obsessively lust . . . leading to orgasm . . . sex . . . sex roles . . . domination . . . of the *passive erōmenos.* The one occasion I heard Sir Kenneth talk on Greek Homosexuality, to Oxford's Gay Society in the 1980s, it was like a lesson in Greek. He covered a blackboard with participles—

"pursuing," "fleeing," *erōmenos,* a "passive" participle. Some members of the audience thought it was a bit technical, but really the grammar of sexuality is as easy as ABC.

Needless to say, the absolutist form of the Sapir–Whorf hypothesis was destroyed long ago, when it was demonstrated that people without the word "green" could still tell the color apart from others, and that Whorf was wrong, perhaps even deceitful, about the Hopi. And I have no doubt at all that if the Greeks couldn't see or be or feel homosexual it was not because they lacked a copy of Krafft-Ebing's *Psychopathia Sexualis* in Greek. This does not, however, mean that Inuit apperceive/experience the environment just as we do or exactly "as it is," and their language and vocabulary are sure to affect the way they make sense of the world. Nor does it mean that the Greeks experienced love and desire exactly as we do or exactly as it is, and the language they spoke could not fail to affect the way they made sense of love. For all the ridicule heaped on the Whorfian hypothesis and the so-called hoax of the Eskimo words for snow, Boas's original article "On Alternating Sounds" still seems sensible and interesting to me.

THE INCREDIBLE "NG"

Sapir himself usually talked of culture, language and individuals in much more subtle, complex and circumspect terms than the "Sapir–Whorf hypothesis" might suggest, and if he is assigned to any particular school it is the one that came to be known as "Culture and Personality," for various reasons probably the most influential of all schools of anthropology in the twentieth century. If Whorf saw language in positive terms, emphasizing what certain words allow people to do and what their absence disallows—words for things, words as labels, words to express things, words to distinguish things—the Culture and Personality school emphasized rigid structures. Culture itself was patterned like a language system, a hard, calcified, slow-moving structure that imprisoned members of a culture within certain roles and values.

Sapir had been very interested in patterns in grammar and sound: Not just what sounds were found in a language but what other sounds they were connected to, whereabouts in words they tended to come—beginning, middle or end—and where they were forbidden to go.

Merely to note what sounds existed, without observing how they related one to another and to words, was like fixing a palette on a gallery wall and calling it a painting. We didn't just learn sounds and words, we got a feeling for the way sounds came together in words. Quite unintentionally, we tended to derive a set of word-making rules from the way our own words were put together. Consequently there were funny-sounding words and normal-sounding words, and it was hard to break the pattern when we learned another language. Thus although we are perfectly able to say "kn" as in "think not" or "Cockney," it sounds funny in English to say "Knorr." Although we can articulate the "ng" sound that you hear at the end of sing, sang, bring, it never comes at the start of a word in English, and so when we learn languages where it does come at the start of a word we find it not hard—for how could it be hard?—but "incredible": the fixed pattern of a language, its *configuration,* produces "misfits."[7]

Another of Boas's students, Ruth Benedict, also at Columbia, applied this patterning theory to cultures as a whole.[8] She argued that when you studied other cultures you quickly found that there was usually more to death practices than mere grief, that agricultural practices were more than just the feeding of a population, and there was more to marriage than sex preference. "Another and greater force has been at work that has used the recurring situations of mating, death, provisioning, and the rest almost as raw material and elaborated them to express its own intent. This force that bends occasions to its purposes and fashions them to *its own idiom* we can call within that society its dominant drive" (emphasis added).

When they moved from one culture to another, anthropologists had noticed that the "personalities" they encountered seemed to change, just as you might notice a change in the people as you traveled from Victorian England, say, to nineteenth-century southern Italy, or to America's Wild West, but much more marked. One tribe might tend to behave in a very shy demure way with strangers, and be very prickly and touchy in response to questions; in another tribe you might meet lots of jolly extrovert types like your least favorite uncle.

Benedict tried to do something with these data—and differences in "personality" between people may be important data and not merely the grounds for amateurish—"Americans, so brash," "The English, so standoffish"—generalization or subjective opinion. Her purpose was to ascribe to different cultures a kind of character type—Apollonian, Dionysian, paranoid, etc.—and to understand the effect those dominant paradigms had on misfits or "deviants" who didn't fit the pattern and were left "outside the game."[9] In 1934 she published *Patterns of Culture,* setting out her findings. According to Benedict there was no absolute category of normal/abnormal, fitting/misfitting. Different cultures validated very different types of personality: someone whose personal character made him stick out, who could be branded a witch in one culture, would be honored and encouraged elsewhere. The Indians of the northwest coast of America had a dominant drive that could be characterized as paranoid: Many of the most valued members of their community would be placed in psychiatric hospitals if they had the misfortune to end up in modern America. Maladjustment meant maladjustment to the particular madness of a particular culture, so to speak. This is an almightily radical idea.

To demonstrate her theory about misfits, Benedict used the example of homosexuals, for since Krafft-Ebing and Oscar Wilde homosexuality had been seen above all either as a mental disease in itself, or as a reflection of mental disorder, or as a condition that led to madness: "Western civilization tends to regard even a mild homosexual as an abnormal. The clinical picture of homosexuality stresses the neuroses and psychoses to which it gives rise, and emphasizes almost equally the inadequate functioning of the invert and his behavior." In other societies, however, homosexuals "have even been especially acclaimed" and have functioned extremely well. Greece is a good example. Just read Plato.

However, often the only response for someone temperamentally out of sync with his own culture is to "do violence to his strongest natural impulses." In the case of homosexuals in an unfriendly environment: "The invert is immediately exposed to all the conflicts to which aberrants are always exposed. His guilt, his sense of inadequacy, his failures, are consequences of the disrepute which social tradition visits upon him . . . The adjustments that society demands of them would strain any man's vitality, and the consequences of this conflict we identify with their homosexuality."[10] The "his" here is significant. Benedict had some very intense relationships with women. Again, though it is easy to ridicule her confident generalizations about the paranoid Indians—

Sapir did—what she says about homosexuals seems very sensible to me, and represents a precocious understanding of the condition of psychopathologized homosexuality. After all, it must have been less stressful, mustn't it, being gay in Greece in the fifth century BC than in twenty-first-century Poland.

The final member of the trio—and they were more than merely academic associates—was Margaret Mead, one of the most famous women of the last century. In 1952, in a brief sketch of the way anthropologists should be trained, she stressed as most important the "*training in the recognition of pattern* . . . Such training may be provided by supervised analysis of any body of cultural materials, by a comparative study of the premises underlying the advertising in *Punch* and the *New Yorker,* a comparative study of the themes of French and British contemporary films, or a detailed analysis of Army training manuals from two different cultures." But best of all was the study of linguistics and the discovery of the grammar of a particular people, especially of the "relationship between a steadily widening perspective of what *may* occur in a language and a precise observation of details from which he will have to construct a grammar of what *does* occur in a particular language."[11]

As early as 1933, Mead was arguing: "The whole of man's life is determined and bounded by his culture and every aspect of it, the inexplicit, the unformulated, the uninstitutionalized, is as important to an understanding of the whole, as are the traditional institutions about which it has been customary to center inquiry."[12] Mead, like many Boasians, was especially interested in the formation and the socialization of children. Her most famous work, *Coming of Age in Samoa,* published in 1928, was a sensation from the start. It was written, she wrote in the introduction, to discover "What is human nature? How flexible is human nature?" In particular she wanted to discover if juvenile delinquency was an American problem or a natural problem. The Samoans, she concluded, were a people almost completely lacking in earnest. They learned not to care from birth, being passed around from one woman to another. They also had a much more carefree and playful approach to sex, even to homosexuality. All this meant that they had few of the neuroses and delinquencies of modern America, including neurotic homosexuality.

Few anthropologists doubt that Mead, though she noted everything she saw and heard honestly, got Samoa rather wrong, if not completely wrong, because she had been too trusting of her informants. In other words the Samoans were "Cretan liars," for if someone lacking in earnest tells you they are lacking in earnest, how do you know they are in earnest? Certainly she had failed to see how powerfully constructed Samoan "playfulness" was.

Hence both Benedict and Mead are often dismissed nowadays as naïve or unthinking, even by fellow anthropologists, although it should be pointed out that the anthropologist who exposed the "hoaxing" of Mead on Samoa was himself soundly hoaxed, or perhaps just caught not paying attention, since in his own work based on several years in Samoa he seemed completely to miss a large group of "woman's way" men, that is, transvestite homosexuals called *fa'afafine*.[13] (If ever anyone says to you, "There are no homosexuals in Spain" or ancient Greece or Renaissance Florence, just remember the colorful, numerous, outrageous and completely invisible *fa'afafine* of Samoa.) But if their stars have dimmed a little or a lot, the work of Mead and Benedict is nevertheless full of insight and intelligence, and they anticipated many of the ideas people think they have taken from Michel Foucault, whose reputation rides as high as theirs is low, despite some equally egregious errors. If the Boasians had spent more time theorizing and less time illustrating with examples and trying to communicate their results to the general public, perhaps things would have been different.

The same applies to a lesser extent to Sapir, whose name has been unfortunately, but not unfairly, fixed to those of Whorf, Mead and Benedict and whose reputation fell a little in the downdraft, though it is now recovering. Sapir "anticipated" many of the ideas of Ferdinand de Saussure, whose work ignited the postmodern revolution in the humanities. But it is Saussure, who wrote next to nothing, not Sapir, who wrote so much, Saussure, whose major work was cobbled together by students after his death, who gets a Modern Master to himself, and has even been acclaimed as the New Galileo, which in many ways he was. The big mistake of the Boasians was that they talked too much. They neglected the symbolic economy of scholarship, the stocks and shares of prestige.

Still, if they are no longer as highly esteemed as they once were, that is in part the price they had to pay for their impact, much more significant in practice, thus far, and infinitely more opportune than any Fran-cophone intellectual for whom they cleared the way.[14] But then the Boasians had help. For there was another reason, apart from a mere love of the exotic, why something apparently so much part of our human na-tures as our sexuality was reassigned to the field of culture. Here Nazism played its part.

A WORD ABOUT OUR ANTI-SEMITISM

At the end of the nineteenth century, Boas noted that you could classify Inuits in three different ways and arrive at three different results.[15] If you measured their skulls, height and nose shapes you came up with one set of groupings, if you listened to and compared their languages and di-alects another set emerged, and if you compared cultural traits, arts and traditions, types of ceremony, style of crafts, content of folktales, etc., you'd be looking at a third set of groupings that would differ again from either of the others. The cross-linkage of languages, physical traits and myths reflected historical movements of people, noted Boas sensibly, as well as exchange over time. There was any amount of evidence for each group producing its own particular transformations of the material it had borrowed or inherited, an ebb and flow of diffusion and integration, like cooks rustling up a meal for a coachload of unexpected visitors from things they found in the cupboard or what their embarrassed guests had brought with them: possibly a banquet, possibly beans on toast with chicken tikka masala and pizza to follow. All elements—language, cul-ture, biological traits and environment—were the product of history, gelling or not gelling, a stable cultural epoch or a flash in the cultural pan.

This research had a direct bearing on an ideology of nationalism that was taking over Germany during Boas's student years. The Germans had started to think of themselves as a *Volk,* in the way that French wine-makers think of Chablis: not the Chardonnay variety of grape, not wine grown on the soil of the Chablis area, not wine made according to the traditional methods of the Chablis region, but an indissoluble eternal compound of all three: Race, Land and Culture. This German *Volk* was a stable, permanent, ancient entity that was most perfectly exemplified not by the superficial *Zivilisations* of feverish cosmopolitan cities, but by

German peasants and German peasant traditions firmly rooted, some-how, in the German soil.

By this time, many middle-class German Jews had assimilated to the degree that they considered themselves completely German, merely practicing a different religion, the religion of Moses. Boas came from such a family, and was grateful to his parents for liberating him from the "shackles" of tradition and "religious dogma." As a student he got into some sword fights that left him with scars. This became a problem when he was measuring American children: "He has scars on his face and head that would make a jailbird turn green with envy. His scalp is seared with saber cuts, and slashes over his eyes, on his nose, and on one cheek from mouth to ear, give his countenance [an] appearance which is not gener-ally considered au fait, outside the criminal class . . ." Would parents "enjoy the hero of German duels feeling their sons' and daughters' heads and bodies over just as he did those of the Eskimaux . . . a hand that fooled around with the topknots of medicine-men and toyed with the war paint of bloodthirsty Indians?"[16] These scars it seems came from fights over anti-Semitic insults, but it seems clear that Boas would have been defending not his Jewish-, but his Germanness, for the ideology of the German *Volk* in its more extreme aspects raised a barrier to assimilat-ing Jews. The admixture of Jews could only spoil Germanness, just as the admixture of Sauvignon Blanc would spoil Chablis forever, unless, of course, you found the errant vines in time and rooted them out.

Already in 1873 things had started to turn nasty. The journalist Wil-helm Marr published a pamphlet on "The Victory of Jewry over Ger-manism" and in 1879 he founded an "Anti-Semites League." He may indeed have invented the term, which sounded less poisonous then, more like a "Family Defense League" than what it sounds like today, a League of Hatred and Evil. In the same year Adolf Stoecker, the Em-peror's Christian chaplain, gave an influential public lecture on "What We Demand of Modern Jewry." What he demanded was that they should accept discrimination: restrictions on their ability to permeate German institutions and society, including strict quotas on public ap-pointments. Otherwise Germany would be Judaized. A few years before Boas left for Baffin Island, Stoecker had been elected to the Reichstag in the constituency next door to Boas's hometown. Hating Jews was a vote winner.

Academics joined in the debate. Heinrich von Treitschke, Professor of Modern History at the University of Berlin, published three articles titled *A Word About Our Jewry* in which he defended German anti-Semitism against the "single-minded contempt" for it of the English and the French. If they boasted of having less prejudice it was simply because they housed fewer Jews. The highly esteemed professor lent an air of respectability to anti-Semitism and helped Germans to stop feeling ashamed of themselves, to dare to take time out from the European Enlightenment. The "unpleasantnesses and lower-class vulgarity" of Jew-haters were justified, he argued.

The year after von Treitschke's "word," his even more distinguished colleague the Roman historian Theodor Mommsen, "greatest living historian," future Nobel Prize winner, produced a rebuttal under the title *Another Word About Our Jewry*. Thirty years earlier, Mommsen had celebrated the Jews in his *History of Rome:* "In the ancient world too, Jewry was an effective enzyme of cosmopolitanism and of the decomposition of nations." Mommsen was horrified to find that he had supplied the anti-Semites with one of their favorite (para)quotations, "enzyme of decomposition"—still useful to Goebbels, with Mommsen of course acknowledged, for that was the point, in his speech at Nuremberg in 1933. Back in the 1880s Mommsen had thought he saw an opportunity to, among other things, set the record straight. He organized opposition to academic anti-Semitism, and argued in his article that Jews were German citizens and should be accepted as such, but he also advised Jews to get rid of their *Sonderart,* their distinctiveness, and to speed up assimilation. Assimilation was an article of faith among all liberals, Jewish and non-Jewish alike, and the irony is that, though one was an anti-Semite and the other the leading anti-anti-Semite, Treitschke (nastily and without much hope) and Mommsen (in desperate earnest) were in practice asking Jews for much the same thing: Vanish. Fast.[17]

DISAPPEARING IN AMERICA

Against this background one can see the significance of Boas's researches in the snow. If even the Inuit—living in the Arctic, for goodness' sake—did not constitute a stable eternal *Volk* compounded out of landscape, race and culture, then how much less *völkisch* must the Germans be. The

Germans were no Chablis. And anyway Chablis itself was no eternal entity but the result of a happy historical meeting of variety, soil, climate and traditions, a Chablis moment. Of course race, language, land and culture were in a state of constant transformation and interaction, and it was the very richness of the mixture, the dynamics of the interflow, that produced the occasional festivals of civilization. People were essentially malleable, plastic and changing, each culture zone a wonderful melting pot, which could change even biological characteristics in a short space of time. Boas's careful scientific measuring of biological traits was crucial to his success. If his cranial calipers and nose-shape-measuring technology—a piece of soft lead impressed on the face—now seem weird, he was only doing what modern geneticists do when they take swabs of cells from inside the cheeks of willing volunteers and come up with similar conclusions about complexity, interaction and flux.

In 1896 Boas, having left Germany, was offered a teaching post at Columbia University in New York. With the background of his immense learning and experience among America's populations, his utter commitment to the scientific method, his enormous database of words and bodily statistics, he was an early, vigorous and authoritative, though at first very lonely, opponent of racism and racial biological determinism at a critical moment in the history of the West, when pseudo-Darwinian views of racial superiority were regarded as incontrovertible, racial degeneration was a major issue in public policy, and eugenics, the control of human reproduction by means that included sterilization of inferior specimens, its most popular solution, not least in Britain and America.

Boas opposed eugenics: "Eugenics is not a panacea that will cure human ills, it is rather a dangerous sword that may turn its edge against those who rely on its strength," he wrote in 1916. He opposed the immigration quotas of the American government, designed to reduce the impact especially of inferior Mediterranean specimens such as Italians on the American population. He emphasized the importance of social factors in the creation of the "problem" of Blacks in the United States, argued against ladders of development that placed European civilization at a more advanced level than barbarous or, worse, primitive cultures, made efforts to reconstruct histories of non-Western peoples, and organized exhibitions to promote understanding of the complexity and achievement of non-Western cultures when seen as an integrated whole, cultures that had been too often nipped in the bud by European colonizers who were not innately superior, just in the right place at the right time. In 1933 everything he stood for seemed threatened by the rise of the Nazis in Germany. He wrote an open letter to President von Hindenburg protesting the appointment of Hitler as Chancellor and wrote letters to newspapers commenting on anti-Jewish legislation in his old country.

If Boas was a formidable and tireless opponent of racial determinism the students he trained at Columbia were a no less remarkable group of people who took his ideas about race and culture and extended them, often with less of Boas's characteristic caution. One outcome of their passionate commitment was that as the debate between racial theorists and antiracists blew hotter, the claims for the power of culture grew stronger. Boas's caveats were sidelined in the battle to counter the claims of racist biology, until culture came to seem almost like a second nature: "Human nature is almost unbelievably malleable," wrote Margaret Mead in 1935.[18]

Another of Boas's students was a PhD student originally from University College London. Ashley Montagu's experience of anti-Semitism in Bethnal Green in the 1920s and 1930s (his name is a neat Englishing of the name Israel Ehrenberg) made him a committed antiracist even in his student days. In 1942 he wrote one of the most successful early antiracist books, *Man's Most Dangerous Myth: The Fallacy of Race,* and he drafted the first version of the UNESCO statement on race in 1950. The transformation of attitudes among the public and professionals was slow and would take many more decades, but things had come a long way since Boas arrived in America in the late nineteenth century. During the Second World War, as evidence of Nazi atrocities mounted, and especially after Pearl Harbor in December 1941, and Hitler's declaration of war on the United States, the tide turned. Once the Allied troops saw what was left of the concentration camps, and had to believe their eyes, professional opposition to antiracism began to evaporate. But it was not the Holocaust alone that eventually discredited racial theory. Its condemnation was also the result of a massive effort spread over half a century, during which Franz Boas and his followers prepared arguments and collected data opposing racial science. Nazism was not only evil, it was, crucially, false.

MARGARET MEAD'S MOMENT

At the end of the war, when she was twelve years old, my mother, like many other children, was taken to the cinema. She remembers a film of happy *völkisch* Germans in dirndl skirts and lederhosen, slapping thighs, laughing and twirling. Quite unexpectedly, and utterly shocking, there followed scenes from the concentration camps, and instead of "The End," "Never Again." She never forgot. And the lesson she learned, remarkably, was not "We must never again let the wicked Germans commit such wickedness," but *We the exhausted victors must watch out for ourselves,* which meant a constant vigilance whenever the subject of people of different race or Jewish people came up in any conversation, in case, from under the pleasant surface of the postwar suburbs, the evil snake of racism was about to come out of hiding. The war was over; the fight went on. It was only through such vigilance, through millions of like-minded gestures, that the anti-Semitism and racism once so normal in everyday life became socially unacceptable in Britain and America, and then sexism, and soon, hopefully, but don't hold your breath, homophobia, may be exiled from nice front rooms.

People sometimes complain about "politically correct" language that it's annoying how the "right" word keeps changing—colored, Black, African American; faggot, queer, homosexual, gay; lady, girl, woman; wife, partner; actress, actor; Moor, Mohammedan, Muslim— or else that all this effort put into *talking right* is distracting from the business of *doing right*. But it was language that inspired the revolution in attitudes, and that revolution never stopped thinking of language as the most solid part of culture. All the same it would be a step forward if a sense of shame were to underpin mere politeness, if people retained a sense of civic embarrassment when they are alone with the ballot paper wondering if they should vote for an anti-Semitic candidate for president of the Republic or vote yes in a referendum to discriminate against faggots.

It has become a commonplace nowadays for some smart critics to mock human scientists for their insistence on believing, without actually believing, Mead's "unbelievable" malleability of human nature, to ridicule Sapir and Whorf, and to talk laughingly of how Mead was "hoaxed" and about the "hoax" of the Eskimo words for snow. Fair enough, but not even scientists work outside history and rhetoric and the symbolic authority of prestige, and they owe not a little to the more humane scientists, and in particular to Boas and his students who managed to steer us out of the mess biologists got us into in the course of the twentieth century. If scientists want to laugh at the follies of all-powerful Superculture, they have a right to—irreverence may even be counted as a duty—but they should, perhaps, pause for a moment before they laugh and briefly present their apologies for past demeanors. An arrogant scientist should send shivers up the spine of anyone who knows anything about the history of the twentieth century.

For it was the discrediting of racial science that cleared the way for culture—the two went hand in hand—and, inevitably, that meant that a way was cleared for the particular conception of culture that had defeated racism, the superstrong culture of the Boasians, the culture that can do anything, that can bend all natures, "unbelievably malleable," to its will, a culture associated in particular with Margaret Mead and Ruth Benedict. They had hardly been ignored before the war, but it was above all in the postwar period that their ideas really began to make the world a better place. *Patterns of Culture* was printed only once in England in the 1930s.[19] It was reprinted in 1945. It had to be printed again in 1946 and in 1949, twice more in the 1950s and four times in the 1960s. Margaret Mead, who lived right into the 1970s, was even more successful with her books, and toured America and the world lecturing to large audiences. She certainly found her way onto the reading list at my mother's teacher-training college in Manchester. Mead from the start had drawn comparisons between the patterns she found on sunny islands and those she found in modern America. Primitive cultures could teach us the most vivid lesson in the malleability of human nature, and could help us to solve our social problems by their example of another way of structuring things.

The British press reviews printed on the cover of Benedict's book were not slow to draw the same conclusions: "Miss Benedict has held up three significant mirrors to contemporary Western civilization"; "The author's conclusions are of great practical interest. It is a book which can be vigorously recommended to the general reader. It is highly encouraging to everyone who seeks to make changes in the prevailing patterns of our own culture." The only problem was that this particular notion of culture as Superculture had been formed under the most unusual circumstances. It had evolved in a racist environment and continued to flex the strong arms it had had to develop during several decades of intense high-stakes antiracist debate.

Boas had always been an extreme assimilationist, both with regard to his own and to others' identity. His main problem with the Nazis at first seemed to be what they were doing to "the old cultural values of Germany." He saw himself as German first and foremost and spoke out against anti-German propaganda during the First World War.[20] He loved Germany and German culture. That may seem odd, considering the amount of anti-Semitism he had witnessed there during the 1870s and 1880s, but there had been something wonderful once about Germany and Boas's attitude was typical of Jewish-German immigrants to America.

In any case, Boas's main scholarly objection to racial prejudice was that it was preventing assimilation, preventing movement and flux. He didn't believe in Jews and Blacks. He wanted them to vanish in the melting pot: "It would seem that man being what he is, the Negro problem will not disappear in America until the Negro blood has been so much diluted that it will no longer be recognized just as anti-Semitism will not disappear until the last vestige of the Jew as a Jew has disappeared." Of course Boas's ideology of assimilation was itself the product of a liberal German-Jewish background, and it was indeed one of the prime objectives of the Nazis in the first place to deanonymize Jews and undo assimilation. But one effect of the Boas position is that Judaism itself was seen as the enemy, shackled by dogma and primitive prejudices and by outdated sexual taboos. The Boasians saw no problem in vigorously attacking racism and at the same time invoking the notion of the "Chosen People" as a prime example of it. Culture, Western culture at least, was supposed to be of the here and now, growing and flourishing on rich loams laid down over the years. It was not supposed to be backward-looking and hidebound; it was not supposed to preserve itself.[21]

WHY HOMOSEXUALITY IS DOOMED

By holding up mirrors to Western society, Mead and Benedict hoped to change its pattern, so that our own misfits might fit a bit better and not stick out quite so stressfully much. Like eugenics, however, culture turned out to be a double-edged sword. Benedict thought our labeling of homosexuals as deviants was merely strength-sapping and led to neuroses, but Mead in 1928 had gone further. Mead seemed to think that permanent homosexuality itself was largely the product of Western hang-ups about casual homosexual behavior, as if being gay was simply a psychopathic syndrome produced by a culture's hostility to homosexual acts. Meanwhile D. J. West, from whom Dover took his ideas about a culture's ability to mold sexuality, drew from Mead's work the lesson that homosexuality might be greatly reduced if not eliminated if we let it all hang out a bit, like the Samoans or the Greeks, and practiced "mental hygiene"—whatever that means.[22] Hard though it is to believe, quite a few people who encouraged a more "Samoan" approach to sex in Britain and America in the fifties and sixties did so in the hope that sexual liberation, the cleansing flood of mere episodic sex acts, would make homosexuals vanish. Some people cherish that hope to this day.

This has led to a paradoxical situation in which the impermanence of homosexuality has come to be an article of faith both for extreme right-wing "pro-family" groups, every bit as bigoted as nineteenth-century German anti-Semites, trying to pressure homosexuals unfortunate enough to find themselves living in their communities to "cure" themselves with "reparative" therapy, and for radical gay activists trying to liberate gay people from gaydom, from the social role that "constructs" them as homosexual. And sometimes it is quite hard to tell them apart. In this respect the most extreme homophobes and the most "pro-gay" activists are as one, though of course there is a very different emphasis— how to be gay, how not to be gay. It is because of this similarity of perspective that Halperin in One Hundred Years of Homosexuality is forced into such an outright vision of the power of culture not merely to construct sexuality but to construct one that cannot be unconstructed, or unlearned by, say, "reparative" therapy. What follows is a far more narrow and inflexible view of what sexuality is in our own or in ancient societies, and a highly simplistic and polarized view of ancient Greece dominated by the phallus, by active masculine roles and by passive feminine roles. Greek sexuality has to be so simple and so strong and to direct its powers so uniformly because this cultural configuration has been given such an awful lot of work to do—the work, that is, of nature.

In fact gay activism has always had close links with the theory that sexualities are culturally "constructed." The gay liberation movement in Britain and the first gay rights marches were in part influenced and inspired by an article by Mary McIntosh, entitled "The Homosexual Role," which came out in the 1968 edition of the journal *Social Problems*. You can perhaps understand the paradox a bit better if you think of these particular radicals as Marxists, and homosexuals as a class, exactly the word Boas liked to use to describe the Jews. Some out-and-proud gay activists have as much love for homosexuals as Marxists do for plebs, fighting on their behalf, but fighting for a new order in which they will disappear, once the sexual class system is overthrown and a new regime of pure polymorphous sexicity, of "mental hygiene," sets about clearing away all the dusty, culturally diseased cobwebs of the oppressed homosexual identity. It is never quite certain if, once liberated from oppressive labels and negative roles, gay people will be simply better adjusted *à la* Benedict or somehow not quite so gay *à la* Mead, or if it will be like Rome in the 1950s before the H-word arrived, with its "innocent distribution of favors" for the price of a cup of tea.

But if this "constructionist" concept inspired some of the most important and energetic efforts on behalf of gay people, and it has, it has also inevitably hampered the fight against homophobia. In her introduction to a collection titled *Margaret Mead Made Me Gay*, Esther Newton can talk of how reading *Coming of Age in Samoa* in 1961 helped her come to terms with her sexuality and to realize that the norms of her American college were not universal, while Robert Kronemeyer can also invoke Mead as the inspiration for his book *Overcoming Homosexuality*. See if you can guess from which side of the "debate" the following statement emerged: "There is this dreadful danger of the homosexual becoming institutionalized."[23] And who do you think cited the Greeks to demonstrate Why Homosexuality Is Doomed in an essay entitled "It's Just a Phase" for a collection entitled *Anti-Gay*?[24]

Of course there is no reason why gay people should see homosexuality as rigidly fixed, serious and eternal just because homophobes see it as an auto-destructive playful impermanent phase, but it is highly suspicious that in its historical development the one—socially formed sexual perversion—shades so neatly into the other—culturally constructed sexuality.

After its comprehensive takeover of the Academy in the eighties the theory that homosexuality was created by culture began to spread into the vernacular. By about 1991 it had got as far as Oxford's Jolly Farmer pub, where it was causing problems in a conversation I had with a student nurse from Bristol on the subject of gay history: "But I thought there wasn't any. It's a modern thing, isn't it, being gay?" she said. "Come again?" "Something that started in the nineteenth century." In the autumn of that year Gilbert and George were getting very agitated over Lynn Barber's astute line of questioning in the *Independent on Sunday:* "In the eighteenth century, every man was bisexual," says Gilbert. "It wasn't even called that; it was just being a gentleman," says George. "He would have a wife and a friend. It's only fashion that makes people think that they personally like this kind of sex or that kind of sex. It's conditioning: people are just dragged along by conditioning."[25]

The best answer to this kind of *mariconada* was given by Edward Sapir himself way back in 1937 in response to Benedict's *Patterns of Culture.* He describes the ultrastrong position:

> Supposedly universal feelings and attitudes, sentiments about parents and children and sex mates, are found to be almost as relative to a culture's set patterns of behavior as fashions in clothes . . . At any rate, this formula of the relativity of custom has long been a commonplace in anthropology on purely descriptive grounds.

While it may be true, he continues, that the character of a culture very largely determines "the externalized system of attitudes and habits which forms the visible 'personality' of a given individual . . . It does not follow . . . that strictly social determinants, tending, as they do, to give visible form and meaning, in a cultural sense, to each of the thousands of modalities of experience which sum up the personality, can define the fundamental structure of the personality . . ." For if so:

> we should be put in the position of a man who claimed, for instance, that the feeling called love could not have started its history, until the vocabulary of a specific language suggested realities, values, and problems hitherto unknown . . . A culture which is constantly being invoked to explain the necessities and the intimacies of individual

relations is like an *ex post facto* legalization of damage done . . . Cultural analysis is hardly more than a preliminary bow to the human scene . . .[26]

II

FOUCAULT'S TRUTH AND STRUCTURALISM

If the notion of an all-powerful Superculture has survived the fall of Benedict and Mead, indeed if it has gone on to prosper as never before in the nineteen-nineties and the noughties, there is one reason for that: Michel Foucault. *The Uses of Pleasure,* volume 2 of his *History of Sexuality,* deals with the classical Greeks and runs Dover's best-known work a close second as the most influential book on Greek Homosexuality. But to rank them like that serves no purpose, since they achieved together far more than either could have achieved on his own. I cannot be sure that they never met, but they functioned, and continue to function, as a kind of duo, combining two different kinds of symbolic capital and credibility, one academic, the other intellectual, the one seen as hugely knowledgeable but not too sophisticated and a bit old-fashioned, the other hugely sophisticated but not too knowledgeable and a bit avant-garde. What made them such a powerful pairing, however, is also what made the pairing so improbable. It should have been Foucault by rights, and going by the evidence of the first volume of his *History of Sexuality,* who took Dover apart. He might have made short work of it, had he felt so inclined. Why he didn't is the result of a series of little accidents: an application, an appointment, a reacquaintance, a spare room, a cheeky invitation, a bad review, a conversation. The key figure here was neither Dover nor Foucault, but the influential Roman historian Paul Veyne, acting as a kind of go-between.

THE TRAGEDY OF M. FOUCAULT

For it is hard to imagine two men more different than Kenneth Dover and Michel Foucault. Foucault the sophisticated Frenchman and harsh critic of claims to truth, Dover the Oxford empiricist, insistent on confessing all; Dover the enthusiastic walker, wanking over mountain scenery, Foucault the "nature"-hater, turning his back on sunsets. While Dover itched to own up to a quasi-"nance," an almost-murder, Foucault was the "man of secrets" determined to bury the confessional project of the age of sexual "liberation," ostentatiously refusing to come out as a gay man and, with less ado, as a person with AIDS. While Dover mounted his quest in pursuit of the penetrating real, Foucault was undermining the certainties of human scientists. Surely Foucault must have seen through Dover's project. Surely he was not about to accept interpretations of Greek sexuality that took as inspiration and support the pseudosexual behavior of monkeys and giraffes, proving the universal meaning of the sexual act as domination . . .

I have called it Foucault's tragedy, because the story conforms so much to the tragic plot, but this is not, I think, a sad kind of tragedy, the tale of a once-muscular intellectual athlete fading in his last years and failing to match his own heroic intellectual standards, but the heartwarming kind of tragedy, the one where the ambitious hero tries to transcend the world and time and finds himself only too human, entangled in the real, in silly human things like friendship and what people think of him. It is the kind of story that leaves the hero humbled but not, I think, humiliated.

And there are a number of points we need to bear in mind. If Foucault, who is often described as a vain and arrogant man, failed with the Greeks, it is in large part because he was not vain and arrogant enough, far too respectful, in fact, of the work of "experts." Perhaps too we have failed all along to grasp what he was really trying to do. Perhaps he wasn't the great cynic of "truth" that people think he was, just a critic of the distracting conventional ones. Perhaps Foucault was much more of a Rankean type of historian, trying with far more verve and élan than anyone ever before to get back to where we once belonged, bringing up the big guns to demolish structures of knowledge and belief that were preventing the facts from speaking for themselves.

And we must also bear in mind the slimmest chance, which I will leave with you here and won't go into, that the greatest critic of games of truth, and in particular of the hazardous game of truth that is the sexual revelation of concrete realities, "the dirty bits" and their relationship to who you really are, did not in fact succumb to the seductions of this, the most blatant of all sex-fact games at all—that he was, in other words, having us all on. Whatever one may think of Foucault, recent work on ancient sexuality provides the most dramatic and convincing demonstration of the truth, the objective truth, of his theories about how truth is never completely objective, of how sexual truth in particular works, i.e., that it is the product of a particular time and place, a particular discourse of experts granted a particular kind of symbolic authority.

PEOPLE IN BOXES

One of the most insistent themes in Foucault's constantly shifting, labyrinthine work had been a view of discourse—words, texts, and/or the unconscious assumptions they depend on—as an autonomous system, a kind of counterpoint to reality, an imposition of taxonomies onto, instead of a mere reflection of, the organization of the world, a structure in its own right. He emerged from an intellectual environment that harbored two competing schools. The "phenomenology" of Martin Heidegger, popularized above all by Sartre, took a question from Aristotle, "What is being per se?" and tried to answer it, stripping from the world all the distractions that since the fifth century BC had hidden "being per se" from view. This grand project of getting back to basics was an almighty effort requiring the lightest touch, for the "being" sought was vanishingly elusive, like Orpheus's Eurydice when she follows him up out of Hades but is lost forever when he looks back to make sure that she is still behind him. Try to capture it in words, and you might lose it. Many consider Heidegger something of a mystic and irrationalist. He is very popular with popes.

"Structuralism" derived from the work of the Swiss linguist Ferdinand de Saussure. He it was who had discovered as a precocious genius, barely twenty-one, the lost "laryngeals" of the prehistoric Indo-European language, the ancestor of Hindi, Iranian, Welsh, Latin, Greek, English etc., which are now labeled h_1, h_2 and h_3, two of which, it has been adduced, must have been found in *erōs*'s Indo-European ancestor *h_1erh_2: Khhergghh . . . Saussure himself did not identify them as guttural throaty laryngeals however. He didn't think it mattered very much what they had sounded like, so long as you knew they had been there, where they liked to go in words, and what traces of their passing they had left in later languages.[27] For he argued that languages were not really what we thought they were, words and sounds, but abstract structures. You might say for instance that you had learned Klingon and then discover that what you thought were words and sounds were in fact color combinations, that the Klingons actually communicated like cuttlefish with a special color organ on their heads, but you could still say you "knew the language," even if you had missed some of the "rhymes," because it was the differences between signs, whether those signs were sounds or colors, and their combinations that constituted the language, the structure. This led to the notion of entities, such as the bishop in chess or the 8:25 from Geneva to Paris, which were meaningful, but not substantial; they only existed as places in a structure—the train system with all its timetables, the game of chess. This was a marvelous antidote to Heidegger's elusive primordial etymological "being per se" hidden by accretions of the hackneyed and conventional; it was a kind of being that was nothing but conventional, contingent and contemporary.

French savants began to apply Saussure's theories to all kinds of things, analyzing the structures of the cultures studied by anthropologists, of the unconscious, of the Mediterranean in the time of Philip II, of Greek myth and religion. Foucault hated being called a structuralist, and sometimes you can see his point, but you can also see why everyone thought he was one. The structures he was interested in, however, were the structures of knowledge, how scientists and experts, in different epochs, different "knowledge regimes" or *epistemes,* ordered their various fields in different periods, how they produced "facts," their games of truth. Scientific "discourse" was itself a system, with its own unspoken grammarlike rules, an artifact, a high-stakes player in power games, achieving things, doing things, not a mere bystander, but a medium to an end. These systems of knowledge, he argued, changed radically and suddenly over time, undermining the notion of absolute scientific truth.

But one of the big ironies of Foucault's work is that a man who argued for the contingency of truth is in fact obsessed with falseness, which should have been an equally contingent notion. What concerns him, it sometimes seems, is not the structures and taxonomies themselves through which the world has been seen—old and new classifications, old and new train timetables—but the mirages these taxonomies create. And the particular kinds of science he was most interested in were "human sciences," sciences that took human beings as their field of knowledge: psychiatry, criminology, education. He wanted to know what it was like to be a subject, an experiencing self, who was also an object of these knowledge regimes, what it was like for a Holy Fool or a Village Idiot to be reclassified as a schizophrenic, and there are times when he seems to think there is in fact another kind of truth somewhere else, an authentic truth hidden or disguised by the frameworks through which we see the world, an originary unshackled unformed untaxonomized primordial Heideggerian being, the primordial unformed trains, before they were bound by train timetables, the primordial bishop before he became entangled in the games of chess, the primordial experience of madness before it was captured by psychiatry, homosexicity before its capture by homosexuality.

In his later work he stressed the violence of these discursive impositions. These academic treatises, for all their tranquillity, did not reside in some quiet backwater of history, some academic grove or cultural lagoon. People did not spend time and effort writing the banal. Discourses were interventions, not glasses for seeing empirically, but guns. They were ideological and polemical even when they pretended to be taxonomical, objective, clinical, commonsensical and mundane. That was why people put so much effort into them. Dividing people into sane and insane, gay and straight, had consequences. Such classifications were active in the field of scientific knowledge, not passive acknowledgments of divisions already there, sorting not sorted. And somewhere along the way, people got promoted or demoted, they got locked up. There was power, even violence, within this mundane ordering, filing and classifying.

Foucault's earlier work had concentrated on a particular type of discourse, the writings of experts, or the silent assumptions that lay under those writings: theories of madness, medical theory, theories of grammar, of economics. In the seventies he turned to more obviously normative texts, those that define and insist upon and coerce norms of behavior: treatises on prisons and punishment, guides to good handwriting, training, pamphlets on factory discipline, on proper methods of raising children. He came to focus on the way discourses produced new practices, new habits, new bodies; how military texts disciplined the movements of soldiers, the activities of laborers, of prisoners, how educational books regulated the postures of children, of the writing hand.

Foucault's next project was a hugely ambitious "history of sexuality." In 1976 he published the first volume, an introduction, titled *The Will to Know* (*La Volonté de savoir*). Originally he thought of calling it *Truth and Sex*.[28] In it he overturned the notion that the Victorians had repressed some preexisting force of sexuality, viewing repression instead as a device for producing discourses, "talk about sex," and the unspoken assumptions that start to break out when people talk about sex. Repression might even *produce* "sexuality," through institutions like confession and psychoanalysis, people talking themselves into being gay. Our modern obsession with sex should not be seen as a liberation from Victorian repression, but as a direct consequence of the Victorian determination to know. As for the homosexual, previously, he argued, there had been only the regulation of forbidden *acts,* like sodomy, and little interest in defining the types who might perform them. In 1869, however, Carl Westphal had written an article on "contrary sexual sensations" and the homosexual became "a personage, a past, a case history, and a childhood, in addition to being a type of life, a life form, and a morphology, with an indiscreet anatomy and possibly a mysterious physiology."[29] This was the making of the modern "homosexual."

Foucault had not finished with sex. On the back cover of the first volume, readers were presented with the prospect of five further volumes in this massive project. The second was titled *Flesh and the Body—La Chair et le corps*—indicating that the starting point was to be the advent of the Christian experience of sexuality. There was no reference to a study of the Greeks, only a footnote anticipating yet another project (never realized) that would examine the uses of torture in Greek and Roman law.[30] It may be that Foucault's research would have led him to the pagans anyway, but in May 1979 he accepted an invitation to speak at a conference that would make that shift much more likely.

Arcadia was France's oldest gay rights group, "dispassionate, serene and dignified," in the group's own words, devoted "to illustrating the homophile problem so that homophiles themselves will live better lives, and so that the heterosexual world will gain a better understanding of what homophiles are and will accept them for what they are, in other words, with their homophile nature." It had been founded in 1954 but its extinction was eagerly anticipated: "because on that day, we will . . . really be side by side with the others, together with the others. There will no longer be any difference between us and the others, and the whole of society will accept us for what we are."[31] Its official title was CLESPAL, an acronym that houses resonances with all we have been talking about—science, the Mediterranean: Club Littéraire et Scientifique des Pays Latins. Unofficially, in the slighting words of Guy Hocquenghem, Arcadia was "a very discreet homosexual institution . . . with a weekly dance and public-information lectures, where people go to look for pick-ups, a fairly bourgeois audience, with quite a few young office workers, some rich old homosexuals, and a small minority of lesbians."[32]

Arcadia's conference took place in Paris on May 24–27, 1979, at the Palais des Congrès under the title "The Gaze of Others," *Le Regard des Autres*. On the day of lectures there were 850 in the audience and four amazingly distinguished speakers, not all of them as "other" as they may have liked the audience to believe: the historian Jean-Paul Aron, Robert Merle talking of "The trial of Oscar Wilde," Michel Foucault talking of the autobiography of the hermaphrodite Herculine Barbin, and finally—the moment that concerns us here—the Roman historian Paul Veyne, giving a paper ironically titled "A historian's heterosexual paper on homosexuality." The irony was not allowed to float in the air for long. We can say that homosexuals (and heterosexuals) don't exist, says Veyne, not merely that homosexuals differ between themselves or that there is a continuum between heterosexuality and homosexuality, but that whether someone is "homo, hetero, or bi" is no criterion for classification, any more than someone's race or the initial of their surname. Nor, by the same token, do heterosexuals exist: "No one loves women in general, for the sole reason that they are biologically of the female sex."

These remarks form an introduction to the theme of sexuality in the ancient world that thus becomes a proof of this point:

I would like to be able to tell you [the Arcadians] that in this happy period there were no prejudices against homosexuals and that Greek civilization was more liberal than our own. But if I said that, I would be lying: the Greeks were unable to be either tolerant or intolerant toward homosexuality for the good reason that they had no idea what homosexuality was. They did not classify sexual conduct according to sex, but according to social class and the categories of activity and passivity.[33]

There are two points to note about this. On the one hand Veyne argues that the Greeks had a different sex timetable, a quite different classification of human sexicities, which proved that the different classifications of different cultures, homo, hetero or bi, reflected nothing but convention. On the other hand, because in the ancient classification sexual activity was all about *roles* in sex—active and passive—about sex per se, the ancients, according to Veyne, seemed to understand better than we do something true about the *essence* of sexuality, that it is not about natures and essences, and who you really are, but a superficial, temporary, changeable, role playing type of thing. All sexualities, even our own permanent and inescapable hetero-, homo- and bisexualities, are, supposedly, the product of particular cultural configurations, but the peculiarity of the structure of Greek sexuality, for Veyne, was that it was so *structural* that it was all about impermanent and inessential positions in sex, like the crossword puzzle clue the solution to which is "SOLUTION." The Greeks had put sexual orientation in its *right* place as a superficial matter of no more importance than the letter that begins your surname. In that respect the Greeks seemed to agree with what Veyne was advocating. With their construction of sexuality as a sexicity of inessential flexible roles, they, unlike us, had got the true, the inessential, nature of human sexuality correct.

The homophiles in the audience who insisted on a separate homosexual nature, who seemed to look on the ancient past as a lost Arcadia free of prejudice, and to idealize, albeit scientifically, the uninhibited sensuality of the Mediterranean, were being taught a good lesson by an expert. The ancient Greeks, the original Arcadians, had nothing to do with them. The Greeks didn't know what a homophile was. In fact Veyne's paper, his "heterosexual paper on homosexuality," seemed to prove the ridiculousness of this entire conference, "The gaze of others." What others? For homosexuals weren't really different from heterosexuals in any significant way. There was in fact no difference, apart from a superficial difference in taxonomy. Indeed the Greeks seemed to prove the nonsense of this entire Arcadian organization with its lectures and dances and absurd pretensions to scientific knowledge. An organization of homosexuals, suggested Professor Veyne, was like an organization of people whose names began with, say, "H." Of course what the bourgeois Arcadians knew, what these "young office workers," these rich old homosexuals, these one or two lesbians, couldn't help but know, was that they were rather more like people whose names began with Ng——.

Veyne's talk was a filleted version of a paper he had published the year before. For by what seems like the most amazing coincidence, in the same year that Dover published his *Greek Homosexuality,* putting sodomy at the center of Greek Love, Veyne had done exactly the same in an article on Roman sexuality in the journal *Annales,* "The Family and Love in the High Roman Empire." Sexual penetration was clearly the presiding spirit of the 1970s; probably it was all those books by Desmond Morris and the sociobiologists. Ancient men may have had sexual preferences, argued Veyne, but they were *inessentielles,* like preferring the racetrack to the stage—just like tea or coffee, perhaps, sugar or no sugar, black or white. Veyne does not follow Dover's distinction between a true heterosexuality and a false homosexuality, arguing that most people may be and always have been bisexual. He quotes an interesting passage from Proust: The days when homosexuality was a custom are long gone; what survives is the hard core who have withstood the obstacles and the shame. Perhaps, suggests Veyne mischievously, this hard core is the ten percent of modern homosexuals, and perhaps for purposes of symmetry there is a similar minority of hard-core heterosexuals at the other end of the scale: "*Voilà qui est difficile à décider, que dis-je: à quantifier.*" It's hard to tell, he says, let alone to quantify.

Like Dover, Veyne insists that there was a crucial difference between activity and passivity. He uses the verb *sabrer,* "to give a hammering to," "shaft." It was fine for slaves, wives and subordinates to submit to "a hammering" from their master every now and again, but quite shameful for free youths to be subjected to such domination. Of course there were times when they did succumb, but nobody talked about it; it was "a taboo subject." Whereas Dover saw subjection as a universal interpretation of the act of sex, Veyne stresses that this active/passive emphasis is culturally specific, a feature of Mediterranean societies in particular, so obsessed with "machismo" and the male role that it produces a kind of naïveté with regard to sexuality. In such feverishly passionate, hot-blooded cultures the gender of the person at the receiving end of one's virility is of no consequence at all.

Veyne introduced Foucault's work into the study of ancient sexuality for the first time. For Veyne had been installed as Professor of Roman history at the Collège de France in 1976, and there established a close friendship with his new colleague M. Foucault, who had just finished the introduction to his history of sexuality, a history that was supposed to start with the Christians. Veyne lived in the south of France and Foucault offered him accommodation for his sojourns in Paris. They spent much time together alone, comparing sexual tastes, straight and gay . . . tea or coffee, sugar or no sugar, black or white. It was almost certainly the arrival of Veyne that changed the course of Foucault's project so drastically. Friends do not always read each other's academic articles, of course, but if Foucault had not heard Veyne's views on pagan sex before, he was certainly listening when Veyne gave an account of them to the conference organized by Arcadia in 1979.

Eight years earlier Veyne had written an important treatise on *How to Write History* in which he had not, oddly, mentioned Foucault at all. But when he got his chair at the Collège de France and began to stay with Foucault, inevitably Foucault started to figure much more largely in his work. Indeed when a second edition of *How to Write History* was produced, Veyne more than made up for his earlier neglect. An encomium, "Foucault Revolutionizes History," was added to the book as an appendix. Veyne's article on the macho hammering world of Roman sexuality should be seen as a similar kind of tribute, for it smiles upon Foucault's work, graciously, in several footnotes, and the entire article can be seen as a demonstration of the truth of Foucault's claim that different epochs produce different sexualities. Once upon a time, in ancient Rome, there had been a different sexual regime. As far as history was concerned, the homosexual did not exist.[34]

Some months after the Arcadia Congress, Veyne elaborated his ideas to a seminar organized by Philippe Ariès, the distinguished historian of childhood. "This is the world of heroic bravado," he said, "with a very Mediterranean flavor, where the important thing is to be the ravisher, never mind the sex of the victim." His emphasis again was on the Roman environment, where only slaves could be subjected to such humiliation—even male slaves, if they were unlucky enough to have oversexed masters. What made the Greek practice different is that they admired the "supposedly Platonic love of adults for *epheboi,* for freeborn youths, who frequented the gymnasium where their admirers went to watch them exercising naked." This is hardly a minor difference. The Greeks had many slaves and women to be sexually dominant over. Why did they subject citizens, their own posterity, freeborn youths, future leaders of the community, to such humiliating, dominating, feminizing ravishment? Veyne does not try to resolve this contradiction himself, but in a note he observes that Foucault's magnum opus on ancient Greek sex, *Aphrodisia,* was about to appear and in the meantime singles out Dover's recent book as "essential."[35] In fact, Foucault's book on *Aphrodisia* had got into difficulties, and would not emerge until his death, as part of his book on the Greek use of pleasure.

By 1982 Foucault was discussing Dover's work himself—"already a classic"—in an interview for a gay journal called *Masques*. He singles out a number of features for his gay readership. Dover had shown that the term homosexuality had absolutely no relevance in antiquity. They had neither the concept *nor the experience*. There were two important issues: whether you played the active or the passive role in sex and whether you had a beard. This led to an extremely complicated and regulated code of behavior. Dover had centered his account on the trial of the politician Timarchus and the law that banned prostitutes from speaking in the Assembly, but a "prostitute" did not incur the charge through streetwalking, argues Foucault; it was the patent fact that he had been passive in sex and an object of pleasure. This was proof that the penetration problem was not easily dismissed by rules about age. It was in fact as unthinkable for the Greeks as for the Romans that a boy who had been buggered could ever assume a position of responsibility in society or the state. Foucault elaborates what Veyne was already hinting. The Greeks got around this problem with lots of guff about an asexual, educational, Platonic love that was simply a façade to cover up the unacceptable physical reality. These texts have been used as evidence that the Greeks were tolerant. In fact they are a sign of their embarrassment. In a review of the French translation of Dover's book for the newspaper *Libération,*

Foucault includes a sideswipe at pathetic creatures who may not agree with this analysis: "Of course there will still be some genial characters good enough to suppose [*esprits aimables pour penser*] that in the final analysis, homosexuality has always existed ... To such naïfs Dover gives a good lesson in historical nominalism ... Dover, one suspects, is having a good laugh at those for whom homosexuality in Greece had been unrestricted." Foucault, one suspects, is using Dover to have a go at the poor deluded homophiles of Arcadia, with their homophile natures.[36]

When Foucault's book on the Greeks, *L'Usage des plaisirs,* eventually came out, it was not surprising that Dover was cited extensively alongside ancient authors. Foucault even uses his ten pages that demonstrate the universal symbolic meaning of homosexual penetration for "the importance of not being dominated and the reticences with regard to sodomy and passive fellation in homosexual relations." He follows Dover's notion of a zero-sum sexual battle between victor and vanquished: "Sexual relations—always conceived in terms of the model act of penetration, assuming a polarity that opposed activity and passivity—were seen as being of the same type as the relationship between a superior and a subordinate ... one who vanquishes and one who is vanquished." As for Timarchus: "In the course of his youth [he] placed himself and showed himself to everyone in the inferior and humiliating position of a pleasure object for others ... What was hard for the Athenians to accept ... was not that they might be governed by someone who loved boys, or who as a youth was loved by a man, but that they might come under the authority of a leader who once identified with the role of pleasure object for others." The apparent double standard in Greek sexual morality—*erōmenoi* like modern girls, encouraged to flee to protect their arses, *erastai* like modern boys, encouraged to pursue in order to demonstrate their virility—has now evolved into "the antinomy of the boy": "On the one hand, young men were recognized as objects of pleasure ... But on the other hand, the boy, whose youth must be a training for manhood, could not and must not identify with that role."

It was this fundamental problem of turning a sexual object, the boy, into a man, a "subject in control of his own pleasures," a "master," that made the homosexual relation a preoccupation for the Greeks of greater intensity than any other. Indeed, for Foucault, the active-passive polarity can be seen as the centerpiece for the whole of Greek morality and the constitution of the Greek Self: "For the Greeks, it was the opposition between activity and passivity that was essential, pervading the domain of sexual behaviors and that of moral attitudes as well . . . In the eyes of the Greeks, what constituted ethical negativity par excellence . . . [was] being passive with regard to the pleasures." Mark Poster seems quite justified, then, in arguing that, for Foucault, "The rudiments of the modern subject can be traced to the Greek problematization of the self in the practice of the love of boys."[37]

Foucault really does say that, I think. Foucault really does think that the modern personage, inasmuch as he is an object of knowledge of himself, inasmuch as there are "truths" about himself that he can avoid or own up to, worried about his weight, thinking he really ought to go more to the gym, analyzing himself, measuring himself, criticizing himself, ambitious for himself, terrified of himself, can trace his origins back to a Greek man c.400 BC wondering whether he should bend over and suffer humiliation and/or whether he should ask the same of his younger boyfriend whom he kind of respects, and kind of doesn't. Buggery; this is where it all began, this is the Fall from Grace and into self-consciousness. Well that's what I think he probably really thought, something like that, at any rate, though he would never spell it out so crudely . . .

In April 1983 Foucault was in Berkeley in northern California giving a series of interviews, in English, about his work. "Sex is boring," says Foucault. "It sounds like the Greeks were not too interested either," says his interlocutor. "No, they were not much interested in sex. It was not a great issue. Compare, for instance, what they say about the place of food . . ." "Yet volume II of *The History of Sexuality, L'Usage des plaisirs,* is concerned almost exclusively with, not to put too fine a point on it, sex." "Yes. One of the numerous reasons I had so much trouble with that book was that I first wrote a book about sex, which I put aside. Then I wrote a book about the self and the techniques of the self; sex disappeared, and for the third time I was obliged to rewrite a book in which I tried to keep the equilibrium between one and the other." In fact when it was published there were lots of other things in *Uses of Pleasure* that are not to do with sex, or not directly.

In the Berkeley interview, Foucault's sodomania seems almost accidental. The centrality of buggery in his work on the Greeks—and it is central—his extraordinary claim that Greek ethics *tout court* is modeled on the ethics of buggery, that self-control and moderation is like being the active partner in sex, that being extravagant and succumbing to excess is like being buggered by your desires, that the Western subject, Western Man as an object of (his own) knowledge, the primordial subject of the Human Sciences, is born from sodomitical anxiety, a struggle to keep your (ethical) back to the wall, so to speak, seems almost to be not so much a linchpin as a mere segue between what had been two separate books, one on sex and one on self-mastery.

But elsewhere in these Berkeley interviews Foucault seems to contradict himself: The Greeks were obsessed with penetration. The interviewers are talking about reciprocity and "friendship": "Both in Aristotle and Cicero you could read it as really being the highest virtue because it's selfless and enduring, it's not easily bought, it doesn't deny the utility and pleasure of the world, but yet it seeks something more." Foucault's interviewers are of course touching on the question of *erōs* and *philia,* ambitious, passionate, expeditionary love and the rock-solid loving intimacy it seeks to establish. We might recall Cicero's description of Greek Love as *amor amicitiae,* a passion for making "friends," i.e., intimate alliances.

But Foucault seems to think *philia* is about being "just good friends" and drives a coach-and-horses, a very Christian kind of coach-and-horses, between *erōs* and *philia,* sex and friendship, drawing a series of distinctions that make no sense in the Greek context, where, of course, sex is conceived in terms of *charis,* the gold-dust of interpersonal relations, the purest kind of delightful unexpected gracious reciprocation. But my book is about sexual ethics, says Foucault; "it's not a book about love, or about friendship, or about reciprocity." Over which I feel like scrawling in red Biro, as my Classics masters quite often did over my proses and unseens, "Aaaaaagggghhhh!"[38]

As he elaborates on the complete one-sidedness of ancient homosex, the apparent lack of sexual reciprocity, the philosopher becomes agitated: "The Greek ethics of pleasure is linked to a virile society, to dissymmetry, exclusion of the other, an obsession with penetration . . . All that is quite disgusting." Interestingly there is a problem here with the transmission of the texts, Foucault's texts, and a little comparison of manuscripts is in order. For Foucault seems to have regretted his outburst. The French translation of the interview—"*Tout cela est franchement répugnant*"—was later amended: "*pas très attrayant.*" Greek sex is no longer "quite disgusting," or even "downright" repugnant, just "not very attractive."[39] But why this ostentatious revulsion for the charming, romantic, self-sacrificing, gracious, lovelorn Greeks? Why does gay Foucault so violently, if momentarily, reject Greek Homosexuality?

Whether or not you agree with Foucault's strange conceit in *Uses of Pleasure,* the metaphor of being shafted by your pleasures and desires, it nevertheless succeeds in putting buggery, rarely mentioned by the Greeks, almost never shown by their image makers, right at the heart of Greek ethics and Greek sexuality, and that perhaps was the whole point. For, as it happens, and for reasons quite different from those Foucault adduced in his book, buggery had been at the heart of work on Greek sexuality for decades: in order to prove that the Greeks weren't gay. For Devereux who hated queers and for Dover who wanted to protect his beloved Greeks from the contempt of people like Devereux who hated queers, buggery, penetration, was a substitute for homosexuality, not psychological but behavioral, it was mere innocent sex acts, "nances," pure insignificant sexicity, episodic, gestural, like animals mounting each other in the zoo, it was a pseudo- or quasi-sexuality and absolutely nothing to do with "fundamental orientations of the personality."

Likewise for Veyne talking to the gay tribe of Arcadia with their homophile "natures," the supposed ancient obsession with buggery proved that the Greeks had nothing to do with them—no, more than that, that homosexuality itself was a pseudo category, like people whose names begin with "H." Like other Mediterranean types, the Greeks were so manly, so macho, so obsessed with their penises and what penises do, that they seemed to be absolutely unconcerned—as innocent, as "naïve" as baboons or Italian gondoliers—about what was actually going on down there, what they were doing with these penises, and in particular about whether they were using them to penetrate a man or a woman, as uninterested a question as whether you like the racetrack or the stage, sugar or no sugar. And of course, long before he thought up the idea of being buggered by desires, Foucault had told the gay readers of *Masques* that "the most important thing" about Dover's work, the most important thing about Greek sexuality, was that they didn't have one: They had sex roles *instead*.

Is it a coincidence that this same buggery, all sex and no sexuality, this sexicity, was again so important in Foucault's own book, but for completely different reasons, or is Foucault, in denying that he is denying homosexuality, as it were, being dishonest? Foucault had made penetration (which in the history of the study of Greek Homosexuality stands for the nongayness of the Greeks) the very centerpiece of their ethics. Penetration, not homosexuality, but mere homosexual behavior, more homogenital acts, is the very origin of the construction of Man as an object of the study of Man, he seems to be saying. In his earlier work, Foucault had located the origin of the homosexual personage in the late nineteenth century. The performer of certain proscribed acts was prodded and poked by scientists and psychiatrists—"Why do you do such things? What's wrong with you?"—until the new entity finally confessed himself: "I am an invert, an erotomaniac, a degenerate type of person, a homosexual, one of them." Now two and a half thousand years earlier the very first words spoken by the Western Self about itSelf, shouting from the rooftops of ancient Athens, seemed to be: It's just sex. I don't even know what "homosexuality" means. The claim that it is or once was or might have been trivial is as airy as a lead balloon, i.e., made *precisely* as uninteresting for them as it is interesting for us. Of course, the question of the historical existence or not of homosexuality was not for Foucault a disinterested inquiry, sugar or no sugar, any more than it was for Dover or Devereux.

Nothing is more guaranteed to cause apoplexy among Foucault's followers, if not to provoke a punch in the eye, than the suggestion that he may not have been completely cool about his own homosexuality, let alone to suggest, as one of the speakers at the Arcadia conference later dared to do, that he was basically a closet case, ashamed of his own proclivities, frightened to "come out," his philosophy of undermining such "truths" motivated by a desire to deny the possibility of one truth in particular: that he, Michel Foucault, could possibly be "one of them," a "queer intellectual," which might tend to diminish his prestige. He could not be a gay intellectual, because there was no such category. It is not just that such timidity would seem to undermine Foucault's claims to heroic status. Since his death an entire industry of academic work on the playfulness, the Greek-style role-playfulness of homosexuality, has grown up. To suggest that in Foucault's case this playfulness was a concession to the homophobia of people like Devereux, *just horseplay, only sex,* an acceptance by homosexuals of their proper place in society, on the margins of earnestness, a surrender of the right to be serious, permanent and real, casts doubt on the radical integrity of these more recent role-playful revolutionaries.

What kind of playfulness is it, this rumpy-pumpy horseplay of the Greeks, the episodic behavior of Dover, the games of Foucault? Is it a jolly game, a relaxed fun-loving sexicity, or is it the determined play that deceived Margaret Mead on Samoa, play with a very fixed grin, a game insisting with nonchalance and gritted teeth that "it's only a game," a desperate recreation, a nervous kind of laughter, a please-don't-kill-me kind of joke? In a different act of the same play, it wasn't only Jews and Gypsies who got sent to the concentration camp. And I forgot to mention something about that "heterosexual paper" that Paul Veyne delivered before the homophile Arcadians. For although his paper was based on the article he wrote for *Annales,* Veyne introduced something new into his discussion when he spoke to the homosexuals. His paper didn't begin by arguing that homosexuals shouldn't exist. It began by talking about the Aryans and the Jews.

Veyne argued that one could defend the Jews in two ways. Either we could say that they are not "monsters and that, despite their race, they have a right to live"—not a completely creditable defense. Or we could say: "There is no such thing." No Jews, no Aryans either. The point of this was that the division of Aryans and Jews was, suggested Veyne, like the division of homosexuals and heterosexuals. And just as we can say that Jews (and Aryans) don't exist, so we can refute the claims to exist of homosexuals (and heterosexuals too). One might pass over Veyne's unexpected comparison as accidental, were it not for a strange piece that appeared a few years later in *Libération.* The subject of the article was the decision of Arcadia's founder, André Baudry, to disband this decades-old organization that had campaigned since the fifties for the rights of gay people, the tribe of homophiles. This bizarre article, which one might expect would be a quiet, moderately respectful survey of the organization, its achievements and its failures, was instead intensely sarcastic. It compared M. Baudry to Moses leading his people out of Egypt.

Now, by disbanding Arcadia, he was abandoning his "people" to the "*stupre des villes*," the decadent fleshpots of the metropolis, while in America the people of Sodom were welcoming fire and brimstone, "the gay cancer," i.e., AIDS, as a punishment from God. "Roll on the day when God becomes a woman and homosexuals finally may be shot of her." Attached to this offensive obituary was the name of the journalist Didier Eribon. Later he said he had not in fact written it, but had merely, with misgivings, put his name to it. It had been written by Foucault himself.

Foucault was born in 1926 in the provincial town of Poitiers. His father was a distinguished surgeon. Foucault went to mass on Sundays, enrolled as a choirboy, was educated by monks in "the most regimented Catholic school [his father] could find" and spent his late teens in Marshal Pétain's Vichy France through the Nazi occupation.[40] It was not uncommon to see German troops arresting people, and the prevailing ideology was all of "Fatherland, Work and Family."[41] Foucault rarely spoke of this period in public but he wondered if he might grow up a German and talked of "very early memories of an absolutely threatening world, which could crush us," of "a private life" that was "really threatened."[42] As Foucault lay dying of a secret illness in 1984, his unfriendly boyfriend the novelist Hervé Guibert kept a secret diary of his last conversations with the great philosopher. The day after the funeral, he wrote a macabre short story. It begins with a brain surgeon cutting into the brain of a certain notorious philosopher, a critic of psychiatry and medicine; inside he finds memories, and hidden in the deepest levels are memories of childhood buried to avoid "the idiocy of interpretations." These memories concern the philosopher's early life as the son of a surgeon in Poitiers. One traumatic scene concerns the war years. Arrogant young refugees from Paris arrive suddenly at the philosopher's provincial school, knocking the local school swot, "the philosopher-child," off his pedestal. He "invites every curse to rain down on them." As if by magic, the arrogant children vanish. It turns out that the children were Jews.[43]

Perhaps in the end then, Foucault's superculture, like that of Franz Boas and Margaret Mead and Ruth Benedict, was an assimilationist kind of process, an antiracist culture, able to combat homophobia, a dream of culture that could help to heal divisions between the mad and the sane,

Aryans and Jews, gay people and heterosexuals, a culture that could be blamed for dangerous differences that seemed so natural. Rigid and prisonlike this culture might be, with its own invisible patterns and grammatical rules, but one day it might be made to undo the differences it had created, to change the timetable, to adjust the configuration, and thereby allow misfits and other structural anomalies to stick out less, to disappear, as Mommsen regretfully and Treitschke vindictively had wanted the Jews to disappear from Germany, as Boas had wanted the Jews and Blacks to disappear in America, but for their own good. This is why it was always so *important* to tell gay readers and gay audiences that homosexuality, their homosexuality, didn't exist. This is why Foucault was so bitterly hostile to the Jew-like gay "people" of Arcadia, under their Moses-like leader, why he rejoiced in Dover teaching a lesson in historical nominalism to the naïfs, to those *esprits aimables* who were nice enough to think that homosexuality had always existed. This is what sodomy had always been for, to disidentify, an enzyme of decomposition. Sodomy was what the Greeks had *instead* of homosexuality, just as the assimilating Jews of nineteenth-century Germany weren't Jews so much as adherents of the Mosaic religion.

Odd, but hardly surprising, that the racial theory of the nineteenth and twentieth centuries produced a strong and equal reaction in theories of culture, but who would have guessed what is so unmistakable in Veyne's "heterosexual paper" delivered to Arcadia in 1979, that the Nazis would help to produce sodomania, that decades after the end of the Second World War we can still trace their influence in a footnote in a book about Greek vase painting where a man is alleged to be drowning through his arse.

And there is an interesting footnote here. Saussure, the man who started all this structuralism, this notion of complex symbolic inessential systems, of structures per se in which the actual elements, the sounds of words, are unimportant, who could write about a long-lost quasi-consonant algebraically as a *"coefficient sonantique"* without trying very hard to say what the letter was like, may also have had a motive in insisting on the abstract. One of the mysteries about Saussure is why he left Paris for the provincial obscurity of Geneva. But among his papers was found a letter addressed to an anti-Semitic journal in Paris complaining about the capital's Jews as "swarms of parasites."[44] He may indeed have been in denial about the substance of sounds as Foucault was in denial about the substance of his homosexuality. For the Aryan quasi-consonants Saussure avoided voicing were not any old letters, but the throaty "laryngeals" typical of Semitic languages such as Hebrew and Arabic, the ones you find in Colonel Ghhhadaffi and Qhhhhatar and al-Qhhhaeda, the letters that framed the root of prehistoric *erōs:* Khhergghh . . . Indeed, one year after Saussure published his research on the unvoiced signs, another linguist, Hermann Möller, suggested they were the long-lost missing link that proved that Aryan and Semitic languages were cousins with a common ancestor (apparently they are not). Perhaps it is just a coincidence that the sound anti-Semitic Saussure could not voice was a Semitic-sounding one, or perhaps he was trying to keep the parasitic Jewish swarms away from the Aryans. At any rate the 8:25 from Geneva to Paris would have to leave without him.

· PART III ·

GREEK LOVE AND GREEK RELIGIONS

GANYMEDE RISING

Ganymede was discovered by Galileo on January 7, 1610, in the direction of the planet Zeus, which we call Jupiter. Galileo was tremendously pleased at his discovery. He thought Ganymede and his companions were stars never seen before by anybody, not even by the great ancient astronomers. He named them, after his patrons, "Medici" stars.

On the night of January 8 Galileo took another look, and found they were not where he thought they would be. The stars had moved. He continued to observe them through his telescope for the whole of the following week. Each night they moved, though never far from Zeus. They seemed to be following Jupiter around. He thought about it and came up with a solution; these were not fixed stars at all, but heavenly bodies of a brand-new kind that orbited Jupiter as Jupiter orbited the Sun. He published the news in March of that year in the *Star Courier*—*Nuncius Sidereus*—and became a famous man.

Astronomy is one of the jewels in the crown of Greek science, one of the Greeks' most astonishing achievements. Looking up without the aid of telescopes they managed to work out that the Earth was round, that the planets (*planētes asteres,* "wandering stars") were spheres in circular motion, and measured with a degree of accuracy the distance from the Earth to the Moon. But being sensible, they thought all this circular motion should have just one center, like a giant whirlpool, and since our Moon did not go around the Sun, that left only one candidate, a fixed nonplanetary Earth. Aristarchus of Samos, it is true, had suggested around 300 BC that the Earth circled the Sun, but no one took him seriously and it just meant that when Copernicus revived the idea 1,800 years later his enemies were well briefed with the arguments of Aristarchus's ancient opponents. Galileo's discovery of bodies moving around Jupiter, therefore, had a major impact. There were other moons now, and for them, manifestly, it was Jupiter not Earth that was the center of the universe.

Galileo didn't have much cause to distinguish between his Medicean stars. In his notebooks he just gave them numbers. Others thought it would be a good idea to name them after different members of the Medici family, Lorenzo, etc., or to describe them as a single microcosmos, a little solar system: Jupiter's Mercury, Jupiter's Venus, Jupiter's Saturn, Jupiter's Jupiter etc. Fortunately this did not catch on. Johannes Kepler, on the other hand, thought of naming them after his patron the Duke of Brandenburg, but he made another suggestion that he passed on to Simon Marius, who was impressed enough to record the occasion:

> Jupiter is much blamed by the poets on account of his adulteries. Three maidens especially are mentioned as having been successfully courted by him in secret: Io, daughter of the River Inachus, Callisto daughter of Lycaon, Europa daughter of Agenor. Then there was Ganymede, the handsome son of King Tros, whom Jupiter transported to heaven on his back, having taken the form of an eagle, as the poets claim, in their stories . . . I will be acting, I think, quite properly, therefore, if I call the first one Io, the second Europa, the third, because of its brilliance and majesty, Ganymede, and the fourth, Callisto . . . This idea, and the assignment of particular names, was suggested to me by Kepler, Imperial Astronomer, when we met at Ratisbon [Regensburg] fair in October 1613. So if, as a joke, and in memory of our friendship then begun, I hail him as joint father of these four stars, that too would be quite proper.[1]

The unmanned spacecraft *Galileo* was launched from the space shuttle *Atlantis* on October 18, 1989. Six years later it arrived at Jupiter and began to orbit this largest of the planets. On December 28, 2000, as the second millennium drew to a close, *Galileo* was programmed to dip within 1,452 miles of the surface of Ganymede as he lay in Jupiter's shadow. Brilliant and majestic Ganymede is the largest moon in the solar system, bigger than Pluto and Mercury, three-quarters the size of Mars. If ever he got knocked out of Zeus's orbit, he would have every cause to be considered a planet in his own right. The purpose of the millennium flyby was to observe the effect of charged particles, trapped by Jupiter, falling onto Ganymede's surface, Ganymede's equivalent of the aurora borealis, since, alone among the moons of the solar system, Ganymede generates a magnetic field. *Galileo* could hear it.

GANYMEDE'S GREAT ADVENTURE

In getting the Greeks a reputation, Ganymede has a lot to answer for, which is ironic, since he wasn't Greek. A prince of Troy, great-uncle to Priam, who was king when the city was sacked, Ganymede disappeared in his youth and was reported to have become a cupbearer to the gods on Mount Olympus. Some insisted there was more to the story than that. Ganymede was very handsome, said Homer, the handsomest boy on the planet. It was because of his beauty that he was snatched away by the gods, and not by any god, it later emerged, but by Zeus himself. Zeus had fallen in love with him. Unable to resist his charms, the king of the gods had flown him up to Olympus on eagle's wings.

This particular image is vivid and has often been imagined and reimagined throughout the long history of European art: the giant bird spreading its feathers behind the long-haired handsome youth.[2] The Trojan prince has been seen on countless cups and vases, cut into precious gems, sewn into fancy costumes, presiding on doors, bookcovers, beds, ceilings and Pompeian walls, in clay, paint and multicolored marble. He is usually naked, but his identity as a Trojan prince is often marked, especially in the later period, by a Phrygian cap, the kind of headgear, limply conical, worn by Delacroix's Liberty as she mounts the Parisian barricades.[3] Sometimes Ganymede also has a cape. It doesn't provide much of a covering for his naked body, but serves to show the swirl of air that must surround him as the big bird descends.

Xenophon, writing around four hundred years before the Christian era, has the philosopher Socrates doing amateur etymology on Ganymede's name (*Ganytai*—"delights in"; *medea*—"thoughts"): "Even in the case of Ganymede, it was not for his body but for his soul that he was elevated by Zeus to Olympus . . . so he is called Ganymede not because of his physical attractions, but because of his sweetness of thought [*hēdugnōmōn*]."[4] This brief passage would eventually become one of the most popular quotes from Greek authors, but not until two thousand years later.

Sometimes the eagle grabs him from the front and Ganymede throws his head back in apparent rapture. More often the eagle is behind him. Sometimes Ganymede is helpless and alarmed, wanting the ride to stop, but afraid of falling. Sometimes he is perfectly composed, as if he knows just what is happening and anticipates the gentlest of landings, like an actor playing Peter Pan, with whom he has qualities in common. Many artists were sensitive to the problem of the eagle's sharp talons digging into the boy's tender flesh: "aware of just what it is abducting in Ganymede and for whom it is carrying him, and which therefore refrains from injuring the boy with its talons, even through his clothing."[5] Some arranged a makeshift harness or hammock formed out of draperies. Others had Ganymede climb on the eagle's back. This is how he was painted on the ceiling of the immense palace Nero built on the area cleared by the Great Fire of Rome, the palace called House of Gold. Ganymede was viewed as if through a skylight, disappearing into the blue. When shown as rider rather than as prey, he tends to look less "enraptured" or "transported," more triumphant and in control, a joyrider. At the very outset it is apparent that the icon of the eagle-borne boy has the potential to veer off toward one of two opposite poles, exaltation or victim.[6] It makes a difference moreover whether you think the eagle is Zeus himself, transmogrified, or a flying limousine sent by the king of the gods to collect the royal beauty.

Two decades or so before year zero, the poet Virgil chose the latter option. He imagined the story in two scenes embroidered on a cloak awarded as a prize in a boat race. In scene one Ganymede chases after fast stags on Mount Ida, hurling javelins and out of breath. Scene two shows the hunter hunted down by a sudden raptor. Already he is rising into the air. Beagles bark, the servants supposed to be tending him reach hopelessly up to the stars, but Ganymede is out of reach. Virgil's imaginary artist was thinking of a nighttime raid. A hundred years later the poet Statius tried to see things from Ganymede's point of view, the ground moving away, a view of the hills and Troy getting smaller.

One image that appealed to the Hellenistic world—the name given to the postclassical phase of a much-expanded Greek world between the death of Alexander in 323 BC and the death of Cleopatra in 30 BC—has the giant eagle drinking from a holy dish (*phialē*) on the boy's lap. There is some debate about what the artists intended. Is this a narrative embel-

8. A miniature Ganymede on the doors of St. Peter's in Rome, one of the few elements of the old St. Peter's to be retained. Antonio Averlino, "*Il Filarete*" (AD 1433–45).

lishment of an episode known nowhere else, which tells not of rape but sly seduction: the boy taking pity on a thirsty bird and about to be repaid unfairly for his act of kindness? Or is it a neat amalgamation of Ganymede's two roles, as cupbearer and kidnap victim? The boy offers the highest bird, the breathless bird, a holy libation for the first of many times.

Ganymede was a popular subject throughout antiquity and wasn't forgotten in the Middle Ages, getting a mention in the works of Ovid, and therefore in the influential fourteenth-century allegorical version of the *Metamorphoses, Ovid Moralized,* as well as in Dante's *Purgatory,* in Petrarch's sonnets and in Boccaccio's *Genealogy of the Pagan Gods* (1375). He even finds his way, in the 1440s, onto the doors of St. Peter's in Rome, where he remains, thanks to the neo-Platonist "Filarete" (see Fig. 8, above).[7] After the Reformation, in the High Renaissance and Baroque especially, his images multiplied. Around the middle of the sixteenth century, Niccolò Tribolo produced an image in bronze with Ganymede riding the bird like a pony, and Benvenuto Cellini, sculptor, jeweler and riffraff, took an antique torso and supplied it with arms, legs and eagle. The raptor stands legs akimbo, looking up at Ganymede who seems to be teasing it with a small bird he holds out of reach, a dangerous game, he should have learned by now.

Around 1530 Correggio did a version for the marquess of Mantua, painted from a precipitous angle as if the artist would still have had time to rescue the boy by grabbing one of his legs, had he not been so preoccupied with painting them. Around the same time Michelangelo did a drawing of Ganymede for his close friend Tommaso de' Cavalieri; what is probably a preliminary sketch survives. Ganymede and the eagle are both full-frontal, twisted around each other in the beginning of a spiral. The youth leans back over the eagle's shoulder, his arms resting on the eagle's neck and wing, while the eagle grabs the boy's legs from behind and wraps his beak across the boy's chest, like a music stand holding a score. The eagle looks dangerous, and has an eagle's evil-looking eye; there is no attempt to soften his beak and claws, but the lovely prince wears an expression of dreamy calm. Michelangelo also sketched in a dog, very faint now in the foreground, not barking in a wild rage, as Virgil described it, but watching quietly, contributing to the dreamy atmosphere, a dog in doggy wonder. Tommaso's thank-you letter survives. He was ill at the time; the drawings inspired him to get better.

In 1564, the year of Michelangelo's death, the counterreformational Council of Trent, which had been meeting on and off for almost twenty years, issued a series of decrees designed to clamp down on pagan license, but baroque artists found it hard to resist a subject so suitable for decorating high interiors. Annibale Carracci painted a Ganymede on the gallery ceiling of the Farnese Palace in Rome, although Tiepolo, heaven-painter par excellence, managed to restrict himself to just one. As visitors mounted the Grand Staircase in the *Residenz* of the Bishop of Würzburg, they found their gaze drawn higher and higher by Ganymede and the eagle. Doubtless many thought of the soul rising up to God, and one or two thought of Nero.

The personal style of religious devotion that developed in the late Middle Ages took the allegory of love very seriously indeed. Dante's beloved Beatrice had taken him as far as Paradise on the wings of love, and for a Renaissance neo-Platonist like Marsiglio Ficino love formed the very centerpiece of his philosophy, the force that made relationships between things, the ties that bound the universe. It was not only that

Zeus, according to Xenophon, loved Ganymede's soul. The image of uplifting in itself encapsulated movement from the worldly plane of physical attraction into the realm of pure celestial joy. This is Eros at his best, that enterprising ambitious love that shrinks the gap between heaven and earth, the pious man always reaching up to the golden apples on the top of the tree of heaven, just out of reach.

Religious emblem books, albums of inspirational talking pictures, which flourished in the first centuries of printing, rammed the message home. The first and most influential was that produced by Andrea Alciato in Augsburg in 1531 and reprinted with modifications in over 150 editions after that. In these books, Ganymede has a starring role. Below the woodcut of the eagle and child are messages, made memorable by rhyme, in Latin and later in vernaculars. "Where did ancient Homer get it from," they ask rhetorically, "this fiction? He who excelled in mind and wise counsel, God's delights, was believed to be snatched away into Jupiter's high presence." It is easy to be skeptical about the spiritual reading of Zeus's love for the handsome prince—many of those drawn to neo-Platonic Ganymede showed more than a connoisseur's fondness for male nudes but these emblem-books became by far the commonest images of the eagle and child in circulation, and the image is, in itself, very powerful.

The emblem of Ganymede had a prominent place near the front of Alciato's *Emblemata,* before all the images illustrating the virtues and the vices, in the preface, as it were, representing "religion" itself, and his motto was *in Deo laetandum,* "God is for rejoicing in." Delight in wisdom and mental excellence, through the medium of imaginative images, was exactly what the emblem-books claimed to promote. Ganymede is the books' advertisement, the soul setting off on a venture into spiritual improvement, the emblematic reader of the emblem-books (see Fig. 9, p. 214). Very often the printers included excerpts of Xenophon's etymology of Ganymede's name in the strange alphabet of the Greeks— "delighting in thoughts." It has been argued that there was a decline in the quantity and seriousness of images of Ganymede after the edicts of the counterreformational Council of Trent, but if there were fewer new oil paintings and frescoes and if a large proportion of those made the Trojan prince an anonymous baby, nevertheless the neo-Platonic Ganymede of Alciato's emblem-books was multiplying through the

9. A Ganymede emblem after Michelangelo's famous drawing for Tommaso
de' Cavalieri with a pointed quotation from Xenophon's *Symposium* 8.30:
"named not for physical attractiveness . . . but mental attractiveness."
Achille Bocchi, *Symbolicae Quaestiones* (Bologna, 1555).

printing press. As a celebration of the high-minded uses of the image,
emblematic Ganymede, lifting off the ground, could stand as the
frontispiece for the whole counterreformational project.[8]

In the eighteenth century, as neoclassicism made its first moves to
clear the decks of rococo swirls, a remarkable fresco was opportunely
found in the new ancient classical style, showing Ganymede offering
wine to Zeus and getting rewarded with a kiss. Johannes J. Winckelmann, founder of the discipline of art history and great fan of the antique, thought it the "most beautiful painting ever to emerge from
antiquity into the light of the present age." On his deathbed, however,
Anton Raphael Mengs, neoclassicism's founder, confessed he had done
rather more than restore the fresco, he had painted it from scratch.

Goethe transformed Ganymede into a rapturous environmentalist,
full of the joys: *Wie im Morgenglänze . . .* —"How, in the flashes of

morning, you wrestle . . ." he wrote, before trying again: *Wie im Morgenrot* . . . —"How, in the blush of dawn, you wrestle me red-faced, O Spring, beloved . . ." In the final stanza Ganymede feels his feet rising off the ground: *Ich komm, ich komme! Wohin? Ach, wohin? Hinauf!* "I'm coming! Whither? . . . where? Up there! . . ." Franz Schubert, not necessarily one for the ladies, and Hugo Wolf, among many others, made the poem into a song. There had already been several cantatas on the subject of Ganymede, and in the eighteenth century he featured in the Spanish operettas called *zarzuelas*. Antoine Elwart's *Uplifting of Ganymede* evoked its subject quite successfully without a text, on piano, cello, violin and clarinet.

Finally in 1959 the pop artist Robert Rauschenberg produced an assemblage that he called *Pail for Ganymede* made, among other things, from an inverted tin can and a tap. Art historians wonder if it isn't a jokey allusion to Rembrandt's incontinent baby; they further suspect that his famous assemblage *Canyon,* a canvas from which hangs a stuffed condor and a bundle on a rope, may be another sly allusion to the Trojan boy. The artist says nothing.

The ancient astronomers who introduced astrology to Europe in the years after 400 BC, starting something of a craze, had identified Ganymede with the constellation Aquarius, arguing that Aquarius's stream of seventeen stars could not be something as ordinary as water but rather resembled the divine liquid served by Ganymede to Zeus. Aquarius was one of that special series of constellations that mark the narrow band of sky to which the sun and the planets confine themselves, that is, the stars that seem to lie level with the flat plane of the solar system as we tilt around the Sun. This means that Ganymede's rising up to heaven carried an astrological significance: "His beauty was it, not the body's pride / That made him great Aquarius stellified. / And that mind most is beautiful and high, / And nearest comes to Divinity, / That furtherest is from spot of Earth's delight . . ." as the Elizabethan poet George Chapman put it in his hymn to Cynthian Diana. It has been suggested, therefore, that Rembrandt's pissing baby Ganymede is a sly allusion to the water-pourer of the zodiac, which also means that Robert Rauschenberg's *Pail for Ganymede* may be a harbinger of the New Age.[9]

For, around 130 years BC, Hipparchus, greatest of Greek astronomers and inventor of trigonometry, was comparing his own observations of the rising and setting of constellations with those recorded by earlier star-gazers in Iraq and made an astonishing discovery: The stars were late. Aries was not where it was supposed to be at this time of year; the celestial clock was losing time, observed Hipparchus, amazingly. Though he didn't know it, he had discovered a wobble in the Earth's axis, like the tiny circle within a circle traced by the axis of a spinning top as it spins, a "precession of equinoxes" that would not see the heavens in their "proper" position again for some tens of thousands of years, a Platonic year. Before very long March 21, the equinox, would see the sun rising in Pisces. That, of course, is exactly what happened; people who say they have been "born under" the sign of Aries because their birthday sun dawned in early April are talking of how the heavens used to be in c.500 BC. That also means that in a few hundred years the spring equinox will see the vernal Sun dawning in the constellation Aquarius, an idea that got some people very excited in the 1960s, and the Age of Ganymede will begin.

TWO GANYMEDES

From the Middle Ages right up until the twentieth century, therefore, the image of Ganymede has recurred in European art and culture, and he has found his way into the very centers of power, into palaces and even onto the doors of the local church of the Bishop of Rome. But there is something quite odd about the prevalence of this lovely boy. For this was a period in which homosexual genital acts were officially an abomination, and those caught committing them were being periodically tortured and/or burned to death, and yet this Ganymede of bishops, popes and kings was also the prime emblem of that vice, the boy who warmed the bed of the king of the gods. Here he was, on the very doors of St. Peter's, in an age when Christians were not supposed even to mention his vice by name.

Perhaps some didn't know what he stood for, but how could they not know? The Greeks had made no secret of it. Some must have read in their copy of Athenaeus that Sophocles in a play had referred to Ganymede's "thighs setting tyrant Zeus on fire."[10] And having been passed through the whispered consonants of the Etruscan language, Ganymede became catamite, then Latin "*catamitus,*" which the *Oxford*

English Dictionary translates as "boy kept for unnatural purposes": a little linguistic shift hinting at many years of knowing interpretation.

In Hellenistic Alexandria the myth of the boy and the eagle was used to flatter handsome youths, the ancient equivalent of "Heaven must be missing an angel . . ." There were several variations on the theme: from the mock-resigned—"Take him, Zeus. I can't compete with the King of Heaven, I ask only that Charidemus kiss me good-bye"—to the mock-hysterical—"Dennis is missing. Is he now Ganymede's second? Does his skin show now the marks where the eagle's claws dug in?"—to the downright manipulative—"Come hide yourself with me, Mysian boy. If you don't, Zeus will swoop down and get you, unless he's very much changed."[11]

The satirist Lucian (second century AD) put Ganymede at the center of his bathetic *Dialogues of the Gods.* In one of these, Ganymede is a simple shepherd boy of no intellectual attainment, who is at first surprised that the eagle has transformed into a man and then further surprised that this man wants to sleep with him. In another dialogue Hera is mad with jealousy. At least the women you seduce stay on earth, she says, but this effeminate Phrygian boy is always around. You can't take the cup from him without kissing him and so you are always taking the cup and drinking more than you need, always from the part of the cup his lips touched. And the other day I caught you, father of all, you with your big beard, squatting down to play knucklebones with him. Don't think you can pull the wool over my eyes. I know what's going on. Why don't you marry him, if he means so much more to you than your wife? This theme of Hera's jealousy was not Lucian's invention. Virgil had made Ganymede's elevation the reason for Hera's hostility to the entire royal family of Troy, the family from which his patron Augustus claimed descent.[12] To make matters worse, this mortal had taken a role away from her own daughter, Hebe, goddess of youthful bloom, who had previously carried the refreshments, but stumbled once.

When the early Christians came along, they were not in a mood to be lenient in their battle to the death with paganism, and zeroed in mercilessly on the faggoty nonsense of Greek religion. Only the first in a long tradition, neither Minucius Felix nor Clement of Alexandria can resist mentioning Ganymede's name, usually as the triumphant climax to a list of the gods' heterosexual seductions—not only was their chief divinity shameless enough to prey on mortal women, he even hunted boys in the shape of an eagle. It was hard to imagine the Christian God doing any such thing, the relationship between heavenly dove and favored Mary being, of course, infinitely innocent; and nothing whatsoever to do with her instant pregnancy.

The dangerous Ganymede of homosexuality proper remained by far the most popular reading of the myth until the Renaissance, and a threat to spiritual Ganymede long after that. In the Middle Ages Ganymede features as the very spokesman of homosexual desire, an alternative to heterosexual reproductive alliances, in direct competition with Zeus's wife Hera, with Helen, the paragon of female beauty, or with Hebe, his predecessor in pouring wine. If in the fourteenth century the Latin *Ovidius moralizatus* by Pierre Bersaire compared Ganymede to St. John and talked of getting close to God, the anonymous *Ovide moralisé* was worried enough to append a condemnation of sodomy as "against law and against nature." Even at the height of the neo-Platonic wave, "spotless" Ganymede never eclipsed the worldly version altogether. Marlowe pays lip service to Xenophon's etymology, by having Zeus describe his boyfriend as *"darling of my thoughts,"* but the boy is clearly a toyboy, playing with Hera's jewelry. Goethe may have made his Ganymede into a sensitive poet, getting high on the beauty of nature, but he was well aware of the toyboy version, and may have been writing in the teeth of it. His friend Christoph Martin Wieland was producing a version of Lucian's dialogues and had already published the one about Ganymede's rivalry with Hera.

From an early date, therefore, we are presented with two Ganymedes. But which one is authentic? Ganymede the catamite kept for homosexual purposes, symbol of the faggoty decadence of pagan religion, or Ganymede the angel rising up to heaven, spotless and pure, model of piety? The answer I think is to be found in his headgear.

GANYMEDE: THE FACTS

"Where did ancient Homer get it from?" asks Alciato's emblem-book under the woodcut of Eagle and Child. There is a short answer to that. Homer didn't get it from anywhere. The father of European literature (conventionally dated 730 BC, though quite possibly writing fifty years later) mentions no eagle, and it was several centuries before artists supplied one. No eagle, then, and Homer doesn't mention love, and it is clear that he lets Zeus himself off the hook. It was "the gods" in general who "snatched up" Ganymede, he says, to be cupbearer for Zeus, leaving open the possibility that the king of the gods knew nothing of the abduction and was simply presented with the Trojan prince at dinner one Olympian evening. What Homer does record is that Zeus felt guilty enough about what the gods had done to give Ganymede's father a team of divine horses as recompense for the loss of his son.[13] In fact, Homer only ever mentions Ganymede when he is talking about these horses. Though there are several scenes on Mount Olympus, scenes of the gods feasting and drinking, Ganymede is nowhere to be found. It is Hebe or even hobbling Hephaestus who performs the cupbearer's role. This is strange. I don't think Homer feels entirely comfortable with Ganymede. So why mention him at all?

After Homer, Ganymede disappears for perhaps a hundred and fifty years, although other Trojan stories were popular. When he puts in an occasional appearance, Zeus is a little more involved. An early religious hymn, the Hymn to Aphrodite, describes how the goddess came in disguise to Trojan prince Anchises and was made pregnant by him with Aeneas, future founder of Rome (hence Julius Caesar's devotion to Aphrodite's Roman equivalent, Venus; she was Caesar's great-great . . . grandmother). In the hymn, Aphrodite is rather ashamed of herself for dallying with a mortal, and comforts herself with parallels such as Zeus and Ganymede: Here it is Zeus himself who snatched the boy because of his beauty to be wine pourer in his house, though he didn't actually lay hands on him, but carried him skyward on a gust of wind.[14] Who was the first explicitly (it is already implicit here) to introduce "*erōs*" to Zeus's appreciation of Ganymede's beauty is unknown, but there is a leading candidate. Many years later, when Zeus's love for Ganymede was a commonplace, someone wrote in the margins of a text that the source for this "snatching" of the boy was one Ibycus of Rhegium, who "flourished" probably around 550–535 BC, though his dates are not certain. Very little of Ibycus's work survives, but we know he wrote about gods and heroes and talked often of his own extreme susceptibility to the charms of boys ("over-Eighteen" *meirakia*, Striplings, adds the Byzantine lexicon, quickly).[15] With the story of Ganymede he could do both at the same time. The reference to the boy being snatched came in a poem dedicated to a youth, Gorgias, it seems; and it is a reasonable assumption that the poet was trying to account for his own susceptibility to male beauty by citing all-powerful Zeus as a precedent.

The commentator notes that Ibycus also wrote of the goddess Dawn, something of a serial rapist, snatching another Trojan prince, Tithonus, and a worm-eaten fragment refers to someone or something "off the earth . . . cutting the thick air." But the evidence stays circumstantial; we have not caught Zeus red-handed yet; there is still the possibility that Ibycus was talking of a gust of wind.[16] A possible contemporary, "Theognis," likewise used Zeus's love for Ganymede to justify his own love of boys: "Even Zeus, king of immortals, once fell in love with Ganymede, snatched him, introduced him to Olympus and made him a god [daimōn] who could hold on to the lovely flower of his boyhood." By the end of the fifth century, in 408 BC to be precise, Euripides wrote one of his nastiest and most cynical plays, Orestes. There he seems to have someone talk of Ganymede as Zeus's "bedmate" or "spouse" (eunetēs), but unfortunately there is something wrong with the text.[17]

Maybe a decade or two after Ibycus, Ganymede makes his entrance into the history of art.[18] It is not a grand entrance. Blink and you might have missed it. Walk and you might have crushed it underfoot: a fragment of a cup, surviving for years on the Acropolis of Athens, where it may once have been left in a temple, hopeful gift for a god. It shows in miniature detail a group of immortals watching Heracles fight the lion. A boy is with them; there is no label, but no alternative identification is proposed; the gods tolerated only one young teenager in the corridors of Olympus; the boy is Ganymede, it seems, for sure.[19]

As we reach the 500th year counting back from Christ's birth, and the end of the archaic period, Ganymede becomes suddenly very popular, just at the point when painters are moving on from the age of black figures incised and into its photographic negative, the age of red figure. Now painters cover most of the vase with that wonderful black metallic gloss they have discovered, but leave areas unpainted that will therefore stand out in the red of pure fired clay. You don't incise details anymore, therefore, you paint them in outline, with an array of fine and finer brushes, to make heavier or lighter lines, painting in relief. And what do you paint? Scenes of love and abduction, loves of gods,

10. Zeus descends with thunder and lightning (the winged object at left)
and drops his scepter in order to abduct Ganymede, whose cockerel crows
in alarm. Impossible to see in this photograph are the surrounding
inscriptions: "The boy is beautiful! The boy is beautiful! The boy is
beautiful!" Cup by Penthesilea Painter (c.470).

loves of Zeus, Ganymedes. Ganymede pouring the nectar for Zeus and
the other gods, Ganymede running from Zeus, Ganymede struggling
with Zeus, Ganymede abducted, Ganymede hanging around.

On a cup by Oltos, a pioneer of the new technique, a boy stands
naked before Zeus and pours liquid for him in the company of gods:
Ganymede (Fig. 11). More gods in procession with Heracles, seen on
fragments of a big-eared cup; one of the figures is a long-haired youth
smaller in stature than the rest; Ganymede again. Now then, a great big
wine bowl of the new simple "bell-shaped" design with a famous image
of a blond boy on one side holding a cockerel in one hand and a hoop in
the other. On the other side Zeus with a scepter strides purposefully and
makes an arresting gesture; Zeus pursuing the Trojan prince. The work
is by one of the great painters of the period. He never revealed his name,
so we have dubbed him the Berlin Painter, after a magnificent piece
of work there. The Berlin Painter must have had some success with
this particular subject—"Let me have something like that one I saw at
Leagros's symposium, please, with Zeus pursuing Ganymede"—and
painted it again, maybe several times; scholars point to four, and a crude

calculation based on a guess at the tiny percentage of Athenian vases that have survived would mean our Berlin Painter originally made many times more, perhaps even hundreds.[20]

By now there is wide agreement first that it was Zeus himself who carried off Ganymede[21]—you can see him with his arms around the boy—and second that it was love that made him do it. How do we know the vase painters think Zeus is in love and not just recruiting a servant? Because now and then we see Eros provoking the action. One of the earliest images, in fact, has a slightly comical scene of a cockerel grabbed at by Ganymede, himself pursued by Zeus, who is being goaded into a frenzy by Eros with a cattle prod.[22] It makes the king of gods look slightly ridiculous, but Eros goading is a symbol of distance, of the space that Zeus has been forced to cross to come down to earth. Even without Eros, love could be read into the scene by an Athenian audience, since the cock is a love gift, as indicative of the giver's intentions as a dinner *à deux* or a bunch of flowers, exactly the kind of present an Athenian of the time would offer to a boy he admired as a sign of his admiration, it seems.

Well, that is the theory, but the drawback here is that though Ganymede very often carries a cock, we never see Zeus hand it over, and it seems to imply too much backstory. If it's a love gift, then Zeus has

11. Ganymede pours immortalizing liquid into Zeus's offering bowl (*phialē*). Hestia (plus Aphrodite, Ares, Athena, Hermes, and Hebe) looks on. Cup signed by Oltos (*c.*510–500).

12. Eros cattle-prods Zeus, who pursues Ganymede, who
pursues a cockerel. The inscriptions are nonsense letters.
Black-figure alabastron by Diosphos Painter (*c.*490).

been courting Ganymede; he doesn't, so to speak, come out of a blue
sky. I think it is better to see the cock as a symbol of the particular
beauty of the male, an *attribute* of Ganymede; on one vase it is noticeable
that whereas boys are handed cocks and even a miniature stag (so obviously not a snapshot of daily life), a naked courtesan is given a hen instead.[23] It is interesting moreover that the gods' other rape victims, male
and female, never seem to have received any presents beforehand. The
goddess Dawn doesn't ply Tithonus with gifts. She just arrives, very
suddenly, and he runs for his life.

Nevertheless, if a seduction seems too much of an innovation, the
amorous motive seems clear. Zeus is pursuing. Ganymede is running.
Some make it a rather stately affair, as if Zeus is calling on others to arrest him. For others it is an energetic chase around the side of the cup.
Finally there are scenes showing Zeus getting to grips with a Ganymede
struggling to free himself. The lightning bolt held by Zeus or thrown to
the ground to free his hands doesn't just identify the god; perhaps here
it represents real lightning, a *katabasis,* a "coming-on-down" of Zeus, as
Ganymede is lifted by the sky god, very dramatic.

Less metaphysical is the abduction represented in a famous pot sculpture from Olympia. First a grimy bearded head was found during German excavations in November 1878 and put in the bottom of the display

13. Zeus abducts Ganymede with his cockerel. The only remaining Ganymede of the three known to have decorated Zeus's sanctuary at Olympia, probably intended for a high place, the pair literally rising into the air. A terra cotta masterpiece of the early classical style (c.470), it was smashed and its fragments dispersed by the Christians when the sanctuary was closed down in the early fifth century AD, and put back together again by the Germans during the Second World War.

cabinet. In November 1938 the Germans found the hem of a long shirt and a statue base, and a few days later its left foot. On January 17, 1939, they found a headless man carrying a headless boy under his arm, as if he were a rugby player about to score a try.[24] Three years later the right foot and the boy's head turned up, and in 1942 the shattered sculpture was put back together for the first time since the Christians had smashed it and used it for groundfill, having closed Olympia down. The statue was of Ganymede being abducted and is now illustrated in every book on Greek art as a prime example of the new classical style (Fig. 13). Here too, what Ganymede is to Zeus, a cock is to Ganymede; as he is bundled under Zeus's arm, he himself bundles a rooster. Most scholars think this particular sculpture was probably placed high up on a pillar or on the roof of a building somewhere in the Olympic complex. In that case Zeus really would be rising through the air, Ganymede watching the world grow smaller.[25]

Centuries later Pausanias, writing a guide to ancient Greece, saw a couple of other Ganymedes at Olympia, a Zeus on a column reaching out with his hand and, opposite, images of Zeus and Ganymede, dedicated by a man from Thessaly around 450 BC. Maybe a decade earlier another Ganymede had been set up; our guide says it was later placed along the side of Zeus's great temple, one of many dedications made by a father in gratitude for his son's recovery from a wasting disease. So all three of the known "Ganymede" sculptures of this early period come from the sanctuary of Olympian Zeus, in the territory of the rich and prosperous and large but not terribly famous community of Elis in the western Peloponnese.

Using the dates provided by the vast *Iconographic Lexicon of Classical Mythology,* we find just six images of Ganymede before 500 BC. Around 490, the time of Marathon, he starts to show up much more often, and over the next forty years, as Athens defeats the Persians and makes an empire of her own out of "the liberated," he puts in almost fifty appearances—not the most popular mythological figure, but up there. Then suddenly, around 450, without any warning, he is gone. After a few decades in the spotlight Ganymede has vanished once more. A century or so later he is back, and this time with a bigger bird than a cockerel, with an eagle, which is first mentioned in a description of a bronze work by Alexander's court sculptor, Leochares. We have no idea at which point in Leochares' long career (*c.* 370–320 BC) he made this famous statue, but it happens that in Italy at about the same time we find vase painters showing Ganymede carried off by a large white swan.[26]

On one point, the vase painters stick closely to Homer's text. Whether or not he was softened up beforehand with gifts, Ganymede was abducted: There is no possibility of him going to heaven of his own accord, prospecting for a job. He is a passive participant in his elevation, and to convey the sense of abduction there must be some running away. Some, however, have seen something less than complete determination in Ganymede's avoidance strategy, even a little coquetry. This may be what's called "blaming the victim," but the question remains: What is Ganymede a victim of?

Of course we are dealing with a myth. In the real world, any Athenian caught assaulting a boy under Eighteen—and that Ganymede is younger than an ephebe is strongly emphasized—could be punished with death on the same day. No defendant would go free who tried to justify the crime by citing the example of Zeus.[27] But if sexual rape is a terrible crime in life, that makes the question of what Zeus is really up to all the more pressing. Does paganism allow its chief god to err so badly? And if it does, are the actions of gods to be abhorred? Euripides, if the text is sound, seems to raise the prospect of sex with Ganymede explicitly, but is he innovating or simply speaking out, tearing back the veils of hypocrisy, voicing the assumption that everybody would make—that Zeus, king of the gods, is a child abuser?

We are privileged to be able to view the myth of Ganymede in a series of snapshots as it evolves over two hundred and fifty years. We don't by any means have the whole story, but apparently we have the critical moments in its evolution, something that could not be said about other important tales. For two hundred years the poets stick to Homer's story: Ganymede is chosen as cupbearer because of his beauty, end of story. Then Ibycus seems to put Zeus in the context of other human and divine loves, and a few decades later the vase painters follow suit. Ganymede's beauty stirs desire in Zeus. Having grabbed him in his fit of desire, Zeus finds him a role on Olympus, serving the wine. Then Euripides stages a play that seems to say that Zeus and Ganymede shared a bed. Are we surprised? Should we be?

What is it that changes over the centuries? The plot or the telling of it? Is myth progressively homosexualized? Or is sex implied already in Homer's version—why else would you have your wine served by a beautiful boy?

HOMER'S GANYMEDE

The first thing we must do is attempt to put Ganymede in contexts. I have argued that Homer is uncomfortable with Ganymede on Olympus: (1) the insistence on a troupe of gods to get him there—normally, when a mortal is taken, there is someone to point the finger at, and of course an enterprising, boundary-crossing *love* is implied in all such abductions, not least if the mortal is outstandingly beautiful, so Homer seems to be avoiding an obvious motive; (2) the careful way Homer, having given him a job, doesn't let him do it, even forcing Hephaestus to perform a comic turn as wine-pourer to distract our attention.

Now there are various reasons why Homer could be reticent. (1) Ganymede is long gone. He came to Olympus, grew old, started spilling wine, was retired, and by now is dead and buried. I really doubt that. One thing that later writers are all agreed upon is that Ganymede was ageless as soon as he reached Olympus, and a crumbling mortal serving immortal gods their wine is not to be thought of. Once you are past the Hours or Seasons who guard the gates of Olympus, you are in a timeless zone. On arrival Ganymede became both immortal and ageless, an eternal Boy. (2) Homer is emphatic about the absolute distinction between mortals and immortals, about the need for Achilles, in particular, to die. A pretty young prince who has escaped death on account of his looks might spoil that vision, detract from the grim facing up to extinction that is the theme of the *Iliad,* for Achilles was terribly handsome too. (3) With the gods plotting the downfall of his hometown, Troy, it might be awkward to have Ganymede overhearing the plans to annihilate his race.

But why then does Homer need Ganymede at all? Well actually, all the early occasions (two in Homer, one in the Homeric Hymn to Aphrodite) on which Ganymede's myth comes up are concerned with Aeneas, and, as it happens, this Aeneas has been seen as one of the few fixed points in the whole of Homer's poem.[28] Unlike most ancient poets writing about the heroic past, Homer has never, or hardly ever, been shown to have an ulterior motive, caught red-handed "zooming" into the present time to say: "And ever since then, the people of X have always sacrificed a peacock to the goddess," or: "And he took the calf which they had made, and burnt it in the fire, and ground it to powder, and strowed it upon the water, and made the children of Israel drink of it."[29]

The major exception is when Homer talks of Aeneas, son of Anchises, a minor Trojan royal, and the goddess Aphrodite. Aeneas is just about to die at the hands of Achilles when Poseidon warns: "Zeus will be furious . . . Aeneas is supposed to survive, so that the line of Dardanus may not perish without seed [*aspermos*] without being seen [*aphantos*] . . . For now Zeus hates Priam's line, and as it stands, it will be the vim [*biē*] of Aeneas that will king it over Trojans, followed hereafter by his children's children" (20.301–308). The prophecy sticks out so sharply from the rest of the text that many have thought Homer must have been working for a non-Greek royal family or a family with royal pretensions that claimed descent from Aeneas, the so-called Aineiadai. It is a neat theory: Homer has been paid to paint a vivid image of Troy by a family claiming descent from the only survivor, and in the course of his poem the poet notes that the role of this family was precisely to ensure that Troy would remain visible, i.e., to pay poets like him for poems like the *Iliad*. Certainly, Homer was composing at an interesting time for the ruined city, a time when the dribble of Greek settlers into the region and onto the site of Troy was starting to look like a more substantial trickle, so it seems entirely possible that Homer's prophecy about Aeneas is informed by Greek exchanges with locals, with current local myths or local politics, even if we don't need to think of him actually pocketing a patron's generous fee for thus flattering "the descendants of Aeneas."[30]

But why would this family of "Sons of Aeneas," if they even existed at the time, insist on a great-great . . . great-uncle in heaven? Well, maybe they had a fine stable of horses that they boasted were descended from those that Zeus gave to Ganymede's father in recompense for the loss of his son. The immortal horses play a key role in the myths about Troy. They had been the cause, years earlier, of the *First* Trojan War, led by Heracles, who considered the horses were owed him for services rendered. Centuries later the locals still refused to honor Heracles because of this first war, although they did honor the heroes of the later expedition, including Achilles. Strabo thought this tradition very odd. Heracles evidently had not damaged the city so badly that it couldn't be destroyed again later in the great Trojan War, but Achilles and his friends had annihilated it.[31] The "horses for Ganymede" were perhaps firmly rooted in local tradition.[32] At any rate, Homer certainly knew of this first Trojan expedition, and by mentioning the horses in the *Iliad* he could subtly recall that First Trojan War, but if he really felt uncomfortable with Olympian Ganymede's abduction, he could have cast a veil over the way the horses had been acquired, or made up another story.[33]

Perhaps it wasn't just the horses. Perhaps to have an ancestor like Ganymede serving the gods was also a mark of distinction. Ganymede can certainly be seen as a reflection of Troy's regal grandeur, increasing the element of tragedy in the fall of the kings of Troy, a family so linked to the gods, at the hands of the gods themselves. Are there any parallels for such a myth in Turkey or the East? In his collection of Levantine myths that look a bit like Greek myths, Martin West matches Ganymede with Elijah, who was walking along with Elisha one day when "behold, there appeared a chariot of fire, and horses of fire, and parted them both asunder; and Elijah went up by a whirlwind into heaven." The people of

Jericho approached Elisha with an offer to send out a search party—
" 'Behold now, there be with thy servants fifty strong men; let them go,
we pray thee and seek thy master: lest peradventure the Spirit of the
Lord hath taken him up, and cast him upon some mountain, or into
some valley.' " It searches for three days without luck.[34] Walter Burkert,
meanwhile, has suggested that Ganymede's eagle finds a parallel in the
old Mesopotamian myth of Etana, whose fall is broken by the bird who
takes him as high as heaven.[35]

But I think we have to seek more local patterns. And they do exist.
From the reports that have come down to us, the area from which
Ganymede disappeared was a veritable Bermuda Triangle for beautiful
young people. We can start with the story of how Aeneas himself came
into the world.

A LAKE CALLED SNATCHING

CASE 1 Anchises, minor Trojan royal, has been left at home while his
companions go cattle herding. He roams around the sheds and outbuild-
ings, strumming his lyre. Suddenly he realizes that he is not alone. A
beautiful woman is standing in front of him, dressed in robes as bright as
fire and intricately embroidered. She is covered in jewelry: twisted
brooches, earrings shaped like flowers, necklaces looped around her
throat. She is noticeably tall. Which goddess are you? he asks. No goddess
at all, she replies, but a mortal, a princess from Phrygia to the east, but I
had a Trojan nurse, in case you are wondering how we can communicate.
I was enjoying the hunt with Artemis and playing with the nymphs when
suddenly I was swept off my feet by Hermes and carried over fields, both
tilled and ownerless, places where savage beasts roam. I began to think I
would never again feel the ground beneath my feet. Then Hermes
dropped me off and went back to Olympus, saying that I should be your
wife. There really is no alternative. Introduce me to your family. My father will be only too pleased to provide a dowry. Then we can start
preparing the wedding. Never mind the wedding, says Anchises, leading
her indoors. She follows him, face averted, eyes downcast.[36]

Now, of course, the woman is Aphrodite and she has been lying
through her teeth, but what is interesting or amusing is the fact that her
elaborate cover story includes being supernaturally swept off her feet

and abducted, as if the poet imagines this is just the kind of explanation a Trojan will find convincing.

CASE 2 Eos, the lady Dawn, was the most successful and notorious of all heavenly abductors. Images of this large winged woman pursuing or grabbing youths are by far the most popular images of divine rape on Athenian vases and a whole range of other media all over the Greek world.[37] She often appeared on the corners of temple roofs, victim in hand. A late source explains her erotic tendency with a story that Aphrodite had found her in bed with Ares, with whom Aphrodite herself was having a fling, and punished her with uncontrollable lust. Uncontrollable she may have been, but Dawn never let her standards drop. She only ever fell for the handsomest mortals on the planet.

Most famous of all Dawn's lovers is beautiful Tithonus, a prince of Troy, in fact King Priam's brother. Dawn abducted him and asked Zeus to make him immortal, which request he granted, but she forgot to ask for eternal youth. When the gray hairs appeared, Dawn stopped visiting Tithonus's bed, and later still she had to make a resolution, put him in a room and closed the door. There he babbles endlessly. Later we hear he was transformed into a cicada, desiccated, senile, endlessly chattering. "Silly woman" Aphrodite calls Dawn in the Hymn as she recounts this sorry tale to Anchises, who having gone to bed with a mysterious Phrygian princess has now woken up to find he is in bed with a gigantic supernatural female.

CASE 3 Among the Mariandyni who lived just north of the Bosphorus they had a festival dirge in which they repeatedly invoked the name of an ancient hero called Bormos.[38] He was the son of a rich and distinguished man, and of surpassing beauty and loveliness. One day he went to fetch water and never came back. The people went seeking him, chanting his name in this dirge, and they are still looking to this day.[39]

CASE 4 On their journey to Colchis to find the Golden Fleece, Jason and the Argonauts stop off in the country opposite Istanbul to make repairs. The youth Hylas, Heracles' boyfriend, goes to fetch water. Darkness has fallen, but the moon is full. He finds what he is looking for, but as he leans over the spring, the local nymph sees his lovely face. Her heart skips a beat. She has found a husband. She reaches out and puts her left hand around his neck, longing to plant a kiss on his tender mouth. With her right arm she pulls him under. Someone hears a cry and rushes to help, but Hylas is nowhere to be seen. When Heracles hears the news he is distraught. Streams of sweat pour off him. His blood boils. Like a mad bull he wanders over the mountain bellowing, but in vain. Hylas has entered another dimension. Eventually Heracles gives up—he has Labors to perform—but before he goes he extorts a promise from the locals to discover the fate of Hylas, alive or dead: "and that is why even to this day the people of Cius ask after Hylas." Another author elaborates: "There is a mountain-ranging festival in which they march in procession and call Hylas, as if their expedition is to look for him."[40]

Cius is now the resort of Gemlik, where the people of Istanbul retreat from the summer heat. Not far away ancient scholars identified the site from which Ganymede disappeared, a lake called "Snatching," *Harpagia,* probably somewhere near Troy or in Mysia.[41] And Aphrodite tells Anchises that when Ganymede was grabbed, his father Tros was seized with "unsoothable grief." He did not know whither the whirlwind had snatched him, and "he was wont to grieve for him, always, all days" (ll. 207–10).

DEAD GANYMEDE

In early Greek poetry characters quite often talk as if the chance of being swept away is a constant risk.[42] At one point in the *Iliad* Helen unwishes the entire Trojan War—she'd rather she had been swept away by the wind into the mountains or into the sea on the day her mother bore her[43]—and Euripides later based an entire play on the premise that only an image of Helen had been taken to Troy while she herself had been whisked off by Hermes to Egypt. Odysseus's wife, Penelope, thinks this must be what has happened to her son Telemachus when she doesn't hear from him for a while, and, when, in despair at her dire domestic situation, she asks Artemis to end it all, she imagines an alternative scenario of being blown away by a gust of wind and dropped into the ocean, just like "the daughters of Pandoreos." These were fair maidens, Penelope informs us, whose father was punished for stealing a special dog of Zeus's from Crete. The goddesses adopted them, gave them many gifts and accomplishments and arranged rather better suitors than orphans could have expected, but on the eve of marriage they were carried off by the Harpies, who are literally "Snatchers," i.e., "snatching winds." Back on Ithaca, "snatched by Harpies" seems one of the more popular theories to explain the continuing nonappearance of Odysseus, the island's king. Gregory Nagy has suggested that these stories of the wind-snatched reveal an ancient conception of death: The soul is caught up and transported to the edge of the world, where it is dropped in Ocean and then makes its way over to Hades.[44]

If being snatched away by winds and deposited elsewhere was seen as a danger that had passed with the heroic age, being snatched by nymphs—nympholepsy—was seen as a real threat in the classical period.[45] The nymphs can inspire a mild kind of possession, or the subject may become prophetic, or epileptic. You might become "happy," says Aristotle, not by nature or by training but by a stroke of luck, like a nympholept.[46] On another level, suffering a "nymph seizure" might involve a physical removal from the world, like someone falling down a well or into a spring, "pulled in by the nymphs," a way of talking of death before time. It is not for nothing that they have given their name to the condition of nymphomania. Theocritus, who says it was not one nymph but several who pulled Hylas under, calls them "dread goddesses."

Ganymede too comes to stand (in) for death, inevitably. On one vase a well-swathed Ganymede has his eyes closed as he is carried off in the arms of Zeus.[47] We can already see that connection perhaps in the statue of Ganymede dedicated at Olympia for the recovery of a son from disease, just as Michelangelo's Ganymede might help to make Tommaso feel better. He becomes a popular figure on Roman sarcophagi and is used as a mythological metaphor for dead children in the work of Nicolaes Maes in the seventeenth century.

TURKISH GANYMEDE

There seem to be two separate elements in all these myths of the Disappeared of northwest Turkey. First a distinctive ritual search for the missing person, who is shouted for or mourned for. The search itself is what matters, and that implies that you don't know where he is or even who he is. Hylas's name, *Hulas,* is nothing more than the sound you utter, Hula, Hula, Halloo, Halloo, as you go seeking him in the mountains: the Cians don't know his "real name," so they call him Cooee! instead. The source and purpose of this ritual practice are unknown. It could be looking for a god to return with—I don't know—the rains, or the new spring growth, or the return of a constellation to the night sky, but it may well be more than a coincidence that the religion of the very ancient Hittites and their cultural descendants in Turkey was characterized by a number of "disappearing" and widely sought deities, not least Telepinu(s) the "noble god," a god of agriculture and fertility. He was eventually discovered fast asleep and woken up by a bee. He returned on the back of an eagle.

The second element is a large body of tales in which everyone knows exactly where the disappeared have gone. They are off with the nymphs, who are always, it seems, raping or seducing shepherds and herdsmen and conceiving children from them, in the area of Troy and indeed all over Turkey. This tradition is probably related to the ancient Mountain Mother of the region, and her nymph companions. She is well attested from the time of the Hittites onward, and often identified with Artemis, as at Ephesus, or Aphrodite, as at Aphrodisias in the south. These are quite different narratives from those myths of chaste nymphs raped by gods that feature strongly in Greek ethnic genealogies. Later authors were able to supply any number of nymphs for the Trojans and their allies to be descended from: "The prominence of nymphs in the resulting Trojan genealogy is unparalleled in Greek myth." Either the locals of Troy, having read Homer, were prompted to start putting as many nymphs as they could into their family trees, or else, much more likely in my view, Homer's references to nymphs in the ancestry of the Trojans and their allies reflect his knowledge of local tradition.

The myths of Hylas and Bormos, according to this theory, represent two distinct traditions of disappearing mortals—either searched for, or else snatched by nymphomaniac nymphs—which were inevitably amalgamated. But it is noticeable that "These tales of illicit love are sternly excluded from the formal genealogy of the royal family, which Homer places in the mouth of Aeneas."[48] And it is also very noticeable that Aeneas is given a true goddess, Aphrodite, as a mother, even though his father must swear, most suspicious this, to pretend it was "just one of those nymphs," if anyone should ask where he got his son from. In other words, it was all right for some minor chief to have a nymph as mother or great-grandmother, but a Trojan prince of the royal line, such as Tithonus, wanted Dawn to abduct him, a kind of supernymph, and the last of the Trojans, Aeneas, had an Olympian goddess, no less, as his rapist mother. It was all right for lesser breeds like the Mysians and Mariandyni to imagine when they reached their own spring or snatching lake that the one they were looking for had gone in there, but for pretenders to royalty in ancient times or in Homer's time, it was a touch of class, perhaps, to claim that their missing boy had been snatched up (from the shores of the lake) heavenward, to live not with some second-class faerie, but with Zeus himself and the family of Olympians.

Homer's prophecy about the special destiny of the line of Aeneas had tremendous consequences for the history of Ganymede, since centuries later, far away in Rome, a number of noble families started to polish up their own genealogies by pretending they were the new Trojans, that Aeneas indeed had refounded Troy in Italy. Among those families were the Julii, who took their name, they said, from Julus, son of Aeneas. And one of the Julii, it happened, was a man named Gaius Julius Caesar. Hence by an extraordinary historical accident, Aeneas, and with him Ganymede, came to be established at the heart of the ideology of the first dynasty of the Roman emperors, the Julii Claudii, "sons" of Caesar. Therefore Ganymede, great-great . . . great-uncle of Augustus himself, took up an important part in the plotting of the greatest Latin "national" epic, Virgil's *Aeneid,* as well as the greatest Greek, the *Iliad.* For why else is the goddess Hera so bitter and vengeful toward the last of the Trojans, if not out of bitterness and jealousy at her husband's unaccountable fondness for that Trojan boy who stole a position from her own daughter, Hebe?[49] And what about Ganymede's other great-great . . . great-nephews, the emperors Tiberius, Claudius, Nero . . . ? Didn't some of them too ascend to heaven after their deaths on eagle's wings, and didn't some of them give Ganymede a prominent place in the decoration of their palaces and grottoes: Nero on the ceiling of his Golden House in Rome, Tiberius above the entrance to his extraordinary cave at Sperlonga? These Ganymedes may well have been read as much more straightforward propaganda, vaunting the right of the Julii to rule.

GREEK GANYMEDE

Although Troy was of course very well established as Ganymede's home by no less an authority than Homer, there are two little references in later literature that locate him in Greece, or should I say her, for in one of these tales Ganymede is Ganymeda, a girl. The main sanctuary on the acropolis of the city of Phlius in the Peloponnese, southwest of Corinth, nestling in a grove of cypresses, was dedicated to a goddess called Dia, also called Hebe.[50] She appears on coins of the city. Our guide to ancient Greece, Pausanias, was told by the locals that she was not really called either Dia or Hebe, most anciently she was Ganymeda, and she too had disappeared, or at least there was no cult image of their most important goddess, not even a secret one, says Pausanias, who adds, most tantalizingly, that there was a "holy story" to explain this strange absence and that the sanctuary was "very very holy-awesome going way back."

The most prominent feature of the sanctuary was its role as a place of absolute asylum. Pausanias saw fetters hanging on the trees of the grove said to have been dedicated by the prisoners who made it this far; they had been lucky enough to reach a place where they too could vanish into thin air.[51] What is interesting about this little piece of gossip Pausanias heard is that it seems to preserve a pattern of thinking well past its sell-by date, a way of imagining deities that can be traced back to the Mycenaean period in the second millennium BC, but that had been more or less eradicated by the classical period and probably already by the time of Homer.

It had long been known that there had been a great Bronze Age civilization in Greece and Crete that had collapsed or been pushed off a steep slope, along with the Hittites and lots of other Mediterranean civilizations, at the end of the second millennium, somewhere around 1250 BC. Mycenae was one of the centers of this civilization, and other great palace-cities were discovered at Cnossus in Crete, Pylos, Tiryns, Thebes and other sites. At Cnossus and Pylos especially the excavators had unearthed numerous clay tablets covered with a strange writing. No one knew what it said. But on April 9, 1954, the *New York Times* announced that the script had been deciphered by one Michael Ventris and that it was an early form of Greek.

Since then scholars have had plenty of time to go over the documents, which are almost entirely Bronze Age red tape—Agamemnon ruled over a nightmare kingdom of accountants, customs officers and quartermasters. But some of the accounts and dockets relate to religious offerings, and some continuities emerge. Many of the later Greek gods are mentioned— Hermes, Hera, Zeus (Dios), Poseidon, Dionysus—but there is something quite unusual. Not only do we find Zeus and Poseidon, we also find Dia, Lady Zeus, and Posidaeia, Madame Poseidon. At least two Greek gods had been worshipped in both masculine and feminine genders. Lady Zeus only survived in a few cults, in Phlius, an out-of-the-way kind of place, and in neighboring Sicyon, where the herb called *paiderōs* flourished.

That the unique female Ganymeda appears in an extremely rare sanctuary of Lady Zeus seems too much of a coincidence. We could generate a nice little tetragram of relationships: Lord Zeus (Dios), his youth Ganymede, Lady Zeus (Dia), her youth (Hebe) Ganymeda. Perhaps Zeus and Ganymede were once aspects of a single deity, like Dia/Ganymeda. The link between them would be obvious at any rate in the city of Aegion, near Patras, where a Boy Zeus (Zeus Pais) was worshipped.[52] And it may well be significant that another strange "unbearded" Zeus, the "Greatest Kouros," a deity widely considered to have deep prehistoric roots, who is invoked in the Dictaean Hymn from Palaikastro on the east coast of Crete, and summoned to come to enjoy the song at the end of the year and leap into flocks, fruits, polities, etc., is described in line 2 of the Hymn as *Pankrates Ganos,* "All-Mastering Gleam," according to the most widely accepted version of the text.[53]

One other Greek place that claimed to have lost Ganymede was Chalcis, on the island of Euboea. Here—and again there is just one tiny haphazard reference—there was a place called *Harpagion,* "The Snatching," which was also a grove: "In this place grow myrtle trees of distinction," says the ancient writer.[54] A statue of a clothed Ganymede carried off by the eagle was found in the 1960s at Nea Lampsakos, about three miles from modern Chalcis on the road south, and it was immediately concluded that the site of Ganymede's disappearance had been found. Now in the National Archaeological Museum in Athens, it is said to be of local workmanship and dated to the fourth century BC, which would make it among the earliest of all surviving eagle and child statues, though stone statues are hard to date.

What more can we add to this? Chalcis had a temple to Olympian Zeus, the god of the Olympic Games in Peloponnesian Elis, the location, you will recall, of all the fifth-century statues of the Trojan boy so far known. And the late skeptical tradition said that Ganymede's remains had been buried by the temple of Olympian Zeus in the Troad. In Euboean Chalcis the temple of Olympian Zeus was used to display important treaties and inscriptions, and it also had a month called, uniquely, *Oly[mpi]ōn,* the occasion for a big important festival in honor of this "mountain Zeus." The festival of the month took place in spring, it has been suggested, just at the time when the myrtle blooms again. Moreover, Zeus's eagle appears flying on Chalcis's coins from a very early date, and on those of her colonies, sometimes snatching a snake. The Greeks usually put their most important city-god on their coins. Zeus of Olympus clearly rated very high in Chalcis, and Ganymede's grove was doubtless connected to the cult as the site where Zeus had come down, whether as a bird, as the wind rustling the leaves, or as a lightning bolt—the Greeks were terribly superstitious about lightning-struck people or places, places where Zeus had "gone down." In Chalcis's colony of Rhegium, hometown of Ibycus, there was a cult of Zeus Lightning (*Keraunos*).[55]

Whether or not one thinks this is important, one must at least give the people of Chalcis credit for hanging on to a counterintuitive version of the myth. For each time they told a visitor that Ganymede had disappeared from here, they must have been met with disbelief: But he's a Trojan, haven't you read Homer? Moreover, although a pair does not make a pattern, it is noticeable that the two places associated with Ganymede on the mainland are sacred groves close to the city, very different from the wild mountains and misty lake shores from which Anatolian youths tended to vanish. If only as an acknowledgment of the tenacity with which the cities of Phlius and Chalcis held on to their beliefs in the teeth of convention and common sense, I'm going to give Ganymede to the Greeks. Ganymede may be an authentic prehistoric entity, closely linked with Olympian Zeus, and through him with the eagle. How did he get to Troy? Maybe Homer put him there, impressed by its traditions of snatched youths. Maybe he arrived with Greek colonists. Maybe it was the place called "Snatching" that suggested a connection. Or maybe it stemmed from a pun. For there are,

oddly, a couple of places opposite "Snatching" called Ganos and Ga-
nias or Ganiai.[56]

Ganymede gets his second big bite at fame in Athens *c*.510–*c*.460 BC,
centuries after his first appearance. New context. New Ganymede. But
what is the context? Well, starting with the randy goddess Dawn, and
moving on from there, this was a period in which "Loves of Gods" enjoyed a sudden startling popularity in art and literature. Why? The
theme represented, on the one hand, a daring elevation of trivial mortal
affairs by association with divine amorousness, very like the *Amours des
Dieux* painted by Boucher and others for the last kings of France in the
eighteenth century—often the selfsame myths, in fact, although rococo
Dawn is not nearly as aggressive as her classical model.[57] On the other
hand, the theme of the gods' loves represented an equally daring understanding of the remote gods in human terms: gods like us. Indeed such
images, it has been said, represent a new religious sensibility at the end
of the archaic period, an unprecedented closeness between the sphere of
gods and the sphere of men.[58] These same gods' loves, however, came to
be viewed by thoughtful pagans and triumphant Christians as the very
epitome of impiety or the amorality of paganism.[59]

Undoubtedly the sudden popularity of Ganymede is part of this pattern of lovelorn gods, but there is more to it than that. The loves that the
painters choose to focus on can be seen as very particular choices, the
product of history, of war in foreign parts, of the coming of the Persians. Despite his long neglect, Ganymede's presence in this amorous
company is almost too predictable. Rampant Dawn and Trojan
Tithonus had long been linked to Zeus and Trojan Ganymede. Tithonus
and Ganymede were relatives; in many authors they are brothers. Then
again, Athens had important links at this time with two important centers of the Ganymede myth. Her most ancient imperial possession was
in the Troy region at Sigeum; indeed it was said that they had built its
walls from the ruins of Troy. Near the time when Ganymede starts appearing on vases, Sigeum was ruled by one of the sons of the dictator of
Athens and provided a refuge for another, the last of the tyrants, when
he was expelled by the new democracy. Moreover, one of Ganymede's
mainland haunts, Chalcis, came to the attention of Athenian foreign
policy at exactly the time he started to flourish on vases. One of the first
great victories of the new democracy in *c*.506 BC was to fight off an in-

vasion from the horse-mad aristocrats of Chalcis, not very far to the north. The Athenians invaded Chalcis, took control of the myrtle grove from which Ganymede had been abducted and resettled the horse-pasturing lands (Hippobotus) of their enemies with Athenian citizens. They set up shrines to their goddess Athena and leased out the rest.[60]

GANYMEDE'S HAT

If we want to explain Ganymede's reappearance in the potters' quarter in Athens in the decades before 500 BC, therefore, we have plenty of good historical reasons to choose from. In those days Athens held two of the places most strongly connected to Ganymede, Chalcis and the Troad. The tyrants had also begun work on a massive new temple to the Zeus most closely associated with Ganymede, Zeus Olympios. But what happens to him now that he has arrived? Most noticeable is his youth. Ganymede almost always looks under Eighteen. He often has a hoop to play with, a game that serves to distinguish older from younger boys—Athenian males under Eighteen were kept so close to their families, and so far away from the world, that they often seem very childish, even babyish, when we get a chance to meet them.[61]

Maybe Ganymede's extreme youth is a function of his service as wine pourer. Euripides was said to have performed the same role for a chorus of well-born youths when he was still "under Eighteen" (en paisin). Sappho, says a later writer, was always going on about her brother Larichus, praising him for pouring wine in the Presidium (prytaneion), the civic mess. She says it was the custom for "nice young nobles" (neoi) to pour wine. And there is some evidence that pouring wine was considered a noble office in the archaic period, that the custom survived in the most ancient and dignified contexts, long after slaves had taken over at the regular drinking party, that these wine pourers were often younger than those they served, and that, if the vase painters are anything to go by, they may sometimes have served stark naked. Under-Eighteens, like unmarried girls, were considered especially pure, untainted by aging and (its powerful agent) sex, and sometimes required to perform special holy tasks, like harvesting the sacred olive at Olympia.[62] Perhaps one of Ganymede's closest cousins in Greek religion is the Theban god or hero known only as Boy who was honored at the strange sanctuary of the

Cabiri. One vase shows him doing Ganymede's job and pouring wine or some other substance for a reclining figure.[63]

But Ganymede's extreme youth also helps to highlight a contrast with Tithonus, his relative or brother. Abducted Tithonus ages but never dies, lingering in eternal decrepitude in Dawn's abode on the margins between earthly and unearthly existence. Abducted Ganymede, who gets to travel right to the heart of heaven, is, by contrast, forever on the brink of maturity, always a boy, a Peter Pan. Both of them are stuck at the opposite ends of the Athenian age-class system that starts at Eighteen and finishes at Sixty.

Greek religion of the historical period makes much of a very stark division between mortals and immortals. All looked human, but crucially mortals must age and die, while gods were ageless and deathless. Mortals came into bloom at Eighteen, blossomed in their Twenties, fruited in their Thirties and Forties and then gradually faded away to a ghostly nothingness. Gods maintained that youthful bloom and supercharged human vigor of Youth (Hebe) forever. This may seem unremarkable, but for the Greeks the relationship between these opposite poles was something of a preoccupation. "Officially" it meant that there was no possibility of resurrection, that no god should ever be said to have "died" or be mourned in ritual lamentation, that once mortals entered Hades they should stay there, and there should be no possibility of apotheosis. There were plenty of exceptions—archaisms, innovations, imports, or just a refusal to play by the rules of the game—but each occasion was recognized as exceptional. That there was a "grave of Zeus" in Crete was considered scandalous. The Greeks were ideologically un-Christian long before Christianity. When the citizens asked a resident sage whether or not they should offer heavenly sacrifice and mourn the "White Goddess" Leucothea, they were told that if they thought she was a goddess they should not mourn her, if they thought she was a mortal they should not offer sacrifice; the logic is impeccable.[64]

The gods maintained their deathlessness in numerous ways, but above all by their diet. When Diomedes wounds Aphrodite in the *Iliad*, as she attempts to shield her son Aeneas, Homer explains that although she seems to bleed it is not really blood, but ichor: "for they eat no bread [*sitos*] and drink no fire-faced wine and so are bloodless and are called the deathless ones." Instead the gods feasted, and feasted and feasted, on nectar and ambrosia, special foods of immortality. "Ambrosia and nectar can be used to feed a newborn god, to change a mortal into an immortal, or even to keep a corpse [Patroclus's] from rotting . . . Ambrosia and nectar could thus be said to be a treatment for immortality, substances that give a body the ability to resist time and defy death. On immortal bodies, a regular application of them sustains beauty, brilliance, and energy."[65]

Once the vase painters started imagining what Homer had spoken of but had not dared to show, Ganymede on Olympus, Ganymede at work, it immediately looked, to any proper Greek, like a job of utmost significance. Indeed he is a unique figure in Greek religion, a mortal on Olympus. It was the very nectar served by Ganymede and the "ambrosia," the food of the gods (ambrosia just means "without mortality"), that kept the gods gods, that kept them up there.[66] The significance of his role is revealed by the fact that it was also performed by Hebe, daughter of Zeus and Hera. Hebe is the personification of youthful "flowering," and as we see in the case of Tithonus it is not just deathlessness but undying youthful vigor that distinguishes gods from men. Her presence on Olympus is terribly important therefore, and when Ganymede takes over her role, he too must be seen to embody the youthfulness he both possesses and dispenses, the fuels of immortality.[67] He is what he serves. He is, precisely, the sap-filled youthfulness that his brother Tithonus, the dried-out cicada, has lost.[68]

For Tithonus's lover, Dawn, represents the edge of day, she is each day. Her rosy fingers streaking the dark at daybreak are the edge of the page of time being turned, the celestial ticking clock. Her ancient Indian cousin Usas—the same word as Greek Dawn (Eōs), many mechanical vowel shifts later—is in fact plural, she is "Dawns," and even Greek Dawn seems to be born again, "born early," each new day. Dawn must stay at the edge of the world, at the boundary between earth and heaven, night and day and keep away from the center of things on Olympus.[69] It is no surprise therefore that living with the succession of days in person, at the edge of the world where the pages of time turn, Tithonus should feel his age.

But the Greeks didn't just let the gods live on with their nectar and ambrosia. They also tried to nourish them with sacrifices. They would kill animals in the open air, and burn the thigh bones, covered in fat, plus the spinal column from horns to tail, on an altar, while eating the rest of the animal themselves. The smoke from the burning remains, encouraged with splashes of wine to make the flames flare up to heaven, also delighted the gods in the sky. And you could see how pleased they were by watching the way the smoke rose and how the tail of the dead animal curled with their delight. The sacrifice was linked to nectar and ambrosia through the nostrils, for nectar and ambrosia are divinely scented substances, and it is the savor of the sacrifice, the tasty smell, that reaches and pleasures the gods.[70]

If you consider Ganymede, therefore, up among the gods, doing his job—and I think that one look would be enough—any Greek would start thinking about the nectar and ambrosia he serves, about immortality, libations and sacrifice. They would see in Ganymede a pure once-mortal boy mediating between earth and heaven, a resonant symbol of human and divine exchange, a uniquely remarkable figure. And when Sophocles wrote of Ganymede "with thighs putting a fire under Autocrat Zeus," I cannot believe there was anyone in the theater whose first, second or third response was not that thighs + fire + Zeus = sacrifice.[71]

The best example of this theme is a cup acquired by the J. Paul Getty Museum in 1984 (Figs. 14, 15, 18), a masterpiece, signed by the painter (or

14. Exterior of the Getty Ganymede Cup. Zeus grabs Ganymede.
Cup signed by Douris ("Doris") (c.480).

15. Interior tondo of the Getty Ganymede Cup. Ganymede pours nectar
and ambrosia into Zeus's cup beside an altar.

painteress) Douris, and cherished by its owner—it was broken once in
the ancient world, and repaired with a piece from another pot stapled
on.[72] It might have come from the Harpagion in Chalcis itself, or from
the sanctuary of Ganymeda in Phlius, but instead it came from nowhere
and was bought by the Getty.[73] On the outside are two rampant deities,
a big winged Dawn swooping on hunter Cephalus, and a Zeus with a
bun and in a negligee arresting a hoop-playing Ganymede. Turn the cup
over and look inside to learn what happens next. Now we see Zeus with
his hair down, sitting on a throne in front of a holy altar, and infinitely
more serious. He holds out his cup. Ganymede fills it with a red liquid
we can see pouring out of a jug, nectarine ambrosia. They are both
wearing the same clothes we saw in disarray on the outside, worn now
in formal fashion. We are allowed this time, I think, to get carried away.
It is hard to think of a more tremendous narrative, a mortal removed
from the earthly sphere and chosen by the most awesome of gods to perform holy offerings in his presence. Here sacrifice and the food of the
gods are as one. It's like having Jesus himself put the wafer on your
tongue.[74]

After that, it is hardly a big surprise to discover that in at least one city, Aegion, an under-Eighteen who had won a beauty contest, a modern-day Ganymede, was chosen as priest of Zeus, probably of Boy Zeus, and discharged from his office as soon as the hair began to darken his upper lip and jaw. On winning the contest he was allowed to take the cult image home with him, a bronze masterpiece by the great sculptor Hageladas, teacher of Pheidias and Polyclitus. Perhaps the contest was like the eyebrow-raising ritual described by Theocritus in Megara. Around the tomb of one "Zeus-famed," Diocles, a foreigner from Athens, "fond of boys" (*philopais*), there was a kissing contest at the beginning of spring. All the youths would gather en masse. Whichever youth (*kouros*) kissed lips on lips most sweetly was the winner, and could run to his mother covered in garlands. "Lucky judge," says Theocritus. I imagine he supplicates "charm-eyed" (*charopon*) Ganymede to give him a mouth like a touchstone that can tell gold from dross. There was a temple of Aphrodite Praxis nearby, full of Erotes, but the name of the hero, the reference to Ganymede and the timing of the festival make it more likely that the selection has something to do with Megara's great temple of Olympian Zeus.[75]

Both Zeus and Ganymede are sporting headgear. They are wearing yarmulkes. It seems these caps were once a sign of holiness all over the Mediterranean. The priest in the Temple in Jerusalem would wear a "non-conical hat . . . covering half the head" when about to perform the sacrifice. A holy priest of Zeus (*flamen Dialis*) at Rome was supposed to keep his head always covered. While performing his duties he wore a special *apex* (skullcap, with a wooden point), which he had to remove before he died, lest he contaminate it with mortality. Greek writers rarely give precise descriptions, talking just of "hats," *piloi,* or "little hats," *pilidia.* When two young riders appear to them wearing caps (*piloi*), the Spartans think they are the divine twins Castor and Pollux; "they bowed down and prayed, thinking that the Dioscuri themselves [Castor and Pollux] had come to their sacrifice"—big mistake; it wasn't them. In Athens wearing a little hat, a *pilidion,* gives you license to say things that otherwise might get you into trouble, indicating an *ekstasis,* a "standing outside of" reasonableness, or "holy talk"—*semnologein.* Wearing one allows Solon to talk of a war it is forbidden to mention, as if "the message had been entrusted to him by the divinity that had invaded him." A *pilidion* also allows the poet Aristophanes (in the person of an actor) to speak out freely against war without fear, "to be as I am, but to seem not to be." When Aeschines slanders Demosthenes with outrageous insults, Demosthenes wants to know where his "little hat" is, that would grant him such license. And when Socrates is forced by his friend Phaedrus to make an immoral speech he covers his head and claims to be channeling the local spirits. At any rate when we find them on statues and in images, skullcaps are worn at solemn moments of revelation with altars at hand and on the heads of seers, indicating a removal to another plane of existence, or alternatively, the immediacy of the divine. And indeed the famous terra-cotta Ganymede carried off like a rugby ball at Olympia, most holy of Zeus's shrines, most holy of shrines, was also wearing a yarmulke when his head was eventually found by the Germans. He is an exact contemporary of Douris's yarmulke-wearing Ganymede, and of Hageladas's *Boy Zeus,* at most a decade later.[76]

If there is a direct and inexorable line then from the abduction of the beautiful Trojan prince to the giggles of Lucian and the condemnation of the *Ovide moralisé,* there are lines no less distinct that run from the royal house of Troy to the court of Charles I of England via the imperial house of Nero, and from the cupbearer of the "highest god" by way of Filarete's doors of St. Peter's to Ganymede as the very emblem of piety at the front of the emblem-books. Ganymede seems to have caused some people discomfort, but shown pouring immortal nectar into the cup of Olympian Zeus, the scene that Homer himself took care to avoid, he *must* have been first and foremost a religious figure; an object of heavenly *erōs,* to be sure, but not a merely trivial pursuit. Maybe he was too serious for Homer's purpose, rather than too raffish a joke.

What is odd is how anyone could have failed to see his importance. In the *Iliad,* on vases, in statues at Olympia beside the greatest altar in all Greece, and later featuring prominently in the imperial propaganda of the Julio-Claudians, the story of the mortal serving immortality to the immortals seems a far more central, widespread and significant myth about sacrifice and the gulf between men and gods than either the myth of Prometheus or the myth of Lycaon the cannibal man-wolf of Arcadia, myths that usually take center stage. Indeed to trivialize such a myth, so ubiquitous and so rich in symbolism, quite unique, takes some doing; the trivialness and frivolousness that seem to attach them-

selves to "gay" things has once again been at work, making it impossible for us to take him seriously. The gravity of the myth of Ganymede's
rising up to heaven proved no match for the levity of a god in love with
a member of his own sex, and so Ganymede has been marginalized in
the histories of Greek religion. Plato, however, certainly knew what he
stood for.

NOONDAY PHAEDRUS. CEPHALUS AT DAWN

Socrates is walking outside the perimeter of the city with his old friend Phaedrus. It is the summer of 404 BC, the year of the surrender to Sparta.[1] Athens had been under siege for years, and at war for decades, but after the surrender the Spartans tore the walls down and cracked Athens out of her shell. Plato describes Socrates as if he is peering out from the confines of the city for the first time, like a citizen of East Berlin walking past the Brandenburg Gate, or a prisoner waking up to find instead of a brick wall outside his window, a view of fields he never knew were there. We could walk all the way to the city of Megara and back, says Socrates, a trip not possible till now.[2]

Both are walking barefoot. Phaedrus is a slightly sad character, not in good health, a hypochondriac perhaps, which is why he is taking a constitutional, but as always in Plato, talking about love. He is always going on about it, says his "companion" (*hetairos*) Eryximachus in the *Symposium*. Phaedrus indeed was responsible for all the talk of love on that occasion too, the "father" of the conversation (*Symposium,* 177d). But that was over a decade ago. By now Phaedrus is about fifty years old, and back, we happen to know from other sources, from a long spell abroad. An inscription records that he was one of those condemned for impiously vandalizing herms, odd statues of the god Hermes that consisted of a square-cut block of stone sometimes inscribed with a little motto, or a thought for the day, surmounted by the god's head, with a beard, often long, and a phallus, often erect.

For Plato's Phaedrus is a historical personage, with a little of that resistance to an artist's imaginative construction of him, his own heft and drag, which is the privilege of real people.[3] Phaedrus is still in search of the same thing, a worthy eulogy of love, as if he had been disappointed by all those speeches made for him in the *Symposium* a decade earlier.

"No one has caused more speeches to be made in your lifetime than you" (*Phaedrus,* 242b), writes Plato, of the insistent, love-obsessed character he has burdened himself with, who demands from off the page, as it were, that Plato, his author, work harder and write more and better on the subject of Love.

Returning from exile, Phaedrus will have discovered a new species in Athens, a group of men who specialize in writing speeches for you, so he has gone to a professional, to Lysias, greatest speechwriter of the day, and finally got what he has been looking for. Lysias, too, is real. He once wrote a speech for Phaedrus's "companion," Eryximachus, fragments of which were first published in 1929. There's just a chance it's not the same Eryximachus, but not many Athenians of this time gave their sons such a name.[4] Lysias himself refers to Phaedrus briefly in a couple (?) of surviving works. In one speech, Phaedrus is represented as a man of good standing but impoverished, through no fault of his own. He had married his cousin, a very common practice, and his uncle gave him a dowry of 4,000 drachmas. By *c.*393 BC, Phaedrus is dead or perhaps divorced, since the girl remarries another important and wealthy person. However, the career of her second husband collapsed. He was convicted and executed by the state and his property confiscated. Since the property proved less valuable than expected, court cases followed. Lysias's speech was commissioned by Phaedrus's cousin and brother-in-law in order to defend himself from the accusation that he and his family had siphoned off money from the estate of his sister's second husband in order to deprive Athens of its due. If my father was so interested in money as to steal from the city, why would he marry his daughter off to his poor old nephew Phaedrus, asks Phaedrus's cousin.[5] Phaedrus's "best friend" and members of his family used Lysias's services, therefore, so Lysias was indeed known to Phaedrus, as Plato claims.

And now on this particular day, walking barefoot with Socrates at the end of the fifth century, it emerges that Phaedrus has spent the whole morning listening to this Lysias, Plato's greatest rival as a writer, talk about Love between men, in a house near the Temple of Olympian Zeus. Phaedrus fell in love with the speech. Socrates wants to hear it. Phaedrus refuses to repeat it; he couldn't possibly do it justice. But then Socrates sees that Phaedrus is hiding something in his draperies; it looks like a document. It turns out that Phaedrus had loved the speech so much, he had had a copy made. Why so coy? asks Socrates. It is as if Lysias himself were here to tell us. Let's find a quiet place and you can read it to me.

A path leads off to the river. It's good we are both barefoot, says Phaedrus, we can wade across, which is especially nice in summer. They find a lovely spot, a spring, a source of the Ilissus with grass in the shade of a plane tree.[6] The cicadas clamor. It is noon, the hottest time of day at the hottest time of the year. Socrates goes into raptures over this lovely spot. Anyone would think, says Phaedrus, you weren't from around here. They notice that people have made offerings at the site, little dedications to minor gods; they read the dedications; the place is sacred to the river spirit Achelous, and the nymphs.[7] Wasn't it somewhere around here that the North Wind abducted Princess Orithyia? asks Phaedrus. Yes, says Socrates, so they say. Was this the actual spot? asks Phaedrus. The water is so clear, you can just imagine girls coming down to play here. No, says Socrates, that's two or three *stades* below where you cross into the suburb of Agra.[8] They have built an altar to Boreas there. Now tell me what Lysias says.

AN INDECENT PROPOSAL

Lysias, it emerges, had launched an ironic attack on the whole culture of Greek love in Athens—mad about the boy, doorstepping, stalking, Don't you love me anymore? Why were you late? You don't pay me any attention. Please, please, please. Oh all right then. He took on the persona of someone who was not an *erastēs,* trying to get a good-looking boy into bed. According to Lysias, the boy should "favor" (*charizesthai*) not the man who is desperately in love with him, but one who is not. Passionate admirers think they are owed a response because of all the trouble they have gone to, the time they have wasted, the disaster they've made of their lives on your account. They freely admit they are mad. How will they respect their former intentions when they recover their senses? Passionate admirers will boast of their conquest, make such a song and dance about their love that everyone will assume the worst anyway if they so much as see you together in intimate conversation. They stop you speaking to interesting and useful people out of jealousy, flatter you into taking the wrong decisions, get upset over trivial slights, fall in love before they know who you really are and lose interest when they've achieved their goal. They are beggars, and you shouldn't reward beggars simply for the constancy of their importunity.

Someone who is cool on the other hand will be able to give you the best advice, will be discreet, assess you and be assessed on merit, as a friend already. Such a man will only get closer through the exchange of mutual pleasures, will get upset only over the most serious offenses, and then only to the proper degree. He'll be as close as a trustworthy friend or a family member, will be constant, providing a better expectation of loving intimacy (*philia,* 231d, 232d) than you can expect from a man riding on Eros's runaway chariot, and what's more, no one will suspect a thing.

Phaedrus cajoles Socrates into attempting to outdo great Lysias on the same theme. He covers his head, and calls on the Muses for inspiration. He begins to suffer a "god condition," a "seizure by nymphs" (*nympholeptos*), talking nearly in the style of the mystical song of Dionysus, the dithyramb (238d). He starts by clarifying the age of the boy in question: "There was this boy, or rather a Striplinglet [*meirakiskos*] and terribly handsome; and he had lots of suitors" (237b). He also reveals that the non-lover is a hypocrite. One of these suitors, as hopelessly in love with the boy (*pais*) as anyone, pretended not to be in love and tried to get the boy to "graciously favor him." This is what he said . . .

Socrates goes on to produce for Phaedrus one of the most brutally realistic and cynical visions of Greek Love to have survived, a passionate admirer pretending to demolish passionate love. Obviously love is some form of lust (*epithumia*), he says, a getting of pleasure. He outlines the relationship between the Eighteen-year-old and his older lover. Such a man is the least pleasant company for a boy. The elder lover will be goaded on toward the prospect of pleasure just out of reach, seeing, hearing, touching, any sensation he can get from his beloved, but what pleasures does he have to offer in return? How will he save his beloved from those same hours that for him are disagreeable, as he looks upon his lover's older face robbed of its youthful blooming beauty—now in his Twenties, or worse his Thirties? So says Sixty-something Socrates to Fiftyish Phaedrus. And what about all the suspiciousness, the alternation of disgustingly fulsome compliments, and foul obscene reproaches when he gets drunk? And if his lover is boring and hurtful when he is in love, imagine what happens when the passion fades. All those promises he made to get him into bed are now exposed as so much bad faith. And the boy will call him to account, while his former lover just tries to get it over with. Serves the boy right. He should have known better than to give himself to a madman, damaging to his bank account (*ousia*), damaging to his once-fantastic body (*sōmatos hexis*), and to his education. Socrates, the cynical lover, concludes: "Admirers love boys, as wolves dote on lambs."

SOCRATES RECANTS

But Socrates recoils from his own success and stops before he starts the more scandalous part of the argument: why the boy should allow himself to be seduced by the *crypto-erastēs,* the "non-lover" who is in fact in love. He has passed beyond dithyramb and is close to epic verse. Transported to this god-inspired condition by the local nymphs into whose clutches Phaedrus deliberately placed him (241e), he needs to escape from the place before his condition gets worse. He knew even as they waded across the river that something this terrible would happen, and now the premonition has been fulfilled. His mood now is quite changed. He realizes he has sinned (*hamartēma,* 242d); he has been playing to the stalls, performing to the audience of men rather than to the higher audience of gods, and winning cheap applause.[9] "That was a terrible speech you brought with you, terrible the speech you made me speak . . . Both foolish and blasphemous, and there is nothing more terrible than that." Eros is a divine being. Lysias made him look wicked, and I too, thanks to you. I must purify myself and make amends. Socrates moves the conversation onto a much higher plane. But first he uncovers his head, no longer requiring the license granted to the holy fool, to say what cannot otherwise be said. This time he will talk of the highest kind of divine possession, possession by Love. It is one of the most influential passages in all of Greek literature.

Socrates goes on to describe the world of the immortal soul in the time before she comes to inhabit a body. This soul has wings and drives a chariot with two horses, one well behaved and one a little frisky. Each day these disembodied souls fly up across the sky, to the very height of heaven, to look at the view, a view of true knowledge of true being

(Heidegger loved Plato), beauty and temperance, which they contemplate with pure sense, *nous,* forming chariot teams following each of the Olympian gods in their ascent, with Zeus's army, of course, at the head. Any soul can join any company; the gods are not jealous. And at the end of the day, the soul unharnesses her pair of horses and feeds them on nectar and ambrosia, as she herself is fed on the sights of truth.

But sometimes souls cannot keep up with the higher trajectories of the gods. They get distracted by the business of driving their horses and forget to admire the view. They shift into a lower orbit, and have to make do with the sights of the inner circle; they feed off the imitations rather than the true entities. Distracted by ugliness and what is bad, they begin to shed their feathers. Fallen to earth they find something solid to hold on to, bodies, and once fallen into bodies they must remain down here for ten thousand years, which is how long it takes for their wings to grow back. The first incarnation in a body is not so bad. Recollection of the visions of the outer universe still linger. This man will be born as a seeker after wisdom and beauty, a follower of the Muses, a man of Love, i.e., a "lover of wisdom," a *"philo-sophos,"* not someone with a degree in Descartes and Derrida but possessed by a passionate desire to know one's self, one's world and its ways. Because he neglects human businesses, people think such a man is off his head, but this is the greatest of all forms of divine madness (248de, 249de).

When at death the soul leaves the body, she goes to the waiting room in the Underworld or in some nicer, more paradisal place, depending on her behavior. There she spends a thousand years before she gets another chance at a body. Eight more levels of incarnation follow that of the Lover/Philosopher in Socrates' description, each less spiritual than the last and more earthly: 2) the king and warrior, 3) the man of affairs, 4) the doctors, athletes and physicians, 5) mystery priests, 6) artists, 7) farmers and artisans, 8) sophists and demagogues, 9) the tyrant. However, a soul can speed up the regeneration of her wings and cut short the ten thousand years of waiting to just three thousand, if she always feeds on wisdom each time she is reincarnated.

This is where Love comes in. In the first place that is not his real name. We call the god Eros, but the gods call him Pt-Eros, Pteros, as in pterodactyl, the winged one, because Love needs must be a "feather implanter" (252b). This Love affects souls differently depending on which battalion they once belonged to during their long distant rides across the heavens in the train of the gods. If they followed in the train of Mars, god of war, their Love will have a martial flavor, even leading to bloodshed and the sacrifice of both. One who was in Hera's queenly train will favor a regal boy, but best of all, of course, are those who once were satellites of Jupiter, and seek a boy Zeus-like in his soul, a lover of wisdom, a leader of men. The soul makes of the beloved a kind of cult image, or a statue resembling the lost divine leader, and will worship and honor him.

As soon as a beautiful boy appears on the horizon and one falls in love, the soul is off on its chariot and pair. And the frisky horse can't wait to cavort with the handsome youth. The charioteer and the good horse resign themselves to some quick fling of passion (or sexual affront of an under-Eighteen) though it is dreadful and illegal (*deina, paranoma,* 254a), and let the frisky horse have his way, but at the last minute, on the brink of outrage, as the boy comes into view his beauty stirs a memory of that other beauty of the outer orbits. In holy awe the driver falls backward, hauling on the reins to set the bit, and the horses fall back on their haunches. The good horse, being good, doesn't mind the pain.

Before too long, when memory begins to fade, the frisky horse charges again, and again the driver, the soul, pulls back on the bit, fighting to keep control, until the mouth of the frisky horse is foaming with blood. This keeps on happening until the frisky horse, like one of Pavlov's dogs, begins to tremble with fear as soon as the boy comes into view. And then, finally, the charioteer can follow in good order, trotting at a gentle steady pace in the footsteps of the beloved.

At first the boy spurns the one in love, misled by his classmates (*sumphoitētai*) or others, who say that it is shameful to "cozy up to" (*plēsiazein,* 255a) one in love with you, but then maturity (*hēlikia*— age-class, coming-of-age) and destiny together lead him to welcome the other's "intercourse" (*homilia*), and when he welcomes that intercourse and conversation, the loved one is stunned by the kindness of the man in love, and sees that all his other friends and relatives have nothing to compare with the *philia* of this friend with a god, Eros, inside him. And if he continues like this, cozying up, and "reaching out to touch" (*haptesthai,* 255b) the man in love with him in the gymnasium or on other social occasions, then does that streaming fountain (*rheumatos pēgē,* 255c), to which Zeus in love with Ganymede gave the name of Himeros, drench the lover until he can absorb no more of it. At this point the fountain of desire splashes back like an echo or a boomerang and returns to its source through the eyes of the beloved. It reaches his soul in turn and nourishes its feathers and gives wings to the boy, and his soul too is filled with *erōs*, as if he has caught a disease. But though the boy is in love, with what he has no clue. He knows not that his lover is a mirror in which he sees himself. He has "love's opposite number," love's mirror image, inside him, Anteros, though he calls it, in error, *philia* (255d). And he shares the lover's longing when he is away and relief when they are together and desires to see, to touch, to be intimate (*philein*—"act fondly"), to lie down next to him, and what follows from that.

The boyfriend (*paidika*) too has a frisky horse inside him, and it makes him embrace his lover and kiss (*philein*) him. When they lie down together it is minded not to withhold the acts of graciousness (*charisasthai*, 256a), though the good horse and the boy's own resident charioteer pull in the opposite direction. And if the better intention wins and a well-ordered daily life of love of wisdom ensues, they spend their lives in a blessed state of oneness of mind, full of self-control and decency: The badness of the soul has been put in chains, and the goodness liberated. When they die the souls of the couple have wings. They have successfully completed the first of the three rounds in the quest to return to heaven, the "true [Olympian] Olympics." And there is no greater prize than that, whether won through divine madness or human temperance (*sōphrosunē*).

Those who don't manage these high standards, who lead day to day a more vulgar life, uncurious about the world (*aphilosophos*) and ambitious (*philotimia*, "devotion to public applause"), and who give their frisky horses their heads in a moment of inattention or drunkenness and "go all the way," will still be good friends. They have exchanged the greatest pledges and will not think it right to be enemies, even when *erōs* has gone. When they die their souls will not have wings, to carry them up, but still they are *eager for wings*, they have intimations of the upper reaches, and so love has given them no small prize. Once the heavenly path stretches before them, their souls cannot return to the darker paths of the Underworld, but shall walk along sharing the "shining (after-) life" together in a state of heavenly bliss (*eudaimonein*). Thanks to Love they too will be of a feather, when the feathers (after further incarnations) come (256d).

And so you should avoid a non-lover because he will leave you in the lower depths and facing nine thousand years of reincarnation, most of which will be spent in the less pleasant nether waiting rooms, until each new body is ready. Socrates finishes his holy speech with a prayer to Eros, whose shrine was in the Academy, begging him to accept his recantation and not to abandon him, calling on him to blame Lysias, "the only begetter of that speech," for the cynical words he spoke at first.

DAWN AND CEPHALUS AND PROCRIS

The dialogue goes on, but Love seems to fade as a topic and there is much more about speech and writing and the inventor of writing, Egyptian Hermes, ibis-headed "Theuth." If there is one theme that unites the *Phaedrus* it is all kinds of divine possession, "enthusiasm," and the truth of enthused speech, in contrast to the carefully composed and loveless writing of cynical, mercenary, Lysias. The dialogue is littered with the abducted or "possessed." From the start we encounter possession: of Princess Orithyia by the North Wind, of Socrates by Nymphs, of Ganymede by Zeus, of a man in love by a god called Pt-Eros, of the one he loves by Eros's reflection, Anteros. And all the while in the background are the little Tithonuses, the cicadas chirruping away, watching mortals closely to see if they will succumb to their Siren charms and fall asleep, or if they will honor properly the Muses of epic and celestial inspiration (Calliope, Ourania) who alone give access to truth, the very Muses who are honored in Socrates' epic celestial speech.[10]

But there is one other abduction at issue here. For Socrates' bizarre and elaborate image of the soul as a female, a winged charioteer, resembles one key character very closely.[11] Only one winged female in Greek myth drives a chariot and pair across the heavens, and feeds them on nectar and ambrosia at the end of the day: the goddess Dawn. The uniqueness of Socrates' allegory of the soul and its precise match to the unique figure of winged Dawn the charioteer, a figure ubiquitous in art, would have made the reference unmissable, even if it wasn't spelled out. What is Plato up to? We might start by looking more closely at the myths of the Dawn goddess and of her Attic paramour Cephalus and his wife

16. The goddess Dawn ("*Eos*") rising over the sea in her winged chariot,
one of the horses labeled "La<m>pon" ("Shining"), a model for Plato's
image of the soul "like the dynamic composite of a pair of winged horses
and a charioteer . . . and she lays on for them ambrosia and nectar to drink"
(*Phaedrus*, 246a, 247e). Stamnos by Midas Painter (*c*.450–425).

Procris.[12] As a bonus it allows us to discover a hidden link between
Plato's midsummer *Phaedrus* and Shakespeare's *A Midsummer Night's
Dream,* also set in Athens; at least, it will give one explanation why his
Bottom is called Bottom.

The story of Cephalus is one of the most romantic of Greek myths,
one of Ovid's favorites and a popular subject in the Renaissance and the
rococo periods. It also contains some of the bizarrest episodes in all of
Greek mythology, which is saying something. But it is an important feature of Greek myth and religion—one might say the whole point of it,
if "point" did not beg too many questions—that there is no Authorized
Version, no Bible, no bishops, no popes, no Koran. That means that the
bits of myth that have survived are rarely singing in unison. Indeed one
would be very surprised to find a myth that came down to us in only one
version, and many of them have many versions, often very different
from one another. But here is a collation or a ragbag of the various stories told by various authors at various times.

Cephalus was the son of Hermes (and/or Deion, for Hermes some-times "co-fathers"!) and a prehistoric Athenian princess, Herse (Morn-ing Dew). When he grew up he married Procris, daughter of the first king of Athens, sister of Orithyia who was abducted by the North Wind. But Cephalus left his new bride in the bridal chamber, after the goddess Dawn abducted him. When he returned, eight years later, he decided to test her fidelity. He pretended to be a stranger and set out to entice her into bed with the offer of much gold: "He made himself fancy [katakosmēsas], and changed his appearance [alloeidē]. [Jealous Dawn was only too happy to help, adds Ovid.] Then, taking ornaments with him, he went home, and tried to persuade Procris to take the finery and have sex. Casting her eye on the finery, and looking at terribly handsome Cephalus, she climbed into bed with him. Cephalus revealed himself and blamed her."[13] Ovid dwells on the difficulty Cephalus has as a passionate admirer of his wife while pretending not to be, when all he wants is to fall into her arms—how often her chasteness rejected my advances, how often she said "I am keeping myself for one alone," but I carried on fighting "to wound myself," increasing the fee, promising a fortune for a night in his wife's company.[14]

Mortified at being caught taking money for sex, and by her own hus-band at that, Procris flees to Crete, where she has some strange adven-tures with King Minos. He has problems with fertility. Whenever he ejaculates (ouresken) he emits little beasties (thēria), scorpions, snakes and millipedes, which attack his women in the joints. Procris invents the femidom, a goat bladder inserted in a woman's "nature." The snakes are captured in the bag, and Minos is cured of infertility, enabling him to fa-ther children, notably Phaedra, Ariadne, Glaucus, etc. As a reward he gives her a magic dog (Laelaps, "Hurricane," later set among the stars as Sirius the Dog Star) and a magic javelin, which never miss their quar-ries.[15] Procris returns to Athens and gets her own back on her hypocrit-ical bridegroom. She dresses up as a man and becomes his hunting companion. Then she makes him an offer he cannot refuse. If he puts out (charisasthai) he can have the magic javelin. They lie down together, Procris rips off her disguise and rebukes her husband for being such an easy lay, for behaving more shamefully than even she had.[16]

The odd couple got together again, finally, many years by now after their wedding night, although the mythmakers don't seem to have been watching the calendar very closely. However, Cephalus is a hunting fanatic, which is why he was so keen to get his hands on the javelin, and on his hunts he loves to take a siesta in a beautiful garden near Mount Hymettus, by a sacred spring. He stretches out and calls on a cloud or a breeze, *aura,* to come and refresh him. It can be very hot in Greece, and Cephalus may have got a bit carried away:

> I looked out for her. She provided relief from my labors. I remember I used to sing out: "*Aura!* Come here, give me pleasure, wrap yourself in my bosom, *gratissima,* and, as you do, please ease this heat with which I am consumed!" Perhaps I did add more sweet nothings (for destiny was leading me on). "You are my great pleasure," I used to say. "You make me a new man. You cherish me. It's because of you that I love the woods and lonely places. That breath of yours is ever on my lips."

But the lonely places were not as lonely as Cephalus thought. Someone had overheard Cephalus's amorous speech to the breezes, and reported back to the wife. Cephalus was up to his old tricks again; it was not Dawn this time, or another man, but some other hussy, a Nymph called Aura.[17]

Procris decided to spy on her errant husband and see for herself. She hid behind a bush and waited to surprise the secret lovers. But she wasn't very good at keeping still. Cephalus saw something twitching and aimed his javelin into the thicket, the magic missile she herself had given him as payment for gay sex, the one that never missed its target. Procris lay dead. Her father the king was furious with his son-in-law, and following a trial at the Areopagus Cephalus was exiled and had more adventures in the islands south of Corfu.

He was the first, it was said, to take a lover's leap from the original Lover's Leap, the spectacular White Rock, topped with a temple of Apollo, that gave its name to the island of Leucas (*leukos,* "bright white"). The Leap was supposed to cure love or at least to put an end to it, and Cephalus was in love with a man called Pterelas ("Wing-Man"). The myth was linked to a ritual:

> The people of Leucas used to have a custom. Each year at the sacrifice for Apollo they would throw some criminal off the headland, for the

sake of averting evil, first having attached to him wings and birds to lighten his leap with wing-power. He would be received at the bottom by a large number of men in little fishing-boats arranged in a circle and they would rescue him and do all in their power to get him outside the borders.[18]

One might have thought it would be "Wing-Man" who would be identified as the one who took the leap, thereby providing a role model for the scapegoat. Quite probably in fact he did so in a sequel. For it is impossible reading this story not to think of the image of the boy falling headlong with two birds in the crooks of his arms at the shrine of Anteros at the foot of the Athenian Acropolis, marking the site where the Turandot-ish Timagoras had thrown himself off and onto the body of his *erastēs,* whom he had told to take a flying leap.[19] No one who had seen the image of the boy with two birds in his arms at the sanctuary of Anteros could have failed to make the connection with Plato's winged Pt-Eros and Anteros implanting feathers in the soul of the beloved.

There is another parallel between lovelorn Cephalus and this unhappy pair. For it seems clear that Cephalus, like Timagoras's admirer, was a "foreign resident," a metic in Leucas, since his home was next door, on the island to which he gave his name: Cephalonia. Either before the leap, if he went to his death, or after it, if he survived, now cured of his love for Pterelas, Cephalus founded a dynasty on the island. His descendants included Odysseus, and here history repeated itself, for Penelope too was abandoned by her husband immediately after her marriage: He was captured by a goddess, Calypso, and kept as her sex slave—Calypso indeed compares herself with Dawn in the *Odyssey* (5.121)—while she had to resist new suitors. And like Procris, strangely, Penelope doesn't recognize her husband when he returns. Unlike her, however, she has a test to guarantee that it really is him before she gets into bed with a stranger. She says she won't sleep with him but she will, if he wants, move the bed outside the bedroom for him. The real Odysseus will know that it can't be moved, because one of its posts is an olive tree.

In the tenth generation, however, Cephalus's descendants were finally allowed to return to Athens, the bloodguilt of his accidental murder of Procris finally cleansed. They were given a sign as they crossed into the plain of Athens, a sign that the crime had been expiated, and immediately built an altar to Apollo at Daphne. Parts of the temple were incorporated into the monastery of Daphne, which now sits on top of its remains. The Cephalids, the "Sons of Cephalus," were in fact an important aristocratic family in Plato's Athens. It is unlikely that Plato, himself of good family, never came into contact with one of them, nor that they were unacquainted with their extraordinary family history, including the tale of Cephalus making the first-ever lover's leap from the White Rock of Leucas, smitten with love for Pterelas.[20]

So much for Cephalus. But what can any of this have to do with *A Midsummer Night's Dream*? Well, first of all, Shakespeare certainly knew the myth, which was one of the favorites of Ovid, his favorite author, and deployed by him more than once. Toward the end of the night, Oberon boasts that unlike the ghosts of the dead, he has no problem with daylight—"we are spirits of a different sort / I with the Morning's love have oft made sport," a nicely ambivalent reference either to Cephalus or to Dawn herself. The myth is referred to more directly in the play by the rude mechanical Bottom. Being a rude mechanical he doesn't quite get the names right and refers to the ill-starred couple as Shafalus and Procrus. But the myth informs the play at a deeper level. Amorous mortal-loving Dawn clearly inspired the amorous mortal-loving fairy Titania. Her name is itself a giveaway, since Dawn is in fact Titanian Dawn, born of the generation of Titans that preceded the Olympians. But the main point is that the rude mechanical she falls in love with, Bottom, is a kind of inversion of Cephalus, whose name in Greek means "Head." Shakespeare's sly error and little joke on words reveals that he is having fun, and very consciously, with the Gods' Loves of *c.*500 BC. The clumsy mishearing of the play within a play, "Shafalus and Procrus," might indeed provide the key to what Shakespeare is up to in this comedy. He is playing games with the very business of learned alluding and reverence for esteemed classical models, with what the Renaissance was all "about." Making no attempt to avoid error, he pleasantly succumbs to it, but in an obvious enough way to make sure no one could accuse him of having made a mistake, instead building something new and different from a classical inheritance deliberately misheard. Racine took a different approach.

And there is another thing, which may be nothing more than a co-

17. The "Blacas Krater." During the dog days of August, Cephalus in the
posture of the constellation Orion with his magic dog Laelaps (Sirius),
rising in the east, fends off the lustful goddess Dawn. To the left, a partly
veiled Moon (Selene) leaves the sky. The ephebic divers to the right are stars
plunging into Ocean. Calyx krater (c.430–420).

incidence. Plato's *Phaedrus* is also set at midsummer, and I think there is
a reason for that. Cephalus was identified with the constellation
Orion.[21] The myth of Dawn's chasing after him and abducting him relates to a specific time of year, the weeks from mid-July onward when he
returns to the sky after a short absence and stretches out on Hymettus
before vanishing in the morning's clutches—around the time, that is, of
the great festival of the Panathenaea and the Athenian New Year.[22]
Maybe Shakespeare just got it from Ovid's Cephalus, crazy about hunting, but what it means is that the love of Titania for Bottom contains,
via the love of Titanian Dawn for "Head," a hidden reference to the
time of year in which the play is set.

PLATO'S ALLEGORY OF ALLEGORIZING

So much for Shakespeare. But what is Plato up to? The image of Dawn,
the winged female in her two-horse chariot, not only informs Plato's
image of the soul as a winged charioteer—a reference that it would be
impossible for any of Plato's contemporaries to miss—but also reminds
us of her most famous Athenian paramour, Cephalus, which happens to
be the name of the father of the orator Lysias whose speech starts the
whole thing off. Indeed Lysias is referred to as "son of Cephalus" in the

course of the dialogue if we needed any reminding (227a, 263d).[23] Perhaps his patronymic is what led Plato to put Lysias in the dialogue in the first place. But once we have started picking up those references to the myth of Dawn, Cephalus and Procris, then those strange speeches about trying to persuade someone to favor someone who is not in love with them must inevitably recall the strange myth of Cephalus trying to persuade his wife into bed for some non-*erōtikos* sex, especially when we recall that in Socrates' version the seducer really is a love-struck admirer who is merely pretending not to be: exactly the position that Cephalus finds himself in, as Ovid brings out so nicely in his version of the tale.

The punch line perhaps comes at 263d, with another sly dig at Lysias. Thanks to my having been possessed by the spirits of the place, my "inspired condition" (*to enthousiastikon*), says Socrates, I cannot recall what I said, whether I defined *erōs* at the beginning of my speech. "And how," says Phaedrus admiringly. "Upon my word," says Socrates, "you rate the Nymphs, daughters of Achelous, and Pan, son of Hermes, more skillful at speeches than Lysias, son of Cephalus." That is how it is normally translated. But this sudden spate of fathers' names is suspicious and the word order is a bit odd. There is a crossword-puzzle clue here, a second meaning in which Plato perhaps provides a key to the puzzle of the loveless speeches of seduction. For one could understand it slightly differently: "You rate the Nymphs, daughters of Achelous, and Pan, son of Hermes, more skillful at making 'speeches of Cephalus' than Lysias." All the sly devices for duping one's fancy into bed could be described as "speeches of Cephalus," in other words, the speeches he spoke to his wife when he was in disguise.

Moreover, Cephalus was connected to a strange and mysterious sanctuary, the sacred spring of Aphrodite at Kaisariani, a leafy foothill of Mount Hymettus on the edge of Athens, and a source of the river Ilissus.[24] Its waters were supposed to be able to cure infertility, as Procris cured Minos's infertility; indeed Greek women were still going there a hundred years ago. "Up to quite recent times the festival was very popular among the Athenians, and sick people were brought for cure at the spring . . . At another branch of the stream nearby women of Athens still go to drink, praying for children."[25] The shrine was known as "Cylloupera," "Club-foot's pouch," a name alluded to by Ovid, who refers to Cephalus as "Cyllenian offspring" when he describes him coming to

Cylloupera for a rest from the midsummer heat and calling on Aura, the breeze, without realizing that he is being spied on.[26] Cyllenian— Cylloupera. Perhaps the hidden reference is a mirage, but it reminds us who Cephalus's father was, Hermes of Mount Cyllene, Hermes the herm with his permanently erect phallus, who had helped at least one Athenian woman, the princess Herse, get pregnant, that very Hermes that Phaedrus had been found guilty of vandalizing, earning that sentence of exile from which he had just returned in *Phaedrus*. A rare fragment of a song with musical notation attached, a real piece of ancient Greek music in which we can pick out the tune, makes a similar connection between Hermes and the fertility shrine. "I've procreated better than [Her]mes," it says, although the text is damaged and "Hermes" is quite probable rather than quite secure.[27] A beautiful white jug may also be connected with this shrine, since it shows Aphrodite and a baby Cephalus. It is hard to think of any other connection between the hero and Aphrodite, never mind babies, other than at her sacred spring at Kaisariani; perhaps the jug was used to hold the magic waters of fertility.[28]

Through Cephalus, at least, the two halves of *Phaedrus,* first about Eros and the soul, then about Hermes and writing, can be joined together, the image of the soul modeled on the image of Dawn, Cephalus's abductor, in the first part, and his father Hermes in the second. But the shrine was also described by Aristophanes as a "brothel." Whatever cult practices he was thinking of when he said that—and we should not rule out the possibility that he meant exactly what it sounds like, for several other shrines of Aphrodite have been identified as brothels, including one discovered during the building works for the Olympic Games—it is impossible not to associate Aristophanes' description of the shrine as a place of commercial sex with the theme of prostitution in the story of Cephalus and Procris, she putting out for finery and a small fortune, he for the magic javelin with which he will eventually kill her.[29] Prostitution is rare in Greek myth; in the story of Cephalus and Procris it features twice.

But is it possible that Plato would actually have set his sublime dialogue at such a place? Well I am not the first to suggest it,[30] and there is not a large number of other candidates. The geographer Strabo names only two main sources of the Ilissus and identifies Plato's lovely spot in *Phaedrus* with one of them.[31] And there may be one final clue right at the end of the dialogue as Phaedrus and Socrates take their leave. For before departing the sacred garden, Socrates offers up a prayer for beauty, but beauty on the inside, and we know that an alternative name for the disreputable spring was the fountain "of Kallias," which sounds pretty much like "Fountain of Beauty," and that the shrine was also proverbial for "unnatural artifice." I cannot quite decide. Plato is certainly capable of extreme irony, but placing *Phaedrus* in a sacred "brothel" might be too much even for him. Perhaps we can say that he put them "nearby."

So what conclusions can we draw from this daisy chain of links? First, Plato's allegory of the amorous soul as a charioteer cannot but refer to amorous Dawn, and therefore to her chief Attic lover, Cephalus, who is linked with prostitution both in myth and through the "brothel" cult site at Kaisariani. Second, even if all of this compels us to speculate beyond what can be proved, it reminds us how much there is to know, and the kinds of things there might be to know, and that we don't know the half of it. Students of Plato may not be able to fully understand the significance of his times and places, but it is far too long a jump from there to concluding that therefore they cannot be important.

Putting the *Phaedrus* into its context, or what we can try to reconstruct of that context, helps to explain some of the oddity of its morality, the competition between "Lysias" and "Socrates" to compose the best loveless speeches to blandish a boy into bed. But how does any of this help us in understanding Socrates' wonderful recantation, his compensatory ecstatic discourse on *erōs*?

Well, for a start, it explains the extraordinary elaborateness of his allegory, the *erastēs* with a soul like Dawn, a three-part soul: the frisky horse, the good horse and the winged lady charioteer. But why choose her? Well, Dawn is mythology's nymphomaniac, thanks to Aphrodite's malignant jealousy. In myth and sculpture and painted on innumerable pots, Dawn is the friskiest of goddesses, swooping down from the higher orbits to grab Tithonus or Cephalus and plenty of others besides. Is that the only point of making the soul in her image, an image of the carnal part of the soul, the frisky, lustful horse? In fact I think we have got things the wrong way around. Plato is not explaining how the soul works by using an image of a Dawn-like charioteer, but explaining the image of Dawn the charioteer swooping down to earth and chasing after boys by interpreting it in terms of the soul.

After their peak of popularity in the decades around 480 BC, there had been an intellectual reaction against myths of Gods' Loves. They were considered extremely disreputable by thoughtful Greeks, not least by Plato, which is one reason why he is so hostile to poets such as Homer and the tragedians who spread such scandalous allegations, and to painters.[32] Plato's Socrates is very respectful of gods, and that includes the goddess Dawn. At least in *Symposium* (220cd) Alcibiades describes how when fighting on a military campaign, Socrates once was seen to fall into deep thought, "seeking," "considering something" as he stood there. Some of the other soldiers were curious and kept an eye on him. He stayed there from early in the day, through the night, stock-still in contemplation, and not "until such time as Dawn came" did he come out of his trance, having prayed toward the rising sun. Socrates, Plato's Socrates, is not only not a "corrupter of young men," he is the most pious man alive.

Socrates has to accept that men think of the gods whom they have never seen "like some animal, having a soul, and a body, in an eternal conjoined growth" (246cd). He doesn't like that idea of gods, but he will move on. And he is not happy about the myth of Boreas, the North Wind, and his abduction of the Princess Orithyia, but he rejects any impious rationalization—those who claim she was just blown off a ridge, and that people said, Oh she's been "taken by the wind." He seeks another kind of truth in such myths: not the truth of events, the truth of himself. Likewise, when he talks of the gods in his inspired speech, there is nothing earthy or lustful about them. Because their horses are superior, the gods can ride high in the sky without exertion. It would be impossible, therefore, for Dawn, since she is a goddess, to fall to earth as the painters suggest, and chase after boys. She is immortal and retains her immortal dignity.

As part of the effort to rescue her from impious slander, Socrates quietly replaces the famous myth that cicadas are the spent and desiccated bodies of Tithonus, one of her rape victims. This is the result of false knowledge, he implies, the knowledge of men lulled into sleep by the cicadas' mesmerizing siren song, perhaps. Instead, ironically, cicadas are the Muses' spies looking out for those who manage to resist their song, keep awake, and speak truly with divine inspiration—that very inspiration, perhaps, celestial and epic, which produces Socrates' story of

Dawn as the soul. This new myth of the soul serves the same purpose as the new myth of the Tithonuses. Both represent the truth behind the ubiquitous images of Dawn's abductions. Socrates does not offer a cynical rationalization of the myth, but the true pious version, the product of divine reason, divinely inspired, a myth that turns out to address the human condition, the lover's condition, oneself. In his myth of the soul, Socrates has been narrating the true *logos,* the true story hidden in the myth of Cephalus.

TRUTH AND ABDUCTION

Although Plato develops the idea that gods' love affairs with mortals are linked to divinely possessed speech, he doesn't make it up from scratch. It is all already there for him, inherent in the popular conception of Nympholepsy. Abduction by Pan or the Nymphs, Panolepsy, Nympholepsy, divine possession, divine inspiration, *enthousiasmos* (the condition of having a "god in"—*entheos, enthous,* "enthused"), might produce babbling nonsense, or lies, but it could mean movement onto another level of reality, lifting the scales from the eyes to reveal the true inner way of the world, or insight into the secret future hidden in the present.[33]

This may make *Phaedrus* seem like a complicated text, and it is somewhat allegorical and elusive, but there are only three main themes to bear in mind in this first part of the dialogue. First, that behind myths about physical abduction by a love-struck god or goddess—Dawn, Nymphs, Zeus—is the story of divine possession or inspiration. Second, that true divine inspiration can give access to true speech, in other words that the truth about the myths is that they are myths about truth. Third is the idea that the man in love is really one who is possessed by a god, Eros, and that this is the best kind of divine inspiration, not really irrational, but a man making a mental leap toward what is beyond reach, stretching up for that dimly remembered vision of true beauty, perceived with true understanding, that the enamored experienced when s/he was a soul soaring above the universe in the train of one of the gods, the truth that is out there.

For what is peculiar to this particular kind of divine inspiration, the possession by the god Eros, is that it is always the shrinking of distances that matters, the action of leaping itself, not the safe landing on the other side. The stress is on seeking truth, not on finding it, on pursuing, not on catching. Socrates for Plato and many of his other followers is first and foremost the *erōtikos,* i.e., amatory, philosopher. That is the most consistent element that emerges about the philosophy of the great man who left no texts of his own, as far as it can be gleaned from the Socratic authors, Plato and Xenophon, and from scraps of several others.[34] And if the *erōtikos* philosopher does indeed represent the true Socrates, Plato has been true to him, since he has written *erōs* into every inch of his work. The dialogues are full of an enterprising love of knowledge, a reaching out for knowledge, but not of pinning it to the ground; he writes, in other words, as dialogue not as treatise. This embedding of love in knowledge is the reason why the lover and beloved who "go all the way" are "without philosophy," and why those who do not are properly philosophical, inasmuch as they are constantly reaching upward, trying to shrink the distance, between themselves, between themselves and the outer limits, without quite closing it. This is why Socrates, the Socrates in Plato's dialogues, never seems to consummate *erōs*—he doesn't find a lover, or enjoy a full-on sexual relationship— because since *erōs* is his philosophy, once the gap has been bridged, his enterprise, which is quintessentially the *activity* of seeking knowledge, is at an end, and there is only dogma and fundamentalism. Those readers of Plato who find they are never quite sure what he is teaching them, what with the irony, the mirages, the different voices, are experiencing his philosophy, which is *erōs,* approaching the object, but not achieving full consummation (or, if you like, penetration), having an intuition of but never fully grasping those truths, which would in Greek be indirect objects taking the genitive case, the ones you "reach for," "aim at," "hit upon," "touch upon," "miss from," "carry a torch for" . . .

The leaping of love, the apparently irrational leap of faith that love implies, is really a leap in the field of knowledge to the long-forgotten truth of the outer limits of the universe. Plato's famous forms, his "ideal" universe, his universe of "basic shapes" (*idea* = "basic shape" or "essential form" of a chair, of beauty, of a table, of justice) which in some dialogues is presented as the only proper object of contemplation, can be viewed merely as a function of this emphasis on an amatory, "erotik," passionately romantic, enterprising search, a perfect object that can be approached as an *erastēs* approaches an *erōmenos,* but that can never fully be grasped. Idealism, in this case, represents not so much a final destination in itself as a wonderful beyond, an ever-receding point, important more for its endless postponing of closure than for any qualities of its own, the promise that serves to maintain the endless activity of the *erōtikos* pursuit of knowledge.

A boy's beauty gets you carried away because it "rings a bell," a distant memory that you cannot quite put your finger on, a memory of a true vision of true beauty. This is how these three recurring figures, the man in love, the man possessed or abducted, and the seeker after the truth of things (the lover of wisdom), are identified as one and the same.

GAY GODS, GRACE AND RAPTURE

Plato's most revolutionary innovation is that, in this narrative, Love has been transferred from the love-struck god who possesses—the nymphomaniac Nymphs, Zeus or Dawn—to the one possessed, the god's passive victim who was minding his own business—Hylas, Ganymede, Cephalus, Tithonus—so that the emphasis is on a reaching up to the divine sphere rather than a reaching down to earth, an enraptured rather than an abducted Ganymede, a Ganymede always rising and rising of his own accord. Plato's unique suggestion in *Phaedrus* that the beloved also has an *erōs,* although he mistakenly calls it *philia,* is an absolute necessity if his argument is to work, if possession by an amorous god or goddess is to be transformed into a higher possession by *erōs.* Ganymede is no longer the passive victim of a love-struck Zeus. His "abduction" is really the feeling of taking flight. The wings do not belong, according to Plato, to Zeus's swan or the eagle who appears in art at exactly the time Plato is writing. They are Ganymede's own, his soul's feathers growing, thanks to the nourishment of *erōs,* the *erōs* that overflows from the Highest God, when Zeus is filled to the brim with love of him. The truth behind the myth of his scandalous abduction is the story of Ganymede's possession by wing-planting Eros, anti-Eros, the reflection of Zeus's Eros, although he does not know what the target of that *erōs* is. Thus Socrates the *erōtikos* is identified with Ganymede the *erōtikos.* Just as Socrates has been first the object of love-struck Nymphs, a nympholept, and then filled with *erōs,* so Ganymede is first the object of Zeus's *erōs,* a theolept, and then is himself filled with *erōs.*

From this perspective *Phaedrus* looks almost like a commentary on Douris's cup in the Getty. On the one side a large winged woman pursuing a youth, like a soul looking for a body; on the other, Zeus arresting Ganymede (Fig. 14). And on the interior Zeus next to the altar on which mortals place offerings that waft up in smoky aromas to the heavens while Ganymede pours down, from his jug of immortality (Fig. 15). For the Love Attack, the *himeros,* that flows from the beloved one when he returns your glance touchingly for the first time or smiles at you to make your heart melt, was invented at the time of that very first look of love, the streaming fountain, a fountain like the one bubbling in the background of the dialogue, that saturated Jupiter when Ganymede succumbed to possession, that stream that Jupiter named for the first time.

Ganymede is the fountain of nectar, and he becomes immortal by means of the splashback from that divine stream. It pours off Ganymede and into Zeus's vessel, until his cup brims over. The very image of pouring comes to be a fine image of unmeasured *charis,* boundless grace, the overwhelming overflow of love, soaking the one in love, and then soaking the one loved in divine nectar, the stream of stars from the constel-

18. The Getty Ganymede Cup, side B. Dawn grabs Cephalus while tribal heroes, King Pandion and King "Cecrophs," all named, look on. The one unnamed figure may be King Erechtheus, Cephalus's father-in-law.
Cup signed by Douris ("Doris") (*c.*480).

lation Aquarius, the shower that waters the wings of the soul, the dew
that silvers the dove's wings, that rouses an ambition to rise up and seek
the sights of those outer reaches that the soul but barely recalls. We don't
have to choose between a Zeus in love and a Zeus who needs a servant.
The love that emanates from Ganymede when he responds to Zeus in
love with him, and the immortal nectar he pours out for Zeus, are one
and the same. But if Socrates is Ganymede, first possessed by the divine,
and then by Love, what is nympholeptic Socrates' equivalent of that divine stream of nectar that pours from theoleptic Ganymede? It is, I suggest, the stream of words, the utterance that flows from Socrates "as fast
as possible," almost unconsciously, as it flows from all those possessed; it
is the lover's discourse.

Does it sound as if I too am getting carried away now by the
Nymphs? Look closer to Plato's day, at the perspective offered by the
fabulously rich and well-connected Jewish writer Philo of Alexandria
(*fl. c.*0–40 AD). What Philo loved was to read the ancient Jewish scriptures, in Greek translation, through the prism of Platonic philosophy.
His particular favorites were the *Timaeus* and the *Phaedrus*. He exerted a
profound influence on both the early Christians and the mystical New
Platonists of the later Roman Empire. According to Philo, God's grace
pours down on us like rain or snow, and greatly superior to the nectar
and ambrosia of the myths. "He to whom God has granted unmixed
draughts of intoxication from the hand of one of his servant angels
whom he has appointed to pour the wine" is not going to be happy
scooping from wells or cisterns. Elsewhere he compares Ganymede, or
rather "God's chief wine steward," to the High Priest, "he who pours
the libation of peace, the truly great High Priest, who first receives the
loving cups of God's perennial bounties, then pays them back when he
pours a libation of that potent undiluted draught: himself." Finally
Philo compares Ganymede to God's divine Reason itself, the *Logos,* the
"Word." "Word" is like the "wine pourer" who pours gladness into the
mind of the righteous man and who is himself the substance (the *Logos*)
that he pours, the ambrosial liquid of grace.[35]

This rapturous, mystical Plato, with his notion of humans who have
inside them a touch of the immortal divine reaching out love-struck to
immaterial forms beyond the mundanities of distracting images and
flesh, has been seen as the ultimate source of a whole chorus of raptur-

ous religious mysticism, not excluding the Sufism of men like Rumi, the abstract Alhambra and the Kabbalah. "Since Plato there has been no theology which has not stood in his shadow. For many centuries Platonism was simply the way in which god was thought of and spoken about, in the West as in the Islamic East . . . Since Plato and through him, religion has been essentially different from what it had been before."[36]

Socrates' Ganymede anticipates the immediacy of personal devotion, devotion without the temple and the priests, the direct line of Protestant grace, the torrent of the waters above provoked by a gracious response to God's gracious love, and its splashback mirror image in the soul of the beloved. Centuries before charismatics produced streams of pentecostal discourse, "tongue-blabbing" *glōssolalia,* centuries before the alienolepts took trips around the solar system, there was Socrates not quite remembering what it was he had just said, and Ganymede "taken" from the myrtle grove three miles south of Chalcis.

PELOPS AND HYACINTHUS AT NEW YEAR

The main concern of Bernard Sergent in his study of *Homosexuality in Greek Myth,* first published in French in 1982, was to demonstrate in upward of three hundred pages packed with references to ancient sources that a body of homosexual myths formed the most ancient layer of Greek myth, that here at last the Aryan, Proto-Indo-European element in Greek mythology, six thousand years old, had been found. They were myths—all of them!—that reflected lost rituals of initiation, involving the marginal passive homosexual phase in a boy's life when he is turned from a boy into a man.[1] Sergent described almost seventy relationships of love between males in myth, of which he decided that nineteen were definitely "very old."

Most British scholars disdain Sergent's Indo-European transitional speculations, and would reduce the myths in his "very old" column to zero—as Dover does, arguing that Greek Homosexuality starts a few decades before *c.*600 BC. Nevertheless he comes up with an impressive array of stories about love affairs between gods and heroes and heroes and heroes told by someone at some point in antiquity. I will focus on those that figure most prominently and try to restore some of the dignity eroded over time.

PELOPS

One myth that gets a tick in Sergent's "very old" column concerns Pelops. He is the true hero of Olympia, not Ganymede, with his two or three statues around the place. The sanctuary of Olympian Zeus, perhaps the most important in all of Greece, lay in the the bosky, hilly valley of the river Alpheios in the northwestern Peloponnese—Pelops's island—where the hills of Arcadia meet the plains of Elis. The Olympic

Games were said to have started when a local king, Oenomaus, a grim son of Ares, god of bloody war, challenged young men from all over Greece to see if they could snatch his daughter Hippodamia from him, and then outrun him in their chariots while he chased in hot pursuit. If he caught them he could kill them for attempted rape. If they escaped he would marry the couple and give them his blessing and his kingdom. Since, however, the king was by far the fastest charioteer in Greece, suitors came and perished one by one. The heads of failed candidates started to pile up, until there were thirteen, perhaps one for each year of the contest. Oenomaus turned them into a monument.

The princess must have fretted. Then one day a prince from Turkey came along. Pelops had already had an eventful life. When he was a boy he had been killed by his own father, Tantalus, and served up to the gods at a banquet. Only Demeter, goddess of agriculture, actually ate the strange meat—she had other things on her mind; her daughter Persephone had been carried off to Hades—but it meant that when the gods put Pelops back together again he was missing a piece of his shoulder, the piece that Demeter had enjoyed. Embarrassed, they made him a new one out of ivory.

Pelops thought he might just be the one who could beat the cruel king and carry off his daughter; an early image showed him with a team of winged horses, useful in a chariot race. Some said they were a gift from his lover, Poseidon. Just to make sure, however, he also took the precaution of having the Gordian knot that pinned the king's chariot to the yoke loosened. There was a terrible accident; the king was killed, Pelops got the princess and the Peloponnese named after him. From then on games were held at Olympia to commemorate Pelops's famous victory. If the organizers of the Olympic Games wanted to promote good sportsmanship, you feel they could have chosen a better foundation myth.

The hero had a tomb in the complex by the altar of Zeus. Heroes as "dead" powers can be seen in some ways as gods' opposites, their tombs linked to the Underworld, as gods' altars are linked through smoky essences to heaven.[2] Witnesses say the ground at Pelops's tomb was drenched with blood. The cult was dark and chthonic, involving nocturnal sacrifices and a black ram, as befits offerings to a dead hero. Modern archaeologists were disappointed when they dug into the "tomb" and found nothing there, nothing even to show that it was very old, though there were several prehistoric buildings around the site.[3] They weren't expecting to find Pelops of course, with or without his shoulder, but they did think there might have been some bones that gave rise to the myth—a skeleton, or perhaps the fossilized remains of some creature—which just goes to show that myths don't need anything in the way of artifacts to give rise to them. In fact by the Roman period the story that Pelops was literally buried in the tomb had been dropped. His bones had been kept in a box, while his shoulder blade, which was fished out magically from the sea near Chalcis, had been displayed separately, like a saint's relic, though it seemed to have faded away to nothing; it was said that possession of the shoulder by Pelops's grandson Agamemnon ensured his conquest of Troy.[4]

In 476 BC, a couple of years after the Persians had been driven from Greece, Hiero, magnificent dictator ("tyrant") of the city of Syracuse and currently in control of almost the entire rich island of Sicily, entered a horse—Pherenicus, "Winner"—in the Olympic horse race and won. If you were rich, it had become traditional on such occasions to commission a poem to make the victory famous. Being very rich, Hiero commissioned at least two. Both survive, by Bacchylides (Ode 5) and Pindar. Pindar chose to sing of the very foundation myth of the Games, the chariot race of Pelops. This had the advantage of enabling him to link Hiero the dictator with Pelops, who was not only a king but a founder of Greek kingship, said to have been given a divine "scepter" that had once belonged to Zeus and later passed to Agamemnon—Queen Elizabeth II has her own bejeweled copy of it—a symbol of his supreme authority. Pindar duly makes flattering reference, in Homeric language, to the dictator's "scepter of right," making Hiero's position mythically official, an outrageous Napoleonic legitimation of illegitimate power.[5]

PELOPS DISMISSED

There were problems, however, in the story Pindar had chosen in order to celebrate the horse's victory; that whole sequence with the gods feasting off Pelops's human flesh for a start. Pindar tries to pass over it quickly. He begins with Poseidon falling in love with the boy as he emerges from the cooking pot with his new shoulder, but, like Socrates in *Phaedrus,* he is clearly disturbed: "To be sure, wonders never cease, but then, too, I think, in the mouth of mortal men, myths are worked up beyond the true story, and deceive with fancy lies . . . Son of Tantalus, what I will say of you, though it contradicts earlier poets, is that . . ." He goes on to tell a different story about a very decent feast with no cannibalism and no cooked Pelops. Tantalus was greatly honored by the gods, says Pindar; in fact most believed he was actually a son of Zeus himself. The gods had Tantalus around for dinner and let him feast off ambrosia and nectar, their immortalizing food. Tantalus invited them back to his house in return. But as soon as Poseidon saw the host's young son serving the wine, he was overcome with desire and carried him off in his chariot to the palace of Zeus—"where Ganymede would come on a second occasion"—to serve wine to the king of the gods.

Meanwhile, back on Earth, the boy's absence has been noticed. Search parties set out but search in vain. His mother is worried. Neighbors, envious of the high status of Tantalus's guests, start putting two and two together. Gods came to dinner and now the son has disappeared. "But I cannot call a god a glutton," says Pindar. "I withdraw."[6] However, he continues, some nectar and ambrosia went missing, and Pelops's father was caught handing it out to his own mortal drinking companions, threatening the immortals' monopoly on immortality. The innocent Olympian cupbearer was sacked and thrown back to live among the mortals, while the father had to endure endless tantalizations—water he couldn't drink, fruit he couldn't eat—as punishment for attempting to spread immortality around, a wonderful image of the love for things beyond reach that is inherent in the separation of men and gods.

Some years later, grown up and anxious to win the hand of the princess of Olympia, Pelops needs a favor. He goes for a walk by the seashore, alone, and addresses the waves. There is unfinished business between us, Poseidon, he says. "If Aphrodite's gifts of intimate love [*philia dōra*] reach some gracious conclusion [*ti . . . es charin telletai*]," come now, I will need the fastest chariot in the world to defeat Oenomaus. Oenomaus is "putting off" the marriage of his daughter and has already killed thirteen suitors. Men have the option of living a quiet life, but since we all die anyway, what's the point of an ignominious old age

19. King Oenomaus begins the sacrifice of a white ram at a finishing post topped by an effigy of Artemis. Above him to his left sits Poseidon with the charioteer, Myrtilus, the constellation Auriga. To the right, an Asiatic Pelops races over the water with his bride, Hippodamia, Oenomaus's daughter. Above them, Ganymede with a hoop is in conversation with Zeus. The scene seems to compress a number of elements in the later history of Pelops. Bell krater by the Oinomaos Painter (c.375).

without noble deeds?[7] I'll enter the contest. You make sure that I win. Poseidon obliged with a golden chariot and horses with wings.[8]

This is a sweet story, but Pindar does seem to say quite clearly that he is making up the story of the abduction. The abduction is needed to provide an alternative explanation for his disappearance, not into the pot, but up there to the banquets of the gods. The whole thing, clearly, is built on the myth of Ganymede. And indeed around the time that Pindar composed his poem, the famous clay sculpture of Zeus and Ganymede was dedicated at Olympia, inspired by him or his inspiration. Poseidon takes Pelops to Zeus's house, and Homer says "the gods" snatched Ganymede for Zeus. Homer also says that Zeus gave Ganymede's father a set of immortal horses in return, and here too divine horses are given, but to Pelops himself. Indeed Pindar adduces the parallel with the Trojan prince explicitly, as if to lend support to his revised version of the myth. The new myth of abduction also serves to put the adversaries of the Trojan War on an equal footing. Priam: "My great-uncle Ganymede serves wine to the gods; that's how royal we are."

Agamemnon: "That's nothing. My *grandfather* served wine to the gods and King Zeus gave him this very scepter as a going-home present."

I don't think making that striking parallel was necessarily Pindar's intention, but the rest of the myth of Pelops made it an easy step to take. You couldn't place any old mortal on Olympus, in the very home of the deathless ones. But Tantalus had been very close to the gods, sharing in their banquets, and it didn't seem outrageous to have the son of such a close friend present on Olympus also. The Olympians were on friendly terms with Pelops's family; he would have known how to behave.

We can look at Pindar's poem as a kind of commentary on the myth of Ganymede and what it meant to the Greeks in this, his second moment of fame, in the late archaic/early classical period. There is the same theme of the cupbearer constituting the very food he serves: instead of being feasted on by the gods, Pelops feasts the gods; like Ganymede, he represents sacrifice in its most immediate sense. The poem also dwells on the closeness between men and gods that is embodied in myths of Gods' Loves. The connection between heroic Pelops and the modern tyrant, Pindar's paymaster Hiero, is stated explicitly. Just as a god's love ensured Pelops's victory, so a "god looking out for you, Hiero, devises [*mēdetai*] ways of achieving your aspirations, and doubtless more in the future, unless he disappears (106–12)."[9] Hiero too must have a god in love with him, which helps him win the grace of victory.

But more important than the closeness is the way the story dramatizes the distinction between mortal and immortal. After the rules of hospitality were broken, all intercourse between men and gods ceased, so Pelops also stands for man's expulsion from divine society, the absolute separation of even heroic mortals from gods, an opposition continually reenacted in the opposed cults of god and hero, Zeus and Pelops, Up and Down, Heaven and Hades, side by side at Olympia. Pelops is not merely mortal, he is literally *removed from* the society of immortals, and his ambition to perform noble feats, immortal deeds, is a kind of compensating for that disaster. Even as mortals are elevated to a closeness to the gods by victory, so their ambition to win, to do something worthy even at risk of your life, is a mark of their mortality, because the alternative is to stew in darkness growing ignominiously old. Hiero comes close to the gods by his victory, his closeness to the gods ensures that victory, but his efforts are the efforts of a mortal man who knows time is running out: "May you walk on high," says Pindar, "for the time that is yours" (115). While flattering "King" Hiero to the skies, Pindar elegantly reminds him that he is only human.[10]

Eros brings men and gods together, for sure, but he brings them together across a deep divide. When you talk of bridges, you must also talk of distances to be bridged.

POSEIDON INTRUDES

But there remain some mysteries about the myth of Pelops. We are missing something. We need to put ourselves back in time, to the days of the ancient Olympics, and look around. It's high summer in August. There has been a night festival in honor of the hero Pelops and the black ram has soaked his tomb with its blood by the light of the full moon, the fiftieth since the last Olympics. We look up at the night sky in all its premodern glory, slowly but noticeably revolving over the hours. It's getting late now. Dawn will be here soon. We look higher still, like cranes mating-dancing, until we see, directly above us, one star in particular, standing out against the starry background, exceptionally bright. It is the star we call Capella.

The main problem with the myth of Pelops's abduction is why it should be Poseidon who abducts. Olympia is not his sanctuary by any means. It belongs to his younger brother, who is nevertheless his brother superior: Zeus. It is Zeus's great altar that stands alongside Pelops's great tomb, putting Olympia midway between the heavens and the Underworld. It is Zeus that Pelops has a relationship with. It is Zeus to whom, like Ganymede, he serves ambrosia and nectar during his time on Olympus. Zeus gives him his royal scepter and the Peloponnese. Zeus stands next to him on the east pediment of his temple. Zeus gives him his victory over wicked Oenomaus, blasting his palace with lightning bolts, and the hand of Hippodamia. If anyone should have abducted Pelops, if anyone should have fallen in love with him, it was Zeus. How on earth did Poseidon seize that role? What does he have to do with anything? Olympia is not his shrine. It is nowhere near the sea. And as one might expect, Poseidon barely registers there. In the myth of Pelops he is an interloper.

One obvious answer is that Poseidon sneaks in thanks to the horses, merely because horses, alongside earthquakes and the seas, are one of Poseidon's special subjects. We could imagine the story having arisen like this: Pelops beats speedy Oenomaus with a speedier team. He must have got such thoroughbreds from somewhere. Poseidon is god of horses. Pelops must have got them from Poseidon. Why did Poseidon give him such a gift? He must have been in love. Where did they meet? At that horrendous banquet of Tantalus.

But Zeus is not short of horses to give people, as he proved on more than one occasion to the Trojans, notably when compensating them for the loss of lovely Ganymede. Both mythologically and ritually speaking, it would have been so much neater if he had been the one to endow Pelops. It could have been Zeus who loved and gave, Zeus who provided the winning team. So why didn't he? Why did Zeus allow his elder brother Poseidon to intrude so significantly on his most important sanctuary, where he seems to have had barely even a toehold?

And there is another question. Why on earth do these horses have wings, according to a tradition that is much older than Pindar even?[11] Not even the Trojans had such horses, not even Achilles was given such horses, and his were actually fathered by a winged creature, Zephyrus, the western breeze. Poseidon has been overgenerous with Pelops. The best chariot team in the world by all means, but surely not horses with wings. And the wings are more than just an archaic way of indicating that something is very fast. This chariot really does fly. Pelops takes it out to sea, without even wetting his axle, we are told.[12] But his rival Oenomaus didn't have flying horses. The race to which he challenged the suitors was land bound. So are we to imagine Pelops racing alongside him, ready to overtake, but suddenly taking to the sky and soaring right over his head? What kind of a foundation myth for the ruthlessly fair Olympics is this?

CRASH VICTIMS: ERECHTHEUS AND HIPPOLYTUS

On the other hand, Poseidon is involved with some other charioteering heroes and some other spectacular crashes, notably Hippolytus, the son of Theseus, falsely accused of seducing his stepmother Phaedra, daughter of Minos, and Erechtheus, father of Procris and king of Athens. The stories are very different. Poseidon is not in love with either of these charioteers, nor the provider of their teams, but their chariots do have one specific thing in common, and something they share with Pelops's.

Erechtheus was believed to have been the man who discovered how to yoke horses to a chariot in the first place, the very first charioteer.[13] Unfortunately there had been a dispute over Athens between Poseidon and Athena. The gods had competed for the city's love by offering different presents. Athena gave Athens the cultivated olive, an enormously useful gift, whereas all Poseidon could come up with was a spring of water, and, what is more, undrinkable water, salty as the sea, a miracle maybe, but hardly beneficial. So Athena won the contest and the city became hers, but Poseidon was not a good loser, and got his son Eumolpus to make war on Athens from neighboring Eleusis.

Erechtheus fought valiantly, but the tide ran against him. To avoid disaster and protect the city his virgin daughters would need to be sacrificed, at any rate those daughters who hadn't, like Procris, been killed by husbands who never erred, or, like Orithyia, been abducted by the North Wind. Athena decided to stellify them, placing them in the heavens as the Hyades, who form the muzzle of Taurus the bull. Finally Erechtheus himself had to die. Poseidon hurled his trident and drove Erechtheus into the earth. Thus Athens was saved and the gods reconciled. As part of the deal and a sign of reconciliation, Poseidon was granted a cult on the Acropolis beside his salty spring. Indeed he was given an odd amalgamated cult with Erechtheus, sharing an altar with the man he had killed, right next to the most ancient and sacred cult of Athena, in the unique sacred building we call the Erechtheum, which was known to the Athenians as "the old temple," a terribly holy place. Among its many odd features is a skylight, a glassless window in the roof.

Hippolytus was also involved in a divine dispute, between himself and Aphrodite, goddess of love.[14] Young Hippolytus, son of Theseus and an Amazon, loved hunting and hated loving. He cared only for sport. Aphrodite decided to teach him a lesson, and Phaedra, his stepmother, suddenly found herself more pleased than she had previously been to see her handsome young stepson. She fell hopelessly in love with him in fact. Hippolytus would have none of it. Phaedra was frustrated, driven quite mad with desire. Eventually she decided to kill herself, but was determined to take Hippolytus down too. Her suicide note contained accusations and Theseus believed them—suicide seemed to be proof enough. Outraged, he called upon his own father, Poseidon, who had foolishly granted him three wishes. He wished his son dead. By this time Hippolytus had taken to his chariot, heading for the coast, driving like a mad thing. Suddenly the sea began to swell and a monstrous bull appeared on the crest of a tidal wave. It spooked the horses, the chariot crashed, and Hippolytus died in the wreckage, while the chariot and the horses vanished, "hidden away along with the dreadful monstrous bull, in the rocky ground, I don't know where."[15] Theseus discovered the truth, that his wife had lied, his son was innocent, and his curse had been only too effective. Poseidon of course would have known all this already, arranging the death of his grandson as a favor to his son, but the gods work in mysterious ways. There is no record of smiling Aphrodite showing the slightest regret.

MYTHS AND CONSTELLATIONS

What these two charioteers have in common is that they were both linked by later writers to the constellation called Reins-Holder, Auriga the Charioteer, distinguished by the very bright star called Goat, Capella, on his reins-holding shoulder, the fourth brightest of Greek stars, which you can see easily even in London if you go outside in winter and simply look straight up.[16] People are often bemused by Greek constellations, wondering how on earth anyone could see a Reins-Holder in the constellation Auriga, for instance. But they are identified not merely, or even not mostly, by what they look like, but by the nature of their movements, especially their first predawn risings, their first predawn settings, their trajectories and the periods when they set "for the last time" and vanish for weeks, nowhere to be seen, and then are suddenly seen rising once more just before Dawn . . . So stories about the Boeotian hero Orion—that he is huge, wades in water, lies on a beach, hunts, is loved by Dawn and killed by Artemis or a scorpion sent by Mother Earth—are in fact stories about what the constellation Orion gets up to: is big, walks over waters, sometimes lies horizontal on the horizon, moves off chasing the Bull or the Pleiades, accompanied by his Dog, Sirius, is chased by Dawn, vanishes from the skies in the spring months "of Artemis," first sets when Scorpion rises from the rocky horizon on the opposite side, etc.

Two features in particular are attached to star myths. Sometimes they are said to be made of metal (they shine), and often they are said to fly (they move across the sky). So Sirius was said to be not just any old dog, but one made of bronze. Aries is the flying golden ram that rescues Phrixus and Helle, dropping Helle haplessly in the Hellespont, and there are no stellar wings to be seen in the constellation Pegasus, nor on the Head of Medusa, nor on Virgo, even if they are represented, e.g., on Versace's Medusa logo, with wings. Those wings just mean Horse-in-the-Sky, Virgin-in-the-Sky, Head-of-Medusa-in-the-Sky; the wings merely identify them as "flying," i.e., as constellations.

The best explanation for how the constellation of Reins-Holder got its name is that it seems to follow a great course, to "drive" right over the top of the sky, like the sun in his chariot, and when it vanishes it does so (in Greek latitudes) only briefly, missing the end of April and the beginning of May, and reappears on the horizon not very far away, like a chariot driving to the very pole of the night sky then turning and returning to earth. That is one theory anyway.

Most classicists don't take star myths very seriously, imagining that they are late and romantic stories with little religious significance, but the popularity of "all-night festivals," *pannychides,* especially in honor of dead Underworld heroes, means that the stars would have been a spectacular part of the sacred landscape. And we can see the way the movements of the stars inform the myths. Anyone in the Erechtheum at night, for instance, would, from the end of August onward, be able to see the brightest star of Auriga, Erechtheus himself, through the skylight above their heads in the hours before Dawn.[17] What is more, many think that is where Poseidon's seawater pool must have been, in the natural rocks left uncovered on the floor of the temple directly below. As the bright white star passed overhead, it would have been reflected on the surface of the water, Erechtheus in Poseidon, a perfect amalgam of the amalgamated god-hero Poseidon-Erechtheus. Moreover, by coincidence Auriga and Taurus, i.e., their brightest and most distinctive stars, set at the same time of year, within days or a day of each other, just as Erechtheus and his daughters, Taurus's muzzle, died at the same time in myth. The strange disappearance together of the monstrous bull from the sea and the chariot team of Hippolytus "in the rocky ground" also makes more sense as an allegory of the setting together of Auriga and Taurus.

The identification of Auriga with Hippolytus was a myth that the people of Troezen told of their great hero with his great sanctuary, but it never caught on elsewhere. Erechtheus did have competition, however, for the handbooks preserve an alternative identification of Reins-Holder with Myrtilus the charioteer, and it is clear that the chariot he was driving when he died and was set among the stars belonged to Pelops. For Myrtilus had been flirting with Pelops's hard-won bride Hippodamia during a ride in the country at Geraistos, the southernmost tip of Euboea (a great place for stargazing) and site of a famous temple of Poseidon. Well, a ride in the country or even across the Aegean Sea! "Myrtilus, sunk in the deep sea, tossed headlong out of the all-golden chariot in grievous outrage . . ."[18] Now is it a coincidence that the coast of Euboea was also where Pelops's prosthetic ivory shoulder was found by fishermen, and that Capella, the brightest star of Auriga, is supposed to form his shoulder? Was there a version of the myth in which Pelops's shoulder was yanked off at the same time?

Here at any rate, on the other side of Greece from Olympia, we have Pelops connected to a sanctuary of Poseidon, at the time of the death of Myrtilus the Reins-Holder. In fact the peculiar features of the chariot, that it is all gold and shiny and flies through the skies, mean that it was probably identified with the constellation Auriga as early as the archaic period, and like the constellation it could be seen to come from the sea, and fly over the sea, without getting its axle wet. During Pelops's nocturnal sacrifices at the Olympic festival, therefore, you would actually have been able to see the chariot, as Auriga, flying directly overhead. This may also help to explain an odd figure on the east pediment of the great temple of Zeus at Olympia. Not only do we find the chariot and Myrtilus the Reins-Holder, holding reins, as well as one of the Pleiads, Sterope, wife of the wicked king, mother of Hippodamia, but a corner of the pediment harbors a crouching boy who seems from images on coins to be Arcas, founder of the race of Arcadians. His presence seems quite inexplicable here until we recall that he was the son of the Great Bear Callisto and that he had another name, Nyktimos, "Nightly One," and was identified with the constellation Boötes, which contains the superbright star Arcturus, second only to Sirius among the stars the

Greeks took heed of. Arcturus would have been setting over the horizon as Auriga rose to the top of the sky, setting perhaps over the "tombs of the Arcadians," who, according to myth, had attacked Olympia but then, inexplicably, fled west, away from Arcadia, terrified when a baby turned into a snake. The pediment can almost be read as an image of the stars during the nocturnal rites. The idea seems to have been picked up by the architects of the Parthenon twenty or so years after the building of the temple of Zeus at Olympia. They placed the Sun's chariot rising on one side of the pediment and the horses of the Moon or Night on the other. The head of the exhausted horse of Selene is one of the masterpieces of Greek art and one of the most celebrated of all the Elgin Marbles. What is more the Sun is about to trample over a reclining ephebe, reclining in exactly the position of Orion on the horizon at dawn at this time of year. No Athenian who had stayed up for the night festival could have failed to notice the similarity. It was as if the triangular pediment was itself an image of the sky, with Athena born from Zeus's head in the middle. Indeed, Auriga may be present on the Parthenon also, since his brightest star, Capella, in Greek *Aix,* was also said to be Athena's aegis.

This then, I think, is how Pelops came to have a relationship with Poseidon, and a golden chariot and horses with wings. Because the chariot with which he defeated Oenomaus was the constellation Auriga the Reins-Holder, and Auriga was connected with Poseidon at Troezen via Hippolytus, in Athens via Erechtheus, and on the southernmost tip of Euboea, where Myrtilus the Reins-Holder died. The link between the god and the constellation was made in the first place, not just perhaps because Poseidon was god of horses, but because he was god of seas and earthquakes and clefts that he makes with his trident, god of those permeable surfaces of the earth from which Auriga rises and into which it disappears. Perhaps, more generally, Poseidon is a god associated with winter. His festivals were often held in winter months, he was said to summer in Ethiopia, and Auriga sits high over the winter skies.

LITTLE CHRYSIPPUS

There is a strange coda to the story of Pelops. The princess he won in the chariot race to the death against her father, and whose honor he so fiercely protected when Myrtilus made a pass, was a dangerous woman. Pelops already had an heir, Chrysippus, a lovely boy by all accounts, the product of some former liaison, not fully legitimate, but kin enough to be a threat to Hippodamia's own children, Atreus and Thyestes. They plotted to get rid of their half brother and threw him down a well. Pelops found out and laid a terrible curse on his sons that would work itself out in the coming generations in horrible crimes committed in the bosom of the family: discovering that his brother has been sleeping with his wife, Atreus serves up the children of this adulterous union to their own father; Thyestes is avenged in the next generation by his son, the son he had fathered by raping his own daughter. This son is called Aegisthus. More adultery, regicide and matricide—Agamemnon, Clytemnestra, Orestes—follow. This is the curse of the House of Atreus.

This version of Chrysippus's demise is attested by historians of the classical period, and Plato thought it was well known. Chrysippus's stepmother certainly fell under a shadow. The women who served the cult of the heroine Hippodamia in Olympia thought her bones had been

20. The beginnings of the Oedipus saga. An ephebic Laius abducts a young Chrysippus who reaches out to his father, Pelops. The old man at top right is the boy's neglectful chaperon (*paidagôgos*). Along with the abduction of Hippodamia, the abduction of Chrysippus was a popular subject among Italian painters. Apulian Bell krater (fourth century).

retrieved from Midea in the Argolid, a Mycenaean site full of ancient tombs. What was she doing there on the other side of the Peloponnese? She was avoiding her husband Pelops. Why was she avoiding him? He was furious with her over the death of his son Chrysippus.[19]

Slightly later we begin to get a quite different story to account for Chrysippus's disappearance. Italian vase painters of the fourth century BC seem to have known a dramatic version of Chrysippus's story in which he appears as a small boy in oriental Phrygian-looking clothing— his father, remember, came from Asian Turkey—being abducted.[20] Both his youth and the criminality of the action are emphasized by the presence of his distraught chaperon, an old *paidagōgos,* whose role in life is precisely to stop this kind of thing happening, and by the sword the abductor sometimes puts to the boy's throat.[21] The vases are illustrating, it seems, a lost play called *Chrysippus,* by Euripides, or another version by some later playwright.[22] In this version, a visitor came to court one day, Laius of Thebes, a young king, about eighteen years old, who had lost his kingdom to a pair of usurping twins.[23] Pelops offered him refuge, but Laius fell in love with his host's son, and when the time came for him to reclaim his throne he decided he would enjoy kingship better if he had Chrysippus by his side.

"You are not telling me anything I don't already know," says Laius to someone in Euripides' version, at the very crossroads, it seems, of his crime, "but though I know what I am supposed to do, Mother Nature has other ideas."[24] Laius pulls Chrysippus into his chariot and races off to Thebes. He regrets his action in similar terms: "Woe is me, when someone knows what is good and doesn't do it, that's the gods' way of bringing evil on men."[25] Hera, however, notices the parallel with Pelops's chariot-racing marriage to Hippodamia, and as goddess of marriage, *gamostolos,* she feels personally insulted.[26] To punish the Thebans for their tolerance, this flouting of her marriage laws, she sends them a monster, a savage lion with the head of a woman and a fondness for riddles. The Sphinx terrorizes Thebes for decades. At the climax of the story, and therefore perhaps of Euripides' play, Chrysippus kills himself out of shame and a messenger gives Laius an oracle from Apollo's sanctuary at Delphi. The gods have heeded the prayers of Pelops and Laius is cursed. He will be killed by his own son. Then his own son will take his place in the marriage bed—the child we know as Oedipus.

The story certainly seems to condemn the rape as a terrible crime equivalent to murder, but the vase painters emphasize the smallness of Chrysippus in the play: This is the rape *at the point of a sword* of an under-Eighteen by a Stripling, Laius, not the abduction of an older son of Pelops by a former marriage. One author seems to have responded by trying to reconcile the two versions of Chrysippus's story, the murder of an older brother and the heir to the throne and the story of the love affair with Laius. The result is sensational. In this version, Chrysippus seems to be older. He is having a secret affair with Laius, but he is discovered by his younger half brothers, who inform their father, Pelops. Pelops, perhaps remembering his happy relationship with Poseidon, condones the lovers because he sees that Laius's love for his son is sincere. Chrysippus retains his status as his father's favorite son and heir. Hippodamia, the wicked stepmother, tries but fails to persuade her sons to kill their rival. She will have to do the work herself. One night she steals into the room where Laius and Chrysippus are lying in bed together. Quietly she takes Laius's sword and uses it to kill her stepson, hoping that his boyfriend will get the blame. Fortunately the boy survives just long enough, however, to identify the real perpetrator and clear Laius's name.[27] This version sounds very much like some lost play. If so, what fun it must have been.

At any rate, just as Pindar substitutes Pelops's abduction to Olympus for his murder, so Euripides, or whoever, substituted Chrysippus's abduction for his murder and Pelops's curse is transferred thereby from his own to another famously dysfunctional family, the House of Oedipus. Greek tragedians frequently commented on each other's plays. They were rivals in competition and these "comments" might be very pointed, satirizing a rival's famous scene, correcting a rival's plot or subverting it with a new piece of information. The target of this rewritten version seems to have been Sophocles' *Oedipus Rex*.[28]

Oedipus Rex was widely considered the greatest masterpiece of Greek tragic drama. Chrysippus doesn't figure in it. The hero, Oedipus, has come to the throne having rid Thebes of the Sphinx that was terrorizing the population, but there is something wrong. Plague stalks the land. Oedipus sends to Apollo's oracle at Delphi to find out what the problem is; the problem is that Laius, his predecessor on the throne, was murdered and his murderer has not yet been brought to justice. A responsi-

ble monarch, Oedipus decides to do all in his power to find the perpetrator and purify his sick kingdom. As his investigation proceeds, he
comes to realize that the culprit is none other than himself, but just as he
is facing up to the horrible truth a further horror is revealed: The king
was his father and his mother is now his wife.

Among the many wonderful things in the tragedy is the way the hero
gradually finds his finger pointing at himself. It is wonderfully plotted,
a hint gradually turning to a revelation, each revelation yielding further
hints, the hero engineering his own destruction in classic tragic style,
but there is something left open at the end. While we are led further and
further on into the truth, and while we are satisfied by the discovery of
a final truth and impressed by the inescapability of the gods' destiny, we
are not entirely satisfied: The gods' logic seems beyond us. While the
play moves toward increasing illumination and the suffering, meanwhile, is piled on, the darkness that covers the reasoning behind the suffering simply grows more and more conspicuous. Oedipus didn't know
what he was doing; he has acted reasonably, heroically, responsibly; it is
all so unfair. It is entirely possible that this mysterious sense of ultimate
dissatisfaction was part of Sophocles' plan. The seductive movement of
the plot toward greater and greater revelation is designed to show up by
contrast what cannot be known. Failing to understand is appropriate for
humans when faced with the workings of the divine. The gods are mysterious; they are not fair. The gods are gods, and for mere mortals there
can be no consummated knowledge of their ways.

With Chrysippus worked into the mixture, we see Sophocles' Oedipus in a quite different light. A new play about a terrible crime committed by Laius unravels this careful distinction between the transparency
of human events and the obscurity of the divine and reduces Sophocles'
great play to an airport novel, the long-ago sexual abuse of a child explaining everything that has happened. Oedipus imagines he has got to
the dreadful heart of things, but one big final secret remains undiscov-
ered. The gods' logic on the other hand becomes instantly transparent.
Laius had committed a terrible crime against a father. The father cursed
him with an accursed child. The gods acted to bring the curse to fruition
in answer to the father's prayers.

Chrysippus's abduction seems on balance—though you can never say
for sure—to be a late myth. There is no sign of it before Euripides'

Chrysippus. The earliest images are later than that and depict a stage drama, later productions, or later versions of the myth. The myth itself seems littered with stage instructions. Moreover, we can see how it was made. Euripides, for he is still the likely candidate, took from Pindar the idea of substituting an abduction for a murder. He gave Pelops a taste of his own medicine by making him the father whose child is abducted, as he had stolen Hippodamia. He turned the chariot-race marriage of Pelops into Laius's chariot-race marriage with a boy, thereby nicely angering Hera and accounting for a Sphinx. And he simply transferred Pelops's curse from one dismal family, his own, the curse of the house of Atreus, to another, neatly avenging Chrysippus's "bad marriage" with an even worse marriage for Laius's son, Oedipus.

The myth of Gay Chrysippus clearly reflects Athenian homosexual anxieties about the proximity of Striplings and Boys in the gymnasium projected onto other nations—the *paidagōgos,* the chaperon, especially seems a distinctively Athenian kind of touch. But I wonder if the apparent popularity of the myth in the fourth century does not also have something to do with attitudes to the specific homosexual practices of the Thebans, with their formal troth-plighting and living as man and wife, practices brought to attention by the startling success of the Army of Lovers whom we will meet later on.

HYACINTHUS

If the gay myths of Ganymede and Pelops have a central role in Greek literature and in reflections on the nature of the mortal condition and sacrificial exchanges with the divine, the love of Apollo for Hyacinthus the Spartan is far more obviously central in cult. According to the myths, Hyacinthus was loved by two deities at the same time, Apollo and Zephyr, the mild West Wind. There was a throwing competition. Hyacinthus let the god go first. Apollo twisted around and launched his discus into the sky with the force only a god can muster, scattering the clouds in every direction. When it came back into view, like a meteor out of infinity, it was heading straight for his boyfriend. Some suspected that jealous Zephyr had blown it off course. Flowers grew from the soil moistened by the boy's dying blood. Apollo was distraught. He made a record of his distraction on the flowers, writing the letters "AIAI," which express grief forever after. Hyacinths you are assuming, and in the end you are probably right, though the flower's identity has been disputed. In fact I think the explanation for the myth about the inscription is simplicity itself. The point is that each hyacinth floret has six petals, petals that used to be narrower and paler and more spread out, like little constellations of stars. There is also often a shadow of a stripe down the center of each of the petals, spelling out as you read around in capital letters Apollo's lamentation "AIAI"—✶—"/|\, /|\"—six down strokes, two groans. Others said that Apollo had written Hyacinthus's initial on the flower. The hyacinth petals are in fact arranged in triplets in the form of two trefoils in a Y-formation, overlaid, and "Y" is Hyacinthus's initial—Greeks tended to omit initial "h."[29]

The earliest *certain* reference to the discus competition and the accidental death comes in Euripides' *Helen,* performed in 412 BC.[30] The story exonerates the god on a technicality, for in Athens, at least, the famous draconian legislation, the "Law of Draco," absolved from the charge of blood-guilty murder anyone who killed an opponent in an athletic competition, following an inquest "at the Delphinium" of Athens, an open-air court by the sanctuary of Apollo Delphinios, "the holiest of all courts and the most shudder-inducing."[31] Others insisted that the discus had hit the ground first and hit Hyacinthus on the rebound; the boy had been too eager to fetch it so that he could have a go. The story of jealous Zephyr serves the same purpose of absolving Apollo, hence in the evolved myth the killing is doubly accidental and Apollo walks doubly free—it was a sporting accident and there was sabotage.

The first definite record of Hyacinthus's youthful beauty is a famous painting by the artist Nicias of the late fourth century BC, known from descriptions: "The Oebalian boy [i.e., Hyacinthus] turns his dying eyes from the unseen discus, Phoebus's fault, Phoebus's pain." The emperor Augustus's favorite painting, he took it as a souvenir from Cleopatra's sacked Alexandria, and after his death and deification it was hung in his own temple.[32] The love triangle with Zephyr and Apollo as rival *erastai* appears toward the end of the treatise *On Things Which Are Hard to Believe (Peri Apistōn)* by the mysterious fourth-century author Palaephatus, Aristotle's beloved boyfriend, but this part of the text was added later, probably much later. At this point, therefore, we could simply remove Hyacinthus from the Very Old Gay Myth column and move on, but

Hyacinthus is an intriguing figure in Greek religion and it is worthwhile to take a closer look at the circumstances in which the story of Apollo's love for him was told. The charming tales told by Ovid and depicted in European art over the centuries have another reality in the religious lives of the Greeks. And there are some strange pictures.

MOURNING HYACINTHUS

Hyacinthus stood at the center of the Hyacinthia, a festival that took place in midsummer, probably in July, some kilometers outside the center of Sparta at a village called Amyclae, "the most treeful and fruitful place in the territory of Sparta . . . containing the sanctuary of Apollo, which is just about the most famous of all Spartan shrines."[33] The festival was famous for a special healing song (and dance) in honor of Apollo, known as the paean, characterized by a ritual bugle-like shout, lingering on the second syllable—I-E-E. It was one of the most important events in Sparta's religious calendar,[34] as a couple of anecdotes will show. In 479 BC, as Xerxes' enormous army, come all the way from Persia, marched for the second time toward Athens, the Athenians begged Sparta to come and save them. The Spartans excused themselves on the grounds that they were celebrating the Hyacinthia.[35] Ninety years later, Sparta herself was in trouble. Corinth, traditionally a staunch ally, had gone over to the other side. The Spartan king Agesilaus was determined to teach them a lesson. Unfortunately it was that time of year again, and some of his soldiers wanted to go home to celebrate the Hyacinthia. This was not the kind of thing a commander wanted to deal with in the middle of a war, but Agesilaus made a concession to those who hailed from the shrine itself: "The people of Amyclae," says Xenophon, "whether they are on campaign or are abroad for any other reason, always go home for the Hyacinthia, so they can sing the paean to Apollo." Agesilaus even arranged an escort for the pilgrims through enemy territory. The escort was massacred, a rare defeat in Sparta's proud history, but an omen of things to come.[36]

At the heart of the festival were three days of feasting, singing and dancing. It is not often that we get to see Spartans having so much fun:

> On the middle day there is a colorful spectacle, and a huge and remarkable gathering of people. Boys [*paides*] with tunics hitched up

play the lyre and sing to the sound of shawms. They sing to the god [Apollo] in a high pitch, singing to the shawm while running over all the lyre-strings with the plectrum [?] to a marching—di di dum, di di dum—beat. Others pass through the theater on caparisoned horses. The entire cohort of Cadets [*Neaniskoi*] enter and sing one of the local [i.e., of Amyclae] songs while in their midst dancers move to the music of song and shawm in the ancient pattern. As for the unmarried women, some ride in wicker carts expensively decked out, others compete in chariot processions. The entire city is given over to the excitement and joy of the festival. On this day they sacrifice masses of victims and the citizens entertain special guests [*gnōrimoi*] at dinner and their own slaves. No one misses the festival. On the contrary, the city is actually emptied for the spectacle.[37]

The wicker floats, topped with arches in the shape of griffins, stags and billy goats, were peculiar to the festival of Hyacinthus and the subject of learned commentaries. Their extravagance is revealed in a flattering obituary of King Agesilaus, who insisted that his daughter go to the festival in the "city-float," as if going in her own float would automatically have involved her father in enormous expense. The floats clearly consisted of something rather more than plant stuff and a lick of paint.[38]

This was day two of the festival. But the other days had a very different character, says our source; it was a somber funereal occasion. Sparta is "in mourning for Hyacinthus; they wear no garlands at dinner, and bring no bread into the dining place, nor do they give out any other baked goods or things which accompany such occasions [?]. They sing no paeans in praise of Apollo and whatever is normal in other sacrificial feasts is banned. Instead they dine very formally and then go home."[39] Our other main source of information for the cult of Hyacinthus concerns the strange monument at its center, the remarkable giant "throne" at Amyclae. The throne doesn't survive, but it was one of Sparta's major tourist attractions and was described by Pausanias in his Roman-period *Description of Greece;* he says he won't go into detail, and then proceeds to give a very long account. Either this is a rhetorical ploy on the part of a notoriously pedantic list maker or the Amyclae throne was even more remarkable than he describes.[40] The most primitive-looking part, to his eyes, was a massive bronze statue of Apollo, forty-five feet high, at a

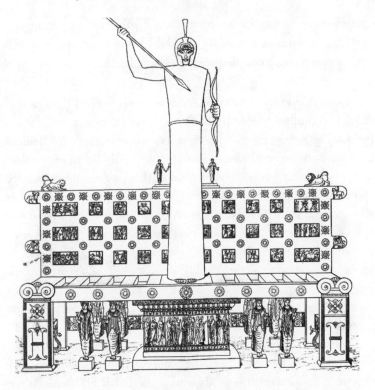

21. Adolf Furtwängler's attempt to reconstruct the Amyclae Throne from
Pausanias's description (3.18,9–19,5). A massive archaic bronze Apollo (*c.*15
meters high) stands on a throne that sits on top of Hyacinthus's tomb. The
tomb showed the dead hero being "translated to the heavens" (*es ouranon*).
The monument was the centerpiece of the annual festival of Hyacinthus.
Bathycles of Magnesia (sixth century).

guess: "Though it has a face, feet and hands, the rest resembles a bronze
column. On its head is a helmet, and in its hands a spear and bow."

At some time, probably in the sixth century, when the first stone
temples were sprouting up all over the Greek world, the Spartans commissioned a sculptor from Magnesia in Asia Minor to make an elaborate
platform or "throne" where the colossus could take his ease, with more
seating provided for other gods or heroes on either side. Bathycles covered the structure with reliefs, drawn from the whole range of myths—
"free association," says one art historian, but there is an emphasis on
Spartan figures such as Menelaus and Helen, and Heracles, a distinguished ancestor, and quite a few constellations.[41] It is worth quoting at

length not only to show what Sparta was capable of but because this is what Greek mythology actually looked like in practice; only Hindu temples are as heavily peopled with gods and heroes:

It is supported in front by two Graces and two Seasons ["caryatids," then] and similarly behind. On the left stand Echidna and Typhos [primordial monsters], on the right Tritons [mermen]. To describe the reliefs one by one in detail would have merely bored my readers; but to be brief and concise—for most of them are familiar: Poseidon and Zeus are carrying Taÿgete [Hyacinthus's great-grandmother, who gave her name to snow-topped Mount Taÿgetus that towers over Sparta, and one of the seven stars called Pleiads, or "mountain Pleiads," daughter of Atlas [archetypal mountain], and Taÿgete's sister Alcyone [another of the stars].[42] There are also reliefs of Atlas, the single combat of Heracles and Cycnus [fearsome warrior who commits sacrilege against a shrine of Apollo], and his battle with the Centaurs at the cave of Pholus.

I do not know why Bathycles represented the so-called Minotaur tied up and led away by Theseus;[43] the dance of the Phaeacians [a chorus of boys entertaining Odysseus at the end of his travels] is represented on the throne, with Demodocus singing [about the affair of Ares and Aphrodite]; and the exploit of Perseus [grandson of Hyacinthus's aunt Eurydice] against Medusa is also depicted. Passing over the fight between Heracles and the giant Thurius and that of Tyndareus [king of Sparta and grandson of Hyacinthus's brother] with Eurytus, one comes to the rape of the Leucippides [by Castor and Pollux]. He has also shown Dionysus and Heracles; Hermes is carrying the former, still a child, to heaven, while Athena is leading Heracles to live henceforth among the gods.[44] Peleus is handing over Achilles [his son] to be brought up by Chiron [the centaur], who is said to have been his teacher too. Cephalus is being abducted by Day [the goddess Dawn] because of his beauty, and the gods are bringing gifts to the wedding of Harmonia [product of the liaison between Ares and Aphrodite]. The duel [narrated in the *Iliad* and in the lost epic *Aithiopis*] between Achilles and Memnon [Dawn's son] is represented, and so is Heracles avenging himself on Dionysius the Thracian and on Nessus [a bad centaur] at the river Euenus. Hermes is leading the goddesses to be judged by Paris [which will lead to Helen's abduction by same Paris], Adrastus and Tydeus are stopping the fight between Amphiaraus and Lycurgus, the son of Pronax. Hera is gazing at Io, the daughter of Inachus, who is already a cow, and Athena is fleeing Hephaestus, who is pursuing her [he will ejaculate, Athena will wipe his seed off her thigh with a piece of wool that will fall on the ground and produce Erechtheus the Charioteer]. Next to them are shown, from the Labors of Heracles, the Hydra and how he led up the dog [Cerberus] from Hades. There are Anaxias and Mnasinous, each on horseback, but Megapenthes, [bastard] son of Menelaus, and Nicostratus [another bastard? son of Menelaus] ride together on one horse. Bellerophon is killing the beast in Lycia [i.e., hunting the Chimaera on the back of Pegasus], and Heracles is driving off Geryon's cattle. On the upper edges of the throne are placed the sons of Tyndareus [Helen's brothers, the twins Castor and Pollux, known as the Dioscuri, "youths of Zeus"] on horseback, one on each side; there are sphinxes beneath the horses, and wild beasts running upwards [?], on one side a leopard, by Pollux a lioness. On the very top of the throne a band of dancers has been made, representing the Magnesians, who helped Bathycles make the throne.[45] Beneath the throne on the inside, away from the Tritons, is the hunt of the Calydonian boar, and Heracles killing Actor's children [fearsome Siamese twins]; Calaïs and Zetes [the Boreads, winged sons of the North Wind] are driving the Harpies away from Phineus; Pirithous and Theseus [best friends] have abducted Helen, and Heracles is strangling the lion; Apollo and Artemis are shooting Tityus [who tried to rape their mother]; also represented is Heracles' fight with Orius the Centaur and Theseus's battle with the Minotaur. In addition are represented Heracles wrestling [the river] Achelous, the fabled binding of Hera by Hephaestus, the games Acastus held for his father [the very famous Funeral Games of Pelias, who had been chopped up and boiled by Medea, to avenge her lover Jason], and the story of Menelaus and Egyptian Proteus [a prophetic protean seal; seals used to be common in the Mediterranean] from the *Odyssey*. And finally there is Admetus yoking a boar and a lion to his chariot and the Trojans are bringing libations to Hector.[46]

The giant statue stood on a strange platform, half altar, half tomb, the central focus of the cult: "and they say that Hyacinthus has been buried in it, and at the Hyacinthia, before the sacrifice to Apollo, they make heroic offerings to Hyacinthus [*enagizousi*], into this altar through a bronze door, which is on the left of the altar."[47]

The altar-tomb itself was also decorated with mythological scenes, and a whole gathering of Olympian gods, including Dionysus and his mother Semele, whom he rescued from the Underworld,[48] and Dionysus's aunt Ino, who likewise escaped her mortality,[49] Demeter, her daughter Persephone and Wealth (Underworld Pluto), then Fates and Seasons, then Aphrodite, Athena and Artemis:

> They are carrying up to heaven [*ouranos*] Hyacinthus and Polyboea, Hyacinthus's sister, they say, who died before marriage.[50] Now this statue of Hyacinthus represents him as already with a beard ["just bearded?"], but Nicias, son of Nicomedes,[51] has painted him in the very prime of youthful beauty [*hōraios*], hinting at the mythical love of Apollo for Hyacinthus. Wrought on the altar is also Heracles; he too is being led to heaven by Athena and the other gods. On the altar are also the daughters of Thestius (Leda, Helen's mother or adoptive mother, and her sisters), Muses and Seasons. As for Zephyr the Wind, how Apollo killed Hyacinthus accidentally, and the story of the flower, that may not be how it was, perhaps, but let the story stand.

HYACINTHUS SUPPLANTED

The ending of Hyacinthus's name, -nthus, comes probably from a non-Indo-European, i.e., non-Aryan language, earlier than Sparta's Dorian dialect, earlier than the Mycenaean language spoken by Menelaus and Agamemnon, earlier, indeed, than Greek.[52] It is a name that seems to belong to an era when Greece knew nothing of Greek-speakers, a name from, say, 2000 BC or even earlier. Moreover, someone was already being worshipped at Amyclae in the Bronze Age by the Greeks who lived in the thick-walled ancient ruins called "Menelaus's Palace." Hyacinthus's shrine, as it happens, is one of the most ancient religious centers in Greece, although there may have been a few interruptions.[53]

To be fair, the Greeks of the historical period seem to have done their best to give him credit for his antiquity. Hyacinthus's great age was acknowledged in symbols of superlongevity; he occupies a position high up in genealogies, preceding Mycenaeans like Menelaus, close to personified geographical features, the most primordial parts of a genealogy, grandson of the nearby river Eurotas, great-grandson of the nymph of Mount Taÿgetus itself, as if he was born out of the very landscape of Sparta; and if there is no bread on his festival day, that may well be because in his prehistoric time bread hadn't been invented—that's how old he is. The combination of great antiquity with the accessories of ancientness is suggestive, and the special place of Amyclae within the Spartan confederation of villages, and the diffusion of Hyacinthus's local cult in cities that spoke in Dorian dialect—lots of "a"s instead of "e"s, Athana instead of Athene—implies that when the Dorians arrived, Hyacinthus was already there, treated with extreme reverence and awe, and the possession of his cult by the Spartans was vaunted as a great achievement. Religion was always very useful in geopolitics, but you couldn't easily fabricate the power of ancient holiness; antiquity has its own weight.

At any rate, evidence for cults involving Hyacinthus is found in all those Dorian places that look as if they dribble out of Sparta into the Mediterranean: the midriff of Crete ("Bakinthos"), Santorini (Thera), Rhodes, Cos, Cnidus ("Iakinthos") and Calymnus.[54] We must imagine that when the Dorians arrived in Sparta they found Hyacinthus waiting for them and adopted his cult as their own, and when some of them emigrated south, they took Hyacinthus with them.[55]

If Apollo was unknown in the Mycenaean period, his healing-dance/song, the Paean, was. For a god Pajawone was found in a Bronze Age list of gods from Cnossus in Crete, when it was part of the Mycenaean (i.e., Greek) second-millennium occupation. Pajawone may be older than that even, since the epiphany of divine powers in rituals of singing and dancing, such as the Paean, is said to have been characteristic of Minoan religion.[56] Pajawone survived the collapse of Mycenaean civilization, for he appears briefly in Homer as Paiēon, a healing god, a distinct divinity, able magically to heal the gods of their wounds. But by the time of Sappho, c.600 BC, he was almost completely subsumed into Apollo, though he still shows through in Apollo's song.[57] One thing we know for sure is that this performance of the Paean, apparently a very ancient element of cult, was heavily stressed in the festival of Apollo-Hyacinthus. Is that a coincidence, that a Mycenaean aspect of Apollo is most evident at a site with clear evidence of Mycenaean ritual? Was it Hyacinthus's wound the song was supposed to heal?[58]

There are some traces of a resurrection. That would certainly explain the joy after the mourning. Euripides' *Helen* pictures the beautiful wife of Menelaus returning to Sparta and "rejoining the revels of Hyacinthus for a night of gladness, he whom Apollo killed with the round discus having contested for the furthest throw, the day of ox-sacrifice in the Spartan land."[59] A Christian bishop talks later of a song of Apollo "in the style [*thesmos*] of Amyclae," which plainly asserts what we always wanted to hear, that "Apollo *reanimated* fair-maned Hyacinthus."[60] Most striking however is the cult of Hyacinthus in Sparta's great Italian colony, Tarentum. Here Apollo and his victim were amalgamated, as were Poseidon and Erechtheus in the Erechtheum, but here there was not an altar, but, shockingly, a tomb, tomb of Apollo Hyacinthus. Buried gods are most unusual in Greek religion, but they are a feature of Phoenician cults, notably of Melqart of Tyre. And one would certainly expect such a god not to stay buried forever, but, like Melqart, to rise.

We could reconstruct the history of the myth as follows, therefore. There was a very ancient pre-Greek "Minoan" deity called Hyacinthus, a vegetation spirit, perhaps, a dying rising god even, a spirit of the agricultural cycle, the spirit of the year. Alongside him a song and dance that was or evoked the healing figure Pajawone, Paean. Superimposed, literally, on ancient Hyacinthus is the god Apollo, introduced when the Dorians arrived. He slipped into the shrine through the healing-song with which he had become identified. The myth of how Apollo killed Hyacinthus echoes the historical events of the Dorian invasion and Apollo's takeover of the old god's sanctuary. When, by the time of Homer at the latest, dying and rising gods came to look un-Greek, the dead and divine elements of the cult were firmly separated into a heroic Underworld mortal element, Hyacinthus, and a divine immortal element, Apollo. After many centuries of celestial service Hyacinthus had been forced out of office, "demoted" from deity to hero. The ritual procession from Sparta to Amyclae, with its marching di-di-dum di-di-dum beat, recalled Sparta's conquest of the indigenous community.[61]

"Yes, but how did Hyacinthus die?" visitors kept asking, and the eyes of the keepers of the sanctuary would rise in the direction of the giant block of metal in the shape of Apollo, who seemed to have swooped like a discus out of the blue, and to have landed on poor Hyacinthus, like Dorothy's house crushing the Wicked Witch of the West. But at some point Amyclae was incorporated into the community of Spartans and a friendlier myth was told. Apollo was sorry, truly sorry. He had been deeply grieved by the death of his predecessor, Hyacinthus. Look, he sends his condolences on the petals of a flower, a veritable certificate of sorrow, "Ai, ai." Later still, a touch of Hellenistic romance was stirred into the mixture, a gentle rivalrous Zephyr, blowing warmly from the west, and Hyacinthus was turned into something worth fighting over, a lovely blooming youth. Thus a new gay myth was born, a myth in which homoerotic *erōs* stands ultimately for the bond between two peoples and their major male divinities, primordial Hyacinthus of the Mycenaeans of Amyclae or even of the people who preceded them, and the Dorian invaders' new god, Apollo.

STAR WARS

Unfortunately, evidence from various sources suggests that this particular neat narrative may need to be modified. For there is something I forgot to mention when I was recounting the fragment of Euripides in which Athena talks of placing the sacrificed virgin daughters of Erechtheus in the heavens. We can work out that she is raising them up as the Hyades, Taurus's muzzle, but she doesn't call them Hyades or Erechtheids, daughters of Erechtheus. Inexplicably she calls them Hyacinthidai, "daughters of Hyacinthus."[62] Indeed she says this is the name they are known by throughout Greece. What is more we know that she is telling the truth, for the tombs of Procris's sisters, of the city-saving virgin princesses, central figures in a major cult to do with war and battles, seem to have been located at a place called Hyacinthion, the Hill of Hyacinthus.[63] One set of myths indeed claimed that Hyacinthus had for some reason emigrated to Athens, and was happy to kill one of his daughters—her name, "Flowery," is preserved—on behalf of his adopted country. By claiming that the starry heroines buried in Athens and so important in war were not in fact daughters of Spartan Hyacinthus, despite their name, but daughters of Athenian Erechtheus, Eu-

ripides was engaging in a bit of nationalistic propaganda, at a time when
Athens and Sparta were at war. From what we can tell from its not in-
substantial fragments, *Erechtheus* is one of the most explicitly propagandistic plays in the whole corpus of Greek tragedy. The tragedian was
nationalizing the heavens themselves. It would be wonderful to know
how he managed to explain why Athenian princesses came to be called
after a thoroughly Spartan hero, but at this point the text disintegrates:
". . . gleam [*ganos*] of hyacinth [or Hyacinthus], saved the land . . ." is all
the papyrologists were able to reconstruct.[64]

Of course the fact that this apparently terribly ancient Hyacinthus with
his pre-Greek name turns up in Athens of all places has provoked a rash of
speculations about prehistoric links with Sparta and the origin of the New
Year festivals, going way back into the Bronze Age, the second millennium BC, the Mycenaean world, and beyond.[65] Those theories may be
right or wrong, but I think the explanation for Hyacinthus and his daughters turning up in Attica is probably much simpler and more mundane. It
is probably nothing more than the result of a visual pun. You will have
noticed that the alternative name for the Hyades, "the Hyacinthidai,"
starts with the same letters. The Romans called the same stars *Suculae*,
"Piggies"—quite inexplicable until you realize that the Greek for pigs is
hyes. Remember too that Apollo wrote Hyacinthus's initial on the flower
to which he gave his name. What links the words and stars and flowers and
names is the letter upsilon, written "Y." For the Hyades are in Y-
formation: the Y-flower and the Y-stars, the hyacinth and the stars known
throughout Greece as the Hyacinthidai. Once the sacrificed heroines and
their stars had become known by that name, it was only a matter of time
before Hyacinthus himself arrived on the scene.

And it seems absolutely clear that the Spartans identified their great
hero himself with a constellation. Unlike the Tarentines the Spartans
seem to have separated the god from the hero and kept the hero, for onlookers at least, properly "dead." The image on his tomb, of Hyacinthus
being "taken up to heaven" with his sister, can only mean one thing
therefore. You cannot be dead and buried, and at the same time translated to heaven, unless you are being stellified. This explains Helen's apparent callousness—"the revels of Hyacinthus for a night of gladness, he
whom Apollo killed." The reason for the night joy is that after all the
sadness on day one, all the mourning for the hero accidentally killed by

Apollo, Hyacinthus was seen to appear again bright and shiny, "resurrected," but in an orthodox fashion.

Stellified as which constellation? That is a harder question. I suppose an obvious candidate for the star associated with the Y-hero of the Y-flower are the Y-stars, the Hyades in Taurus. I am not sure about that, however. Athena seems very insistent that these were known as the Hyacinthidai, "Hyacinthids," "Daughters of Hyacinthus," not as "Hyacinthus" himself, and there does seem a consistent tendency to identify them with multiple females. Another candidate is Auriga the Reins-Holder, simply on the Athenian analogy: Erechtheus fathers the Erechtheids = Auriga fathers the Hyades, so if the Hyades are really "daughters of Hyacinthus" (*Hyacinthidai*), Hyacinthus must be Auriga. There is a very late reference to Hyacinthus driving Apollo's swan chariot, another chariot that flies.

But then one night I saw an apparition, and a quite different solution suddenly made itself known to me. It was the end of August. I was staying at El Rosal, near Buenaventura, in the middle of the Iberian Peninsula, opposite the Sierra de Gredos. Our host switched off all the outside lights and we lay on the loungers in our coats, around the swimming pool, staring at the stunning sky. Amazed at the spectacle, I got up to walk around, making sure I didn't trip over anything in the darkness, and there on the northeastern horizon I saw what looked like the vividest image of Hyacinthus: Orion, flat on his back, directly above him the giant ➤ of the flowery Hyades, daughters of Hyacinthus, and directly above them the Pleiades, looking for all the world like a discus lying on the ground. This was exactly what Euripides' Helen and the Spartan maidens would have seen as they danced in deep Lacedaemon, during the Hyacinthia festival's "night of gladness." It was impossible that they would not have made the connection between the story of their dead hero and these constellations, when it now seemed so apparent to me.

But we have not examined a most important feature of the story, the balmy westerly breeze called Zephyr, and some images on Athenian pots that the experts are absolutely convinced are images of Hyacinthus, some of them clearly in a rather amorous situation. And there is something else that stars resemble, something sticky and droplety and white.

RANDY ZEPHYRS

The meager data on the love story of Apollo and Hyacinthus would be greatly increased if we included some mysterious Athenian images. These come in two groups. The first shows a Boy, under Eighteen, sometimes carrying a piece of stylized vegetation, riding on a giant swan, sometimes over water. Is this "Swan-Boy" Hyacinthus? Several of these images were painted around 500 BC, during the Loves of the Gods craze, and then a few more in dribs and drabs over the next one hundred years. In at least one of the more rapturous versions, the boy is wearing a dark yarmulke, which implies the presence of the divine, i.e., an abduction or a theolepsy. Pure white swans are often linked to pure Apollo. Hence the images were identified with the myth of Apollo and his most celebrated love, Hyacinthus.

One of these Swan-Boys is being gestured at by a young winged Stripling. Zephyr, like all wind gods, was normally represented with wings, and unlike most winds he was represented as a blooming youthful wind, a Stripling. So if Swan-Boy was Hyacinthus being abducted by Apollo in the form of a swan, it might seem reasonable to identify the winged Stripling with Zephyr, jealously trying to prevent the abduction. That single vase in turn has allowed iconologists (students of *eikones,* "likenesses") to infer (a) that the myth of Zephyr and Apollo fighting over Hyacinthus was well-known in Athens centuries before

22. Swan-Boy (Hyacinthus?) rides the waves on the back of a swan (Apollo?). An inscription in the background proclaims "The Boy is Beautiful." Cup by Apollodorus (*c.* 500–490).

any text informs us of the fact, and (b) that therefore all the Striplings embraced by winged Striplings on Athenian vases are images of Zephyr and Hyacinthus, even if a giant swan is nowhere to be seen.[66] On the other hand, there is no trace in written sources of an *abduction* of Hyacinthus by a swan, and there should surely be some positive indication on the part of the painters to show that Apollo is involved. What a great god to paint as an *erastēs*! Why make the viewer guess? It looks to me as if Swan-Boy represents a myth we haven't discovered yet; the theory that Swan-Boy is Hyacinthus must to my mind remain "dubious."[67]

The other character, however, the Stripling pursued by a Stripling with wings, deserves closer consideration. For a Stripling with wings is very probably Zephyr. Cults of winds were perhaps more central in the religion of the Mycenaean period. A "priestess of winds" is recorded in the bureaucracy discovered at Mycenaean Cnossus, and the name Zephyrus is found in the Mycenaean accounts from Pylos on the west coast of the Peloponnese. Later, in Athens, we find priestly families of Eudanemoi (*anemos,* "wind") who made prayers to the gods responsible for winds and had a role to play in the cult of Demeter at Eleusis, and Boreasmoi (Boreastai?) who made sacrifices to summon up winds, and in Corinth a family of Anemokoitai, "Wind-Consorts," "consort" being a term with strong sexual connotations.[68]

Often winds are invoked and propitiated in general terms, but by the time of Homer, at the latest, they had acquired individual characters based on the time of year or time of day on which they blew, their intensity, direction, temperature and effects. Of all the named winds, Zephyr has the most attractive character, although in early writers he can be as violent as any of his brothers. He is first and foremost the wind that blows in the dark (*zophos*). On the mountain-surrounded plains of Greece, cooling breezes will often descend from the heights at the end of the day, and it is this effect, probably, that gives Zephyrus his gentle sweetness. As the wind that blows at sunset he is also the wind that blows from the sunset, from the west, so he alone is kept out of the bag of winds in order that Odysseus can sail home to Ithaca from the western Mediterranean. He is also the wind that blows *in* the west, on the paradisal Isles of the Blessed for instance, later identified with Madeira and the Canaries. He also seems to be associated with spring; this is a connection that is particularly emphatic in the Roman version of Zephyrus,

Favonius, who starts to blow at the same time each year, on February 7, officially announcing the start of spring.

He is also therefore associated with spring flowers. Indeed it was Zephyr who married the Pale Green Nymph Chloris and turned her into the nymph of flowers, in Rome the goddess Flora—"formerly the earth was a single color."[69] Zephyr can be seen performing that transformation in Botticelli's allegory of spring, the *Primavera*. The marriage of Zephyr and the goddess of flowers produces Karpos, "fruit," "harvest," and hence Zephyr is an agricultural deity, the god who separates the harvest from the chaff as the wheat is winnowed. This makes him "fat-richest of all the winds" (*piotatos*).[70] He was believed to be super-fertile himself, *genitabilis aura*, "fecund breeze," *genitalis spiritus mundi*, "the generative breath of the world." He often seems to mate with horses, producing the quality in Erichthonius's magnificent stable at Troy. Way out west on the banks of the encircling Ocean he had sex with the snatching wind, the harpy Podarge, and sired the immortal horses Xanthus and Balius, which pull the chariot of Achilles, horses who suddenly acquire the power of speech in a famous scene in the *Iliad* and briefly take the hero by surprise. Because of this procreative tendency Vitruvius advised that you should not build a library open to the West Wind, since he would generate worms to eat the rolls of papyrus. Christians used this well-known example of spontaneous generation to make the pregnancy of the Virgin, through the Holy Gust, seem less unbelievable.[71] Attica had a cult of Zephyr a short distance from the city on the Sacred Way from Athens to Eleusis. It was linked to a shrine of Demeter and Persephone and to the tomb of the hero Phytalus (*phyton*, "tree," "growing thing"), first cultivator of the fig. Zephyrus's cult was perhaps administered by Phytalus's descendants, the Phytalidai, whose myths made them seem terribly ancient.[72]

Zephyr is also on show in another Botticelli painting, the *Birth of Venus*, since it was he who blew ashore the foamy genitals of castrated Heaven (Uranus, Ouranos), out of which Aphrodite grew.[73] Sweet cooling breeze of evening, the wind that ruffles the flowers of spring, so important to Aphrodite, which lend color to the seductive dresses of women and especially courtesans, Zephyrus is a bit of a wafter—"womanish wind"—and seems bound to take on an erotic disposition. Indeed Sappho's contemporary Alcaeus says he is father of Eros, and that Eros's mother was not Aphrodite but Iris, the rainbow.[74]

Zephyr appears on the Tower of Winds in Athens as a beardless young man, a Stripling carrying flowers in the folds of his drapery. Since Eros too is often represented as a winged Stripling and is fond of flowers, it is very hard to tell them apart in art, but Zephyr is the most likely candidate for the amorous winged Stripling who appears on Athenian vases and yo-yos or "bobbins," chasing young men. Eros in love would be freakish, like a thunderstruck Zeus or a plague-stricken Apollo, though of course it was not beyond the ingenuity of Greek myth to give a god or goddess a taste of their own medicine. Unlike other amorous deities who chase or abduct, however, this god is shown in action, pressing his groin into the other's, a proper *anemocoitus*. Zephyrus was showing a passionate interest in the Spartan hero two centuries before the first amorous Apollo. And Hyacinthus does not seem to be resisting Zephyr's advances on the vases. One would love to know what the comic poet Anaxilas did with Hyacinthus in his play called *Hyacinthus (or) the Pimp*.[75]

But the myth of Zephyr and Hyacinthus is strongly marked as Spartan. Is there any evidence from there? There were sacrifices of horses (most extraordinary) to Sun and Winds on Mount Taÿgetus, and in the town itself a sanctuary of Zeus Euanemos, "Nice Wind." A paean sung in praise of Eurus, the Southeast Wind, as "Savior of Sparta"— hopefully? thankfully?—was found in a papyrus anthology. Those are

23. An ephebic Zephyr grabs an ephebic Hyacinthus carrying Apollo's seven-stringed lyre in one hand and attempting to pull his cloak around himself with the other. An inscription on the border proclaims "The Boy is Beautiful." White-ground yo-yo or bobbin by the Penthesilea Painter (c.460–450).

quite good finds. But much more striking and obvious than these bits of antiquarian information is the fact that archaic Spartan pottery is strewn with small winged creatures. Some of these are definitely identified as the Boreads, that is, the two sons of Boreas the North Wind and Orithyia, the Argonauts Zetes and Calaïs, who fight against the stormy snatching winds, the Harpies. The others ought really to be winds also. These winged demons seem to have a role to play in cult. One vexingly fragmentary cup has a whole host of them surrounding a large female figure, a goddess, probably, who seems to be holding branches and flowers. Some of these figures are beardless; flowers and winged Striplings immediately suggest Zephyrus. One of them attempts to crown a young man on a horse, which reminds us of the procession of boys on horseback through the theater during the Hyacinthia. Along with Sirens, these little winged figures hover around at some kind of ritual banquets, where men and women mix. Their role here is clearly erotic. Zephyr has become Cupid.[76]

Nothing would be less surprising therefore than to find Zephyrus playing a role at the sanctuary of Hyacinthus either in imagery or even in cult. Indeed, that Zephyrus had been present at the Hyacinthia for as long as the Hyacinthia was celebrated cannot be in doubt. The festival probably took place, remember, at the hottest time of year during the annual two-month-long drought. In Ovid's version of the myth, the discus accident takes place at noon when Titan (Sun) is in the middle of

24. Zephyr in intimate embrace above the horizon with "fair-tressed" Hyacinthus, who carries Apollo's lyre. There are a few very similar scenes painted in the last decades of the archaic period. Cup in the manner of Douris (c.490–80).

the sky—"Apollo-Struck," *Apollōnoblētos,* is the same as "Sun-Struck," *hēlioblētos,* a later author points out helpfully . . . perhaps Hyacinthus had sunstroke, perhaps Apollo's discus is the sun itself. Temperatures can reach as high as 40°C in the Spartan summer, but because of the extraordinary wall of mountain that towers over the plain on the western side, the breeze from the west was especially dramatic when it arrived at sunset: "On summer evenings katabatic winds gravitate down the slopes of Taÿgetus to Sparta and accelerate the cooling of the air, which begins in earnest when the sun disappears behind the mountain and suddenly swathes the town in shadow."[77] This piece of evidence lets Zephyr off the hook. The sunset wind will have arrived too late to have been involved in the noonday killing of Hyacinthus. Zephyrus was framed for the murder of Hyacinthus, in order to let a more important divinity off the hook. Or was he?

ORION'S THREE FATHERS

Perhaps we can look again now at those images of Zephyr and Stripling Hyacinthus (Fig. 24). They seem quite different from the images of other divine abductions—Dawn chasing after and grabbing Cephalus or Tithonus or indeed anyone male and with two legs, Boreas chasing after and grabbing Orithyia, Zeus chasing after and grabbing Ganymede and then rising into the air. It does not look as if Hyacinthus is being taken anywhere in fact. The wind god seems to be hovering in midair, keeping him off the ground. It seems impossible not to put such an image alongside the image on the altar, which is probably very close in date, of Hyacinthus going up to heaven. I concluded that such an image must refer to Hyacinthus himself being put among the stars alongside his sometime daughters, the Hyacinthidai of Taurus. So after the heat of the day of mourning the death of Hyacinthus, as the sun sets, winged Zephyrus sweeps down from Taÿgetus, bringing a cooling, healing breeze. At the same time the star or stars of Hyacinthus come out, as if Zephyrus is hovering with him in the air. As a wind of the west, where souls go, the wind that blows on the Isles of the Blessed, it would look as if Zephyrus had fetched Hyacinthus back, rescued him.

But perhaps all these loves of the gods are sounding rather too lovey-dovey. What really happened? It may be flattering to have a god pas-

25. A unique image showing Zephyr and Hyacinthus, who holds a seven-
stringed lyre, engaged in midair Spartan-style sex: ". . . everything apart
from the deed (*stuprum*) itself . . . they sanction embraces and sleeping
together, but with cloaks placed between . . . a meager barrier indeed!"
(Cicero, *Rep.* 4.4). The almost completely destroyed inscription above the
lyre probably proclaims "Chaerestra]tus is Beau[tiful," since, with at least
twenty-six surviving acclamations, Chaerestratus is by far the most often
vaunted of Douris's *erōmenoi*. Fragment of cup by Douris (*c.*500–490).

sionately in love with you, but just imagine what the sex would be like,
or the half-sex. For on one fragment of a vase Zephyrus is caught in a
state of sexual excitement, screwing, it would seem, Hyacinthus's
draperies. We might well think this was a painterly error or a symbolic
gesture, were it not that this strikingly Spartan hero is being abused in a
notoriously Spartan way, "with the cloak intervening." Zephyrus really
is having sex with Hyacinthus while he still has his clothes on.

Now perhaps we would prefer to leave the scene, but we have to put
delicacy aside and picture to ourselves what happens next: a spatter of
white droplets onto fabric. We have been here before. One other constellation, Erechtheus the Reins-Holder, was the result of a similar ejaculation that missed. It landed on the leg of Athena, who wiped it off
with a piece of wool and dropped it on the ground. The first recorded
representation of that myth was on the great Throne of Amyclae over
Hyacinthus's grave. And there is another story, a version of the birth of
Orion, a hero from Tanagra in Boeotia. His future father Hyrieus invited three gods around for dinner, Zeus, Hermes and Poseidon, and

killed a fatted ox. That was delicious, said the gods. Make a wish. I've always wanted a son, said Hyrieus. "They assented. All stood by the hide of the ox—to say anything further is shameful. Then they covered up the moistenings they had scattered over the surface [*superiniecta . . . madentia*] with earth." Ten months later, Earthborn Orion emerged.[78] The myth was mentioned by Pindar, we are told, in his dithyrambs.[79] Hermes in particular is interesting. The son of a star, the Pleiad Maia, and escorter of souls, he was also the (co-?)father of Cephalus, who was also identified with Orion, of Myrtilus, identified with Auriga, and of the lyre identified with Lyra.

So myths made at least two constellations the product of gods' sperm, but we can go further than these. For some people, it seems, the notion that the night's white brilliance was god-spattered seed was taken for granted. We know that thanks to the extraordinarily accidental survival of an extraordinary esoteric text. It was placed on the pyre of a dead Macedonian, but as viewers of forensic crime series are aware, in any given conflagration lots of things don't burn, and by some such fluke this papyrus text did not only fail to burn properly but survived intact for more than two millennia. It came to light again in January 1962. This "Derveni Papyrus" is a commentary probably from before *c*.400 BC. It quotes one line from an even earlier mystic poem: "[Zeus] swallowed down the penis which first ejaculated the aither." The commentator comments: " 'ejaculated' what is whitest and brightest [i.e., the starry aether]" and interprets the "penis" as the sun.[80] The general idea seems to be that the stars come from the direction of the sun, from where the sun will later rise. This is why some authors made Dawn not a star-chaser, but mother of the stars, as if they were emerging from her womb. In the Derveni Papyrus the sun is the procreative organ, once affixed to the body of Heaven (Ouranos), but now unfixed (castrated), which is why, presumably, it could move *across* Heaven in the course of the year. When Zeus swallows it (i.e., the sun, Ouranos's penis), the sun's starry ejaculate, "the whitest and brightest," is revealed.

My point is a simple one: that there may well be some more esoteric doctrines in Greek religion that never make it into the record, but that are suddenly revealed in chance finds of unique works such as the Derveni Papyrus.

Or perhaps the point is simpler still. The gracious exchanges of *charis* in passionate relationships between Greeks involved, it would appear, one kind of encounter in particular: nonpenetrative "intercrural" rubbing between the thighs, sometimes even with a cloak between the two bodies. That could only produce one result when satisfaction was reached and the rubbing stopped, leaving the rubbed one with a little constellation of his own. Any Spartan who happened to find himself in the potteries of the Ceramicus and saw Zephyrus hovering while having sex through the cloak with Hyacinthus, and who also remembered that Hyacinthus on his tomb was shown being led up to the stars, would surely be able to make the connection.

After all that religion and exaltation, perhaps it is time for a change of scene. We shall descend to the mortal sphere for a tour of different homosexualities in Greece—Spartans, Cretans, Thebans, Macedonians, men in uniform. We may even find words to say about the "utterly reprehensible" activities of the Eleans who hosted the Olympic Games. But to soften the transition from heaven to earth, as mediators on our journey we shall look first, if briefly, at Heracles and Iolaus, and above all at Achilles and Patroclus, men in chariots. These I perceive as the true originals of Greek Homosexuality, and ascribe to them a very ancient history.

· PART IV ·

MEN OF WAR

10

ACHILLES AND HERACLES

I

ACHILLES AND HIS LOVERS

ACHILLES LOVES PATROCLUS

The plot of the *Iliad,* most accessible of great books, is easily summarized. The Homeric warriors who have distinguished themselves earn special perquisites. In particular they are awarded prizes from the booty, including booty of the female sex. To Achilles, the greatest Greek warrior, a woman called Briseis was awarded. To Agamemnon, the highest-ranking lord, went a woman called Chryseis. But King Agamemnon chose badly. This piece of living plunder was the daughter of a priest of Apollo. Not happy to see his daughter become a captive concubine, the priest invokes Apollo and asks him to intervene. Apollo responds. The god of plague shoots plague arrows onto the Greek camp. The Greeks start dying. This is how the *Iliad* opens.

Whenever there is a plague the Greeks know that it has a cause. The gods must be offended. They quickly learn the nature of the offense: The priest of Apollo wants his daughter back. Agamemnon refuses to give her up. Achilles says Agamemnon is useless anyway and didn't deserve his prize. Agamemnon says in that case he will indeed give up his girl, provided he can have Achilles' concubine to replace her. Achilles is grossly insulted by this assault on his privileges. He retires to his tent, refusing to fight. Patroclus and all the other warriors he brought with him, the Myrmidons, will not be fighting either.

Achilles' mother meanwhile, Thetis, goddess of the depths of the sea, asks Zeus to make her son's absence more noticeable, by tipping the balance of victory in Troy's favor. Zeus agrees. The gods who favor the Greeks, notably Hera and Athena, are appalled by this. Discreetly, or fairly discreetly, they do everything they can to defy Zeus. Eventually Zeus demands obedience. What he has assented to must be achieved. Soon the Trojans are gaining the upper hand. They drive the Greeks far from the walls of Troy. Indeed they are closing on the Greek ships, threatening to destroy any chance they have of going home, and to slaughter the entire army on the shore. Just as Thetis anticipated, emissaries are finally dispatched to try to soften sulking Achilles' bitter wrath. They offer him compensation, if only he will return to the fight and help to save them. Achilles still jibs. His strike will continue. However, seeing the state of his former comrades, the dead and wounded being carried from the front, he begins to show some concern.

In book eleven out of twenty-four, Patroclus goes to help dress one of the warriors' wounds. When he returns to Achilles in book sixteen he is in tears—like a precipice dark-streaked by a mountain stream, says Homer. Like a little girl tugging at her mother's dress and begging to be carried, says Achilles. Patroclus suggests that he at least could do something to help, even if Achilles won't. Achilles consents, but only as a damage-limitation exercise. Achilles lends him his armor and his chariot and sends them off. In private Achilles takes out a special cup he uses only to make libations to Zeus, who loved his mother once. He would like everyone to see that Patroclus is a great warrior even without him, the great Achilles, by his side, and prays that Patroclus will come back to him. Zeus agrees to half of this.

Patroclus is tremendously successful, and not only turns the tide but actually reaches the walls of Troy. At this point things start to go wrong. Apollo throws him off the wall, and makes sure that an arrow strikes its target. Then Hector dispatches the wounded man with a sword. After his moment of glory, Patroclus is dead. When he hears the news, Achilles goes out of his mind with grief. Briseis too is grieved beyond endurance when she is sent back to Achilles' tent and sees the body. She has seen her betrothed killed by Achilles, her three brothers dead, her city sacked, and now Patroclus too, who was kind to her, and promised he would make her Achilles' wife, and arrange a marriage feast for her in Thessaly.[1] The other women of the camp also wail when they see the body: "Patroclus the pretext," but really for their own misfortunes—the phrase became proverbial.[2]

Achilles dresses for battle, and in book twenty embarks on a killing spree; he fills the rivers of the Trojan plain with cruel blood. But it is Hector he has in his sights, the Trojan champion, Priam's fond son, a gentle husband, a proud father, and Patroclus's assassin. Here there is a drawback: once Hector is killed, Achilles' death is destined soon to follow. And Achilles knows this. In book twenty-two, Hector finally turns up, wearing the armor Achilles lent to Patroclus. A brave provocation, but then his courage fails him. He runs around the city walls trying to escape an almost demoniacal Achilles. Zeus weighs the fates of the two warriors in his golden balance, and it is Hector's fate that sinks down. After killing him Achilles drags the corpse around the city until it is disfigured and filthy. Then he attends to Patroclus, book twenty-three. He sacrifices twelve Trojan prisoners in his honor and holds funeral games. The last book has Priam coming to visit Achilles to ask for his son's body back.

US TWO FOREVER

Clearly the love of Achilles and Patroclus is central to the plot of the *Iliad*.[3] Homer uses it to get Achilles back on the battlefield after twenty books on strike. His love explains Achilles' bloody revenge, and his atrocious treatment of Hector's corpse. Achilles sulks hard, loves hard, and wages hard war when the object of his love is taken from him. The conclusion of the *Iliad*, when he gives up Hector's body to Priam, is not the end of the war, or of Achilles, it is the conclusion of Achilles' grief over Patroclus, a coming to terms with his friend's death and, beyond that, his own. The relationship is by far the most emotionally intense in the poem, and the climax of the *Iliad* is engineered around it. In book sixteen, as Patroclus prepares to go into battle, Achilles advises him not to be too successful:

> Return to me directly you have swept the Trojans from the ships. Even if thundering Zeus offers an opportunity of winning glory for yourself, you mustn't take it. You must not make war without me against these warlike Trojans—you will only reduce my glory . . . Ah Father Zeus, Athena and Apollo, I pray that not one Trojan may get away alive, not one, and not a Greek either, but we two [*nōïn*, dual] survive the massacre and unfasten Troy's holy battlements alone.

Of all the passages that deal with the relationship, this was the one that stood out for later scholars, suspicious that it had been added "by those who believe Achilles was in love with Patroclus."[4]

When he hears of Patroclus's death, Achilles pours dirt over his head, covers his face with it and sullies his fragrant robes with ashes. The messenger clings to his hands to prevent him from killing himself. In the deeps of the sea his mother hears his dreadful cries and hurries to see what pains him. Patroclus meant as much to him as his own life, he tells her. If you kill Hector, you are doomed to die soon afterward, she says. Let me die, is his response to that, since he wasn't there to help his friend when he needed him. Thetis goes to order a new set of armor from Hephaestus to replace the one Achilles lent Patroclus and that Hector has despoiled. When it is ready she brings it to him. She finds him wrapped around Patroclus's corpse, wailing.

Later Patroclus's ghost appears. It is a strange and eerie moment. All he wants, having died, is please to be buried. He accuses Achilles of neglecting him as he never neglected him in life. Don't have my bones buried apart from yours, he says, but together, just as we grew up together in your halls, when my father led me to your place, when, as a child, I killed a boy over a game of knucklebones (oblong sheep bones with different scores for each of the four long sides) and Peleus, your father, brought me up and named me your attendant. "Let a single tomb hide the bones of us two in its embrace: the double-handled golden amphora [*ostea nōïn homē soros amphikaluptoi chruseos amphiphoreus*] your lady mother provided for you."[5]

Why have you come here to tell me to do these things? Achilles asks Patroclus. Of course I will do everything properly and I will obey your commands. He uses the dual form again, the more than single and less than plural forms of a noun, used to refer to things that come in pairs, like ears, and hands and feet: " 'But stand closer to me; so we may take our fill of the delights of deathly lamentation, *us two* with our arms thrown around each other [*amphibalonte*] even if only for a little while.' So saying Achilles reached out with loving arms, but took nothing in them. The spirit was gone like smoke, creaking underground."[6] At the funeral itself, Achilles cradles Patroclus's head in his arms, in just the way Andromache will finally cradle the head of her husband Hector. Patroclus's corpse is covered in locks of hair cut off in mourning by his com-

rades. Finally Achilles cuts a lock from his own head. He had dedicated
it to the river Spercheus, vowing to grow it until he returned safely
home, but now he will not be sailing anywhere.[7]

Achilles is still crying after all the funerary carnage and the funeral
games, but the gods have had enough of Achilles' demonstrations of
grief by now and want Hector's body returned to Troy for something
like a decent burial. Thetis sees what she can do. Her son has not been
sleeping. He can't get his dear companion out of his mind. He remembers occasions when they fought together. He tosses and turns "longing
for Patroclus's manliness and spunk" (*potheōn androtēta te kai menos ēu*).
Menos refers to spunk in the broad sense of courage or mettle, but in 1974
a long fragment of Archilochus was published that revealed unequivocally that it can also mean spunk in the more specific sense of semen.[8]
Again ancient commentators objected, mainly on the grounds that
Homer was the epitome of elevation and dignity in style and these lines
were "cheap" and "over the top," but there are also signs of a debate
over their rampantly homosexual (cinaedic) implication: "because it's as
if he longs for him like a bedmate, something unworthy of [effeminate]
demi-men let alone demi-gods. Since, if you had to go the whole hog in
one's conjecturing, Patroclus would be his *erastēs* on the grounds that
Achilles is younger and very much more beautiful."[9]

The critics were not past the rapids yet. More indignities lay in wait.
For Thetis tries to console her son. "My child," she says, "how much
longer are you going to eat your heart out in grief and agony, forgetful
both of food and bed? It is good to have loving intercourse even with a
woman."[10] This remark in particular has caused plenty of squirming on
the part of commentators both ancient and modern: "quite inappropriate that a mother says to her son that it is good to have sex with a
woman. What's more . . . it is quite the wrong moment, not least for
men going out to battle; for you need to be in good condition with lots
of puff."[11] The ancient critics at least make one thing clear: The language is straightforward, even if the precise implications are not. In the
first place, when it is qualified by *philotēs*—"love"—*misgesthai* must
mean *sexual* intercourse. It seems to pick up "bed" in the previous sentence and refers back to Achilles tossing and turning and longing for Patroclus's *menos*. Thetis is worried that her son has been depriving himself
of loving intimacy since his friend's death, and so when Priam arrives to

collect his son, he returns to both food and bed, and, after a meal, ends up sleeping with Briseis in a corner of the hut.

Debate has concentrated on the phrase *"gunaiki per,"* "with a woman even," but again this construction is paralleled in many other passages and seems transparent, which leaves few ways out.[12] One sidestep is changing the text, which most have been unwilling to contemplate. Another is to treat the statement as a generalization: "Sex (with women) is good even though they are only women." But when Achilles is missing a man, the phrase "even with a woman" acquires a more specific and pointed relevance. The comment should refer to Achilles' particular circumstances. Achilles is being prodded by his mother to move on: having taken a husband, now to take a wife.

In this heroic syzygy Patroclus is older and wiser than Achilles, but lower-ranking. He is officially designated his *therapōn,* attendant, by Achilles' own father. Patroclus does indeed attend, making food and preparing beds for visitors, but the word and the role it denotes has a more positive connotation in Greece, used of "worshipping" gods and performing devotions—"devotee" rather than "servant." The most interesting parallel for the relationship is provided by Meleager and his wife Cleopatra. The myth is told as a story within a story, in fact as a parable to try to persuade Achilles to end his battle strike. Meleager has refused to fight in the war to possess the hide of the Calydonian Boar, since his mother has cursed him for killing one of her brothers. Everyone tries to persuade him, but it is only his wife, evoking images of the horror of sacked cities, who finally gets him back to work. Homer gives two names for Meleager's wife, and most agree that he has invented one of them, the name "Cleopatra," in order to make a connection with Patroclus, for the name is a simple inversion of that name, a mirror-image. However, when the Trojans approach the Greek "city," the encampment by the ships, and threaten to burn it down, Patroclus plays a different role from Meleager's wife. He doesn't persuade Achilles to go out and fight, but fights himself, as Achilles' substitute. Unlike Cleopatra, Patroclus is a man, after all, and a warrior in his own right.

Indeed, as has been pointed out on different occasions, Patroclus is best seen as Achilles' body double. Marriage it may be, but this is the marriage of a homozygous, not a heterozygous, couple, and gender will out. Patroclus stands for Achilles as a warrior, as Cleopatra could never stand for Meleager. He is dressed in Achilles' armor. His death stands for Achilles' death. His funeral games foreshadow those of Achilles, whose own end is often anticipated in the *Iliad,* but only realized in the period after the poem concludes. Patroclus is "pretext" not just for the wailing women of the camp to mourn their own miseries, but for the poet and the audience to mourn Achilles, a pretext indeed for Achilles himself to face up to his own mortality.[13]

As well as dearest comrade and "devotee," Patroclus is described as Achilles' "Reins-Holder," and when Patroclus appears in Achilles' armor with Automedon as his charioteer, the Trojans think it is Achilles and his *therapo⁻n,* as Patroclus would normally be by Achilles' side. But in the *Iliad* the heroic pair is broken. The bond between Achilles and Patroclus is made manifest, not in scenes of them fighting together in real time, but in tragic separation, loss and absence. The teamwork of Achilles and Patroclus is the stuff of nostalgia for the past and fantasies about the future. It appears only in Achilles' tortured dreams, the memory of when together they sacked cities, the wish for them both alone to sack Troy, with everyone else dead. It is only Achilles' taking to his tent that enables Patroclus to step out of his shadow for the first time. Achilles is even a little worried that his friend's success might reduce his own value to the Greek army. But it will be a disaster for Patroclus to fight alone as the poet points out the moment Patroclus suggests it. Together they have survived countless battles and sieges. Separately each is doomed. The relationship is most intense in absence and loss, and is made most poignant when Achilles tries to embrace the ghost, desiring, reaching out for the image of the other half but embracing nothing. Achilles and Patroclus will embrace only in a vase and in a tomb, although when Homer has gone, and has stopped enforcing the rules of mortality so strictly, we will find them embracing once more on the White Island, as two ghosts, substantial at least to each other, or walking somewhere, not in Hades and not in Heaven either, along Plato's shining path, waiting to grow similar-looking wings.

READING ACHILLES

It is hard to overestimate just how central Homer was to Greek culture. And with Homer went the love of Achilles and Patroclus. We are therefore in the fortunate position of not only having the original text in front of us, but a host of ancient Greeks over a long period reading it for us and not infrequently commenting explicitly or implicitly on what they thought it meant.[14] Their classic love features on one of the oldest masterpieces of Greek vase painting, the unique archaic "François Vase" in Florence, covered in miniature friezes depicting different scenes from myth and handily inscribed with its own profuse labeling. In one prominent frieze, Achilles, bereft, waits at the finishing line to hand out prizes at the funeral games of Patroclus. Cleopatra's husband Meleager is above him, hunting the Calydonian Boar. Below him is a flashback, the procession of gods who attended the wedding of his parents, Thetis and Peleus, many years before. One of the guests is Dionysus. As befits the god of wine he brings a two-handled amphora, but it will contain most famously something other than wine: the bride's as yet unborn son. It is the selfsame amphora in which Achilles and Patroclus will be co-interred, the homotaph itself. It seems a brutal gift: "Congratulations, Thetis! I am so happy for you! Do I hear already the patter of tiny feet? Well, when you can hear them no longer, you can put your dead son in this."

The François Vase was itself used for burial, hence the theme of its decoration: mortality, death. Probably it was commissioned for that purpose. The unknown Etruscan who chose to be buried in it must have known at least what the myths meant. The question is, did he also know of the love story covertly insistent behind it? When it was smashed up and scattered by ancient tomb robbers, oblivious of the pricelessness of the vessel and only interested in what might be inside, did the remains of one body or two drop out?

The tragedians of course kept coming back to the Trojan War to provide material for their dramas. Often they skirted around the episodes great Homer had already dealt with, but not always. A play by Aeschylus focused on the mission to Achilles to persuade him to call off his strike, and in *Myrmidons* he dealt with the love of Achilles for Patroclus in what appears to be an unmistakably sexual fashion. If Homer described Achilles tossing, turning and longing for Patroclus's manliness and *menos*, Aeschylus showed him rebuking his dead friend for getting himself killed. We lack context, but the idea may be that though it was kind of Patroclus to come to the Greeks' rescue there are things apart from one's loyalty to one's army that also deserve respect. What about showing "reverence for awesome thighs, oh how ungrateful you proved [*duschariste*] for kisses thick and fast," thighs that at some point had been involved in "god-fearing intercourse [*homilia*]."[15] Several hundred years later the passage was still being cited as proof of the raciness of the Greeks of yore, especially when it came to homosexual intimacies.[16]

This play of Aeschylus attracted comment much sooner, however, from Plato, writing around a century after its performance. The comment comes in that part of the *Symposium* when Phaedrus takes issue in the strongest terms with the esteemed old dramatist's treatment of the affair: "Aeschylus is talking rubbish." The problem seems not at all to do with the sexual nature of his description, but with the fact that Aeschylus had made Achilles "in love with Patroclus" instead of the other way around—"Achilles who was not merely more beautiful than Patroclus but than all the other heroes, not even with a beard even, younger, *much* younger, according to Homer."[17] The comment comes in the context of Phaedrus's special spin on Eros.

For Phaedrus Love is all about honor and self-sacrifice, people to die for. A true *erastēs* would feel more ashamed of doing something cowardly ("unmanly") in front of his beloved than in front of his own father or his comrades. But a beloved equally would feel especially ashamed if seen doing something shameful in front of his *erastēs*. The pair might even compete for each other's esteem. It matches what Homer says about the god breathing spunk (*menos*) into warriors, only the god in question is Eros. So what a good idea it would be, suggests Phaedrus, if you could have an army composed entirely of *erastai* and *erōmenoi*. At the time of writing, of course, precisely such an army was beginning to acquire a reputation for itself in Thebes.[18]

But Phaedrus hasn't reached his climax yet. He is on a roll. It's not just a question of not doing something cowardly, nor of competing for honor in the eyes of the other, nor of getting worked up on berserker love. You see Love's power especially in the fact that it makes people ready to die for each other. A woman, even a woman, gets an honorable mention here. Alcestis was prepared to give her life for her husband when Death came knocking at the door. No marks for Orpheus, however. It's good that he went down to the Underworld to bring back his Eurydice, but it isn't exactly self-sacrifice if you try to come back alive.

He wasn't prepared to die for her. So what do you expect of a minstrel?[19]

But the supreme example for Phaedrus is Achilles. He did something even greater than Alcestis and he reaped in the event a greater reward. He knew that he would die if he killed Hector. Still he came to assist (!) his *erastēs* Patroclus, to avenge him, not merely to die "for him" (*huperapothanein*), but "to add his own death to the dead man's" (*alla kai epapothanein teteleutēkoti*). That is why the gods gave him such an extraordinary reward in the afterlife, because he esteemed his *erastēs* so highly. "But Aeschylus is talking rubbish, claiming Achilles was in love with Patroclus, etc." In Phaedrus's view, it was precisely the fact that Achilles was not inspired by *erōs* for Patroclus that made his devotion all the more amazing. For although the gods honor virtue that emerges from *erōs* (*hē aretē hē peri ton erōta*) more highly than other kinds of virtue, they are even more impressed by an *erōmenos* who dotes devotedly (*agapai*) on his *erastēs* than by an *erōs*-inspired *erastēs* who dotes devotedly on his *erōmenos*. And that is why Alcestis, inspired by *erōs*-derived *philia*, was merely brought back from death, whereas Achilles was placed in the Isles of the Blessed.[20]

Phaedrus here provides a wonderful example of perverse sophistic logic: What is wonderful about what Achilles does is precisely that he *doesn't* do it out of *erōs*. How like the kind of argument Phaedrus will produce (with apologies to Lysias) years after *Symposium* in *Phaedrus*—that you should put out especially to someone who is not in love with you. There is probably a pattern here, an in-joke about the historical Phaedrus or his relationships, and "not being in love." We should certainly not read it as Plato's reading of the relationship. Quite possibly it is an example of how *not* to read the *Iliad*—for Socrates will dispute Phaedrus's theory. But we can take it as an example of how a Greek might *possibly* read the *Iliad*, or rather of the problems and questions the narrative raised for Greeks of the classical period, three hundred and fifty years after the *Iliad* was put together. The relationship does not seem to fit the forms of Greek Love in classical Athens very neatly. Patroclus clearly loves Achilles, and asks to be buried with him in a single grave, but it is Achilles' love for Patroclus that is most intense, Achilles who remembers most nostalgically past adventures and who anticipates most startlingly a world in which they are the only two survivors, even though he is the younger and prettier of the pair.

About thirty years or so after Plato wrote *Symposium,* Aeschines also
discusses their relationship in his long attack on Timarchus as a "common whore." The defenders of Timarchus have brought the subject up.
They will not be claiming that Timarchus did not have boyfriends, but
rather will insist that they were of the honorable kind based on *erōs,* not
payments. Aeschines is anxious to show that he is not against Greek
Love, just whorishness. Indeed the suspicion that he might be against
same-sex Love in general seems to jeopardize his case, and he makes
some efforts to forestall any such argument, delivering quite a discourse
on Greek Love to rival the one he thinks Timarchus's allies are preparing. He actually reads from Homer in the courtroom, quoting at some
length passages of poetry written in archaic epic dialect, and then commenting on them.[21] It is not the kind of speech for the prosecution you
are likely to hear in any modern court:

> And since you remind us of Achilles and Patroclus, of Homer and the
> other poets, as if the jurors were completely uneducated, while you
> pretend to be men of refinement with a knowledge of history supe-
> rior to the people's, then we will tell you something else about these
> men, so you may know that we too have heard of them and are not
> completely ignorant. They endeavor to reveal the names of wise men
> and to seek refuge in words spoken in verse, so feast your eyes, Athe-
> nians, on these poets who are by common consent good and worthy
> men and see how great a gulf they thought lay between upright
> [*sōphrones*] men and men in love with such men, and the improperly
> self-indulgent and abusers [*hubristai*]. I will speak of Homer first,
> whom we place in the ranks of the oldest and wisest poets. He refers
> on many occasions to Patroclus and Achilles, yet he keeps their *erōs*
> out of sight and refrains from giving their love [*philia*] a specific des-
> ignation, assuming that educated listeners would immediately per-
> ceive their extraordinary fondness for each other.[22]

It has long been recognized that here and elsewhere the distinction
that Aeschines seeks to draw between good and bad homosexual
relationships—upright men in love with upright men, such as Achilles
and Patroclus, and the uncontrolled and (their) abusers, such as
Timarchus and his boyfriends—cannot be a contrast between those who
have no sex and those who do.[23] But Aeschines is also *not* saying that

Homer keeps *sex* out of sight. In fact he gives a wonderful illustration of what features of a narrative of a relationship would lead a classical Greek to infer that it was a relationship founded on *erōs*. To prove it he quotes a passage from the end of the *Iliad* where Achilles is in the throes of grief. Achilles regrets especially that he has broken a promise he made to Patroclus's father to bring his son home safe and sound, if he would but let Patroclus come with him.[24] "This makes it quite clear," says Aeschines, "that Achilles took on his commission of care because of *erōs*."[25] The most conspicuously *erōtikos* bit was in the past, he infers, in the winning of Patroclus with his father's consent.

Next, Aeschines cites the fact of Achilles' self-sacrifice, determined to avenge Patroclus although he was warned it would mean his own death, "putting his pledge [*pistis*] to a dead man before his own safety." In particular a pledge not to bury Patroclus until he had cut off Hector's head and put it on his pyre.[26] Aeschines continues: "When Achilles was sleeping by the funeral pyre, the poet says, the image of Patroclus stood in front of him and stirred up such memories and asked such things of him, that reading them we are moved to tears and think we should emulate their virtue and their love [*philia*]."[27] Patroclus wanted them to be buried together, says Aeschines, translating Homeric into classical Greek as if from memory:

In grief going over the times they shared when living he says, "No longer in great councils will we sit alone together apart from the other friends, as we used to, taking each other's counsel," thinking I suppose that it was this trust and affection they would long for most . . . Read now what Patroclus says in the dream about the homotaph and the times they spent together: "Alive no longer, no longer will we, sitting apart from our dear comrades, counsel each other with counsels . . .[28]

ACHILLES DOES SOMETHING FOR SOMEONE ELSE

So much for reading and responding to Homer's Achilles and Patroclus, but Achilles has a place in Greek culture that reaches far beyond the *Iliad*. He seems to have been quite an important figure in Greek religion and in religious thinking, and that allows us to wonder about Homer's

sources, how this same-sex passion came to be at the center of the greatest epic in the Greek language, how his readers might have responded to
this relationship in Homer's time—whether with nodding familiarity,
or surprise. Or did they find themselves reading around it and into it
some other things not mentioned that everybody knew? We might even
get a glimpse of what Homer himself was up to.

A huge, exceptional and very strange cup in Berlin by the "Sosias
Painter" shows Achilles and Patroclus together.[29] On the interior
Achilles seems to have removed an arrow from Patroclus and is bandag-
ing the wound, while Patroclus holds the bandage in place with his
thumb; the episode is found in no myth that I know of. Achilles is a
beardless adult, a Stripling, but with the beard already appearing by his
ears; indeed he seems to have raised his cheek-guard to show us his age.
He kneels between Patroclus's open legs. Patroclus is a bit older, bearded
but not luxuriantly. If you have read very much at all about Achilles,
you will find it completely amazing to see him so meekly and mildly
being unselfish and kind.

It is a remarkably careful piece of work. Patroclus's genitals are
prominent and the anonymous artist has taken great care to show the
loose skin around his testicles, like an art nouveau flower design on a
stained-glass window in Brussels, Barcelona or Prague. He has shown
the knuckles on the back of Achilles' hand, and the folds of his palm just
visible on the other. The pleats on Patroclus's chemise are especially
finely done. It is possible to make out the emblem of a tripod on the
shield on which Patroclus is sitting.

The overall composition is no less astonishing. You notice the contrasts of detailed miniaturist painting and the unpainted areas of flesh,
and the further contrast between heavy metal armor and the flimsiest,
lightest pieces of chiffon side by side. Patroclus places his foot against
the round picture frame as if to brace himself, but not quite, for there is
a little gap between his foot and the border, like a thickness of glass.
They occupy a circular space defined by the shape of the round interior.
That artificial space, the cup, is real to them, and they are protected by
an invisible barrier from ever being in danger of escaping into our
world. But nor is there any sense that we are viewing them through a
keyhole into an encampment extending in all directions around them,
beyond what we can see. They belong to their own world, wrapped up

in each other, not even looking at anything that lies outside the frame. It reminds me of that scene at the end of Tarkovsky's *Solaris* where the spaceman seems to have returned to the place of nostalgia, the dacha with the shallow stream, and then as the camera recedes you see that he is not back on his world, but on a slice of it grafted onto the surface of another planet. And since, according to Homer, these two will actually be buried together in a two-handled vase, it's almost as if we are watching them in death together like two genies in a flask, thus reversing the startling wish of Achilles in the *Iliad* that they be the only two left alive and everyone else be dead.

Well, maybe I am getting carried away. After all, that arrow must have come from outside the frame.

Not necessarily. There is a wound, and an arrow we presume to have caused it, but there is also a quiver on Patroclus's shoulder that we would assume the arrow had come from. And a Greek seeing Achilles in this role would immediately think of another myth in which Achilles heals and cures. Telephus of Mysia had a wound in his thigh that wouldn't heal. It could only be cured, he was told, by the wounder: Achilles.

26. The huge Sosias Cup in Berlin. Achilles tends to Patroclus (both named). On the outside Heracles hails his father as "Zeus, my friend" from the back of a long procession of gods. Cup by the Sosias Painter (*c.* 510–500).

Achilles denies all knowledge of healing, but Odysseus understands that the wounder was not in fact Achilles, but his spear, and Telephus's wound is cured by Achilles using rust from the blade.[30] It would occur to any Greek viewing this scene, I think, that the painter was alluding to friendly fire.

The tail end of the plume of Achilles' helmet is bent a little out of line by the collar of his fish-scaled cuirass, and repeats the shape of the circular tondo. In contrast to these curves are some straight-ruled diagonals slicing up the circle, notably the platform on which they are squatting and, at an angle to it, the removed arrow, which leans against the tondo's glass lining but seems to penetrate through the base on which Achilles is crouching, making a line that seems to continue into the palmettes below. This diagonal is paralleled by the angle of Patroclus's leg and that in turn is exactly paralleled by a line running from his upper arm through Achilles' bent lower leg, which slices the circle in two, at 45 degrees from the horizontal. Perpendicular to that line, squaring it off at the top, is another diagonal formed by the line of Patroclus's gaze turning away in pain from the wound and fixating upon the feathers of the arrow that caused it. The composition is centered perfectly on the perfect right angle made by Patroclus's elbow. Here right through the middle of the disc Achilles pulls up a white bandage, as if to draw the whole thing together. What is especially admirable is the way that all these lines are given force, a force of dramatic significance and physical tension at the same time, pushing and pulling and bracing and turning away and tightening. It is like a kind of elasticated cat's cradle. Very formal and geometrical, and yet somehow quite natural.

The outside of this cup, no less breathtaking and intriguing, shows an assembly of gods on Olympus, standing and sitting, holding out gold and silver dishes, *phialai,* to make or receive offerings, poured out by a winged goddess, who may be Hebe—an "E" of her name survives, even if the wings would be most unusual. Among the gods is a ram-bearing, wing-booted Hermes, a figure associated in cult with Striplings like this Achilles and with averting plague.[31] Strangest of all is a figure labeled Artemis, who carries a tortoiseshell lyre and looks to all intents and purposes like her brother, i.e., a boy of Eighteen, a Stripling, a *meirakion.* Behind her is a white-spotted fawn. Several of the gods are seated on thrones covered in what appear to be the skins of spotted lions, or maned leopards. The three Seasons, the *Hōrai,* the Times, guardians of the gates of heaven, who represent the cyclic passing of the seasons, stand out in front on one side. Heracles is here too, though with so many gods with their backs to him, it can hardly be a scene depicting his being welcomed to Olympus.

He seems to be calling on his father as "Friend Zeus." We know it's a speech bubble and not a misplaced label, because it is in the vocative case "Zeu Phile." This address brings the two halves of the exterior together, a shout from the end of the line to the head of the line, going all the way around the outside of the vase. It surely also brings the inside and the outside together. One theme of the cup, then, seems to be *philia,* an intimate love between warriors, between a Stripling and an elder battle comrade, emblematized in the tender care of Achilles for his wounded comrade-in-arms, Patroclus. A few years after the cup was made (*c.*500 BC), the poet Simonides wrote a song in celebration of the victory of the Greeks over the Persians at Plataea. It opens with an address to Achilles: "Hello, Achilles." Once again Achilles and Patroclus were celebrated as archetypes of comrades-in-arms, buried in a common grave, like all warriors who died for their country.[32]

The assembly of gods with distinctive cult attributes and pouring libations would seem to indicate some religious festival, but which, where? The find-spot does not help, since the vase came from yet another tomb of a whispering Etruscan in faraway Vulci.[33] Nor does the address to Zeus Philos help necessarily, since this is not quite a cult title, "Zeus Philios," but a common invocation of Zeus as friend. Indeed cult titles are rare on Greek vases. It was the attributes, like carrying a ram, which indicated a particular Hermes, "Ram-Carrying Hermes Kriophoros" for instance. It is just possible to detect a little eagle on Zeus's scepter like the one held by Olympian Zeus at Olympia. There are other clues. In particular under one handle of the cup is a round head of the goddess Selene, a full moon, setting the scene for whatever is going on. It ought therefore to be a festival in the middle of the lunar month, and indeed the nocturnal portion of it. Since Achilles is a dead hero, the offerings may have something to do with him. The tripod on Patroclus's shield may be another indication. This is a victory tripod awarded at festival competitions. There is one competition festival where Achilles, Heracles and Olympian Zeus come together in the middle of the month: Olympia.

A WHITE ISLAND IN THE BLACK SEA

Precisely thirty days before the Olympic festival, at the full moon that preceded the Olympic full moon, all the athletes had to gather in Elis, miles away from the Olympic Sanctuary, to be inspected by the Greek Justices. This inspection was done in an ancient gymnasium complex, lined with plane trees, which had a separate running track, *dromos,* used only for competitive victory-bringing sprint races, not for practice or for the sprints of pentathletes. This running track was called sacred by the locals. The sprint really was one of the "holiest" events in Greece. The inspections were performed at a place called Acre (Plethrios, in fact two-thirds of an English acre, a "yoke-pair" plot, a *zeugos* or *jugerum*), which was evidently very famous. Near the gymnasium complex was a sanctuary of Artemis surnamed "Who Loves Eighteen-Year-Olds," Philomeirax, because she had got a position so close to the gymnasium, said Pausanias, who, given the reputation of Elean Homosexuality, is treading very carefully through a rather dangerous zone. In the gymnasium were images of Heracles, and in the wrestling pits a relief of Eros holding a palm branch, while Anteros, "Love's opposite number," was trying to get it off him.

When the Olympic Committee, the Greek Justices, arrived to view the competitors, they had to take a prescribed route into this gymnasium, a route that had to pass over the "Tomb" (*taphos*) of Achilles. First they compared the runners and matched them for age (and ability?). This had to be done before sunup.[34] Finally the Games themselves were opened with a ceremony in Elis where the women did honor to Achilles, in particular with the custom of beating their breasts, an act of mourning (*koptesthai nomizousin auton*). Achilles was not actually buried in this tomb, said Pausanias; it was a cenotaph, a memorial established by mantic runes reading (*mnēma ek manteias*).[35]

It is fairly straightforward to explain why the Olympic Games should start with Achilles. First of all he was a national Greek hero who had fought against barbarians, and Olympia was a self-consciously Greek site: All Greeks and only Greeks were allowed to attend, though exceptions were sometimes made for a people like the Romans, whose language and cults seemed not so very different if you squinted, and whom a refusal, more importantly, might offend. But Achilles' place was also secured by profounder, more cosmological reasons. Olympia was dominated by the Mountain of Cronus, Zeus's father. He was supposed to have had a temple built for him there by the Golden Race of the first humans, who knew nothing of aging and reproduction. But to preserve his rule Cronus was forced to eat his own children, to stop them from succeeding him. Zeus escaped by a ruse and overthrew his father. Indeed they had a wrestling match at Olympia and Zeus won. The Golden Age was over. Men would henceforth grow old, although Cronus was still held in honor on Mount Cronus and still ruled over the Isles of the Blessed. And Zeus is often referred to as Son of Cronus, as if to remind him of where he came from, and, naturally, what might lie in store for him also: succession.[36] Zeus's rule was threatened in its turn by the son he was about to father on Thetis. To forestall any possible divine rival, he forced her to yield to a mortal, and so Achilles was born with a fatal, crucial flaw. He would die. And Zeus was saved. Alongside Cronus, therefore, a dead Achilles represents the maintenance of the current order at Olympia, the old epoch surpassed, the surpassing of the Age of Zeus postponed, until, of course, another son of the highest god might emerge.

Naturally there was a lot of debate over the cosmic status of Achilles—a mortal, yet his mother had been immortal. Achilles' fellow countrymen, the Thessalians, hedged their bets and brought a Black victim to offer to the dead mortal Achilles and a white one for his other half, hero and a god, but not at the same time. But at Olympia, of all places, which celebrated the continuity of the Age of Zeus, it was critical that Achilles was dead and no threat to the status quo. Hence there was not even an altar to him at Elis, though even dead heroes could have an altar sometimes, and the mourning and beating of the breasts underlined the point. Achilles was dead and buried. The Age of Olympian Zeus was secure.

The Eleans would perhaps have liked to lay plausible claim to the actual body of the hero, but Achilles was widely believed to have his tomb near Troy. For those who believed that he was more than mortal, however, his ghost was neither in heaven nor among the ordinary ranks of the dead in the Underworld (where Homer had placed him, very insistently, in the *Odyssey*), but on the White Island, the island of Leuke in the Black Sea, which lies off the coast of Ukraine, opposite the Danube delta, a block of solid white limestone rising thirty meters sheer out of the sea. It was (and remains) a small island, full of snakes, planted with white poplars and kept clean and tidy by white birds. Sacrificial victims wandered about. If you were forced to land on the island by accident and had no offering to make, you could pay money "to Achilles" and when he thought you had donated enough, one of the animals would come toward you, driven by the strange invisible unheavenly god. No one was allowed to live there and the island was evacuated at sunset. The island is no fantasy—it really does exist—but naturally in these circumstances it became a place of fantasy. Sailors reported seeing Achilles aboard their ships as they approached, and strange sounds were heard of Helen and Achilles, the two most beautiful Greeks at Troy, singing about their own fame.[37] One man claimed to have met Achilles himself on the island and spent time with him. Achilles blessed his business prospects and asked him to bring to him a certain woman of Troy, the last remaining descendant, little did people know, of Priam. The woman had to stay on the ship because women were not allowed on the island. Achilles did not like women, generally speaking. Helen, it seems, was a different matter. But on this occasion Achilles told the visitors to leave the last of the Trojans behind with him when they departed. As they sailed away they heard screams and saw Achilles tearing her limb from limb.[38]

On the island there was indeed a temple of Achilles made of rough-hewn blocks of limestone. Some of them were still standing in the early nineteenth century, but are now obliterated by a lighthouse. Among the finds were lots of little clay discs inscribed with Achilles' name. The finds go back to the seventh century BC. The shrine was probably founded by the city of Miletus, which dominated the area, one of the greatest of all Greek cities in the archaic period until it was reduced most dramatically by the Persians.[39] Achilles was terribly important for Miletus's Black Sea colonies. One of them, Olbia, honored him on a very long and narrow spit of land called the Running Track of Achilles. Miletus's own god "Luke," the White God, *Leukos,* was perhaps identified with the Achilles of the White Island.[40] The British Museum's famous Portland Vase from the decades around the year 0, inspiration for Josiah Wedgwood, may in fact depict Achilles in his island paradise, against a background of white poplars. The artist made a vase of cobalt blue, and then dipped it in molten smoky white glass, and then carefully cut into the ghostly shell to reveal the blue underneath, producing a beautiful cameo scene; this is extremely difficult to achieve, and a modern replica took about two years to make. The vase probably shows the wedding of Thetis and Peleus, and on the other side their son Achilles perhaps, sitting on white slabs of rock next to a white temple, while beautiful white Helen reclines beautifully. There is a lot of support for the idea that it is indeed Peleus and Thetis who are shown on one side, and it seems quite plausible to me that it is Achilles on the White Island who is shown on the other. The whiteness of the Portland Vase, the whiteness of Wedgwood vases therefore, is full of meaning. The white stuff: The material is the message.[41]

When his countrymen, the Thessalians, made the annual sacrifice to Achilles at Troy, they brought everything with them from home including firewood and fire. Before they made landfall they sang a special hymn to his mother: "Dark-blue Thetis, Pelian Thetis, who bore great Achilles . . . Troy was allotted a share of him as much as his mortal nature held sway, but what is deathless about him is held by the Deep Black Sea [pontos] . . . get yourself over here, no tears, get yourself over here and Thessaly with you, Dark-blue Thetis, Pelian Thetis." After singing the song, when they were actually approaching the tomb, they struck a shield and cried out loud, rapidly and rhythmically, repeating Achilles' name. They dug offering pits and slaughtered a black bull as to one who is dead, and "they summoned Patroclus to the feast, doing this as if Achilles would receive the gesture graciously." They also perhaps ran a sprint in the nude at Achilles' tomb, since we are told this was "traditional." Then on the beach they sacrificed to him as to a god and toward dawn sailed off with the animal so as not to eat it on enemy territory.[42]

Here at least there is a cultic connection between Achilles and Locrian Opuntian Patroclus, with whom, ethnically and culturally speaking, the Thessalians had nothing to do. And this extraordinary practice of making an offering to a foreign hero who was not even buried on their soil whenever they made an offering to their own hero at Troy would have informed the experience of any Thessalians listening to Homer's lines about the pair, even if it did not inform Homer himself when writing of their relationship. For this account comes late, and refers to a practice that happened in "the olden days." Alternatively it could be this bizarre ancient cult practice—no Thessalian must make offerings to Thessalian

Achilles unless he offers something to Locrian Patroclus too—that provided all the inspiration Homer needed for the relationship between the two heroes in life. It is a nice way of underlining, at least, how Patroclus's death stands for Achilles', that he is associated with one of two aspects of the hero, the dark dead Underworld side, rather than the heavenly luminous sacrifice side. The pair were also thought to be together on the White Island, however, for someone saw them there.

A man from the colony of Croton on the instep of Italy, famous for its Olympic sprinters, Pythagoras and doctors, had got wounded in battle, and the wound wasn't healing. He had been fighting against the splendidly named Epizephyrian Locrians (i.e., colonial "Out-Western Locrians"). In preparation for the battle, the Epizephyrians had sent home to the motherland to fetch the hero Ajax for assistance. There are two Ajaxes in the epic tradition ("the pair of Ajaxes"): (1) Big Hard-Done-By Telamonian Ajax of Salamis, a Goliath and a Rock who rescues the dead body of Achilles; he watches as Odysseus snaffles Achilles' precious armor out from under his nose, and then commits suicide, and has the Larkspur—*Consolida ajacis*—named after him; and (2) Nasty Little Locrian Ajax, whom Homer makes slip in excrement during the funeral games of Patroclus, who rapes virginal Cassandra in the temple of Athena, knocks over Athena's statue, comes within an inch of being stoned to death by his comrades, and is drowned by Poseidon when the gods have had enough of him, the main cause in some versions for the scattering of the Greek fleet after their victory, which gave so many of them such meandering returns home (*nostoi*); clearly a hateful scapegoat figure—they should, said Alcaeus, have stoned him.[43]

We should certainly not strive too hard to distinguish the two Ajaxes, however, unless the sources insist. The Ajaxes are confused by us, they were confused by ancient Greeks, and there is a good chance that the man from Croton has here confused them.

The Locrians acknowledged their hero's wickedness every year with extraordinary expiations for the rape of Cassandra and the affront to Athena, which I won't go into here, but that they claimed to have been performing for hundreds of years ever since Troy was sacked. But presumably they also found something good to say about him, or at least had found a way of putting the hero's nastiness to good use. If not, they could always confer him on their colonists, on loan as it were, when they requested him for an important battle, with no great urgency perhaps to send him back.

It is this latter Ajax, the Nasty Little One, that we seem to be dealing with here. The Epizephyrian colonists having acquired him from their founders, in the form of an image of him, presumably, or a relic, stationed him in the front line. The man from Croton discovered where the hero was stationed and deliberately launched an attack there. Not surprising, then, that he got injured. To cure the wound, Delphi told him to go to the White Island and Ajax would cure him. He did and was cured of his wound. But he didn't only see Ajax and Achilles. Patroclus was there too, he insisted.[44]

All this may help to provide more context for Achilles at the Olympic festival. The wood at Olympia was supplied by an official, the "woodman," who was no ordinary lumberjack. He alone was allowed to take something away from Pelops's gloomy sacrifice of a black ram—the neck—a substantial cosmological burden. This woodman provided all the fuel for the holy mantic sacrifices at Olympia, selling it to visitors at a fixed rate. Only the wood of the "White," the *Leukē,* the white poplar, tree of Achilles' island, could be used in sacrifices to Zeus. Pausanias does not know why and speculates that it is because the first sacrifice was made by Heracles, who found the tree growing beside the Underworld river Acheron. The tree grew by the banks of the river that bounds the Olympian shrine. When young it has a green-white bark and the pith in cross section makes the shape of a five-pointed star.[45] In March or April the white poplar produces spectacular drifts of cotton-covered seeds made famous in films by Italian directors. When the poplars were snowing, the White Island must have been an even more ghostly place, with its own permanent fluffy dry ice. The tree has conspicuous two-tone leaves, dark green on top and downy white underneath, like the black-and-white, night-and-day opposition between Olympian Zeus and Underworld Pelops.

SONS AND MOTHERS AND MOTHERS AND MOTHERS

White Achilles also has an opposite at Olympia. Black Memnon was an African from the Sudan ("Ethiopia"), who came to Troy and had the temerity to kill Achilles' beloved Antilochus, who provided consolation

once Patroclus was gone. And Antilochus, son of Nestor of Pylos, oldest of the Greeks, is something special, one of the most likable heroes in
the *Iliad,* a three-dimensional character and almost "normal": the epitome of *charis.* He has good legs and can run fast, bounding around the
battlefield, brave and enthusiastic. For he is also "youngest" of all the
Greeks at Troy and both he and his companions constantly draw attention to the fact.[46] He leaps on Trojan Melanippus like a hunting dog
upon a wounded fawn and then when he sees Hector approaching escapes like a wolf who has killed a guard dog or a herdsman, at the approach of a band of men.[47] He is a skilled charioteer and he learned his
skills from two remarkable teachers, Zeus and Poseidon, both of whom
"loved him" (*philēsan*). Poseidon especially, who is his great-grandfather,
keeps an eye out for him on the battlefield.

It takes a while for Antilochus to learn that Patroclus has been killed,
and he is shocked by the news. He is chosen to run back to camp to tell
Achilles. Sobbing himself, he has the presence of mind to hold Achilles'
hands, to stop him slitting his throat in grief. At the funeral games of Patroclus he competes, in the chariot race, of course, but proves to be
something of a boy racer. He shouts at his horses—How will you be
able to look the other horses in the eye, beaten by a mare? If you don't
go faster I'll have my father have you knackered. They hear and respond.
But now the road narrows, with room for just one chariot. Antilochus
goes off road to overtake Menelaus, who is forced to slow down to prevent an accident: "Antilochus, you are the most appalling driver in the
world."[48] Antilochus comes in second, but Achilles proposes giving his
second prize, a mare, to Eumelus, whose chariot had crashed spectacularly thanks to the wicked work of Athena, leaving him grazed and
bruised and having to pull his chariot on his own two legs.

Antilochus is furious. You can't take my prize away from me. Eumelus should have prayed harder to the gods. Give him some other
prize, Achilles, not mine. You're not exactly short of things to bestow.
Anyone who tries to take my prize will have to fight me for it with his
fists. "Achilles smiled, pleased to see [*chairōn*] Antilochus, because he was
his dear companion . . ."[49] He sends for an even more splendid prize to
give to Eumelus. But Menelaus can contain himself no longer, and accuses Antilochus of reckless driving, challenging him to deny it on oath.
Antilochus confesses, and after a gracious speech acknowledging

Menelaus's seniority and royal dignity, he hands the mare over at once. Menelaus melts. Antilochus can keep the mare, but as a gift from him.

Antilochus also competes in the footrace against Nasty Little Ajax, who is "a bit older than him," and Odysseus, a generation older. Athena makes Ajax slip in the dung left by all the sacrificial cows brought in for the funeral of Patroclus. He is covered in the stuff, in his mouth, his nostrils, everywhere. He cannot catch Odysseus but nor can Antilochus catch him. They cross the finish line in reverse age order. Ajax ironically wins an ox and, leaning on its horns, spits out mouthfuls of cow-dung, cursing and swearing. Antilochus, the youngest and the fastest, really should have won, but when he comes last he makes another gracious speech. Smiling, he marvels at the way the gods honor old-timers. The only man who could have beaten Odysseus would have been swift Achilles. Achilles doubles his prize to a talent of gold and puts the money in his hands himself. Antilochus receives it with pleasure (*chairōn*).[50]

That is the last we hear of Antilochus in the *Iliad,* but other sources tell us that he got closer to Achilles, and did not survive the war, but died trying to defend his father. Memnon should have known better than to mess with one of Achilles' dear companions. Achilles would surely avenge the death of Antilochus as he avenged the death of his previous boyfriend. But Memnon was not any old hero. He had a mother, Dawn, who was every bit as distinguished as Thetis, if not quite so bright. His father it seems was the Trojan prince Tithonus, already well on his way to becoming a wittering husk.[51]

27. Hermes weighs the fates of Achilles and Memnon while their mothers, Dawn and Thetis, plead with Zeus. Cup signed by Epictetus (*c.*525–500).

Memnon had an epic dedicated to his story, the *Aethiopis,* ascribed not to Homer but to one Arctinus of Miletus. From what we are told its climax was a duel between Memnon and Achilles, by general agreement the two most beautiful men at Troy. Both wore armor made by Hephaestus the divine blacksmith, and, as they fought, their divine mothers, Thetis and Dawn, stood behind them on either side, standing in for mothers of heroes everywhere. In these scenes Dawn is often shown wingless to indicate her mundane powerlessness to uplift her son or whisk him away. Thetis seems to have had a useful piece of information that she whispers into Achilles' ear; it is probably something important, but we don't know what it is—perhaps foretelling what will happen next.

Both mothers pleaded with Zeus to save their sons, but Zeus put their souls, or more pedantically, since they weren't dead yet, their fates, *kēres,* represented as little sprites, in the scales, where it was Memnon's fate that sank, and with it his mother's heart. The duel was shown on the Amyclae Throne over the tomb of Hyacinthus, and artists especially loved the "Psychostasia," the soul weighing, and painted it on several vases. Playwrights, including Aeschylus, who wrote a whole Memnon

28. Dawn tries to raise her dead son, Memnon, his feet crossing the frame, his hands behind it. There is a *kalos* acclamation (probably commissioned by an *erastēs,* since it is, so far, unique in Douris's oeuvre)—"Hermogenes is Beautiful"—and an indecipherable comment "?ENEMEKNERINE," perhaps mistranscribed from a text given by the purchaser. Cup found at Capua and signed by "Doris" (Douris) (c.485).

trilogy, put it onstage, with actors, when technology allowed, actually standing in the scales perhaps. The sequel—Dawn, alone, with her wings restored, but still finding it hard to lift her dead son, his ordinary weight now given special significance—was turned by one artist into a pre-Christian pietà (Fig. 28). Memnon's feet cross into our world. His hands remain in his, an indication of a three-dimensional perspective the artist was not quite technically capable of rendering. There is no weighing of souls here, but the effort of lifting him, against the force of gravity, inevitably recalls the moment just before, when his destiny still hung in the balance. This is not a mother removing the body of her dead son; Dawn is rehearsing Memnon's last minutes of life, and what she might have done differently to save him.[52]

Dawn cried a lot and the morning dew commemorates her tears. In Egyptian Thebes a colossal statue of Memnon (in fact Amenophis III), damaged by an earthquake, "sang" when he saw his mother each morning, until he was repaired by a visiting Roman emperor in AD 200. After Egypt was conquered by Alexander many Greeks visited to pay their respects to Dawn's son and covered his monument with interesting graffiti. We should mention at this point that the *Aethiopis* claims a happy ending. In the Milesian version of the tale, Achilles went to the White Island and Memnon himself was eventually immortalized.[53]

There seem to have been several prominent Achilles vs Memnon images at Olympia, one on the ornate Cypselus Chest, which was said to have been the cradle of the eponymous dictator who seized Corinth in 657 BC. In reality it was probably a Corinthian dedication of eighty years later and therefore contemporary with the François Vase.[54] Equally extraordinary is what seems to have been a statue group on a semicircular plinth in blue-black limestone from the archaic period, one of the stones having MEMNON carved on it in very antique-looking letters, although Pausanias missed it when he visited, so we cannot much elaborate on this; no tourist sees everything, and sometimes the managers of the site removed and buried things to make way for others.[55] Pausanias did however notice a later version, hard to miss in fact: a series of thirteen bronze statues ranged on a white, shell-bearing-limestone semicircle, thirteen meters across, next to the shrine dedicated to Pelops's wife Hippodamia.[56] In the center: Zeus. On either side of him, the two mothers pleading for their sons' lives and for the other mother's son to

die. At the two ends of the semicircle, Memnon and Achilles in opposition, Achilles presumably on Zeus's auspicious right. The other figures
were also pairs, one Greek, one "barbarian" from Troy. Menelaus was
opposite Paris, who stole his wife; Clever Odysseus was opposed to Helenus, Priam's clever son; Diomedes to Aeneas, whose team of horses,
sired by Ganymede's compensatory stable, Diomedes grabbed; and Ajax
(Big Hard-Done-By) to Deiphobus, each Greek-Barbarian pair becoming more extremely opposed until we reach Achilles and Memnon at the
very extremities of the semicircle. Pausanias, however, mentions no
weighing of the fates. The monument itself is a three-dimensional
weighing machine, with Zeus enthroned on Olympus as the heavenly
pivot and Achilles and Memnon at the farthest points, on the battlefield
down below.

The statues themselves are long gone, of course, probably ripped off
their plinths by Christian-converted Greeks and melted down for
crosses or bullion. Cheap terra-cottas had a much better chance of survival, more breakable but also more indestructible, for oven-baked pot
cannot be turned back into clay. Resilience comes in many forms and
pride comes before a fall. The vanished statues did however leave foot-
prints where they had been in the stone, which allows us to work out
that Zeus was enthroned, and the mothers on their knees. And the van-
dals also left parts of the dedication, which shows once more that Pausanias was quite a good transcriber, though, as usual, smoothing out for
his readers some of the "archaisms" and local accent, as Aeschines did
when quoting Homer. The people who dedicated it in fact were from
Albania, from what Cicero describes as the "dignified and noble" city of
Apollonia, where Octavian attended school with Athenodorus, who advised him to recite the alphabet before lashing out in anger—the anger
of the future emperor Augustus needing more time to abate than a mere
count from one to ten would provide. The city was founded opposite
Brindisi, where the Adriatic is at its narrowest, in 588 BC by the great city
of Corfu (Corcyra), itself a colony of Corinth, which may have assisted
in the foundation, like a helpful grandmotheropolis.

New colonies always liked to show off to older cities, to write themselves brashly into history without waiting for historians to catch up.
Often they built massive temples at conspicuous points and within
decades of their foundation. In fact in 1997 an Albanian family building

a new house stumbled across the massive foundation stones of an ambitious new temple, forty meters long and fourteen meters wide, which must have been built only a generation or two after Apollonia came into existence. Excavation began in earnest in 2004, and the provisional results are causing a certain amount of excitement. To whom the great temple belonged however has not yet been determined.

There was an alternative way of making your mark in the Greek world and that was by causing a splash at a site where all the Greeks came together. From the sixth century onward it was colonial cities that showed off most conspicuously at Olympia, building monuments, making lavish offerings and building treasure-houses to keep them in, training hard to win as many victories as they could in races. The first thing visitors would observe, therefore, as they passed along the path in the years around 440 BC and saw a brand-new monument on a semicircular platform that hadn't been there at the last Olympics, was simply its extravagance, provoking the thought: "Golly, that's impressive. Thirteen bronzes. Those guys must be doing well for themselves. I wonder who they are." As he—and it would be a he—read the inscription, he would hear the statues themselves speaking to him: "We have been put up here as monuments of Apollonia . . ." Apollonia? Where's that? Of course. The city founded by Corfu. Wrong answer. ". . . the city that Phoebus Apollo, who lets his hair grow long, founded in the Ionian Sea [*pontos*]." The statues fall silent in the second distich and a third-person voice takes over, more like a museum label: "Those who captured the borders of the Abantid land stood these things here together with the gods, a tenth-tithe from the plunder of Thronium."[57]

It should be said that in art Memnon is no more Black than Achilles is White, or than his parentage would demand, but he does have Black attendants.[58] For the opposition is not a racial one between Caucasians and sub-Saharan Africans but a neatly structural one founded on a cosmic white-black opposition with deep roots in religion—gods and heroes, heavenly and "chthonic" offerings, day and night, up and down—an opposition between Achilles of the White Island in the north of the known world and Memnon from Aethiopia, the "Burnt-Faced" country in the far south. The group itself emphasizes structuralism, for although the three central figures of Zeus and the mothers and the two end figures of Memnon and Achilles make up a "real" scene, a group

often represented in two-dimensional art, now rendered in three dimensions; the other figures do not belong to that scene. They win their
places on the monument simply on the quasi-algebraic principle of
Greek-Trojan, Greek-Barbarian dualism.

If the opposition isn't "racist," it is certainly "ethnicist." For the
Apollonians it seems had been raiding the local Epirotes of Thronium
and had built this anti-Barbarian monument from the spoils. But who
counted as a Greek was not always clear-cut. The Epirotes certainly
might have had something to say about being placed implicitly on the
Trojan, left-hand, Barbarian side, the dark side.[59] And there is always a
barely hidden anxiety, or a touch of wishful thinking in the Greek vs
Barbarian opposition, because the greatest enemies of Greeks were almost always other Greeks, who often show no hesitation at all in siding
with local barbarians in order to bring down a rival faction or a rival
city, especially one that is expanding into a region they might consider
their own sphere. Indeed, soon after the monument was dedicated in-
ternecine conflict broke out within this cozy Corinthian family of all-
Greek colonies in the northwest corner of mainland Greece. Trouble
may well already have been brewing when the great monument to
Achilles was erected.

Epidamnus, Apollonia's sister-city, farther up the coast, had not been
doing nearly so well against the locals; in fact rather badly. Eventually the
city split into factions. One faction stirred the natives up further. Corfu,
the mother-city, wouldn't get involved. Corinth, the grandmother-
city, would, and both Elis, which controlled Olympia, and Apollonia
sent assistance.[60] Corfu suddenly rediscovered an interest in her daughter-
city, once her own mother started interfering. Before too long the
whole family—mothers, grandmothers, sisters and granddaughters—
were at one another's throats, fighting among one another as only relatives can, with shocking cruelty and disregard for the rules of normal
behavior and some of the biggest and bloodiest sea battles Greece had
ever known. At one point in the argument Corfu fatefully asked Athens
to intervene, and so began a conflict that involved the whole of Greece
for nearly thirty years: the Peloponnesian War.

Most Greeks who came to Olympia and saw the monument during
those years would not think: "Golly, who made that?" but: "I wonder
whose side they're on." And anyone from Corfu who saw it might

think: "Look at the Apollonians, trying to filch a little reflected glory from the heroic age to add luster to their upstart history. They might at least have given a little credit to the city that bore them. Phoebus Apollo did not found the city on his own." Olympia in other words was full of jabs and jibes, as well as boastings thinly veiled with pious modesty and Team-Greece propaganda, and most Greeks had a great deal of practice in seeing through the veils. There was also not a little outright rubbing of others' noses in the dirt. Not only would other Greeks read the lavish Greeks vs Barbarians monument set up by Apollonia as something other than a celebration of Our innate superiority over Them, some would definitely read it in rivalry: an indication of uppishness, a warning, or even a provocation.

So in art there was a more famous standoff between Achilles and someone from the Trojan side, a more famous weighing of fates in the balance. Not Achilles vs Hector in revenge for the death of Patroclus, but Achilles vs Memnon in revenge for the death of Antilochus. The duel is another image of Achilles as a fierce lover of his own sex, therefore, putting his life in the balance for the sake of a man he was passionately devoted to. But what is interesting is that the opposed warriors also stand for the greater opposition of Greek vs Barbarian. The Greekest Greek is not uxorious Odysseus, nor cuckolded Agamemnon; it is a man avenging his boyfriend. The Memnon myth puts Greek Love right at the heart of Greekness. The Barbarian just does not seem to get it.

PRECURSORS AND FORESHADOWINGS

The question is which of Achilles' two suicidally avenged beloveds was the original? Since Homer is the first literature, and pot painters of his time preferred to cover their pots not with informative scenes from myth but mostly rather abstract geometrical designs, that is a difficult question. But there are clues in Homer himself as to the myths that were already in circulation, myths he alludes to implicitly and explicitly. This practice of his has led to an entire "neo-analytical" school devoted to seeing back through Homer's "layers." There are also a few images from the period immediately after Homer that reveal the kinds of myths in popular circulation, and one can, more subjectively, assess myths themselves for their neatness and tidiness, which ones are "mythic" in the vernacular sense, which are "good stories," i.e., which ones look as if they would be good to recount around a fire, without the aid of a master poet, and which ones, by contrast, look as if they wouldn't make it on their own. And from all this, there seems no question at all that Homer knew the myth of Memnon killing Antilochus and of an enraged Achilles resolving on vengeance, even at the cost of his life.

Antilochus is mentioned four times in the *Odyssey,* which is a very different kind of epic from the *Iliad,* a scene-, voice- and time-shifting, multiframed tale of the aftermath of Troy. On coming of age, Odysseus's son Telemachus sails across the sea to Pylos south of Elis to visit Nestor the old trooper and to ask about the war that finished ten years ago and for news of his father, whom he has never known. We left so many good men behind there, says Nestor: Ajax; Achilles; Patroclus; Antilochus, my own son. Telemachus stays the night, but he is not put up in the spare bedroom. Two beds are prepared, and while Nestor goes to sleep with his wife, Telemachus sleeps alongside Antilochus's younger brother, still unmarried, his own age. While Nestor beds down with his wife, Telemachus beds down with Pisistratus.[61]

Pisistratus, Nestor's son, in fact accompanies Telemachus on his mission to Sparta and back. They travel as a chariot pair, like Achilles and Patroclus. They make an overnight stop with one mysterious Diocles at "Pherae" and then on to Sparta and the palace of Menelaus and Helen, not far from Hyacinthian Amyclae. Over twenty years after she was seduced and got carried away by Paris, Helen is nevertheless no Norma Desmond: a little ashamed of all the heroes who died for her, to be sure, but bitter, surely not, and she's still got it—whatever it was she had— wonderfully charming and mysterious, quietly self-confident, and ever so slightly from another planet. She divines straightaway from his resemblance to Odysseus that Telemachus must be the son of the father he never knew. She begins to cry and they all do. But Pisistratus is thinking of his brother Antilochus, "whom the splendid son of shining Dawn killed . . ."[62] Memnon. Antilochus questions their host about his elder brother. Menelaus, you would have known him. I never met him. They say he was something, my brother Antilochus. Menelaus praises the bachelor-boy's speech but tells him nothing more, nothing about the chariot race, his reckless driving, the altercation, his brother's charm, the mare. Having started all the weeping, Helen puts an end to it. She slips a drug into everybody's drink, a powerful anodyne that would guard against the deepest misery, even if your parents had just died, even if you saw your own brother or your own son put to death right in front of you. Then they bed down for the night, Telemachus, once more, on purple bedding beside Pisistratus.

Meanwhile in another location Odysseus is visiting the Underworld. One by one the ghosts of his former comrades-in-arms come to speak to him. He is surprised to find Agamemnon down there, thinking that he at least must have got home safely. I did, says Agamemnon, but my wife Clytemnestra had a nasty surprise in store. They shed tears together. Women? Treacherous bitches, all of them. But Odysseus's wife Penelope is not like that. You think? Next up, the same, it seems, quartet that Nestor had spoken of, if in a slightly different order: Achilles, Patroclus, Antilochus and Ajax, but this, it seems, is Big Hard-Done-By Ajax. He still cannot believe how he, after carrying Achilles' dead body from the battlefield like a fireman single-handed, over his shoulder, missed out on Achilles' famous panoply. He will not speak to Odysseus.

Finally, right at the end of the *Odyssey* in its mysterious book twenty-four, Hermes is taking all the wittering souls of Penelope's massacred suitors to the Underworld. There on the Isles of the Blessed is the familiar quartet in the same order: Achilles and Patroclus, Antilochus and Ajax, apparently the Big Hard-Done-By one again, who committed suicide at Troy. "They were gathered in association around Achilles' (*peri keinon homileon*).[63] Agamemnon arrives, and Achilles questions him. He tells him what happened after his death. "Your mother gave us a golden two-handled amphora. A gift from Dionysus she said it was, the work of celebrated Hephaestus. In it your white bones were put, glorious Achilles, mixed with those of already dead Patroclus, son of Menoetius, and separately those of Antilochus, whom you esteemed most out of all the rest of your comrades after Patroclus, him being dead." Then a mighty mound visible for miles around was piled up on them.[64]

From this it seems clear that the White Island quartet was known by tradition to be associating somewhere in the afterlife—Achilles, Patroclus, Antilochus and an Ajax—and that this association was linked to shared tombs and tombs at Troy. Homer, and therefore presumably his audience, certainly knew the story of Memnon killing Antilochus, so they would be able to read foreshadowings of that story in the fact that it is Antilochus who brings the news of Patroclus's death and in the clear affection Achilles shows him at Patroclus's funeral games. In fact it seems very likely that when Homer in the *Iliad* describes Zeus weighing the souls of Hector and Achilles, an unequal contest, he has stolen it from Memnon's story, where it is more central and the result less predictable, and there are some early images of myths connected to the *Aethiopis* that suggest they were circulating widely around this time, while Achilles fighting Hector over Patroclus takes a long time to catch on, and even when Homer has become the national poet, never manages to take over, as if Homer's fate-weighing episode is still not canonical. In fact the theory that Antilochus-Memnon-Achilles is the original myth from which the Patroclus-Hector-Achilles myth drew its inspiration has long been accepted by neo-analysts, enough to provoke a splendidly sharp and sarcastic rebuke from Denys Page in 1963.[65]

Such an original myth would be neater in other ways. It would wrap up the story of Achilles more tidily, since in this version he dies soon after he avenges his beloved: "Then they bury Antilochus and lay out the corpse of Achilles."[66] It always had seemed odd that Patroclus does not receive final burial, that his bones would be disturbed, that he might be dug up again to be reburied with Achilles. The dream in which Patroclus's ghost makes this request for a homotaph could also be seen as Homer licensing the desecration by having the corpse himself request it.

In fact the greater popularity of non-Homeric myths of Troy in representations continuing long after Homer has become the canonical Greek epic poet, this and their neatness of conception—High Concept—are not separate issues. Some myths are better than others, better to represent, easier to remember, more forceful and with more satisfying closures: the tale of the Trojan Horse and the Sack of Troy, the duel between Achilles and Memnon with their divine mothers interceding on their behalf as their fates hang in the balance, followed by the death of Memnon and then of Achilles in quick succession, Meleager returning to battle and certain death thanks to his mother's curse, how Achilles provoked Apollo and was shot by an arrow in the foot. Homer alludes to more cohesive myths, and by alluding to them ties his long narrative to pithier, more resonant and more final tales, but the *Iliad* is not High Concept; it feels like an episode in a serial. It doesn't seem to have a crystalline center, which is one reason why we love it so much. It reads like proper literature, a great poet creating his own narrative. Even tragedies seem to have better bone structure. What, after all, is *the* myth of the *Iliad*? Sing, O Muses, of the time when

Achilles was cross for a long time and stopped fighting and then stopped being cross and started fighting again? When students of mythology turn to the *Iliad,* when later authors summarize the story, it feels as if we are in a quite different world from the world of other myths. When artists turn to the *Iliad,* they always look as if they are illustrating a text, not making a resonant myth with an independent life of its own manifest in paint or stone.

So I think it's quite a cogent argument that Patroclus is secondary to Antilochus. That would mean, of course, that just when we are about to start chasing after some theory to explain why the Greek Love of Achilles and Patroclus is so un-Greek in structure, Achilles the beardless beauty passionately devoted to older Patroclus, we discover an earlier version of Achilles' love that conforms more neatly to the "canonical model." Which just goes to show. Perhaps Homer's audience would also be wondering like Phaedrus: "What on earth is going on between these two?" Where are Memnon and his Aethiopians?

ACHILLES AND THE BOY

But in fact there is another myth just as neat, with roots equally deep and a history in art no less long, about Achilles and an underage Boy. It shows the same combination of love and raging hate, but its object here is one and the same, for he is a Trojan and his name is Troilus.

Achilles may be mightiest of warriors, but he is particularly famous for his extraordinary fleetness of foot: "like Ares in the power of his hands, like lightnings in the power of his feet," says Themis, in her warning of a threat to Zeus should he go ahead and seduce Thetis, instantly pouring cold water on Zeus's lust for Achilles' mother.[67] This particular ability revealed itself prodigiously when Achilles was only six and still living with Chiron the centaur. Already "fast as the winds," he would "kill boars and deal death to savager lions, bringing them to Chiron, still trying to get their breath . . . Artemis and bold Athena were amazed to see him killing deer without the aid of dogs or tricky traps; he preferred to overtake them on foot."[68] Gregory Nagy has counted over thirty references to Achilles in the *Iliad* as "swift of foot," over twenty calling him *podarkes,* "relying on his feet," and over twenty "swift-footeds," and this of a man who spends most of the poem sulking in his tent, the irony, the contrast with Achilles' immobilization, probably not unintended. Achilles is the only hero so designated. It is his defining characteristic. One might imagine that when most of the fighting in the *Iliad* is in the form of individual duels and most of the movement is in chariots, speed of foot would come way down the list of qualities a warrior might pray for, most useful for a rather unsuccessful warrior, perhaps, always losing duels and falling off his chariot, one who runs away. But, like Superman, Achilles' extraordinary speed is a mark of his general forcefulness, his impetus and impact "faster than a speeding arrow."[69]

Achilles' speed comes to the fore in book twenty-two, in the climactic scene of Homer's *Iliad,* a scene cruel and ridiculous at the same time. Gone berserk after the death of Patroclus, Achilles is wreaking havoc on the flower of Trojan manhood. One Agenor stands fast and strikes Thetis's son with his spear, on the shin below the knee. The missile however glances off, no match for Hephaestus's armory. Achilles turns to see from where the missile came and pursues his attacker across the wheatfields toward the river Scamander. Achilles, about to catch up, thinks at any moment he will catch up, being so fast on his feet must catch up, but never catches up with his attacker, for it is Agenor no longer, but the god Apollo in disguise. "Why, pray, are you chasing me, with your fast feet, son of Peleus?" Achilles "swift in foot" is "very cross indeed," but wastes no more energy on the god and speeds off back toward Troy: "As easily as a prize-winning horse in a chariot race putting on a plain-shrinking spurt, with just such a whoosh did Achilles deploy [*enōma*] his feet and knees" (22.22–24). He is spotted by Priam, the bronze on his breastplate flashing like the Dog of Orion that comes in ripe August and, though it is bright, brings plagues. Finally Hector comes out and Achilles chases him around and around and around the walls of Troy.

This famous scene is not the one that Clitias chose to show on the François Vase, however. Two men running around and around would bring out the absurdity but not the pathos of Homer's description. Instead he has chosen an episode Homer doesn't cover, but one that encapsulates the speed (and violent impact) of Achilles more graphically: his murder of Hector's brother Troilus. The basic story is a simple one, but very neat and tidy. Troilus is an underage Boy. He takes a horse and goes to fetch water at a fountain house outside the city walls. Achilles is waiting for him. Although the details of where and how he actually kills the boy are variable, one feature is fixed: Troilus is on horseback and Achilles runs him down on foot.[70] Indeed it seems from one image that he cut the boy's head off and waved it in the face of his brothers. Out of all Achilles' exploits at Troy, Clitias has chosen to picture this one, not glorious at all, but a feat that has the advantage of showing to a viewer the unique quality the poets never tire of celebrating: Achilles' phenomenal speed. It is also the feat that will lead to his death, for Clitias has shown Apollo watching in some agitation. Either the crime itself, or the fact that Achilles took the boy to the sanctuary of Apollo, or even killed him on Apollo's altar is what finally led to Achilles' death, according to one prominent tradition. And it was an outraged Apollo who guided the arrow that would kill him. All terribly neat. Achilles' most amazing ability, his speed, is precisely what undoes him, and when Apollo shoots him, where does the arrow pierce him? In the foot.

This is a detail well established at an early date.[71] Later mythographers did not really grasp its significance and told stories about the ankle as Achilles' only point of vulnerability, something that Homer and the earlier poets do not mention. Achilles is certainly not invulnerable—that's why his mother goes to so much trouble to get him a piece of armor—but the symbolic significance of Achilles, "swift in foot," being fatally wounded in the foot needs no further explanation. The arrow guided by Apollo quite literally pins the fastest man on the planet to the ground, it stops him dead. There is irony then in the fact that on each handle of the François Vase Achilles' corpse is carried from the battlefield at a run. His own legs quite useless to him now, he depends on those of Ajax, the Quick and the Dead.

The story that Achilles was in love with Troilus is told first in the second century BC in the impossibly obscure and allegorical prophetic "monodrama" of Cassandra (*Alexandra*), "quite the most repellent poem to survive from antiquity," composed in iambic trimeters and ascribed to the Hellenistic poet Lycophron.[72] The prophetess is apostrophizing, addressing now her little brother, young Troilus, whom she sees in strange visions of the future: "Lion-cub you, who shot the wild dragon with fire-bearing love-charm of arrows, and wouldn't let go of smitten him, holding him in snares inescapable, for a scant loveless time, yourself untouched by the man you had subjected, you will bloody your father's altar cut off at the head." "Untouched," literally "unwounded," i.e., unattracted to Achilles, is a play on the paradox of the "captor" "captivated"; it could easily be read more graphically, "unpenetrated."[73]

29. Achilles kills Troilus at the altar of Thymbraean Apollo. The cockerel indicates an erotic motif. What was the warrior who commissioned such a relief thinking of? Shield band discovered at Olympia (c.580).

An ancient reader offered some helpful notes in the margin of the text: Troilus had taken refuge in the sanctuary to escape Achilles' advances. Unable to get him to come out, Achilles goes in and kills him. A commentator on Virgil's *Aeneid* adds more detail: "Led on by his love for Troilus, Achilles held out to him some doves, of which the boy was very fond, but as he reached out to take them, he was captured by Achilles and died in his arms."[74] This is all very late, but the abduction, the doves, and hence probably the love motif appear in paintings of the scene as early as the sixth century.[75] I think it would be impossible for a Greek, knowing Achilles' tendencies and seeing an image of him as a Stripling chasing down a Boy, not to adduce an *erōtikos* motivation. The myth, of course, has a roller coaster of an afterlife. The heterosexual element in the love triangle, Achilles' Iliadic concubine Briseis, enters the story in the twelfth-century *Roman de Troie* of Benoît de Sainte-Maure. His "Briseida" becomes "Criseida" in Boccaccio's version, Criseyde in Chaucer's and Cressida in Shakespeare.[76] Thus a homosexual dyad is transformed into a heterosexual triad.

The myth encapsulates more economically the fighter-lover character of Achilles, the fierce intensity of the hero-god's black-white two-sided character expressed both positively in his devotion to Patroclus and An-

30. Achilles taunts Hector with the head of his little brother, Troilus.
Achilles will pay for this. The hatched mound is Apollo's "altar," as the
inscription (BOMOS) helpfully points out. Black-figure neck amphora
("Tyrrhenian") by the Timiades Painter (c. 560–550).

tilochus and negatively toward the Trojans. And Homer's audience
might well find echoes of that myth when Achilles tells of chasing down
Hector, Troilus's big brother, and cutting off his head, almost as if he has
separated the white and the black. It is this duality that makes Achilles
the Greekest of heroes, loving his own side as much as he hates the
enemy, a perfect inspiration for all Greek hoplite warriors, lovingly devoted to those alongside and nursing equal hate for those ranged opposite: the enemy, the Other, the Barbarian. Perhaps when they thought
of Achilles it would not seem as strange to the Spartans and the Cretans
as it does to us to offer sacrifice to Eros before going into battle.

II

HERACLES AND IOLAUS

HERACLES' LITTLE HELPER

One thing we don't see in the narratives of Achilles and Patroclus and
Antilochus is any instance of teamwork. Achilles and Patroclus never

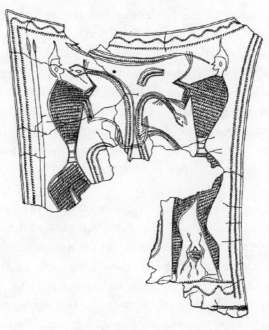

31. Heracles and Iolaus fight the Hydra. One of the earliest identifiable
images from Greek myth, Iolaus with his long machete helps Heracles
kill the many-headed Hydra in the marshes of Lerna.
Boeotian "safety-pin" (*c.* 710).

fight together as a pair in the *Iliad*. That is merely something they recall
with great nostalgia as happening in the past, or look forward to happening in the future, all the Greeks and all the Trojans dead. For teamwork we must turn to an equally famous same-sex pair: Heracles and
Iolaus. For Heracles did not perform all his famous Labors on his own.
If same-sex-loving Achilles indicates verve and spunk, sharp fury and
the blistering energy of a forceful revenge attack, this couple indicates
steadfastness, two men enduring long toils together, spread over a long
time. So these two are utterly different, except for two things: They belong to the same Aeolian cultural group as the Thessalians, Achilles and
Patroclus, from a little farther south, from the great and ancient city of
seven-gated Thebes; and they journey together in a chariot.

Iolaus is above all the youth or man (for usually in art he is shown
bearded) who helps Heracles with his Labors, in particular the killing of
the great many-headed snaky Hydra of the marshes at Lerna, on the
coast opposite Nauplion, where a bottomless lake reached all the way

down to the gates of the Underworld. Iolaus is first found on two brooches from Thebes dating to around 700 BC, among the very earliest of all recognizable mythological scenes in Greek art, helping Heracles in his battle with the Lernaean monster. Brooches connect, and these brooches show a strong alliance. One of them indicates a figure rather smaller than the great hero. When inscriptions start appearing on Corinthian vases around the end of the seventh century, Heracles' assistant is named "Wiolawos" or "Violavos"—the ancient sound v/w, represented by the letter "*F*," was preserved in Dorian areas such as Corinth.[77]

The Lernaean Hydra was particularly tricky to take on single-handed because of all its heads, which in later authors grow back fast and multiply when severed. Iolaus's role was to sear the stumps: "If one miscreant dies, two politicians spring up. For there is no Iolaus in Athens to cauterize the politicians' heads."[78] Later he uses torches applied directly to the bleeding neck. In the early versions he is using a jagged-toothed sickle heated in a fire that burns in the background. This sickle or machete, the *harpē,* seems important in Iolaus's myths and cult. Just as a sickle cuts heads of wheat, so Iolaus cuts the Hydra's snaky heads, and ultimately the head of Eurystheus, deadly enemy of Heracles and his sons and the man who had set him all these supposedly impossible tasks. Perseus, an Argive hero who comes from the region around Lerna, uses the same instrument to cut the snake-tressed head of Medusa, and Iolaus's mother was a mysterious Automedusa.

Because Heracles had Iolaus's help here, some say that the Lernaean Hydra didn't count as an accomplishment and the original Ten Labors were increased to Twelve.[79] In depictions of other Labors therefore, Iolaus takes care to do nothing: He stands around, chatting to a god, while Heracles gets on with it, or revs up the getaway chariot so that Heracles can make a quick escape and move on to his next quest. This role made him one of the most famous mythological reins-holders, first victor in the first chariot race at the Olympic Games, dressed sometimes in the driver's peculiar elegant costume. On some later vases he drives Heracles all the way up to heaven, providing an interesting parallel with Poseidon's transport of Pelops. For it is hard not to see in such an image the heavenly constellation of the Reins-Holder driving from the bottom of the night sky, from the edge of the horizon, to the uppermost height of heaven. On some vases there is a little crab trying to pinch the hero's foot, the only member of the animal kingdom that would help the poor Hydra save its heads. Hera, city-goddess of Argos, who hated Heracles, her husband's son by another woman, liked what the crab was doing and placed it among the stars as the constellation Cancer.

In the earliest source, "Hesiod's" *Shield of Heracles,* tentatively dated 580–570, Iolaus is "dearest of all mortals" to Heracles and son of his estranged half brother Iphicles, an early example of sons cultivating alliances their fathers incautiously neglect. There is no extended narrative to compare with the *Iliad* describing their exploits together, but Iolaus was a very familiar figure in painting, thanks to the enormous popularity of the Labors. One of the most charming passages in Euripides describes viewers' responses to these images. The viewers are a group of women visiting Delphi in attendance on Creusa, queen of Athens, daughter of Erechtheus, and sister of Orithyia the wind-snatched and Procris, whose husband was seduced by Dawn. Creusa has come to consult the oracle. Her attendants, meanwhile, go to see the sights, amazed to find things worth looking at outside their own grand city. Euripides is perhaps gently mocking the Athenians' nationalistic parochialism in what seems on the face of it a nationalistically parochial play.[80] The first thing the women see is Heracles and the Hydra—"Take a look at that, my friend." "I see it. And next to him there is someone else, raising a fiery torch; it's that man in the story, isn't it? We do him in my weaving session, shield-bearer Iolaus, the man who undertook to share the Labors with Zeus's son." "That's all very well, but take a good look at this man on a flying horse over here . . ."[81]

It was something of a *coup de théâtre,* therefore, when Euripides opened his *Sons of Heracles* at Marathon, with Marathon's cult hero Iolaus no longer the fresh youth, nor even the vigorous Reins-Holder, but a decrepit old man.[82] With Heracles in heaven married to Hebe the goddess of youth, his archenemy Eurystheus decides to destroy Heracles' line, root and branch, and invades Attica where his sons have sought asylum. With the help of a servant, Iolaus goes out to help defend his uncle/lover's offspring. His shuffling exit is unpromising. He is so slow that you really think the battle will be over before he arrives—not that his absence seems likely to alter the outcome. "Put a pointed spear in my right hand, and let me lean on you with my left arm, as you guide my

32. A mature Iolaus assists a lion-skin-dressed Heracles to kill the Hydra.
Red-figure stamnos by the Syleus Painter (*c.* 500–475).

feet." "Must I take the hoplite in hand then and lead him like a child?"
"Get on with it. It will be terrible if I miss the battle." "You're the one
who's holding us up, not me." "You'll change your tune when you see
me there . . ." "Doing what exactly?" ". . . plunging a spear through
the shield of one of the enemy." "If we ever get there . . ."[83]

Some time later a messenger comes back from the front with a report.
There has been a miracle. As Eurystheus raced past, Iolaus grabbed the
reins of a chariot and raced after him. He prayed to Zeus and Hebe to
give him back his youth just for a day. Two brilliant lights appeared over
the horses' yoke. It was Hebe and her husband. A thick cloud covered
the chariot. When it cleared, the reins-holding arm of Iolaus was restored to youthful vigor, as if through a force transmitted up the reins
from the bright lights on the yoke. Eurystheus was doomed.[84]

BINDING AND BONDAGE

Apart from the images and the passages in literature, this relationship
was one very much informed by and informing cult and cult practices.
The hero Iolaus seems to have been something of a Theban mascot, as
important to the city as Hippolytus was in Troezen. Aristophanes char-

acterizes a Boeotian not only by a funny accent but by his swearing an oath in Iolaus's name. It seems that Heracles' Theban sanctuary, incorporating a training ground, guarded the southern approaches to the city. Iolaus's sanctuary lay eastward, outside one of her seven gates, the Proetidian, which leads out to the island of Euboea and Chalcis. There was a training ground here too, a stadium and a racecourse. According to Aristotle, it was here at the tomb of Iolaus that Theban same-sex pairs plighted their troths, the hero presumably invoked to guarantee these oaths of faith as he guaranteed all oaths, and to punish faithless lovers.[85] Theban couples seem therefore to have exchanged their vows in a thoroughly sporty atmosphere, surrounded by naked youths, building muscle. Iolaus's Theban festival, the Iolaieia, was an important athletics meeting, although not in quite the same league as the four great pan-Hellenic occasions, Olympic, Nemean (in Argos), Isthmian (Corinth) and Pythian (Delphi), and Pindar often mentions it in his celebrations of sporting victories. Here newly crowned Alexander set up camp when he came to besiege the city in 335. The outcome was a massacre and the complete destruction of Thebes. Pindar's hundred-year-old house was spared out of finer feelings.

In cult Iolaus is "altar-partner," *symbōmos,* of Heracles and got a sacrifice at the shrine of Heracles at Marathon in the lunar month around January, and a whole sheep at Sunium around April (alongside Heracles, his grandmother Alcmene, and the "Hero at the Salt-Flat" etc.), apparently a big occasion. He was also offered cult alongside Heracles in the Athenian gymnasium of Cynosarges. Indeed co-cults seem to have been typical: "Heracles had 68 sons, but loved his nephews as well as any of them," says Plutarch, a fellow Boeotian, in his treatise *On Brotherly Love.* "To this day his nephew Iolaus shares a common altar with him and they are invoked in prayer together, Iolaus under the designation Heracles' Comrade."[86]

But as one might expect from a traveling couple, Iolaus pops up in all sorts of places. He is very important out west it would seem. He is a significant figure for the Etruscans, who called him Vile (two syllables; in the west, Greek influence was Dorian Greek influence, and the Dorians brought their v/ws with them), and in the hometown of the historian Diodorus of Sicily. Agyrium lay inside the island, west of Mount Etna, a city of native Sicels, later taken over by Greeks. They thought they were the first to offer sacrifices to Heracles as a god before his death, and they had a track of fossilized cow hooves called Hoofs of Heracles to prove it. One of Heracles's Labors was to steal the cattle of the three-bodied giant Geryon, who lived way out west—a myth that gets students of comparative mythology tremendously excited. Driving his cattle through Agyrium they left imprints in solid rock, a clear indication that an apotheosis was afoot. In gratitude for their divine honors Heracles built a lake in front of the city, almost 900 yards in circumference, and it too was called Heraclean.

He also set up a hero shrine to Geryon, says Diodorus, and a sacred precinct to Iolaus, who had accompanied him of course, ordering annual honors and divine sacrifices (*thusias*) for him. The inhabitants grow their hair from birth in Iolaus's honor, says Diodorus, who had probably done it himself, until omens show they have sacrificed magnificently enough to have rendered the god (Iolaus? Heracles?) propitious. So great is the holy majesty of the sanctuary that those Boys (*paides*) who fail to complete the accustomed sacrifices are paralyzed like corpses and speechless, although a vow to complete will effect a cure—how you make a vow if you cannot speak, he doesn't say. An Italian vase from Caere made by immigrant Greek panel painters from the eastern Aegean shows a young Iolaus with his long hair knotted into a bun with a tail. The annual festival at Agyrium included athletics and horse races.[87] This haircutting ritual certainly must be related to coming-of-age, but the idea of delaying citizenship for whatever reason is quite alien to Greek age-class systems, which were obsessively policed according to natural, physical, bodily age, thoroughly automatic. We have two options, it seems to me. Either in Agyrium, as in some other places, Japan for instance, or Rome, coming-of-age was a movable event, depending on various things having been achieved, or else Iolaus was deemed capable of arresting development. Is that what Diodorus means when he says he could freeze boys? Possibly the idea of "freezing" is a way of shifting from one type of variable-age initiation based upon the performing of various vows to another based on natural development. But we notice once more the strong links between Iolaus and pledges. He is almost the hero of steadfastness and keeping one's word, something he shares with Heracles, whose Labors, of course, are a case of dutifully doing what he is oath-bound to do, at the request of his archenemy.

IOLAUS THE PHOENICIAN

Iolaus also turns up in the extraordinary contract of friendship arranged between Hannibal the Carthaginian and the Macedonian King Philip V—Hannibal's crushing victory over the Romans at Cannae had made the Greeks sit up and take notice. In the contract, Hannibal and Philip swear to be "friends, kinsmen [*oikeioi*] and brothers," sealing their alliance in the name of a whole list of gods and heroes arranged in threes. After Zeus, Hera and Apollo comes Divinity of Carthage, Heracles and Iolaus.[88] Now, for a Greek, Heracles and Iolaus would be the most suitable powers to invoke in a binding oath of intense fraternal and enduring (military) pact; Hannibal and Philip would, in the eyes of Greeks, be assimilating themselves to the Theban lovers pledging themselves at Iolaus's tomb in the fourth century. But the document must have been bilingual, and what is interesting is the attempt to find important metaphysical powers that might be taken seriously both by a Greek and by a Phoenician from Carthage.

Heracles was an obvious choice. He had long been identified with the Phoenician god Melqart of Tyre, the metropolis of Carthage, a proper "dying rising god" who was buried and resurrected, or "awakened" (*egersis*), like Jesus Christ. Since Sir James Frazer identified lots of dying rising gods, including Hyacinthus, students of religion have tightened up the requirements considerably, some of them hoping to squeeze all such divine figures, bar one, out of existence. They cannot be Underworld deities such as Osiris or Persephone, with little celestial presence, but who are said once to have been alive and to have returned. Nor can they be mere stellified heroes, or heroes dead in fine places like the White Island or the Isles of the Blessed, nor demigods worshipped as both celestial and chthonic powers, nor celestial divinities who visit the Underworld as tourists. They have to be celestial divinities a central part of whose myth is that they died, really died, lights-out died, were buried, properly buried, went to the Underworld like any other person, spent time down there, were mourned and then, normally three days later, came back, were revivified, reawakened to everyone's amazement and general celebration, and having been resurrected went up to heaven, where they are important, until next Easter, when the whole drama happens again. Melqart was such a one, and Jesus Christ another, and

Heracles through his links to Melqart was such a one in fits and starts, though mostly, like Achilles, he alternated the roles of god and hero, up and down. Whether Heracles' myth ensured the connection to Melqart or whether the connection to Melqart produced the myth is something that people, obviously, debate. At any rate, in this *interpretatio graeca* of Phoenician myth, crypto-Phoenician Iolaus in revivifying crypto-Phoenician Heracles with the smell of roasted quails is performing a terribly important role in Melqart's cult, and a role often filled, it seems, in practice by a priestlike human personage or a king.

So the Pillars of Heracles at the entrance to the Mediterranean are in fact the pillars of the great temple of Melqart built by the Phoenicians at Cadiz; one author says the pillars were of silver blended with gold and stood about one and a half feet high, "like anvils."[89] It is the fact that he was identified with Melqart that explains why Heracles has such far-flung adventures in the western Mediterranean; he has purloined Melqart's sanctuaries it would seem. It also has something to do with Heracles' ability to go into the Underworld and return and his receiving the honor, along with only Ganymede, who did not ever die, of being translated to Olympus. Not even Achilles managed such a feat. There is no doubt that Iolaus too was identified with a figure from Phoenician religion. This connection would explain why he was so popular in Italy, Sardinia and Sicily, but especially Sardinia. Most interesting is a Greek myth about Iolaus leading a prehistoric colony to Sardinia, giving his name, Iolians, to the native population and creating all kinds of monuments, statues—still standing, says Diodorus—and structures, "Nuraghic." He was worshipped by the natives as Father Iolaus.

Who, then, is the Phoenician Iolaus? The most popular candidates are the healing god Eshmoun and Sid (in Greek "Sardus" as in "Sardinia," "sardine"), and it is beginning to look, unfortunately, as if Sid is the likeliest candidate. "Vile." "Sid." Iolaus did not translate well into other languages. But this much seems clear: In the friendship pact between Hannibal and Philip, the three powers named—Divinity of Carthage, Heracles and Iolaus—represent either a nice symbolic triangle of the ancient Phoenician territory in the west—Carthage, Sardinia and Melqart's Cadiz—or a colonial family tree, respectively the god of Carthage, the god of her mother-city Tyre, and the god of her Sardinian daughter-colonies, currently in revolt from Rome.[90]

Through these undeniable and widely accepted links with Phoenician myths and deities in which chariots also figure, Iolaus, it seems, comes to represent leafy fruitfulness and greenery, or well-wateredness in general if you want to be reductive, the life-giving function that re-erects Heracles-Melqart destroyed by Typhon-Seth, the desiccated (Sahara) Desert. Caution would stop me right here, but I can see something very intriguing peeking out from around the next corner, one of the most scabrous gay myths I know of, and curiosity entices me on.

DIONYSUS AND THE DILDO

The Hydra of the infernal bottomless lake of Lerna became an important part of the crypto-Phoenician myth of dead-but-risen Heracles-Melqart, for in one version Heracles got fatally stung by the marshy monster and could only be cured by a magic plant. The plant was brought. Heracles was cured. On some Phoenician coins from Tyre and elsewhere this plant that saved the dying god is positively brandished. It is probably safe to assume that, with Heracles incapacitated, it was Iolaus who fetched it.[91] This is not quite a death and resurrection of Heracles at Lerna, but it comes close—a near-death and a recovery from it—and, given the context, it may well have been a death *tout court*. The crypto-Phoenician myth of Lerna is in fact the model for the subsequent episode of Melqart-Heracles' death and resurrection, or, at the very least, a dry run, a dress rehearsal. The Hydra is the daughter of Typhon, a foreshadowing of Typhon-Seth-the-Sahara-Desiccation—the Very Devil.

Now we might like to leave it like that. But there is another myth of Lerna that has nothing to do with Heracles and Iolaus, but that involves death and resurrections, and re-erections of the most straightforward kind. It involves an even greener god, Dionysus, he of the nonstop ever-growing vine. A Christian is denouncing pagan religion:

But those contests and phalluses consecrated to Dionysus were a world's shame, pervading life with their deadly influence. For Dionysus ["Bacchus"] burned with desire to descend to the Underworld [*ad inferos*], but did not know the way. A man called Prosymnus offered to tell him, but not without a fee [*merces*]. The fee was no honorable one, though honorable enough for Dionysus: it was a sexual favor [*gratia*] that was asked of Dionysus.

The god was not averse to the request, and promised on oath that he would do what Prosymnus wanted if he returned. When he had learned the route, Dionysus went off. He returned but did not come across Prosymnus, for Prosymnus was dead. Then indeed, in order to pay off his debt to his lover [*amator*] he took himself off to his grave [*monumentum*] and burned with desire to suffer womanish things [*muliebria patiendi desiderio flagrat*]. When therefore Dionysus had cut a branch of the fig-tree, he made it into a substitute male member and sitting on it [*ei insidens*] fulfilled his promise to the dead man. And this deed [or "crime," *facinus*] they commemorate with mystical rites [*mystico ritu*] when they erect phalluses to Dionysus through almost all the cities of Greece. "For," to quote Heraclitus, "it would be utterly shameless if it was not Dionysus to whom they make the procession [*pompē*] and sing the hymn to the genitals [*aidoia*]; and Hades [lord of the Underworld] and Dionysus, for whom they rave and celebrate the Lenaea, are the same man."[92]

"Greeks" are the "Heathen," the "Gentiles." St. Clement of Alexandria (*c.*150–*c.*215), we happen to know, is talking of the myth of Lerna, and from Pausanias and some other sources we can reconstruct something of what went on at this spooky snaky infernal marsh. In a seashore sanctuary with a sacred grove of plane trees our guide saw a statue of Prosymnaean Demeter, a Dionysus, and on the shore itself an Aphrodite. Demeter had a festival with rites said to go back to a son of Apollo, but an ancient scholar had established that since the words of the rite were in Dorian dialect they could not have preceded the Dorian invasion. There was also a temple of Dionysus Savior (*Saōtēs*) with an image of the seated god carved in wood. Farther on there was the small Alcyonian lake, a bottomless pool of water surrounded by reeds. Emperor Nero had tried to plumb the depths with ropes of many fathoms but could not find the bottom. Anyone who tried to swim across was sucked down. As Pausanias heard the tale from the people of Argos, it was through here that Dionysus entered the Underworld to lead up his mother Semele. Pausanias feels it is not holy (*hosion*) to write down for all to read the things that are done at the lake each year at night, a touch of discretion that has fostered some wild speculations. A fragment from a treatise on priests by a local Hellenistic antiquarian is more forthcoming. It talks of the worshippers revealing trumpets concealed in fennel-stalks, thyrsi. With these trumpets they summon Ox-Born Dionysus from the depths of the waters, and throw a lamb into the lake to appease the Guardian of the Gates of Hell. It was not Semele but Dionysus himself who was drowned in the lake, adds another source, and the god was murdered by the hero Perseus; Dionysus Savior, therefore, is also Dionysus Saved. A late author says there was a grave of Pluto at or in the lake, and even a grave of Poseidon.[93] It has been suggested that some of Pindar's dithyrambs were written to be performed at this terrifying spot.[94]

What do sodomy and erections have to do with a trip to the Underworld and back? Some classicists fancy that "initiates" at Lerna were sodomized just like Dionysus,[95] but there is no evidence for that, and surely the Christians would have mentioned it. Another gay—or "same-sex sexual"—myth was told in Attica to explain the same practice of carrying phalluses for Dionysus. The hero called Icarius possessed a rich sanctuary—a bank-statement survives—in the ignominious Attic country village of Icarion, which sits on the slopes of Mount Pentelicum overlooking the bay of Marathon.[96] This rustic village claimed to be the true birthplace of drama, both comedy and tragedy. Some said Susarion, the first comic poet, had come from here, and Thespis himself, the original thespian, was also claimed as an Icarian. A Hellenistic poet refers to this early type of theater as "rustic mimes" and "visiting revels" (kōmoi).[97] Scholars are not sure they should believe in Icarion's claim to be the birthplace of European theater, but Icarion certainly did, and continued to organize its own dramatic festivals in a primitive kind of theatrical space arranged so that the performances could be viewed by (Pythian) Apollo, whose temple had a great view of the stage.[98] There was also a temple to Dionysus: Icarion's colossal cult image of the god has been found.

According to the foundation myth of the cult, Icarius was taught the art of the vine by Dionysus himself. This was the first epiphany of the new god on Earth and it was acknowledged as such by Delphi.[99] Watching his first vines grow, Icarius was vexed that a goat was nibbling the first shoots, so he killed it, made a balloon out of its skin and danced around it, hence in the words of the great Eratosthenes (c.285–194 BC), who wrote a much-admired poem, "Erigone," about the myth, "Men first danced around the goat of Icarius" (not much more of the poem has survived).[100] This was the start of European drama, according to the villagers of Icarion. Tragedy is *tragōidoi,* billy-goat songs.[101]

Now Icarius had a daughter, Erigone. She had a dog, a bitch called Maera, and the whole party traveled around the countryside by oxcart with this new invention of wine, spreading the word and proselytizing (hence in Attic myth Icarius was stellified as Boötes, the Wagoner), and with this wine he got all the Attic shepherds drunk, so that they talked of unseemly things and lay down all over the place in a drunken stupor. The other shepherds were alarmed when they saw this and thought Icarius had poisoned their friends, so they killed Icarius with clubs. Some say they buried him under a tree. But then, miraculously, Icarius's victims woke up and said they had never slept better and wanted to thank Icarius for his gift of alcohol. Ah, said the other shepherds, there's a problem.

But the faithful hound Maera knew where the body was buried and howled and howled and pulled at Erigone's garments until she followed her to the site, marked by a tree, where her father was buried. Then Erigone hanged herself from that very tree and the dog, distraught, jumped down a well. Erigone was stellified as Virgo and the dog as the Dog, either Canis Major or Canis Minor (Prokyon, the pre-Dog Star). A whole series of terrible things happened on account of the murder. For the shepherds of Icarion itself, however, Dionysus had reserved the most terrible punishment of all; he made himself sexy:

> He approached them in the form of a beautiful boy [*pais*] and drove them out of their minds with the urge for sex [*pros hormēn mixeōs*]. And indeed they wanted to debauch him [*diaphtheirai*]. But then, suddenly [the gorgeous boy] disappeared, while they, because Dionysus had promised he would let them fulfill [*ektelesai*] their sexual urge, continued to be fired up to the very brink of sexual action [*hōrmēkesan achri kinēseōs*] and remained thus the whole time, thanks to Dionysus's anger, full of this never-ending urge. So they placated the god, on the advice of an oracle, by making clay images of such a kind [i.e., of their own incessant erections, phalluses], and they stopped the madness by dedicating the phalluses as proxies for themselves [*anti heautōn*].[102]

Both these admittedly very late-mentioned myths construct the phal-luses carried in processions all over Greece as images of frustrated male lust for Dionysus's body, desire for the god to return. In Euripides' *Bac-chae,* too, Dionysus transforms himself into a handsome effeminate youth. The same comedy of now-you-see-him-now-you-don't seems to have been reenacted every year at the very ancient festival of the An-thesteria, which consisted of three days called "Jar-opening," "Jugs" and "Vessels," *Pithoigia, Choes, Chutroi.* It was centered on the temple of Dionysus-in-the-Marshes, which, like the marshes of Lerna, some-how gave access to the Underworld, since it is from here it seems that Dionysus sets out to Hades in Aristophanes' *Frogs* to fetch back Euripi-des. Like the unique temple of Hades in Elis, the temple was open only one day a year, *Choes,* the feast of Jugs, which included competitive drinking straight from the jug at the sound of a trumpet. Like All-Souls Day it was a day when fates or spirits of the dead, *kēres,* were abroad. All other sanctuaries were roped off, and Athenians put black pitch on their doors. What is strange is that, from what we know, there were only gatherings at the temple on Days One and Three. They would arrive. The temple was closed. They would leave. The temple opened. They would return. The temple was closed again for another year.[103] It is the same pattern of frustrated desire for the god that we see in the myth of Icarion, which looks like a myth about the Anthesteria.

Other myths constructed the phallus as an image of Dionysus him-self. Dionysus was son of Zeus and the mortal Semele, one of the daugh-ters of Phoenician Cadmus. Unfortunately her sisters didn't believe that Semele's lover was a god and got her to have him appear in all his glory. Since Zeus in all his glory is thunder and lightning, Semele was burnt to a crisp, and Zeus had to sew his unborn son into his own thigh, until at the right moment Dionysus emerged out of Zeus's loins, born again. The image of Zeus's Birth-Erection is beautifully captured in the name vase of an archaic painter christened the Diosphos Painter. Zeus in tra-vail sits down. His wife Hera dances in front of him. There, straight out of his crotch, is Dionysus, looking exactly like Zeus's erection. The painter has called him Diosphos, "Light of Zeus," and he carries two torches like a star.[104]

So the phalluses at Lerna relate in two ways to Dionysus's trip to the Underworld and back, saving his mother, and saved himself after sickle-wielding Perseus had killed him. First they represent the desire of Prosymnus and thereby all male worshippers for the god to return, a desire that is somehow fulfilled when Dionysus somehow or other reappears from the lake to the worshippers. Remember that a still, small pool at night would provide a sparkling image of the night sky in which a Dionysus "Light of Zeus" might well be thought to appear amid the Derveni Papyrus's "whitest and brightest," the starry ejaculate of Heaven.

Second, the images of the phallus represent it as Dionysus himself, rescued from death and reborn, as Dionysus was reborn from Zeus's thigh, the phallus as an all-powerful liberating Dionysus, a bonds-busting Shiva-lingam, the Pankratic penis, which, in the words of Plato, desires "to overpower all" (*pantōn kratein*).[105] For both forms of phallus—those of the frustrated worshippers and the phallus of Dionysus himself breaking out of the gates of Hades to be born again—combine in the idea of Dionysus as the Irresistible One.

Any connections between these extraordinary myths and cult practices of Dionysus at Lerna and Heracles and Iolaus at Lerna are completely circumstantial. Perhaps the only purpose they serve is as a reminder of more sexual and esoteric possibilities in the myth. But certainly when we recall that Iolaus and Heracles were models for real Theban homosexual couples who really did have sex, and when we put the extraordinary and explicitly sexual myths of Dionysus's trip to the Underworld and back alongside the crypto-Phoenician myth of Iolaus bringing his *erastēs* back to life, releasing him from the Underworld, it is not fanciful to read something more into it. First, and obviously, that Iolaus desires Heracles to come back to him, that as his boyfriend he arouses Heracles; then again that the unbreakable bond between them survives even when one of them has crossed into Hades, for Heracles too has a phallus. And there is one very interesting element in the Dionysus myth that connects sodomy to a pledge, which is one of the key features of Iolaus and his relationship with Heracles. Dionysus's outrageous act of sitting on a dildo on Prosymnus's grave indicates an absolutely unbreakable promise: No matter what it is that he has vowed or the apparent impossibility of fulfilling it, nevertheless the god will fulfill, not unto death, but even after death. And there seems to be unequivocal evidence for precisely this act, of a Stripling sitting on the erection of another Stripling, and it happens in a religious context.

CONCLUSION

These myths and legends of same-sex-loving heroes and the cult practices that go with them have a very different flavor from the Gods' Loves
myths of Ganymede and Pelops. Those latter reflect upon the central
questions of Greek religion: the gulf between mortals and immortals,
and exchanges between those two spheres in the central practice of
sacrifice. Such questions are by no means absent from the myths of
heroes—Achilles' mortality was central to the theme of his possible succession to Zeus, and is dwelled upon by Homer in both the *Iliad* and the
Odyssey. But for others it was more complicated. He was worshipped as
both immortal god and as dead hero by his own people, the Thessalians,
and the people of Miletus found a kind of halfway house for him, somewhere between heaven and hell, with his remote temple on the White
Island opposite the Danube delta in the Black Sea, almost as if by its very
remoteness the question was put slightly beyond reach. Heracles too,
the only hero who found, probably in the course of the sixth century BC,
and quite possibly thanks to Phoenician influence, a place on Olympus,
also plays with the cosmic boundaries. He becomes a proper god, with
cults in many places, but is also worshipped as a hero.

But for most of the time, and especially in the ubiquitous images and
songs relating to their loves and partnerships, the hero-loving heroes
represent relationships between men, an image of the warrior community. That does not exclude in either case a reputation as "woman-
haters," misogynists. No women were allowed on the White Island and
women were also strictly barred from many cults of Heracles.

These two heroic pairings have a lot in common. Above all they both
involve great warriors, great foes of Troy, even, and their Drivers or
Reins-Holders, Patroclus and Iolaus. There is a relationship almost of
substitution between them. Iolaus by helping Heracles with the Lernaean Hydra is performing his Labors for him, and in some versions that
means that Heracles has not been performing them himself and must
therefore take on more of them. Iolaus also takes Heracles' place as husband of his former wife and watches over his children like a substitute
father when Eurystheus tries to wipe them out. Patroclus famously
fights as a substitute for Achilles, wearing his armor and being mistaken
for him. In cult it seems he emphasizes the dead, heroic aspect of

Achilles, and his funeral and funeral games act as a substitute for those of Achilles himself, shortly to come.

But in other ways these pairings are very different, even contrasting or opposed. Achilles and Patroclus are fighters and killers. It is their isolation together from the rest of the community that is emphasized by Homer and the painters, in the image of their bones mixed up together and apart from anyone else in the golden amphora, the homotaph. It is a relationship that zooms in on itself, that eclipses the rest of the world. And there is a danger in it. Achilles' fierce love is directly connected to his fierce hatred of the enemy. It is the same force, the same intensity, which is Achilles' defining characteristic, but sometimes in a positive— Us Two . . . —sometimes in a negative form— . . . Against the World. This love-hate combination is perfectly clear in the *Iliad* but is configured more vividly and economically in the myth of Achilles chasing down Troilus, which ends with him ripping the boy's head from his body.

The myth of his confrontation with Memnon to avenge the death of Antilochus, on the other hand, places the Greek at the heart of Greek Love—Achilles the passionate lover of someone with whom he has no links of family or ethnicity, someone from the diagonal opposite of mainland Greece in Pylos. They don't share a tent, or ride together in a chariot; their one connection is through a boundary-crossing love. Here the aloof Achilles of the relationship with Patroclus becomes a pan-Hellenic hero, a model for all Greek warriors fighting barbarian enemies, even the people of Apollonia fighting the natives in Albania: a national representative. In fact we should not draw too strong a contrast between these two aspects of Achilles, for the aloof Achilles cut off from the rest of the world, buried away from nation and family with no one but his companions, also stands for all Greek warriors buried in a single communal grave.

The myths of Heracles and Iolaus could hardly differ more. They are as expansive as Achilles and Patroclus are inward-looking. Their relationship is pictured as enduring through thick and thin; those of Achilles are enacted in short, sharp shocks. While he and Patroclus are confined in their golden vase, Heracles and Iolaus are driving all over the Mediterranean, from one end to the other, a team bringing benefits to all mankind, slaying monsters and demons and generally making the world a safer place. This is helped by and helps their early assimilation to the gods of other peoples, so that they can even figure in a treaty of friendship between Hannibal of Carthage and Philip V of Macedon. Forget about Greeks vs Barbarians. Here Greek Love is going global and providing a model for a geopolitical alliance.

What part does sex play? The question is incongruous and in many ways quite meaningless. We are not, probably, talking about historical figures, and if we are we are unlikely to unearth new evidence from either Heracles or Achilles in the near future. Greeks who saw Achilles tending to Patroclus on the Sosias Cup, or who read about his vengeance for the death of Antilochus, or his slaughter of the Boy Troilus, would interpret these accounts against the background of what their own experience told them about Greek Love. Thebans who pledged themselves at the tomb of Iolaus, Athenians who honored Heracles and Iolaus in the gymnasium at Cynosarges, or made joint offerings to them as "altar-sharing," would simply assume that it was the same kind of relationship as the ones they had, and those relationships were by no means asexual. One may imagine that individual writers or artists had different ideas and that they tried to emphasize chasteness, but in fact there is no sign of that. Quite the opposite. Homer, for instance, goes out of his way to stress the exceptional love between Achilles and Patroclus, and makes it clear that it is a physical intimacy Achilles is missing and longing for. He even draws parallels with husbands and wives, with Meleager and Cleopatra, and Hector mourned by Andromache. This is not the way for an author to pour cold water on an audience's wilder conjectures.

But if the absence of explicit evidence is equated with evidence of absence, then the only remaining possibility, so Kenneth Dover and David Halperin suggest, is that there has been a terrible misunderstanding, that Greek Love was twice born, first in an entirely asexual but nevertheless intensely passionate form of abstinent heroes and their just good friends, and second, shortly before 600 BC, in an entirely sexual way, centered on sodomy and "homosexual submission." From such a perspective, Homer did not need to pour cold water on any intimations of homosexual sex, because it never once occurred to him or to his audience that two warriors passionately in love with each other might have sex. He was innocent of homosexuality, or homosexual sex was still "in the closet" in some way, not celebrated or publicized as it was by people like Solon and Theognis a century later, an absolute secret. But it seems to me that the relationship Homer describes is on exactly the same wavelength as the later discourse of Greek Love, which always was about passion and pledges and another person meaning more to you than your own life. That is precisely why the myths remained so resonant. Greek Love in the classical period, while not all about sex, was all about Love-not-excluding-sex, and in that respect Achilles and Patroclus are all about Greek Love.

If the doorstepping and pursuing and wooing and seducing that took up so much of a classical *erastēs*'s time and money are absent, where would one expect them to appear? These men are comrades already, sleeping in the same tent. They have a history. It would be ridiculous for Patroclus to be pursuing Achilles or for Achilles to be bringing Patroclus flowers and courting him. They have a whole history together. Their *philia* has long since been achieved. The only hint of such a wooing *erōs,* as Aeschines notes, is when Achilles recalls going to ask Patroclus's father, many years previously, to send his son with him, although there are hints of the classical practice perhaps if we think that the birds seen in early images of Troilus at the fountain house are love gifts, and that Achilles may perhaps be seen in the first stages of wooing Antilochus when he doubles his money and hands over to him in person a talent of gold. We would hardly expect Homer himself in his own voice to sing of boys he loves, as Solon does, or Theognis, or Ibycus, or as Sappho sings of girls. He is writing epic poetry, not love songs.

For a notoriously homosexualizing society to also have a passionate homosexual relationship at the core of its national epic, and for same-sex couples all over the Greek world to have heroic models already provided for them, is simply too great a coincidence. There is no evidence at all for this prior asexual version of Greek Love. For rigor's sake, let us be economical. There is but one single phenomenon.

The main reason why I think the Greeks of Homer's time would read the relationship of Achilles and Patroclus in the same way that the classical Greeks would read it is because I think the phenomenon was already around in 700 BC, and the main reason I think that is because it appears in so many different places in so many different forms with so many peculiar practices. So we should now survey that diverse world of Greek Love, embark on a tour of Greek Homosexualities, and then perhaps we can also discover if sex was not just assumed or an optional extra, but an intrinsic, necessary part.

CRETE AND SPARTA

I
CRETE

You are a young man who has been to watch the dances. Now you are walking home with your "friends." On the path, before you reach the junction, you see a group of men coming toward you. One of them you pick out at once. It's the one who is always going on about his grandfather's role in the last war . . . if you want to call a skirmish a war. You caught him staring hard at you during last month's festival, when your group came in second in the dance competition, though you really should have won, and then he was hanging around again during one of the fights; it was distracting and cost you a black eye, which spoiled your looks for a while. Your father says you ought to be more friendly, considering who his grandfather was, and that there is such a thing as taking modesty too far. You move to one side to let him pass. He stands in your way. Your "friends" shout at him to clear off. He still won't let you pass. He grabs you. You resist, but he's bigger than you are. Your "friends" try to free you, but they can't seem to manage it. He is pulling you down the path that leads to his Men's House. You realize what's going on. You are going to be raped.

This is embarrassing. You dig in your heels and hold on to your "friends." A crowd has gathered. People are watching. This will be even more embarrassing now. The idiot should have checked with your "friends" first to find out if you were amenable. Now, he is going to be shown up. Considering his family and the pride he takes in it, this will probably be traumatic for the community. So what? It is hardly your fault that he's an idiot; you have done nothing to encourage him, unless you count that look you gave him during the boxing match just before you got that black eye.

Then you notice that even as they abuse him with shouts and oaths, your "friends" are in fact smiling. Your heart sinks. He did check with them first.

TO THE MEN'S HOUSE

Plato could never really work out what to do with the myth of Ganymede. In his final attempt to imagine a perfect practical constitution, his massive "dialogue" known as *Laws,* he claims that the story was invented by the Cretans as ideological support for their own peculiar practices: "Everyone accuses the Cretans of having made up the story of Ganymede. Since they believe their laws and institutions come from Zeus, they added this slander against Zeus to mythology, so that it would be as the god's disciples, forsooth, that they would be enjoying this *pleasure* too."[1]

Plato provides no details about these laws and institutions, but his contemporary Ephorus is on hand to help out. Ephorus was a historian, the most famous son of Cyme, a city on a peninsula projecting from the Turkish coast toward the island of Lesbos. Unhappily his history is lost. It was huge and ambitious, thirty volumes long. (Herodotus, by comparison, took nine books for his rambling study of the Persian Wars, and Thucydides, for his partial account of the Peloponnesian, eight.) Nor did Ephorus write the history of mere wars or single nations, or important periods in human history. He covered "the whole lot," a universal (in Greek *catholik*) history of everything that had happened in Greece and outside Greece from the age of the sons of Heracles, approximately dated to 1069–68 BC, up to the siege of Perinthus, near Constantinople, carried out by Philip of Macedon in 340 BC. Ephorus was also, by all accounts, a pretty good historian. Ancient writers rated him high, and although modern historians sometimes think they have enough evidence to demur from that opinion—Wilamowitz thought his work appealed to the same sentiments as the fifth act of a bad tragedy—there would be great excitement should he be rediscovered—not top, but somewhere close, in the wish list of those we would like to bring back intact from some rescue expedition into the book-burning past.[2]

In the meantime, well over two hundred fragments of Ephorus survive in the work of other authors. There are even a couple of likely scraps of him from the deserts of Egypt, discovered in provincial Oxyrhynchus's useful dumps of waste papyrus. One of the longest fragments, preserved in Strabo's *Geography,* concerns a homosexual custom (*nomimon*) in Crete. Ephorus called it "peculiar." So it is. In Crete, says Ephorus, they win the beloved boys not by persuasion, but by abduction.[3]

The boy's admirer notifies the "friends," *philoi,* of an intention to abduct a few days before.[4] If they approve of the abduction, they put up a show of resistance for form's sake, grappling with the abductor but "only moderately," and ultimately letting the boy go. If they deem the boy unworthy of his suitor, i.e., not "manly" enough or "proper"— someone who is exceptionally handsome (*kallei diapherōn*) doesn't automatically pass the test, notes Ephorus—they keep him away from the place of rendezvous. This is a black mark against the boy, and a reason for shame—what kind of "friends" are these, you may well ask, who may decide among themselves that their "pal" isn't worthy of someone who has fallen in love with him?

If, on the other hand, the "friends" think the *admirer* is unworthy, i.e., "beneath" the boy in social status or "other regards," their efforts to resist are more than a sham and they prevent the abduction—you don't want any Tom, Dick or Harry going about snatching boys.

The "pursuit" does not end until the boy is taken to the Men's House (*andreion*), the military mess of his abductor.[5] Then, after giving the boy presents and a "welcome," the abductor takes him away to any place in the country he wishes, and those who were present at the abduction follow after them. After feasting and hunting with them for up to two months (the legal maximum), they return to the city. The boy is sent off with traditional gifts of (1) an outfit of a warlike character (*stolē polemikē*), (2) an ox and (3) a drinking cup, plus a whole load of other things so numerous and costly that the friends make contributions toward the expense. The boy sacrifices the ox to Zeus and entertains those who returned with him at a feast, and there he reveals whether or not he is happy about the association (*homilia*) with his admirer. In this way the law gives him an opportunity to avenge himself and be acquitted, if the snatch was effected through force. It is disgraceful, says Ephorus, for those who are good-looking (*kalos tēn idean*—Ephorus isn't contradicting what he said before, about looks not being everything) or of distinguished ancestry to fail to obtain admirers: There must be something wrong with their character. The abducted are known as "associated" (*parastathentes,* literally "set up beside") and receive honors. In both dances and runs they occupy the most honored positions,[6] and are allowed to dress in better clothes than everyone else, in the apparel given them by their lovers; and not only then, but even after they have grown to manhood, they wear a distinctive dress, which announces the fact that each wearer has become "famed," for they call the beloved boy the "famed" and his *erastēs* the "lover" (*philētor*).[7]

AGE-CLASSES AND MASS MARRIAGES IN CRETE

Ephorus seems to show something straightforward and easy to get to grips with, and modern scholars have used him to prove very different things about the true nature of Greek Homosexuality.[8] The late John Boswell in his book *Same-Sex Unions* thought it was evidence that Greek males didn't just have sex with one another, but could have long-term meaningful relationships. He compared it to a marriage ceremony and found traces of similar same-sex weddings all over Europe right up until the Renaissance.[9] Few have followed him down that path. Mostly they have seen in this Cretan custom an antique ritual of initiation into adulthood. For these scholars Ephorus's "peculiar custom" is the pristine form of Greek Homosexuality, the phenomenon at its most primitive, anthropological and original, a trace of the lost ritual that the Ganymede myth reflects.

We need to explore what is really going on there. But where is "there?" Ancient "Crete" was not a single entity, in fact it was an island of many and quite different cultural affinities, one of the most mixed communities in Greece of the first millennium BC. Ephorus was generalizing from a knowledge of at most a few communities out of very many, above all those that spoke the Dorian dialect and were supposed to be closely linked to Sparta, which is not very far away by boat. The two most important cities, the old-fashioned-looking ones to which ancient authors generally referred when discussing origins, were Lyctus (which lies southeast of Heraklion as far inland as Crete allows) and Gortyn, its next-door neighbor to the west.[10] For various reasons, we are unusually well-informed about these two cities, which in other respects lie way off the beaten track of Greek history.

Gortyn is famous above all for the collection of laws inscribed in zigzag formation—written left to right, then right to left, and so on: *boustrophedon,* "as the oxen wend"—on the walls of a building built specially for the purpose in the mid-fifth century.[11] It makes a nice stop for tourists by the side of the road that leads from Heraklion to the Minoan palace of Phaistos. In Greece, the writing of laws in metal, wood and stone has often been seen as a democratic measure that acted to open up the law to public scrutiny, but the laws of Gortyn—like most Greek laws, in fact—were designed to keep things in their place, and they seem to have served that function as intended.

This great monumental wall of carefully chiseled letters telling people what they can and cannot do, or rather, exactly what penalties await them if they transgress, reveals a society carefully divided according to status into several different groups to whom different provisions and different penalties apply for crimes we would view as identical. The laws refer, for instance, to people called *apetairoi,* "those not members of a Men's House [*hetaireia*]."[12] So the crime of seducing a free woman incurs a fine of one hundred Aeginetan staters, a considerable sum—say, "thousands of pounds." But there is a fifty percent discount if the seduced woman is outside the family home; she is half-asking for it, something of a hussy. And the fine is reduced to a mere tenth if she is of more lowly status, a woman belonging to "someone who isn't a member of a Men's House." The law doesn't seem to mind where such a woman is seduced. If the seducer is a slave and his victim a free woman, on the other hand, the fines are doubled. But if the culprit is a slave and the victim too, there is a fine of not one hundred but merely five staters. The law doesn't seem to entertain the possibility of a crime involving the seduction of a slave woman by a free man.[13]

The great wall of Gortyn mentions other more mysterious categories of person, some of which can safely be interpreted not as social but as age categories. An adult male, it seems, was officially called a "runner," *dromeus,* or "member of the *dromos,*" a Cretan word for the gymnasium. A male below that age was *apodromos,* "not qualified for the running-track." This may be another term for an *agelaos,* "herdsman," i.e., under Twenty.[14] "Up until Seventeen," the dictionaries inform us, you were an *apagelos,* "not [yet] a member of a herd," also called *skotios,* which means "dark, shadowy, obscure, unknown."[15]

About a hundred years after this amazing outburst of early Cretan lawmaking, of which the Gortyn Wall is only the latest and most monumental example, we start to get ethnographic fragments about Cretan customs. Ephorus is the earliest and most extensive. They add color and form to the skeleton of categories we find in the laws without contradicting the image they represent. The impression we get is of a system developed and fixed in law during the sixth and fifth centuries BC, in isolation from the mainland, being rediscovered in the fourth.

The society they rediscovered was, we learn, an aristocratic society dedicated to communal living. The "associations of comrades," *hetaireiai,* were physical entities, also called *andreia* (Men's Houses, Men's Rooms). All the citizens of Lyctus belonged to one; otherwise you weren't a citizen. Here the men dined every evening, possibly all together under one roof, watching carefully what rival associations were having for dinner on the neighboring table, or, more probably, in their own several Men's Houses, which might well be alongside one another, as at Sparta, and on view to the world. There was always a dormitory next door for "guests" of the House, *xenoi,* a way to prevent individuals from fraternizing with outsiders, perhaps.[16] Every man contributed a tenth of his crops to his Men's House, and there were further subsidies from the public revenues.[17] It is interesting that a woman was in charge, with three or four assistants.[18] She goes around and takes the best food (or the best from each table) and gives it to those who have distinguished themselves in war or wisdom. After dinner they talk about politics and heroic deeds.

In the Men's House the different age-classes are carefully kept in their place. According to Ephorus, when they are young, Cretans sit together on the floor in shabby clothes and wait on the others, who sit on chairs. Others confirm this but add that the "younger men" sit with their fathers and receive only half a ration of meat and none of the "other" items. Those without fathers get the full amount, but miss out on the "trimmings."[19] The boys of Crete were rough. Boys from each Men's House fight with each other and contest with boys from other clubs; they actually bear scars, says Ephorus, of punches and metal-inflicted wounds. But when they are bigger, ephebes, Striplings, they attend (*phoitain*) a herd (*agela*) with the most powerful and distinguished boys as leaders, each assembling as many boys as he can.[20] There are battles within herds and between herds. The father of the assembler of the herd is the herd's ruler (*archōn*), and he takes them on hunts, organizes races and issues punishments. If all of this sounds a bit like a scout troop or a British public school, it is probably not a coincidence. When they graduate or rather are "selected" to graduate, they all "get married" to girls en masse.[21] But they don't take the girls (*paidas*) they have married home until they are more mature, "sufficient for house management." This probably refers to a custom—"marriage of approximation"— well-known from other parts of the world, in which older men lie beside their child brides and then leave them, and then begin to visit them like legalized adulterers in the night.

A LESBIAN STRIDES LIKE A MAN

From Ephorus and the other fragments we are able to distinguish at least four key stages in the life of a Cretan boy during the decade or so between mid- to late teens and mid- to late twenties.

1 Boys sit on the floor of their father's club and their existence is centered on the Men's House. The boys of one Men's House sometimes fight with boys from another.
2 In their late teens they join "herds" who are "fed at public expense." The implication is that they leave the Men's House of their fathers and their rations are provided by the entire community.[22]
3 Then there are the massed ranks of newly-"weds." Probably these mass weddings to "underage" girls represent a kind of graduation ceremony from the "herds" and entry into the ranks of "runners."[23] After the "wedding" there is a period of semi-marriage, living apart from wives until the girls are old enough. The Gortyn Law Wall talks of heiresses being "married," *opuiethai,* at Twelve, but this is no mere engagement: It refers to "sex in marriage," consummation, and may have occurred some years after the collective "wedding" ceremony.[24] These "semi-married" Runners, *neoi,* Young Men, are one of the most interesting and mysterious categories. They are the backbone of the army, living, probably, a very intense competitive existence. It is most unlikely that they lived alone in their own "bachelor pads," waiting for their wives to grow up. Either they are living at their own family home again, or in some kind of communal barracks that have

escaped the mention of our sources. These recent graduates of the herds are probably the "Younger Men" we hear of who sit next to their fathers in the Men's House, receiving half portions: half-married, half-members, half-citizens, half-hungry.[25]

4 It is perhaps only when they take their wives home that Cretan men cease to be counted as someone's son and take up full membership of the House and of the community in their own right.[26] For, Ephorus says, membership is for full adults (*teleioi*) only.[27] Doubtless after taking a wife home, age continued to be a factor in deciding when you retired from the regular levy and when you were eligible for magistracies and councils. The dictionaries mention the word "Ten(-year) runner" and an inscription refers to "Fifteen(-year) runner," which implies, as one might expect from the example of other Greek cities, that important boundaries of qualification/disqualification were crossed at around Thirty and Thirty-five.[28]

At any rate Crete was undoubtedly a society in which age-classes were important. The course of one's life was very much of the canal rather than the river type, with growing up structured around a whole series of transitions from one level to another. Doubtless there were rituals that accompanied the movement from the floor of the club to a herd, from unmarried to married status, on first entry to the running track, on induction into the Men's House, from married to living with a wife, from half-rations to full rations. Perhaps some of these rituals involved strange behavior, mask wearing and dances. Perhaps some of them involved rituals of separation and mourning, jumbling up, and joyous reincorporation.

In particular, inscriptions seem to refer to a kind of stripping-off ceremony on graduation from the herd—"those stripping off at that time," "the herd then stripping off."[29] The running track, *dromos,* was the Cretan equivalent of the gymnasium, which means "place for stripping off" (*gymnos*—"undressed"), and it is likely that, just like the Athenian Council's physical inspection of naked boys who applied to be Eighteen, physical inspection was the basis of graduation into the ranks of adults. So it is entirely appropriate that entering the ranks of Runners at around Twenty could be described as stripping off. However, the marriage festival called "The Doffing," Ekdusia, at Phaistos, reveals a rather more complicated symbolism.

This festival is connected with a myth recorded by Ovid about a woman of Phaistos, a city on the site of an ancient Minoan palace complex, married to Ligdus (i.e., Lyctus?). She gives birth to a girl and decides not to expose the child, against her husband's command. In a dream, the goddess Isis/Io reassures her. She pretends that the child is a boy and calls her Iphis, a name used by both sexes. The girl grows up, and at thirteen finds herself strongly attracted to another girl called Ianthe, who eagerly starts anticipating their marriage. Ovid goes to town on Iphis's distress: "What is to be the end of this for me, caught as I am in a strange and unnatural kind of love, which none has known before? . . . Cows do not burn with love for cows, nor mares for mares. It is the ram which excites the ewe, the hind follows the stag . . ." She recalls that Pasiphaë, wife of Minos and mother of the Minotaur, committed adultery with a bull, but "at least he was male!" Her mother delays the marriage on various pretexts, but eventually runs out of excuses. In desperation she prays to Isis. As she leaves the temple and is walking along with her daughter, she notices that the girl's stride is longer, her hair shorter, her face darker, her features sharpened and that she has a lot more energy than a woman has, for she is no longer a woman but a man. The happy couple bring gifts to the temple and commission an inscription: "The tributes Iphis promised as a maid / By Iphis, now a man, are duly paid."[30]

Another author tells the same story with different names. Here Iphis is called Leucippus and the goddess is Leto, mother of the youthful Apollo and Artemis, instead of the Egyptian import, Isis. In this version it is above all the girl's womanly beauty as she reaches puberty that threatens to give her away. The author adds: "The people of Phaistos commemorate the change to this day and sacrifice to Plant Leto [*Phytia Leto*], for she planted genitals [*mēdea*] in the girl. And they call the festival the Stripping Off, since the girl stripped off her dress [*peplos*]. It is the custom in their marriage ceremonies to lie down beforehand by the statue of Leucippus."[31]

THE FRIENDS

The Cretans therefore lived in a highly structured age-class society, and there were some strange rituals connected with transition from one age-class to another, notably a kind of heterosexual marriage that was not one, on initiation into the proper age-class system at Twenty. However, the homosexual abduction ceremony described by Ephorus is not presented in any sense as a "coming-of-age." There is not the slightest hint that it is a *mass* ceremony for all boys in an age-class. Quite the opposite. The boy is decidedly on his own on his own unique occasion. Moreover, we are told perfectly clearly that the boy continues to wear a special costume *even after* he becomes a full adult, which is a pretty straightforward indication that the abduction itself doesn't make him an adult. In fact the glorious group of abducted boys *maintained* the age-class distinctions within its elite ranks. At first the boy "is allowed to get dressed up [*kosmeisthai*] in the exceptional costume, that is the one given him by his abductor, and not only then but when they are full adults they wear distinctive clothing." In other words he wears a costume that marks his status as a glorious abductee when he is a warrior, but this is not the costume he was given during the ceremony itself.

Despite all this, modern scholars insist on reading the abduction ceremony not as the beginning of a long-term relationship, but as a critical, supposedly sexual, supposedly violent, moment in the life of a Nineteen- or Twenty-year-old, designed to turn him from a boy into a man, although to this general tendency one must mention an honorable exception: Kenneth Dover.[32] The abduction itself, they say, is a graduation and/or an initiation of the boy into the Men's House of his abductor. The hunt is an initiation into hunting, the warlike costume an initiation into war, the cup an initiation into drinking, the sacrifice an initiation into sacrifice. And all of this is symbolic of initiation into adulthood, a kind of graduation *summa cum laude;* the boy is a kind of representative of his age-class, a sacrificial virgin.[33] The abduction can be an initiation into almost anything, it seems, except what Ephorus tells us it is: an initiation into a homosexual relationship, a *homilia,* a homosexual *wedding*.

Despite the insistence of scholars, then, not only is there nothing in the account of the Cretan abduction that mentions the boy's coming-of-age, but we are informed quite plainly that he doesn't come of age. Drinking, hunting, fighting and feasting were part of the life of all boys, and there is no sign that this boy is doing any of them for the first time. In fact it seems that the abduction has nothing to do with the communal system and its ladder of progressions. It is individualistic rather than collective, concerned with distinction rather than with sameness, with particular "friends" not age mates or tribes. It sets a boy apart from his contemporaries.

But the fact that he doesn't answer *our* questions doesn't mean that Ephorus isn't informative. Close reading, in fact, reveals much of interest. So what are we to make of this ritual rape? We know, to begin with, that the boy is a "Boy," which means someone under Twenty with no proper beard yet. One author calls him *meirakion,* Eighteen-plus.[34]

What of the abductor then? He, it seems, is not a "Boy," and as a graduate of the herds he will have "married" a little girl at a precisely appointed time alongside his coevals. He may be only a couple of years older than the boy, then, or several years, or only a few months. But he is a member of a Men's House. For what it is worth, a late author tells an anecdote about a Cretan lover who was a very valiant warrior, but unlucky. Having tripped over a corpse in battle, he was about to be dispatched with a thrust into his back. Just before the enemy struck, his victim turned and asked him to make sure the wound came from the front, so that he would appear to his beloved to have died an honorable death, not stabbed in the back as if running away. Otherwise the boy might feel ashamed to lay out his corpse. Here the lover is described as a "young man" (*neanias*), a term that in Athens was used for Striplings.[35]

The great mystery concerns the group of "friends" who seem so important to the whole ritual. One salient point is that in this society, so full of formal associations of men, they constitute an *informal* body. They are neither relatives nor clan members nor coevals, nor members of a single Men's House. Yet they are closely involved in the whole process. They not only have to make sure the boy is at the assignation point at the stated time and place, they have to decide if the match is suitable for both parties, and they play a key role in the ceremony itself. They have to accompany the pair on their hunting trip, up to two months long, and make contributions to the lavish gifts the admirer offers to the boy. They must therefore have property and be in a position to spend some of it. What informal group of men would go to all that trouble to help two other males get together?

These friends are clearly a recognized group of men. The potential admirer advises them of his intentions three days *at least* before the abduction. Following the formal proposal they have, it seems, three options, and three days in which to choose which option to pursue. (1) They can take the boy to the assignation point and after some half-hearted resistance allow the abduction to take place, requiring a great deal of time and money on their part, and finally a formal public acceptance of the relationship. (2) They can take the boy to the assignation point and make sure he is not abducted. This would mean, apparently, that in their view the suitor was not up to the boy's standard, which would have been extremely humiliating for him, a spectacular loss of face in front of the community. (3) On the other hand they can keep the boy away from the meeting point altogether. Ephorus emphasizes that this would be extremely scandalous, implying that the poor innocent boy, not the admirer, was unworthy.

The "friends," I suggest, are a kind of group of *erastai* of the wolf-pack, guard-of-honor, fan-club type. At any rate one source probably says that in Crete a boy considered it special to have "as many *erastai* as possible."[36] It makes no sense to suppose that each of these many *erastai* of a single boy had to keep on repeating the whole abduction ceremony, that the boys would want to be snatched as often as possible. The whole system would have collapsed. There would have been endless expenditure, daily abductions. But if it means that it was a mark of honor to be chaperoned by as many "friends" as possible, that seems completely plausible. When you were abducted you wanted a whole crowd trying unsuccessfully to rescue you from the arms of that violent, intemperate, reckless young captor.[37]

When a young man of suitable status, perhaps an especially elite young man of a particular elite group, announces his intention to abduct, they must, it seems, make sure that the boy turns up at the rendezvous, or else face scandal. An admirer has the right, in other words, to his tug-of-war. Presumably during the three days word gets around about the assignation and a crowd will gather to watch the ritual, to see if the admirer is successful. Presumably they didn't just watch in silence but shouted their approval or not of the abduction, telling the friends to let it take place or booing out their objections.

The next crucial stage is the kiss. Let's say that the admirer succeeds in dragging the boy to his Men's House. Here, thanks only to the inadequate rubbings-out of Christian monks short of paper, we now know that "he embraced the boy." I think this is probably a critical moment, a public display of affection in front of the community, a proclamation of admiration for the boy's worthiness. Some think the boy is now formally introduced into the new Men's House of the abductor, transferred, so to speak, from one House into another.[38] But this can't be so. First, the boy is not old enough yet, and second, he hasn't said anything about what he thinks of the whole business. The admirer is not home yet. The *erōs* of the *erastēs* may not be matched by *philia* in return.

FORCED SEX

Following the public embrace, a hunting expedition. It is important, I think, that the admirer is allowed to go *anywhere* "in the country [*chōra*]" he chooses. The rite-of-passage advocates would like this to be the Cretan equivalent of the jungle or the bush, but Ephorus is not talking about some untamed wilderness. The Greek "country" is simply the territory outside the town, that is, the landed estates attached to individual citizens and worked by native Cretans on behalf of their Dorian masters.[39] You can see now why there is such insistence on this in our historian's account of the custom. If the party were going off into no-man's-land there would be no point in saying they had permission to do so, nor in insisting that the license would expire after two months. In no-man's-land you can do whatever you like for as long as you like. This provision, therefore, to go not merely anywhere in the wilds, but also onto anyone's property, represents an amazing degree of freedom granted to the hunting party. Elite young men are allowed to turn settled, farmed areas into a game park. Doubtless this was something of an imposition, to put it mildly, on the landowner and especially on his serfs, who might notice smoke rising from a campfire one cool evening, and would know that a germ of disorder was honeymooning in their midst.

Honeymooning? Was it at this point that sexual intercourse took place? Most scholars are in no doubt that sex is the centerpiece. The Cretan boy has been sodomized ad nauseam in modern accounts of the hunting expedition. But what kind of honeymoon is it where your "friends" tag along? Did they wait outside the leafy bivouac while the boy was deflowered and offer a round of applause as the abductor emerged? When at the feast the boy reveals his feelings about the association or intercourse (*homilia*), is he supposed to give his abductor marks out of ten for his skills in buggery? Ephorus, of course, doesn't mention sex, and it is noticeable that the boy and his abductor are *never* left alone. Maximus of Tyre insists that unlike the dreadful Eleans, about whom he will remain silent, the Cretan custom of "compulsion" is praiseworthy: "for a Cretan Stripling [*meirakion*] it is shameful not to be the object of passionate love, for a Cretan Cadet [*neaniskos*] it is shameful to lay a finger on his favorite [*paidika*]. O what a custom that mixes modesty and *erōs* so beautifully/nobly!"[40] What I suspect is that the boy had to be of such a character that no one would dare to suggest he was easy, and the friends were there to make sure that he wasn't forced. For what if, when it was all over, the sodomized boy took the opportunity granted by law to denounce the association and to insist that he was not content, that the whole thing had gone on against his will, to announce in front of the whole community that he had indeed been raped in the modern sense of the term? What if he took up his right "to be avenged" (*timōrein*)?

This is not to say there was anything chaste and pure about the Cretans. They were notorious for their homosexuality. Some said they had invented it.[41] Plato blames the myth of Ganymede on them as concocting a divine precedent for this *pleasure*. And he talks about the Cretans as if homosexuality was a defining feature of their culture, a homosexuality of a very physical, lustful and sexual nature.[42] Aristotle likewise says the Cretan lawgiver Minos instituted "intercourse [*homilia*] with males" as a method of population control. And the name Meriones (*mēria*, "thighs") given to the charioteer of the Cretan King Idomeneus in Homer was believed to be an allusion to the Cretan practice of intercrural sex.[43] These references to Minos and Zeus are not casual chat. Unusually for the Greeks, the Cretans, like the Jews, insisted that their laws and customs had come from the Highest God himself. Their ancient king Minos, says Ephorus, used to go up to the mountain every nine years, spend time with Zeus in a cave and leave with a list of commandments drawn up. Perhaps one of these commandments laid down the rules for sex between the thighs.[44]

NOT BEFORE MARRIAGE

We can at least construct something of the background landscape of sexual expectation. The Gortyn Law Wall, in fact, has much to say on the subject of sex, for before the provisions concerning seduction comes a whole series concerning "rape":

> If someone forcibly has sex with[45] a free man or a free woman, 100 staters; but if with a man who is not a member of a House [*apetairos*], ten; and if a slave [forcibly has sex with] a free man or woman, the fine is double [i.e., 200 staters]; and if a free man [forcibly has sex with] a male serf [a *woikeus* working an estate] or a female serf, five drachmas (*c*.2.5 staters); and if a serf [forcibly has sex with] a male serf or a female serf, five staters.[46]

There are some interesting points here. The Gortynians seemed to define a crime that comes fairly close to the modern definition of rape. From Athens, the city whose laws we know best, we know of no such clear-cut offense of forced intercourse, although the sources do talk of "abduction" (*ean d' harpasēi tis* . . .) with "use of violence" (. . . *kai biasētai*) against a free woman, and of the "violent shaming" (*aischunēi biai*) of a free man or boy. Quite possibly a raped Athenian would have had recourse to a "private suit" (*dikē*) against general "acts of violence" (*biaiōn*) or a "public suit" (*graphē*) against abuse, "hubris."[47]

We also notice that the crime is considered the same crime and of the same seriousness whether committed against a man or a woman. This may seem like common sense, but it is in striking contrast to many modern jurisdictions. In Britain, men were only included in the remit of the law governing rape by the Criminal Justice and Public Order Act of 1994. Until then there was no such crime as male rape. The British Act defines rape as "vaginal or anal penetration to the slightest degree." The Gortyn Code seems to talk simply of "forced sex," *oipēi*.

Exactly the same penalties were laid down for *moicheia,* seduction of a woman in the house of her husband, brother or father.[48] *Moicheia* is best seen as a kind of sexual burglary, invading someone's house to get at his woman, with a reduced penalty if she was not at home with her family, since in that case the family home had not been similarly defiled. Rape was originally defined in contrast to this crime of sexual burglary, which is why we find references in Athens's early law code to the "snatching," *harpazein,* of a free woman, that is, her forcible removal. Indeed *rapere* is simply Latin for "seize" or "snatch." Since snatching was part of a respectable ritual in Crete, this must be one reason why rape in the modern sense had to be more precisely defined.

The boy's mock rape, then, the whole two-month process, is best seen as a way of dramatizing the extremely delicate issue of the boy's consent in an elaborate fashion. It is only on their return that the couple can have sex with impunity. After the boy's speech agreeing to the *homilia,* claiming he was content, that he had not been forced, it would be impossible for him in future to bring a charge of rape against this particular man. He couldn't change his mind. The speech serves to make him sexually available to his lover. This may be why Plato thought the Cretans had invented the myth of Ganymede to license *pleasure.*[49]

Ephorus's rather embarrassed reference to the boy's looks also has relevance to the question of sexual lust. In Athens, by the time he was writing, it had become very difficult to separate "beauty" from "sexual attractiveness" and "sexual attractiveness" from sexual lust. Xenophon goes to some lengths to argue that it was Ganymede's beautiful mind Zeus was interested in, not his physical attributes, and he insists that the Spartan lawgiver took measures to deter lovers who were attracted by a boy's body. This context, I think, explains Ephorus's squirming. On the one hand it is clear that the abduction was expected to select "the beautiful," or at least, any *kalos* boy who was not selected would automatically be placed under a cloud of suspicion as to his moral character. On the other hand he says "they consider charming [*erasmion*] not the strikingly handsome, but the strikingly brave and respectable."[50] What he wants to avoid is the notion of the abductor drooling over the boy.

After the hunting, more presents. In Gortyn, at least, the cup given to the boy was of a unique type, a deep goblet of bronze called a *chonnos,* going in at the waist, possibly of elaborate manufacture, and similar to a cup used in pledges. Its primary significance, probably, is as a symbol of the relationship between the boy and his lover, a guarantee of loyalty and faith; very probably it was used in the ceremony in a ritual to bind the pair; certainly it will have been distinctive enough to reveal its possessor thereafter as "Famed."[51]

In many modern accounts, a second gift, the "costume of military character," *polemikē stolē,* has transmogrified into a "set of armor." But not only does *stolē* imply something rather more dressy, but we are told by another author that it is in fact "clothing" (*esthēs*) that is at issue, and the boy was supposed to wear it all the time.[52] Far from being a run-of-the-mill hoplite uniform, the costume of the "Famed" was, above all, *distinctive*. We should not doubt the militaristic nature of Cretan society, of Cretan values, and Cretan love, but "warlike" in this context means simply that an imaginative observer, pressed to explain the odd getup, was able to justify it in terms of a symbolic connection to war. Xenophon uses the same kind of argument to explain the color of Spartan cloaks. A red cloak is "most warlike," he insists. Others explained that red was the color of blood. Similar arguments were used to account for the odd shape of Spartan cups—very useful for scooping water from a muddy stream while on campaign—and their famous long tresses, beautifully combed before battle—very terrifying, "rather like gorgons," says Xenophon, implausibly. The "military costume," then, could be anything: a cloak fringed with the scalps of the enemy or a floaty dress embroidered with a sword-and-shield design.

We can go a little further, I think. Whenever Sparta's supporters take time out to justify Spartan trappings in terms of their military function, it is always with regard to things that appeared to other Greeks as elaborate, effeminate, luxurious and/or decadent: long hair, deep cups, rich dyes. I strongly suspect that this is what has happened with Ephorus's Cretan costume.[53] On his return from the hunt, the boy discards the shabby garments he wore on the floor of the Men's House and walks around in something rather fine.

Finally there is the present of an ox that the boy must sacrifice to Zeus in a feast for the hunting party on their return.[54] Sacrifice, for the Greeks, is the most basic religious ritual, used to bring people together in the presence of gods. The significant thing is not that a sacrifice has taken place, but who provides a sacrifice to whom, for whom, of what. What is sacrificed is an ox (*bous*), an expensive victim, indicating, as if we didn't already know, that this was a very important occasion. It was sacrificed to Zeus, and almost certainly to a particular Zeus, but which one—Zeus of Clans, of Clubs, of Friendship (the most likely), of Good Advice, of Completion—we aren't told. Unlike sacrifices to Ares, say, or Aphrodite or Demeter, a sacrifice to just "Zeus" has rather a broad frame of reference. What is relevant is his responsibility for social order or social cohesion: "Zeus has a special concern for the relations which bind strangers to one another: guests, suppliants, and those bound by oaths . . ."—very appropriate, then, in the context of a relationship of trust established between men of rival houses.[55]

Whose sacrifice is it? Originally, of course, the abductor provided the victim. It was one of the presents he was required to give to the boy, but it is the boy who gives it to Zeus and the hunting party. If anyone is the host of this feast, at any rate, it is the boy, who is therefore in the position not of adoptee but of adopter. The abductor who originally provided the animal is now the honored guest. The feast, therefore, can be seen as doing with food what the boy does in speech, retrospectively consenting to the relationship. If the boy repudiates the rape as forced on him against his will, it is hardly conceivable that the abductor would be sharing in the sacrificial meal. The elaborate formalities of the ritual are designed to make sure that such a disastrous eventuality happens as rarely as possible.

The boy is henceforth one of the "Famed." On public occasions, they have a position of honor in dances and races. Is that it? Is that the only role they play in society? Ephorus briefly mentions one other elite "office" (*archē*) in Crete, that of the *hippeis,* Knights or simply "Horsemen." Could these be the Famed? Ephorus compares them with the Spartan Knights, a group of three hundred select troops in their Twenties. The Cretan Knights are the originals, he argues, since they still had horses: "Just as some like spades to be spades, so Ephoros looked for horses for his Knights."[56]

We are also told of a battalion of Beauties. "The Cretans marshal the most beautiful/noble of the citizens in the front [?] lines and these sacrifice to Eros on their behalf."[57] We know from Ephorus that it was very shameful for a beautiful boy (beautiful *in appearance*) not to be abducted, so it is fair to assume that the corps of the most beautiful men, arrayed in the battle lines, who sacrifice to Eros before a battle, was recruited, automatically or in practice, from the corps of "Famed" who enjoy most honorable positions in races and dances. In Thessaly those with positions of honor in dances, the "dancers in front" (*proorchestēr*), were also battle champions. Lucian records an inscription on a statue that commemorates a Thessalian who had just been "judged to be frontline dancer by the city." Perhaps he too had been "Famed."[58]

All this seems to me to be pointing in one direction: The Famed are being selected for bravery, beauty and decorum, in order to form the ranks of the Beauties who make sacrifice to Eros before battle. The Beauties need not necessarily fight together in a single body. They are perhaps the front line spread through the army, the "champions." Here perhaps another piece of evidence comes in handy. Maximus in his celebration of the wonderful modesty of Cretan custom seems to say that the *erastēs* is a *neaniskos*, a Cadet, the *erōmenos* just a Stripling, a *meirakion*. In Athens *neaniskoi* are the young men who go around on horseback, Aristophanes' *Knights*, and those two young men in *Lysis* with their terribly horsey names. Was the battalion of Beauties selected by the battalion of Knights, therefore? Did the "stood by" have "reins-holders" as their partners, just as Idomeneus had his beloved "Thigh-man," Meriones, as Heracles had his Iolaus, and Achilles his Patroclus? Did Cretan couples too model themselves on the heroic chariot pair? At any rate, that special day, those wonderful two months, free to go anywhere you wanted, all those presents, the great feast, all that attention, gallivanting in distinctive costumes, pushing past your age-mates to take your place of honor at the front in the dances and the races, might be considered fair exchange for a life now likely to be shorter. "Fame" is a guarantee of *remembered* glory . . . glory after death. In Crete, in other words, fame cost.

HOMOSEXUALITY AND THE CRETAN POLIS

The Cretan abduction ritual, then, was a major event involving great expenditure on the part of the participants and some, perhaps much, inconvenience to the community. According to the sources it does two things, one very personal and private, one very public and political. In the first place it formally inaugurates a relationship between two men, one perhaps in his Twenties, already in the ranks of the Knights, or a Cadet, the other under Twenty. At the end of the process the teenager makes a formal declaration that he has not been taken by force and that he accepts the relationship with this man. They are pledged to each other, sexually available to each other, beyond the reach of the law on rape. Aelian talks of the Cretan beloved laying out the body of his lover, as Achilles does for Patroclus, as Andromache does for Hector, as wives do for husbands. Perhaps that was the norm. This coupling function of the ritual is symbolized by the bronze chalice. The abductor is from a different club, and taking the boy to his social home, his Men's House, and publicly embracing him is the climax of the abduction phase of the process. It means in the first place that there is a kind of incest avoidance going on: You can't have relationships with boys who belong to your own social family. Secondly it has the interesting consequence that the boys of one House must depend for their elevation on the admiration of a man from a rival House. Finally it means that the most distinguished members of your dining society are pledged to, are "stood beside," someone who belongs to another such society, or simply an outsider.

At the same time, however, the abduction initiates the boy into the ranks of a conspicuous group of citizens who are called "Famed." These are men of various ages who wear distinctive costumes and occupy positions of honor in performances of dance and running. They are supposed to include the most splendid men of their generation who were not excluded on grounds of bad behavior. They must have been quite a sight.

Solely or largely drawn from these splendid specimens were the ranks of Beauties through whom sacrifice was made to Eros on the battlefield. This erotic/political function, the selection of Beauties to represent the city, is symbolized by the gift of the warlike costume.

The abduction brings rival men together and establishes relationships among the worthy and distinguished. It uses the boundary-crossing power of *erōs* to stitch the city together with love. The "Famed" represent a splendid and vivid cross section of the community, the cream of several herds, several Houses, the flower of the manhood of Lyctus or Gortyn or wherever, a rare and spectacular image of a group that now represents no group but the polis per se.

II
SPARTA

Our best early source for Sparta is the Athenian Xenophon, who went to live among the Spartans as an exile and wrote in the early fourth century BC. He even put his sons through the Spartan "education system," we are told. He probably thought it was good for them. At any rate he had by far the best opportunity to be our most informative source, even if he didn't always take it.[59] Other writers, notably Plutarch writing centuries later at the end of the first century AD, provide more details, which are good fun, but which may reflect Sparta's endless attempts to turn the clock back and restore the old ways. Moreover Sparta was for a long time one of the most or the most powerful and important city in Greece, and for much of the classical period it stood in opposition, an ideological and structural opposition, to Athens, the other important city, a situation not unlike the standoff between Soviet Russia and the USA for much of the twentieth century. The combination of huge symbolic significance and little firsthand knowledge lends a slightly mythical or "mirage"-like atmosphere to the city.[60] The sources sometimes seem inconsistent, and we have no idea if that inconsistency is because they are talking of different Spartas, the classical one, the Hellenistic one, the Roman-period one, or if it derives from "spin-doctoring." What we really ought to do is to take the primary classical source, Xenophon, as the gold standard, but there is a problem with that. Xenophon seems to say that in Sparta there was no homosexuality at all: Here *erōs* was completely chaste. Nobody, for excellent reasons, believes that. But in that case what on earth was he up to? Was he, in fact, saying something more precise, not lying through his teeth, but misleading?

THE SYSTEM

Authors refer to Spartan *erōtikos* practices in the context of the System. This System was conceived as a Thing that had not evolved but which had been instituted in its classic form by someone in particular at a particular time: Lycurgus. It was often compared with Crete's system and has provoked much more discussion than any other. There is still dispute about its terminology, although the basic structure seems clear.[61] A lexical commentator on Herodotus refers to six junior age-grades: "Among the Spartans in the first year the *pais* is called *rhobidas,* in the second year *promikizomenos,* in the third year *mikizomenos,* in the fourth year *propais,* in the fifth year *pais,* in the sixth year *meleirēn.* And among them, the *pais* is in ephebic training [*ephēbeuei*] from Fourteen to Twenty."[62] All except the first grade, which may refer to all those under Fifteen, are found in modified but recognizable form in inscriptions. The grade following in the same series will be *eirēn,* to which Plutarch gives an age of Twenty(-plus).[63]

But underneath this complexity we can detect a more familiar system of (1) Boys under-Eighteen, (2) Striplings without citizenship or "Sturdy Boys," and (3) "Males," *eirenes,* or "Bloomers," *hēbōntes*—adults.[64] Plutarch talks of a tomb called in Sparta "Of the Earthquake" (*Seismatias*) said to be that of an entire age-class of ephebes who died together when the gymnasium collapsed on them during the earthquake of 464 BC. The Cadets (*neaniskoi*) escaped because they were oiled up and when a hare appeared they "ran out playfully in pursuit" (*meta paidias ekdramein*), while the ephebes were "left behind." These are not old Spartan terms but Athenian/Hellenistic age-terms, and since *neaniskoi* are subadults but always older than ephebes when the two terms are found together, it probably means those of Eighteen and Nineteen, *paides* and *meleirenes.* Very probably the legend relates to graduation. "Run out" seems to have been the technical term for graduation in Crete, and naturally those unable to graduate are "left behind."[65] The least we can squeeze out of the legend of the Earthquake Tomb is that visitors to Sparta could be shown a grave in the center of the city exclusively filled with the bodies of a single narrow age-grade.

As in Crete, boys are said to be organized in "herds" (*boua*—Spartan for "herd [*agelē*] of boys") under the leadership of a *bouagor,* Spartan for "herd leader, the *boy* who rules the herd." But they were also organized in "companies," *ilai.* These herds seem to have been almost like children's secret societies, fiercely competitive rival gangs: *sumbouai:* "Conspirators—those sworn together [*sunōmotai*]"; *sumbouaddei* (i.e., *sumbouazei*): "This is Spartan dialect for 'fights for one's side [*hupermachei*].'" There seems to have been intense identification with the gang and the gang leader.[66]

Xenophon says a single "Boy-magistrate" (*paidonomos*) was in overall charge of boys and that he was assisted by keen young adults, armed with whips, who were put in charge of each mysterious "company," *ilē.* These Young Men presided over their collective dinners.[67] The Spartan system reveals much more polis control of boy-herds than in Crete and dispenses with the power and prestige acquired by the father of the Cretan herd leader. Moreover "any citizen present had authority to direct them in anything he thought good . . ." This probably means that any

citizen could go to where the boys were encamped and ask them to perform a traditional song or dance or recite a speech in praise of some
deeds of their ancestors or some such thing. A very similar custom is
practiced by the Shavante of Brazil, although the ethnographer observed, what must have been the case in Sparta also, that it would be a
way for one of their Seniors to show off his own stature in the community: "A man who is shy about pushing himself forward will not be the
one to go and order out the boys, especially if it is a cold night and they
are liable to come out reluctantly, muttering and grumbling."[68]

Plutarch seems to confirm much of Xenophon's picture and adds
more details. He says that Spartan boys were put in these gangs as early
as age Seven. In Crete this happened only when the boys had reached the
equivalent of ephebe status, which probably means Eighteen. He says
these herds served as play teams and sports teams, that the brightest and
most fiery of the boys was appointed ruler of the gang, that the members "shared the same laws" and had to obey him.[69] At Twelve, he continues, they slept together "by gang and by company." He confirms
Xenophon's information that a Twenty-something *eirēn* was put in
charge of the boys "in their gangs."[70] The Young Man commands them
in mock battles. He is served by them, demands from a boy speeches on
a certain topic or a song—so perhaps by Plutarch's time the custom that
anyone could order the boys about had been forgotten. Now these boys
under the command of the Young Man are clearly not all the same age.
The Young Man with the whip is not a "form master," because he gives
different duties to "sturdy boys" and to "littler boys," i.e., in Athenian
terminology, the Young Man is in charge of both Striplings and Boys.

Putting all this together, the only sensible conclusion is that these
gangs (*agelai, bouai*) are teams of coevals, forming a powerfully self-
identified and properly incorporated subset of a particular year, like,
e.g., third-formers from rival schools, but actually sworn together and
under the leadership of a coeval, the gang leader, *bouagor*. At some point,
they are put with older gangs to make an age-grade-differentiated company that fights together.[71] The companies would therefore form a junior version of the multi-aged messes and fighting units of adults, a
rehearsal for adult age-classed society, well drilled in the system of different "years," acting together and on different instructions from other
"years" in their unit. It seems likely, therefore, that for any given year

the number of gangs equaled the number of companies and that the companies, like schools, had a permanent existence, renewing themselves when their senior herd graduated and was replaced by a more junior herd. This seems to have no parallel in "Crete"—i.e., those southern Dorian cities of Crete, supposedly colonized by Sparta in the early first millennium BC—and we can understand why Ephorus emphasizes that the Cretan gang leader tried to get as many boys as he could into his herd, and his father was given control over it; he is showing how different it was from Sparta, much more ad hoc.

Xenophon emphasizes that Boys had one cloak that they wore throughout the year, even in summer, the better to prepare them "also for summer-heats [*thalpē*]." Plutarch says tunics were banned from Twelve, they had one cloak for the year, and boys did not bathe or anoint themselves, except on certain days of the year.[72] All of this seems perfectly consistent: Spartan Boys, like Cretan Boys, kept their kit on. Now also perhaps we can understand why the legend of the Earthquake Tomb makes such a play of the Cadets having stripped off and run out to exercise all covered in oil. That "stripping off" and "running out" must, as in Crete, have been the ceremony of leaving boyhood and entering into adulthood, just like the ephebes of Athens at the Panathenaea running naked from the altar of Eros to the altar in the city, carrying torches.

We are given little other information directly about the transition from junior age-classes to adulthood. Of course, several festivals specified particular roles for particular age-groups, and we could reconstruct a sequence of initiation rituals if we knew when the human year, i.e., New Year, began in Sparta. What is clear is that high summer and early autumn were critical. According to a Hellenistic antiquarian, "at the time of the *Gymnopédies*," which Plato calls "trials of fortitude of those combating the strength of stifling heat [*pnigos*]," "[three] choruses" performed: in front, a chorus of boys (probably here under Twenty); next, though this is merely a plausible emendation, one of old men, *gerontes* (Sixty-plus), on the right; and finally one "of men [*andrōn*] on the left dancing naked and singing songs of Thaletas and Alcman and the paeans of Dionysodotus the Spartan."[73] The same festival has been linked to Plutarch's reference to a performance of three choruses "in the festivals" organized "according to the three age-grades [*hēlikias*]." The old men first sang: "Once we *were* bold Young Men [*neaniai*]"; then the chorus of men at their peak: "We *are;* if you are up to it, look"; and finally the boys, *paides:* "And we *will be,* mightier much."[74] Significantly it was the Ephors, the "lookers at," who presided over the *Gymnopédies,* and if one demurs at the idea of old men cavorting naked and singing and accepts that Boys always wore a cloak, one could infer that the Men alone are naked, which would, of course, give greater point to their challenge: "Look!"[75]

Plutarch says elsewhere that "in the *Gymnopédies*" unmarrieds (*agamoi*) were banned from looking (*thea*). Perhaps they attended, but kept their eyes shut, perhaps they are the ones who might be "unwilling" to look.[76] Around the same time there was also the great festival of Hyacinthia, which involved the whole community. Boys played the lyre and sang "high-pitched"—voices unbroken therefore—to the shawm, and a full complement (*pamplētheis*) of Cadets singing and dancing entered the theater and sang the local songs; this was probably the entire (graduating) age-class.[77] One or two months later, in the *Karneia,* another big festival, selected unmarrieds chased a man covered in woolen ribbons bringing "good things" to the city if they caught him.[78] The race probably took place on "the running-track" (*dromos*), which was where the Young Men in particular did their running, at one end of which was the temple of Apollo Karneios. This seems to me the likeliest place for the stripping off and running out of the Earthquake Tomb legend, in which case it wasn't a hare but this strange man clad in ribbons that they pursued.[79] But that role was reserved for select unmarrieds. So who were these honored, and apparently plentiful, racing bachelors?

Spartan "marriage" is a minefield.[80] Nevertheless, Xenophon clearly states that Lycurgus "put a stop to men taking [*agesthai*] a wife whenever each wished and laid down that they celebrate weddings [*gamous poiesthai*] at their bodily peak."[81] The "Sayings of the Spartans" insists that Lycurgus "defined the time of marriage for both males and females [*gamesthai, gamein*]," to make sure that matured parents, *teleioi,* would produce strong children, and Hermippus of Smyrna (third century BC) says that in Sparta "all the girls were shut in a dark building and the unmarried Cadets were shut in with them. Whichever girl each one laid hold of he led away [*apēgen*] without dowry." The great general Lysander broke the rules, he says, which means it must still have been the practice in the later fifth century BC. Not liking what he had picked from the bran tub, he changed his mind.[82] All this fits together, I think. Xenophon is referring to the practice Hermippus describes: that in Sparta there were mass-"marriages" on graduation, exactly as in Crete and in many other age-class societies. In this context, "unmarrieds" is just another term for Cadets or *meleirenes* ("intending to be adult males") on the eve of their graduation. Plutarch, writing three hundred years after Hermippus, seemingly dissents from these authors, but there are some agreements on detail. At any rate the bride, we are told, was taken "by abduction" like a Cretan boy. The "abducted" girl was put in a room on a pallet, her head shaved and wearing a man's cloak and shoes. A Young Man came in having dined with his mess-mates, loosed her belt (*zōnē*), a highly symbolic gesture, lifted her in his arms and "transferred" her to a couch (*klinē*). He spent time with her there—"not much time"—and went back to sleep with the other Young Men.[83]

There seem to have been so many different definitions of "marriage" in Sparta—successful production of children was one of them, it seems—and so many different kinds of heterosexual relationships, that it is hard to say what "marriage" means on any particular occasion, and it is quite possible that Plutarch got confused. But even Xenophon says the Spartans don't follow the System as they used to, and many other authors point to general and specific changes in Spartan society during the years of wealth and imperialism after they had defeated Athens in the Peloponnesian War. In particular the numbers of "Spartiates," the full citizens, shrank, revealing a drastic narrowing of the elite. It must have been hard, especially, to forgo advantageous marriage alliances, and especially the dowry. Perhaps the custom was modified to the extent that when the bridegroom went into the dark room there was only one girl there by prearrangement, so the custom could be kept and the randomness got rid of.

The "Bloomers" might go on for years like this, sleeping in barracks and only visiting their wives at night and in secret. For like the Cretans, Spartans did not move in with their wives straightaway:

> Lycurgus noticed that among the rest of the Greeks, where a woman got married and moved in with her husband, the husbands were having immoderate amounts of sex with women immediately after the

marriage. He decided to do the opposite of this. He laid it down that the husband be ashamed of being seen to go in, and ashamed to be seen to be leaving. Thus necessarily intercourse between them would be more full of longing, and the children conceived more robust, than if they were fully sated with each other.[84]

Plutarch seems to concur about the nature of these postmarital visits—"secretly," "with meticulous care," "full of embarrassment," "afraid in case someone inside should notice." How could residents not notice so frequent an intruder? The Spartans did not live in mansions, with "wings."[85]

Similar customs are known in many other places. Laura Graham provides a vivid account of going to stay with a Shavante family in 1984:

> Long after I thought my housemates had gone to sleep, I heard the door creep open and the mysterious sounds of someone slipping in. Palm fronds rustled—the intruder must have adjusted the sleeping mat as he lay down. For a while all I heard was the steady breathing of those who still slept a sleep untroubled by the appearance of this stranger in our midst . . . Then I saw . . . Aracy silently cross the room to . . . where her daughter slept . . . She whispered, loud enough for me to hear . . . "My son-in-law is here!"

In the morning after one of these visits, the father would address his daughter's husband neither in the second person, "Do you . . . ," nor by name: "Does he like rice?"[86]

Two decades earlier another ethnographer had discovered a great deal of embarrassment and a lot of teasing:

> They take a delight in opposing the young man's pretensions to chastity by telling in circumstantial detail how they see him come to their household by night, how long he stays, when he leaves, and how he is so sluggish and sleepy that he slinks away when the rest of the household is already astir. The man himself strenuously denies it all, usually maintaining that he has no wish whatever to sleep with any woman . . . and that if he had, he would know how to come and go like a shadow in the night without her household being so much as aware that anyone had intercourse with her.[87]

These sons-in-law are coming from their own houses, however. An even closer parallel is provided by another Brazilian community, the Kayapo, where men live in a communal Men's House in the middle of the village. They were filmed for *Man Alive,* and the film includes an interview in which a son-in-law describes leaving the Men's House to visit his wife.[88]

Some Spartan men might even have children before they saw what their wives looked like in the daylight, says Plutarch.[89] We also hear of social penalties for "late marriers." If they had no choice about when to marry, how can they "marry late," one might wonder. Again, it might be a penalty for those who didn't produce children, or a change of custom over the centuries.

A very distinctive custom was the polyandry attested by Xenophon. Again there is inconsistency in his account. On the one hand, as in Crete, men were forced to marry at their peak. On the other hand, if an old man had somehow managed to get himself a young wife, he was obliged to get a young man whose qualities he admired to father children for him. And if a man didn't want to live with a woman, he could impregnate someone else's wife, with the husband's permission—a woman of noble birth and good children, says Xenophon, of course. The husband would not object because his sons would have brothers who shared in the "power" of the family while not diluting their inheritance. It appears, from what Xenophon says, that there was an element of choice in deciding whether you wanted a home life or a barracks life, and that once children were born a man was expected to live at home, unless he made other arrangements. The Spartans had the reputation of being least interested in "guarding" their women. Xenophon is such an apologist for Sparta, and the custom would look so outrageous to other Greeks, that we must accept Spartan wife swapping as gospel truth.[90]

Probably on graduation as an adult you applied to join one of the messes (*pheiditia, syskania*) grouped along the Hyacinthian Road between Sparta and Amyclae. The mess proper was a group of just fifteen men drawn from all age-groups, which must mean, unless there is an error, that there were hundreds of these messes along the Hyacinthian Road. They dined together "in the open" every single day. Membership in a mess was a requirement for membership in the citizen-body and was paid for by contributions of barley, wine, cheese and figs, but also by money to pay for special dishes like the famous pork-blood stew. Both the necessity of paying your subs and, probably, the election for membership were distinctive features of Spartan as opposed to Cretan custom, and many believe these distinctive features were the cause of the shrinking of the elite in the course of the classical period. Sparta's decline was caused by excessively fussy rules for membership of dining clubs.

Most Greeks shared food, picking it from a plate with their fingers. In Sparta each member of the club was served individually, in the modern "Russian" manner. The pork was a regular feature and Spartan dinners were notoriously meager and uninteresting. Well, yes and no. For, just as there were several different definitions of Spartan marriage, there was more than one definition of "dinner." After the "Spartan dinner" they had another one. This was supplied by one of the members of the club and prepared at home. These second dinners were an occasion for showing off. If you were wealthy you might provide something from one of your own estates, some lamb or a kid. Otherwise you might offer something you had caught while out hunting. For after this prolonged youth of intense physical competition and barracks living, you were allowed, after Thirty probably, to let yourself go a bit and spend your time killing wild animals. We hear of fish, hares, geese, ring-doves, turtle-doves, thrushes and blackbirds. "The cooks announce the names of those who are contributing anything, so that the whole company may know of the effort they have put into hunting and their enthusiasm for their fellow diners." Again it sounds excruciating.

What you didn't do was go and buy something from the marketplace. Xenophon says this dining in the open was designed to counter greed, but whenever he justifies any Spartan custom we must prick up our ears. It is not hard to see how eating in the open might in fact have offered the chance to show off. Just imagine a series of al fresco dining societies along the route to Hyacinthus's tomb, putting on a display of what they are having for dinner and even having it announced down the road. "Did you hear that? Splendidas is giving them roast boar. Mmm, I can smell it from here. He cannot have caught them himself. He's no good as a hunter, and I saw him very deep in conversation with the pig seller in the marketplace this morning."

At any rate the Cretan custom of selecting from the common table the best food for the most distinguished members presents quite a contrast, one that is probably intended to emphasize how superior Crete was in comparison to Sparta. The members voted for or against the admission of new members by placing a piece of barley-cake (or barley-dumpling), *maza,* into a bowl. You made your rejection known by impressing your piece, and the result must be unanimous, so that one single thumb impression could rule a candidate out. One imagines the selection committee wondering whether they should recommend inducting this rather impoverished but athletically quite distinguished candidate who might struggle to keep up his contributions, or wait for so-and-so's son to apply next year, the one with vast estates and splendid horses, the one who could provide wheat bread and wild boar every evening, with fish shipped in from the coast on special occasions, even if he was rather fat.

The point about these tiny private multi-aged dining societies that would only be able to take a new member once every few years is that they will have served to break up the intense loyalties of the gangs and companies in which Spartans had been living for so long, and replace them with completely new bonds to a new group of men, from the horizontal and coeval to the vertical and political. People often assume that amatory connections will have abetted membership applications. They probably had influence, but maybe not much. If numbers really were so tightly controlled, you could never guarantee there would be an opening for your boyfriend when he graduated.

BREEZY RELATIONSHIPS

As elsewhere, there is a great deal of evidence that Spartan *homoerotikos* relationships between males had "a public and official character."[91] In other words, like Cretans, males were somehow recognizably wedded to each other. In the first place there was a technical term (an "Amyclaean" term) for the admirer, *eispnēlas,* which sounded like "Inspirationist."[92] Dover has shown cogently that this probably means he is inspired by the *erōmenos,* not that he inspires the *erōmenos*—by which some people would like to infer "inseminates," since one author tells us that Spartans used the word *eispnein,* "breathe into," for "to be in love," *eran.* This can only mean that the boys required their admirers to be "inspired" with love. We also hear of a term for the beloved, *aïtas,* which probably comes from the verb "to blow" and is cognate therefore with the word *aētēs,* "breeze," or "gust."[93] The beloved is the Blow therefore, the "Inspirationist" the one who is blown into, or inspired by him.

Both of these words relate to movements of air, winds and breathings, and we cannot forget that winds had a prominent role in Spartan culture and indeed in cult. Wing-shod Boreads of one kind or another, sons of the North Wind, were all over Spartan pots. At some time the Spartans sang a healing song, a paean, in praise of Eurus, the East Wind, as Savior, and of course the most amorous, charming and fertile of all the inspiring winds, the *Aētēs* Zephyrus, the West Wind, the wind who blew speed into the horses of the kings of Troy and of Achilles and used to come down to Hyacinthus from Mount Taÿgetus at the end of hot summer days and quickly reduce the temperature at Amyclae. Winged creatures who look exactly like winds are a characteristic feature of Spartan art, sometimes fluttering around what look like goddesses, perhaps even bloody Artemis Orthia herself, trying to steal her cheeses, and this must be related to all the breathing and blowing metaphors in Spartan homosexuality. Looking at a handsome winged youth on a cup, a Spartan might easily have said: "Look, it is an *aïtas,* a breezy inspiring boy."

On at least one cup, showing men and women at a drinking party, these little winged youths alternate with images of feminine seduction, Sirens, and they probably represent by contrast an image of a love for boys in particular, homosexual fairies. And let's not forget that the windy winged image of the god of love himself was probably born in Sparta. In Sparta especially it seems impossible to separate the beloved boy, the "Blow," from that Eros who, according to Phaedrus in the *Symposium,* blows *menos* into warriors, inspiring them to great deeds. So an image of a winged Stripling could at one and the same time be read as a breezy inspiring *erōmenos,* as an inspiring Eros, or as Hyacinthus's lover, and Eros's sometime father, breezy Zephyrus. Like the Cretan battalion of Beauties, the Spartans sacrificed to Eros before war. I would be amazed if these two rituals, the only military sacrifices to Eros hitherto known, are not related. They must have a common origin, going back to the early first millennium at least. That sacrifice must have connected Eros to Achillean martial energy, inspiring the warriors, filling them with spunk, and how much more vivid that sense of inspiration would have been in Crete, with the beautiful brigade, probably manned partly or wholly by the beautiful "Famed," each of them formally tied to an *erastēs,* coming forward to make the sacrifice.

Apart from the formal titles for *erastai* and *erōmenoi,* we hear of specific rights and responsibilities that depend on the notion of formal, publicly recognized attachments between males. We hear for instance of an Inspirationist who was punished because his Breeze cried inappropriately when he was in one of the fights. Later authors talk of laws governing these relationships. A gentleman, *kalosk'agathos,* could be punished if he didn't get himself into a relationship with one of the "beautifully formed boys," *kalōs pephukotes,* a term that seems to refer to natural physical attributes. He was punished because "though worthy [*chrēstos*] he was not in love with anyone." On the other hand, if one of the beautiful boys chose a rich *erastēs* instead of a poor but worthy (*chrēstos*) man he could be fined.[94] The law would need to know whether or not this relationship existed; there must, as in Crete, have been a formal wedding.

Did abduction occur in Spartan Love customs too? Well, there is one strange legend that involves a homosexual abduction. It is supposed to be set in history, but the story is attached to a legend about vengeful female ghosts, the ghosts of women raped once upon a time by Spartan young men (*neaniai*). They are the spirits who famously helped to cause the disastrous Spartan defeat at Leuctra. So history it is not.[95]

The story about the girls is juxtaposed with a story about a boy similarly raped by a Spartan. It is set in the city of Oreus at the top of Euboea. In the legend the city is under Spartan control, and the victim is the narrator's son, "a subject of Sparta."[96] The Spartan governor, Aristodemus, showed himself criminal and raw. He fell in love with the Stripling. However, he was:

> incapable of persuading him, so he *put his hands to forcing him,* and to leading him from the exercise ground [*palaistra*]. The trainer prevented him and many Cadets came to help, and forthwith Aristodemus went away. But the very next day he came with a ship and carried off the boy and crossed to the other side from Oreus and put his hand to outraging him. Since the boy did not concur he slit his throat and crossed back to Oreus and enjoyed a feast.

This sounds very much like a tug-of-war.

Other things we hear are that no proper Spartan was allowed into the marketplace until he was over Thirty. His kinsmen or *erastai* would go instead, a nice case of inherited and "made" forms of kinship placed together.[97] A boy might have more than one admirer, and not only was there no rivalry between them, the admirers were joined in their common admiration and interest for the boy. Were they all punished therefore if the boy was a wimp?

INTERPRETING SPARTAN HOMOSEXUALITY

All of this is at first very hard to make sense of. In particular, sometimes the sources seem to imply lots of admirers, sometimes only one. I think the whole thing needs to be read against the background of other systems, and especially the institutions of Crete. In Athens, as we have seen, there are two types of *erastai:* the group of men who follow behind a boy and write his name on walls, and someone who is in a recognized relationship, like Harmodius and Aristogiton, the Tyrant-Slayers, the *erastēs* who "has" the boy, in the words of Thucydides, a term used of husbands "having" wives. This is what Plato means when he talks of his two sexual lovers who wait together on the shining path for reincarnation as men "who have exchanged the greatest pledges," or when Pausanias in *Symposium,* alluding perhaps to the Tyrant-Slayers, talks of a *koinōnia,* a federation, a commonwealth between the pair, a love for life.

Likewise in Crete, although, according to Ephorus's account, there is only one *philētor* who has been through the abduction ceremony, there are many *philoi* who "follow" the pair hunting and make contributions to all the gifts. This must be what Nepos refers to when he says that in Crete boys thought it was a good thing "to have as many admirers as possible." He wanted to be attended by as many "friends" as possible during the tug-of-war and the hunt. It is easy to see how the group of "friends," the fan club, could be seen as bonding together around the boy in the way Xenophon describes in Sparta, and that their love establishes a relationship not just between each of them and the boy, but between each other, just as it does in the potteries of Athens, the workshop of Fans of Leagros, or Fans of Athenodotus etc. . . . Again, unity through homosexuality.

Crete also helps to explain the strange laws about compulsory homosexual relationships. The reference in Maximus of Tyre to the Cretan *erastēs* as Cadet (*neaniskos*) might imply that the abductors were drawn from the elite, the ranks of young knights or horsemen. A similar provision in Sparta would help to account for these odd laws. In other words, the "Inspirationist" had to come from a particular recognizable class, one of the *chrēstoi,* the "worthies," or the *kaloik'agathoi,* the gentlemen, who were required by law to form a homosexual alliance. This class must have overlapped considerably with the three hundred Spartan Knights-with-no-horses who had already been selected for their excellent qualities. The law could be interpreted as meaning, first, that these elite warriors had to have a boyfriend, and second, that they alone could establish relationships of *eispnēlas* and *aïtas.* A boy at any rate could not have an inspirationist who was not a member of the "worthies."

Note that the "worthy" also had to choose a boy who was not *necessarily* a gentleman himself but "beautifully made." Again, if we follow the Cretan example, which, I have argued, selected the Famed to serve in a distinct battalion of Beauties who made the sacrifice to Eros on behalf of the whole army, then we can perhaps explain Xenophon's outraged criticism of the Thebans and Eleans, that they slept together *and fought together,* that they placed their boyfriends *alongside them* in the ranks. Clearly in Sparta boyfriends did not fight together. One possibility is that there was a large age difference, so that the boys were too young to fight with their partners at first, and by the time they were old enough to fight their partners had moved on, but we know of one relationship, between Archidamus and Cleonymus, which cannot have included so large an age gap, perhaps just five years or so. But what happens, then, if a Knight chooses a partner who is also chosen as a Knight some years later? Boyfriends would end up sleeping together and fighting together exactly as in dreadful Thebes.

The two partners must, I think, be drawn from separate groups. Of necessity *erōs* in Sparta, according to Xenophon, serves to form a bond between different parts of the army. We also hear, however, that the reason the "worthy" had to make a homosexual attachment was in order to "make a boy the same as himself," *homoios,* i.e., "worthy," "gentlemanly." Is there a bit of social recruitment going on here, the induction of beautiful boys who may or may not be classy and turning those who are not gentlemen into gentlemen? Simply by going to the marketplace for him, the *erastai* were making the boy more respectable. Moreover in Crete, we notice, a great deal of property is handed over to the Famed boy, so much that the admirer cannot afford it himself and needs the friends to have a whip-round. Is there some kind of sponsorship of promising, handsome but not necessarily classy boys going on?[98]

DID THEY OR DIDN'T THEY?

Did Spartan men have sex with each other or not? This is a terribly ancient question, seemingly, and one that remains unresolved. Basically, several ancient authors on Sparta—Xenophon, Plutarch, Aelian, Maximus of Tyre—*seem* to say that they didn't at all, absolutely not. But the word *lakonize,* "make like a Spartan," could be used to mean precisely "use favorites," and Plato assumed that they were always at it, just like the Cretans, full of homosexual lust, absorbed in homosexual pleasure. Almost all modern scholars, for good reason, agree with Plato's version.[99] But it makes me uncomfortable to discard the best source according to Rankean principles, the most primary source, so unceremoniously.

Xenophon is an operator, and elsewhere he certainly makes claims about himself that cannot possibly be true, but those are (usually) Socratic fictions, not meant to deceive—for this is the man who is often credited with inventing the very notion of narrative prose fiction, when he wrote the *Cyropaedia,* the *Formation of Cyrus,* which doesn't even pretend to be factual and historical. But granted that he is not a completely reliable narrator, I don't think when he is in nonfictional mode he is so outrageous a liar either. It's just that his readers need to keep their wits about them.

According to Xenophon, the *custom* in Sparta, as laid down by *Lycurgus the lawgiver,* was quite contrary to what happened elsewhere in Greece, notably among the dreadful Boeotians and Eleans—by this time I have to say I am beginning to share the general disdain for whatever it was the Eleans got up to, even though I have no idea what it was. But Spartan practice, he says, was also quite different from what happened in those prudish places where *erastai* were forbidden to talk to Boys, i.e., Athens. We notice that when he introduces the marriage customs with the same remarks, it means that he is about to side with Sparta. By analogy with his comments about marriage customs and wife swapping, we might interpret the formula more like this: "Although Spartan Homosexuality looks very peculiar or even immoral to most Greeks, if you think about it, it turns out to be much better than elsewhere." And note also that the reference to some cities preventing even speaking to boys implies we are talking about Boys, under-Eighteens, because that, it would appear, is the group it referred to in Athens.[100]

Xenophon, in fact, writes very allusively, almost in a kind of code, with a great deal left between the lines. So you have to pay close attention to exactly what he says. First the *erastēs* had to be the right sort, "the type of person it is necessary to be"—more confirmation that not anybody could be an *erastēs*. This is Xenophon's way of saying he was a "worthy," presumably, or "gentleman." And then: "if he delighted in a boy's personality [*psuchē*] and made an attempt to turn him into the finished product of his unblamable *friend* [*amempton philon apotelesasthai*] and be with him [*suneinai,* "have intercourse with him"], Lycurgus praised the fact and considered this the most beautiful training [*paideia,* not "education" so much as "formation" in general, *Bildung*]."[101]

This strange and stilted language may indicate a formal process of friend-making initiation into a relationship, for *apoteleō* refers to arriving at an end product; he must be talking of establishing an "intimate friendship." But note too that if Xenophon is talking, as he seems to be, of underage Boys, it would be utterly shocking to an Athenian audience that Spartan men "had intercourse" with them, sexual or otherwise, any intimate intercourse, even a tête-à-tête. And this fact is confirmed by Plutarch, who says that *erastai* were allowed to associate when Boys were as young as Twelve, not just contrary to Athenian practice but ringing alarm bells all over Greece, only too aware of the dreadful crimes that Striplings could perpetrate with under-Eighteens: Laius and Chrysippus, Achilles and Troilus.[102] This is the point of *kallistos,* "most beautiful," which means "not ugly and shameful at all, but on the contrary very beautiful." In other words Xenophon is protesting very much. However:

> if someone was seen to be reaching out to touch the body of a boy [*paidos sōmatos oregomenos phaneiē*], he laid down that this was most shameful/ugly and made it that in Sparta *erastai* keep away from favorites [*paidika*] no less than parents from children and brothers from

brothers as regards sex [*eis aphrodisia*]. That these things are not believed by some people, however, is no surprise to me; in many cities the laws/customs do not run contrary to desires [*epithumiais*] toward boys.[103]

The contrast between those two formulations—allowed to "be with . . . most beautiful," but not allowed to "reach out to touch a boy's body . . . most ugly"—reveals the heart of Xenophon's anxiety. Spartan boys had no *paidagōgoi* and did not live at home but in boarding schools under the supervision of a Young Man. Moreover, other Spartans, even *erastai,* could associate with them and "be with them." How outrageous. "No, no," says Xenophon. "I know what it looks like, but it really isn't like that at all."

He returns to his defense in his *Symposium,* which is written in response to Plato's *Symposium.* Again the contrast is explicitly with Phaedrus's talk of the Army of Lovers, and the appalling customs of Elis and Thebes, where men fight and sleep together, apparently: "The Spartans believe that if anyone even reached out to touch a body [*orechthēi . . . sōmatos*] he will no longer achieve any deed [worthy] of a gentleman . . . For they worship the goddess Sense of Shame [*Aidōs*] not the goddess Shamelessness."[104] As for Armies of Lovers sleeping in the same tent . . .

If the strange repeated formula about "being seen to reach out to touch a boy's body" arouses our suspicions, it is the final sentence that gives the game away, for there was indeed a cult of Sense of Shame, *Aidōs,* five kilometers outside Sparta; it was said to be a statue of Penelope veiled.[105]

The key it seems to me is the hermeneutic—reading and interpreting—tendency that runs so deep in Greek talk about themselves and others. We might refer to this tendency more specifically as "ecphrastic"—describing, narrating and interpreting a visual image. We have already come across many examples of this, when the Greeks read the stars, for example. "The hero Orion was killed by a scorpion, sent by a hostile goddess Earth" is a reading of the night sky: It tells as a story the fact that the constellation sets when the constellation Scorpio rises on the horizon. "The problem is that authors do not always tell us this is what they are doing. In one famous example, Pausanias in his Guide to Greece mentions that there was a statue of the great sixth-century BC wrestler Milo of Croton and then goes on to tell some stories about his great feats of strength:

> The following stories are told . . . He would hold a pomegranate in such a way that nobody could take it from him by force, and yet he did not damage it by pressure. He would stand upon a discus covered in oil and make fools of those who charged at him and tried to push him off the discus. He used to perform also the following feats for show: he used to tie a cord round his forehead as though it were a bandanna or a crown. Holding his breath, his lips tightly closed, and filling the veins of his head with blood, he would break the cord by the strength of these veins. It is also said that keeping his upper arm by his side he would stretch out his lower arm from the elbow, fingers stretched out, with his thumb on top and the others lying on top of each other. And no one could force his little finger, at the bottom, out of alignment. (6.14, 5–7)

It is only when Philostratus in his *Life of Apollonius of Tyana* (4.28) describes what the statue of Milo at Olympia actually looked like, standing on a rounded platform like a discus, wearing a headband, with its arms stretched out, the left holding a pomegranate, the right with fingers fused together, that we realize that Pausanias's anecdotes are in fact ecphrastic, that he was describing and interpreting the statue in front of his eyes, without telling us that was what he was doing. In the biography, Apollonius goes on to produce a superior interpretation of the statue, concluding that it represents Milo as a priest of Hera, standing not on a large discus but on a small shield, to offer prayer. Had this full account of the image and its interpretation not survived, however, we might simply hear that, according to Philostratus or Apollonius, "Milo was a priest of Hera." In fact it seems that a lot of the stories in Pausanias, and in Herodotus and lots of other authors, are in fact disguised ecphrasis, readings and interpretations of monuments, which were familiar to everyone—"And it is said that Nelson used to climb to the top of the ship's mast to look out over London and was attacked by pigeons"—"And it is said that Lincoln used to take his armchair outside and sit with his back to the river."

But this tendency goes beyond mere reading of visual images and extends to reading and interpreting all kinds of prominent texts and artifacts or conspicuous cult practices or customs. This broader kind of hermeneutics we might refer to as an "archaeological" tendency: treating a contemporary culture, even one's own, as an archaeological site with certain prominent objects, buildings, images and texts, but also conspicuous cult practices and customs, which are read and interpreted in order to prove certain general conclusions about that society as a whole. If you visited a city and found streets lined with public bars, you might conclude the population drank a lot. If it was temples that caught your eye, that they were very religious. Again we have already come across lots of examples of this: The fact that there is a cult of the Three Graces, according to Aristotle, is an indication of the importance of reciprocity. We can see it also in the work of his student, the author of the Athenian Constitution, in his account of how the age-class system works. He doesn't just say, "Persons Fifty-nine years of age serve as Dispute-Settlers," which would presumably be a well-known and unexceptionable fact, he goes on to "show it," to demonstrate and prove it, almost as if he were an ancient historian: "as appears from the regulations for the archons and eponymous heroes," going on to describe the whitened age-set lists and how they take the "one at the end" in order to select the age-set of Dispute-Settlers. It is rather as if someone were to say: "Britain is a democracy as can be seen from the signs called 'Polling Booth' that are put outside public buildings every five years, and the ballot boxes."

Such an archaeological focus on institutions, laws, artifacts and tangibles is naturally open to misinterpretation. One could easily imagine an ancient Greek Constitution of Great Britain that got it all wrong: "The country is ruled by the monarch, and her servants whom they call 'ministers' must do exactly what she says. Indeed she summons them annually and reads out a list of instructions before many witnesses, telling them what she requires of them in the course of the year." We tend to think of history as starting out as wild gossip and gradually coming to terms with artifacts and documents and other kinds of proof, terribly impressed at the scientific approach of historians of many years ago, who are modern and Rankean enough to cite the texts of treaties. Rather it seems that history starts out with artifacts and documents and proofs. What changes is the nature of the artifacts, the kinds of stories told about them and the ability to read them. Certainly the Greeks are not sociologists or anthropologists or surveyors with clipboards and impertinent questions, trying to find out the truth about what other Greeks really get up to in their spare time.

We can see this archaeological tendency, this focusing on particular rituals and customs, throughout the discourses of Greek Love. And when Xenophon talks of Spartan *paidikos erōs* he is clearly talking about *institutions,* specifically Lycurgan laws and customs, just as the thieving and whipping refer to the sanctuary of Artemis Orthia, just as his reference to Lycurgus ordering that it be shameful for husbands to be seen entering or leaving the wife's home refers to a specific marriage custom, a tangible, demonstrable practice, just as he uses the fact that there is a veiled statue of "Sense of Shame" to make a point about Spartan modesty. It is only because of other references elsewhere that we would ever have realized that that is what he was doing on each particular occasion. If not for Pausanias we would think he was just talking figuratively and rhetorically rather than referring to a specific cult of *Aidōs* centered on a veiled woman.

So what was this institution lurking behind Xenophon's claim that it was *laid down* as most shameful "to manifestly reach out to touch the body of the boy"? Other later authors seem to be describing something similar. It was permitted to be in love with the soul, but not "to be physically intimate [*plēsiazein*] . . . on the grounds that they were in love with the body and not the soul; anyone even *accused* of physical intimacy directed at shamefulness was deprived of civic rights for life." "If any Stripling went so far as to submit to abuse [*hubris*], or his *erastēs* to abuse him . . . either he left the country, or, in more heated cases, abandoned life itself." We are left then with not just a slight disagreement but an extraordinary conflict in the sources, some saying that there were heavy penalties against the slightest touch, others that the Spartans were so much into homosexuality that they became a byword.[106]

Cicero explains all. Following his repudiation of the "libido that has a sanctioned license" in the customs of Elis and Thebes, he comes to Sparta. In the love of young men the Spartans permit everything, he says, apart from *stuprum,* "the dirty deed" itself (*omnia concedunt in amore iuvenum praeter stuprum*), for "they put a fence between themselves"—

dissaepiunt. What this means, he explains, is that in Spartan custom "they sanction embraces and lyings down together, but with cloaks placed between." But what can you do, which is not full sex, when a boy's body is completely shrouded in fabric apart, perhaps, from the head? Well, there is that fragment of a vase, which most people think is an image of Spartan homosexual myth, a winged male abducting a boy, Zephyrus abducting a Stripling Hyacinthus. And the winged male has a very prominent erection aimed at the boy's thighs, but the boy is wrapped up in a cloak. And we also recall the insistence in our sources that Cretan boys and Spartan boys had one cloak in summer and winter and that they *kept their cloaks on all the time*. Spartan boys it seems kept their kit on even when having sex. This then must be the Spartan institution Xenophon is alluding to, which involves no "reaching out to the body of the boy," with extreme penalties for anyone who does. Full-on intercrural sex, but with a piece of fabric intervening. "A meager barrier indeed," notes Cicero. Indeed.[107] There was certainly something very unusual about sex "the Spartan way." When Theseus abducted beautiful Helen, we are told, he had sex with her, *kusolakōn,* the "Spartan cleft."

We can perhaps detect a similar description of the custom in Maximus of Tyre:

> I do not speak of the things the Eleans do, but I do speak of the things the Spartans do. A Spartiate man is in love with a Stripling of Laconia, but he is in love with him only like a beautiful statue, and many can be in love with one, and one with many.[108] The pleasure that comes out of abuse is not shared with each other [*akoinōnētos*]; but the *erōs* of the eyes alone is shared [*koinōnikos*], reaching all those naturally disposed to *erōs*. What could be more seasonably beautiful than the sun, and what for *erastai* is more watchful than the sun [*poluderkesteron*].[109] Yet the eyes of all are in love with the sun nevertheless.[110]

The boy having sex the Spartan way would indeed be like a statue, immobilized and wrapped up in his cloak, and the pleasure would certainly not be shared, but the same practice would serve to isolate the boy's face, *erōs* through the eyes and perhaps his breathing mouth. I wonder if Plato is not hinting at something similar in his description of the infamous *Spartanizer* his uncle Charmides, whom all the Boys gaze at "as if he were a statue," for there is the same face vs body emphasis: "If you saw his body you would forget about his face." And Socrates supposedly compared the love of Charmides' guardian Critias for the boy Euthydemus to a pig's desire to scratch himself on a stone. Again if we recall that Critias was an even more notorious *Spartanizer,* and what Spartan Homosexuality actually consisted of, such an image becomes infinitely vivider and more pointed.[111]

A HOLY ACT IN A HOLY PLACE

Drawing on such oblique or coded evidence, perhaps it is rash to try to reconstruct the Spartan homosexual wedding ritual, but I am quite certain there was a ritual that made a relationship public and formal, that the powers-that-be not only had a tangible, archaeologicable relationship in mind when the laws were passed but were archaeologists of Love themselves. If someone accused someone who ought to have had a boyfriend according to law of not having one, and the powers-that-be summoned him for a hypothetical interview, I doubt very much that they could be fobbed off merely with protestations of devotion—"No, I assure you I really do have a boyfriend. The vendors will tell you how much I spend on sweetmeats and flowers. What more proof could anyone need? What? I still have to go through with it? With the cloaks intervening and everything? For goodness' sake, this is the Iron Age."

For what was in question was a public ceremony of some kind, visible from afar. Some tangible archaeologicable relationship, I am fairly sure, is what Cicero, Xenophon and Maximus are alluding to, and so we might as well have a guess as to what that formalization might have looked like, always with the abduction ceremony of the Spartans' cultural cousins, the Cretans, in the back of our minds and the strange story of the governor of Oreus.

For to say nothing is also to say "a nothing," i.e., something that might be misleading, like a biopic of Louis Quatorze that is filmed against plain white backgrounds whenever there is dispute among his scholarly biogaphers about what exactly was on the walls, or a biopic of Shakespeare that left him and Her Majesty's courtiers speechless for fear they might say the wrong thing. Sometimes wrong stuff is much less misleading than blank space and silence, because at least it offers something substantial to stand for the stuff we know was present. Even the faultiest reconstruction reminds an audience that life was lived in all its dimensions, then as now. I understand the practice adopted by the managers of rococo palaces in Germany. When the ceilings have been lost, they neither fake a reproduction nor paint it white, they cover it with something abstractly rococoey.

With that proviso, I can shade in my conjectural reconstruction of Spartan homosexual custom. Contrary to Athenian practice, Spartan men over Twenty are allowed to go where the Boys are, perhaps from as young as Twelve and upward. During this time they form fan bands, like the Cretan *philoi* or the potters of the Athenian Ceramicus, clubs that establish ties between themselves along the horizontal axis as well as ties to the boy himself. When the boy is the age of a Stripling, *meirakion,* or *iuvenis,* a homosexual wedding to an individual who will thenceforth be personally responsible for the boy's actions is in the cards.[112] The *erastēs,* who must come from the right class or the right part of the army, goes into the training ground. There is a threat of violence or indeed there is violence, a clash with the *erastēs* on one side, the Cadets on the other, and the Stripling in between. The boy as always is wrapped up in a cloak. There is an embrace and the two lie down together, doing everything but the deed itself, but with no touching of bodies, and preservative cloaks always between.

Well, that is the best I can do. But I really feel as if I am answering one of those photo questions on a quiz show, where the screen shows a tiny part of a big object, or a shot taken from an angle that no ordinary eye could look from. The camera zooms out and out until we all get the picture. Only this is not so easy. This close-up from an odd angle is of an object no one living has ever seen; there is no perspective to zoom back to. And yet here I am extrapolating upon what is left to see. It goes without saying, in other words, that there was a teeming world back then in ancient Sparta, lots of colorful and complicated things, of which mostly we haven't the slightest idea, that I am looking at a detail on a horse from a carousel and trying from that to reconstruct a fairground.

But why do I think this cloak-wrapped practice belongs to a particular occasion rather than to a broader pattern? It might well refer to a common practice of Men visiting their boyfriends just as they visit their young wives at home; a practice does not have to be restricted. But in fact the brief visit to someone wrapped up in a cloak most resembles what Plutarch tells us about the inter-sex marriage ceremony, the girl on the bed in the male cloak, etc. And how would anyone be able to know if someone had touched flesh? How would anyone know if a boy had not kept his kit on—just a cloak, after all? Where is the shame if it's something that goes on in private and/or the dark? Again we have to read Xenophon most carefully. It is most shameful, he says, "if someone *is seen to be* [or even "makes a display of"] reaching out to touch the body of the boy." It sounds, in other words, as if there were spectators.

An archaeologicable ceremony also means of course that once the boy was Boy no longer, the cloak could come off, and Spartans could enjoy, like other Greeks, the pleasures of the flesh. For Spartan *erastai* were surely no more permanently prevented from touching than Athenian *erastai* were permanently prevented from "conversing with" their boyfriends.

But if this sex with cloaks on was a necessary part of the ceremony of wedding, if a wedding was necessary for a legally recognized relationship, and if a relationship was necessary for certain men, that would also mean that some kind of rolling about with a boy wrapped up like a present was also necessary for certain men who wished to retain their status. If that was the case, I would be surprised if a bit of friction would be enough. There really ought to have been some kind of climax to the friction. I will leave it at that, except to say that one might hope at least that, once the ceremony was over, Spartan *erastai,* like Cretan *erastai,* gave their newly wedded *erōmenoi* something to wear afterward.

I have certainly deployed a lot of ifs, and it may seem extravagant to reconstruct such a bizarre sexual act from two lines of Cicero and a little piece of pot from a city some distance away, but it is far more extravagant simply to delete from the corpus of evidence the most primary primary source for Spartan Homosexuality, Xenophon; that is moving the goalposts. Cicero was telling what he thought was the truth, and we need to go with him and take him seriously, if only because he explains so much and because it is so hard to imagine such a man inventing it. He thought he was just repeating what everybody knew. It would not be the first time that it was an Italian who gave away a secret about what had been happening in Greece.

Perhaps what is most obvious and striking about Spartan Homosex as

Cicero describes it is the way it takes the asymmetry between *erastēs* and *erōmenos* to the extreme: The boy really would be coolly gazing on his lust-drunk admirer, not just frigid but frigidized. It is hard to imagine a more solipsistic sexual experience, or a more sublime communion with Eros, the utterly one-sided Greek Love.

And we need to recall two further things. First, that as in Crete and in the Sacred Band, these weddings, whatever they were, need not have been very frequent at all. If it was only the three hundred "Knights" who made such formal compulsory alliances, perhaps Spartan Homosexuality consisted of thirty sexual acts per year (perhaps even mass homosexual weddings, like the mass marriages to girls). For, second, these weddings would by no means be identical with Spartan same-sex loves or same-sex sex. Ceremonial Spartan Homosexuality in its spectacular, official and bizarre, that is in its archaeologicable form, would not have been the same as everyday homosexuality in Sparta.

But where did all this take place? And what would you call such a sexual act, with cloak intervening? Could you call it "having sex with" or "screwing"?

Theocritus refers to the term *eispnēlas* as "Amyclaean," and the only representation of the sexual practice seems to portray Hyacinthus of Amyclae. Were the gods or heroes also invoked in this wedding, as witnesses to pledges, for instance? That would seem highly plausible. Did they wed in church, so to speak, at Amyclae? Did they consummate even in a sanctuary? Precisely such a thing has been suggested for another community of southern Dorians: the boys of Thera on the island of Santorini, which is basically the remains of the vertical walls of the crater of the volcano that exploded in the second millennium BC.[113] And here sex becomes highly archaeologicable, for high on the rocky and spectacular southeastern promontory there are inscriptions, cut into the mountain itself in big deep letters, and judging from the letter forms, some of them are among the oldest inscriptions from Greece.[114] Most of them are certainly archaic and some may date from well back into the seventh century BC, beginning not long after the foundation of the community, which was probably in the eighth century BC and, according to legend, from Sparta, a story confirmed by the existence of Spartan cults, such as Karneios, and political institutions on the island.[115] The promontory seems to have been a sacred area for sacrifices to several divinities, but above all to Apollo, who eventually had a temple built for him, about 50 meters away. There was also a gymnasium and a dancing ground.

The inscriptions are often just isolated names, but some are in praise of the carver and others as "good dancer," "best dancer," "good" (*agathos*), "first" or even "very first," which may be references to dancing in the front line. Someone also wished to record the fact that so-and-so "is in love with [*eratai*] Phanocles."[116] Despite the awesome and sacred setting some of the graffiti sound very rude. The important word is *oiphei,*[117] the same word when joined with "by force" that is used to indicate rape of male or female in the Gortyn law code, but *oiphei* does not seem to need an object. It is not necessarily something you do to someone but something you can just do. In fact three people can do it at the same time. "Crimon *oiphed* Amotion," "Euponos *oiphed,*" "Pheidippidas *oiphed*. Timagoras, Empheres and I, we *oiphed*." The most famous concerns one Crimon: "Yes, by [Apollo] Delphinios, Crimon here *oiphed* [so-and-so . . .] son of Bathycles, brother."[118] Nothing would be less surprising than to discover that the people of Thera imported Spartan Homosexuality, sex in cloaks, along with other Spartan institutions. Perhaps then the best translation is "to spunk": "We spunked," "I spunked the son of Bathycles." And it really does look as if this activity happened right here, on the rocks, a stone's throw from the altar of Apollo, and that it was recorded and the god Apollo Delphinios was called to witness it, or rather to assure the reader that the statements written in stone were also true.[119] It was indeed an initiation, but it was an initiation not necessarily into a new age-grade, but into a relationship, as seemed quite obvious to the scholars who first wrote about the inscriptions at the turn of the last century: "marriage before divine witnesses."[120]

But what about that mysterious "brother" in Crimon's inscription? It is very unusual to describe someone as someone else's brother, when you are chiseling into solid rock you need to be especially economical, and there is no sign of any name after the word "brother." You cannot simply take texts you don't like and add things to them until they mean what you want them to mean. As it stands it can only mean "his brother," "Crimon's brother," not a reference to homosexual incest but the name Crimon uses to describe the son of Bathycles he had "*oiphed* here." Once again we need to read Xenophon most carefully: "Lycurgus made it that in Sparta *erastai* keep from favorites [*paidika*] no less than parents from children and brothers from brothers as regards sex [*eis aphrodisia*]." Once again, it seems, he is using an archaeologicable fact about a Spartan institution, that wedded boyfriends called each other "brother," to argue for the nonlascivious character of those relationships, at least in the intention of the lawgiver. For how else can a lawgiver make a relationship like brothers unless by making a relationship of "brothers?" And that would be most interesting, because it would mean that Spartan same-sex pairs did not model themselves on Zephyrus and Hyacinthus necessarily, nor on the loves of Achilles, who also enjoyed cult in Sparta, but on the brothers of Helen, the devoted twins Castor and Pollux, stellified as Gemini. And what Xenophon was afraid others might think is nicely illustrated by some visitors to the rocks of Thera several centuries later. Instead of praising and celebrating they wrote "Whore," "*Kinaidos.*"[121]

POLITICS AND SPARTAN HOMOSEXUALITY

The fact that Spartan warriors in their Twenties still had their shopping done for them by their *erastai* certainly implies, as in Crete, that the relationships established had consequences well into adulthood. And, again, it certainly was not *all* about sex, nor even all about war, even in Sparta. Indeed Suda, the Byzantine encyclopedia, translates the Spartan word for *erōmenos—aeitēs—*"companion" (*hetairos*).[122] It has long been recognized that these amatory and sexual relationships played an important role in Spartan society and politics and foreign policy. Indeed homosexual relationships seem to play a crucial role in most of the major turning points in Spartan history.[123]

1. "KILL THE MESSENGER"

Sparta first came to great-power status at the end of the archaic period when Athens was really nothing more than a minor power with an important ceramic export industry. Under the leadership of the Agiad king Cleomenes, the Spartans started intervening in the politics of other states, which meant that when the Persians invaded to put an end to the

archaic period and to inaugurate the classical in 480, Sparta had no serious rival to the claim of leadership of the Greek resistance. The Spartans
earned enormous credit for their brave stand under Cleomenes' brother
and successor Leonidas at Thermopylae in northern Greece, and eventually in 479 for their success in the great land battle at Plataea in Boeotia,
just over the border from Attica, which sent the Persians scurrying out
of mainland Greece forever. The man who took credit for this remarkable all-Greek victory was Pausanias the regent, who kept the Agiad
throne warm for Pleistarchus, Leonidas's young son. He even went so
far as to put his own name on the dedication of a victory tripod commemorating Plataea. The Spartans scratched it off and replaced it with a
list of all the Greeks who had contributed, which was wise.

Within a few months, however, Pausanias squandered all the credit
Sparta had earned and allowed Athens to take over the continuing fight
to liberate the Greeks of Asia Minor. The problem was that Spartan
kings—there were two of them at any one time—were not very kingly,
more like "generals-for-life." Seeing what proper kings looked like, not
least the King of Kings, Xerxes, Pausanias thought he could strengthen
his regency and began to behave more monarchically. He started to wear
expensive Persian clothes, enlisted an escort of Egyptians and Persians,
cut himself off, shockingly, from ordinary access, and began to hold lavish banquets in the Persian manner.[124] This last was especially alarming.
The Persian "King's Dinner" was notorious throughout Greece, since it
seems that part of the Persian tribute had been presented as presents for
his table. One such dinner had nearly ruined the rich city of Thasos. The
Greeks of Asia Minor did not like the idea of exchanging a Persian king
for a Spartan king in Persian clothing, and preferred the newly democratic Athenians instead, little realizing that democracies too can put on
airs and graces and generally behave in a dictatorial manner. Reports of
what the regent was up to reached Sparta, and Pausanias was recalled to
face various charges and to be reminded by the fact of being recalled that
Spartan kings were not so very kingly after all.[125]

Moreover, the Greeks were archaeologists of people as they were archaeologists of peoples and of the past. Someone who looked like a Persian obviously had a Persian side to him, and indeed it was suspected that
Pausanias's liking for Persian stuff reflected treachery and intrigue with
the Persian side, that he was working with the king of Persia so that he

might become with his assistance king of Greece. Nevertheless Pausanias obeyed the order to return home to face charges. There was not yet enough hard evidence against him and he was acquitted, but relieved of his command. It was difficult, however, for a man credited with saving Greece in her time of greatest danger to stay at home, so Pausanias mounted his own expedition, says Thucydides, and sailed to where all the fighting was, hoping to make some contribution. The Spartan ephors recalled him once more, and when he returned threw him in prison; jailing kings was one of their special powers.

But all they had against him even now was his dress sense. Pausanias somehow got himself out of prison and offered to answer any questions, confident that there would be no evidence against him. Nor would there have been had he treated his boyfriend better. For now a man of Argilos, an important city way up north near the Chalcidice, came forward with information. He had once been Pausanias's beloved (*paidika*) and was now the man he trusted most (*pistotatos*).[126] He had indeed been involved in secret negotiations with the king of Persia, and in particular he had been entrusted with the last letter Pausanias had written to the king. However, he had noticed that the servants Pausanias usually sent out with his secret correspondence never came back, so he made a copy of Pausanias's seal, opened the letter and saw at the bottom "P.S. Kill the messenger." Feeling terribly betrayed, he handed the letter over to the ephors. Still they didn't feel that this treacherous letter with the sender's own seal was enough evidence to move against the regent, so they got the former *erōmenos* to go down to the temple of Poseidon at the tip of the Mani promontory and seek sanctuary there. This was another of those seaside places that gave access to the Underworld. Indeed it was here that Heracles had emerged from Hades with Cerberus, the three-headed hound of Hell.

When Pausanias was informed he wondered what the matter was and went to see his messenger and current confidant in the sanctuary. His former favorite accused him of betrayal. In all the negotiations he had always been faithful, and now Pausanias had repaid his loyalty by treating him like one of his servants. Pausanias confessed, asked the man not to be angry, pledged his safety and asked him to make haste and close the deal.[127] All this time the ephors were listening, hidden behind a partition. They did nothing. Pausanias returned to Sparta. But soon after that he saw the ephors approaching. One of them may have tipped him the wink. Knowing his time had run out, he fled to the temple of Athena of the Bronze House and made a home for himself there. The ephors sealed the doors and took the roof off and watched him slowly dying. When he seemed on the point of death they removed him so as not to pollute the shrine. They were in the nick of time. As soon as they got him outside he breathed his last. Or perhaps they came too late, for subsequently a curse fell upon Sparta, and they had to make expiations and offer Pausanias heroic honors along with his uncle Leonidas.[128]

This account comes from the usually impeccable Thucydides, but it is a very odd story for him, expressed in unusual language and style, and one might well suspect that even Thucydides has been misled by an odd artifact at Taenarum, say, or Argilos or the temple of Athena of the Bronze House at first-, second- or thirdhand. Perhaps the most intriguing possibility, since Taenarum contained an oracle of the dead, is that the regent's former favorite had indeed delivered the letter and been killed, and that the ephors overheard Pausanias talking to his victim's ghost, his boyfriend denouncing him from beyond the grave.[129]

What counts for our purposes, however, is the picture of Spartan Homosexuality that Thucydides found quite plausible: a former *paidika,* now transformed into an intimate confidant of the most dangerous secrets, only betraying his trust when his own is betrayed. It is also interesting that he thought Pausanias could have formed an attachment with someone so far away from home, someone he presumably met while on an expedition fighting against the Persians.

2. PUTTING AN EX ON THE THRONE

We move forward to the end of the century. Sparta was knocked off her perch and suffered the earthquake that killed the ephebes who were not stripped down for exercise and were buried in the gymnasium. That set the helots off, and then there was the uncomfortable experience of watching lowly Athens rise to become one of the most glorious, rich and powerful cities in Greece. But now, after a long struggle with Athens, Sparta was entering what looked like a second period of even greater preeminence.

In the spring of 400 BC, while Sparta still basked in its recent defeat of

Athens, one of the Spartan kings died, this time not an Agiad but a Eurypontid. He had a son, but it was widely believed that the boy's mother
had ventured into Spartan polyandry and that his real father was none
other than Alcibiades of Athens, who had lived in Sparta when Athens
threw him out after the Hermes-bashing scandal. Apparently there had
once been another tremor while this interesting and useful Athenian
exile was resident in Sparta, and as people ran out in their night clothes
it was noticed that Alcibiades ran out of the wrong bedroom, the king's
wife's. When she got pregnant later, people did their calculations and
discovered that the earthquake must have coincided with the child's conception. A later version of the story is more amusing. It was the king
himself who was having sex when the earth moved. He was so terrified
that he refused to sleep with his wife for a whole year, a period during
which she managed to get pregnant, "perhaps the greatest domestic
scandal of all Spartan history."[130]

At any rate, for those who believed that the heir to the throne was illegitimate, there was another candidate, the dead king's younger brother
Agesilaus, now pushing forty-five. But Agesilaus was short and lame,
and someone produced an oracle that spoke darkly of "sure-footed
Sparta" and the dangers of a "lame kingship." No, no, a lame-footed
kingship means a bastard kingship, said one of Agesilaus's supporters,
and quickly got to the point: a bastard kingship . . . like that of the heir
apparent!

The speaker was not any old Spartan, however, heckling from the
back row. This was none other than Lysander himself, Sparta's Welling-
ton, the general responsible for conquering Athens's dreadful pride, a
Machiavellian character who just three years earlier had had the fore-
sight to have Alcibiades, the other candidate's alleged father, the man
who might settle the issue of legitimacy, murdered.

People listened to Lysander. Agesilaus took the crown. Now, according to Plutarch, who had done some research into Agesilaus, the relationship between the prince and the general went back a very long
way.[131] Lysander was a *mothax,* which meant he had to be sponsored by
another family to get through the system, i.e., he was poor. But he had
worked hard to overcome any disadvantages, and rose to the top of
Spartan society. He started early, it seems, by becoming *eispnelas* of the
king's short lame younger son, Agesilaus (*erastēs tou Agēsilaou gegonōs*).[132]

Of course he could never have imagined that he might actually be able to put his former boyfriend on the throne, but for someone like Lysander a prince was a notable catch by any standard: "That Lysander was in a position to woo and win the most eligible boy of his age-group argues powerful character and powerful contacts, which is what we would expect from the evidence of his career after 408."[133] But perhaps in so body-fascistic a society as Sparta, in which men had to strip off for physique inspections each decade of the moon, and where short lame Agesilaus had been demoted from front row to back of the boy band in case he gave Spartan boys a bad reputation, perhaps the talented Lysander was not such a bad catch either. And there must have been luck in it too: Agesilaus reaching the right age for being someone's boyfriend as Lysander reached the age for thinking he should have one.

The *homoerōtikos* relationship between himself and Lysander was believed to have secured Agesilaus the throne, but if Lysander expected to pull the new king's strings, he was soon less deceived. The first move Agesilaus made was to undo the power network that Lysander had spun for himself around the Mediterranean when he had conquered each of Athens's allies and replaced their governments with ten-man juntas.[134] And Plutarch, for one, thought that the shenanigans between these two former lovers—and they probably were "lovers" in this case, once, at least—were what led to Sparta's subsequent decline. For Sparta was about to throw it all away again, and again it was same-sex loving that was to blame, not on the part of Agesilaus, this time, but his son and heir.

3. TEARS FOR FATHER

King Agesilaus was still on the throne some twenty years later, when Sparta sent ambassadors to Athens for some delicate negotiations. It was another tense moment in history. Suddenly and unprecedentedly Sparta's dominance on land in Greece was being seriously threatened by friendly relations between Athens and Thebes, traditional enemies, an alliance that Sparta must scupper forthwith. This was the task of the ambassadors. One of them was a friend of Agesilaus, and it looks as if the embassy was on the king's initiative. Unfortunately, at that very critical moment for international diplomacy, something very undiplomatic occurred. A Spartan general called Sphodrias staged an unprovoked attack, aiming to capture Athens's port, Piraeus. The Athenians were furious. They arrested the Spartan ambassadors, eventually releasing them, but only on condition that the Spartan general who had violated the territory of another nation would be tried and punished.

Sparta did put their general on trial, as the Athenians insisted, but the defendant didn't turn up. Surely the verdict must go against him. No, the absent general was acquitted, to the chagrin of the Athenians whose sole reason for freeing the Spartan ambassadors had been the promise of a proper trial. Their good faith had been shockingly betrayed. The nontrial of the general Sphodrias went down in history: "And it seemed to many that the decision in this case was the most unjust ever known in Lacedaemon." It also crippled the whole of Sparta's and in particular Agesilaus's foreign policy strategy for the next few critical decades. Why on earth did the Spartans do such an idiotic thing? Xenophon supplies the "cause" (aition).[135]

Sphodrias had close ties with one of the two Spartan kings, the "superior" Agiad king from the line of Cleomenes, Leonidas and Pausanias the regent, but he needed the votes of Agesilaus, the Eurypontid king, to ensure acquittal. His son Cleonymus, Eighteen, had just graduated from the ranks of the Boys and was something of a star—in Xenophon's words, "the most beautiful and the most esteemed of all his age-class." He probably had plenty of admirers, but he used his charms to strengthen his father's support, having cleverly made an alliance with the son of Agesilaus, Archidamus, then about Twenty-two years old. Xenophon, who completely ignores the fact that Athens was at this very moment reconstructing a naval alliance against Sparta in the face of Spartan aggression, spends pages on this sentimental episode in the politics of Spartan Homosexuality.

Cleonymus paid a visit to his admirer, Prince Archidamus, son of the swing voter who might decide his father's fate, and there this boy, the most esteemed of his graduation class, bravest, toughest, finest figure of a man, broke down in tears, says Xenophon. Archidamus was moved by this combination of the athletic and the pathetic and promised to talk to his father. Of course, he didn't abuse his position, says Xenophon, the apologist. He waited until he saw Agesilaus emerge from the house in the morning and took his place with all the other pe-

titioners, even foreigners and servants; it took him days even to broach
the subject.

Meanwhile Archidamus had stopped hanging out with his boyfriend.
Sphodrias's supporters noticed the absence of the prince and were getting worried. Finally one of them bumped into one of the friends of
King Agesilaus. "I suppose Agesilaus and his friends will vote to condemn," he said. "Not if we follow Agesilaus," was the reply. The general was in the clear. Agesilaus's votes were decisive. Cleonymus went to
thank his lover: "Now we know that you really care for us . . . we too
will try to make sure you are never ashamed of our love [*philia*]." The
acquittal was such a disaster for Sparta that it wasn't too long before
Cleonymus had the chance to keep his promise. Following the miscar-
riage of justice, Athens helped Thebes become a formidable new power.
Thebes took on Sparta at the battle of Leuctra in 371 BC and inflicted a
great defeat. Sparta's legendary invincibility was at an end. Cleonymus,
now about Twenty-five years old, was one of those who died in the
slaughter. He died well. Archidamus grieved, nevertheless.[136]

What is so extraordinary about this unique digression is that
Xenophon obviously thinks he is putting a positive spin on a case of injustice and betrayal. Instead of compounding the corruption, he seems
to think that *erōs* excuses it. Archidamus had no choice, it seems. It was
honorable for him to ask his father for a favor on behalf of his boyfriend.
This entanglement of conspiracy, nepotism and corruption with *erōs* is a
common feature of Greek Love. It crops up again in Athens a couple of
decades later in the trial of Timarchus, when a "general" defends the accused politician against the accusation of political corruption and mercenary relationships with a speech about the glories of boyfriends,
Achilles and Patroclus, Harmodius and Aristogiton, etc. *Erōs* is the opposite of corruption. It is uncalculating, blinding, altruistic Love.

Spartan Homosexuality obviously has something institutional about
it, but far from being a formality, it is the informality of these *erōtikos* affairs that stands out in a society full of automatic socializing. We
shouldn't think of these relationships as *only* political. It was just that
they might come in useful politically, not just for the individuals concerned but for their fathers and families. You couldn't just go through
the motions when you made an alliance with another male, as the law
required: it had to be proper, passionate, devoted, impervious to reason.
Sentimentality was just as much of a necessity as sex.

4. THE PERSIAN BOY

Agesilaus even uses this characteristically Greek relationship as a tool of foreign policy. Immediately after the defeat of Athens, when Sparta still aspired to the role of Liberator and Agesilaus had secured the throne, he had crossed over the Aegean Sea and was making hay in the sunshine of Sparta's renaissance, as well as wreaking havoc, in the Persian domains of Turkey. His "friend" Lysander was still on the scene, still pumped up with the glory of his great victory, still hoping to pull some strings. And Lysander had discovered that one very distinguished Persian, Spithridates, felt he had been insulted by the satrap Pharnabazus, who had had the gall to ask him for one of his daughters to use as a concubine while he arranged a proper marriage with the daughter of the Great King (of Persia) himself. Lysander persuaded Spithridates to get his family and his movable property together along with two hundred cavalry and come over to the other side. He then took this new ally on a journey so as to introduce him to his king and former beloved Agesilaus—a gift for an old friend.

For Spithridates had a son, Megabates, a "beautiful Young Man" (*kalos, neos*) says a history found on a papyrus in Egypt, "extremely beautiful," *kallistos,* says Xenophon, who knew Agesilaus better than anyone whose writings survive, though not perhaps quite as well as he claims. Says Xenophon: "Agesilaus was very pleased with what Lysander had done" and immediately started to interrogate Spithridates. "He took them up because of the boy," says the papyrus, "it is said he was extremely infatuated with him. Spithridates [was a secondary consideration], yet . . ." It is significant that Xenophon chooses this apparently notorious affair between a Spartan king and a Persian boy to prove Agesilaus's phenomenal powers of self-control. Once again Xenophon has a case to make. Once again he omits the preamble—"Although what follows looks bad and everybody says there was something of a scandal, in truth it was quite the opposite." We see now the point of the superlative: To any normal man, Megabates was irresistible. On one occasion he attempted to plant a kiss on the king—a Persian way of showing honor, Xenophon explains—but Agesilaus through a massive effort of will resists the advance. Megabates is deeply offended—the family is touchy about honor—and there are negotiations to get the boy to kiss him again. The sticking point is Agesilaus's refusal to promise to kiss him in return. After another insult, when father and son are relieved of some booty they think by rights is theirs, they pack their bags and leave. Agesilaus is tremendously upset.[137] A kiss in public between a Spartan king and a Persian Young Man would be a highly political gesture. Agesilaus would be taking on a role that would involve loyalty and favors for the foreigner. Sometime later a more famous king and general, Alexander the Great, would do the very opposite, and show favor to a Persian by kissing him not once but twice in public.

In his efforts to prove Agesilaus's chasteness, however, Xenophon reveals that more than a kiss might be at stake, even the prospect of sex with the Twenty-something Persian boy. For Agesilaus went to extreme lengths, apparently, to avoid suspicion, even sleeping in the open. Evidently even Spartans would make assumptions about what Agesilaus might get up to at night with Megabates if the couple were left together behind closed doors.

A little later Agesilaus tries to land an even bigger fish, Pharnabazus himself, Spithridates' bitter enemy, and a useful ally when Sparta and Persia fought together against Athens. It was he who had had fugitive Alcibiades murdered at Lysander's request.[138] There is an international conference. Agesilaus and the Spartans are lying on the grass. Grand old Pharnabazus approaches, luxuriously dressed, and servants start spreading out the kind of soft rugs on which the Persians sit. Seeing the Spartan austerity, says Xenophon, the satrap dispenses with the carpets and sits on the grass. But Pharnabazus is far too close to the Persian king to betray him, unless of course he finds himself insulted in the future. He is more interested in complaining about all the burning and looting and ravaging, the destruction of his lovely parks and palaces by the Spartan army. The conference ends. Pharnabazus rides off. His son, however, "still handsome," stays behind. "Agesilaus, I should like you to become my friend [xenos]." "And I am happy to be your friend." "Remember, now," says the boy and gives Agesilaus a javelin. Agesilaus gives him a magnificent horse-trapping—not his own but his secretary's, adds Xenophon quickly, always eager to forestall accusations of luxury. And Agesilaus did remember, because he left the territory of Pharnabazus, and when the boy was later driven off his lands by his brother, he was in a position to help him. In particular, he tried to get the boy's Athenian boyfriend into the stadion, the oldest race at Olympia. He was technically a boy, but big for his age. In fact he was "the biggest of the boys," says Xenophon.[139]

As in Crete, Spartan love affairs stand outside the System, a personal relationship between one individual and another, recognized but voluntary, entered into with someone you chose. This was a "made intimacy," not one you inherited thanks to your familial or tribal connections, or your class or age-set. And in Crete, at least, the whole business of choosing was emphasized most elaborately. And yet all these relationships seem to have been extremely useful and convenient. Although Agesilaus's relationship with Pharnabazus's son was not "*erōtik*"—a *xenos* remains an "away friend"—there is a nice parallel with the relationship between Archidamus and Cleonymus. The sons' relationships supplement their fathers', providing a kind of insurance, without compromising their fathers' loyalty to other kings. As in Crete, Spartan *erōs* enabled cross-links to be established between the otherwise monolithic blocks of Spartan society: the son of a member of one faction and the son of the leader of another; boys of high status and men of lower status but distinguished; gentlemen and boys who were not gentlemen; between one gang, one mess, one age-class and another; a short lame prince and an ambitious aristocrat fallen on hard times, a regent plotting to make himself king of Greece and a most trusted go-between. Love was love, but it was also a social and political, geopolitical glue. Indeed what made Love so functional was precisely, it seems, its dysfunctionality. For what could be more objectively practical than the hyperbolic subjectivity of a hopeless devotion? What could be more calculating than utter and total besottedness?

THE SECRETS OF ELIS, THE SACRED BAND
AND ALEXANDER: REGIONAL VARIATIONS

It has been worthwhile to linger with the southern Dorians because they were believed—by, for instance, Timaeus (fragment 144), Aristotle (*Politics* 1272a) and Plato (*Laws* 636ab)—to have been founders and originators of Greek Homosexuality and because we have some startling pieces of evidence about the way those relationships were formed and how they operated. We are much less well-informed about how things happened among the soldierly same-sex lovers of other nations, but we can use what we have learned or deduced from Crete and Sparta to supply some of the missing details. Nonetheless, it is clear that Greek Love varied considerably from place to place—sometimes they even seem to be *trying* to be different—and there remain some intriguing mysteries. In particular, what was so appalling about the practices of the Eleans who ran the Olympic Games? How could there be an army like the Theban one, entirely composed of *erastai* and *erōmenoi*? Or is it just a myth? Why were so many kings of Macedonia assassinated by former boyfriends? What was Alexander up to with his beloved Hephaestion?

I

UNSPEAKABLE ACTS

But there are some other mysteries that are not tied to any specific polis, and not least among these is a unique scene of homosexual sex painted on a vase, a wine bowl in the British Museum, in its own way just as extraordinary as the inscriptions from Santorini. It is dated to round about 430 BC. On one side, three modestly dressed boys wrapped up in cloaks and with thin woolen headbands are deep in conversation. One of them is gesturing. An oil bottle suspended indicates that this is a gymnasium. On the other side, a beardless youth sits on a bent-legged chair with his feet on a platform. His draperies are open and he has an erection. Another youth, completely naked, holds what looks like a spear. He holds it by the very point and is using it as a prop to lever himself onto the ready lap of the other.

A pillar painted white separates the couple from an older man with a beard who seems to be waiting. Behind him a woman looks on from behind a door, the top half of which is open. All the male figures have elaborate headgear: The two boys about to have sex are wearing crowns, the older man has a long thick piece of material tied around his head, arranged in two loops at the sides and then hanging down. The great connoisseur of Greek vases John Beazley referred to it, apparently, as

33. Two crowned ephebes are about to engage in an unusual sexual act in a marble-columned interior, while a man with a festival headdress listens, and a woman leans on the sill of a half-door. There are some inscriptions, one of them representing a public inscription, but all now sadly illegible. On the other side, three well-wrapped ephebes wearing headbands converse in a gymnasium with an oil bottle suspended on the wall. Bell krater by the Dinos Painter (c.430).

"Life in the Socratic Circle." It sounds as if he was joking, but some jokes tell the truth.[1]

SILENCE AND THE ELEANS

Elis may not be as famous a polity as Sparta, Athens and Thebes, but situated in the northwest segment of the Peloponnese between eight and ten o'clock, it was one of the largest, wealthiest and most successful of the Greek communities, one of the last to develop a metropolitan urban center, but with very ancient settlements going well back into the second millennium BC. It occupied some of the best land in Greece, although its position laid it open to attack and there seems to have been a long period of depopulation in the early first millennium BC.[2]

It was at Olympia in the bosky hinterland of Elis, and only there, that statues of Ganymede are known to have stood in the fifth century, next to the altar of Zeus, including that statue pieced together by the Germans at the end of the Second World War, where Ganymede, holding a love gift, a cockerel, is carried off under the arm of the highest god. It was here that Pindar translated the boiling and eating of Olympia's great hero Pelops into a *homoerōtikos* abduction by Poseidon, and here too that young Laius had forced Pelops's even younger son Chrysippus into his chariot, so offending Hera, goddess of marriage, and leading him to produce a son who was far too precociously fertile for his own good.

There was no Athenian complexity of manners, no "contest" of "pursuit" and "flight" involved in Elean Homosexuality, says Pausanias in Plato's *Symposium*. Outside Athens the custom is easy (*rhadiōs*), the "lines are drawn in a straightforward fashion" (*haplōs*):

> In Elis and Boeotia and where they aren't clever [*sophos*] at talking, it is laid out straightforwardly by law that it is beautiful [*kalon*] to graciously favor [*charizesthai*] and no one, neither a young man nor an old man, would say it was shameful, in order that they don't have to go to the trouble, I think, of making an attempt to persuade [*peirōmenoi peithein*] young men [*neous*], because they don't have the capacity to talk [*adunatoi legein*].

Xenophon, a bitter enemy, who had owned an estate not far from Olympia, was equally appalled. The customs of Elis are the complete opposite of Spartan customs, where it is shameful to be seen to reach out to touch the body of a boy: "The men of Elis make intimate use of the seasonal bloom [*hōra*] through gracious favoring [*dia charitōn*]." Elsewhere Xenophon attacks the men-together-against-the-world speech of Phaedrus in *Symposium*.[3] This man had vaunted the notion of armies of lovers, claims Xenophon, and he had cited as proof the men of Elis (and Thebes) who slept with boyfriends and then stood them beside them in the battle line. But what they do in those places may be "customary for them, but for us [Athenians] it is something utterly reprehensible."

Whatever the Eleans got up to they were still doing it in the first century BC. "I will pass over the Eleans and Thebans," says Cicero, "among whom, in their love affairs with free-born citizens, even lust [*libido*] has a license, both sanctioned and without restriction." Even in the second century AD it is still spoken of in the present tense: "I censure the Elean custom, for its license . . . I don't speak about the things of the Eleans . . . ," says Maximus of Tyre, who thought the Thebans weren't quite so bad.[4] Sometimes you wish the sources had been a little less discreet. Where is the Greek Ezekiel to denounce the Eleans in full technicolor detail? Because of all these decorous omissions it may be too late now to recover anything of these dreadful Elean boys, who were once so infamous. But I will do my best. We should notice one thing, at least: that the inability to speak that characterizes Elean Homosexuality according to Pausanias in *Symposium* seems to have infected Maximus and Cicero too.

Most straightforwardly, we can infer that the Eleans maintained an elite battalion, two of them indeed, one of four hundred and one of three hundred. This latter was probably organized like the Theban Sacred Band (*Hieros Lochos*) of three hundred, with each member formally wedded to another man, perhaps in the same battalion, a hundred and fifty pairs, "sleeping together" in Xenophon's words. So in Elis, according to Xenophon, they had a battalion composed like the famous Sacred Band, a Boyfriend-Band.[5] Perhaps that is all there is behind the rumors: an Elean army of lovers with unorthodox sleeping arrangements. Because the men of Elis (and Thebes) did not segregate soldiers who might love each other, the rest of the Greeks fantasized about what might go on in those deviant encampments.

PHAEDO WAITS FOR CLIENTS

But I think the sources so scandalized by the customs of the people who ran the Olympics are offended by more than grown men having sex with each other. When Socrates discusses his gay couple in *Phaedrus,* he assumes that *they do indeed have sex*—"the two of them coming together and making that choice which the multitude think of as most blessed [*makaristēn*] and going all the way [*diepraxasthēn*] and having gone all the way continue with the practice, but sparingly, because what they decide to do is not done with the consent of the entirety of their thoughtful mind." Yet this couple, though not as good as the philosophically minded chaste couple, will nevertheless end up walking not in the Underworld but on the shining path, while waiting for wings to fly back to the outer heavens.[6] Cicero on the other hand insists that Greek Love in Elis included some kind of "lust" having "license," "*sanctioned.*" And while in the *Symposium* Pausanias maintains that in Elis it was *kalon,* beautiful, noble and in no sense shameful to graciously favor admirers, Xenophon insists that what in Athens was most reprehensible was "customary" there.

These references to *nomos,* custom or law, in Plato's and Xenophon's accounts of Elean Homosexuality, to "license sanctioned" in Cicero's, should be taken seriously. We are talking of something formal and "legislated," another archaeologicable institution. What kind of utterly reprehensible sexual transaction is easy and straightforward? Let me think . . .

While I am thinking let me introduce you to one more bad boy from Elis. Phaedo gave his name to another of the most famous of Plato's dialogues. The *Phaedo* is an account of Socrates' very last hours in jail. It reflects on the lesser status of the mere mortal body and the immortality of the wonderful soul. Of course such a belief is not irrelevant to Socrates' circumstances, and at the end of the conversation the poison, the hemlock, gradually numbs his extremities until it smothers his life and he can say nothing at all. All in all this not entirely tasteful description of Socrates dying has moved and provoked a large number of people very profoundly. But one thing they tend to ignore in their discussions is the long-standing public rumors about this Phaedo with whom Socrates shares those last hours on Earth talking of immortality. Phaedo is a male prostitute. Later writers, especially early Christians, saw him as a kind of Mary Magdalene character, a reformed call girl of *c*.400 BC.

Phaedo had been a member of the old noble families (*eupatridai*) of Elis, we hear. He was captured in war, a "spear-point captive," and "forced to station himself in a cubicle" (*stēnai ep'oikēmatos*), "sitting in a cubicle," but "closing the little door he got involved with Socrates instead" (*meteiche Sōkratous*), who got his friends to pay to free him. There are even more bizarre elaborations. Phaedo was captured by "Indians" says one! He was sold to a pimp who placed him in Athens for prostitution. Socrates "took him from the cubicle and converted him to philosophy"; "he transferred him from the brothel [*lupanari*] where he served the lust of many because of the cruelty and greediness of his master" etc. And yet this man was considered worthy to star in Plato's dialogue on the soul! Few modern commentators accept this version of the biography of Phaedo of Elis.[7] Like Xenophon's remarks on Spartan men not reaching out to touch a boy's body, so Phaedo's life as a whore has simply been deleted.

The story is not impossible. Greek cities often went to war with one another. Once they had captured another Greek city they might indeed exceptionally sell the inhabitants into slavery. Pimps might buy them. They might end up in a brothel. Theoretically. But if so, we hear very little about them. There were not large numbers of Greeks working openly and recognizably as slaves in Athens. Greeks generally assumed that slaves were foreigners with thick accents, and that any Greeks you came across were free. I cannot think of another example to compare with this Phaedo, a man from the top echelon of a famous Greek city working in the great Greek city of Athens, not only as a slave but as a prostitute, not even a high-class male escort working under contract, but the kind who sits in a cubicle. Why, moreover, would Plato have made such a statement, giving pride of place to a male prostitute in a dialogue about the immortal soul?

When you look at the story, cracks appear. The sources for the tale are very late. No one knows when and where Phaedo was taken prisoner, nor by which city. No one knows who freed him. Sometimes it is Alcibiades, or Alcibiades' party, or Crito's, or Cebes. And did Socrates really visit male prostitutes in order to talk philosophy? Why?

On the other hand what we do know about Phaedo is that he was a proper Socratic philosopher of the early fourth century, who actually founded a school of philosophy known as the School of Elis. After Socrates' death he wrote some of the very first Socratic dialogues. One or two fragments survive. Also there seems to have been a bit of tension between upstart Plato and Phaedo, both of them claiming the laurels of Socrates, Phaedo with an a priori superior claim. Plato, who was thought by later writers to be a malicious man, was said to have charged Phaedo, the aristocrat of wealthy Elis, with being a slave. Phaedo for his part claimed that Plato's docufictional *Phaedo* was all lies; the last moments of Socrates were nothing like that. So perhaps what happened is that the whole sordid story is simply derived from an accusation, made at a time of fierce rivalry over the inheritance of Socrates, that Phaedo had been a slave or slavish. From that, the rumors spread of their own accord, about what kind of work a male slave might be involved in, ending with a neat inversion of the charge on which Socrates was condemned. Instead of corrupting the youth, he was rescuing a youth from a life of prostitution!

There are certainly signs of tension between Plato and the Eleans detectable in Plato. It is extremely provocative, for instance, for Plato to write that the men of Elis are not "clever [*sophoi*] at speaking," "incapable of discourse" (*legein*), at a time when one particular man of Elis had been publishing philosophical discourses with Socrates. And when Plato goes on to argue that this inarticulacy is a cause of the fact that boys of Elis are, so to speak, "easy," it is pointed in the extreme. What I suggest is that the strange story of Phaedo of Elis "serving the lust [*libido*] of many men," which some writers also make a play of refusing to talk about—"I will not say it," says Julian—is a reflection of the licensed lust of Elean homosexual custom that authors also love not to talk about. The straightforward utterly reprehensible homosexuality customary in Elis could be compared to male prostitution, perhaps because it involved some ritual in which boys sat in cubicles and waited for visitors. Or a visitor.

BUGGERY IS BEAUTIFUL

The Eleans were consistently the worst of the worse, but the Boeotians, and especially the men of the great Boeotian city of Thebes, ran them a close second. "Among other Greeks, among the Boeotians, for example, a man and a boy associate together once they have been conjugally yoked [*suzugentes homilousi*]."[8] Like the Eleans, "they sleep with them and nevertheless put boyfriends [*paidika*] in the battle line alongside."[9] This sounds like proper married cohabitation. For *suzeugnumi*, "to make a yoke pair," a syzygy, is a common term for "wedding" or "marriage" and is usually so translated. An Athenian would give his daughter "for the ploughing of legitimate children," and "yoke together" is in fact the term used in the famous passage in the gospel of St. Mark that fulminates against the very idea of divorce: "What therefore God yoked together [*sunezeusen*], let not man put asunder."[10]

Xenophon here seems to be making a clear reference to the Sacred Band of boyfriends that was currently cutting a swath through Greek history, putting an end once and for all to the preeminence of Sparta, helped in part by the ruinous leadership of Agesilaus and his son Archidamus and their phony trial that let an acknowledged miscreant walk without even having to bother to show up. The Sacred Band (*Hieros Lochos*) is described at length only by Plutarch, a local from Chaeronea, but one writing about four hundred and fifty years later, long after the Band had disappeared.[11] The Band was founded, we are told, around the time Archidamus was getting sentimental with Cleonymus, whose father had wrecked Spartan foreign policy with his disastrous raid on Athens. Three hundred men were selected (*epilektoi*). They were fed at public expense and encamped on the acropolis of Thebes, the Cadmeia. They were also called, most significantly, the Band *from the City*. "But some say it was composed of *erastai* and *erōmenoi*." Plutarch seems to see these two options as alternatives, either "selected" from the best or "*erastai* and *erōmenoi*," but this is a false opposition. We have seen that in Sparta and in Crete great care was taken as to what kind of person an *erastēs* had to be and what kind of qualities his "Stood by" or "Famed" or *aïtas* must have. Through groups like the "friends" in Crete and through public rituals like the abduction, a public tug-of-war, announced at least three days in advance, the entire community would be able to make its feelings known about the suitability of the selection. One thing is clear, at least: Plutarch seems certain that it is a question of *recruitment*.

A Theban called Pammenes, says Plutarch, was quoted as saying that when Nestor in the *Iliad* argued that armies should be formed of clans and tribes, he was wrong. It was better to draw up *erastēs* next to *erōmenos*. For a band held together by love-inspired attachment (*erōtikē philia*) would be unbreakable, the one group because they love (*agapōntes*) their *erōmenoi*, the others because they feel shame in front of the men who love them. The contrast between a group drawn from the whole community formed according to private personal *made* ties, and one made from tribal and clannish *inherited* kinship, is of course highly significant. Once again, just like the Cretan battalion of Beauties, by creating a band of champions drawn from the entire community, those men most esteemed by other men for physical splendor, might and excellence, *erōs* dissolves other allegiances and unifies. They are not just the band "from the polis," they are the most visible image of the human city as a single undivided collective. And the composition of the Sacred Band might even have been visible to those who fought against them. For Theban *erastai,* we are told, gave a panoply of armory and weaponry to their beloveds when they became Men, which could mean either at Eighteen or Twenty.[12] If the shields they gave were decorated with their own insignia, you would be able to see the pairs as you fought against them. Perhaps also the Sacred Band contained Striplings, a group who were segregated elsewhere and deployed especially for patrolling the borders, but who were not allowed to go on expeditions. Is this the source for some of the scandal about the Sacred Band, that they deployed Eighteen and Nineteen-year-olds alongside bearded men?

Few believe that Pammenes actually created the band of champions. Indeed some decades before the Army of Lovers we hear of an elite platoon of Thebans, three hundred front-row "champion" fighters, divided into two groups, "Reins-Holders" and "standers-by," *parabatai,* an allusion to the chariot pair of Driver and warrior, although in fact they are fighting on foot. That this is a prototype of the Sacred Band seems obvious.[13] So why all the fuss? What changed? Originally, we are told, the Sacred Band was distributed right through the army, not unlike the Cretan "battalion of Beauties" who come forward to make the sacrifice to Eros. The crucial change was in getting them all to fight together, crack troops of the front line. Pelopidas, who carried out the reform, compared them to horses: On their own they never run as fast as when they are harnessed to a chariot, because then they compete with each other in rivalry—another allusion to conjugality, yoke-pairs, syzygies.

An epigram written in the next century to accompany a dedication to Apollo in a shrine outside Thebes gives a little more information and is the earliest Theban source for Theban Love. "Direct the arrow of Eros at these here bachelors [*ēitheoi*], that, bold in the love of youths [*philotati kourōn*], they may defend their fatherland; for it [the dart] fires boldness and of all the gods he [Eros] is supreme at exalting [*aexein*] the front-line champions [*promachoi*]."[14] Let us not forget that Thespiae too, homeland of Narcissus and Eros, is a Boeotian city. What is said about the reprehensible Thebans applies to them too. And if the Eros of the temple of Eros in the center of the city was strangely disarmed, he could still shoot arrows through the eyes, and there seems to have been at least one other Eros of Thespiae who dwelt high on Mount Helicon near the woods that Ovid describes as giving shelter to lovers, around the pool where a handsome boy is in love with himself while the crescent moon of fourth-born, born-on-the-fourth Eros smiles at its own reflection. And this Eros according to Hadrian was certainly armed with a bow: "O Boy, Archer, son of the clear-voiced Cyprian goddess, you who dwell in Heliconian Thespiae beside Narcissus's flowering garden, be merciful."

This notion of *erōs* somehow or other making men better fighters, breathing *menos* into them, in Phaedrus's words in the *Symposium,* is by now completely familiar to us. And it is impossible not also to recall that image of Achilles and Patroclus on the Sosias Cup. The epigram allows us now to read that arrow as a love-arrow: Patroclus was indeed wounded by friendly fire, by Achilles, in the same way that little Troilus wounded Achilles. That love arrow shot from Troilus led to a less figurative arrow that wounded him in his foot: Troilus "who shot the wild dragon with fire-bearing love-charm of arrows, and wouldn't let go of smitten him, holding him in snares inescapable, for a scant loveless time, yourself untouched by the man you had subjected." So now on the Sosias Cup Eros has breathed *menos* into Patroclus and soon, "bold in the love of youths" and of one *kouros* in particular, Achilles, he will go out to fight in full berserk mode, inspired by that *menos* that is white sperm in Archilochus's description of himself ejaculating into the daughter of his political enemy, or "what is whitest and brightest" ejaculated from the phallus of Heaven in the Derveni Papyrus to produce the stars, *menos* as white and bright as the bandages Achilles applies to his *erastēs,* and that stands out vividly in Patroclus's gritted teeth. You think I am getting carried away? I don't.

The Army of Lovers enjoyed precisely forty years of fame, and with numbers limited to three hundred it was never more than a small part of the Boeotian war effort, which counted thousands. They came to Greek notice when the Thebans liberated themselves by throwing out their impious Spartan occupiers in 378. Then they fought a series of combats with Spartan Agesilaus and his son and his generals who were trying to get Boeotia back under their illegal control—almost as if, it was said, Agesilaus was giving them practice in fighting Sparta: Agesilaus "who with his continual assaults and expeditions into Boeotia had equipped the Thebans for the role of Sparta's sparring-partners."[15] They not only survived repeated onslaughts, but began to clock up some fateful victories against the undefeatable Spartans, until they helped Thebes secure a "Theban Hegemony" that perfectly bridges the gap between the old Greek world of classical states headed by Sparta and the new Greek world dominated by Macedonia, a new era that within a decade opens out onto a newer one, the Hellenistic era of Alexander and his successors all the way to Cleopatra and Augustus and the Romans.

In fact, famous though it is now and was then, the Army of Lovers is associated with but three battles, two phenomenal victories at Tegyra (375) and Leuctra (371), where Cleonymus died and Sparta was finally eclipsed, and one absolute defeat at Chaeronea (338), where Philip's Macedonian cavalry led by the promising Prince Alexander outnumbered and overwhelmed them and wiped the Army of Lovers off the face of the planet. Each of these battles, one should note, took place on homeland territory, in Boeotia, as did the fifth-century battle at Delium, where the band of Reins-Holders and Chariot-Warriors (*parabatai*) fought. Both homeguard and vanguard, the Army of Lovers, the Battalion of the City, the Sacred Band, was ready to stand and die for Boeotia.

They currently reside in the basement of Athens's National Museum. As to how they got there, we can let the garrulous self-publicist Frank Harris tell the story:

Everyone knows that in our day there was a gigantic marble lion at Chaeroneia. The Turks in their time had heard that there was money in it, so they blew it up to get the treasure, but they found nothing, and no one could understand what the lion of Chaeroneia was doing in the center of a deserted plain, far away from any village.

At a big meeting of the Classic Greek Society, I declared my belief that the lion of Chaeroneia was an excellent specimen of antique work carved in classic times. I believed it had been erected over the barrow of the "Sacred Band," and if the excavations were carried out, I felt sure that the grave of the heroes would be discovered. Greek patriotism took fire at the suggestion; a banker and friend offered to defray the expenses and we went up to Chaeroneia to begin the work . . . On studying the ground closely, I was insistent that a long grass-grown depression in the ground near the lion should be laid open first, arguing always that the lion would prove to have been erected on the grave itself; and soon the barrow was discovered.

Four stone walls a foot or so broad and six feet or so in height had been built in the form of an elongated square, resting on the shingle of an old river bed, and therein like sardines we found the bodies, or rather, the skeletons of the "Sacred Band." The first thing we noticed was the terrible wounds sustained in the conflict; here, for example, was a skeleton with three ribs smashed on one side while the head of the spear that killed him was jammed between a rib and the backbone; another had his backbone broken by a vigorous spear-thrust and one side of his head beaten in as well . . .

We counted two hundred and ninety-seven skeletons, and in one corner there was a little pile of ashes, evidently of the three who had survived the longest and were finally cremated. At one side of the oblong enclosure there was a solid piece of masonry some ten feet square, plainly the pedestal of the lion which was placed there *couchant,* looking away over the bodies of the dead toward Thebes in eternal remembrance of the heroism of the youths who had given their lives in defense of their fatherland. A "Sacred Band" indeed!

So, the poetic legend that this modern historian and that could not even take seriously was found to be strictly and exactly true, a transcript of the facts. It all helped to make the work of the writer precious to me and vivified the past for me in such a way that I began to read other books, and notably the New Testament, in a different spirit.[16]

Harris is a notorious vaunter of himself and a bit slipshod with the facts. It was not the Turks but Odysseus Androutsos, one of the heroes of the Greek War of Independence, who blew up the lion with gunpowder to get at treasure supposedly inside, and the excavation of 1879 revealed not 297 skeletons, but 254, plus the ashes of a couple. So forty-four got away. The bodies were without their weapons, but they did seem to be planning on doing some exercise in the afterlife, since they were buried with their strigils, used to scrape oil off anointed bodies.[17] The lion, sixteen feet tall, still stands at Chaeronea, successfully reconstituted by the true excavator whose name is not mentioned by Harris, Dr. Georgios Soteriades: "All the fragments of the lion fit together wonderfully . . . its gaze is turned slightly toward the tomb of the Macedonians."[18]

Plutarch says that Philip was walking over the battlefield afterward. When someone told him that this particular pile of corpses belonged to the Band of Lovers, he wept: "May they suffer evil destruction those who surmise these men are doing or undergoing something ugly." You might imagine, as Plutarch perhaps imagines, that this means Philip was insisting that the Sacred Band were just good friends. But this is a strong curse to protect the reputations of dead enemies, and why is it in the present tense?

Once more, it is not by dismissing the sources as gossip and rumor, or propagandistic fictions, but by taking them more seriously and more literally, that we will discover apparently inconsistent pieces of the puzzle, one seeming to insist on total chastity, the other on sexual license, fitting together most neatly. According to Pausanias, remember, in Plato's *Symposium,* in Boeotia and Elis: "It has been *straightforwardly laid down by law* [*haplōs nenomothetētai*] that it is beautiful to graciously gratify *erastai,* and no man, neither young nor ancient would/could say that it was ugly."

In other words in these cities it was *illegal* to say that homosexual sex was not beautiful. How on earth could such a law work? Well, Philip I think reveals how. He may even be giving us an echo of that very "legislation." In other words, at the time that the homosexual alliances were being made, while the Young Men and their boyfriends were actually doing the do even, there was not only a grand insistence on not saying something you were not supposed to but quite possibly public curses were laid on anyone who so much as ventured to conjecture that there was anything ugly about it: "May they suffer evil destruction those who surmise these men are doing or undergoing something ugly." This is what Pausanias means, perhaps, by his references to "straightforward legislation."

TEACHING IT TO THE CHALCIDIANS

Another nearby city throws more light on what we might call a structural problematization of the beauty of Greek Homosex. Pausanias goes on to make another claim commonly dismissed by scholars: that the Ionian cultural group, especially those living in modern Turkey, had neither gymnasia nor homosexuality, which was why they suffered tyrannies and foreign rule. But this unlikely assertion gets some support from a legend of Chalcis, a community of Ionians in Euboea, the island that lies along the eastern coast of mainland Greece, separated by a tiny channel. The Ionians of Chalcis—the same city that claimed to have the myrtle grove from which Ganymede had been abducted, the city that seems to have had as its major civic cult the cult of Ganymede's admirer, Olympian Zeus—used to hold homosex in contempt, as something deserving "invective," *psogos*.

However, during the great legendary war with their neighbors over the Lelantine plain they were converted and practiced homosexuality thenceforth with the zeal of converts, so much so that they became proverbial for it, and "make like a man of Chalcis," *chalcidizein,* meant "to practice the love of boys."[19] There are two accounts of this conversion. In one, the horsemen, the Knights, of Chalcis were not prevailing in battle, although the foot soldiers were fighting excellently. The men of Chalcis called in the help of a man of Thessaly, from Pharsalus, called Cleomachus, Battle-famed. Cleomachus showed the Ionians of Chalcis how Knights fight better if they have a boyfriend. He brought along his own boyfriend, a Cadet, a *neaniskos*. He asked if the young man would be witnessing the battle. He said he would. They embraced publicly and then the young man handed him his helmet. Cleomachus was filled at once with the necessary ardor and took the best of the Thessalians and charged at the enemy, routing them completely. He himself was killed. The men of Chalcis made a hero-shrine for him right in the middle of the city, in the agora, the marketplace. The tall pillar they erected there was still standing in the time of Plutarch, around 100 AD. From then on the men of Chalcis embraced the practice of falling in love with boys and honored it even more than others did.

Now Cleomachus might seem to have quite a good claim as the man who introduced gay love to Chalcis. His tomb was in the town center of Chalcis, and presumably this tale was told to explain to visitors why Chalcis offered hero worship to a Thessalian and why a great pillar reared up from the hero's tomb. I am reminded of the fig-wood dildo that stuck up out of the tomb of Prosymnus at Lerna, and the outrageous myth that Dionysus on returning from the Underworld came and sat on it.

Aristotle, however, told a different story, says Plutarch. He said that the hero was not Cleomachus but another man of Chalcis, who hailed from her colonies in Thrace. This was "the man who was kissed [philēthenta] by his erōmenos," a man who came as help (epikouros) for his kinsmen. He cites a popular song of Chalcis that commemorates the event: "Boys, you who have won the lottery of graces and good [esthloi] fathers, don't begrudge us good [agathoi] men intercourse [homilia] with your seasonal beauty. In the cities of the men of Chalcis limb-loosening Eros sprouts, in union with manly courage." This "Aristotle"—probably, in fact, another student—or his source, Dionysius of Corinth, a thoroughly mysterious epic poet, adds one other fascinating detail, the names of the two men of Chalcis who initiated homosexuality: they are Anton, from the colonies abroad, and Philistos. These are clearly "speaking names," and the work of Dionysius was called Origins (Aitiai), just-so stories told to explain how ritual practices came about. Philistos is a superlative of philos, meaning "Most Full of Loving Intimacy," or just "Dearest." Anton is more interesting. It means "He Who Is Coming to Meet Face-to-Face." The locals are represented in Chalcis's myth by utterly loving Philistos, the exotics by Anton who comes to meet Philistos face-to-face. Maybe it was just a public kiss that was commemorated, but the Chalcidians also had a reputation for full-on sex, "intercourse with seasonal beauty."[20]

At any rate whether or not the men of Chalcis were persuaded at some point to change their attitude toward homosexuality, they believed they had once held it in contempt, and had introduced it in order to make their Knights into better fighters. Here, perhaps, they were highly self-conscious about their outrageous homosexual practices, whatever they were. For one thing, again, is sure: The references are not to homosexuality in general but to an institution that was inaugurated at a particular moment in time, to "Chalcidian Homosexuality" or "Homosexuality Chalcidian-Style." The same kind of problematic can be seen both in Philip's statements after Chaeronea bringing curses on those who surmise anything ugly, and in Pausania's references to the people of Elis and Boeotia *legislating* that homosex was beautiful, as if they knew it might be considered ugly by other Greeks, such as Xenophon. Not for nothing was the Army of Lovers so notorious among some people called by the Thebans "the *Sacred* Band."

THE STREET OF SILENCE

Let us return now to the wine bowl in the British Museum with the Stripling with the erection sitting on a chair and another Stripling about to sit on him. Once again the location of the find won't help us, for like so much X-rated data about the Greeks—the most horrific myths, the most explicit acts—this bowl comes from Italy, from Capua in Campania. There is evidence for a text on the vase, the traces of some lost letters—"horizontal, above the heads: dots, vertical strokes and once an imitation inscription: above the seated youth: three strokes and two dots. Above the mounting youth: $\lambda(\lambda)(.)(.)(.)$. Above the bearded man three dots and a stroke"—but they are not very informative, though that may change with the help of new imaging techniques. Which means of course that any conclusions I draw must be provisional.[21]

It has been suggested that this scene shows a prostitute awaiting a client. It certainly looks like prostitution, for we do *seem* to hear about male prostitutes sitting in "cubicles," *oikēmata,* awaiting clients. They are mentioned by Aeschines in his denunciation of Timarchus as a male whore, although in fact he is very careful to be gender-nonspecific:

Put before your eyes those who sit in the cubicles, unarguably doing the do [*tēn praxin prattontas*].[22] However, whenever they become engaged in this necessity, they nevertheless put up some barrier in front of the shamefulness and close the doors together. And if someone asked you as you go along the street, what is that person doing? immediately you could say the name of the action [*ergon*], though seeing nothing and not knowing who it was who had gone inside, but aware of the purpose of the individual's activity [*ergasia*], you recognize what is done.[23]

He seems to provide an excellent description of the scene on the vase. A boy in an interior with another, and a man very interested about what's happening inside, surmising.

But it would be a lucky prostitute who had so handsome a client and one his own age, flourishing in the bloom of youth—yet another nail in the coffin, one might hope, of the notion of Greek Homosexuality as a matter of old Greek pedophiles penetrating "young boys"—and the fillets around the head show beyond doubt that this is a festival of some kind, a ritual sexual transaction, a holy act in a holy place, just like the boys *oiphing* each other "by Apollo Delphinios," near the temples and the gymnasium on Thera. Indeed the white Doric column must be a marble column, a succinct enough way for the artist to indicate a temple. As for the crowns the couple are wearing, we know from gymnasium regulations that crowns were awarded during some gymnasium festivals for the winners in certain competitions. The boy Lysis was wearing one he had won, presumably, in some competition at the festival of Hermes described by Socrates in *Lysis*. Victors should wear crowns on that day, so say the gymnasium rules from Beroea, but others were allowed to wear thin headbands (*tainioun*) if they so wished.[24] The boys on the other side of the vase wearing mere headbands in the gymnasium have not won anything, therefore. The boys about to have sex have won some kind of victory in some kind of contest, beauty contests being by no means ruled out, for we hear of these in several places—the contest to be priest of Boy Zeus in Aegion, for instance. Elis too had such a contest. The winner carried "the goddess's [Athena's] gear [*teuche*]," the second-placed led the ox, and the third put the preliminary offerings on the fire. What is the goddess Athena's gear? A helmet? An aegis? A spear?[25]

The vase therefore shows prize-winners taking up their ritual prerogatives, like Prom Queens or May Queens, or the Pubilla Major of the cities of Catalunya. That is the only way to read the crowns, and it

shows how, as in Crete, homosexuality and selection need not be mutually exclusive. The bearded man with the elaborate headgear must also
be involved in the ritual. Involved how? He does not seem to be observing exactly, if he is outside and they are within. And this pose of hand
on hip and leaning seems to be used elsewhere to indicate "listening."[26]
He is eavesdropping. Look at the vase again and we notice a contrast between the two sides. The well-clad boys in the gymnasium are making a
noise, gesticulating, talking. This draws attention to the contrast on this
side of the vase. Here no one is saying a word. You could hear a pin
drop.

Of the three main candidates, there is only one where gracious favoring was "noble" according to legislation, where homosexual lust was
sanctioned, where utterly reprehensible acts were considered customary
and beyond reproach, and that was also the homeland of an aristocratic
young man who once "sat in a cubicle" waiting for sex: Elis. Is the
seated boy in fact a "Phaedo captured by the Indians?"

Let us see how far we can get. The unspeakable acts that no one will
go into must have happened somewhere in Elis. The vase associates the
ritual with the gymnasium shown on the other side, and on Thera too
the *oiphing* recorded on the inscriptions took place not far from the gymnasium. So the area near the gymnasium of Elis must be a good place to
start. Here Pausanias saw altars to Eros and Anteros and to the chthonic
Cretan Heracles, here called *Parastas,* "Standing By." The pair of Erotes,
Eros and Eros Opposite, clearly point to some kind of *erōtikos* pairing, as
does the nickname of Heracles, when we recall that the married *erōmenos*
on Crete was called *parastatheis* (Stood-by); the same trio, Eros, Anteros
and Heracles, also featured in the gymnasium reserved for ephebes.
There was no altar to Achilles, however, as Pausanias the Periegete
points out, because he had a cenotaph instead. Indeed one way into the
gymnasium of Elis lay right over the "grave" of Achilles. And this was
the route the Greek Justices had to take when they arrived before Dawn
to match the Runners. The route they were not allowed to take was the
entrance that led from the "Street of Silence."

Given Athenian Pausanias's emphasis on the easiness of the boys of
Elis being, in some mysterious way, a result of the inability of the Eleans
to speak—"They are incapable of talking," or even "It's impossible for
them to talk," *hate adunatoi legein*—it is very interesting to find a street

with such a name right outside the gymnasium of Elis, with its altars to Eros and Anteros, and it is clear moreover that the silence was a very pregnant one. The name of the street commemorated a legend about a spying expedition at the time when the Eleans first arrived in the city of Elis from the north. They made a pact to keep quiet so that they could listen and note what was happening on the other side of the wall. The Street of Silence, the Street of Hush, is a Street of All Ears, so to speak, quiet so that you can hear everything happening inside. There seems no doubt that this is an *aition,* a just-so story for some ritual silence of some kind, and it is that ritual silence probably that is echoed by authors falling silent about Elean Homosexuality—"I do not tell the things in Elis," or even Julian's refusal to speak of Phaedo of Elis sitting in the cubicle. Here too was the temple of Artemis Stripling-Lover, *Philomeirax,* so-called because of her proximity to the gymnasium. This area must be the prime candidate for the site of the Eleans' notorious practices. Is it possible that they actually took place inside the temple of Artemis? If the Street of Silence is a Street for Eavesdropping on what's happening on the other side of a wall, is it what is happening inside the temple of Artemis Stripling-Lover?[27]

I wonder also if Aeschines might be talking about some specific ritual rather than commercial sex—though sacred male prostitution was by no means unknown in the ancient world: It used to take place on the Sacred Mount in Jerusalem until Josiah "brake down the houses of the sodomites." Some of Aeschines' language is obscure. The prostitutes are "engaged in this necessity." He refers to the "purpose of the activity." He talks of "putting [two] doors together," and seems to think it might be important to know "who it is who has gone in." Even more extraordinary is a strange episode in a comedy of Aristophanes, *Thesmophoriazusae,* which manages to combine silence, the sacred, a frontline champion and homosexual sex behind a door. The comedy opens with Euripides and a mysterious "in-law" going to find the poet Agathon. Agathon will enter later dressed as a prostitute, the courtesan Cyrene. He will emerge not from a door, but from a little door, a *thurion,* like the "little door" (*thuridion*) Phaedo pushed to when he was sitting in a cubicle. Not only does the scene juxtapose sacredness and prostitution, but it could be describing what is happening on the London Vase painted just two decades or so earlier. "Do you see that little door?" "By Heracles, I think I do." "Quiet now." "I am keeping silent about the little door." "Listen." "I am listening and I am keeping silent about the little door."

Eventually, enter an attendant holding fire (*pur*) and myrtle (the plant of Aphrodite). He offers up a highfalutin archaic-sounding prayer, which begins: "Let all the people say nothing they are not supposed to [*euphemos*, "speak well," "utter no words of ill-omen"], shutting together their mouths." He elaborates on the quietness of the whole planet, of the sea, of the air, of birds, of beasts in the forest. "For our champion [*promos* = *promachos*] is about to . . ." "Be sexually pleasured." "Who has uttered it?" The attendant continues with more mysterious descriptions of Agathon's activity behind the little door, words that might refer both to poetic and to sexual activity: ". . . and he is wax-melting, and he is making round, and he is casting [the molten liquid] . . ." ". . . and he is cocksucking." "What peasant [*agroiōtas*] approacheth the wall?" etc.[28] That "peasant" is not in Attic dialect, although it could identify the attendant as an Elean. That would be ironic, of course, because the attendant of Agathon whom Aristophanes is satirizing with this pompous speech seems to be Agathon's partner Pausanias, the very one who denounces Elean custom so insistently in Plato's *Symposium*. This is another of Aristophanes' brilliant *eikones*, the putting on stage of a vivid literal metaphor. Agathon's poetry is meretricious and whorish, and here his act of composition is directly compared to the act of sex. But why all the sacred language? Is Aristophanes satirizing people who take Agathon too seriously? Is he saying Agathon is overly revered by his priest, his attendant, by Pausanias? If there is ritual sex in ancient Greece, and the nearly contemporary vase seems to make that a pretty sure thing, then surely that is what Aristophanes is satirizing. And why else is Agathon a "frontline champion," a *promos*?

But what possible significance would the Eleans see in so bizarre a ritual? Well, Pausanias the Periegete relates the name of the Street of Silence to the foundation myths of Elis, the arrival of new immigrants to a settlement already inhabited. These myths insisted on the friendliness of the takeover. The two peoples, the indigenous Greeks and the exotic Greeks, were said to have been full of brotherly love for each other. Pausanias saw an image that looked to be of two armies coming together to fight. He was told that on the contrary it was the invaders being wel-

comed by the locals. When they "met" they recalled their original ethnic connection and therefore demonstrated kind favor for each other
(*genous . . . mnēmēi tou ex archēs kai eunoian . . .*).[29] According to the
foundation myth, two champions were chosen from each community to
decide which community would supply the king. For the indigenes,
Degmenos, for the exotics, Pyraichmes. Degmenos shot arrows at
Pyraichmes. Pyraichmes, using a slingshot like David, showered Degmenos with stones, normally a weapon used against traitors and scapegoats. Pyraichmes won, and so the leader of the immigrants became
king.

So perhaps the boys are crowned as representatives of each community engaged in friendly (re)union. They are, so to speak, taking on the
roles of the legendary champions Degmenos and Pyraichmes at the in-
ception of Elis. Indigenous Degmenos, which means "Receiving" or
"Welcoming," must in that case be represented by the boy waiting in-
digenously in the cubicle, and the other one must represent the exotic
Pyraichmes, "Fire Spear-point," which may be what the other boy is
clutching in his hand.[30]

But as it happens there is one other famous male pair in Elis, a very
ancient mythological pair, the very earliest heroes identifiable in Greek
art, going way back to before Homer in the eighth century BC, depicted
on Boeotian brooches and Attic pots. They are the terrible conjoined
twins called the Sons of Actor, or the Moliones, fearsome world-beating
warriors of the ancient indigenous population of Elis, the "Epeians,"
and like Achilles and Patroclus a chariot pair. In fact they provide the
model for the story of the invention of Eros as told by Aristophanes in
Symposium. Originally, in the golden age of Cronus, everyone was like
the sons of Actor, fused bodies. Then Zeus separated them and now
everyone is looking for their other half. That is what sex is for, to enable
the two halves to reconjoin.[31]

If you think—as anybody might—that this idea of representing political or social union in terms of homosexual sex and the literal fusing
of bodies is all too much, it might help to consider some parallels. The
Greeks, like lots of other peoples, regularly conceived of the act of sex
as a mixing, a conjunction, a coming together. This, for instance, is what
Artemidorus, interpreter of dreams, writing in the second century AD,
thinks a dream of homosexual incest signifies: "To have sexual inter-

course with one's son, if he is already a grown man and is living abroad, is auspicious. For the dream signifies that they will be rejoined and live with each other because of the word intercourse [*sunousia,* "coexistence," "being together," "sex"]."[32] The whole of the myth of Aristophanes in *Symposium* depends on this idea of sex as a conjunction of bodies. Sex is a kind of temporary return to that unity, and what lovers most desire is to be conjoined forever, in life and in death. Our splitting from the other half is an injustice, like the splitting of the people of Arcadia from each other by the Spartans! The men of Arcadia in other words want to reunite politically, and this is comparable to a homosexual couple having sex, and fusing themselves together like the sons of Actor. One can quite see how resonant Aristophanes' myth about their Siamese twin heroes would be to the combined populations of Elis.

Ultimately, of course, I have no idea whether the vase in the British Museum depicts Elean Homosexuality or not. Possibly it shows the ritual originated by Anton coming from the Chalcidian colonies to join his Chalcidian boyfriend Philistos, or some Theban practice. Perhaps it represents a practice from a different city entirely, or even from Athens. Elis is simply my best guess based on what we know about Elis and the strange story of aristocratic Phaedo sitting in the cubicle. But even if this is not what Elean Homosexuality looked like, it shows us the *kind* of practice that might well have given the Eleans so base a reputation, i.e., a very formal homosexual institution. For whatever is going on on the London Vase, it is clearly something very elaborate. How did the boys win the crown? Who is the woman leaning over the sill of the half-door? What are the boys debating on the other side?

II

TOFFS AND KINGS

BEAUTY A BLIND MAN CAN SEE

Thessaly, homeland of Achilles and of Cleomachus, who taught homosexuality to the Chalcidians, was another place with a particular homosexual reputation. We learn that here too the *erōmenos* was given a special title, *aitas,* which sounds similar to the breezy or blowy Spartan one, presumably awarded when he entered into a formal relationship and became *hetairos*.[33] We also know that at some point in history when the Thessalians made offerings to Achilles as dead hero at Troy, they also offered something to his dearest companion Patroclus, a foreigner from Locrian Opous, to please him (*es charin*), a practice that beautifully configures a same-sex love beyond the grave.[34] We might also expect that Thessalian homosexual customs had some affinities with those of the Boeotians their kinsmen, some way to the south, from whom they were separated by other peoples; it has been suggested that the very name "Thessalians," which is, believe it or not, related to *pothos,* "longing," is Boeotian and refers "to their longed-for brethren who remained in their original homeland."[35] The Thessalians and the Boeotians did not always behave like brothers, any more than Corinth, Corfu and Epidamnus behaved like mothers and daughters, but they both belonged to the Aeolian cultural group, and Aeolian Homosexuality does seem to have had certain characteristics, or to have underlined certain elements in a relationship, as we will see when we come to the other famous Aeolians on Sappho's Lesbos.[36]

But Thessaly seems quite odd in many ways, a different Greece from the Greece we are most familiar with, a kind of cultural halfway house on the road from the world of the city-states to that of Macedonia.[37] They had different burial practices and were famous for their witches, though this may be the Greeks being archaeological again, for the reputation may derive from nothing more than the fact that Thessalians gave special honors to the goddess associated with witches and ghosts, Hecate. The famous Georgian witch Medea of Colchis also spent time here when she returned to Mycenaean Iolcus with Jason, and then arranged to have his usurping uncle Pelias boiled to death by his own daughters, though one of them, Alcestis, demurred. Some said that Medea dwelled with Achilles on the White Island. Certainly the strange status of Achilles as a kind of ghost-god may have looked slightly less strange in Thessaly. Like Cleomachus who taught the Chalcidians, Achilles was associated especially with the area of Phthiotis in the south of Thessaly, the country around Pharsalus that honored his mother the goddess Thetis at the Thetideion. It is at this sanctuary of Thetis that Euripides' *Andromache* opens with the widow of Hector, now the sex slave of Achilles' son Pyrrhus, pregnant and afraid about the future.

Same-sex loving in Thebes, Crete and Sparta seems to have a great deal to do with social and political structures, an integral part of a "System," and in their politics and society too the Thessalians were rather different. The Thessalians, it seems, were aristocratic horsemen who, like the Spartans and some others, ruled over a variety of variously subject peoples or even "serfs," known collectively as *penestai*. The country was much greener than its neighbors to the south, the olive and the vine were rather less visibly in production, and its aristocrats were famously wealthy, putting on lavish feasts, entertaining visiting writers and intellectuals, almost like medieval barons with mini courts in mini palaces. They feuded like barons too, competing for preeminence, especially for the title of "Tagus," the ruler of Thessaly's four "quarters."[38] Sometimes it seems the Thessalians who ruled Thessaly were not just aristocratic but superaristocratic, Top Toffs, with "free agoras" for instance, where vulgar traders were not allowed unless they had permission from magistrates to set up a stall.[39]

The different style of Thessalian Love can perhaps be detected in the career of one particularly famous Thessalian. He was, according to some very good sources, one of the most handsome men in history, and he was not shy of using his looks. Like Achilles and Cleomachus, Meno came from Pharsalus, most likely from its ruling or leading family, and was probably very rich. It seems that an ancestor of the same name had once been able to provide the Athenians with the financial backing, and 300 horsemen, "his own serfs," for an expedition up north. For that he was rewarded with Athenian citizenship, a very rare privilege. Demosthenes was still talking about it well over a hundred years later, presumably because the grant was commemorated somewhere, i.e., he was archaeologizing.[40] In 431, at the start of the Peloponnesian War, another Meno arrived from Pharsalus with cavalry to assist the Athenians. This may well have been Meno's own grandfather.[41] Our Meno, Meno III, was one of the five commanders who at the very end of the fifth century BC led the "Ten Thousand" mercenaries right into the heart of Asia on Cyrus the Younger's unhappy campaign to seize the throne of Persia.[42] Pro-Athenian, anti-Spartan, terribly rich and powerful, terribly young and handsome, and the owner of lots of horses, it would be hard to design a character better able to antagonize Xenophon. But Xenophon had one thing that Meno lacked: a pen and the skill to use it.

Meno also stars in one of Plato's dialogues, the *Meno,* where he has several slaves in attendance and a friendly if imperious manner. Meno was so good-looking, says Socrates there, that he even sounded good-looking: His beauty would not escape the notice even of a blind man. Because of that he *still (eti)* has admirers moreover (a remark that implies he is in his Twenties, when one would normally assume all the wooing and courting would have ceased), including Aristippus of the great family of the Aleuads of Larissa in the north of Thessaly. Aristippus is also called Meno's "companion" (*hetairos*). Here we can perhaps see evidence in Thessaly for the same two types of Greek Love: the wolf pack of multiple admirers and a one-to-one relationship of *hetaireia*.[43] Aristippus had obtained money from Cyrus the Younger to maintain a small army that he was using to feud against a rival. But the army was on loan, as it were, and when Cyrus wanted to march against his brother and seize the throne of Persia, the loan was recalled. Instead of taking command himself, Aristippus sent his beloved, Meno.

Xenophon, who had marched under Meno's coleadership on the expedition of the Ten Thousand, painted the most vicious portrait when he came to write his obituary. After referring to Meno's greed he begins to archaeologize, that is, publicly to surmise and offer implicit proofs for things that cannot be known from what is known: "As for the invisible aspects of his life, though it is possible to tell lies [*exesti pseudesthai*] about him, nevertheless everyone knows this much": (a) still in possession of youthful charm (*hōraios*), he got Aristippus to transfer to him command of the army; (b) he enjoyed a very close association with Ariaeus, Cyrus's second-in-command, though Ariaeus was Persian and took pleasure in the company of handsome Striplings (*meirakia kala*); (c) he kept Tharypas as his favorite (*paidika*), though Tharypas had a beard while he himself did not.[44]

Attention has focused on the last of these insinuated crimes and what it says about the rules of penetration. But again such discussion distracts from the fact that the relationships Xenophon infers are all of great significance in Meno's career and the history of the Ten Thousand, and quite probably in the history of Greece. The allusion to his relationship with Aristippus casts aspersions on the way Meno got his command in the first place. We might, of course, put a quite different spin on this. Aristippus did not want to leave Thessaly with his enemies still at large, and might have been very happy to see Meno take on the burden of obligation he had incurred in his friendship with Cyrus. This way he could remain on good terms both with the Persian king and with his rival to the throne at one and the same time, thanks to his boyfriend acting for him. Meno's relationship with Ariaeus is also significant, since Ariaeus was no ordinary Persian, but had been Cyrus's second-in-command before his death, whereupon he had transferred his allegiance back to the Great King. There had moreover been some kind of conspiracy that led to the death or arrest of all the mercenary leaders, a conspiracy for which Meno was blamed. So the pivotal episode in the story of the Ten Thousand, a band of errant soldiers suddenly leaderless in the middle of enemy territory, finds the relationship between one of the generals, Meno, and the Persian Ariaeus at its very center.

And note how keen Xenophon is to cast aspersions on Ariaeus's sexual proclivities. He surrounded himself with handsome Striplings. In exactly the same way, Aeschines casts aspersions on "the whore Timarchus" by noting that he went around with Misgolas, who was always surrounded by handsome cithara-boys, that is, slaves or ex-slaves selected for their beauty. Ariaeus and Misgolas are rampant homosexuals, it is strongly implied, and so they seek only one thing from the men they associate with, from handsome Meno and nearly as handsome Timarchus. Here homosexual lust is contrasted with the honorable hopeless devotions of Greek Love, which Xenophon had trumpeted with tearjerking sentimentality in his account of the outrageous nepotism of Archidamus, and how his beloved Cleonymus's father came to get off scot-free.

Xenophon really is being malicious about proud Meno. Perhaps it was not just politics and envy. Perhaps Meno did turn out in the end to be a notorious blackguard and traitor, and it was that that earned Xenophon's malice, but in that case why would Plato be so kind to him? Either way, in Xenophon's obituary you can see, perhaps for the first time in history, a historian brimful of hate and setting out, self-consciously and deliberately, to blacken a dead man's name, to try him after the fact and most unfairly.

What about the mysterious Tharypas? Well, in the course of the Peloponnesian War, sometime between 428 and 424, one Tharypas or Tharyps arrived in Athens for an education. He was boy-king of the

Molossians, the people of Epirus, opposite Corfu, breeders of the famous Molossian hounds, and belonged to the dynasty that eventually supplied Philip of Macedon with one of his wives, Princess Olympias, mother of Alexander. Tharypas's regent, Sabylinthos, had allied with Sparta,[45] and it may well be that Tharypas arrived as a refugee. Athens did not look this gift horse in the mouth and offered him citizenship, young though he was—an even more exceptional honor, therefore, than that awarded to Meno of Pharsalus half a century earlier. Euripides' *Andromache,* set at the sanctuary of Thetis, the Thetideion in Pharsalus, was written to flatter him, for it ends with Thetis as a goddess *ex machina* predicting that the child of Pyrrhus, grandson of Achilles, sole survivor of the line, will rule in Molossian Epirus. If it was not a commission from the Molossian king, it may have been a case of Euripides doing his bit for the war effort.[46] Eventually Tharypas returned to his kingdom and was credited with transforming it into a civilized, i.e., Hellenized, nation, with laws and a constitution, and doubtless plenty of Euripides, although he did not give up the kingship. Archaeology does nothing to contradict the impression of a transformation; Epirus looks much more Greek after Tharypas than it did before. The friendly relations between Athens and the royal house of the Molossians continued well into the fourth century.[47]

The Greekness of the Molossians was not an uncontroversial subject. Neither Tharypas nor Sabylinthos is a Greek name, and the variety of spellings—Tharyps, Arrhybas—seems to reveal that the Greeks could neither decline them nor even pronounce them properly. We can see a little tussle of identity going on here, with people like the Molossians claiming descent from both Greeks and Trojans, from Achilles and from Hector's widow Andromache, and the "pure-bred Greek" colony of Apollonia a little farther up the coast emphasizing division and opposition, nicely represented by Apollonia's great victory monument at Olympia, with Greeks versus Barbarians, Team Greece of course headed by Achilles avenging his beloved boyfriend Antilochus by fighting Memnon to the death.[48] Euripides' play could almost be seen as a rejoinder: The Molossians alone continue Achilles' line, and they are descended from Trojans too.

Perhaps Xenophon's Tharypas is not King Tharypas, but another Molossian entirely. But the name seems to belong to the Molossian royal line, and when Tharypases are so extremely precious it would be only economical to identify the two. It's a little as if modern historians were to discover that Roosevelt had a relationship with someone called Stalin in the 1940s, and then merely to speculate about whether that meant that Roosevelt was gay, and what that says about gender relations in the mid-twentieth century. Xenophon certainly seems to expect us to know who Tharypas was; so far as we know there was only one man with that name. Perhaps I am missing something, but it seems likely that Greek historians have overlooked a major geopolitical fact, lurking right under their noses, an alliance between Epirus and Meno of Pharsalus.

So perhaps Tharypas's relationship of Greek Love with Meno was another part of his program of Hellenization: to become Greek, first find a boyfriend. And here is something interesting. If Tharypas is indeed the Molossian king, then Meno and his favorite probably had a common descendant many years later in the third century, grandson of yet one more Meno of Thessaly. I am talking of the nearly great general Pyrrhus, named after the son of Achilles, the man who invaded Italy and invented the Pyrrhic victory, and who may have had more than a negligible role in provoking the Romans to empire.[49]

That assignation of Molossian and Pharsalian genes took place nearly a century after our Meno met Tharypas the Molossian. Clearly marriage and other alliances between Pharsalus, homeland of Achilles, and Epirus, land of Achilles' only descendants, were part of an enduring program of contacts. When the Thessalians went to consult the oracle about the kind of cult they should offer to Achilles, it was not to Delphi they went, but to the Molossian oracle at Dodona. It would not be very surprising if the house of Meno of Pharsalus, ancestral friends of Athens, had had something to do with introducing Athens to this new and very useful friend from Epirus, whose guardian and regent was so unfortunately pro-Spartan. Of course it was a bit odd for handsome young Meno to play the role of *erastēs* to bearded Tharypas, who must have been at least ten years older, but perhaps Meno had helped him out in some way, or showed himself by his actions his passionate fan and self-sacrificing devotee, or perhaps he was in the role of patron to Tharypas, for the Molossians later appear as client allies of Thessaly. But who, seeing such a relationship between a man of Pharsalus and a man of Epirus, would not have thought of one other controversial relationship between a beardless handsome youth and a bearded *erōmenos:* Pharsalian Achilles and Patroclus? If such a relationship was un-Greek it was also the Greekest.

At any rate we can see in Meno's amatory alliances an extraordinary network that links Pharsalus to the Aleuads of Larissa in the north of Thessaly and to the descendants of Achilles in the far west. And finally it provides a platform for some shady dealings with the Persian Ariaeus. But there was clearly something striking about Meno's youthfulness, mentioned by both Plato and Xenophon. It is not impossible that he really was a Stripling when he assumed command, or at least in his early Twenties, as most concede, something that would in itself have been quite startling for an Athenian such as Thucydides, who hinted that even Alcibiades—then in his Thirties—was too young for command.

But in this Thessalian world of dynasties there was no room for obedience to rules about age. Dynasties and age-class systems simply don't sit well together. The Athenians implicitly acknowledged this when they gave citizenship to the boy-king Tharypas. Meno was not going to wait until he was Thirty before he could take command, nor, if a useful *erōtikos* alliance presented itself, would he wait for his beard to grow. If there was an age-class system in Thessaly, either Meno did not participate or it was not policed very strictly. In the far north of Greece, with its acres of grass, its palaces, princelings and kingships, they didn't seem to pay much attention to age rules or to love rules at all. Some of them, it seems, even shaved.

MURDEROUS MACEDONIANS

During their years of dead-end ascendency, the Thebans concentrated most of their energies first on rebuffing Agesilaus and his Spartans and then on invading the Peloponnese and actually separating Sparta from Messenia, homeland of Nestor and Antilochus, which Sparta had held since well back into the archaic period. But they were not unaware of their northern neighbors either, and in 368 BC the Thebans marched in the other direction, as far as Macedonia. They returned with a very useful captive, a Macedonian prince called Philip, a hostage for good behavior. He must have been in his mid teens and may have been adopted as an *erōmenos* by that selfsame Theban Pammenes, who was so eloquently theoretical about an Army of Lovers. Such "geo-erotikal" alliances are, hopefully, less surprising by now. Pammenes may even have thought Philip would thenceforth prove a loyal friend to Thebes, rather than her nemesis.[50]

At any rate, after a couple of years Philip was allowed to go home. When he succeeded to the throne, as Philip II, in c.359 in his early Twenties, he quickly set about reforming the army, improving on the Theban model of the deep phalanx. He also expanded the elite force of fighting courtiers known as the Companions of the King (*Hetairoi*). If Philip walking among the corpses at Chaeronea leaves us in the dark about what it was exactly that suspicious minds might "surmise" about the bodies of the Sacred Band, "all mixed up together," the contemporary historian Theopompus has left a vivid account of the kind of scurrilous gossip that was being published about his own Macedonian men at around the same time:

> Did not some of them continue to shave and to keep themselves smooth into manhood? While others were brazen enough to practice "insurgency" on each other, even though they had beards. They took around with them two or three male prostitutes and they served others in the same capacity, so that we would be justified in calling them not *hetairoi* but *hetaeras,* not marchers, but streetwalkers, for they were man killers by nature, but man whores in their way of life.[51]

The passage neatly encapsulates the fantasies of brutality and pornography, the giggles and terror such successful elite troops might inspire.

The events leading up to Philip's assassination by a member of his aristocratic bodyguard, one Pausanias, throw a little light on what actually went on at the Macedonian court and help to explain where Theopompus was coming from. The fullest account of the affair is given by Diodorus, whose chaste vocabulary is thrown into comic relief by the graphic tale he tells. Pausanias I, it seems, had been Philip's boyfriend—"became his intimate friend because of his beauty"—but noticed that the king was turning his affections—*agapōmenon*—to another, also called Pausanias (II). He insulted his usurper by calling him effeminate (*androgunos*) and a whore—"one ready to accept amatory approaches from anyone interested." This was upsetting to the second

Pausanias. He made a plan. To prove himself and his honor, he would throw himself in front of Philip in the middle of a battle to receive all the missiles designed for the royal body. He confided his plan to one Attalus, carried it out and died. The incident was widely discussed, and Attalus resolved to avenge the poor man. He invited Pausanias I to dinner, got him drunk and then had him thoroughly sexually abused by his muleteers, the lowest possible kind of slave—"handed him over to the muleteers for abuse and drunken lawlessness of a whorish character."[52] Now it was Pausanias who felt aggrieved. He complained to King Philip that Attalus had arranged for him to be gang-raped, and not just by slaves, but by vile muleteers. Philip gave him presents and promotion but refused to punish Attalus, who was very useful and a close relative of his new wife. Pausanias bided his time and then assassinated his former lover and king.

Aristotle seems to refer to these events in his *Politics,* leading some scholars to see it as an "official version," but this was not the only homosexual scandal he brought back with him from his time at Philip's court. There were some old stories about earlier kings: Amyntas the Little, who boasted loudly of his success with regard to Derdas's "youthful prime"—Derdas killed him—and Amyntas's father Archelaus, who maintained a splendid court in the later fifth century and provided refuge for both Euripides and the fancy wide-arse poet Agathon, who perhaps had found that Aristophanes' depiction of him as a cock-sucking courtesan had made Athens a less pleasant place to live, together with Agathon's long-term companion, that other Pausanias who was so eloquent on the subject of Greek Love in *Symposium.*

Plato claims that Archelaus had been illegitimate and came to the throne by doing away with his legitimate rivals, pushing one of them down a well and claiming that the boy had been chasing a goose. He was assassinated finally by a conspiracy mounted by two former boyfriends and a man called Decamnichus, who had taken offense after insulting Euripides' bad breath and being turned over to the poet for punishment. One of the lovers, Hellanocrates, was an exile from neighboring Thessaly, probably an Aleuad and a relative therefore of Aristippus of Larissa, which Archelaus had occupied.[53] The king had enjoyed his maturity (*chrōmenos autou tēi hēlikiai*) but then reneged on his promise to restore him to his lands. Hellanocrates realized therefore that the intercourse between them had been based not on "love-inspired desire" (*erotikē epithumia*), but on *hubris* ("abuse"). His ally was Crateuas. Unlike Hellanocrates, Crateuas was never happy about the royal intercourse, more precisely, the sexual favors (*aphrodisiatikē charis*) the king had enjoyed, but put up with it because Archelaus promised him the hand of his daughter. When he broke his promise, he killed him.[54]

It seems as if the kings of Macedon who were descended from Heracles actually had a family of institutionalized boyfriends, or seconds, who may have claimed descent from Iolaus. These so-called Iolidae not only functioned, when adult, as the kings' "deputies" or seconds-in-command, probably since the fifth century onward—one of them, Antipater, was left in charge of Macedonia when Alexander went off conquering Persia—but also as boys and/or Striplings they served as the kings' chief wine tasters and wine pourers, like Ganymedes to Olympian Zeus. In fact at Alexander's last banquet the son of Philip of the line of Heracles was served the fateful cup that killed him, the "cup of Heracles," by one Iolaus, son of Antipater. That an Iolaus should be found serving a descendant of Heracles a cup of Heracles on the night of Alexander's demise will appear an amazing coincidence only to those who have not been following the plot of Greek Love and the insistence of its mythical models.[55] Many suspected Iolaus of having poisoned the king. The Athenians suggested he and his brother be given divine honors. When Iolaus the wine pourer died, Alexander's mother is said to have desecrated his grave.[56]

Philip himself established a special corps called the Royal Boys, perhaps based on his Theban experiences.[57] This was an elite troop of sons of courtiers on the verge of manhood, i.e., Striplings (*meirakia*).[58] They can be seen on the mosaics and frescoes from the royal Macedonian tombs at Vergina and from Pella and also (with their sideburns carefully engraved) on the amazing "Alexander Sarcophagus" in Istanbul, which is in fact the tomb of the new governor of Sidon, decorated with scenes of Alexander killing Persians and animals. They took it in turns to guard the king's bedchamber, dined with him, accompanied him while out hunting, brought him his horses, and escorted him in battle. Every day, in other words, they more or less monopolized close contacts with the king. It seems quite likely in fact that Philip *reestablished* this institution and that both Crateuas and Decamanichus had been Striplings when

34. Macedonian "Royal Boys" slaughtering a deer. Mosaic from
Pella signed by Gnosis (*c*. 300).

they hunted and dined with King Archelaus fifty years before.[59] The
king alone was allowed to whip the Royal Boys, an outrageous thing for
a free Greek to undergo.

This corps seems to have been a breeding ground for a potent mix of
aristocratic pride and intense homosexual relationships. Alexander punished one of the Striplings, Hermolaus, for spearing a wild boar that was
charging the king before the king himself had had a chance to strike.
Hermolaus was whipped in front of the other boys and had his horse
confiscated. His *erastēs,* a boy of the same age-group, vowed revenge:
"Sostratus saw the body he loved to distraction lacerated" and enrolled
Hermolaus in a plot to kill the king, after exchanging pledges.[60] Alexander was saved on this occasion by that love of drinking that eventually
killed him. The Royal Boys planned to attack him in his sleep when they
were assigned to guard his quarters, but on that night Alexander was out
carousing until late. They waited outside the party for Alexander to appear, so that they could escort him from the party to bed and an evil end.
Time ticked by, and the king lingered on. One of his most apologetic
historians says that he did try to leave the party, but a woman who reg-

ularly hung around inspired by gods and uttering rambling prophecies fell at his feet and begged him to return to the drinking. If the gods so wish, said Alexander, I guess I must, and went back inside to get more drunk. He praised the Royal Boys for being so dutiful and gave them a tip. Their replacements arrived and they were dismissed. A conspiracy that had lasted until the night of action did not endure beyond it, and one of the Striplings, Epimenes, imagining the gods were against them, told his own *erastēs* what was afoot. His boyfriend told Epimenes' brother. The brother revealed the conspiracy to the bodyguard Ptolemy, soon to be king of Egypt and our ultimate source for the whole affair. Ptolemy told Alexander. Hermolaus and his colleagues were stoned to death, although Epimenes and his brother were spared.[61]

But homosexuality and plotting was certainly not confined to the men and Striplings around the king, a fact that stands out in one of the most mysterious and central episodes in the history of Alexander, the downfall of Philotas, "Love," son of Parmenion. Parmenion was the greatest of Macedonian generals. He had probably been preeminent even before Philip came to power, and with Philip was responsible for some of the key victories during the extraordinary transformation of

35. An Asiatic with one of the Macedonian Royal Boys in a Royal Hunt. "Back" side of Alexander Sarcophagus (*c.* 320), from the "Royal Necropolis" in Sidon, Lebanon.

Macedonia from a marginal power on the brink of collapse to the greatest power in the Mediterranean world. He remained in his post after
Alexander's succession and came with him to Asia. Naturally Parmenion's son was by virtue of his father's status not someone to be taken
lightly:

> He had self-importance and great financial resources, and a personal
> fastidiousness and way of life that, found in an ordinary man, aroused
> resentment. At that particular time, too, his high-handed and swag-
> gering manner was particularly tasteless; in fact, he had no charisma
> ["without graces"], and cut a rather gauche and affected figure. He
> thus provoked suspicion and antipathy, to the extent that Parmenion
> once said to him: "Son, please tone yourself down."[62]

Philotas had apparently been boasting to his mistress that Alexander
was but a Stripling who owed his success and his rule to himself and his
father. The mistress mentioned it to someone who mentioned it to
someone and she was called in for questioning. Alexander made no
move as yet, but sent the woman back with orders to report back at regular intervals. Philotas carried on vaunting himself and denigrating
Alexander, quite unaware that his mistress was keeping a mental record.
   Then when the army was in Phadra (probably modern Farah in
Afghanistan), an obscure Macedonian called Dymnus or Limnus or
Dimnus hatched a plot. He had an infatuation for a young man called
Nicomachus. This boy is also described as his erōmenos, but the most
elaborate and lurid account of the affair by Quintus Curtius describes
him as his whore, Dymnus's male prostitute (exoletus, scortum).[63] Dymnus was "bound [vinctus] to the boy by the sexual ministration of a body
given over to him alone."[64] He took him into a temple with no one else
present and said he had secrets to tell that could not be divulged. He
asked him on account of their mutual love (mutuam caritatem) and pledges
they had made each other to swear an oath of silence. The boy swore and
Dymnus revealed that there was a plot to kill Alexander in two days'
time involving members of the bodyguard and several Royal Boys. He
invited the boy to join the conspiracy. Nicomachus refused. He was a
good prostitute. Dymnus, mad with passion and fear, threatened him
and insulted him as an effeminate, a coward, a traitor to his lover, and

then made extravagant promises. He would give him the world, and put his rent-boy on the throne of the Great King. The young man was not tempted but pretended to go along.

Immediately after the interview Nicomachus went to tell his brother Cebalinus, which sounds like a Macedonian name. Cebalinus told him to stay "in the tent" (*tabernaculo*), because it was not usual for the rent-boy to enter the king's presence, and the conspirators would get suspicious. Cebalinus was stopped at the entrance to the king's tent by Philotas, the only one on duty . . . "for some reason." Cebalinus told him what his prostitute brother had learned from his lover. Philotas said he would tell the king, but didn't. Cebalinus tried again the next day; Philotas said he was dealing with it. But now it was the day of the assassination and the boy was suspicious. He mentioned the plot to one of the Royal Boys, Metro. Metro took him inside, hid him in a cupboard, and went straight to the king, who was having a bath. Alexander gave orders for Dymnus to be arrested and went in to where Cebalinus was hiding. Cebalinus was overjoyed: "You are alive! I have saved you!" "Why did it take you two days to reveal the conspiracy?" Alexander asked. "Well, I told Philotas," said the boy. "I thought it was just a squabble between a lover and his whore," said Philotas.[65] Dymnus was brought in to the king, but he had stabbed himself and was in no condition to speak (*iam defecerat vox*).[66] But now everyone suspected Philotas and all kinds of accusations were made and recollections of his arrogance rehearsed. He was arrested and tried, tortured and stoned to death, though not before he had implicated his father, Philip's grand old general, who could now be removed. Alexander sent a man on a camel to where Parmenion was fighting with orders for his subordinate generals to kill him: "For the troops there was temporary disbelief, then resignation: they had witnessed a cabinet shuffle, Macedonian-style."[67]

The whole story of the boy prostitute holding the futures of the best of the Macedonians in his hands, able to implicate any one of them thanks to what his ignominious boyfriend had told him, stinks to high heaven, but it does seem as if Curtius used "a source that had a great deal of precise information."[68] What is salvageable is that a boy with no access to Alexander came forward to claim that he had been told of a plot by his boyfriend, a man also of no great account, and that this denunciation was thought to be substantial enough to enable their enemies to put paid to Philotas for active involvement or for passively not taking it seriously enough, and even to remove his father, mighty Parmenion. The place where the plot was foiled was thenceforth known as "Anticipation."

GAY ALEXANDER

A more uplifting, but equally over-the-top example of Macedonian *erōs* is Alexander's relationship with Hephaestion. Certainly, if we are looking for homosexuals in history, Alexander is the one to put your money on, producing any amount of scandal from which his apologists, who ended up almost monopolizing the historical record, would rather not have had to defend him. Athenaeus, a late anthologist, summarizes what he has gleaned from his reading on the subject: "Alexander was insanely fond of boys [*philopais d'ēn ekmanōs*]."

A contemporary, he notes, Dicaearchus, a student of Aristotle, claimed that Alexander kissed the handsome "eunuch" Bagoas in public, was applauded and kissed him again. Bagoas had been the last Persian king's beloved "eunuch" too; Alexander was always anxious to step into the former monarch's shoes. Plutarch adds that Alexander had first been carried through southern Iran on a float built for continual drinking parties. When they arrived at the local palace he watched, drunk, his *erōmenos* Bagoas win the singing and dancing competition and process through the theater in festal costume to Alexander's side.[69]

Then Athenaeus quotes Carystius of Pergamum, writing two hundred years later and trying to prove Alexander's self-restraint. He tells a story of a Chalcidian named Charon who had a beautiful boy who was devoted to him. Over drinks at a symposium in the house of Craterus, Alexander expressed admiration for the boy, who was clearly in attendance, and not as a servant but sitting or reclining. Charon bade the boy give Alexander "a proper full-on kiss" (*kataphilein*). Alexander refused: the kiss would pain Charon more than it would give him pleasure.[70] This pair may be the couple called Charus and Alexander who led a brave assault of thirty young men at Aornus. This Alexander was killed, and Charus rushed to his body to avenge him, killing left, right and center, until he was overwhelmed and fell on top of his boyfriend's body.[71] Carystius adds that Alexander also resolutely kept his hands off the daughters of Darius.

Elsewhere Athenaeus is discussing Alexander's drinking problem; maybe this is why he had no urge for sex. Aristotle says that drinking makes your sperm watery, he notes, and Theophrastus is quoted as saying that Alexander was in poor shape for sex. His mother arranged for Callixeina, a very beautiful Thessalian courtesan, to recline beside him and often begged him to have intercourse with her. Philip was also "in the know" (for they were worried that he might be womanish, "*gunnis*")—sometimes you think the Greeks would have benefited from an understanding of sexual orientation. Theophrastus is an excellent source for such a tale, by the way, since he was a close confidant of one who should know, namely Alexander's tutor, Aristotle. Plutarch has Alexander saying that heterosex makes him think of death, since reproduction (*genesis*) is the displacement of something of one's own elsewhere and its destruction.

Soon after his death, it seems, letter forgers had Alexander being offered handsome slaves and indignantly writing to turn the offers down:

When Philoxenus his admiral wrote that he had with him one Theodorus of Tarentum, and that Theodorus had two boys for sale, really extraordinary physical specimens to look at, and he wanted to know if he should buy them, Alexander was furious and cried out to his friends repeatedly, asking whatever ugly thing in him it could possibly be that Philoxenus had recognized to set himself up as his commissioner for such reproachful things. And he reviled Philoxenus himself in a letter and bade him deliver by all means Theodorus— deliver him to perdition, him and his cargo. And he was apoplectic with Hagnon also when he wrote that he wanted to buy Crobylus and send him to him, Crobylus being highly esteemed in Corinth.[72]

I would love to believe these letters are authentic; they are so hilarious. I do not doubt, moreover, that they are informed by historical particulars, simply because the circumstantial detail is so oddly specific.[73] But if you are going to buy Alexander the Great a present, you just do it. You don't call up by mobile, so to speak, and say: "Hey Alexander, er, mighty King and all that, look, your birthday's coming up and I was wondering what to get you and I'm with this guy called Theodorus now, and he has these two absolutely stunning boys in tow—I mean, you have to see them to believe them, real knockouts. So, would you like me to buy them for you or not? I mean they aren't cheap." But what is even more extraordinary is the fact that these letters did actually exist, available to Plutarch or his source to quote from. In other words someone really did think it worthwhile to forge such extraordinary correspondence in order to quash rumors, albeit in the crudest fashion: "Dear Philoxenus, How dare you offer to buy me boys, even if they are amazing to look at? When I received your letter I shouted out to all my friends, 'What shameful thing does Philoxenus see in me, to write such things?' I am not like that at all. I am very self-restrained, and I don't have a drinking problem, or anger-management issues either. Yours sincerely, Alexander the Great." If anyone anywhere has ever protested too much, it is in this forged Alexander of Plutarch's correspondence.

If we compare Xenophon's defense of the Spartan King Agesilaus's fawning over the Persian boy Megabates, without any hint of what the papyrus history attests, that it was a notorious affair, it seems likely that there were specific reports about Alexander's harem of handsome slaves. His Persian predecessor had had beautiful women sent to him from all over the empire, just as he collected the best of the empire's trees, fruits and fauna. Remember Theopompus's comments on Macedonian courtiers—"They took around with them two or three male prostitutes and they served others in the same capacity."

HEPHAESTION

From the sordid to the sublime, the love of Alexander's life: Hephaestion, his chief of staff or grand vizier, his best man and his brother-in-law, the man whom "Alexander loved most of all" (*ephilei malista*).[74] The pair of them are found drinking together a lot—an activity full of implications of bonding—but the relationship was most demonstrative after Hephaestion's death—from too much drinking. Alexander mourned him extravagantly and expensively. It was another scandal.

Here is Arrian, a late historian, but the most serious, reviewing what earlier historians, some of them eyewitnesses, said in their accounts:

> That his grief was great all have related, but there are differences over what actually happened, depending on their good will toward He-

phaestion or envy of him, or indeed their good will toward, or envy of, Alexander. Among those who record excesses, some seem to have thought whatever he said or did in extreme pain over his dearest of all mortal intimates could only be taken as decent [es kosmon], for the others, as shameful, improper for a king and certainly for King Alexander. Some say he lay prostrate over the body of his companion weeping for most of the day and wouldn't move, until he was forcefully extracted by his courtiers. Others, that he lay prostrate on the body the entire day and the following night.

Arrian gives us a selection of other things he found in the histories. The doctor was hanged either for incompetence or because he had not stopped Hephaestion from drinking. Like Achilles, Alexander cut his hair over the corpse—Arrian allows this. He drove the hearse himself— definitely not. He had the local temple of Asclepius the doctor god razed—Arrian will not have that either, although he did talk of resentment toward the god when an embassy came from the god's shrine at Epidaurus. Alexander ordered heroic sacrifice—a general consensus that this is true; the Athenians were appalled. Tried to get divine sacrifices for him—request denied, although Lucian talks of people reporting epiphanies of Hephaestion in dreams, offering prophecies and cures— examples of the grossest flattery, according to the author—and says that someone who was observed weeping as he passed Hephaestion's tomb, as if Hephaestion were dead, came close to being sent to the lion's den, until another courtier claimed a vision in which Hephaestion had recommended mercy. Lucian says Hephaestion did receive divine honors both as paredros and alexikakos theos, "best man and evil-averting god," terms that reflect Hephaestion's position with regard to the king.[75]

All agree, however, that Alexander neglected himself and food and drink for two days, ordered a pyre to be built at Babylon, fifty miles south of Baghdad, costing ten thousand drachmas (or more), and held a festival of athletics and music in Hephaestion's honor with three thousand performers. Others give more details: the making of little images of Hephaestion in ivory and gold by members of the court, the quenching of the sacred fire all through Persia, a mark of respect for the death of kings, and a bad omen for the king therefore, a nice example of a lover as a second self. One of the very first and very negative histories of

Alexander, written by the Chalcidian Ephippus of Olynthus after his death, actually paired the couple up: *The Last Days of Alexander and Hephaestion*.[76]

As for the pyre itself, there survives a detailed description or blueprint. One of Babylon's great brick walls was to be knocked down, an allusion perhaps to Achilles' wish in the *Iliad* that he and Patroclus might alone be left standing and together might loosen the battlements of Troy. The base of the pyre was approximately 220 yards square, or about ten acres. Its seven layers were built up out of palm trunks. The first layer had 240 gilded ship prows, with archers and warriors onboard and red felt in between. Then a layer of torches with snakes around the base looking up at eagles looking down over the flames, then hunting scenes, then—level four—a battle with centaurs in gold, then lions and bulls alternating, also in gold, then weapons, both Persian and Macedonian, and finally Sirens, hollowed out so that people could hide inside and sing funeral laments. The structure was around 250 feet high. Ten thousand animals were to be sacrificed. But it never was put to the flame. On his way to Babylon, Alexander received warnings from Babylonian astrologers, who had by now got the entire Zodiac sorted out. Alexander should avoid the city or approach by a more difficult route. Alexander tried to comply, but the more difficult route proved too difficult and he entered by the orthodox road. He died soon afterward in the Palace of Nebuchadnezzar, and the Macedonians decided not to proceed with the elaborate funeral for Hephaestion, plans for which were found in Alexander's papers.[77]

Hephaestion's modern obituaries are less extravagant. "Perhaps of all his officers Hephaestion was at the last the only one whom Alexander could fully trust." "Nothing suggests that his abilities were outstanding."[78]

I

DID THEY OR DIDN'T THEY?

Alexander seems never to have behaved inappropriately in public with Hephaestion. We would know about that if he had; a public kiss would have caused ripples. The relationship may quite possibly never have included a kiss even in private, but it was presented as a deep amatory attachment, and that attachment was certainly presented by later writers as conventionally *erōs*-derived, i.e., not excluding sex, although we should not be surprised to find that the sources normally use *philia* words rather than *erōs* words to describe a relationship that had long achieved intimacy. Alexander was not carrying a torch for Hephaestion nor Hephaestion for Alexander. Things had gone much further than that.

But once again we have to separate "Alexander Homosexuality" from Alexander's homosexuality. The sources seem to see a notable and exceptional homosexual proclivity in Alexander—"insanely fond of boys"—and an exceptional performance of love for Hephaestion, but the one need not have anything at all to do with the other. Alexander seems to have been gay, in other words, but he was not *necessarily* gay with his boyfriend.[79]

It seems that Hephaestion was a coeval of Alexander and had been brought up with him as one of his father's Royal Boys. He was taller than Alexander, and quite striking in a youthful way. At some point he was made one of the Seven, the inner core of royal bodyguards, who slept inside the king's bedchamber while the Royal Boys slept outside. As a bodyguard he therefore held the same position with Alexander as the two Pausaniases had with his father Philip, probably much closer in fact.[80] It seems, moreover, as if he was the first of Alexander's "own people" to be appointed to the Seven, and it probably happened in the first year of the campaign after the capture of Halicarnassus; he was already special, if not the most special of Alexander's special friends therefore.[81]

The first direct evidence for a relationship comes very early on in the campaign in 334 BC. Alexander was a descendant, through his mother, of Tharypas the Molossian, and therefore of Achilles. Achilles of course was his favorite hero, and it seems quite likely that he deliberately set out to emulate him, even risking his life to perform bold heroic acts. At least one attendant poet cast Alexander as Achilles in an epic poem, for on the eve of Alexander's Persian expedition a statue of Orpheus was seen to be sweating, a sign, obviously, that praise singers everywhere were about to be given some praising to do.[82] But we can see what Achilles meant to Alexander in his actions. In these initial phases he looked back, over and over, to the Trojan War, and to Achilles. After celebrating the Macedonian festival of Olympian Zeus, which had been inaugurated by

Archelaus at the end of the fifth century, Alexander set off. According to Arrian, he made sacrifice at the tomb of Protesilaus, first of Agamemnon's army to land, and first to die, in the hope that the same thing would not happen to him.[83] Then Alexander crossed the Hellespont into Asia, sacrificing to Poseidon and to the Nereids, i.e., to Thetis and her sisters, in midcrossing. He was himself the first off the ship, and clad in full armor. (This was not necessarily very brave, for we are not informed of any army of Persians waiting on the shore.) So, just a beach, a boat running up it till the prow will go no farther, a short warrior leaping out, hoping he had not misjudged the depth, armored from head to toe, probably spectacular armor covered in scenes, a beautiful work of art in fact of the kind that present-day museums would pay vast sums for, and, from the crew, lots of shouting and whooping and weapon clanging.

After landing, Alexander headed straight for Troy. He made offerings to Priam, hoping to expiate the pollution his Molossian ancestor Pyrrhus, son of Achilles, had incurred by murdering the old king on his altar throne. He also, however, gave honors to the modern city of Troy in memory of his other ancestor, Hector's widow Andromache.[84] He went to the main temple of Athena and dedicated his armor to the goddess, and also removed some of the armor already dedicated there by the heroes of the Trojan War itself. He gave these antiques to his shield-bearers to carry in front of him in battle. It seems likely that Hephaestion was by now one of these, at the very least.

Then Alexander anointed the tomb of Achilles with oil, a regular offering of a relative, and ran a nude foot race with his companions "as is the custom." Then he crowned the tomb of Achilles, and remarked that Achilles was "blessed to chance upon a trusty intimate [*philos pistos*] while still alive, and after death a great proclaimer." The neatness of the antithesis and the fact that more than one source has the same or a similar phrase makes it seem probable that it is a genuine quote, and probably well rehearsed.[85] Here Hephaestion steps in, for "allegedly" he crowned Patroclus's tomb at the same time. The "allegedly" shows the source keeping his distance from the fact, but it is not in itself improbable. According to the Thessalian custom, whenever they made offerings to Achilles as hero they also invited Patroclus to share in the feast, so it would be appropriate for Patroclus to receive a crown if Achilles received one. As soon as Alexander crowned Achilles' grave—a very plausible thing for him to do—and remarked upon Achilles' good fortune in finding a trusty intimate, the implications must have been obvious, and one thing Hephaestion was not was slow-witted. We might even imagine a scramble for Patroclus, among all those in Alexander's entourage who felt they had some call on his affections. Hephaestion might well have been among them. The only thing that prevents me from concluding that the popular story is true is that it really should have been Alexander himself who made the gesture to Patroclus in that case, and that it would have been a very loud and presumptuous act on Hephaestion's part to show his hand and advertise his ambitions before his position was secure; unless, of course, his position with Alexander was in fact secure, and the whole thing was staged as a piece of theater to advertise the beginning of the takeover of the new men. But what has happened, we may ask, to the homotaph, the single grave of the two heroes?

At any rate our historian, a contemporary of Hadrian from over four hundred years later, notices this gesture of Hephaestion's in response to Alexander's remark and takes his cue. If Hephaestion will step into Patroclus's shoes and become Alexander's trusty intimate, then he himself will step into Homer's shoes and become Alexander's great "proclaimer."[86]

The next significant mention comes after the second of Alexander's three great battles against the Persians, at Issus, in 333 BC, right in that farthest corner of the Mediterranean where Turkey bends south toward Lebanon. It is the famous episode painted by Veronese that hangs in the National Gallery in London. Issus was the first time the Great King Darius had bothered to come to a battle, and he suffered a great defeat; he also lost track of his mother, who was captured by the Macedonians along with his wife and daughters and his tent. Thinking that Darius himself had been killed, they began to wail. Alexander went in to reassure them, with Hephaestion in attendance. Since he was taller and better-looking, Darius's mother made obeisance to Hephaestion. He drew back, and one of her eunuchs whispered that she had got the wrong man. What a gaffe. But Alexander graciously remarked: "This one too is Alexander."

Arrian cannot be certain the story is true, but it doesn't matter, he says. If it is true, it shows Alexander behaving most graciously; if not, then it shows that the historians thought it was plausible for Alexander to behave graciously, which comes down to the same thing.[87]

By the time of the third great battle at Gaugamela in 331 BC we find Hephaestion as "Leader of the Bodyguards," a role that got him wounded. Then he begins to show his dark side, leading some to view him as a quarrelsome, spiteful or even sinister character, playing not so much a gentle Patroclus to Alexander's Achilles as a Beria to his Stalin. There seems little doubt that in the plot to remove the graceless Philotas, Hephaestion, who had long hated him, played a leading role. Indeed he is said to have supervised the torture of the man. Curtius in Jacobean mood claims that he actually took part, "with their own spears stabbing him in the mouth and eyes."[88] Another of the torturers was Philotas's own brother-in-law, Coenus, which reveals that a willingness to attack Philotas may have been a way of demonstrating loyalty at an extremely dangerous time. Hephaestion was only doing his duty as a bodyguard or even Leader of the Bodyguards by gathering all the information he could about threats to the king's life. He was also making himself unpopular with the rest of the army, putting all his money on Alexander's survival: "He was attractive to no one else, and therefore to Alexander alone."[89] I think perhaps the sinister side of Hephaestion has been overdone. Given the fate of so many previous Macedonian kings, including Alexander's father, assassination was a real and present danger. Hephaestion would not see that happen on his watch. No wonder there were rumors after his death that Alexander wanted to deify him as "Evil-Averter."

Nevertheless, Hephaestion was a direct beneficiary of the demise of Philotas, since he took over half of his job as commander of the cavalry of Companions, but in lands that dwarfed Macedonia he seems to have been more of an organizer than a warrior, now playing production manager to Alexander's director, building bridges and cities, managing fortifications and harbors, arranging the terms of settlement for conquered peoples.[90] He had one major rival as closest to Alexander, the more military-minded Craterus. At one point way out east they came to blows and both drew their swords. Alexander intervened and told Hephaestion publicly that he was nothing without him, Alexander, adding that Craterus was a king-lover but Hephaestion was an Alexander-lover: "No two individuals are more aptly characterized . . ."[91] The drawn swords are probably real, the rebuke possibly. But it would be remarkable that Alexander should say such a thing to a proud Macedonian like Hephaestion in front of the army. Perhaps it was the kind of thing he could say only to Hephaestion. Perhaps only Hephaestion would take it. Following this public rebuke from Alexander he is Alexander's indisputable second. Hephaestion now even "Alexandrizes," follows Alexander in his adoption of Persian costume and Persian ways. Imitating someone's habits and ways is always seen as both flattery and affinity in Greece, but it is quite possible that Alexander was following Hephaestion's advice in the first place.

It seems to me that all the modern histories of Alexander fail in one key respect, that they trivialize his Second, distracted by the question of whether and to what extent Hephaestion was Alexander's boyfriend, and caught up in the romance of war. Hephaestion may have been no great warrior, but Alexander was warrior enough. Hephaestion played a different and no less important role as Alexander's perfect foil and complement. Looking at what is ascribed to Hephaestion, we find that he was constantly at work, from the time that the "Old Guard," Parmenion and Philotas, met their end, and probably from well before. He dealt with complex tasks of organization and administration, and he seems to have achieved them, over and over again, and in good time. We really should look at Alexander's conquests as a team effort, the work of Alexander and Hephaestion too. Hephaestion is a serious man in the histories of Alexander. He needs to be taken more seriously.

With his quite exceptional mourning and the quite exceptional honors paid to Hephaestion after his death, Alexander was passing judgment on their relationship. We don't have to choose between affairs of love and of state. Here they are one and the same. Alexander was mourning both his prime minister and his lover. And he may well have died not so much from drinking too much, but of a broken heart.

Alexander's relationship with Hephaestion really does stand out. The combination of same-sex love and politics was already well established in the court of his predecessor Archelaus, both in domestic policy and in international relations, but these royal relationships were always unequal. We hear of Philip having a relationship with Pausanias, who fought as his bodyguard, and with his wife's brother, the Molossian Alexander of Epirus, but not with Parmenion or with Antipater. That would be another thing entirely. What is unusual about Alexander's love for Hephaestion, his coeval and someone he had been brought up with, first of his friends to be given a place close to the center of power, is that it evolved from an unequal relationship, perhaps quite comparable to Philip's relationship with Pausanias, into a true partnership, as Ephippus acknowledged by writing his unique joint history of the couple. This was an extraordinary thing for a king as all-powerful as Alexander, to allow one man to become his other half. It is also perhaps a reflection of the great political change in the course of Alexander's reign, the replacement of the "Old Guard," with its independent power blocks and resources, by "New Men" and a new style of politics in which power derived from closeness to the king. Hephaestion exemplifies that change.

But perhaps we could also see that development as the replacement of one model of Greek Love derived from Alexander's ancestor Heracles and Iolaus his helper, who looks after Heracles' business and his interests when his friend is no longer around, by a more passionate and intense model of Us-two-against-the-world, together in life, together in death, which looks instead to Achilles and his mother's side.

CONCLUSION

What is most striking about Macedonian Homosexuality is its infinite variety. Here above all we can see that Greek Love could be a very flexible thing, deployed in a whole range of equal and unequal, vertical and horizontal relations. Perhaps that was what Theopompus was getting at in his notorious description of the promiscuous chaos of their sexual relationships. Like the Theban Sacred Band, the Band from the City all gathered on the great citadel, the Cadmeia, the Royal Boys, the Stripling sons of the nobility who mustered at court around the king, created a specifically Macedonian corps that transcended geographical and familial divisions. Just as Striplings were used elsewhere in Greece to protect the homeland, so they fought around the king as if he were a homeland on the move. The vertical relation between the king and the men who accompanied him reached both ways. On the one hand the Boys and the Bodyguards, the group to which they often graduated, were supposed to behave like the king's devoted admirers, ready to demonstrate their love as Pausanias II did for Philip by putting himself in the way of a missile, rather as Pericles wanted Athenian men to be uncalculating *erastai* of Athens. On the other hand they were like the king's *erōmenoi,* clients of his patronage, engaged in relations of *charis.* So Craterus thought he would reap a rich return, the hand of the king's daughter, by having sex with Archelaus. But like the Elean and the Theban men who fought together and slept together, they also clearly had relations between themselves, as the conspiracies reveal. There were formal one-to-one relationships within the Boys, with both *erastai* and *erōmenoi* fighting together, like Hermolaus and Sostratus, coevals like Alexander and Hephaestion. For one set of practices that seem to have lost their sway were the age-rules: "Did not some of them," in the words of Theopompus, "continue to shave and to keep themselves smooth into manhood? While others were brazen enough to practice 'insurgency' on each other, even though they had beards." And that also means that there is not much sign of Athenian-style wooing and courting.

Then again, like Meno of Pharsalus and his relationships with bearded Tharypas the Molossian on the one hand and with Aristippus of Larissa on the other, same-sex love could also be used to forge relationships outside Macedonia, like the one between Archelaus and Hellanocrates of Larissa. These are almost like marriage alliances, though rather more dangerous for the king if he paid too little heed to questions of honor and graciousness. Such relationships indeed could be made even with Persians, as Alexander observed by giving a very public kiss to Bagoas, his predecessor's favorite eunuch, and probably the master of the Persian court. Nor can we ignore those two or three male prostitutes that the Macedonians were said to take around with them, a practice that may be reflected in the posthumous forging of letters from Alexander refusing to take his pick of beautiful boys. Such boys were symbols of wealth, to be sure, trophy boys, decorative objects like fine costumes and gold cups, but also reflections of sheer commoditized homosexual lust.

SYZYGIES

I hope it is clear by now why I prefaced my grand tour of Greek Homosexualities—Sparta, Thera and Crete, Elis, Thebes, Thessaly and Macedonia—with an account of the heroes Achilles and Patroclus, Heracles and Iolaus. The heroes, whether as sung about in epics, painted on pots, configured in bronze in great sculptural groups or crafted on small ancient brooches, provide a series of spectacular and widespread models of male bonding. And those pairs also figure in quotidian cult practices: "altar sharing" Heracles and Iolaus worshipped together at Marathon and at the gymnasium of Cynosarges; the Thessalian practice of offering something to foreign-born Patroclus whenever they offered something to dead Achilles, the native son. These instances by no means complete the list, however. There were other male pairs in myth and cult. In fact they abound.

Apart from Heracles and Iolaus, there was another pair of semi-legendary male lovers buried at Thebes. Aristotle says Diocles was a Corinthian. He was victor in the most prestigious event at the Olympics of 728 BC, the *stadion* (about 200 meters), and eloped with his lover Philolaus to Thebes in order to escape his mother's incestuous passion for him.[1] Their tombs were pointed out by the Thebans. They lay close together, but Diocles' was in a place from which Corinth couldn't be seen. Philolaus drew up laws for the Thebans, says Aristotle, concerning provision of sons (*paidopoiia*) and adoption. His concern was to preserve property holdings.[2] Only in Greece, you can't help thinking, would locals point out the grave of the ancient heroic lawgiver who established unique measures for the production of children (*paidopoiia*) and then show you his boyfriend's memorial nearby. The date of Diocles' victory in 728 BC is close to the conventional (early) date of Homer: *c.*730. The couple look like the very oldest "historical" homosexual couple in Greece.

Another example is the pair of Theseus and the king of the Lapiths of Thessaly, Pirithous. Together they snatch Helen and fight the Amazons, and together these two try to rape Persephone, awesome queen of the Underworld. For that egregious error, one of them, Pirithous, has to stay behind in Hades.

The son of Agamemnon, mother-murdering Orestes, also has a right-hand man, Pylades—"a pair of brothers [*adelphō*] in loving affection [*philotēti*] but not born brothers [*kasignētō*]," says Euripides. Orestes stays with Pylades when wicked Clytemnestra exiles him, and it is with Pylades that he returns to kill her. Pylades eventually marries Electra. Euripides' *Iphigeneia Among the Taurians* tells of their expedition to steal the image of Artemis from the Crimea and take it to Attica. There is a catch, however: In these parts the goddess receives human victims—"Is that the altar from which Greek blood drips, Pylades?"—and the priestess is none other than Iphigeneia, Orestes' other sister, supposed to have been sacrificed herself by her father, Agamemnon, but in fact transported here by the goddess. Iphigeneia doesn't recognize Orestes, but offers to save him so that he can take a letter to her brother Orestes telling of her survival, but only if Pylades agrees to be sacrificed. Orestes refuses— "his life means as much to me as my own"—and offers himself as a victim; Pylades will take the letter for her.[3] When Orestes discovers I am alive he will be overjoyed, says Iphigeneia, about to kill Orestes. This is dramatic irony, Greek-style. Then Pylades says he won't leave Orestes and will die with him so they can be burned on the pyre together. Orestes says the best thing he can do is look after his sister Electra, despite her tainted family, and rear children who will be a memorial also to their uncle. There is a great recognition scene when Iphigeneia carefully repeats to Pylades the contents of her letter to Orestes and gets testy when Orestes tries to interrupt her.

"A pair of brothers in love" could also be a pair of brothers in blood. In a highly competitive field, the most famous same-sex pair is probably that of Orestes' uncles, Zeus's *kouroi,* the Dioscuri, the brothers of Helen and Clytemnestra: Castor and Pollux (in Greek, Polydeuces). They were supposed to be buried or living underground half the time at Therapne in Sparta, where they slept in a coma; the rest of the time they spent in heaven. In myth they sidle into the anyone-can-join expeditions—voyage of the *Argo,* Calydonian boar hunt—but they also rescue their sister Helen from Theseus and take Theseus's mother back to Sparta with them for revenge. They do a bit of raping themselves, their victims the two daughters of Leucippus, "daughters of bright white horse," but the girls' cousins, yet another pair, take revenge and kill Castor. His brother Pollux, who turns out to have been the immortal half of the pair, offers to share his immortality, a glorious example of brotherly love.

The Dioscuri are strongly associated with Sparta, and if an Athenian wants to do a quick impression of a Spartan he just inserts the oath "by the male pair of gods," *nai tō siō,* "by the twain."[4] They were, however, worshipped all over Greece, and, from an early date, in Rome. A peculiar ritual was to lay a table for them in a private house, and votive reliefs sometimes show them galloping in to partake like Santa Claus greedy for mince pies. In Attica in the village of Cephale, and elsewhere, and

36. The superb "Ildefonso" group, representing Orestes and Pylades,
"brothers in love," sacrificing together at an altar. Others have suggested
it represents Castor and Pollux. Eclectic, classicizing,
marble group from Rome (first century AD).

also in Argos, they were called Anakes, which on Mycenaean tablets means "Lords." The Twins were widely associated with horses and celestial light. Eventually they became the constellation Gemini. St. Elmo's fire, a luminescence that appears around a ship's mast in a storm, was said to be their epiphany, and they often served as saviors at times of crisis, on hand to help sailors in trouble at sea, very much like St. Nicholas, who succeeded them. They could turn up anywhere, as a famous anecdote nicely demonstrates.

The poet Simonides was commissioned to write a poem in praise of a victorious boxer, another Thessalian noble. He presented his piece at a banquet, but the host was not pleased. He had digressed "as poets generally do" into myth and spent too long eulogizing Castor and Pollux, a famous heroic boxer. The patron refused to pay the full price. Maybe the Dioscuri would pay the balance. Simonides would get no money for his money-box and no *charis* either for his *charis*-box. Not long after this shocking demonstration of stinginess, Simonides was called to the door. There were a couple of men on horseback wanting to see him as a matter of urgency. Simonides made his excuses and left the room. As he crossed the threshold the ceiling collapsed. The two men on horseback were nowhere to be found.[5] In Sparta the Twain were associated with a strange wooden structure called *dokana,* two parallel uprights bound by two parallel crossbeams—"may perhaps be understood as a gate in a *rite de passage,*" "a consistent connection between them and a particular age group cannot be observed in cult"[6]—but all kinds of pairs were associated with them, including the Spartan dual kingship. Images of the Dioscuri were taken into battle, but if one king stayed at home so did one of the Dioscuri. The people of Epizephyrian Locris in southern Italy asked Sparta for help in their war against Croton, thinking that Nasty Little Ajax might not be enough. The Spartans gave them the Dioscuri. During the battle two gigantic youths in strange clothes were seen fighting with the Locrians, who won.

If a Theban swore "by the pair of gods," *nei tō thiō*—note the subtle difference of accent—he was referring not to Castor and Pollux but to Amphion and Zethus. Another pair of sons of Zeus, born in a cave, it was they who built the walls of seven-gated Thebes, the Theban version of Romulus and Remus who built seven-hilled Rome.[7] This alternative Theban royal family, which seemed to have little to do with the family of Cadmus, Laius, Pentheus and Oedipus, caused headaches for poets. They are the main reason why Oedipus's father Laius has to vacate the throne and spend some time in Pelops's palace, to clear the stage for them, so to speak. Their main myth was to rescue their mother from the wicked usurping Queen Dirce, whom they killed by tying her to a bull. The famous sculpture known as the "Farnese Bull," a copy of a second-century BC group from Rhodes that once was admired by visitors to the Baths of Caracalla, shows them in action. Their own tomb was probably just to the north of the Cadmeia citadel. But it was a great secret where they had buried Dirce. Only the Captain of the Theban Knights knew, and each passed the knowledge on to his successor. Together they made a secret offering to her and then carefully hid all traces of it: more enforced discretion. A guard was mounted at the tomb of the Twins

37. The Theban twins Amphion (with the lyre) and Zethus tie wicked Dirce to the Bull (Taurus). Roman copy of a Pergamene (?) bronze of (165–59) or of a Rhodian monument by Tauriscus and Apollonius of Tralles (c.150). From the Baths of Caracalla in Rome.

"when the Sun traverses the Bull in heaven," i.e., when Taurus (Hyades and Pleiades) is invisible. The Twins were also identified with Gemini, and they were born on Mount Cithaeron to the daughter of "Nocturnal" Nykteus, the "brother" of the constellation Orion and son of Hyrieus, the son of the Pleiad Alcyone.[8] Perhaps they are the Boeotian "stellar" royal family therefore.

Another fine pair are Cleobis and Biton, used by Herodotus to illustrate the motto "Call no man happy till he be dead." The story, which sounds very much like the explanation for a ritual, tells of two young men of Argos, great athletes, who yoked themselves to an oxcart when the oxen didn't show up to take their mother, a priestess, to the great sanctuary of Hera, ox-eyed, ox-offered, goddess of the yoke of marriage, surnamed Zugia and Zeuxidia, eight miles outside the city. When they arrived, men congratulated them on their strength and women

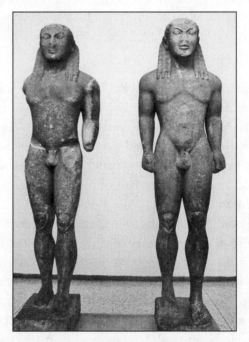

38. Giant twins unearthed at Delphi, probably supposed to represent the Argive brothers Cleobis and Biton, who pulled the oxcart of their mother, the priestess of Hera, and died peacefully in the sanctuary. Work signed by Argive [Poly?]medes (c. 580).

39. A warrior slices up the Siamese Twins known as "the Twain of Actor,"
"Aktorione," an unbeatable chariot pair from Elis. Bronze safety pin
from the cave of Zeus on Mt. Ida, Crete (c.700).

kept telling their mother how lucky she was to have such sons. Overjoyed, she asked Hera to grant her sons the greatest blessing that can fall
to mortal man. After the sacrifices and the festival celebrations the two
boys fell asleep in the temple and never woke up—"a most enviable
death, a proof from heaven that it is better to be dead than alive . . . The
Argives, considering them to be best of men, had statues made of them
which they sent to Delphi."[9]

Indeed they did. The statues, twins, were discovered complete with
the signature of the Argive artist and are now in the local museum.
They look as if they could pull an oxcart. Indeed Herodotus was probably being archaeological when he told the story, looking at the statue
and surmising. When you stand in front of them, the taped guide talking in your ear and explaining, you are very probably sharing an experience with Herodotus. Pausanias saw another statue of them
complete with oxcart in Argos, and they seem to have been a popular
subject.[10]

But there can be a closer pair than twins. For the extreme point of male bonding must be the Sons of Actor from Elis, with their bodies fused together (Fig. 39). And then again, maybe we can trump even the Sons of Actor if we think of Narcissus by his pool high on Helicon and love reflecting love, Eros and Anteros, Eros and his opposite number. We can construct an opposition between superclose pairs like Castor and Pollux at one end and superdistant pairs like Achilles and foreign Patroclus, or Timagoras and Meletus the resident alien, at the other, along with a whole host of other same-sex-loving resident aliens entombed in city centers among foreign populations. The one type embodies bonding, togetherness, the other the process of bonding, of coming together, which is understood as soon as anyone says: "What is he doing with him?" And images and configurations of the bond are everywhere: the use of pairs on bridging brooches, the invocation of their names in oaths, the stories about them exchanging pledges right until death, or being enclosed in a golden jar with two handles, or in the *dokana* of the

40. Yet another Boeotian same-sex pair. The caryatidic figures of the ephebes Kitylos and Dermys in an arm-around-the-shoulder pose borrowed from Egyptian sculptures of wedded couples, with inscriptions: "Amphalkes put it up for Dermys and for Kitylos" (*IG* VII 579); these strange names may indicate that they are divine or heroic figures, like the later Cleobis and Biton. From the cemetery of Kokali in Tanagra, ancestral homeland of "the glamorous Gephyraioi," the family of Harmodius and Aristogiton (*c.*590).

Dioscuri, the double-doubled figure of Ⴞ, or the image of Cleobis and Biton literally submitting to the yoke. Indeed, transport seems closely connected. A large number of these pairs are chariot pairs: Heracles and Iolaus, Castor and Pollux, Achilles and Patroclus, the pair of Sons of Actor.

· PART V ·

EROS OFF DUTY

SAPPHO, SAMOS AND THE TOMB OF THE DIVER:
LYRICS OF GREEK LOVE

After all this blood and death and heroics, it is something of a relief to spend time in more civilized company. Remove the straps that bind you to your bloody shield—if it's too heavy, just leave it lying on the ground, there are more important things than a shield—unbuckle your buckler, ease your head out of your tight-fitting helmet and kick off your greaves. No more tough-guy relationships played out in risk and jeopardy. Here love and wine reign supreme. Here in the flickering lamplight a charming voice and the pluck of soft lyre strings drown out the sounds of war. If the heart beats faster it's because you love the singer singing this song, not because some overgrown man-tank is bearing down on you at full speed. Have a bath, wash the blood off and slip on something more comfortable. We are going to a drinking party.

THE TOMB OF THE DIVER

Paestum is an ancient city in Italy, 60 kilometers south of Naples. It started life as a Greek colony part-founded by Sybaris about 600 years BC, and grew fast in its first hundred years. Nicely placed on the edge of territory controlled by Etruscans, it prospered from trade and from the rich agricultural land of the bay below the Bay of Naples. As if anxious to make a statement about the Greek presence in Italy, it erected a series of great temples, massive and stocky in the Doric style. A temple to Hera rose in the north of its territory overlooking native settlements on the other side of the river Sele, and another dedicated to Poseidon marked its territory in the south. Building activity soared toward the end of its first century, around the same time, coincidentally, that

Sybaris, Paestum's mother-city, famous for its love of luxury, was being razed to the ground.

In 410 BC, however, the city was overrun by "Italians" and never recovered. The population began to forget the Greek language, it was said, and the Greek way of life, and soon all that remained was one Greek festival in which they came together once a year not to celebrate their ancient identity, but to mourn the loss of meaning that had once made some sense of these words ritually intoned. At least that's what the other Greeks maintained about them, exaggerating perhaps the swiftness of Paestum's fall into multiculturalism. Two thousand years later, writing from Alexandria in Egypt, Constantine Cavafy wrote a poem about it, "The Inhabitants of Paestum" (*Poseidōniatai*), in his native Greek.

In 273 BC the Romans conquered the Italian conquerors and sent out their own military settlers—four thousand, we are told. Paestum pros-

41. Detail from the symposium depicted on the Tomb of the Diver (*c.*470). The left-hand figure is flicking the dregs from his cup at a target (see front papers). His companion is calling for more wine. What appear to be precocious portraits of real individuals are really portraits of age-classes; great care is taken to indicate tiny differences in development of the beard, always said to creep down "by the ears," despite what happens in nature. Here the most developed of those "Off-a-beard" (*ageneioi*) reclines with the most full-bearded of the Young Men (*neoi*).

42. On the east end of the tomb, a naked wine pourer prepares to refill the
cups of the north-side drinkers from a barely visible jug. Behind him a
volute krater holds the wine mixed with water. There are five more fronds
to distribute to the singers on the south side of the tomb when they have
completed their contributions of song (see front matter).

pered once more, on and off, but in late antiquity it was abandoned.
Malaria had arrived and was killing the population. The temples it built
in its first century and a half still stand, however, in an impressive row,
one after the other, markers laid down, early on, of great expectations.

The temples have long made Paestum a fixture on the cultivated
tourist circuit, and in 1968, as if to stimulate this interest, the city yielded
more treasure. A tomb was discovered, nothing but a stone box (*c.*220 ×
110 × 80 centimeters) built out of slabs of limestone, enough only to
keep soil off the skeleton, but the slabs were painted—a hint, like gold,
of the great lost masterpieces of classical Greek fresco, much talked
about, often celebrated, but rarely found. Around the sides of the tomb
a party was taking place, a drinking party, a *symposion,* men only, some
older, some younger, some very young and acting as attendants. The
men lie mostly two to a couch, flirting. One makes a pass at the most
beautiful of the young men. He defends himself. Two of the men have
lyres they aren't playing, with sound boxes made out of tortoiseshell.

43. At the west end of the tomb is the exit from the Men's Room (*andreion*).
The two men, of identical height, but one a beardless ephebe, the other a
recently bearded young man (*neos*), probably represent the "first" and "last"
banqueters waving good-bye, having abandoned their couch companions
and taking with them the "*aulos*-girl" (of lesser size = of lesser status),
her tune now taken up by one of the guests. That would mean that
one of the departing had finished his three rounds of elegies, and the
other was leaving "incomplete." Some think the central, naked,
blue-cloaked man represents the occupant of the tomb.

One plays the double-piped *aulos,* a kind of oboe or shawm. One sings,
one flings the dregs from his wine cup at a target, having called on the
name of a beautiful boy, a peculiarly Greek party game—kottabos—a
game of *erōs,* crossing a trajectory, like one of Love's arrows; if it hits,
success. Two of the guests have no one to share their couch. Their companions are seen leaving, on the western wall, the "first" and "last" of
this sympotic community—one having finished his three rounds of elegies indicated by the fronds below each banqueter, one "incomplete"—
and taking the *aulos*-girl with them.

The Tomb of the Diver takes its name from none of these scenes, but
from the image on the lid of the box. There in a sparse landscape with
two trees and a high platform, a naked youth, a diver, is suspended in
midair, about to plunge, carefully aligned according to the points on the
compass, like a star rising in the east and setting into the western ocean.

44. The extraordinary lid that gave the Tomb of the Diver its name,
generally interpreted as an image of death. The tomb is carefully aligned
with the points of the compass, so a preliminary translation of the image is
"an ephebe, on the vault above, dives into the west." The ephebe probably
represents a star, like those diving off rocks on the Blacas Krater (Fig. 17);
the water, therefore, would represent the western horizon, the "encircling
stream" of Ocean that divides the living from the dead. In that case, the
pillars will indicate the Pillars of Heracles in Cadiz (Gades), which mark the
western edge of the world (= the temple of the Phoenician god Melqart
who died, was buried, and was then, after an interval, resurrected in an
annual ceremony). The diver seems to be diving over the pillars from a
sheer cliff like the white rock of Leucas, from where, according to
tradition, lovesick Sappho and Cephalus (Orion) leapt, and sundry
ritual scapegoats. The idea of the "stars bathing in Ocean," of dead
souls being dropped into Ocean, and of stars as the bright representatives
of the heroic (or ordinary) dead is an ancient one.

There is nothing special about this drinking party, no special sign that
it belongs in a tomb, no particular eschatological significance; the subject of death seems to be avoided. Indeed the tomb seems to celebrate
ephemeral moments—a departure in the middle of a round of singing, a
pass made, a pass rejected, a toss of wine that may or may not hit the target. The only thing that is unfaithful to life is that this nocturnal event is
so full of whiteness and light, although of course when the tomb was
sealed the symposium would be plunged into darkness, with the only

light provided by the diving star in the night sky above. And in life it is rare to see so many vivid moments at any one time, rare that someone arrives to find a party so absolutely in full swing. And if this is true, there is a toughness here in these instants of chosen trivia that commands the greatest respect, not merely to celebrate and commemorate the life he has lost on the walls of a dead man's tomb, but not to flinch from its fleetingness.[1]

THE SOUND OF CUPS

The Greek drinking party or "symposium" (*sym*, "together," *posium*, "drinks") was a far cry from what goes by that name today—a days-long series of academic seminars and lectures followed by twenty minutes of questions—although, to be sure, speeches, argument and close analysis of texts were also woven into its culture. A symposium, basically, is the second half of a Greek banquet for guests. After the food, eaten with the fingers, has been consumed and the debris thrown on the floor, hands are washed, floors swept, perfumes applied, foliage crowns the head, cups are distributed, and slaves serve wine from a large bowl in which it has been mixed with at least an equal amount of water, normally much more. All of this takes place in a guest room, called after the number of couches it contains—three in a *triklinion*, seven in a *heptaklinion*, with double that number of men, two sharing a single couch like a charioteer and his standby. Sometimes it is simply called the "men's room," *andrōn*, like a private version of the ancient men's mess (*andreion*) of Crete and Sparta. We have some idea of what might go on in these evening rooms from accounts in ancient literature and from cups and crockery, which often show scenes of the drinking party that was taking place around them.

The rooms are found in houses of the classical period all over Greece. Not every house had one, but they were far from rare. They are generally very small rooms. Sometimes they are right by the entrance, a kind of anteroom, but often they are well inside, across the central courtyard, but always with a window, a small high window opening onto the street. They were decorated with painted crockery displayed on the wall, with tapestries, and in some later examples with frescoes and mosaic floors. Sometimes the *andrōn* itself had a little anteroom. Archaeologists can identify them because a small ledge runs around the wall, and here couches were placed, two on each side, except for the short side where the door was. The guests reclined on the couch on their left elbow. Usually another man was reclining alongside. Sometimes he might be an admirer of yours, or a young man you admired, or someone you had never met before, but to lie horizontally he had to be Eighteen or over.[2]

As the Tomb of the Diver shows so nicely, there was singing. We can see guests singing on vases. Typically they put their right hand on their head, throw back the neck, and sounds come out. Sometimes the artist shows actual lyrics, emerging letter by letter, sometimes just a series of "o"s. Often a shawm player accompanies them. Sometimes the artist tries to depict the sound of the instrument as it leaves the pipe. From a shawm, something nasally resonant, *NETENARENETENETO,* showing that the shawm players used their tongue. From a trumpet, not a sympotic instrument, *TOTOTE TOTE.* One particular *meirakion* is shown singing a line to the music of a lyre: *mame ka poteo,* ". . . and I am longing . . . ," which means he is singing the personal lyric poetry of Anacreon, Ibycus, Alcaeus etc. It might just possibly be a misspelled and/or misremembered line of Lesbian Sappho: *kai maomai kai potheo,* "and I am yearning and I am longing" (cf. fragment 36).[3]

Over the last twenty years or so, a consensus has begun to emerge that not only Sappho but the great majority of all early Greek songs were composed for performance in a symposium, with the exception of dance songs ("choral" lyre songs, or, in drama, "choral" shawm songs), which can usually be differentiated by their fancy footwork (i.e., complex rhythmical structure) and generic themes.[4] Such a theory begs a lot of questions and tends to make the notion of "sympotic poetry" more fuzzy as a category in itself.[5]

US:SONGS AND ME:SONGS

Perhaps it is most useful to distinguish between broadcast and narrow-cast drinking-party songs. The former is designed to go from group to group, it is not too specific in content or difficult in vocabulary and form, and it tries to get the whole community singing from the same song sheet at the same time.

"How much longer is it going to last, your lying down on the job? When will you pluck up the courage, Young Men? Don't your neighbors make you feel embarrassed about this utter negligence of yours? You seem to be enjoying peaceful repose, but the whole country is in the grip of war . . ." One can imagine Callinus's opening lines from the seventh century BC spreading around the dining rooms of Ephesus and making all the Twenty-somethings (neoi) feel distinctly uncomfortable as they recline on their couches.[6] We find something like this at a later date in Hellenistic Alexandria, where a general learned of the universal praise he enjoyed, the toasts poured in his name in symposia, the flattering graffiti and the paignia (musical mimes) being sung in his honor throughout the city "thanks to the entertainers at dinner [akroamata]."[7] It is not surprising then to find that some of these early songs, some of them quite charming, have been described as "propaganda."[8]

Poets sometimes describe their songs as "aerodynamic"—the song is a wing, or the blade of an oar: "I have given you wings, Cyrnus, with which you can fly over the big deep sea and all the land, soaring with ease. You will be there at every banquet and celebration, coming to rest in the mouths of many. Of you, Young Men [neoi andres] of charm and beauty will sing with lovely resonant voices to the accompaniment of little resonant shawms, and with all elegance and propriety."[9] Both these examples are in elegiac couplets, which means they consist of a full dactylic hexameter line of six feet, Dumdidi dumdum etc., followed by a broken or mid-paused hexameter, Dumdidi dum . . . PAUSE . . . Dumdidi.[10] These meters were standard—Homer used hexameters— and simple to remember, using the standard Ionic dialect of epic, and with elegies you only had to concentrate on singing, while a professional shawm player, probably a girl, accompanied you. The shawm-girls were an important part of the traveling part of the symposium, the kōmos, which took drunken revelers out into the streets on visits to other houses, joining one group to another. Elegies were used for a wide range of subjects—politics, exhortations, war—but there was also the elegiac elegy, the songs of commiseration and loss, songs for which the shawm might perhaps be played in a sustainedly mournful, rather than a staccato rhythmical fashion. These are underrepresented in surviving literature, but a few of Archilochus's elegies are on the subject of his brother-in-law's death at sea, and one of the grandest and most influential of all ele-

gies, Antimachus's "Lyde," of about 400 BC, seems to have been a consolation on the death of his mistress or wife, Lyde. Elegy became the standard format for tomb inscriptions, one of which actually has its score
inscribed, to remind us that it is not just a text. Both of these examples
have a jolly "enjoy it while you can" approach to looming death, but we
are also told that the competition for mournful elegies at Delphi was soon
terminated because they were thought to be gloomy and inauspicious,
and songs of commemorative lamentation were banned at around the
same time in Athens, which may help to explain why so small a proportion of the surviving examples of "elegy" show anything of the funereal
tone conjured up by the English word elegiac and the Greek *elegos*.[11]

Narrow-cast song on the other hand means distinctiveness, personal
autonomy (you can perform it on your own), freedom, class and individ-
uality; it circulates in the first place within the group gathered together
at a drinking party. It may contain irregular, immoral or controversial
sentiments that reject the values of the communal and collective; it may
present itself as expression rather than communication, as solitary
thoughts "overheard" by the other drinkers, feelings made visible, rising
up from the interior into the surface of the world. More positively it
may describe the poet's very particular feelings about a particular named
person or situation. In various ways, it may be quite difficult to remember and perform, using uncommon meters, unexpected or uncommon
words in local dialect, surprising combinations, distinctive poetry for
amateurs of distinction.

This kind of Me-Song also went out into the world, bringing fame
willy-nilly, to its poets, as well as to the maidens and youths, the ideas
and values that it celebrated, but it was probably quite pleased, on the
other hand, if it didn't reach too wide an audience. It wanted its fame,
perhaps, at the right kind of parties, not best pleased to grace the mouth
of some low-life drunkard sprawled on a rubbish heap singing the
praises of an aristocratic youth to shoppers, or performed in a brothel
for its clients.

Theognis, quoted above, a poet of the sixth century, hopes that the
people who sing of his beloved Cyrnus will be fine Young Men with
lovely voices, at a symposium "of elegance and propriety" (*eukosmiōs*).
He is anxious about his name and reputation as a composer, and "signs"
or seals (*sphrēgis*) his poems as a defense against pirated copies: "Their

theft will never pass unnoticed, and no one will take something of inferior quality, when something good can be had. So everyone will say:
'They are the verses of Theognis of Megara; his name is known
throughout the world' " (ll. 19–23). But if Theognis is anxious, that is
because he needs to be. He wrote simple songs in popular meters to the
accompaniment of professional shawm players that anyone could hire.
Anyone could sing his songs and fashion their own variations. Surely,
soon after Theognis fitted it with wings, Cyrnus's name came to rest in
the mouth of someone inappropriate, and despite his attempts to copy-
right his material his songs were debased by spurious imitations, so that
nowadays no one can be sure which of the poems ascribed to him belong
to him and which are copies, and some have gone so far as to say that
poor proud Theognis is nothing more than a brand name. The problem
is that his poetry is structurally promiscuous.

On the other hand, Sappho and Alcaeus of the island of Lesbos, all
but contemporaries, took measures to ensure that their songs would not
fall into the wrong hands by making them in narrow-cast format, i.e.,
lyre songs. There were various kinds of lyre in ancient Greece. The
most elaborate and difficult was the cithara (whence "guitar," "zither"),
with a sound box made of wood by "cabinetmakers" and inlaid, occasionally, with ivory and precious jewels and metal, the instrument of
professionals.[12] Ladies and gentlemen, however, seem to have played the
simple tortoiseshell lyre with seven strings, or the *barbitos,* an elongated
version with longer strings, lower pitch and softer tone, associated especially with the island of Lesbos. It is possible to extend the range of such
instruments to two octaves by gently touching the vibrating string at
midpoint.[13]

Still within the range of an amateur, and not needing hours and hours
of rehearsal like the dance songs, it nevertheless took practice and skill to
tune, play and sing to the lyre, which was supposed to be an aristocratic
accomplishment, achieved through years (Plato advises three years) of
training with a paid music teacher. Lyre singers had to do several things
at once: play with both hands, tap out a rhythm with the foot, remember the words and carry the song. In *Frogs,* Aristophanes has Euripides
imitate Aeschylus's monotonous lyre songs by ending each line with a
strum, "*phlatto-thratto-phlatto-thrat.*"

Already in Homer, Achilles, best of Achaeans, and Alexander (i.e.,

Paris) prince of Troy know how to play the lyre. Paris's lyre looks as if it already functions as an instrument of softness and loveliness, most unwarlike, the instrument of a seducer. For Achilles too it seems unwarlike, an instrument he plays to himself while sulking on strike, with only Patroclus present. But Achilles' subject matter is rather different from that of later lyre players, more epic and heroic; he sings not of his feelings, but of war and glorious deeds.[14]

The aristocratic associations of the amateur lyre persisted into the classical period. Plato's supremely well-born schoolboy Lysis can be assumed to be taking lyre lessons. So too Alcibiades. Others, of less refined background, haven't a clue. "Forgive him, he can't play the lyre" was the ancient equivalent of "Forgive him, he didn't attend a private school." Comic poets developed an equivalent for the lower orders: "Forgive him, he never learned to dig."[15]

We have a vivid account of Alexander the Great being brought in by his father to perform on the difficult cithara in front of a delegation of middle-aged Athenians come for peace talks in the spring of 346 BC, among them Aeschines and Demosthenes—a nice example of the Macedonians buying into the aristocratic culture of the Greek city. This is Alexander's first appearance in history. He was coming up to his tenth birthday, an early age to be learning an instrument. One later writer, who has his extreme youth right at any rate, suggests that Alexander's music master might not have been too keen to correct the young prince, conscious of the fact that young Heracles had killed a critical lyre teacher with his plectrum. At any rate, it is safe to assume, or we surely would have heard all about it, that nine-year-old Alexander was no prodigy on the lyre, any more than at making speeches, another thing his father asked him to do in front of the visiting dignitaries. But if the ambassadors clapped and applauded, as they surely did—the talks were going well; peace was coming—it need not be put down to sycophancy; it was probably quite remarkable to see a nine-year-old Macedonian prince play anything at all. I wonder what he was playing.[16]

NOT ABOUT THE WAR

A lot of the archaic song that survives is sympotic in the narrow sense, songs about the world of the drinking party, songs about drinking and love and boys. And this song seems to have a quite different tone from what has passed for poetry hitherto, all that torrent of Homer, arrows through eye sockets, goddesses bleeding on the battlefield, the relentless weighty hexameter, line after line . . .

> I am not fond [*phileo*] of the man who talks about quarrels and tear-jerking war, while he wine-drinks with the wine bowl standing full right next to him. Give me someone who mixes the lovely gifts of the Muses with the gifts of Aphrodite, someone who makes us think of passion and pleasure.

> Boy! Bring water! Bring wine! Bring flower-garlands for us. Fetch them at once. I am going into the boxing-ring with Eros.

> Come on, boy, bring us a wine bowl, so I can drink a toast in one draught.[17]

Already, just from these few fragments of Anacreon, it is possible to detect a distinctive mood in the sympotic poetry of the symposium, not just avoiding the topic of heroic deeds but opposed to it. Lying with their feet off the ground, Young Men were deliberately creating a world that was not the world of running and leaping and charging. It isn't impossible that they are taking time off from the responsibilities of their age-class, the martial character the age-class system has thrust upon them. The archaic songs of off-duty hours have a flippant tone, irresponsible even. Shields were heavy, for instance, but hoplite warfare demanded that each citizen-soldier stand fast in the phalanx, a cog in the citizen machine, maintaining a solid wall of armor to protect his next-door neighbor as he in turn is protected by the man next to him. What Archilochus says here, therefore, is quite shocking: "Some member of the Saian tribe is enjoying my shield that I left behind by a bush, not that there's anything wrong with it. I didn't leave it willingly. I saved myself. Why worry about a shield? Let it go. I'll get another, just as good" (fragment 5).

Archilochus of Ionian Paros is the earliest of these poets to survive in any quantity, so early that we have little idea of where he was coming from, although we do know that he sometimes took on the voice of particular characters, so maybe this is a bad man or a coward. But Alcaeus of

Lesbos wrote something not dissimilar, half a century later. In 607/606 there had been a battle against the Athenians over the land around Troy opposite Gallipoli. When the Athenians started winning, we are told, Alcaeus quickly shed his gear and fled. He sends a poetic dispatch from the front line to his companion (*hetairos*) Melanippus: Alcaeus is safe, but his arms and armor are trophies, hung on the walls of the temple of gray-eyed Athena by the men of Attica.[18] Plutarch accuses Herodotus of spite for even mentioning Alcaeus's "shameful" action.[19] But Alcaeus writes a poem about it and signs it with his own name. What must it have sounded like at the time?

The Homeric ethos centers on the glory, the fame, the never-forgotten name, that comes only from great deeds and a heroic death. Archilochus begs to differ: "When you're dead there's no respect, no talk about you in town. It's the gratitude of the living that we, the living, pursue. The dead get things that are worth nothing."[20] Alcaeus addresses his friend Melanippus on a similar subject:

Drink and get drunk with me, Melanippus; once you have crossed to the other side of great eddying Acheron, do you think you will see the clean light of the sun again? Come, don't be ambitious for great things. King Sisyphus, let me tell you, Aeolus's son, had more big ideas than any other man . . . but for all his cunning plans he too crossed eddying Acheron twice, forced by fate, and King Zeus, Cronus's son, thought up something to keep him well occupied under the black earth. Come, don't hold out for these things. We are young. Now's the time, if ever there was a time, passively to put up with whatever god puts in our way.[21]

It is quite amazing to have such voices preserved from so long ago, for the earliest lyric poets lived in a world that is ancient even for ancient historians, a world where much of what we imagine when we imagine the ancient world—splendid cities, marble temples, bronze statues, histories, great all-Greek athletic contests, images, texts—don't exist, or rather are only just beginning to appear. We know very little about how these people lived, the geopolitical situation, their religious beliefs, their stories, the type of communities they lived in, but we seem to know them intimately because of the intimate-seeming poetry they left behind. They left nothing, it seems, apart from their innermost thoughts and feelings.

In *The Times* of May 14, 1906, archaeologists announced the discovery of a library in the sand drifts that had buried the ancient provincial city of "Sharp-snouted Fish," Oxyrhynchus, in Egypt, with significant indications that the owner of said library had possessed several manuscripts of Sappho. Sappho was no slacker; her complete works constituted a nine-volume set, a fat paperback if published by Faber and Faber today. But in 1906, something like 99 percent of Sappho had not reached anyone's ears for over a millennium. The poems had survived more or less intact until the sixth or seventh centuries AD, but little seems to have reached the ninth century, and by the twelfth century scholars in Constantinople were mourning the loss. What happened during those fateful two or three hundred years was not a determined attempt to wipe out pagan literature, let alone lesbian literature, just a catastrophic change in priorities; not book burnings, but a few hundred years of neglect, just enough of a distraction of attention to break the chain that was Sappho's lifeline into the future.

Time and again, a manuscript of Sappho's songs or of Strabo or of Archimedes, one of only two or three copies in the world, or one of only one, was allowed to rot in the book box, while the scribe spent his precious hours making yet another copy of the painfully awful Greek prose of the evangelists. Or worse, the priceless thousand-year-old text was systematically erased and overwritten to make a private copy of the more polished pieties of some bestselling Christian sermonizer. Where the reused manuscript survives, the original underneath can often be reconstructed, as scholars have recently reconstructed the ghostly rubbed-out text of Archimedes' *Method of Mechanical Theorems,* also rediscovered in 1906, but this time under the pages of a book on a shelf in a library in Istanbul. But if, after some centuries of use, the reused pages were themselves copied, then the ugly old volume written on secondhand parchment was thrown unceremoniously in the rubbish, along with the priceless text hidden underneath, organic matter after all and biodegradable.

In one comedy, written about two centuries after her death, Sappho starred in her own play, a comedy in which she posed a riddle: "She is female in nature and keeps her offspring under the fold of her bosom, and they, though voiceless, raise a loud cry over the swell of the deep sea, over the landmass to reach whomever they want to even those who are not present can hear, yet at the hearing the audience is deaf." Her interlocutor thinks the answer is a city, its politicians and the public that ignores them. "What a lot of nonsense," says Sappho, the answer is "a letter" holding voiceless characters in its envelope that speak to someone who is not present, while someone standing next to the reader hears nothing.[22] When the papyrus hunters eventually excavated the private library in 1906, her words seemed prophetic, but in a way the author had not intended. The little library turned out to be badly damaged. As they dug in they discovered that most of it had decomposed; letters and words littered the surface of the soil.[23] Every letter might have been preserved and every word lost, or every word preserved and every poem lost, for alphabetic scripts depend on their ordering to make any sense; otherwise it's just scrabble and fridge-word-magnets. But at least one substantial combination of letters and words had managed to hold its formation during the centuries under the sand. Finally at least one more of Sappho's missives would reach its destination, albeit a little disheveled:

> Some say there's nothing lovelier to look at on earth's dark face than a division of cavalry, or an army, or a fleet, but I say lovelier than anything else is what the heart desires. It is perfectly easy for everyone to understand what I mean, for Helen, whose beauty far surpassed everyone, left her perfectly good husband and took a boat for Troy, her child, her dear parents, even, not crossing her mind; she was led astray by . . . lightly . . . which reminds me of Anactoria who isn't here. Her charming way of walking, her bright flashing face, not rows of Lydian chariots, not armed infantry, is what I'd like to see. (fragment 16)

The poem has attracted much appreciation, and it is worth reading again in slow motion, as all Sappho's songs are, and just trying to write down your impressions of it, your sense of it, your understanding of what's going on and what's coming next line by line, being as honest with yourself as possible.

Her songs are like short stories in that respect. You are launched into a situation and then realize it is not quite the situation you thought it was, and then gradually released from the poet's grip with some kind of ending. All I would like to point out is that here she expresses not just a personal preference but a poetical one, for Sappho is a maker of images as well as a connoisseur of them. Homer, say, gives us scenes of armies and fighting, cavalcades and arraignments, but all these scenes are simply epiphenomena of Menelaus's desire to see his wife again, a wife who left the husband arranged for her in favor of a Trojan called Paris, who took her fancy.[24] Homer showed the solitary lyre as an unwarlike instrument and put it in the hands of Helen's seducer. But for Sappho all the action of the *Iliad* is really just a reflection of the action of *erōs,* private *erōs* undermining public relationships of family and tribe, the same opposition between clan ties and ties made through *erōs* that underlines all aspects of the ideology of Greek Love. Sappho prefers to put more important things before her audience's eyes—love, beauty, beautiful girls she loves, and some extremely complicated feelings:

> I think he's like the gods, that man who sits across from you and hears close up your sweet intonation and loving laugh, by god, it makes my heart thump against my breastbone; for when I look at you only briefly, my voice is gone to nothing. Instead my tongue buckles. Before I know it a bushfire has sprinted under my skin, vision fails, ears hum, down me runs a trickle of sweat, and trembling seizes the whole of me, greener than grass am I, I'm dead, nearly, I think. (fragment 31.1–16)

Ricocheting, the poem shifts quickly from one point of view to another, around the girl whose shape appears in the responses of those around her. Sappho begins with what the man seems like to her, what the girl sounds like to the man, what she herself would feel like were she in the man's position, what she would look like then to others, what she seems like to herself. As we cut through these different perspectives, zooming in and out, our mood changes. We think she's admiring the man, then we realize that she only admires him because she admires the girl he's talking to. She is jealous, but not of the girl, of the man's *composure.* She seems to speak to us and says she can only speak because she is not speaking to the girl, although in fact she seems imaginatively to shrink the distance, putting herself right there in front of the girl, heart pounding, ears humming, tongue tied, which makes us suspect that this voice we hear, our text, her song, is really a voice in Sappho's tongue-tied head. And if talk of desire, as many suspect, is a way of paying a compliment to someone's loveliness and beauty, then Sappho's original compliment to the godslike man comes to seem somewhat backhanded. The girl makes less of an impact on the composed man who is close to her. It is the woman who is watching from a distance who reflects her lovely charm, her true charm, most forcefully, so forcefully she is about to faint.

Another famous poem starts off more formally:

Undying Aphrodite, cunning daughter of Zeus, cunningly enthroned, don't crush me into submission, I ask you, with all this anguish and ache, come and see me, if ever my voice managed to reach you in the past, some distant place on the other side, and you listened and came, leaving the gold house of your father, chariot all yoked up; and quick sparrows, wings blurring, flew you handsomely over earth's dark loams, from heaven by way of air, to their direct destination; and you, O happy one, with a knowing smile on your undying face, asked what the matter was with me this time, why I was calling, what was the object of my zealousness.

"Who is it this time I must persuade to take you into her affections? Who is it, Sappho, who has injured you? So she avoids you, in no time she'll pursue; so she turns down your gifts, instead she'll give them; so she doesn't like you, in no time she will, whether or not she wants to."

Come to me again now. Lighten my anxious load; and what my heart longs to see accomplished, accomplish for me; stand with me, you yourself, my allied. (fragment 1)

The same juxtaposition of objective distanced exterior with subjective solipsistic interior, but instead of the ricocheting of fragment 31, the main feature of this poem is the sense of steadily increasing presence. Again Sappho adopts the device of projecting herself from the present into another prospective reality, in order to create a vector of movement. In 31 she placed herself imaginatively next to the stunning girl. Here she imagines Aphrodite coming to her in the past, getting closer and closer, talking to her first in indirect then in direct speech, crystal clear, addressing her by name, even predicting the future. As in fragment 31, which begins "I think he is like . . ." and reaches closure with "what I am like," *phainetai . . . phainomai,* there is a neat circular construction, but whereas that poem spirals inward to greater intensity, fragment 1 ends where it began. Suddenly the fantastic vision is gone and the goddess is distant once more. Sappho stands alone, back where she started, summoning her "mistress."

One thing missing in translation, of course, is the noise of the accented Greek. Sappho's Hymn to Aphrodite was selected by the ancient critic Dionysius of Halicarnassus as a supreme example of the inlaid, i.e., carpentered and decorated style. He notes especially the euphony and charm of the joinery, the way "The Songstress" juxtaposes and interweaves words according to their relatedness and the natural bonding (*syzygias*) of the letters. The poem is full of clear patterns of sound. The first stanza sounds something like

> *poikilotron' atanat aprodita*
> *pai Dios doloploke, lissomai se*
> *mē m'asaisi mēd' oniaisi damna*
> *potnia, tumon . . .*

There is plenty of rhyme and assonance, tripping runs that alternate simple vowels with simple consonants or smooth consonant blends, followed by long vowels, diphthongs, and nasal combinations. Not a single "b" is to be found in the whole poem. Probably this is because the b-sound wasn't appropriate to the aural impression Sappho wanted to create. Others wrote poems that avoided, a more difficult exercise, the letter "s"—but it is also possible, beyond letter games, that the letter "b" had some significance.[25] Most astonishingly, at the beginning of the last century Antoine Meillet demonstrated that the eleven-syllable line used by Sappho for all the songs in book one and most notably in this song, her Hymn to Aphrodite, which probably headed the entire collection—

> *kai gar ai pheugei, tacheōs diōxei;*
> *ai de kōra mē deket', alla dōsei;*
> *ai de mē philei, tacheōs philēsei*

> So she avoids you, in no time she'll pursue;
> so she turns down your gifts, instead she'll give them;
> so she doesn't like you, in no time she will . . .

—had close similarities to the meters of the ancient Indian Rig Veda, composed by *c.* 1200 BC; the specific forms used by the Rig Veda and Sap-

pho probably had a common origin, therefore, before *c.*2000 BC. Which is
a little bit like discovering a late Roman tradition of the late eighteenth-
century limerick—"There was an old woman of Croydon . . ."—not
perfectly but 90 percent identical, and perfectly recognizable.[26]

There is a whole corpus of ancient hymns to gods written in Homer's
weighty long hexameters. A few of these, probably, were composed by
Sappho's contemporaries. They celebrate the gods' important myths,
their cultic epithets, their cults, but they have none of this feeling we
find in Sappho's Hymn to Aphrodite, of a familiar, slightly witchy, or
mantic, seerlike, relationship with a divinity. Ancient critics described
them as "cletic" songs, "calling" hymns or "invocations," a kind of private version of the anonymous hymns in epic hexameters. In their invocations, the poets summoned lots of gods from lots of places, Artemis
from many mountains and cities, Aphrodite from Cyprus or Syria or
Crete. They might vividly describe the places from which the gods were
summoned, the particular temples and gardens. They might describe the
loveliness of the place from which they were speaking, to which the god
was being called. Most of Sappho's hymns were like this, apparently: in-
vocative. Another, which survives substantially, evokes a beautiful
shrine watered by icy springtime streams, where incense smoke wafts
from altars into apple trees and mixes with the sounds of water, breezes
grace a meadow where horses could graze, shade is provided by roses
and slumber slips down through leaves. It "displays, perhaps for the first
time in European literature, the 'sentiment of place'—not just a 'feeling
for nature,' but a feeling for what it is like to be in a *particular* place at a
particular time." The personalizing tendency in lyric poetry specifies not
just the individual speaker, but the place and time in which she speaks;
it is not just me-song, it is here-song, and now-song.[27]

CONJUGAL LESBIANS

The authenticity of Sappho's desires and feelings has often been called
into question. It should be enough, perhaps, that she is an authentic
writer. She may or may not have been a "lesbian" but she was perfect at
imagining herself one and, witch that she was, everyone who sang her
songs became something of a lesbian too. Greek men did not generally
respect the talent of Greek women enough to give them opportunities
to explore and develop their potential, but they accorded Sappho a very

high degree of respect, not merely as a really good "lesbian" poet, or woman poet, but as a really good poet, *thaumaston chrēma,* "a wonderful phenomenon." In just the few bits of her that remain we see striking examples of that strange coming together of art and belief that makes all the great "makers" precious enough to preserve and reproduce; there really was something badly wrong with those few centuries when, disastrously, book lovers neglected to reproduce Sappho.

Sappho frames her imagining with a confession that she is only imagining—what seems, what she calls to mind, what she remembers— that it's not real, but in each case she imagines so well that her confession seems less like a concession to the demands of realism and truth, an honesty, than a permit to take her whole self with her to somewhere she's not, into the gradual presence of a metaphysical Aphrodite, right into the garden to which she is calling her, right up close to a girl she watches from a distance. Sappho may or may not perfectly fit her poetic "I," but she inhabits her poetic "if" with absolute conviction. If, after all that, you want the real Sappho too, I am happy to oblige. A papyrus informs us that she had a figure "very much to be despised," was "extremely unattractive," "dark in complexion" and "tiny" . . . "apparently."[28]

It seems to me, once more, that those who wish to separate Sappho's same-sex *erōs,* like those who wish to separate the same-sex hopeless devotion of Achilles and Patroclus, from the culture of Greek Love, on the grounds that there is no active and passive penetration, are being deeply perverse. Sappho in the female gender conforms beautifully to the pattern of Greek Love or, more specifically, of Athenian Love, which we know from so many examples in the male gender. We might say they were copying male same-sex relationships. But since women's worlds were generally left alone by men, and since women's rituals seem in reputation and in fact to have been more respectful of tradition, less politically public, generally less visible and vulnerable to the impositions of new male regimes, it seems just as likely that they provide a more original and authentic version of the phenomenon. The Lesbians used Aeolic dialect, like the Thebans and the Thessalians; indeed a high percentage of the tiny number of lady poets in Greece come from the Aeolic cultural zone. And just like those of her cultural cousins way back home in Thebes, the relationships between women on Lesbos are described as *conjugal,* yoke-pairs. Sappho herself uses the word in her own dialect: *syndygos.*

But at least one Dorian city also seems to have had conjugal women. We are told by Plutarch that the maidens of Sparta were loved by gentlewomen (*kalaik'agathai*) in the same way as the men, which implies formal, publicly recognized same-sex unions, the female equivalent of *eispnēlas* and *aïtas*. Indeed one of the "Maiden songs" from the great male poet Alcman (fragment 1), of the generation of poets that precedes Sappho, contains words written for Spartan girls in which they passionately admire each other's beauty and fantasize about admiring other girls who are strangely off-limits to them: "Nor will you go to Aenesimbrota's and say, 'Could Astaphis be mine, might Philylla gaze in my direction, and Damareta, and lovely Wianthemis.' But no, Hagesichora is watching me [*tērei*]" (ll. 73–77). The song involves the carrying of a plow (*pharos*), we are told, through the night, in honor of the goddess at Dawn, Aotis, the goddess of the Rising, Orthria. Two women are especially prominent, Agido and Hagesichora. This latter is "leader of the chorus," evidently, keeping a jealous eye on her girls. Agido, exactly like Maximus's Spartan *erōmenos* on whom all eyes are turned, is compared to the sun—"So I sing of the light [*phōs*] of Agido. I see her as I see the sun, which Agido summons to shine on us as our witness . . ." This must be a reference to some binding pledge they are about to make, since the all-seeing eye of the sun was often invoked as a witness to oaths. The girls also compare themselves to Sirens, who alternate, as we have seen, with handsome young winged males, like breezes, on a Spartan cup. And if we concluded, uncontroversially, that the winged males represent male Loves, if not male beloveds of men, the Sirens should indicate, controversially, female Loves. I am not sure who is about to be pledged to whom under the morning sun's watchful eye, whether Agido to the whole chorus, to Hagesichora, to a maiden (*parsenos*) who speaks, as if a lone maiden, self-deprecatingly, at one point in the song, or another girl to another girl entirely, under the auspices of Hagesichora.

Despite over a hundred years of debate about the meaning of this mysterious song, there is one rather straightforward interpretation, which is, naturally, the one classicists have been most reluctant to consider: that it celebrates an *erōtikos* yoke pairing of two Spartan women, if not the ritual of yoke pairing itself. It is a lesbian, if you like, wedding. Indeed there seems no possibility of women pulling a plow without a "yoke pairing" of women being put on public display. And there is something terribly intriguing about this particular ritual, which is one of the oldest, if not the oldest, of those directly attested in Greece by a primary document relating to a contemporary practice. It is also one of the extremely few rituals attached to the obsolescent goddess of the dawn, Eos, who, along with Zeus and Helios, the sun, is one of only three Greek divinities with impeccable Indo-European origins. And it relates to a same-sex pair, one of the few quite distinctive features of Indo-European religions that Greek historians are prepared to accept as surviving in Greece, not least in Sparta, in the persons of the Dioscuri, Castor and Pollux, the chariot pair of the "Divine Twins," the "Horse-Pair Twins," who as Asvins were intimately associated with Dawn, Usas, in the earliest Indian literature. Most classicists prefer not even to touch upon the possibility of any Greek rituals reaching as far back in time as the Aryans *c.*4000 BC, but if you are not so fastidious, a predawn wedding of women might not be the worst candidate.

It is also interesting to note that the only proper "modern-style" lesbians in ancient Greek literature, who appear in the fifth of Lucian's *Dialogues of the Courtesans,* are also described as married, and that one of them is also from Lesbos. Here's a filleted version of this fabulous text. A friend is talking to her girlfriend Leaena, a courtesan: "We hear novel things about you, Leaena, to the effect that Megilla that rich Lesbian woman is in love with you as a man is in love, and that you have intercourse with each other, doing I don't know what with each other . . . You don't love [*phileis*] me or you wouldn't keep such things from me." "I love you as I love any woman. But this woman is terribly manlike." "I don't know what you mean, unless you mean she happens to be one of those women with a tendency for female comradeships [*hetairistria*]; for they say in Lesbos there are women with a male countenance, who don't like undergoing it at the hands of men, but get off by cozying up [*plēsiazousas*] to women in the way men do." . . . Well, "She and another woman, Demonassa of Corinth, put a symposium together. Demonassa is also rich and of the same accomplishments as Megilla."

At this particular symposium it transpires that, after Leaena had played the cithara for them, the two women invited her to lie between them. "At first they kissed me like men, not simply touching lips but with open mouth, putting their arms around me and fondling my breasts. Demonassa even bit me amid the kissing . . . In time Megilla, getting a little heated, removed her wig, which was very realistic and close-fitting, and revealed a skinhead like the very manly athletes . . . and she said, 'Have you ever seen so beautiful a Cadet?' and I said, 'I see no Cadet here, Megilla.' 'Don't feminize me,' she said. 'I am called Megillus, I have been married to Demonassa here [gegamēka] for donkey's years, and she is my wife . . . I was born a woman like the rest of you women, but my mind [gnōmē] and desire [epithumia] and everything else is that of a man.' 'And is the desire of a man sufficient for you?' 'Give me a chance, Leaena, if you don't believe me,' she said, 'and you will come to recognize that I lack nothing of what men have. I have something instead of the man's thing. Give me a chance and you will see.' Well, I did give her a chance . . . I put my arms around her just as if she were a man, and she began to do the do and to love and to pant, and to reach the very peak of pleasure, apparently." "Began to do what, Leaena, how? Tell me this, above all." "Don't ask for details, for they are ugly/shameful things; in the name of heavenly Aphrodite, I won't tell."

There are good grounds for thinking that all three of these relationships between women that we know about—the Spartan women, Sappho's syzygies, Megilla and her married wife Demonassa—involved formal bondings. Whether there was some kind of sexual mixing of bodies of women during the ceremony of bonding, I have no idea, but I would be surprised if there was not some public gesture. These relationships could serve any number of purposes, exactly like male same-sex homo-erōs. It could be a way of selecting beautiful girls for dances or rituals, a way of recruiting beautiful nonelite women into the elite. But just as with the men, the main point is to establish boundary-crossing personal "can't-help-myself" ties, to bring the women of the polis together through erōs, or even, in the case of Megilla and Demonassa, to establish international relations, through a special made kinship.[29]

Certainly it would seem that locally, on the eastern seaboard, Aeolian Lesbos stood out for its lesbianism. There seems to be no other way to interpret this poem dating from about fifty years after Sappho, by the amorous poet Anacreon, originally from Teos, an Ionian city on the mainland to the south of Lesbos:

Again long-gold-haired Love, tossing in my direction a scarlet ball, sends me an invitation to play games with the girl with the fancy footwear. But she says she doesn't like my hair, "because it's white," because she is from beautifully colonized Lesbos, and is gagging for another of her sex.[30]

The poem is not without its richness and complications, colors and tresses, bouncing balls, like a gossipy haiku. One might infer, at least, that there is a contrast between the kind of things Eros normally shoots at people, i.e., arrows that pierce the skin, and a soft round ball that bounces off. Anacreon is not smitten by love, it just rebounds. And there is also a lovely image of uninvolvement. He wants to join in the ball game when the ball comes his way, but the girl doesn't want to play ball, or, rather, not with him. But for all the sophistic squirming of some scholars—"another of her sex" might refer to any object of the female gender, like long hair (komē, fem.), so "she is all agog for other tresses"— there seems no way out of the fact that the girl is said to reject him because she is from Lesbos. Indeed one can see a little sharp rejoinder. She says there is something wrong with Anacreon's hair: its color. He says there's something wrong with her nationality: Lesbian. Some ancient readers thought it was a fantasy about being rejected by long-dead Sappho herself. But really it is the archaeological tendency again. Lesbos stood out for its female syzygies. It was this institution of amatory pairing of women on the island, a hard fact to stub one's figurative toe on, that grabbed attention and gave the island its reputation.

A MALE LESBIAN

It is in narrow-cast format, the lyre songs of the symposium, that the first intense love poetry written by men about boys materializes, sometime at the end of the seventh century. It is a fair assumption that the boys referred to are the kind who go to symposia. They do not seem to have chaperons, and unless the rules have changed, that means they are over Eighteen or slaves.[31] Occasionally the sources who quote the fragments insist on this, talking of "Striplings."

Among the first to survive is Alcaeus of Mytilene, who was writing around the same time as Sappho and probably in the same city, though it is possible that Sappho was born in neighboring Eresos and belonged to a slightly later period. Highly esteemed by the ancient critics, he was sometimes criticized for preening himself too much on his own pedigree and for a threatening tone. His poems show him to be almost as intense as Sappho, just as careless of the rules and just as meticulous in his constructions, and quite concerned about the weather:

Let's drink, for the Dog Star is coming around . . .

Wet your lungs with wine, for the Dog Star is coming around, it's a dangerous time of year . . .

It's raining, and out of heaven the storm is of a size; flowing streams are frozen stiff . . . Let the storm fall over our heads. But pile up the fire in the meantime, mix the honeyed wine without stint, make your head comfy with cushiony fluff.[32]

The Roman poet Horace had a near-death experience and imagined—as only he would—how close he was to meeting Sappho and Alcaeus in the Underworld. In his fantasy he awarded the latter a "golden plectrum." Quintilian confirmed the award, especially for his attacks on tyrants, but he notes sadly that Alcaeus also "messed about and descended to love poetry, though he was better suited to grander themes." "What things wrote Alcaeus about the love of young men [*iuvenum*]!" gasped Cicero, and I doubt that he means holding hands. Unfortunately those things Alcaeus wrote did not survive, apart from a cheeky condition set for his acceptance of invitations: "I ask people to invite Meno, who is enchanting, if the party's to have any pleasure for me" (fragment 368). Although Alcaeus was still being sung in Roman Egypt, and we have lots of scrappy fragments, all of the love poetry from his corpus must at best still be lying under the desert or has disappeared for good. Thanks to Horace, however, we do know the name of one of Alcaeus's youths: Lycus. Lycus had black hair and black eyes, and was lovely to look at, as one might have predicted.[33]

The world of Sappho and Alcaeus, the world of the archaic symposium, is not a different place, but the flipside of the world of heroic warriors. It is self-consciously off duty, a place for not competing, for not fighting, for hard warriors to allow their bodies to unwind and to take time off from the system. But the symposium brought something else with it, pleasure, and eventually a market for pleasure, for professional performers, even professional boys, the most beautiful money could buy.

AT THE COURT OF THE TYRANTS OF SAMOS

In the century after Sappho and Alcaeus, in the decades around 550 BC, two poets in particular became famous for their celebrations of youths. With Alcaeus they sometimes form a kind of homoerotic trio. "And we can see," says Cicero, "that the loves of these three were lustful." There are two big differences between Alcaeus and his two successors, however. The new songwriters are not independent aristocrats, singing to themselves, but courtiers or guests, or even "poets laureate" singing for their supper at the court of the tyrants of Samos in the Aegean. And like Samians, Chalcidians and Athenians, and unlike Thebans and Sappho and Lesbians, they are all Ionians, which means, among other things, lots of long "e"s. First up is Ibycus, originally from the Chalcidian colony of Reggio di Calabria in southern Italy and probably from quite an important family. Despite fierce competition it was Ibycus who earned the title "the *most* crazy about boys" (*erōtomanestatos peri meirakia*); he flourished sometime around the middle decades of the sixth century. "Truly, he was consumed with love more than anyone," says Cicero, which means of course that he was more convincing when he wrote about what it was like to be consumed.[34]

Again, however, the papyri of Ibycus are in tatters, and reading them is like listening to a weak radio signal from the depths of some vast forbidden country: ". . . in it I will hymn a boy . . . eye . . . whit- . . . Dawn climb . . ."; ". . . soul-biting of boys . . ."; "about the man . . . oath . . . curl . . . loveliest of boys"; "pray . . . came . . . most handsome of admirers."

On a few occasions, we get something much clearer, quoted by another author. Here is a lovely garden like Sappho's, only this time the poet is outside it:

In spring, the Cretan quince, irrigated by river-currents, where the pristine garden of maidens is to be found, and the grape-flower too, swelling under parasols of leafy vine, can put on a spurt of fresh growth, but for me fierce passion never lets up at the appropriate season. Like a wintry Thracian wind it rushes down from the Cypriot love-goddess, lightning-blasting, burning, in secret, shameless, drawing thirst and raving in its path, and it shakes the very heart of me powerfully from its roots. (fragment 286)[35]

One fragment refers back to the old idea of lovers as chariot pairs, but with a new twist:

Love again shoots a melting glance at me from dark-lidded eyes, lures me with fancy enchantments and throws me into the endless nets of the Cyprian, Aphrodite; My god, I am frightened of him marching all over me, like a yoke-bearing, prize-winning horse in old age, reluctant to enter the race again, pulling the swift chariot behind me. (fragment 287)

Sometimes we get the name of the boy in question. One Gorgias is mentioned a few times, Polycrates, and Euryalus, "leafy shoot of gray-eyed Graces, darling of the fair-tressed Seasons, you whom the Cyprian goddess, and the easy-eyed goddess Persuasion brought up amid rose-flowers" (fragment 288). One particularly interesting feature of Ibycus's poetry is his mixing of love and myth. The poetry of love and drinking parties had often eschewed gods and heroes as belonging to a different, more elevated, genre. To be sure, Dionysus and Aphrodite, Graces, Seasons, Helen of Troy, etc., sometimes feature and Sappho had written of the goddess's love for Adonis and/or Phaon the ferryman, whom Aphrodite rejuvenated and beautified because he had been kind to her when she was pretending to be an old woman, and also the love of the Moon for Endymion.[36] Ibycus, however, seems to have gone much further, providing the first signs of that explosion of images of the loves of the gods that became so obvious in Athenian painting in the next generation. He was the first perhaps to have Zeus rather than the gods in general drawn to Ganymede, and may have placed that affair in the same amorous category as the famed love of Dawn for Tithonus. He celebrates the boy Polycrates by putting him alongside a whole series of beautiful heroes, including Achilles' beloved victim, Troilus, without quite saying that Polycrates is as beautiful. Polycrates was a member of the ruling family, a prince, and soon took power, establishing an even more brilliant and famous court.[37]

Ibycus had an interesting death. He was said to have been murdered by pirates. They took him to an isolated beach, where cranes came flying overhead. "They will be my avengers," said Ibycus. The pirates murdered him, nevertheless. Sometime later they landed in Corinth and went to the theater, as pirates do. One of them noticed some cranes flying overhead and said: "Look, the 'avengers of Ibycus.' " Someone sitting close by heard him and drew a conclusion. The bandits confessed and paid the penalty. The story tries to explain the proverb "cranes of Ibycus," which refers to people who give themselves away by revealing too much knowledge of a crime, like the suspects in modern crime novels who know details never given to the press.[38]

Ibycus's successor as songwriter of the court of Samos was Anacreon, from the grand city of Teōs near Ephesus, one of the most popular of all songwriters, and much imitated. He seems to have tried to surpass his predecessors in coming up with novel metaphors for love, but he has a lighter, cleverer, defter tone. In one poem he managed to get in a reference to wealth "tantamount to all the talents of Tantalus," which is even more of a jingle in the Greek (fragment 355). He was represented as a jolly old man, full of love and alcohol, and his poems reflect that easiness and facility, not to everyone's taste: "The emotions which Sappho and Alcaeus had treated so candidly and so seriously, were now largely the subject of fancy and wit."[39] Instead of Ibycus's stormy north wind with all its flashings of lightning, Love is . . . like someone playing a game of knucklebones, each haphazard toss corresponding to "madnesses and affray" (398) or a blacksmith "hitting me with a big hammer all over again, and plunging me into a winter torrent for tempering" (413). As for Ibycus's former chariot-racing champion, "O boy, blinking like a virgin, I'm after you, though you don't pay any attention, unaware that you hold the reins of my soul" (360). Sappho may have written a song about jumping off lover's leap by the temple of Apollo where the island of Leucas dropped sheer down to the sea. Anacreon followed suit, more metaphorically speaking: "I've taken off once more from the white cliff of Leucas, diving into the white-haired wave, drunk on love" (376). Another echoes Sappho's Hymn to Aphrodite, starting formally with invocations to a god whose identity is revealed in the last line: "O Lord, playmate of Eros the Conqueror, of navy-eyed Nymphs and scarlet Aphrodite, you who haunt the pinnacles, I beg you on my knees, please be kind and come to me in answer to my prayer. Talk it over with Cleobulus like a good friend, that he welcome my love, O Dionysus" (357).

Cleobulus features in other poems. Ancient readers especially remembered one about his eyes. Another clever fragment runs through a declension of his name in the genitive, dative and accusative cases: "With Cleobulou I'm in love, for Cleobulo I am mad, at Cleobulon I stare" (359). But Cleobulus was not the only one. Savage-sounding Smerdies from Thrace had long hair but cut it off, much to Anacreon's annoyance. Bathyllus was a great beauty and played the shawm. With Megistes, Anacreon talked class and politics. Anacreon mentions girls too. One was like a frolicsome pony that he threatened to tame. He also mentions a woman called Eurypyle, "Wide-Gate," who was fond of the whoremonger Artemon, who liked women so much that he started to look like one. Eurypyle may have joined Anacreon in the symposium, and also Gastrodora, who sounds somewhat stomach-oriented—surely not respectable women. These individuals, whom we glimpse, despite the gaps in the texts, as vivid—some of them Greek, some foreign, some low-class, some with nice eyes, some with nice hair, some admired, some advised, some abused—look like the colorful cast of a series of artificial little sympotic dramas.[40]

Samos in the archaic period must have been quite a place. The island's old-world aristocrats rivaled the rich new cities of Sicily and Italy—Syracuse, Siris, Sybaris—in putting on a show. Greece in the century before the classical period looks a bit like Europe in the late Middle Ages, the court of Burgundy, the painting of International Gothic, the music of Josquin Desprez, arrayed in lavish surface patterns of cloth and paint. Archaic Greece even had the same noses and the same mysterious smile as worn by the angels on Gothic French cathedrals. The presiding deity of Samos was Hera, who seems to have been the queen of archaic luxury and whose festivals looked like nothing so much as fashion parades. At Samos's ancient sanctuary, the Heraion, built a few miles west of the city on a site that had first been occupied way back in the third millennium BC, the Samians celebrated the goddess's birth and marriage. Excavations have turned up large numbers of exotic objects from Egypt and the Near East, gods and gold, alongside Greek imitations.

And the well-born lords of Samos, known as the "Land-lots," used to wear bracelets when they went to her church. They let down their hair and combed it over their backs and shoulders: "Just as before, when they would comb their tresses and make visits to the sanctuary of Hera, swathed in finery, trailing snow-white tunics over the wide surface of the earth. And on them were golden head-pieces in the shape of cicadas; and their manes waved in the wind amid their golden fetters, and bracelets of cunning craftsmanship were all about their arms . . ."[41] These golden cicadas were popular among the old-time Greeks of the sixth century, and the fashion reached Athens too. Thucydides mentioned them as out of date.[42] But we should not be too taken in by this image of the Samians in their wizard-white wardrobes; it seems highly likely that these refined aristocrats were what we would call pirates. Many of the oriental goods the archaeologists discovered were probably loot.

Amid these people Polycrates established his court. Samos was at the height of her power, terrorizing the merchants and cities along the coast of Asia Minor, not unlike the English in the Renaissance. Polycrates came from a dynasty of "pirate kings"—his brother and grandfather probably went by the name of "Syloson," "Plunder-oson," and his father, probably, Aeaces, left behind an inscription on the throne of an outsize statue of Hera, noting that the dedication was paid for from the proceeds of piracy (sylē).[43] Polycrates built a large fleet, manned by a thousand archers, and went raiding all over the place. There were no "letters of marque and reprisal" of the kind that made modern privateers and corsairs unofficial warriors against the enemies of their state. Polycrates was a proper pirate, allowing raids on all alike, friend and foe, although if it was a friendly nation that had been robbed he might return the stolen goods in expectation of gratitude. On one occasion he defeated the entire fleet of Lesbos, which had come to the assistance of rich Miletus. Polycrates put the captives to work on one of his many building projects. Perhaps, while they learned to dig, the refined Lesbians sang some of the songs they had learned to sing to the tune of the lyre.[44]

From Polycrates the city of Samos got a magnificent set of fortifications, some still to be seen to this day, and a vast artificial harbor made of marble blocks that were reused when the modern quay was built over it in the nineteenth century. An extraordinary tunnel one kilometer long was built through the acropolis. The diggers worked from both ends at the same time and managed to arrive in the middle only meters apart; archaeologists are still quite puzzled as to how they managed it. Finally the temple of Hera, already gigantic, was rebuilt on a slightly more gigantic scale, following a fire. Over one hundred meters in length and over fifty meters wide, sitting fat on a high pedestal, and surrounded by double rows of columns, its scale defeated even Polycrates' ambitions, and like the cathedral of Siena, among others, it was never finished. Now only one column still stands. Aristotle thought there was a political purpose behind the "Polycratean projects," which he compared to the pyramids of Egypt and the temple of Olympian Zeus in Athens. These massive endeavors were designed to make sure that the subjects of despots and kings had no time to think seditious thoughts.[45]

If Polycrates did his bit for Samos, he didn't exactly stint on his own behalf. Even before he came to power he had sumptuous fabrics made, and cups that he lent out to others for weddings and larger receptions.[46] The materials (*kosmos*) that decorated his men's room were magnificent. He built a pleasure quarter, the *laura,* said to be a hangout for prostitutes, but probably more like a Persian imperial paradise or park, and he paid generously to get the best engineers, artists, doctors and poets to come to his court. There were debits as well as credits on Polycrates' culture ledger. He was one of those tyrants said to have tried to suppress love affairs with boys, "for loves like these are at war with men like those." Tyrants viewed the gymnasia that usually lay outside the perimeter "as counter-walls of their own citadels," and some even razed them to the ground, as Polycrates did.[47] This may be how he lost Pythagoras, the mystic mathematician, who went into exile in Italy. Under Polycrates, Samos produced some of the greatest archaic sculptors, among them Theodorus, who spent time studying the techniques of Egyptian stonecutters, made advances in bronze casting, produced the first self-portrait, and cut for the tyrant a splendid emerald that he wore on his finger and that was his most precious possession.[48]

The songs of Ibycus and Anacreon and all their mad passions and beautiful boys were part and parcel of this splendor. Anacreon's work was said to have been "full of reference to Polycrates," though the writers who preserved Anacreon's fragments seem to have overlooked these.[49] Polycrates, who cannot have been much below the age of fifty when he came to power, and was married with children, seems to have been fully involved in the homoerotic world described by the court singers.[50] If he crushed civic homosexuality, he was all in favor of the courtly kind. He had been compared to beautiful heroes by Ibycus in his younger days, and a later writer describes him as "passionately devoted to intercourse with males" (*peri tas arrhenōn homilias eptoēmenos*), in competition with Anacreon; indeed "it is surprising that he is nowhere recorded as having summoned women and boys to his court."[51] Well, on that matter, there are stories that Smerdies the Thracian—how did he get to Samos?—was in fact Polycrates' favorite; Anacreon calls him "thrice-swept," i.e., "thoroughly abused," which could be a vulgar reference to sexual violation or alternatively to his famous haircut . . .

An anecdote claims that the tyrant was jealous when Anacreon, who loved the Stripling "for his personality [*psuchē*] not his body," praised him extravagantly and found the boy loved him in return (*antiphileisthai*) as a result. Polycrates had the boy's hair cut off in revenge. It was a mark of Anacreon's tact, they said, that rather than the tyrant he blamed the boy for his brazenness and "lack of education" in "arming himself" against his own beauty—"You have cut the flower of your soft hair, though it did nothing wrong" (fragment 414).[52] The anecdote is probably nothing more than a fantasy built up around a famous poem, but a fantasy based on a more comprehensive understanding of Anacreon's world, deriving from all of his songs. Ancient readers saw more than fancy and wit in Anacreon's charming poetry; they saw power and necessity in the background, looming large.[53]

That there were sensitivities and jealousies at the court of Polycrates, that relationships of power might sometimes intrude on the playfulness of Anacreon's poetry and the culture of love, that something was at stake in all this homo-amorousness and self-conscious besottedness, and that Anacreon's drunken stumbling was in fact the most careful choreography, seems quite likely to me. Another of Anacreon's boys, the shawm player Bathyllus, was also said to be loved by Polycrates. There was a statue of him dedicated by the tyrant in the temple of Hera, singing a song of Anacreon "for the sake of friendship." Perhaps we should see Anacreon's songs as images and representations like this statue, in the same way that Xenophon's Autolycus is like the statue of *Autolycus* by Leochares. Perhaps we should see these lovely boys as

merely more soft furnishings, more *kosmos*, an early example of the decorative young men and women who will grace Callias's dinner party a
hundred years later. Perhaps Polycrates loved Smerdies or Bathyllus in a
way not unlike the way you love your expensive car, perhaps in a way
not unlike the way you love your lover. Or perhaps his attentions
amounted to less than love.[54]

Somewhere around the year 522 BC, a messenger, it is said, came into the
men's room in Polycrates' palace in Samos. He brought a message from
the Persian satrap who ruled the province across the strait in Turkey.
Polycrates was reclining with his face to the wall. Anacreon was with
him. The messenger read out his message. Polycrates, it is said, did not
even look at him while he spoke. The message was an invitation to make
an alliance that would leave Polycrates in control of the whole Aegean.
Polycrates was more interested than he seemed and took the matter further. There were bad signs and oracles, his daughter had had a strange
dream, but he went to see the satrap, taking much of his court with him.
It was a trick. Polycrates was crucified. Some said that the messenger had
reported to the satrap on the uncouth way he had been received—
Persians were world champions when it came to taking offense—but
still there were better reasons. At any rate, the fabulous furniture of
Polycrates' banqueting room ended up like so much other lost property,
decorating Hera's temple; no one records what became of the beautiful
boys.[55]

Suddenly Anacreon's world collapsed; the brilliant court closed
down. He was around fifty at the time. Fortunately Hipparchus, one of
the tyrants in Athens, sent a warship to rescue the tipsy old man and
took him across the Aegean to safety. Anacreon seems to have carried
with him all the decadence of the Asian style of living from the very epi-
center of this late archaic movement. Either he had a big impact on the
city or perhaps he arrived at just the right time. At any rate, in the thirty
years after his arrival the culture of the symposium, of love of boys and
of amorous gods seems to have reached another spectacular climax in a
city hitherto of only moderate interest, but that was on the verge of
doing momentous things.

In these years, moderately interesting Athens sent out cargo after cargo of drinking cups and mixing bowls decorated with visions of lovely youths and covered in written declarations of love and admiration for specific real-life boys. The Athenians filled the Mediterranean with images of love and wine, announcing the virtues of their local beauties to drinkers and collectors from Tuscany to Anatolia, who probably could not even read Greek, but especially in Tuscany, whose Etruscan inhabitants took these inscribed drinking cups to their graves. This amazing efflorescence of Greek Love may or may not have something to do with the docking in Athens of fun-loving Anacreon, aged fifty, in *c.*522, but a series of odd vases from around the year 500 seem to reflect a more direct connection. They show figures with long beards playing the long decadent *barbitos* of old Lesbos, while wearing hairnets and earrings and long flowing robes. Women playing citharas and shawms accompany them. At first it was thought that these anomalies were transvestite men, then it was suggested that they were women with false beards. It seems, however, that their dress celebrates nothing more than Asiatic Ionian decadence. These odd characters are shown singing at drinking parties or going on festive *kōmos* processions into the street. One of them actually has the name Anacreon inscribed on his lyre, identifying either the singer, or the author of the song that someone less famous is singing. This was reason enough for the great twentieth-century connoisseur of vases Sir John Davidson Beazley to label them all Anacreontic. Anacreon does not explain everything about them, but certainly they are redolent of him. And surely when Anacreon arrived he brought with him his whole cast of characters: Thracian Smerdies with his catastrophic haircut, lovely Bathyllus, greedy Gastrodora, transvestite Artemon the whoremonger and wide-open Eurypyle.[56]

WORDS AND PICTURES: THE ATHENIAN SYSTEM

There ought to be more to be said about Athenian Homosexuality than about any other variety in the ancient world. The chattiest, noisiest, showiest Greeks left lots of words and pictures. The main problem is that the words say one thing and the pictures show something else. And not all the texts seem based on the same assumptions. There have been many solutions proposed to account for the discrepancies—that there was a revolution in attitudes between the two eras that produced the pictures and the words, that the aristocracy thought one thing and the common people something else. But the contradictions are not nearly so mutually exclusive as they may at first seem. Once again the answer is to be found in careful reading.

Back, therefore, to Plato's *Symposium,* to see what Pausanias, so dismissive of the Boeotians and Eleans, has to say about his own people.

THE WEIRD WAYS OF THE ATHENIANS

Phaedrus has neglected a crucial point, Pausanias begins. There are not one but two goddesses Aphrodite: Urania, Heavenly (or, we might add, born from Uranus's foaming genitals), and Pandemos (here meaning Vulgar, Common).[1] The vulgar sort is carnal and opportunistic, directed toward sexual gratification. It affects people with love for women just as much as for boys, and generally for people with more physical than mental attractions. This Aphrodite is the younger of the two. Daughter of Zeus and the goddess Dione (Homer's alternative version of Aphrodite's origins), she has both male and female elements.

Uranian Aphrodite, however, was born from the male element alone (i.e., from Uranus's bloody genitals). She is older, more mature, and hence has nothing to do with abuse (*hubris*). Uranians are "male-oriented," inasmuch as the male, like Uranian Aphrodite, is stronger and has more sense. But that doesn't mean that all those attracted to the male sex are inspired by her, unfortunately. Even among those who admire boys, there is carnal desire; what's more, one can tell which of the two kinds of love provides the motivation. For high-minded (heavenly) lovers don't fall for boys, unless for those getting their beards, i.e., Eighteen. By falling in love with someone at that age, they show that their intention is "to be together for as long as they live, living together in common" (*ton bion hapanta sunesomenoi kai koinēi sumbiōsomenoi*).[2]

In fact love of under-Eighteens should be illegal. It would save a great deal of wasted effort, since at that age you don't know how someone will turn out, kind or unkind, attractive or not, in character and looks. Good men follow this rule anyway, and it should be imposed also on the sexually motivated lover, just as free women are protected from seducers. Those who care only for sex give homosexuality a bad name, so that some, looking at these inopportune and irregular associations, make so bold (*tolman*) as to suggest it's simply wrong for males (meaning even over-Eighteens) to favor lovers, when there is nothing wrong with any behavior, so long as it's done in a proper fashion.[3] There certainly were, Pausanias is saying, people who disapproved of homosex. But this is a "daring" thing for them to suggest, and he is certainly not one of them.

Pausanias turns his attention toward the usual trio, the men of Sparta and Thebes and Elis. It's all terribly straightforward there. It is equally straightforward for the Greeks who live under the Barbarians on the coast of Asia Minor: they have no love of gymnastic culture or of discussion (*philosophia*).[4] This is due to the oppressive nature of their dictatorial regimes. There is no advantage for rulers if the ruled get "big ideas" or develop those "strong intimacies and confederacies" (*philias ischuras kai koinōnias*) that *erōs* especially tends to implant.[5] The reason those societies condemn favoring admirers therefore is threefold: the poor condition (*kakia*) of their institutions, the aggrandizement (*pleonexia*) of the rulers, and the unmanly cowardice (*anandria*) of the ruled. In places where putting out is considered a good thing full stop, with no need for elaborate rituals of courting, this is due to "mental laziness" produced by their institutions.

In Athens, on the other hand, the way it has been laid down is "elaborate" and "hard to understand," but far lovelier (*kallion*) than elsewhere. Pausanias now does some archaeology on his own society to work out and to prove what Athenian Homosexuality is like, constantly referring to *nomoi,* "the rules," customs, laws, institutions. We like love to be open and not concealed, especially if its objects are the most noble-born and persons of the highest quality (*aristoi*), "even if they are relatively ugly." The man in love is marvelously encouraged by everyone as if there is nothing remotely wrong with it. If he makes a catch, it's a good thing; if he fails, bad. We applaud the most extraordinary behavior, promises and oaths, sleeping in doorways, voluntary submission that would be considered disgustingly servile for someone who just wanted money, some political appointment or power. A lover is given extraordinary license. He can even break promises, "lover's oaths," which for anyone else would be considered an impiety. So you would think that in this city it is considered absolutely splendid both to fall in love, and to become intimate friends with admirers (*to philous gignesthai tois erastais*).

But you would be wrong. When you see how fathers go out of their way to protect their sons from admirers, and order chaperons to prevent any words being exchanged between them, when you see that if anything like that does happen, the boys are abused by their age-mates and friends and no one tries to prevent the abuse, then you would think, on the contrary, that here it is considered not the most beautiful thing but the ugliest. Yet no action is intrinsically "ugly" or "noble"; it just depends. "Obliging a vile lover [*poneros*] in a vile fashion [*poneros*] is ugly, obliging a worthy man in a noble fashion is noble, and the vile man is that pandemic lover whose interest is in the body more than the personality [*psuche*]. And he is not constant, because what he is devoted to is not constant."[6] As soon as the body's blossoming fades, which is what attracted him, then he is gone too. The ardent fan of someone good, however, is constant for life, because he is "welded" to something constant—the goodness of a good man does not fade with the beauty of his features.

What Pausanias is saying here is simply that if you fall for someone just because of their physical beauty you are falling for something that changes, and when physical beauty fades, so will your love. This is especially obvious in the case of men who chase after boys under Eighteen and women, i.e., courtesans. They can only be interested in physical charms because such people have no developed character. If you fall for someone because of their personality, their soul, their inner qualities, then it doesn't matter what happens to their physical beauty. But these men have to wait until the boys are Eighteen, at least, the age at which you can tell what someone is like.

So this explains our complicated arrangements. Our custom is designed to thoroughly test admirers, to discover which are for responding to, which are to be shunned. The ardent fans are encouraged to chase, the objects of their devotion to elude them. It's organized like a game (*agōnothetōn*) or a test (*basanizōn*). For the pursued to get caught quickly is considered bad, because it is generally true that time must elapse in order to test things properly.[7] To get caught thanks to offers of money or political power is also bad, if the pursued should crumble under pressure and not stand up for himself, or if he fails to turn his nose up at the offers of money and opportunities to "achieve political ambitions" that are used to tempt him. For there is nothing certain or constant about such things, and no "high-born love" (*gennaia philia*) has ever grown out of them.

So if you should not oblige a lover for financial or political reasons, then what should persuade you? Here Pausanias's argument takes what for us seems a rather unexpected turn. Just as the *erastēs* can submit to slavery when it's for love, so the object of that passion can submit for one thing only that does not incur reproach: for excellence (*aretē*). For the only other occasion when we accept voluntary servitude is when someone wishes to be an adherent (*therapeuein*, "honor," "look after," "pay court"), thinking he will improve himself in specific knowledge (*sophia*) or in some other aspect of excellence. This kind of voluntary slavery is not considered bad or obsequious (*kolakeia*).[8]

So a kindly response to a lover is good only when each of the partners is following his proper rule. The lover is right to subject himself (*hupēretein*) to any degree of servitude for a favorite who has favored (*charisamena paidika*). The favorite is right to render service (*hupourgein*) to someone who is making him wise and good, taking into account also that the lover is able to make a contribution toward practical wisdom (*phronēsis*) and other kinds of excellence, and that the boyfriend requires education and other kinds of useful knowledge (*sophia*, used of medical art, carpentry, poetic technique, etc.).[9] Then and only then is it right to give a lover a favorable response. It doesn't matter if the boy gets it wrong, for if a boy does favors because he thinks his admirer is rich and he isn't, it is shameful, since he has shown what type of person he is, but if he responds to a lover on the grounds that he will improve himself through fond association (*philia*) with a good man, and his admirer turns out to be a bad man, at least he had the right intention.

PAUSANIAS AS ARCHAEOLOGIST OF ATHENIAN LOVE

We need to separate two elements in Pausanias's speech: what he says happens in Athens that is different from other places, and what he reads into that.

I. WHAT HAPPENS

1 The first thing he draws attention to is the publicity and showiness of Athenian Homosexuality. It really does seem as if the noisiness, the public nature of *erōs,* the following and acclaiming and sleeping in doorways, are a distinctive feature. That is one reason then why we have so much information, in stark contrast to the more secretive practices of elsewhere. Wooing is characteristic of Athens, not necessarily of anywhere else.

2 The next thing is that boys are not necessarily selected for their looks, but especially for their nobility of birth and their "quality." Other places, we recall, had beauty competitions for boys, and beauty was an important factor in Cretan Homosexuality to the extent that beauties who were not abducted had a stain on their character. There was also some evidence that *erastai* in those societies had to belong to a particular class, while the boys need not be so distinguished, which would open up the possibility of elite men choosing boys from outside the elite on the basis of their physical attributes. Maximus, for instance, distinguishes Spartan and Cretan *erastai* ("Spartiate," "Cadet") from *erōmenoi* ("from the Spartan territory," "Stripling"). When Theban *erastai* gave their beloveds a panoply or when Cretan *erastai* gave their beloveds all those presents so lavish that the "friends" had to chip in, they may have been giving them to boys who were not already rich. So one distinctive Athenian practice perhaps is that here *erōs* celebrated classiness. Pausanias may even be talking of boys from a particular social group, the horsey class called "Knights." It does at least seem as if

he is talking of the type of boys who go to the gymnasium, and is probably alluding to gymnasium rules in particular.

3 The slavishness of the Athenian *erastai* is also notable according to Pausanias. He goes on and on about it, the servility they display toward the *erōmenoi*. Here he does seem to refer to some law or custom that guarantees such behavior is not blameworthy. Perhaps you could not have an *erastēs* removed from the door. He also goes on about *erastai* alone being allowed to break oaths; again he insists on a specific Athenian rule, "a *nomos* here," and one that is sanctioned by the gods, for the Greeks normally take oaths very seriously indeed. Perhaps he just means there is a popular saying in Athens "no oath of Aphrodite." Certainly it was considered extraordinary to swear an oath in the Assembly in the goddess's name, and probably extraordinary for any man to do so at any time.[10]

4 Next Pausanias cites the Athenian institution of the *paidagōgoi* who are specifically employed, he says, to prevent beloveds conversing with (*dialegesthai*) *erastai*. This seems to be a direct reference to Boys who go to the gymnasium and to under-Eighteens. Pausanias seems to see this extreme protection of Boys as distinctively Athenian. In Sparta, certainly, this was not the case.

5 Finally he notes the fact that the Boy is insulted by his age-mates and companions if they see such a conversation, and no one does anything to prevent the abuse and rebuke the other Boys for getting things wrong. This seems to be a direct reference to gymnasium rules. For where are his coevals going to see the Boy chatting to his admirer, unless his admirer is one of the Cadets who train in the gymnasium, but without mingling and at the opposite end, throwing their javelins at a target near the Boys? Perhaps the gymnasium regulations at Athens made specific provisions for the denunciation of such fraternizing and formally released any informer from liability to a charge of slander.

II. WHAT IT MEANS

In typical Greek fashion Pausanias then interprets these visible practices almost as evidence in a court of law that Athenian Homosexuality is of the Uranian personality-focused beautiful kind, rather than the Vulgar body-focused ugly kind. The period of enforced separation is a way of revealing the constancy of the *erastēs,* forcing him to wait until the Boy is Eighteen, and also a way of guaranteeing that they get to know each other's personality. The rule about waiting until a Boy has reached the right age also brings out the importance of personality, since Eighteen-year-olds have more developed personalities. One might of course object that Eighteen-year-olds also have more developed muscles as well, and are generally considered at the very peak of youthful beauty, and that you are not going to get to know a Boy if you are prevented from conversing with him.

Pausanias then goes on to think about the "voluntary slavery" of the *erastēs,* all the things he does for the boy, and thence of the motives a boy *ought* to have to agree to favoring, which is now considered a similar kind of service. What kind of relationship involves voluntary servitude that is not a creepy and fawning relationship? We recognize only one kind of relationship, he concludes, that of someone out to acquire a particular learned skill (*sophia*) from someone. He seems to be thinking of an apprentice submitting to a master to learn a trade. We might think of Timarchus becoming an apprentice of the doctor, or Euathlus, or Critobulus or Alcibiades learning sophistry supposedly from Protagoras or Socrates. Pausanias might be thinking of himself sitting at the feet of Prodicus, or Phaedrus and Eryximachus following Hippias of Elis discoursing on philosophy. But it is clear that Pausanias assumes that a boy would in fact very often be tempted to put out because his admirer was rich or could offer him political office or the achievement of political ambitions.

AESCHINES AND THE LAWS

Much of what Pausanias points to as distinctive about Athenian custom is confirmed from other sources. We also see elsewhere the same deep-rooted hermeneutic tendency to read things and reach conclusions about the meaning and intent of institutions. Here is Aeschines in his speech against the "prostitute" politician Timarchus, going through a whole series of laws relevant to the protection of *paides:*[11]

(9) In the first place, look at what the law says about teachers. Now these men, to whom we are obliged to entrust our Boys, depend on good behavior to survive. If they behave badly, they are ruined. Even

so, the lawgiver does not trust them. He makes detailed provisions as to what time of day is appropriate for a freeborn Boy to go to school, how many Boys must go with him and at what time they must leave. (10) And the teachers are not allowed to open the schools, nor sports trainers the training ground before dawn and they must be closed by sunset. The lawgiver considered dark hours and lonely places very suspicious indeed. And as for the Cadets who frequent these places, he specifies which ones are allowed and which year-groups [*hēlikias*] and which official supervises these things.[12] He provides for supervision of the slave chaperons and of the festivals of the Muses and of Hermes, in the schools and the training grounds respectively. He is even concerned, finally, about those occasions when the Boys get together to perform in the circular boy bands. (11) For he lays down that the sponsor, a man who is spending his own money for your sake, must be over Forty years old when he does this, to make sure he has already reached the age of greatest self-restraint when he comes into contact with your sons. The clerk will read you these laws and you will see that the lawgiver thought that a Boy brought up properly would, as a Man, be an asset to the city. But what about those occasions when a man's nature makes a false start and veers toward vileness [*ponēran archēn*] at the very beginning of its development? From Boys raised improperly, thought the lawgiver, there could only be citizens such as this Timarchus here. Read them these laws. [LAW][13]

(13) Next, men of Athens, he made laws concerning crimes that though appalling, do nevertheless occur in the city, or so I am led to believe. Indeed it was because things that should not be done were being done that they made laws to prevent it. The law, at any rate, is quite explicit: if anyone is "hired out as an escort" by his father, his brother, his uncle or guardian or by anyone else with authority over him, then the Boy himself must not be indicted, but rather the man who hired him out and the man who hired him. The former, because he put him on hire, the latter, because he hired him. The penalty is the same for both. Moreover, when the Boy comes of age [*hēbēsanti*] he is relieved of any obligation to look after his father if his father hired him out as an escort; he owes him only a burial and the normal rituals that accompany it. (14) See how well-made the law is, depriving the parent when he is alive of the benefit of parenthood, just as he deprived his son of the right to be heard in the People's Assembly [i.e., if a Boy was

forced into prostitution . . . tough; the point is to protect the political decisions made in the Assembly from meretriciousness, not to punish the meretricious], and awarding him burial and traditional rites in deference to custom and religion, only when he is dead and cannot sense the good that is being done to him. Is there another law to guard your Boys? Yes, the law against procurers, which stipulates the heaviest penalties for those who prostitute Boys of free status or women. (15) Is there yet another? Yes, the law against abuse [*hubris*][14] which covers all offenses of this kind under one heading, expressly forbidding an act of abuse—and there can be no doubt that hiring someone is an act of abuse—committed against a boy, or a man or a woman, whether free or slave, in fact forbidding any kind of felonious [*paranomon*] behavior against such persons, making the perpetrators liable to a prosecution for abuse and laying down the punishment they must suffer, the price they must be made to pay. Read out the law. [LAW][15]

(17) Perhaps when you hear this, men of Athens, some of you will react with amazement. What on earth is this clause about slaves doing in a law about *abuse*? But if you think about it for a moment, you will see that this is in fact the best part of all. The lawgiver was no campaigner for the rights of slaves, but wanting to put the crime of *abuse* against free men beyond the pale, he forbade it even against the unfree. In sum, he considered a man who commits *abuse* an unsuitable candidate for participation in a democracy, no matter what the status of his victim.

(18) Allow me to remind you, men of Athens, that at this point the lawgiver is not yet addressing himself to the Boy in person ["to the body—*sōma*—of the boy"], but to his immediate circle, his father, his brother, his custodian, his teachers, to those, in short, who are responsible for him.

Later in the speech, as we have seen, Aeschines returns to his theme, this time defending himself against an anticipated countercharge of being a pest himself, i.e., an *erastēs*—something he is not remotely ashamed of, of course. There is no law against being in love with, associating with (*homilein*) or following (*akolouthein*) a Boy around, he says. And it does no harm. Indeed it allows the boy to make a show of chasteness (*sōphrosunē*). But Aeschines does imply, though he doesn't go into it, that there were laws against intimate conversations with Boys:

So long as the Boy is not yet his own master and is as yet unable to judge who is truly and who not really sympathetic to him [*eunous*], the law imposes moral restraint on the man in love [*ton erōnta sōphronizei*] and puts off discourses of *philia* to a later time, until the Boy has reached a more sensible and senior age-class. But he thought that following after Boys and watching them would provide the Boy with a garrison, a guard of his honor [*sophrosunē*].[16]

This is probably what Xenophon is referring to when he notes that, in stark contrast to the Elean customs, some cities "completely forbid *erastai* from conversing with boys."[17] When Pausanias in the *Symposium* says that Athenian boys are reproached for having dialogue with *erastai* we should take him seriously. Plato in *Lysis* calls it a law against "mingling," in *Phaedrus* he says "sex talk" is illegal, and the Beroea gymnasium inscription from Hellenistic Macedonia forbids Cadets to "chat" with Boys.

All strict and consistent, therefore, all terribly proper. But then there are the pictures. What they show happening seems utterly different from what the texts seem to say.

THE CUP OF PERSUASION

In particular there is a famous drinking cup of roughly 500 BC, nearly a century before the date of the *Symposium*. It is signed by one Peithinos, and is now in Berlin. It shows what scholars call—ahem—"a courting scene."[18] There are sponges, bulbous oil bottles with leather thongs, and curved channeled oil scrapers, like the ones with which the Sacred Band were buried, hung up on the wall, indicating that this is a gymnasium. On one side a youth with sideburns leans on a stick, his right hand on his hip, his head bowed. Behind him is a stool covered with the pelt of a spotted male lion. In front of him are four couples, each made up of a Cadet and a Boy. All carry knobbly walking sticks, some entwined with string at top, middle and base, and three wear wristbands; all of these details probably said something once about each young man. They all wear sandals and cloaks.

The Boys on the other hand are all barefoot and their cloaks come right up to the top of their heads in elaborate pleats, but their bodies are exposed. Whereas the Cadets are the same height and the same stage of puberty, the same age-group, the same year-group, the Boys are all sizes and shapes, an undifferentiated mass of Boys. Two of them are blond. The first Boy tries to take a fruit of some kind from the youth who has his hand behind the Boy's head. The next two Cadets are both wearing their cloaks open at the front, exposing themselves, like the Boys. Both of these youths attempt a tight clinch, moving their hands toward the Boys' genitals. One of the Cadets has an erection and bends his knees so as to enjoy a more intimate form of intercourse between the Boy's legs. This is the kind of sex called a *diamērion,* which is normally translated into Latin as "intercrural," between the thighs, the Princeton rub, frottage.

45. One side of the Peithinos Cup. *Neaniskoi,* identical in height and with beards beginning to grow down from the ear, have come in off the street into the gymnasium where the underage and underheight Boys exercise, perhaps during the festival of Hermes when alone Boys and *neaniskoi* are allowed to "mingle." The scene (and its inscriptions—"Beautiful . . . the Boy is . . . yes indeed," etc.) reads from left to right and is introduced by a grand leopard-lion-skin–covered stool, although its important occupant has gone missing. The artist is careful to indicate degrees of encirclement and danger. Three of the *neaniskoi* use their staffs to block or half-block the Boys' escape routes. The Boys modestly resist or anticipate their assaults. The dog, symbol of shamelessness or dog-day lust, introduces the scene on the other side, where *neaniskoi* with bowed heads modestly resist in their turn the seductions of courtesans labeled "beautiful." Giant cup signed by Peithinos (*c.*500).

If this is a "typical" scene from the gymnasium, a scene reflecting elite values, how things were supposed to be, even, then it seems there must have been a complete revolution in sexual attitudes between this cup and Plato. The mingling of over-Eighteens and under-Eighteens in the gymnasium in what looks like festive dress and fancy hairdos immediately suggests the Boys "dressed up to the nines" in the festival of Hermes described in *Lysis*. With their walking sticks and sandals the Cadets look as if they have arrived from outside into the barefoot space of the Boys like the Cadets in *Lysis*. They are visiting the Boys, not training themselves. But the festival of Hermes was an occasion, we are told, on which Boys were especially carefully supervised. Here the gymnasium looks more like an occasion for a teen orgy. How on earth can we square this image with what the authors have been telling us, with all that talk of strict supervision of morals, the admirers forming an honor guard of modesty, the cousins and slave chaperons, the nervousness about intimate conversations, never mind full-on frottage in a public place?

Once again, the Athenians are all at sea. One day they tell us one thing, all modesty and propriety, the next they seem to show us something completely different: anything goes. Far from being so utterly decent, in 500 BC the Athenians seem even more scandalous than the Boys of Elis. How times had changed. Let's not be too prudish about this. Boys will be boys, and this is more or less what you would expect, isn't it, in a culture of homosexual *erōs,* despite all the law's good intentions? Look what happened in the upper-class English public schools, despite all the school uniforms and Leviticus and St. Paul. Just imagine what would happen if you had a group of randy pagan teenagers spending all day in the hot sun, oiled up, wrestling and naked.

And 500 BC is a very different world from that of the 350s, the world of Plato and Aeschines. Athens had been transformed by a century and a half of democratic reform, prosperity, empire and history and with all that came some dramatic social, religious, cultural and intellectual changes, including at least one law that seems to have raised the age requirement for the man who sponsored the Boys' boy bands to Forty. The cup may very well be much closer to what actually happened in Athenian gymnasia back then, what the blond crowned Boy Lysis and his admirer the Cadet Hippothales really got up to. But painted images are not documentary photographs; they are neither reflections of reality, nor panoramic views of a cultural mentality, this one least of all. They too need to be read, and I mean that literally.

The scene comes complete with a running commentary. Behind the solitary youth, written over his bent arm, the artist has offered some consolation: "*kalos,*" which means he is "beautiful," or "a splendid example" in terms of his facial appearance, his physique, his moral character and his social class, all of those things together, the opposite of *aischros,* "ugly," "shameful," "low-class." In front of him another inscription drips from the strigil and sponge: *kalos* again. But the commentary this time seems to be part of a phrase and a conversation with the reader, continued on either side of the first couple: "beautiful . . . the Boy . . . yes indeed . . ." (*kalos . . . ho pais . . . naichi . . .*). The commentary continues to the next two couples, the most sexual, where gropes and more are attempted and arrested. Thus between couples two and three there is another . . . *kalos* . . . , with an inscription between couples three and four, "beautiful . . . the Boy is" (. . . *ho pais . . .*). With the final nongroping couple, both youth and Boy get a . . . *kalos* . . . each: ". . . Beautiful! . . . Beautiful!"

Sometimes it is impossible to relate the artist's comments to the scene, as when a real-life individual is named but no human figure is depicted; after all, you don't have to draw a picture of your heartthrob every time you write his or her name on a wall. But on the other side of this cup there are women trying to seduce Cadets in turn, and they too are described as "beautiful"—*kale,* with the gender changed—though judging from their forward behavior they are courtesans, and beauty is the beginning and end of their virtues.

So, by a lucky chance, our first instinct happens to be right in this case; the inscriptions comment directly on the figures we see before us. And in this context *pais* does not refer, as it usually does on vases, to some anonymous love object in the outside world under Twenty, but specifically to the age-class of "Boys" under Eighteen, these Boys here in front of you.[19]

"*Kalos* inscriptions"—"Lysis is beautiful," or simply "The boy is beautiful!" (*ho pais kalos*)—are found scrawled neatly over a large minority of all vases in this period, thousands of them, acclamations from the ceramic industry located in the Ceramicus district of Athens that travel the length and breadth of the ancient world. But those we have here are not regular *kalos* inscriptions. They are different: *kalos* descriptions, specifically attached to the women, the Boys and the Cadets the artist has painted.

What other information do we have to help us make sense of this cup? There is some more helpful writing. To start with, the name of the artist himself on the interior, Peithinos. Unfortunately that does not get us very far. The name is found on only one other vase, and anyway it sounds like an assumed name. *Peithō* is a forceful kind of "persuasion," i.e., "persuasiveness," "winning over" or "seduction," regularly person-ified as a goddess associated in cult, of course, with Aphrodite and Eros. So the artist wrote something like "Persuader drew it," "Seductive drew it."[20] "Seductive?" Does this low-class artisan fancy himself as one of the swanky gymnasium boys? Or is it us that he aims to seduce, the viewers, or, entirely possible, the judges in a drawing competition? Well, it is indeed a very fine piece of work. The great connoisseur of vases Sir John Davidson Beazley described it as "an exceptional piece, among the most elaborate of all cups (and among the most affected)." Maybe that's what the hypothetical judges said too, back in 500 BC. But a certain Etruscan traveler from miles away over in Vulci, north of Rome, was captivated by it, cherished it and took it home with him, which is our good fortune, since the Etruscans in general and the people of Vulci in particular loved to be buried with their collections of pottery, thereby preserving Peithinos's masterpiece for two and a half thousand years until it saw the light of day once more in a dealer's shop in 1833.

On the interior of the vase is more information, a regular *kalos* accla-mation: "Athenodotus. He is beautiful!" We don't know very much about Athenodotus, except that he was one of the hottest things around in 500 BC, and that about two decades earlier his arrival kicking and screaming into the world answered a prayer, since his name means "Given by Athena."[21]

At least fifteen other pots from this period, several of them remark-able for various reasons, proclaim this particular fine young man's virtues to the art markets of the Mediterranean. He seems to be a mas-cot of one particular group of artists, which included Douris, the one who painted the Getty Ganymede with yarmulke.[22] Indeed Douris's hand has been detected on another cup vaunting Athenodotus in which an Eighteen-year-old (fully grown, no sideburns yet) is about to pour a libation with a cup at an altar. The cup the youth holds has Douris's name on it. Douris has painted himself into the boy's life. Athenodotus's name is also written emerging from the forehead of an Eighteen-year-old tying up his penis with a "dog-leash" to prepare for the long jump (the hand-weights on the wall are for swinging to give extra thrust). The space around the boy is filled with *kalos, kalos, kalos,* three times "beautiful." I think this is certainly supposed to be Athenodotus himself. If so, it will be "iconic," meaning not a realistic portrait, not even an attempt at a likeness, but an image that identifies Athenodotus by attribute, i.e., very probably he was a star of the long jump.

One estimates that approximately, very approximately, around 0.5 percent *on average* of Athenian vase production survives, which means that something like three thousand vases may have been painted to proclaim Athenodotus's virtues to the world.[23] Perhaps this particular workshop turned out one vase a day inscribed with Athenodotus's name for several years, or perhaps they made a batch during some athletics competition, when everyone was showing support for him. You out there have qualities too. Probably some of you will be locally famous for your looks, your nobility, your athletic prowess, or your great body. Some of you might outclass Athenodotus in some or all of those things, were he still around to compete. But in the year AD 4500, when you have been dead and gone for centuries, will anyone have the slightest idea that you were once anything at all?

Although we know nothing about the mysterious painter who hides behind the name "Seductive" therefore, we have a pretty good idea of his imaginative world and the world of his colleagues, a world of clever ironic jokes, friendly or perhaps unfriendly rivalry, an extremely high level of artistic merit in terms of composition, innovation and execution, an attention to subtle symbolic details, and a tendency to declare admiration for a particular elite youth, membership of a particular fan club to which some colleagues in the Ceramicus belonged and some definitely did not. Peithinos and the other fans of Athenodotus painted hundreds of cups for the drinking parties of rich young Athenians, and on those cups they celebrated the world of these young men by painting symposia and scenes of athletics and the gymnasium. These pot painters, indoor, sedentary, hardworking laborers, sweating all day by the kiln, established, through their cups, relationships with these leisured youths of freedom of movement and outdoor exercise, youths who lived at the opposite end of the scale of physical values, completely asymmetrical relationships, but relationships nonetheless, with no kind of affinity or intimacy, but with a newfound political connection, thanks to the democratic revolution. And perhaps while posh Athenodotus stretched out his athletic young body on a couch, waiting to have this gigantic cup filled at a party to celebrate his victory in the long jump, he might casually read what was written inside, as one reads the writing on a cereal packet, and see the name of this artist from the potters' quarters, and read what he had written about him, and he might say to himself "Gee! Thanks, er, Peithinos! I am quite something, actually, aren't I . . ."

JUST SAY "NO!"

This, therefore, is a cup that speaks about, speaks to and is probably aimed at the elite Cadets, the elite Striplings, the pinups of Athenian society, celebrating and reflecting their values. It is demonstrably a showpiece, much larger than normal, 34 centimeters in diameter, the size of a large flat fruit bowl, very difficult to drink from, made for passing around the entire company reclining on their seven couches, for downing in one in a dangerous drinking contest, for dedication as a gift to a god or to hang on a wall or in a shop. It must have taken many manhours to complete. It is special, valuable, something painted with meticulous care, by no means destined for a bottom drawer or a secret cabinet. There is nothing jokey or comic about it, no sign of a satirical attack on the elite, or pornography for young men to giggle at.

What else can we extract from it? Well, let's take a step back and look at the rest of its pictures. The center of all these circles of images is the interior of the cup. Here we see the "persuading" of the protean sea goddess Thetis by the hero Peleus. Peithinos has shown the moment immediately preceding the conception of Achilles, at the goddess's lair on Cape Cuttlefish (*Sēpias*) in Thessaly. In the myth, Thetis transforms herself into various creatures to escape Peleus's clutches. Here Peithinos has shown the creatures shooting out from her. Snakes sink their fangs into Peleus's heel and his forehead. A miniature male lion emerges from her right sleeve. This is an excellent lion, beautifully detailed, but it is not, obviously, a realistic snapshot of what happened at the Cape. Rather it uses pictures to narrate a story.

If the struggle is fierce, it ought to be. There is a great deal at stake. For Thetis, you will recall, was nearly the lover of Zeus, until it was revealed by the goddess of the Current Order (Themis) that Thetis's child would be greater than his father, that if Zeus was the father of her son, in other words, then a greater than Zeus would come into the world and the whole of the cosmos would be thrown into revolution, as once Zeus had overthrown the order of his father before him, bringing an end to the ageless Golden Age of Cronus. Anxious to preserve the Present, Zeus had to make sure that Thetis's son, Achilles, was no powerful god but a paltry mortal, who might be the greatest of mortals, but whose passing, *qua* mortal, was ultimately assured. He chose Peleus for the job of inseminating her and moderating the sting of her pregnancy with mortal sperm. Thetis, we can see, was not pleased.

The ambush of the sea goddess at Cape Cuttlefish was a popular one in painting, but only Peithinos has really grasped the full implications, the seriousness of the situation. Note especially the way that one of the snakes sinks its fangs into Peleus at precisely the point at which his son Achilles, the swiftest of the Greeks, will finally be pinned to the ground, and meet his mortality. The outcome of the struggle is by no means a foregone conclusion. Peleus had wrestled a woman once before in competition, and some said he had lost.[24] This time he holds on with the tightest grip imaginable, padlocking her in his arms. The world as we know it depends on that handlock, that *symplegma,* that "entwining," which means both a wrestling grip and the knot of bodies of those engaged in sexual intercourse. Peleus's handlock must remain absolutely secure while the goddess runs through the gamut of her transmogrifications. That handlock binds immortal Thetis to a mortal mate; it produces her son Achilles, greatest of heroes; it secures his death, and for his mother a great deal of mourning; but it also secures, through that death, a safe future for the current cosmic regime, the regime of endless mortal successions.

Peithinos has used that same stylized handlock to encircle the whole image, and the same design appears again on the outside of the cup to make a ground line. And so that conventional bit of decoration, a neat Greek key or meander around the margin of the scene, has been integrated with the scene itself. Indeed it has been brought into the very center of the image, the focus of all the tension and thereby loaded with significance. We see it no longer as an attractive abstract pattern, there-

46. Foreplay at Cape Cuttlefish (Sepias), at the foot of Mount Pelium in
Thessaly. Moments before the conception of Achilles, the *neaniskos* Peleus
holds on tight to the sea-goddess Thetis (both labeled) as she transforms
herself into savage beasts, a snake sinking its fangs into Peleus's foot at the
point where their son will be killed by an arrow. The design of Peleus's
handlock is continued around the border in what would otherwise be seen
as a merely decorative meander. An inscription—"Athenodotus is
Beautiful"—acclaims a pentathlete, favorite of the painter Onesimus
and his circle. Interior of the Peithinos Cup (*c.*500).

fore, but a chain of mightily interlocking hands. Peithinos, "the Persuader," locks in his images, just as Peleus the Persuader locks in the
goddess Thetis. Within that locked frame, on the inside of the cup,
transformations appear, as they do between Peleus's determined arms—
lion, snakes, woman, impossible images, imagined images taken from
the world of stories. Outside that tight impassable circle, on the outside
of the cup, we are in a different world completely, the world of the present, and everyday realities, the world of mortal generations; Peleus's
handlock marks the meeting point of the world of myth juxtaposed
with the world of now, the mortal world that it ensures.

Peleus has been given sideburns, making him the same age precisely as
the Cadets on the exterior, making them the stars of the cup. That's one
element that links the inside and the outside, the mythic past and the

present. There is another obvious connection: entrapment. But where is the artist going with that? Is he making a comment about the advance of civilization, "contrasting Peleus's violent, heroic-style abduction with his own culture's more civilized preference for persuasion, not force"?[25] Rather I think the interior establishes a heightened and epic version, a full-color myth-heroic version of a theme that finds echoes in the contemporary. Peleus represents the most strenuous and inescapable entrapment, Thetis the most extraordinary and fierce resistance. Their struggle is reflected in less operatic terms among the today folk on the outside. This is the story Peithinos is telling. This is the plot. Not rape, but making an erotic conquest and resisting defeat.

We turn the cup over. Scene 1—Boys and girls—is introduced by a dog sitting under the handle. The dog sets the tone straightaway, for it is a symbol of shamelessness and dirtiness, and sometimes it stands, more particularly, for the heat, the sexual heat, the on-heat of the dog days in August. As we pan from left to right, we see three Cadets subjected to the wiles of feminine *peithō,* the arts of visual seduction. The women approach in all their elaborate finery, offering bits of foliage or a flower, very common in erotic scenes, emblematic of youthful bloom, or perhaps a seductive sweet perfume. Courtesans are compared to Sirens, Sphinxes, sea-swallowing Charybdises, hunters with nets and potions. The Cadets are the prey, and very much in danger. They wrap up tightly or press their chins into their chests, bowing their heads to indicate *aidōs,* a sense of shame, that sense that dogs don't have. They are fiercely resisting the temptation of the lovely brazen ladies.

I doubt very much that you would find women like that walking the streets of Athens barefoot in 500 BC, offering flowers and bits of foliage to loitering youths, and if they did, you would not find many Cadets behaving so modestly. This is simply a representation of the seductive power of courtesans and the danger they represent to Cadets in particular—a danger they seem well aware of. They resist seduction.

The gymnasium scene on the other side is preceded by an object, a lion-footed stool draped in a spotted lionskin. Just as the shameless dog sets the tone and gives a context for the encounters between women and youths, so this piece of furniture introduces the gymnasium. What does it mean? The vases found in both Greek and Etruscan tombs very often come in pairs, matched in size, shape and quality, and also, very roughly, in types of figure and imagery.[26] And there is that other remarkable cup in Berlin, the Sosias Cup, which shows white-toothed Patroclus being bandaged in white by Peleus's son Achilles, the product of the ejaculation at Cape Cuttlefish, both of them with those peculiar big round eyes.[27] Achilles has reached the age of the Cadets, the same age as his father now wrestling Thetis.

The Sosias Cup is also exceptionally large, in fact its proportions are almost identical to those of the Peithinos Cup. It is of around the same date, c. 500 BC, and was found at the same site, Vulci, five years before the Peithinos Cup turned up in a dealer's shop window in Rome. The two cups have nearly identical zigzag folds falling down on drapery, and the same elaborate flared and pleated sleeves worn by Thetis are worn here by wounded Patroclus. On this cup too are those lion-footed stools covered in pelts of the same strange lion with both spots and a mane, very nearly but not quite identical to those of Peithinos; "affected" Peithinos has put spots within his spots. Perhaps there really was a subspecies of spotted lion once in the lands of the eastern Mediterranean, until the market for their skins drove them into extinction, or perhaps these impossible lions remind us once more that we are not seeing a drawing from life. On Sosias's cup, however, the stools are being sat upon, by gods and goddesses. Lion pelts really were used on religious occasions. Remains of several of them, i.e., skull and claws, have been found in the sanctuary of Artemis at Ephesus.[28] They must have been brought out for festivals.

Once we put the two vases together, the empty lionskin-covered stool, provided by the Sosias Painter for the use of eagle-sceptered "friend Zeus" and all the other gods receiving libations, seems a highly significant object. If the precise meaning of it escapes us, we know one thing for sure, that it is made for a very distinguished spectator—if not a god, then the boss of the gymnasium, presumably, the one who was responsible for enforcing the strictures of the law about contact between under-Eighteens and their elders, probably the kosmētes, "supervisor of decorousness." Well, whoever he is, he isn't there now. The expensively draped but empty seat indicates a decisive absence, one that sets the tone for what follows.

While the cat's away . . . the Cadets subject the Boys to the same test

47. The Gotha Cup. Like the Peithinos Cup, it shows a Boy fenced in by
the staff of a *neaniskos* in the gymnasium as if he were a caged hare slavered
over by a dog. Red-figure interior of white-ground cup from Cape Colias
in Attica by Euphronios(?) or one of his circle (*c.* 510–500).

to which they themselves have been subjected by the seductive courtesans on the other side. How do they fare? Peleus's handlock grip on the
interior establishes an extreme point of strong persuasion, and allows us
to plot the other entrapments along a continuum. In particular the positioning of the walking sticks by the Cadets looks much more precisely
modulated, like leaving a gate more open or more closed. On the far
right, couple number four, the least degree of compulsion, the Cadet
keeps his walking stick well removed, behind him; the Boy is under no
pressure and is free to walk away; and in tune with that, there is no grop-
ing and no tight clinch. Balancing this couple stands couple number one,
where more persuasion has been brought to bear. The Boy has been offered a lure of fruit, and meanwhile the walking stick of the Cadet has
moved in behind him to block one exit route. But when we come to the
central part of the series, couples two and three, the situation has deteri-
orated. The Boys are completely encircled, and, in line with that, they
have been drawn into much greater sexual intimacy. This is not a
panorama of Greek Homosexuality, Boys at various stages on the road
to getting laid. Rather it shows varying degrees of entrapment and re-

48AB. Details of the Peithinos Cup. The oil bottle introducing the most
determined *neaniskos* tips over dangerously of its own accord, on the brink
of spilling its contents. By contrast, the bottle introducing the most upright
couple stays emphatically upright. No danger of spillage here.

sistance, each degree carefully articulated. It may seem slight to us, but
seen in the light of their time I think there is a world of difference between what couples number two and three are doing and the more
proper behavior of couple number four. One cup in Gotha (Fig. 47)
shows a Stripling "gating" a Boy in just this way. In the background a
dog is barking hungrily at a caged hare.

And here's another nice little sequence. Reading from left to right on
the Peithinos Cup, each couple is introduced by a gym kit, consisting of
sponge, strigil, and a round anointing flask of olive oil, fixed to a kind of
peg. This tells us we are in a gymnasium, but you don't need *four* gym
kits to get that message across. Four gym kits, four couples. I am not the
first to think that they are used to signify something about what is going
on: "The Painter has included these oil-sets for a reason."[29] The three

oil flasks introducing the first three scenes of clinching couples are tilting over dangerously.[30] Any farther and they will spill (Fig. 48a). The last one, introducing the most decorous couple, is emphatically level, *orthios,* "upright," its three strings properly spread, the fringe around the rim nicely spaced out (Fig. 48b). Perhaps that is just a haphazard detail, a touch of realistic variation, but there is no variation in the previous three, and one thing we should have learned by now is that this artist leaves nothing to chance, from the choice of the meander to decorate the border, to the exact location of the snakebite on Peleus's foot. See then how each of the bottles hangs on a peg bang in the midpoint of the strap, carefully emphasized, but the strings are not taut, but loose and twisted. The bottles have not been hung at an angle. They are tipping of their own accord!

The practice of covering oneself with olive oil in the gymnasium was a symbolic act, making the body shine with brilliance and beauty, "anointed," "oil-smeared," *christos.* Even the mixture of oil, sweat and dust scraped off beautiful Boys with the strigils was considered special, and gymnasia seem to have collected and sold it. "Boy gunk," *paidikos gloios,* was an ingredient in beauty treatments. Moreover, in Athens the olive tree had tremendous symbolic value. It represented the very life of the city, and an olive branch was placed on the door of the house to indicate the birth of a new Athenian boy. The olive tree was Athena's gift to Athens, the bribe that enabled her to beat Poseidon in the contest for the city, the gift that made it the city of Athena. This divine gift still grew on the Acropolis in the sanctuary of Poseidon/Erechtheus, the Erechtheum. When the Athenians came to inspect the devastation wrought by the Persian occupation, they were amazed to find that although the tree had been burned in the conflagration, a brand-new shoot was already sprouting out of its charred remains. All over Attica there were holy olive trees that it was forbidden to touch, even if they seemed to have died, just in case they should burst into life once more. From these sacred trees olive oil was collected to be offered as prizes to athletes during the great All-Athenian festival that marked a new civic year. The oil was placed in special amphoras, called Panathenaic. Several of those discovered were painted by someone we have christened the Eucharides Painter. He often included an image of the goddess Athena on these sacred jars, next to a column with a cockerel on top. The cock-

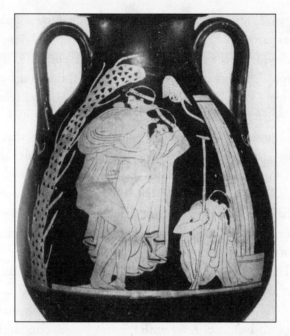

49. A Man has intercrural sex with a *neaniskos*. In the background, an oil
bottle with gym kit (sponge and oil scraper) has tipped to horizontal,
exposing its opening to the viewer and spilling its contents.
The tall pedestal has lost its victory monument. A friend or attendant
looks away or misses what is happening while he dozes off.
Pelike by the Eucharides Painter (*c*.490).

erel, as we have seen when it is shown with Ganymede, symbolizes the
triumphant beauty of the male, *kallos*.

This same artist also painted one of the most flagrant scenes of homosexual copulation (Fig. 49). It shows a Stripling with a headband actually allowing an older man, also wearing a headband, to pleasure
himself between his thighs. Another Stripling crouches on the ground,
with his head in his hands turned away and his eyes closed. Is he just nap-
ping while his friend or his slave-master has a bit of fun, as many have
suggested? Or is this "to suggest that the seduction of young men is not
entirely beautiful to see?"[31] Behind him is one of the painter's column
stands, but there is no beautiful male bird on top of it, another significant absence. And here too is an oil flask, full—or it used to be full—of
Athena's olive oil . . . For not only is it not upright, but it has tipped

right over to the horizontal, spilling out. Moreover, most unusually, it is drawn full-frontal, the hole in the top exposed to view.

If we put this oil flask in a series with the flasks on the Peithinos Cup, therefore, we have a direct correlation between the degree of tipping and the degree of sex, from upright-distanced-admiring, to dangerously tilted seductions, to complete and utter spillage. Steady. Going. Going. Going. Gone. One must note especially the oil flask in the shape of genitals, with a scene of importuning and the signature of the potter Priapos.[32]

The stop-it gesture the Boys make on the Peithinos Cup is absolutely standard, found in a majority of "heavy petting" scenes, where Boys and Cadets resist a kiss or a grope, and also on the walls of the Tomb of the Diver at Paestum in Italy, for instance. It is a meaningful gesture, I think, as the way an artist depicts that most important virtue, *sōphrosunē,* modesty—how else would you advertise a determination to defend your reputation, unless there is something to defend it against? According to Aeschines that is what all this courting was about. The lawgiver didn't ban erotic stalking, he says, precisely so that a boy could demonstrate his *sōphrosunē.* And let us not forget the moral connotations of *kalos,* "beautiful," "noble," "good," the opposite of *aischros,* "ugly," "shameful." Pausanias in the *Symposium,* remember, says that responding to an admirer's advances beautifully is beautiful, responding in an ugly fashion is ugly. Socrates noted that since his cousin was present it would not be ugly (*aischron*) for the handsome Cadet Charmides to speak to strangers at the gymnasium. And Aeschines claims that the essence of the gymnasium was to create *kalon,* "the beautiful," which was why it was off-limits to slaves.[33] What we see on the cup is behavior that Plato, Aeschines and Socrates would have no problem labeling alternately "ugly" or "beautiful," "shameful" or "impressive," *aischros* or *kalos.*

On this cup, as we have seen, the *kalos* inscriptions are gender- and age-specific. And the term Boy, so common in formulaic acclamations of general application with no relevance to the scene in question, is here used only on that part of the cup where the under-Eighteens are, and never where they aren't. The viewer must refer it to the figures we see before us. On the other side of the cup each Cadet, so utterly modest, so implausibly abashed by the forward ladies, has his own *kalos,* which in this context must be seen as a commendation of their admirable modest behavior—indeed there are a couple of extra *kaloses* decorating the field. And even the ladies have their own *kalē* in the feminine, though here I think it refers to their physical attractions only, and the word is written backward, like an emanation or a charm, as if the beauty of the women is talking from their bodies. On the gymnasium side, however, there are not enough *kaloses* to go around. Nine males but only five "beautiful males" between them. It is not that there is too little space, because the artist has filled it with emphasis— "yes indeed," *naichi,* etc.—and designations—"the Boy"—which ought not, according to the modern interpretation, to be necessary. Four of our Athenian teenagers, therefore, seem to have been deliberately denied approbation, the only figures on the entire cup who lack a label. Which four? The three well-behaved boys at either end of the frieze seem safe. In their little tableaux, separated off by the sponge kits, they have one *kalos* each. And the two remaining "beautifuls" belong explicitly to Boys, whose efforts to resist have merited the stamp of approval. So it seems as if three of the Cadets in the middle zone are not "to be admired," and perhaps one of the Boys too has not tried hard enough: a budding Timarchus, off to what Aeschines calls a "lewd start."

The primary theme of the cup, then, is erotic persuading and resistance, presented in three different scenes: on the mythological level, the erotic conquest of Peleus and the fierce resistance of Thetis; then the feminine ensnarement of the courtesans and the resistance of modest Cadets; and finally the Cadets putting pressure on under-Eighteens and the Boys defending their honor. The scene at the gymnasium is as highly stylized as the others on the cup, and I think I can guarantee that if you went back to Athens in the year 500 BC you would not see Nineteen-year-olds walking in off the street and having sex with Boys in the public open-air space of the gymnasium, with or without supervisors present. In no Athenian text is there the slightest hint that rubbing your penis between the thighs of under-Eighteens is normal, praiseworthy, or just one of those things, while several texts express the strongest disapproval of Boys who concede intimate contact, both from the Boys' schoolmates and from their parents, as well as utter condemnation of the villainous men (*ponēroi*) who press them to concede.

In Athens, even conversing with older males to whom he was not related could compromise a Boy's reputation if chaperons were not present, and Pausanias, one of the speakers in Plato's *Symposium,* thinks that the same law should condemn seducing Boys as condemning those who seduce freeborn women, one of the most heinous crimes a Greek could think of, one that incurred the heaviest fines or, if caught in flagrante, instant death.[34] Yet at the same time older teenagers like Hippothales and older men like Aeschines would openly declare their love for under-Eighteens by following them around, writing elaborate love songs and, doubtless, graffiti, performing the role of the Boys' passionate admirers. That this was "complicated" and "not easy to understand," in contrast to the way things were in less sophisticated cities, was stated explicitly by that same Pausanias in the *Symposium.*[35] Images like that of the Peithinos Cup must be viewed against this background; they are from Athens too.

Now it is quite possible that seducing under-Eighteens was a matter similar to the question of taking drugs in our own society, that there were ferocious laws against it, universal condemnation, yet still it took place on a large scale. But the Peithinos Cup is not a window on reality, a news report. It is a work of art that demands to be read in context. It belongs to the same world of values as the texts, and cannot escape from it, any more than some modern portrait painter, dependent on aristocratic clients, who painted a huge exhibition canvas of schoolboys at Eton shooting up could escape from the context of the "War on Drugs." Perhaps he might paint a true picture. Nevertheless it would be a gross error for future generations to interpret his image as a straightforward documentary photograph, a window on how things were. It would be, in other words, A Statement.

If we go back to the problem we started with, the contradiction between the gymnasium as it was supposed to be according to the institution of slave chaperons, the testimony of Aeschines, Plato and the law, and the gymnasium as it seems to be on this cup right there in front of us, we can see in fact that they respond to the same society. The later obsession with the honor of elite boys is already much in evidence here, a century earlier. Peithinos the Persuader, in other words, has shown us in a stylized and symbolic fashion what the law rules out: the fantasy ever present in anxieties about the honor of under-Eighteens when they come into contact with their loud admirers, the danger that *must* arise when Boys mix unsupervised with those gallant young Cadets, who are allowed to keep company with them on the occasion of the festival of Hermes.

EUPHRONIOS THINKS LEAGROS IS FANTASTIC

Another vase in the amazing collection of new discoveries that arrived at the Getty in the eighties shows more clearly than any that the purpose of depicting so-called courting couples on Athenian vases is to represent admiration for them. Unlike the other vases we have been looking at, this is no masterpiece, it is a cheap product, representing few man-hours, or even a sketch, a practice piece. It was made by an artist called "Little," Smikros, which could be the name of a citizen, or a nickname, but more likely indicates he is a slave whom one of the potters has bought to work beside him. This is how ancient tradesmen invested and expanded their business; they bought labor-saving people. As on the Peithinos Cup, the vase shows a series of courting couples. Most of them seem to be members of the gymnasium, the elite, but one of these elite boys, Leagros, is being admired in a self-controlled way by someone from a different class altogether. The admirer is Euphronios, one of the most famous and celebrated of all the pot painters, quite possibly the artist's boss, master to Smikros's apprentice; probably his owner.

We know that Euphronios liked Leagros because he wrote "Leagros is Kalos" on his own vases, which now fetch extravagant prices at auction, but there has been much debate about what this scene showing these two males from quite different age-classes mixing socially implies. Some think that perhaps these workers, these pot painters and potters, *banausoi,* were not in fact as socially excluded as others have supposed. The little potteries on the margins of the city in the Ceramicus, right next to the great Double Gate of Athens, surrounded by bathhouses, brothels, and the dead, dominated the Mediterranean trade in fine ceramic ware for decades. Their artistry may have been ignored by people who wrote histories and songs, but it was highly valued by their customers, not least by Etruscans. Unless they were the most naïve businessmen, with such a huge international market for their goods, money must have poured

50. The vase painter Euphronios respectfully admires Leagros (both labeled), whose hand is modestly wrapped in his cloak. Leagros and his son, Glaucon, members of the elite family of the parish *Kerameis,* home of the ceramic industry, were much acclaimed as "beautiful" on the vases that were produced there and exported to all corners of the Mediterranean and the Black Sea. Euphronios and his "artistic circle" (workshop?) seem to have established some kind of special relationship with the family around the time of the overthrow of the tyranny (*c.*510) and the early years of the "democracy." In the aftermath of the Persian wars (the year 465–446), *Kerameis* helped to elect Leagros to a generalship that ended in disaster at "Nine Roads" near Argilos in the northwestern Aegean. A century later, Leagros's grandson (Leagros 2) was mocked by comedians as "a cuckoo-brained naïf with the calves of a eunuch melon" (Plato Comicus 65 K-A). Here the artist has almost certainly "youthened" Euphronios and shown him as a beardless *neaniskos,* one of those allowed into the gymnasium with the Boys. Psykter (wine cooler) attributed to the painter Smikros, Euphronios's colleague and, quite possibly, his slave (*c.*510–500).

into the workshops. You do not find such trade without profits being made. As among other skilled workmen, dramatists and comic poets, the pot-painting industry seems to have been a family affair, a household business passed down from father to son. The painters or potters must have got rich, therefore, off the backs of their slave assistants. Indeed some of them may have got rich enough to make dedications on the Acropolis.

But it didn't matter how successful the *bauausoi* were in business, because it was not poverty that made them inferior, but their bodies, deformed or even "mutilated" by their sedentary occupations, sitting by the furnace indoors, the polar opposites of the gym boys. I don't think Euphronios actually courted posh young Leagros. I would be very surprised if the two of them ever socialized at all. A more likely explanation is that the painters are playing social games. Elsewhere too they show themselves mixing with the elite. Even slavish Smikros is shown as a beautiful young Cadet reclining at a symposium. Early poets loved to make themselves vivid participants in imagined scenes—Archilochus seducing and ejaculating into a girl while he plays with her yellow hair, Sappho being visited by Aphrodite and describing their conversation. So this image of Smikros's master courting a member of the elite may be a fantasy about Euphronios, his role model, who is so obviously enamored of Leagros, achieving his impossible dream— "what success—wild, impossible success; success worth emulating— might be like."[36]

I think, rather, that the vase is simply a visual representation of the fact that Euphronios celebrates Leagros so often on his vases: "The picture renders iconic what is in most cases a merely textual message: the exclamation of 'Leagros *Kalos*' that appears on so many Euphronian pots."[37] The image does not show Euphronios trying to seduce Leagros, it shows him as an *erastēs,* an admirer, a fan. That gesture of a youth standing at a distance from a Boy, which we saw on the edge of Peithinos's gymnasium scene, here means simply that the "youth acclaims the boy as fine and noble—*kalos.*" The youth is a fan of the Boy. Just as on Peithinos's cup, the good Euphronios, standing away from Leagros, leaning on his stick and merely reaching out to his chin—the chin of a Boy dressed extremely modestly, with his hand even inside his cloak—is contrasted with the next couple, a draped youth with his arm locked around a youth of similar age, and touching him not on the chin but on the genitals. Smikros has painted no upright *orthios* oil bottle to indicate upright behavior, but the contrast is still very marked, indicating Euphronios's propriety as a fan of impeccable Leagros, a local aristocrat.

Euphronios's whole factory was a factory of the fans of Leagros, a man who belonged to their own parish, the Ceramicus, and their own

democratic tribe, "of Acamas."* Naturally for a man to praise the qualities of a boy who might win victories, "beautiful victories," for the tribe
in any one of countless terribly important tribal competitions, singing
and dancing contests, or athletic contests, for a voter to praise the wonderfulness of a boy he might later be electing to the office of generalship,
is not without political ramifications. Apart from many other things, the
badly drawn vase (Fig. 50) shows a supporter honoring a future candidate. It may not look like it, but it is a little like a contributor to the Re-
publican Party in the 1980s depicted honoring George W. Bush.

In case this seems a far-fetched comparison, the potters of the Ceramicus did indeed, some years after this vase was painted, help to elect Leagros general to lead them into battle in the north. This was unfortunate;
it was a disaster. Many members of the tribe were killed, and Leagros
too probably, but there was a consolation. Leagros had a son named
Glaucon. And at around the time of the great tragedy the jury gave a
victory to the tribe of Acamas in, probably, the Dithyramb contest, the
important contest of circular Boy bands said to have been invented by
Arion, of dolphin fame, a century and a half earlier. We know this because the painters painted the trophy, a victory tripod. To vaunt their
own victory in this way, so directly, is most unusual for the painters, but
these were perhaps unusual times. Normally such a monument displayed on the pedestal the name of the elite man who sponsored the performance. Leagros's son does indeed appear on the pedestal, but instead
of "Glaucon was the sponsor," the painters have changed the inscription
to "Glaucon Kalos," "Glaucon is Beautiful."[38] I don't think we should
necessarily imagine that either Glaucon or his father was particularly
good-looking, though after all those hours in the gym they were doubt-

---

* Under the democracy, the c.139 parishes (demes) of Attica were divided among thirty
"thirds" (trittyes). These "thirds" were sorted into three equal-sized categories: of the City,
the Coast or the Interior. Then, ten "tribes" (phylai) were formed by joining three thirds, one
from each group, and assigned one of ten "eponymous heroes," chosen by Delphi. These
phylai, each originally representing Athenians from all over Attica, were the major administrative units of the democracy, used in military levies, jury service, membership of the
Council of Five Hundred (fifty Councilors per phylē) and to make competitive teams in races
and dances at major festivals. Akamantis, the phylē of Acamas, who, according to myth, was
one of the sons of Theseus, united the city-parish of the Ceramicus (Kerameis) with Coastal
parishes in the far south of the Attic peninsula, e.g., Thoricus, and Interior parishes in between.

51. The winged goddess Victory (Nike) at a monument
commemorating a choral victory: AKAMANTIS ENIKA PHULE,
"The tribe Acamantis won." Acamantis was the tribe to which the
potters and painters of the Ceramicus (*Kerameis*) belonged. Where the
name of the sponsor (*khoregus*) would have appeared there is an
acclamation—"Glaucon is Beautiful"—the artist using official Attic
lettering for the formal inscription and Ionic (ordinary
"handwriting") for the personal acclamation. This unusual
example of boasting may be explained by the recent defeat
(465–464) at "Nine Roads" under the leadership of Glaucon's
father Leagros, who probably died in the rout. Nolan amphora
from Nola by the Nikon Painter (*c*.460).

less quite something without their clothes on. Acclamations of beauty
here indicate quite unequivocally a homo-*political* relationship, a tribal
bond. In this case, at least, "Glaucon is beautiful" is a way of saying
"Glaucon Forever."

We have no idea if Leagros really was an under-Eighteen at the time
Smikros showed him being admired by Euphronios, but it seems very
unlikely that Euphronios was so young. He seems to have been active for
some time before the vase was painted. Smikros has made him the right
age to be shown courting a Boy, as a *meirakion,* or a *neaniskos,* just as Peithinos has shown only Cadets courting Boys in the gymnasium in *Lysis.*
If Smikros is prepared to show an outrageous mixing of social classes, he
is unable to break the law and show a mixing of inappropriate age-
classes; that would have been an insult to both Leagros and Euphronios.

One vase however, the Brygos Cup, breaks this rule in a very dramatic fashion.

THE *KINAIDOS* AS A PEDOPHILE

Again the vase is highly unusual for the period, but it has been taken as typical of Greek pedophilia, proof of it, despite all the laws and all the slave chaperons we know of. I think, however, it shows the very opposite of what it has been supposed to show: not approval but rejection, a cautionary portrait of that most despised and vilified of characters, a *ponēros*, a *kinaidos*, a sex pest.

On the inside of the cup, which is in Oxford, a man with a hairy chest, a full beard and an erection bends his knees around a Boy who makes no effort to resist and even seems to put his hand behind the man's head.[39] The gesture is the exact opposite of what the good Boys, the "*kalos*, yes indeed" Boys of the gymnasium, do in Peithinos's scene. He is not resisting beautifully. He is behaving badly. Again the sponge and strigil, as well as the nudity of the Boy, indicate a gymnasium, and again the gym kit seems to be tipping over at a precipitous angle, although the opening of the oil bottle has been hidden. The youth of the under-Eighteen is emphasized notably by the bag of knucklebones that he carries, a typical pastime of Boys like the Boys in *Lysis*. The man has come in off the street with his walking stick, now leaning against the wall, and still with his shoes on. A man his age should not be in the gymnasium at all.

Pausanias, as we have seen in his speech in *Symposium,* argues fiercely against those who chase lustfully after Boys when they have only physical beauty and no properly formed character or personality, when they are like women. The law should be used to discourage such predators, just as it does the seducers of freeborn women. He is referring to the set of laws regulating heterosexual seduction, *moicheia*. This is the same perspective as when Plato's imagined *erastēs,* represented as a charioteer, first encounters his beloved, who has not yet reached the age-class system, *hēlikia,* i.e., under Eighteen. The modest part of him refrains from leaping on the boy, but the frisky part gallops straight at him, to make "mention of *sexual* favoring," *tēs tōn aphrodisiōn charitos*. The frisky horse is so strong that the charioteer is compelled to resign himself to "dreadful and illegal things" (*deina kai paranoma*). Only at the last minute does the charioteer haul on the reins and save the situation, which leads in the end to a quiet trotting behind, like a good little *erastēs* forming a kind of conga of honor, following an *erōmenos* around and not talking about sex.[40]

Finally there is that interesting joke in Aristophanes' *Birds,* where Euelpides is asked what kind of city he would like to live in, his version of Cloud-cuckooland, and he describes the kind of city where the father of a boy of seasonal beauty would complain to him because he had met the boy, coming home, having washed at the gymnasium, but didn't kiss him, or speak to him, or embrace him, or go for his balls (*ōrchipedisas,* a unique verb: "to testicle him")—"What kind of a family friend are you?" The joke is that an Athenian father would be outraged at such a thing, of course, and the meter builds up to this five-syllable neologism, *ōrchipedisas,* the outrageous climax of the inversion of values in Euelpides' utopia.[41] Euelpides is being characterized as a villainous type. Even in this fantasy there is no question of the man actually going into the gymnasium, like the man on the Brygos Painter's cup, but only being encouraged to grope the Boy as he leaves. Our painter, on the other hand, has shown a mature man, a Senior even, with his pectoral muscles having dropped to mid-chest, a trespasser, doing precisely what Plato calls "terrible and illegal things."

The vase painters of the early fifth century do not show us a world of Athenian Homosexuality utterly different from the writers born a generation later, utterly different from the world of the laws, which were thought to go back to *c.*600 BC. They show precisely what the law explicitly forbids, a Senior entering a gymnasium, Cadets mingling with Boys. These are cautionary images, images, in other words, of anxiety. There seems no reason, therefore, to postulate a great rupture in Athenian Homosexuality in the mid fifth century. It is a single thing, with its own shape and form and distinctive practices, centered above all on wooing and the service of the *erastēs* to the *erōmenos*. These practices create the same kind of asymmetry we found in the Cretan abduction, or Spartan sex through the cloak, or the Boy sitting in the cubicle on the London Vase. But in Athens stringent protocol put a literal distance between the underage Boy and his admirers, a kind of public seclusion guaranteed by the slave chaperons and the gymnasium rules. On the one side, noisy praise, worship from afar, acclamations; on the other side a refusal of intimacy.

The central cultic manifestation of this Athenian Homosexuality took place at the shrine of Eros and Anteros at the foot of the northern side of the Acropolis under the Erechtheum, and its central myth told about the foundation of the shrine. For the tale about the indifferent Athenian youth Timagoras and his resident alien suitor Meletus, who fetched hunting dogs, horses and finally a pair of cocks, all to no avail, is a good story of Athenian Homosexuality, centered on the process of seduction. The other characteristic feature Pausanias identifies, the utter servitude of the *erastēs,* is also expressed in the myth of Meletus, who obeys to the letter his *erōmenos*'s injunction to take a flying leap. But perhaps the most interesting feature of Athenian Homosexuality is the marking of a boundary at Eighteen, the sense of new citizens "coming out" like debutants onto the scene, and coming out, it would seem, in the most spectacular fashion, with the nude streak from the gymnasium of the Academy into the city the night before the Panathenaea. Athenian Homosexuality is constructed, therefore, as the frustrated longing of citizen males for Boys to be among them, for Boys to become men, a sense of great anticipation at the start of the New Year when the Boys shake off their chaperons, their clothes and their privacy and become Striplings, and members of the polis.

THE FOURTH CENTURY:
POLITICS AND THE PROFESSIONALS

But if Athenian Homosexuality could be presented as timeless and unchanging, recognizably the same thing in the sixth, the fifth and the fourth centuries BC, homosexuality in Athens—something rather different—had changed. Homo-whorishness, *porneia,* had arrived in the city in spectacular fashion, in the form of sex slaves who might serve their masters as live-in lovers; handsome cithara-boys of notorious reputation who entertained at drinking parties; and mercenary politicians, chief among them Timarchus, even more infamous now than he was in the fourth century. Himself once as handsome as a cithara-boy, he seemed to have chosen his Greek Lovers for all those wrong reasons his contemporary Plato had Pausanias denounce in the *Symposium:* money, position.

It was just these changes in homosexuality in Athens that seem to have provoked so much discussion among fourth-century Athenians—Plato, Xenophon, Aeschines—about what Greek Homosexuality was supposed to be, discussion that has proved so illuminating and at the same time so confusing for all those in later periods who wanted to understand what exactly "the Greek custom" was; we were eavesdropping on a debate. For streams of discourse tend to be generated when questions are raised about things that were previously taken for granted. Foucault thought the problem was a systemic one, the problem that an adult citizen who was an active, victorious, penetrating sexual subject, a master of others and a master of himself, had once been a passive, vanquished, penetrated sexual object; the impossibility of imagining that a boy once penetrated could ever assume a position of dominance in the state. All this theorizing about true love accompanied by "reticence" about sodomy, he argued, was designed to render the love of boys acceptable, by denying what actually happened; it was a sign not of tolerance but embarrassment.[1] I would see all this discussion, rather, as the result of what we might call a *charis* crisis, related to much broader changes in the social, economic and political history of Athens. The ineffable exchanges of gracious favoring seemed a lot less ineffable when it came to sex between prostitutes and their patrons, or between men and the boys they had acquired through purchase. The commoditized bodies of handsome slaves, the politicians whose prominence seemed to owe less to their talents as statesmen and public speakers and more to the physical talents with which they had charmed their political masters, the puppeteers who pulled their strings, were collectively calling Eros's bluff. Greek Love was looking more and more like Greek Lust. And already, it seems, there were people calling for an end to it all, men who condemned homosexual sex altogether, who "had the audacity," in Plato's words, "to say putting out is ugly," no matter what the circumstances.[2]

BOYS FOR PLEASURE

One of the most startling avowals of this new lust comes right at the beginning of the fourth century, *c.*390 BC, in a speech written by Lysias: "Against Simon." The speech paints a picture of Greek Love that immediately seems a world away from all the courting, acclaiming and songs of praise that are associated with the gymnasium elite: "We both fancied [*epethumēsamen*] Theodotus," says the speaker, bluntly. He is telling the story of his dispute with Simon over the boy, referred to insistently as "the Stripling." This dispute had ended up with the speaker in the dock on a charge of attempted murder ("wounding with premeditation").[3]

We have no idea who the speaker was, not even his name, only that he was getting on in years and was rich. But we can attempt to piece together what happened by reading between the lines of his heavily biased account. Theodotus seems to have been "a live-in rent-boy."[4] Simon, it would seem, had paid three hundred drachmas, much more money than he could afford, to hire him under contract.[5] Then, before the period covered by the contract had expired, the nameless speaker had come on the scene and had taken the Stripling off with him. Simon had gone around to the speaker's house looking for Theodotus. Finding no one inside apart from some female relatives, he tracked the couple down to where they were having dinner and called the speaker outside. There was a scuffle and Simon threw stones. He missed the speaker, the speaker notes, and hit one of his own friends instead. The speaker emphasizes the slapstick nature of this first street battle as another indication of the ludicrous nature of the dispute. The speaker decided it would be safer to take the boy out of Athens altogether, and they went to live abroad for a while.[6]

When he thought Simon had had enough time to forget about Theodotus, he brought the boy back and the two of them took up residence in Piraeus, the port of Athens. But however much time they had spent abroad was not long enough. There was another more serious scuffle between him and Simon, this time in front of Simon's own house. It was here that Simon claimed the speaker had wounded him with intent to kill. According to the speaker, Theodotus had then slipped out of his cloak to escape Simon's clutches and run away, taking refuge in a fuller's shop. Simon and his friends had grabbed him and dragged him out. The speaker had run off in the opposite direction, but came by chance across the would-be kidnappers in a street on the other side of town. There was another scuffle, but with the help of bystanders the speaker managed to retrieve the boy, and that, so he thought, was that. It seems to have been something of a surprise, therefore, when, four years later, Simon charged him with attempted murder and had him called before the Areopagus.[7]

The speaker's account of what happened on the crucial morning does not really add up. It is clear that the brawl that led to the charge took place outside Simon's house. What was the defendant doing there? He claims that although he was living with Theodotus in Piraeus he had nevertheless installed the Stripling at the house of a friend in the city, a friend who just happened to live next door to Simon, the very man he claimed to have been avoiding.

Simon, he alleged, was having a party in the early hours of the day. He had posted some lookouts on the roof, and as soon as they saw the couple leave the house, the defendant with Theodotus in tow, Simon attempted to grab the boy. It seems much more probable that the speaker was outside Simon's house because he had paid him a visit for some reason. So why bring Theodotus along, after all that had happened? Was he rubbing Simon's nose in it? Well, there is a hint that Simon would be arguing that Theodotus was not living with the defendant at all, but had gone back to live with him, his ex-patron.[8] This makes a much more plausible story. The lookouts were there to watch out for the speaker when he discovered that Theodotus had absconded and came to remove him in a jealous rage. This may also account for the carousing. Simon was celebrating the boy's return. It may also explain the boy's state of undress—a solid fact, it would appear, that the speaker has to account for.

Who was Theodotus? The speaker refers to him as "the Plataeic [Plataïkos] Stripling," a most enigmatic term. The only other boy so called is another handsome Stripling, Aristion, alleged to be Demosthenes' live-in lover, and later a confidant of Alexander the Great.[9] One thing is clear: Theodotus is not a "citizen of Plataea" (Plataieus). The speaker also claims that he could not have done anything felonious because, if he had, the boy could have been tortured to provide evidence against him. This makes it seem very likely that the boy was a slave—under Athenian law, a slave's testimony was only valid if it had been extracted under torture—as most commentators have, in fact, concluded.[10] Simon, then, will have paid the three hundred drachmas to Theodotus's master, when he hired him out under contract. And the speaker will then have bought him outright. Otherwise he could not, surely, have taken Theodotus abroad. This would also explain how the speaker managed to get Theodotus back so easily, when he seemed to be outnumbered. He was simply reclaiming his rightful property.

So, if the alternative version of events I have outlined is correct, Theodotus was a runaway slave who sought refuge with a former client/lover. He did not get separated from the speaker accidentally during the street battle. He was trying to escape from him. Where was Theodotus now? It seems that the possibility of him giving evidence against the speaker was a hypothetical danger now past. Perhaps Theodotus was now serving another master, a long way from Athens.

Whatever happened, it is clear that Simon claimed in court that he had been "in love with" Theodotus; he had hired him under contract simply as a way of protecting himself from the dreadful allegation of abusing the boy, a charge that could be leveled even if the boy was a slave apparently; for Theodotus's original owner could not bring charges of rape and assault of his slave if a document proved that he had hired him out as an escort.[11] We know that Simon had talked of *erōs* because the speaker disputes this lover's discourse; it is impossible, he says, for someone like Simon, a pettifogging extortionist (*sykophantēs*), "to be in love" (*eran*). Nor do "people when they are in love" (*erōsin*), and deprived of what they desire, wait four years before seeking redress.[12] The word used to describe the origins of the dispute—"we both lusted after Theodotus"—is carefully chosen therefore. The only difference between him and Simon is that he thought he would make the boy his intimate friend (*philos*) through benefactions, whereas dreadful Simon thought he would force him to do whatever he wanted through acts of criminal abuse. It is true that the speaker claims to be embarrassed at having got mixed up in such a petty and squalid dispute at his age, but pettiness and squalor was his main defense strategy, and his supposed embarrassment over the episode explains why he himself did not bring charges against Simon, despite extreme provocation. It was like a squabble over a courtesan, he claims, something trivial and commonplace, and not a matter for the venerable Areopagus to concern itself with.[13] Perhaps he really was crazily in love with his slave Theodotus but wanted to play it down. Simon's version of his actions implied that the speaker had been "out of his mind" (*eis touto manias*). Eros would have provided all too plausible a motivation for a reckless murderous assault.[14]

Many decades later, probably in the 320s, a plaintiff called Epicrates tries a quite different approach, insisting upon his love for a slave.[15] In fact he was so in love that he paid a small fortune for him, 4,000 drachmas, and for his father and his brother too. The boy, he claims, insisted upon it, saying he would not "be with him" (or even, "have intercourse with him," *suneinai*) otherwise.[16] Unfortunately the boy's slave father, a perfumier called Midas, turned out to be saddled with a large number of debts. The purchase contract listed some of these debts for which Midas's new owner would be liable and referred to others not listed. The speaker did not read the small print and only later discovered that his love for the slave would cost him more than a small fortune; it would ruin him. He sued in order to annul the purchase or for compensation.

Once again there is plenty of room to doubt the speaker's version of events. The story about the boy's emotional blackmail sounds intrinsically unlikely. Would a slave really make so bold with a man who was about to become his master and who was promising to free him or have him freed? It would moreover be hard to verify. The story makes one thing clear, however: It was Epicrates himself who first suggested to the boy's owner, Athenogenes, that he buy the whole family off him, which meant, in effect, buying the entire perfume business. Athenogenes, it seems, was initially very reluctant. Epicrates' only defense is to say that the whole thing was a setup. Athenogenes, he claims, was merely feigning reluctance, and in fact had sent the boy to visit him to demand that Epicrates pay for his father and brother too.

It seems much more likely that Epicrates bought the perfume business not absentmindedly but quite deliberately, and then regretted his decision and looked for any possible means to renege on the deal after it had been signed and sealed. His vaunted *erōs* for the boy is simply a way of explaining to the jurors why he had not read the contract carefully or made inquiries about the nonspecified debts. The business was the last thing on his mind, he claims; he was thinking only of being with the boy. Although there is no mention of it in the surviving fragments—the speech was discovered on papyrus after two thousand years in the desert and sold to the Louvre for 1,500 francs in 1888—the jury might well have wanted to know what the boy had to say, or if Epicrates refused to surrender him for torture, whether that meant he was hiding something. A passionate love might also, therefore, have provided a plausible explanation for the absence of the boy's testimony: It was not that Epicrates had anything to hide or that he thought the boy might not corroborate his version of events, it was simply that he could not bear to think of his beloved in pain.

Whether pretending to be in love and not being, or genuinely in love and pretending not to be, both these relationships between master and slave clearly belong to quite a different world from that of traditional Athenian Homosexuality. There is no talk of *erastai* and *erōmenoi,* and, of course, no courting, acclaiming, writing songs of praise. Instead reference is made to *erōntes,* "men in love," or *hotan erōsin,* "men when they are in love," emphasizing a mere helpless subjectivity beyond culture, ethnography and custom.[17]

RENT-BOYS

Buying your own private sex slave was an expensive business. For those who wanted to spend a little less or to enjoy a range of the goods on offer, there seems to have been quite a well-developed homosex market in fourth-century Athens. Aeschines provides something of a list of famous rent-boys. He briefly mentions one "orphan," Diophantus, who had brought a claim, shockingly, against a foreigner for the sum of four drachmas, under the law that protected fatherless citizens. Other male prostitutes whom Aeschines brands as notorious at the time were Cephisodorus, "known as the son of Molon," and Mnesitheus, known as "the butcher's boy," and countless others he is pleased to forget about.[18] Both may have been slaves or former slaves. Aeschines also refers to an unnamed politician—perhaps, as one ancient commentator plausibly surmises, the statesman and historian Androtion—who had brought the institution of homosexual sex contracts to public notice by making such a contract in his youth. Aeschines provides enough particular details—the name of the man with whom the contract was deposited—to make the claim seem superficially convincing.[19]

A special group of sex slaves were the cithara-boys, the closest male equivalent to female courtesans. The reason for the fascination with them is that they were probably chosen in the first place for their looks: boys of such innate charm that their master had thought it worthwhile to pay for cithara lessons for them. The cithara was a box lyre. Unlike the *aulos* or shawm it was a noble instrument, the kind that might be seen in the grasp of a god such as Apollo. But, as mentioned earlier, one reason for its exalted status is that it was difficult to play, let alone to play and sing to. It might take well over a year's worth of lessons to train a slave to perform to an appropriate standard.[20] That meant that it was costly to turn a slave-boy into a classy cithara-boy, and there was no point in spending so much money on slaves who would never attract a wealthy clientele, so that their owners could recoup their investment. Doubtless not all handsome slaves would prove adept at the instrument, but there was no point spending money on a slave who was not good-looking in the first place. He might not get many invitations to perform.

One man in particular, Misgolas, was believed to be especially addicted to these fancy slave-boys. In fact his predilection for them was satirized in several comedies of the mid fourth century, fragments of which survive.[21] We get a closer look at another cithara-boy, terribly handsome, who plays for Socrates and the other guests at Xenophon's *Symposium*. And playing the cithara is not all he can do. He can also dance and even performs a little dinner-theater, taking on the role of Dionysus making love to Ariadne on Naxos. The choreographer, a Sicilian, is also one of the guests, almost certainly the boy's master. In the course of the conversation he reveals that he sleeps with the boy "every night and all night." The assiduousness of his attentions is explained by the fact that some men, he fears, are plotting to "corrupt/destroy" the boy, at which point ironical Socrates, who will soon receive several lectures on what it means "to corrupt Young Men," overreacts to what he thinks is a plot to assassinate the boy. When it is patiently explained to him that "corrupt/destroy" means "convince him to sleep with them," he marvels that the boy has not already been corrupted by sleeping with the Sicilian. You must be very proud, suggests the philosopher, not so much of the beautiful boy, but of your uniquely uncorrupting flesh.[22]

THE LAW AGAINST PROSTITUTES BEING POLITICIANS

Misgolas and his cithara-boys also feature in Aeschines' long speech demolishing poor Timarchus "the whore," which we should now look at in its proper context in more detail.[23] The legal basis for Aeschines' prosecution of Timarchus in the winter of 346–345 was the so-called scrutiny of speakers, *dokimasia rhētorōn*.[24] This was a modified version of the normal scrutinies of magistrates and officers of the polis, who could be examined not only after their term of office was complete—the *euthynai*, "settling of accounts"—but also before they even took up office—the *dokimasiai*, which would normally amount to no more than a straightforward eligibility check: taxes paid, military service rendered, parents and grandparents full citizens, etc. Now since a "speaker" was merely "one who speaks at public meetings" and since, theoretically, that could mean "anyone who wanted," a "scrutiny of orators" was problematic; you couldn't hold an examination of each man who stood up to have his say in a debate before he could open his mouth, and yet it might seem especially urgent that a man who advised the people was the right sort of person, a citizen in good standing. So what happened, in ef-

fect, was that those who spoke had to perform a little self-scrutiny before they launched forth, and woe betide anyone who cheated on his
self-examination and dared to speak when he was disqualified from
doing so. He was open to prosecution. His life would be raked over and,
if convicted, he would be deprived of civic rights, *atimia,* a kind of ret-
rospective imposition of the punishment he should automatically have
imposed upon himself. A peace treaty with Philip of Macedon, which
Aeschines had helped to arrange, was in the process of being finalized
when Timarchus started stirring things up with speeches in the Council
and Assembly, panicking the country, throwing out accusations of
treachery and corruption against Aeschines, threatening to impeach
him. The scrutiny of orators was a very effective way to shut him up.

The relevant legislation comes as the climax to Aeschines' survey of
the laws. He has gone over laws relating to Boys and to Striplings. Now,
following in the footsteps of the lawgiver (by which he means revered
archaic Solon), he comes to the other age-classes. These laws are headed,
he says, with the rubric "On Orderliness" (*Eukosmia*), and they begin
with the proper conduct of assemblies, the purifying ritual of pouring a
circle of pig's blood, the herald announcing prayers, then business to do
with ancestral religion, then the receiving of heralds on business from
elsewhere, and ambassadors, then secular matters. After all that the herald asks "who wishes to speak from those at least Fifty years old . . . he
summons them to the speaker's platform with the label of the entire age-
class." Then, when they have spoken, he invites any other of the Athenians to speak of "those to whom it is permitted."[25]

Aeschines briefly digresses on the modesty of orators in former times,
how they used to speak with hand inside cloak, the archaeologicable
"proof" of which is the statue of Solon erected (many years after his
death!) on Salamis.[26] How different Solon is from Timarchus's lewd
style of off-the-shoulder delivery. Then he returns to the phrase "those
to whom it is permitted," as if picking up from where the lawgiver left
off, and elaborates:

Who did he think ought not to speak? Those who had lived ugly [*ais-
chrōs*] lives, that's who. And where does he show this? "Scrutiny," he
says, "of Orators: if someone speaks among the People, who beats his
father or mother, or doesn't look after them, or provide a home for

them." That this man be not suffered to speak. Beautifully said, say I by Zeus.[27]

He lists further grounds for disqualification, discussing each in turn: cowardice in battle or evading military duty. It is the two final provisions that most concern him, "wasting one's patrimony" and prostitution: "If anyone has prostituted himself or served as male courtesan [*ē peporneuomenos ē hētairēkōs*]."[28] This is the clause he will use to attack Timarchus and to rake over decades of ancient scandal.

A PROSTITUTE'S PROGRESS

He provides a short biography of Timarchus the whore, starting from his coming-of-age—for Aeschines will grant him an amnesty for the vile indiscretions of his Boyhood. First Timarchus left home and went to live down by the harbor in Piraeus with a doctor called Euthydicus. Timarchus, it seems, reasonably claimed that he went there as an apprentice to learn the doctor's trade. In truth, says Aeschines, he wanted to capitalize on his youthful charms—other evidence confirms that Timarchus was a very handsome young man.[29] He went to the port to set himself up as a rent-boy, with the doctor's surgery supposedly operating as a front for a clandestine brothel where Timarchus prostituted himself to "merchants" and other foreigners as well as to "our own" Athenian citizens. But Aeschines won't name names; he doesn't want to go into too much sordid detail. He will concentrate instead on those men Timarchus actually went to live with.

First up, Misgolas, who had by the time of the trial, though probably not when Timarchus met him twenty-five years earlier, acquired his reputation for preferring the company of cithara-boys. He seems to have been a man of some wealth and standing in the city. He is described as *kalos k'agathos,* "smart (in dress, manners and class)."[30] When Misgolas discovered what was going on at the doctor's house, he bribed Timarchus to move out and live with him, "since he had a good body" (*eusarkos,* "nicely fleshed out"), was young, "lewd" (*bdeluros*), and amenable to the act Misgolas was inclined to do and Timarchus prepared to have done to him.[31] Aeschines is not, one should note, implying a sexual predilection as such on the part of Timarchus, whose sexual pro-

clivities are characterized, in contrast to Misgolas's, as thoroughly heterosexual. Rather, Timarchus was enthusiastic because he needed the
money to pay for all the luxuries and debaucheries his wastrel nature was
addicted to: fish consumption, expensive dinners, gambling, courtesans
and shawm-girls (*aulētrides*). Aeschines is able to call witnesses to the fact
that Timarchus lived with Misgolas, so it was probably true. People
might remember these events of several decades earlier because such cohabitation looked anomalous or even slightly scandalous: Misgolas was
not a friend of Timarchus's father, observes Aeschines, nor an age-mate,
but older than him, and had certain unchecked predilections, while
Timarchus was still a Stripling at the time.[32]

There is an important problem with deciding quite how old Misgolas
was, since he was in the same age-set as Aeschines, and that set was
Forty-five at the time of the trial, whereas Timarchus's set must have
been Forty-five *at the very minimum,* according to Aeschines' own information. If that information is correct then far from being so much
younger when he met Misgolas, Timarchus would have been the same
age or older. Moreover, it would not have been as amazing as Aeschines
insists for Misgolas to have no head of white hair (he has been dyeing it,
implies Aeschines) if he was only Forty-five. Various solutions to the
problem have been suggested.[33] Perhaps the easiest solution is a scribal
error. Aeschines and Misgolas were not Forty-five but Fifty-four, which
means Misgolas's age-set could have been anything up to nine years
older than Timarchus's.

We can confidently surmise that Misgolas lusted after handsome
Timarchus, but the precise nature of the arrangement between them
cannot now be recovered. If it was as scandalous as Aeschines claims,
they were presumably not "out" as a couple and there will have been
some other excuse, a blind for the anomalous cohabitation. And it may
not have been quite so scandalous after all. Timarchus's father died when
he was young, and if Misgolas was not a friend of his father he was a
friend of Phaedrus of Sphettos, who seems to have acted *in loco parentis.*

For Aeschines has some more mud to sling. It was the time of the
great city-festival of Dionysus, which included a riotous procession and
the carrying of a great pole-like phallus with an eye painted on it, followed by lots of comedies and tragedies in the famous theater attached
to Dionysus's temple at the foot of the Acropolis.[34] Young Timarchus

was supposed to process but he was nowhere to be found. He was eventually discovered breakfasting in a tenement house with some "foreigners." Misgolas threatened to denounce them for "having corrupted a free Stripling" and they ran off. This "laughable" incident seems to be true, since Aeschines can call Phaedrus of Sphettos as a witness, a distinguished member of Timarchus's own parish. We can be fairly sure that Timarchus had indeed had a role in the ceremony, that he did not show up, that he was discovered in the company of some foreigners and that they were threatened with the charge of corrupting him.

So much for the facts. What Aeschines makes of them is highly questionable. It could be considered potentially "ugly" for a boy to be seen unchaperoned in the intimate company of Athenians he had no formal relationship with, even for a Stripling such as Charmides, talking in public with Socrates in *Charmides*. It looks all the worse if a handsome Stripling is discovered at a daytime feast behind closed doors with complete strangers, men with whom he has no relationship at all, perhaps not even Greeks. So Aeschines clearly wishes to imply "corruption" in the sense of "they had got Timarchus into bed (for money)." But we also remember that in the trial of Socrates the charge of "corrupting the youth" referred to Socrates "not believing in the gods the city believes in but in other divinities, brand-new ones," and influencing the Young Men to do the same. This must be the ground on which the charge could be brought against the foreigners: They had taken Timarchus away from his place in the worship of City Dionysus. To use a more familiar analogy, it is rather as if Timarchus had forgotten to go to church at Easter and take his place as, say, an altar boy, and was then found in the company of non-Christians. Aeschines is simply taking this incident, which would count as "corruption" according to one definition, and hinting at a quite different form of corruption.[35]

Aeschines now raises the stakes. Terrible as it was for Timarchus to be Misgolas's paid live-in lover, it might not be so bad had he stayed where he was. Had that been the end of Timarchus's affairs, Aeschines would have accused him merely of being a "male courtesan."[36] The reason why he can, why he must, go further and accuse him of being a "common prostitute," a *pornos,* is that he left Misgolas and went off with many different men for money. Aeschines, one cannot help noticing, seems to have forgotten about Timarchus's time in Piraeus before Misgolas discovered him, serving the needs of commodity traders from all over the world, evidently something for which he had no evidence at all.

Aeschines first "passes over in silence," a very noisy silence, Timarchus's dealings with the "beastly savage men [*agrioi*]" Cedonides, Autoclides and Thersander. Harpocration, a learned imperial tutor of the second century AD and a little better informed than we are, claims that the beastly triumvirate were "extreme boy-admirers" (*paiderastai sphodroi*).[37] For it seems that the development of the homosex market had had another consequence: It had made it obvious that some men were especially prone to homosexual lust. This is obvious from Aeschines' characterization of Misgolas as "enthusiastic for this thing like one possessed [*peri de to pragma touto daimoniōs espoudakōs*] and accustomed always to have around him certain cithara singers or cithara players [*kitharōidous ē kitharistas*]."[38] One of the comic fragments adds that he was not interested in female courtesans.[39] It seems clear that Aeschines is using Misgolas's perceived sexual proclivity to infer something about the nature of his relationship with Timarchus. Likewise his emphasis on Timarchus's fondness for shawm-girls and courtesans and other men's wives is designed to characterize him as heterosexual, with the added implication that he was only "gay for pay." It seems quite likely that a number of the other men he links with Timarchus had acquired a similar reputation as "extreme boy-admirers." Xenophon has already used the sexuality of Ariaeus, always surrounded by handsome Striplings, to suggest something of the nature of his relationship with handsome Meno.[40] And Aristophanes in his speech in the *Symposium* had famously narrated his myth of the origin of Love as the splitting of four-legged human beings into homosexual women, heterosexuals, and homosexual men, born respectively from the all-female, the androgynous and the all-male originals, each half desperately seeking to reconnect with its other half.[41]

Next Aeschines turns to one Anticles, a man from a distinguished and probably wealthy family.[42] Timarchus moved in with him next, he claims. He would like to say more, but unfortunately Anticles can't be with us to testify. After these unsubstantiated slanders, Aeschines comes to one of the strangest of all allegations: that Timarchus became the live-in lover of a slave. Pittalacus, according to Aeschines, was a "public slave" who ran a gambling joint for dice throwers, cockfighters and quail tappers.[43] From this he made plenty of money and took Timarchus to live with him. Timarchus did not care what this public slave Pittalacus did with him but Aeschines has heard of certain "abuses" (*hubreis*) committed against Timarchus's body and "sins" (*hamartēmata,* "errors") so awful that he cannot say what they are. He would rather die first, "by Olympian Zeus." And yet these things he dare not mention, Timarchus was happy actually to do, so long as Pittalacus was prepared to subsidize his own disgusting habits (i.e., gourmandise, affairs with courtesans, shawm-girls, etc.). But then one Hegesander arrived on the scene, says Aeschines, a man with lots of money that he had embezzled during his position as treasurer of the general Timomachus who served on the Hellespont in 361/360 BC. By that time Timarchus's age-set was at least Thirty.[44]

Hegesander took Timarchus away to live with him. The so-called slave Pittalacus could not bear the idea he had spent so much money in vain and started to visit them, making such a nuisance of himself that they decided to teach him a lesson. One drunken night they raided his gambling den, killed his birds, smashed his dice boxes and tied Pittalacus to a pillar and whipped him, his cries waking the neighbors. Next day Pittalacus stripped off his cloak to show the whip marks and sought refuge at the sanctuary of Cybele, the "Mother of the Gods," in the agora. Crowds gathered. Terrified in case their guilty secret got out, Timarchus and Hegesander persuaded him to come away, Timarchus actually touching him on the chin in supplication. Now Pittalacus resorted to a lawsuit against each of them. In retaliation Hegesander laid a charge against Pittalacus, that he was his own runaway slave. Another citizen, one Glaucon, stepped in to help Pittalacus and restored his "freedom." The lawsuits were submitted to arbitration, but the arbitrator, who came from the same parish as Hegesander and had had relations with Hegesander ("used him") when he was in his prime, did nothing. Meanwhile Hegesander and his brother Hegesippus were becoming important public figures. Finally Pittalacus gave up.

What can Aeschines produce to substantiate these allegations? Well, it's common knowledge, is it not? But since this is a court of law he will call as witness Glaucon, who restored Pittalacus to freedom. In addition, we can assume that Aeschines would not have dared to invent the very public scene of Pittalacus seeking refuge at the altar of Cybele in the agora. And Timarchus's touching him on the chin is one of those little details with a ring of truth. So what seems to have happened is that there was a violent dispute between Hegesander and Pittalacus, just possibly a turf war in the gambling business. In the course of the dispute, Pittalacus's status, as public or private slave and/or as freedman, was called into question. From Timarchus's public gesture of chin-chucking and perhaps his frequenting of gambling dens, Aeschines has simply invented a love affair between them, and made this the origin of the dispute. Aeschines anticipates the retort that he has no evidence. "They will say I must produce witnesses to testify to every little detail, where he used to practice, how he used to do it, who saw him, in what manner it was done, an act of shamelessness in itself for them to say such things, in my opinion."[45]

POLITICS AND *PORNEIA*

After the Pittalacus affair, Aeschines turns to what I think is the more substantial part of his accusation of prostitution, Timarchus's political relationship with Hegesander. This apparently is what the audience has been waiting for: "I am quite aware that you are amazed I have not mentioned him long before now."[46] Their relationship seems first to have come to public attention in 361/360, when Timarchus had been allotted one of his parish's five seats on the Council of Five Hundred. At this time, Hegesander was his tribe's representative on the board of the ten "Stewards of Athena," in charge of Athena's substantial properties, which doubled as a Treasury of Athens.[47] The lottery, one should note, was not a random selection from all citizens but was drawn from a short (sometimes very short) list of volunteers. One could normally occupy one of these annual posts only once in a lifetime, and there is evidence that some boards could not always fill all their ten positions, while a number of men seem to have held an awful lot of different posts in their careers.[48] The board seems to have been supervised by the Council, and Timarchus, who before or afterward served as an auditor of magistrates' accounts (*logistēs*), may have played a leading role in the supervision.[49] But one day in the Assembly an old enemy of Timarchus stood up and claimed that far from overseeing the board, Timarchus was in cahoots with one of the stewards, Hegesander. Together they were embezzling

1,000 drachmas from the city. To describe their relationship, as we have seen, he used an odd expression: the embezzlers were a couple, "a man and his wife," Hegesander being the husband. The informer added the apparently irrelevant information, according to Aeschines, that Hegesander had been a wife too in his own time, "wife of Leodamas."[50] Clearly this man had some grudges against Timarchus and some other axes to grind, and nothing came of his accusations, though Aeschines claims Timarchus was nearly voted off the Council.

To describe Hegesander as "formerly Leodamas's wife" certainly implies a formal relationship between the two. What is interesting is that Leodamas, a very important politician in his time, seems to have been a friend of Boeotian Thebes, visiting frequently as an ambassador, and, as Xenophon had observed around that time, in Boeotia "men and boys associate with each other once they have been conjugally yoked," relationships that were on display every time the Sacred Band drew up in battle, as it had done famously in recent times, as it was to do for the last time at Chaeronea just seven years after the trial of Timarchus.[51] The odd accusation against Leodamas and Hegesander must in my view be put alongside this characteristic feature of Boeotian Homosexuality. And now Timarchus too is implicated in this political lineage of serial same-sex monogamy. Leodamas, Hegesander and Timarchus are sexual Thebanizers. Aeschines uses another term to describe the wicked cooperation between Hegesander and Timarchus, *mala philetairōs*, which can be translated as "very buddy-lovingly," clearly not a term of flattery. They were *hetairoi*, companions, like Phaedrus and Eryximachus the herm bashers of *Symposium*: "companion lovers."

But this by no means exhausts the vocabulary of invective directed at the relationships between these three. Hegesander was also Leodamas's "whore," and Timarchus was Hegesander's, so he had effectively "prostituted himself to a prostitute."[52] Hegesander in fact had narrowly escaped being himself accused of prostitution, allegedly.[53] Time and again, therefore, Aeschines explains collusion between politicians, or even the delaying tactics of an arbitrator, as the result of sexual and mercenary relations between leading members of the state. He will pursue the same theme when he turns to his great enemy, the predatory *kinaidos* Demosthenes, his relationship with Aristarchus, assassin of one of his enemies, whose admirer he pretended to be, promising him a preeminent position in politics and even showing him a mysterious "list," and his relationship with "Plataeic" Aristion, another great beauty who lived with him "doing what, having what done to him, it's hard to be certain."[54]

But how did the accused in these cases respond? They did not it seems always deny the charges of having an amatory relationship. Instead they claimed they had been relationships of *erōs*. This is why Aeschines spends so long in his speech talking of the exemplary romantic loves between Achilles and Patroclus in the *Iliad,* determined to show the difference between true love and whoring, the beautiful and the ugly faces of Greek Homosexuality. For Timarchus's defense it appears will be a defense of Greek Love, led by "one of the generals . . . coming over like a man long familiar with the wrestling grounds . . ."[55] Doubtless some of this would be broad in its scope, but much of it must also have been to the point, designed to prevent Timarchus's conviction on charges of prostitution. Clearly, therefore, some of Timarchus's loves were quite public, or at any rate they lacked deniability.

Which ones? I wonder. His relationship with Misgolas must be a prime candidate for an amatory defense. There were witnesses to their association and Timarchus was still a Stripling at the time, the perfect age for having *erastai*. But Aeschines makes such a play on his relationship with Hegesander, with the informer in the Assembly calling Timarchus "Hegesander's wife," that that too may have been a publicly acknowledged relationship, a traditional amatory tie, in which case, doubtless, its origin will have been backdated to long before 361/360 when Timarchus was at least Thirty. Quite possibly Timarchus, whose family was probably not very wealthy, and whose father had died when he was young, but who had family links to the gymnasium business—his uncle had been an athletic trainer—had infiltrated, so to speak, the ranks of the leisured "beautifuls," the *kaloi,* the "body-stars" of the gymnasium. This, as others have suggested, may be one reason why Aeschines provides a list of such famous beauties whose reputation was unsullied; Timarchus, he implies, must have done something wrong to acquire his reputation, apart from being a star of the gymnasium and having many admirers.[56] But in truth Timarchus acquired his whorish reputation through unequal political relationships.

COMMODITIZED BODIES

Traditional Athenian Homosexuality, centered on the gymnasium, with its ritualistic practices of courting, praising, sleeping in doorways, following at a distance, and discreet gracious favoring, seems to have continued as before right through the fourth century. Such practices are referred to in Plato's dialogues. The dialogues are set a generation earlier, of course, in the fifth century, but there is no need to think they were practices that had become obsolete in Plato's own lifetime. They still seem relevant to his discussion. There is little hint of nostalgia for a vanished world of Athenian Homosexuality. Timarchus and his allies were indeed going to use it as part of their defense, wheeling in "the general" to remind the Athenians of the ancient love-ways of the training grounds. And Aeschines is not only able to point to elite *erōmenoi* among his contemporaries who had managed to make their way through the labyrinth of Athenian Love with their reputations intact, but is happy himself to confess to being an *erastēs,* bothering boys at the gymnasium in the good old-fashioned style. Nevertheless, the Athenian variety of Greek Love no longer had same-sex loving to itself. It was now confronted with a very different image of homo-amorousness: the naked homosexual lust that was made manifest in the market for handsome slaves, those who served as their masters' live-in lovers, or who danced and performed for appreciative audiences at symposia, and the well-developed market for male prostitutes, both slave and free. That is not to say, of course, that male slaves had never been chosen for their looks in the past. It seems likely that some of the beauties at the court of Polycrates on Samos, lauded by Anacreon, were slaves or former slaves. But in the fourth century the market in handsome males seems to have become more obvious, more visible, more talked about.

This other kind of homosexuality is what made it so easy for Aeschines to reclassify Timarchus, who probably thought of himself as an *erōmenos,* as a whore. His audience would know what a male prostitute was. They would have seen examples of same-sex lust and mercenary same-sex relationships. A window had been opened through all the purple smoke that seemed to shroud the hyperromanticized and overly courtly *erōs* of boys, an opportunity finally to ask the impertinent question, not "What exactly did you do?" but "What exactly did you do it for?"

52A. Much reproduced in antiquity as today, the (second) monument erected in the agora to honor the heroic martyrs of the foundation of the Athenian Democracy, the "Tyrant-Slayers" Harmodius (a beardless *neaniskos*) and Aristogiton, his well-bearded, rather older *erastēs*. Harmodius's sword-wielding arm was restored incorrectly and should be much farther back, his elbow near his temple, his sword parallel with his back, in preparation for a murderous slashing movement. According to tradition, they killed "the tyrant" Hipparchus on the morning of Great Panathenaea of 514; after the eventual fall of the Tyranny (510) they were reburied together in a tomb just outside the Academy gymnasium, near the altar of Eros at the start of the Panathenaic torch race. Roman copy, made for the emperor Hadrian's villa at Tivoli, of an Athenian original (after 480) by Critius and Nesiotes, made to replace an even earlier monument looted or destroyed by the Persians during their occupation of Athens in that year. Some said Alexander returned the original (first) monument, when he conquered the Persians (Arrian *An.* 3.16, 7–8). If so, it left no traces.

———

52B. A bit of the original metrical inscription that accompanied the monument was found in the agora on March 23, 1936. Thanks to an ancient quotation in a treatise on metrical difficulties, it can be partly restored: "[Truly a great light dawned for the Athenians when Aristogiton and] Harmod[ius two together killed Hipparchus and their fath]erland made . . ." (*IG* I³ 502).

The workings of the democracy had also probably played a role in fostering cynicism. It was not, as some have argued, that the ordinary people of Athens rebelled against the elite aristocratic practices of the gymnasium.[57] That much is clear, not just from the fact that the same-sex *erōs* of the training grounds was clearly going to be an important part of Timarchus's defense strategy before a jury of ordinary Athenians, but from Aeschines' own efforts to preempt that defense with extravagant praise of the *erōs* of Achilles and Patroclus and of Athens's own tyrant-killers, Harmodius and Aristogiton; even in the second half of the fourth century BC, attacking same-sex *erōs* was not a vote winner.

Indeed this latter couple, who had been presented as altruistic, honor-obsessed, self-sacrificing, same-sex wedded lovers since at least the time of Thucydides at the end of the fifth century BC—Aristogiton "was Harmodius's *erastēs* and *had him to spouse*" (6.54)—had enjoyed something of a national revival following the end of the short-lived oligarchies and the restoration of the democracy. Their statues still stood in the city center, the agora, as they had since before the Persian invasions. The honors they had enjoyed since shortly after the foundation of the democracy were still paid to them, but in 410 the newly restored democracy demanded that every Athenian citizen must come to the agora under the gaze of the statues of the two men and swear to honor any future tyrant-killers in the same way as they honored Harmodius and Aristogiton.[58] And this same-sex couple in their emblematic poses now started to appear on the shield of the goddess Athena. Far from being representatives of an alien aristocratic lifestyle, these two were model democratic citizens.

But it was precisely the disinterested, altruistic and self-sacrificing nature of their *erōs* that made the tyrant-killers such democratic paragons. Unlike monarchies and dictatorships and oligarchies and aristocracies, democracies must have a special antipathy toward cronies and favored friends. Democracy is nothing if it does not rule out special interests.

Our best source for this democratic anxiety, the *charis* crisis in politics, is a passage in Plutarch where he addresses the issue directly, citing lots of sources from archaic and classical Athens, half a millennium before his own time.[59] We may not credit his sources, but anecdotal literature—encounters with famous men and what they said—is one of the earliest genres of prose literature, and the anxieties the stories reveal seem very much of their time. One that probably should not be credited dates from around 600 BC and claims that revered Solon informed his friends about one of the reforms he was planning, a cancellation of debts. They borrowed huge sums and made a fortune from this insider knowledge, becoming great landowners with big houses. More possibly genuine is a statement of Themistocles, who played the role of Athens's Churchill during the Persian invasions and who declared: "May I never sit on the kind of throne that means those who are my intimates will not have more from me than those who are not." But Themistocles too was forced into exile, later disgraced for having dealings with the Persian enemy. If he said this at all, the throne he was thinking of sitting on was probably that of a sub-satrap of a crony of the King of Kings. More politically correct is what he is said to have said to the mercenary poet Simonides: "He is not a serious poet who sings against the song, and he is not an even-handed magistrate whose favors [*charizomenos*] break the law."

Elsewhere Plutarch, who is evidently very interested in the topic, notes that Pericles, a radical democrat in his time, avoided socializing while he was in political life. This it would seem is the context for Pericles' extraordinary call for the soldiers of Athens to think of themselves as the city's *erastai,* hopelessly devoted admirers, not of a handsome member of the elite, but of an abstract nation-state—a nice way of democratizing Eros. Eros had an unusually prominent position on Pericles' Parthenon, leaning on his mother Aphrodite and looking out northward over the gathered citizens to where his two sanctuaries lay: the niche-pocketed sanctuary of Eros—Anteros at the foot of the little cliff below the Erechtheum and beyond to his altar in the Academy where the ephebes lit their torches for the race that opened the festivities of the Panathenaea. This democratic transposition of *erōs* from the personal to the political was also a revolutionary notion, inasmuch as it provided, perhaps for the first time, a clear vision of the state as an entity quite separate from the citizens who constitute it. Plutarch ascribes a similar democratic antisociability to the wealthy general Nicias of the generation that followed Pericles.[60]

More drastic was Nicias's elder contemporary, the radical demagogue Cleon: "When he first decided to get into politics, he gathered his intimates together in one place and broke his intimacy with them on the grounds that *philia* often undermines or distracts from making the right and true decisions."[61] This may well have gone hand in hand with Cleon's suspicion of homosexuality. So, in Aristophanes' *Knights* of 424 BC, blustery Cleon boasts of having "put a stop to the buggered, when I removed Gryttus from the citizen-rolls." To which the Sausage-Seller retorts: "Wasn't that clever of you, getting to the very bottoms of the matter? Without a doubt you were jealous of your position and 'put a stop to them,' lest they become politicians."[62] Perhaps it was Cleon in fact who introduced the provision banning male courtesans and whores from being public speakers. Either way, here we have a magnificent example of the true sexual interest—i.e., buggery—and the true political interest—power and influence—conjoined. This was what all that *erōtikos* purple smoke was obfuscating: sex and politics.

In fact the whole plot of *Knights* is based on the premise that only a sleazy market trader like the Sausage-Seller, by no means a member of the gymnasium elite, and with a willingness to put out at every opportunity, can rival vile Cleon as a star of the speaker's platform. A Big Man among the orators had already spotted his potential when he saw him, while still but a lad, shoplift a piece of meat and stick it up his perineum: " 'For sure, this boy is going to be a Statesman' . . . And he was spot-on. But, come on; he had had some strong hints: you had filched, you had forsworn yourself and you had got a piece of meat properly fixed up your arsehole—a politician, QED."[63] The very trade of the (Blood)-Sausage-Seller, who hawks his wares alongside the whores of the red-light district in the Ceramicus, refers straightforwardly to male prostitution: "selling his big salami."[64] Indeed Aristophanes makes the Sausage-Seller's maiden speech a kind of prolonged sexual grunt: "I bent over and thrusting with my arse I cried out . . ."

Over thirty years later Aristophanes' "Women in Parliament" (*Ekklēsiazousai*—"Women Attending the Assembly") make the same joke. The men have made such a hash of ruling that their wives decide to take over and establish a juster, more communitarian society with property shared more fairly, which means, for instance, that the sexual services of handsome young men are awarded according to the naturally equitable age-class system: Old hags get first refusal. Whereas Lysistrata's sex strike was presented as a form of violent extortion equivalent to a women's tyrannical coup, a seizing of the citadel of the Acropolis, these women prefer more constitutional revolution.[65] They dress up in male drag, with tanned skin and false beards, and pack the male Assembly to vote women formally into power—a nice example of characters taking on another identity in order to speak on behalf of themselves. The play opens with a dress rehearsal. Some of the women are worried that they will not be any good at public speaking and that their ruse will be seen through. Their leader, however, points out that women have a natural advantage, because they are regularly "pounded." For it is those of the Cadets (*neaniskoi*) who are most often buggered who prove cleverest at speaking.[66] The theme is not merely Aristophanes', but crops up in fragments by his comic contemporaries.[67]

Plato puts similar assumptions into the mouth of his own Aristophanes in *Symposium:* the boys who love having sex with men are not brazen shameless hussies but macho guys who love embracing what is male like themselves. "The big proof? Such boys alone turn out to be Big Men in politics [*mono . . . eis ta politika andres*]."[68] Similarly in *Phaedrus* the *erōs*-possessed and their responsive boyfriends, who reject a chaste relationship and philosophy, choose instead sexual consummation and "a life of civic ambition [*diaitai . . . philotimōi*]."[69] That these are not merely generic slanders or vague allusions is made clear in the *Symposium* by Pausanias, who is much more concrete when listing all the wrong reasons for putting out: "to gain some office or some other power" (*archēn arxai ē tina allēn dunamin*); "for the achievement of political ambitions" (*eis diapraxeis politikas*).[70] And Aeschines claims that Demosthenes tried to seduce his *erōmenos* not merely with the promise of swift advancement but by showing him that mysterious list.

So although I see no evidence that ordinary people reacted against the supposedly alien homosexual practices of the elite, I do think the democracy created an atmosphere of paranoia and suspicion, and that all were constantly on the lookout for any hint of collusion between politicians and of corrupt backroom deals. This paranoia seems to have become especially intense in the radical democracy of the second half of the fifth century, when Cleon made his theatrical gesture of breaking with his intimates and somehow or other "put a stop to the buggered." It is no coincidence that it is at this time that the comic poets start talking of politicians as if they were all in bed with one another, as if all of them were whores.

HOMOSEXUAL ANXIETIES

In my view, therefore, the new anxiety about same-sex *erōs* that seems so obvious in the works of fourth-century Athenians, and that provoked so much discussion among them about what Greek Love was or ought to be, was produced by the confrontation between centuries-old traditional practices of same-sex courting, praising and bonding, and a new world of commoditized homosex and democratic paranoia about politicians getting into bed with one another literally and figuratively. This double onslaught on ineffable *erōs* from two rather different directions—from the slave market on the one hand and the speakers' platform on the other—produces that chimera who is the beautiful Greek Lover's ugly twin: the prostitute politician. It is rather as if the homosex market, which challenged the principle of gracious discreet *charis* in affairs of Love, and the democracy's paranoia about favors between those in positions of influence, which challenged the principle of gracious *charis* in the field of politics, provoked both the insistent question: "What exactly did you do it for?" and the bizarre answer: "Sex and power." This is why the *erōs*-inspired Lovers of Plato's *Phaedrus* seem to have two options: either to abstain from sex altogether and pursue philosophy, or to consummate their relationship and pursue civic ambitions. This is why in Aristophanes' speech in the *Symposium* the male-seeking males, two halves of the all-male original, not only consummate their desire physically to reconnect but also become Big Men in politics. For the truth behind Eros's clouds of purple smoke, the secret that one might "know," could be buggery, political collusion or payment for services rendered, one after the other or all at the same time. This is such a dizzying spiral that one has to take time out to remind oneself that in fact Love is not the same as Sex, which is not the same as Prostitution, and that neither Love nor Sex nor Prostitution need have anything to do with getting on in life or making a career for oneself.

This may also explain why some people, according to Pausanias, had the audacity to declare that "putting out was ugly" without reservation. Indeed Plato himself would, finally, make so bold as to suggest such a thing. For around the time of the trial of Timarchus, Plato's last dialogue, the *Laws,* his longest work, was beginning to emerge into the light of day.[71] It was discovered, according to tradition, among his papers after his death in 347 BC, scratched onto wax tablets and waiting to be transcribed. In the dialogue, an anonymous elderly "Athenian Guest" (*xenos*), in conversation with an elderly Spartan and an elderly Cretan from Cnossus, suggests some laws for the refounding of the city of Magnesia in Crete. For Cnossus has been put in charge of the refoundation, and the Cretan is on the committee for drawing up a constitution. Naturally the topic of same-sex *erōs* comes up, but the Athenian warns his friends that he is about to suggest something very "audacious," something that both Sparta and Crete will vehemently oppose.[72] He toys with the idea of legislation like that which Pausanias ascribed to Elis and Thebes: "If we were to agree to legislate that [homosex] is beautiful and in no way ugly," what contribution to virtue would it make? "None" would seem to be the answer. So the Athenian suggests instead that they should encourage the Magnesians to say that same-sex sex is like incest: "utterly unholy, odious-to-the-god(s) and ugliest of ugly things."[73] The Cretan reserves judgment.[74]

Plato is not suggesting a ban on homosex with penalties attached. Much more shocking and sinister in fact is that, speaking from a world in which same-sex sex was conventional, something to admit to or even to vaunt in court cases, Plato seems to describe a deliberate and self-conscious plan to make homosex socially, morally and religiously unacceptable. It is almost like discovering a secret blueprint for a remarkably successful and thoroughly deliberate geriatric conspiracy to repress gay people over the following millennia. It is no consolation that he would like to discourage *all* sexual intercourse outside the confines of marriage between partners who are selected not out of love but from careful consideration of the needs of the state.

So, just decades after that declaration of a sheer, unadulterated, squalid and "embarrassing" homosexual desire in Lysias's speech "Against Simon"—"we both fancied Theodotus"—and just a few years after Misgolas and Ariaeus were brought to public notice as homosexuals, or rather as men with a striking, toe-stubbing archaeologicable fondness for the company of handsome Striplings, "enthusiastic for this thing like one possessed," audacious men started muttering that homosex was ugly, until finally Plato himself seems to have had the audacity to join them. Greek Love was one thing. Homosexual lust was something else entirely.

That was by no means the end of the Greek custom. It was still going strong centuries later, when Hadrian came to Thespiae to pay honors to Eros, and later when he expressed his love for the boy Antinous in a fashion so spectacular—with countless statues erected after his death in the Nile on October 30, AD 130, a city named after him, festivals in his honor, and even deification, complete with temples and priests—that it made the *kalos*-acclamations of the archaic and classical periods look lukewarm by comparison. But I do not think it is merely hindsight to foresee in Plato's encouragement of condemnation pagan homosexuality's ultimate demise. Eros's bluff had now been called, the ineffable exchanges of gracious *charis* had been well and truly spelled out. Same-sex loving would never be quite the same again.

But there was always, surely, something slightly preposterous about the whole phenomenon in the first place, the phenomenon of a culture that seems, from other perspectives, as predominantly heterosexual as ours is, a culture that seems to have had no problem in heterosexually reproducing itself, the population steadily rising during our period until settlement reached levels of density that would not be matched again until the nineteenth century AD, a culture where feminine Aphrodite also held sway, where courtesans and shawm-girls were far more numerous than cithara-boys and hardly short of clientele, a culture that nevertheless made Homosexuality the monumental centerpiece of its public identity.

One may with some justification ask if Greek Love was ever really taken for granted, something it never occurred to anyone to question; legislating, like the Thebans and the Eleans, that homosex is "beautiful" must always have implied, must it not, the possibility that some would say it was nothing of the sort.

CONCLUSION: A MAP OF GREEK LOVE

I started this book by observing that Greek Love was a knotty subject. I even suggested that partly because of the rather different approach to same-sex loving promoted by the Christian imperial successors of Constantine the Great, and the great schism that opened up within the space of a hundred years between post-pagan and pagan antiquity, Greek Love may be one of the knottiest subjects in all of Western history. Such a claim is not incontestable, but I have found no cause to change my mind. Certainly it has been one of the most difficult subjects I have tackled as a modern historian of ancient Greece—elusive, complicated, hard to fathom—which is precisely what makes it so fascinating a subject to explore.

In the previous chapters I have traced a few of the more notable strands that go to make up that knot, though I have not and could not trace them all. The Latin for "knot" is *nodus,* which gives us the English word "nodal"—"designating a center of convergence or divergence"[1]—and if Greek Love is a knotty subject in the sense of "tangled," it is also knotty in the sense of "tying lots of things together," not merely a junction that is difficult to navigate, but one where many different routes to many different destinations converge, a distinctive feature of Greek art, Greek society, Greek philosophy, poetry, history, what ties the court of Polycrates, archaic tyrant of Samos, to the courts of the kings of Macedon, what ties Hyacinthus, the hero mourned at Sparta's most important shrine, to Pelops, hero of Olympia, the most important shrine in Greece, what links Aristophanes' *Knights* to Sappho's Hymn to Aphrodite, the pot painter Euphronios to the praise singer Pindar, a Cretan abduction ceremony to the Sacred Band of Thebes . . . A full investigation of "the Greek custom" and all its ramifications would not merely take at least a lifetime, therefore; in the end it would resemble something not very far from a full-scale social, cultural and political history of that loose cultural federation of polities that we call "ancient Greece."

That is another bold claim, but I doubt that there are many, if any, students of the Greeks who would deny either the knottiness of the subject or its nodality. Those who specialize in Attic vases can hardly avoid the topic, nor those who specialize in Plato or lyric poetry or Sparta or Alexander the Great. What they probably would deny is my claim that it is a subject that has been neglected. There are still many, admittedly a diminishing number, who would claim it had all been settled once and for all by Sir Kenneth Dover in AD 1978. But the problem is not that there have not been books and articles about the Greeks with "homosexuality" in the title, nor that students of Alexander deny that he probably had male lovers, for instance, nor that students of Greek religion claim that Zeus's interest in beautiful Ganymede was (believed to be) innocent. What blocks one's view is that the business of deciding whether or not these relationships between real or imaginary members of the same sex were or were not sexually consummated has monopolized debate, serving to trivialize Greek Love, to cut it adrift from mainstream topics and to distract scholars from the business of exploring the implications. It is rather as if students of the Middle Ages neglected Christianity except insomuch as they debated whether or not people in the Middle Ages really believed in transubstantiation and whether, in that case, they really believed they were eating the body of Christ. Not only would it be impossible to reach any definite conclusions, it would also miss the point: the central role played by Christianity and Christian institutions in the medieval world and its *imaginaire*. So while few students of ancient religion would deny that imagined Zeus was in homosexual love with imagined Ganymede, almost no one has properly explored the extraordinary resonances of the myth of the mortal kidnapped in order to serve the gods their immortality (*ambrosia*). While it is hard nowadays to find any modern scholar outside Greece itself who disputes the proposition that Alexander the Great had sex with men, few have explored the politics of same-sex *erōs* at the Macedonian court. While everyone assumes that an Athenian Timarchus or a Cretan abductee was thoroughly buggered by his boyfriend, almost no one has explored the implications of visible and monumental—"archaeologicable"—same-sex couplings in the Athenian democracy or an oligarchic Cretan state.

From such wide-ranging explorations we can draw one uncontroversial conclusion straightaway: There were lots of different kinds of homosexuality in ancient Greece rather than one single *mos Graecorum*. It manifests itself differently in different materials, in paint or in poetry; in different places, Elis or Macedonia; in different times, fourth-century Athens or archaic Lesbos *c*.600 BC. It is a rather different thing when the lovers are Spartan women, gods and heroes, comrades-in-arms or master and slave. There is the bloodthirsty self-sacrificing love of Achilles for his "dear companions," the sweet and playful *erōs* of the lyric poets, the patriotic *erōs* of Pericles' funeral speech, the *erōs* of Plato's Academy, ambitious for knowledge, the *erōs* of the potter's quarters, exporting to the four corners of the ancient world acclamations of the beauty of local boys, the *erōs* of the monument to the Tyrant Slayers, the whorish homosexuality of Aeschines' speech "Against Timarchus," and of the strange letters supposed to have been written by Alexander, forcefully rejecting ill-conceived offers to send him the most beautiful boys in the world, the squalid, squabbling, homosexual lust of Lysias's speech "Against Simon," the rampant *katapugones* of Aristophanes and the writers of graffiti, the monstrous, seductive, predatory *kinaidoi,* the rather too obvious sexual proclivities of Misgolas and Autoclides mocked in the fragments of the comic poets of the fourth century BC, the same-sex sex acts Plato would like to discourage in *Laws* on the grounds that they don't conform with nature.

But if a single "it's all about" solution to the phenomenon of ancient same-sex *erōs* still eludes us—what Meier in 1837 referred to as "understanding the thing," *die Sache begreifen*—we can do a little better than "it's all very various."[2] Having traveled so far on our explorations of the subject, we can at least attempt to draft a provisional map of the landscapes we have explored, even if it may resemble one of those premodern not-quite-right maps of the planet, in which Australia was a series of disconnected coastlines and California an island.

So here I present some principles and provisional conclusions, or what the French call a *Vers un* . . . . : a "Toward a solution of the Greek Knot." There are three overlapping questions we can usefully ask: What was it? What was it for? Where did it come from?

I
WHAT WAS IT?

The first distinction we need to make is that between Greek Homosexualities and homosexuality in ancient Greece. It is the former that have left most traces in the sources and that demand most attention.[3]

LOCAL LOVE-WAYS

Greek Homosexualities are the peculiar and specific same-sex love-ways associated with different communities. They are invoked both in generalizations about Homosexuality in each community and in comparisons with the love-ways of other Greeks. Were we able to go back in time two and a half thousand years we would probably be able to identify scores of different varieties, not impossibly hundreds, but in our sources the Homosexualities of five communities in particular are regularly compared and contrasted. Sparta and Crete were considered by some the most ancient practitioners of the "custom," and/or the communities that were most attached to it. More particularly they were those that would be most opposed to discouraging same-sex sex, according to the Athenian Stranger in Plato's *Laws*.[4] Elis and Boeotia were considered by Athenians and later writers to encourage a particularly libidinous or no-nonsense variety of Greek Homosexuality, while Athenian Homosexuality was typically viewed (by Athenians) as the "most beautiful" and "complicated" Homosexuality of all, "not easy to grasp."

One problem is that for most of the period we are concerned with, two of these communities are not in fact political entities at all. When Crete emerged from the disturbance that ended its Bronze Age glory days, it was said by Homer to be a cultural mishmash of peoples "speaking many different languages," including "Achaeans," "Dorians" who claimed to be colonists from Sparta (Lyctus, Gortyn) or from Argos (Cnossus), and even "Eteocretans" of Praisos who claimed to be the original inhabitants of the island and who occasionally wrote inscriptions in their own language (still undecoded) to prove it.[5] By "Cretan Homosexuality" our authors are probably referring above all to the culturally dominant Dorian cities of central Crete, especially

Lyctus, but they might be referring to island-wide love-ways, which would raise interesting questions about the origins of the "Greek custom."

Boeotia, on the other hand, is the region north of Attica. It belonged to the Aeolic cultural group, to which Lesbos and Thessaly also belonged, and was first and foremost a cultural and religious federation of fiercely rivalrous cities, including Plataea, which was long allied with Athens; Tanagra, original homeland of the family of Harmodius and Aristogiton the Tyrant-Slayers; Thespiae, home to Narcissus and the center of Eros's most important cult; Orchomenus, home of the Three Graces; and, of course, mighty Thebes. When they were not trying to eradicate one another, the cities of Boeotia sometimes coalesced or were coerced into a political federation, notably during the Theban hegemony of the fourth century, which lasted about forty years, c.378–c.338, the period during which many of our writers were writing. Authors refer to "Boeotian" Homosexuality or "Theban" Homosexuality alternately, as if talking of the same thing. Probably they mean to infer a cultural institution shared by all or most of the cities of the region, but found most famously at Thebes. Boeotian Homosexuality, therefore, was a sign of cultural identity, like the Boeotian dialect.

There is another intriguing possibility. The first indications of a peculiarly Boeotian Homosexuality are to be found in the band of same-sex couples, the three hundred champions called "Reins-Holders" (hēniochoi) and "Chariot-Fighters" (parabatai), who make their one and only appearance in the pages of history at the battle of Delium in 424 BC.[6] They are often viewed as the prototype for the famous three hundred same-sex couples who formed the Sacred Band of Thebes half a century later. But this original band of champions that fought at Delium is not said to be from any city in particular and is strung along the front line of the entire Pan-Boeotian army, which means that both the Sacred Band and this prototype are only mentioned fighting in battles within the confines of Boeotia (cf. Ath. Pol. 13.22). There may have been a time, therefore, when Boeotian Homosexuality was Boeotian in the full sense of the word, not merely an expression of a cultural identity but of a territorial identity too, uniting men from all over the region in opposition to outsiders, an image of the collective manhood of Boeotia itself.

LAWS, LAWGIVERS AND DIVINE SANCTION

These local love-ways are often described as distinctive "customs" or "laws" (*nomoi*) or even as the result of "legislation" (*nomothetein*) on the part of lawgivers (*nomothetai*). They are often included in general accounts of a particular "constitution" (*politeia*). Ephorus's account of the "Cretan custom" of mock homosexual abduction was included as part of a general account of the "Cretan system," and one of Aristotle's pupils seems to have included something similar when he came to write his "Cretan Constitution," probably using Ephorus as a crib.[7] Plutarch, himself a Boeotian, insisted that Theban Homosexuality was not initiated by Laius's outrageous rape of Chrysippus, but was a deliberate policy on the part of the Theban lawgivers, seeking to temper their citizens' violent nature.[8] Xenophon includes his defensive account of Spartan Homosexuality in his *Constitution of Sparta* and he claims it was the great lawgiver Lycurgus who made Spartan Homosexuality what it was.

One reason why the Athenian Stranger in Plato's *Laws* is so hesitant when about to launch his "bold" and "solitary" attack on same-sex sex is that he sees it as an attack on the institutions of his Spartan and Cretan interlocutors, which were believed to have been sanctioned by Apollo on the one hand, speaking from Delphi, and by Zeus himself on the other, via his son King Minos, who went to consult him Moses-like in the cave on Mount Ida every nine years. Because of this, there was a law that Young Men in these Dorian cities had to agree "with one voice" that all the laws are beautiful "inasmuch as they are laid down by the gods." This seems to apply equally to their local love-ways. The Cretans indeed claimed to be following Zeus's example when they abducted boys as Zeus abducted Ganymede.[9] Therefore the Athenian may only criticize homosexuality because there are no Young Men around to hear: "for we are alone."[10]

Their distinctive love-ways, therefore, were regarded as central, even foundational, elements of a community's institutions: ancient, unchangeable, even divinely sanctioned, not just "cultural," but a fundamental part of a city's self-conscious cultural identity.

"ARCHAEOLOGICABLE" FACTS

When ancient authors refer to "the laws here" or "what the Spartan lawgiver laid down," they are referring to a whole host of very different things: a Spartan cult of *Aidōs,* "Modesty" or "Sense of Shame," the existence of slaves called *paidagōgoi* whose job it was to chaperon Athenian Boys, a gymnasium law forbidding Striplings from mingling with Boys. This is a crucial point, and one of the keys to resolving some of the contradictions in the sources on Greek Homosexuality. The distinctive *erōs* of a particular city or community—"what the lawgiver laid down concerning *erōs*"—is in fact an artificial composite of distinctive institutions, practices, rituals and rules, written or unwritten, which magistrates can enforce.

These are what I have called "archaeologicable" facts, by which I mean institutions that outsiders might find noticeable and distinctive, like some artifact or edifice stumbled upon by an archaeologist, an artifact which can then be "read" and interpreted by the ancient "archaeologist of *erōs*" to draw general conclusions about the nature of, the attitudes to, Greek Love in this particular community, even the local moral landscape. This peculiar hermeneutic tendency runs deep in Greek culture, and we even find locals doing "archaeology" on themselves—when Pausanias, for instance, in Plato's *Symposium* looks at the distinctive and peculiar features of his own Athenian Homosexuality as if as an outsider, or when Aeschines in his speech "Against Timarchus" examines the laws governing gymnasia, supposedly laid down by Solon, in order to draw conclusions as to what Athenian Homosexuality was supposed to be, what the lawgiver laid down it should be. Such a hermeneutics is just another aspect of the Greek concern with tangible "proofs," *tekmēria,* which has been seen as characteristic of whatever is scientific about Greek science and of whatever is objectively realistic about "realism" in Greek art.

Sometimes, as with the speeches of Pausanias and Aeschines that outline the *nomoi,* "the rules," of Athenian Homosexuality, we can watch the whole process from beginning to end: the reading of the artifact or the "artifactual" regulation, practice or institution, and the general conclusion derived from that reading as regards Athenian attitudes or morality. But the process of reading archaeologicable monuments and creating new "monuments" out of those readings (when the interpretations are published and thereby "monumentalized" in their turn) is not always explicit and can be subtle and complex. Aristophanes refers to rival poets using their recent victories in the comedy competition to win over the beautiful Boys of the gymnasium. We might think it was a trivial throwaway remark, the kind of thing Aristophanes thinks a comic poet might do. Or we might think that he was laying an accusation against a poet whom witnesses had seen going down to the gymnasium after a victory. But, as it happens, we know from other sources that Aristophanes was commenting on a claim his rival, Eupolis, had made about himself in one of his own plays. What looks like an instance of observation or generalization is in fact a comment on a comment that had served to monumentalize Eupolis's triumphal visit to the gymnasium—quite possibly a self-deprecating joke with no basis in reality—into an artifactual factoid.[11]

In his speech "Against Timarchus" Aeschines notes that Misgolas is always surrounded by certain cithara-boys. As it happens, in *c.* AD 200 Athenaeus collected some fragments of comic poets of the fourth century BC that ridiculed Misgolas for his fondness for cithara-boys. Either Aeschines' remark had made Misgolas's predilection for cithara-boys into an artifactual factoid for the comic poets to play with when his speech was published, or, more probably, the comic poets had recently monumentalized Misgolas's predilection in their comedies, perhaps following a particular incident or trial, enabling Aeschines to make use of a piece of gossip that had recently been concretized, i.e., that had recently become a useful archaeologicable "fact" about Misgolas.

Understanding this often hidden process of reading the artifactual proofs represented in specific monuments and institutions is fundamental to an understanding of ancient statements about the laws or customs of Homosexuality in different states. When authors seem to be making ridiculous generalizations about local attitudes, as if they have been wandering around observing or handing out questionnaires, they are really engaged in crypto-archaeologizing. When Xenophon defends the Spartans by observing that "they believe in the goddess Modesty [*Aidōs*], not the goddess Shamelessness," it sounds like a generalization about Spartan morality, albeit one couched in a rather poetically figurative style.[12] Fortunately Pausanias, the author of the *Guide to Greece* written centuries later in the reign of Hadrian, allows us to see that Xenophon was, on the contrary, being quite literal, using the Spartan cult of a personification of *aidōs* as archaeologicable proof.[13] When Xenophon says, referring to Spartan marriage, that the lawgiver "laid it down that the husband be ashamed to be seen going in and ashamed to be seen leaving his wife" it sounds as if there was a decree written down somewhere in which the lawgiver declared: "Let the husband feel shame when he is seen . . ." or else as if Xenophon had interviewed Spartan men about having sex with their wives and they responded: "I am ashamed to be seen entering the marital bedroom, in accordance with the laws . . ." But thanks to Plutarch's rather more detailed description of the strange Spartan practice of nocturnal visits to the marital home, and to modern descriptions of just such practices of "marriages of approximation" in numerous communities all around the world, we can see that Xenophon is in fact taking a peculiar, distinctive, highly archaeologicable custom, ascribing its invention to the great Spartan lawgiver, and reading into it conclusions about Spartan attitudes to marital sex. We do not *need* to postulate one single Spartan husband feeling genuine shame on visiting his wife. The very practice of nocturnal intrusions into the house where the wife slept said it all.

Again, when Xenophon insists that "some cities entirely prevent *erastai* from conversing with Boys" it seems impossible to believe.[14] Yet Aeschines concurs that the Athenian lawgiver "postpones words of intimate love [*philia*] until the age of sensibleness and greater maturity."[15] But in that case how is it possible for Callias in Xenophon's *Symposium* to converse with his *erōmenos,* Autolycus, who had won the Boys' all-in wrestling contest? The answer is that these statements are alluding to much more specific institutions, the *paidagōgoi* who chaperoned Boys in Athens, and laws forbidding Cadets to "mingle" or to "chat" with the Boys who shared their training grounds, unless the festival of Hermes was being celebrated.

There seems no doubt to me that this is how we must interpret Xenophon's most controversial statement about Spartan Homosexuality, one that has been greeted with disbelief by modern scholars, just as Xenophon anticipated it would be greeted with disbelief by his own contemporaries: "If someone was seen to be reaching out to touch the body of a boy, [the lawgiver] laid down that this was most ugly and made it that in Sparta *erastai* keep from favorites [*paidika*] no less than parents from children and brothers from brothers as regards sex."[16] The formula in the first part, which Xenophon repeats elsewhere—"if anyone even reached out to touch a body"[17]—must be a reading of an archaeologicable practice, the practice of sex (*omnia praeter stuprum*) "with cloaks intervening," as described by Cicero and as depicted by one Athenian red-figure vase painter in a scene of the Spartan Hyacinthus with winged Zephyr, a practice probably referred to as "Spartan cleft" (*kusolakōn;* see Fig. 25).[18] Xenophon may have been trying deliberately to mislead his fellow Greeks, but in his defense he could argue that he was also being literally correct.

The second part of Xenophon's statement—"[the lawgiver] made it that in Sparta *erastai* keep from favorites no less than parents from children and brothers from brothers"—should be interpreted in exactly the same way, as a reading of a Spartan institution, most straightforwardly the practice of addressing same-sex lovers as "brother." That is a guess on my part, but one informed by the fact that "brother" could often be used of intimates to whom one was not related, just as Hannibal of Carthage makes a contract of "friendship, kinship and brotherhood" with Philip V of Macedon, sworn in the name of Heracles and Iolaus (among others), just as the Spartan hero Orestes is "brother in love" of Pylades, as Crimon seems to have referred to his same-sex sex-partner, the "son of Bathycles," as his "brother" in the inscription cut into the clifftop rocks of the Spartan colony of Santorini, five or six or seven centuries BC, as Petronius's debauched "Greek" satyrs refer to each other as "brothers" all the time in the first century AD.

If I seem to be laboring the point it is because it has important consequences, and not only for understanding the strange generalizations in our sources and the apparent contradictions between them. When authors refer to "Cretan Homosexuality" they may be referring, and sometimes clearly are referring, simply to the "Cretan Custom" described by Ephorus, no more and no less. Such an expensive and tumultuous occasion cannot have been a daily occurrence. Quite possibly in any given city, "Cretan Homosexuality" happened only a dozen or so times per year. It may also mean that being a lover meant the performance of a defined role, a set of distinctive actions. So Plato and Aeschines can talk of someone not really in love but a "pretend" (*prospoiētos*) *erastēs,* or, as in Socrates' indecent speech in *Phaedrus,* someone who does not perform the role of *erastēs,* but who really is, secretly, in love.

COURTING, COUPLEDOM, SEX

When authors compare and contrast same-sex *erōs* in one city with same-sex *erōs* elsewhere, they are referring to a very wide range of amatory and amorous relationships. This is one reason why Greek Love can appear sometimes so terribly respectful, formal, even passionless, and sometimes so terribly crude. They are talking of a whole gamut of relationships from the most distant to the most intimate: courting, coupledom and sex.

I. "FAN CLUB" ERASTAI It was the first element, the practice of admiring and pursuing, that involved the largest number of people and that was spread most broadly through a community. It is this aspect of Greek Love that has left most traces in the materials, especially those from Athens, so that Greek Homosexuality is often and mistakenly confused with "Athenian Same-Sex Paying Court": the songs of praise known as "Boy-Hymns" like those in honor of Lysis with which his *erastēs* Hippothales has been bothering his friends, the countless images of gifts of cocks and hares and other things on late archaic and early classical Athenian vases.[19] It was the following and pursuing and sleeping in doorways, the slavish importuning, that seemed to Pausanias the most visible and remarkable aspect of Athenian Homosexuality, and it was this that Roman observers such as Nepos were referring to when they explained to their readers the peculiar "custom of the Greeks": "When [Alcibiades] reached Striplinghood he was loved by many according to the Greek custom."[20] The "sweet little Stripling" (*meirakiskos*) of Socrates' impious speech in *Phaedrus* has a whole gang of competing admirers, as does Charmides in *Charmides,* while in Sophocles' lost *Erastai of Achilles,* the young hero was pursued by a group of competing satyrs. It must really have looked very much like what Aeschines calls a "guard of the Boy's honor," trotting behind him.

But if it was in Athens that paying court was most spectacular and prolonged, we also hear of multiple admirers in Sparta, and the "friends" of the Cretan Boy seem to be in a similar role. There is less evidence from other places, but, for what it is worth, the myth of Narcissus of Boeotian Thespiae refers to several admirers who eventually tire of his disdain and "cease being in love with him," all but one, who commits suicide, and, dying, brings a curse down on Narcissus's head.

One of the characteristic features of admiring was writing an acclamation of a Boy's beauty (*kallos*) in a public place. The *kalos*-acclamations that cover Athenian vases therefore make the painters into *erastai* of the boy they praise, as is nicely revealed by Smikros's image of the painter Euphronios, probably his boss/owner, respectfully admiring Leagros, the parish's local posh boy, whom Euphronios acclaims on his finest vases. Painters indeed seem to have been loyal to individual boys, so that some anonymous artists have been named from the boy they praise. The Epidromos Painter, for instance, is so called because he seems to have been almost the only man in the Ceramicus who saw something worth admiring in Epidromos. Usually it would be more accurate to talk of serial loyalty, which means that the names of the admired can be used to date a vase painter's works. Since painters are rarely loyal to more than three boys in the course of their painting career, the period during which a Greek man could be acclaimed was probably much longer than merely a couple of years and very probably extended into adulthood. Moreover, typically a boy would have more than one painter celebrating his beauty, and often these fellow admirers show other signs of affinity in their style of painting or their subject matter, or simply by naming each other on their pots, as Smikros names Euphronios. This has allowed connoisseurs to identify a "Leagros Group," for instance, a group of black-figure artists of very similar style, united in their admiration of Leagros. An extraordinary feature of the commercial workshops of the Ceramicus *c.*540–460 BC is that they seem to have been organized as if they were rival fan clubs, groups of *erastai* devoted to particular boys.[21]

It is hard to believe that the despised *banausoi* of the potters' quarters of sixth-century Athens had very much at all to do socially with the elite youths of the gymnasium who passed by on their way to the gymnasium of the Academy. The same surely applies to the quarrymen who celebrated the beautifulnesses of the boys of the island of Thasos in the fourth century.[22] It must be the case that the "beautifuls" often did not even know the identity of all the *erastai* who vaunted their respective virtues in songs, graffiti or paint. Likewise when Isocrates and Lysias, both by that time mature men, are called the "favorites," the *paidika,* of Socrates and Phaedrus respectively, it seems to mean simply that their writings were admired by them.[23] Perhaps the vase painters really were hopelessly in love with Leagros, an elite boy who belonged to their own parish of Ceramicus (*Kerameis*), whom they later helped to elect as general to lead them, disastrously, in war. But when one of them acclaimed Leagros's son Glaucon as *kalos* on an image of a tripod commemorating his successful sponsorship of their tribe Acamantis in a festival competition (Fig. 51), it surely meant no more and no less than "*Viva* Glaucon! *Viva* Ceramicus! *Viva* Acamantis!"[24]

2. WEDDED COUPLES If paying court has left the widest wake in the sources and involved the broadest range of people, the oldest manifestations of Greek Love are the same-sex couples. The couple made up of Heracles and Iolaus, his little helper, who appear together on Boeotian brooches dated to *c.*700 BC (Fig. 31) are among the earliest characters from myth recognizable on artifacts. Not long before, according to the traditional date of *c.*730 BC, Homer had put the complicitous and devoted intimacy between Achilles and Patroclus at the heart of the plot of his *Iliad,* probably borrowing from an even older myth that presented Achilles as the self-sacrificing devotee of the younger Antilochus. Such same-sex couples in a one-to-one relationship remain prominent right through the period: Orestes and Pylades, brothers-in-love, Harmodius and Aristogiton, Phaedrus and Eryximachus, Pausanias and Agathon, the Regent Pausanias and the man from Argilos whom he betrayed with a postscripted "Kill the messenger," Cleonymus and Prince Archidamus, Leodamas and Hegesander, Hegesander and Timarchus, to name a very few. In the *Symposium* and *Phaedrus* Plato assumes a lifelong relationship of "steadfast partnership" (*koinōnia*) to be the ideal, and not merely lifelong but continuing into the grave, in the golden homotaph that Patroclus will share with Achilles, for instance, a wedding present from Dionysus to Achilles' mother, and beyond the grave, in the land of the shades or on Plato's "shining path" or on the White Island off the coast of Ukraine.

These relationships could be publicly and officially recognized. By far the most extensive account of such a pairing is Ephorus's description of the Cretan abduction ceremony, which culminates in a formal and public acceptance of the association (*homilia*) by the abductee at a sacrificial feast in honor of Zeus. He would, from then on, be allowed to wear a distinctive costume, and another distinctive costume when he came of age at Twenty. He was also accorded the privilege of a special place in dances and races. The finalization of the relationship meant the conferring of special titles—*philētor* for the abductor, *kleinos,* "Famed," for the abductee. Other members of the community had a say in sanctioning a relationship that would have consequences for the respective status of other members of the population. The Boy's "friends" (*philoi*), probably his fan club, had to announce the point of abduction at least three days in advance. Probably the crowds that would undoubtedly have gathered would be able to influence the outcome, giving strong hints to the "friends" as to whether or not the community thought the Boy was worthy of the status of *kleinos* and all the symbolic privileges that title entailed, and whether his abductor was an appropriate *philētor*.

We would know as little about Cretan modes of homosexual pairing as we do about pairing rituals elsewhere, had a monk not chosen to copy Strabo, had Strabo not cited Ephorus, had Ephorus not digressed. But other communities must have had similar public rituals of one-to-one association. That much is clear from what we hear of the rules that compelled certain Spartan men to contract a same-sex relationship and made them responsible for the behavior of their *erōmenoi;* the fact of pairing and the identities of any particular pair must have been known to the authorities; by some signal means or another, each same-sex relationship must have been concretized as a public and archaeologicable fact. We have more information about Thebes. There, according to Plutarch, who claims he got the information from Aristotle, the formalization involved exchanges of oaths at the tomb of Heracles' constant companion Iolaus. We also hear that the *erastēs* gave his one-and-only a gift of weaponry on coming-of-age. The formal, slightly mysterious, titles for same-sex couples we hear of from Sparta and Thessaly—"Inspirator" (*eispnēlas*) and "Blow" (*aïtas*)—and from fifth-century Boeotia—"Reins-Holder" and "Chariot-Fighter"—were also probably conferred following the formalization of a relationship.

Such intrasex marriages were rather different from ancient intersex marriages, which were often arranged by families with no wooing and courting of the girl and little concern for love on the part of the bridegroom, nor even for liking on the part of the little bride. Eros was supposed magically to appear at the ceremony itself as the bride was unveiled and, hopefully, fond intimacy (*philia*) and domestic harmony (*homonoia*) would follow. In that respect ancient same-sex weddings were more like modern marriages, associations of individuals who had come to know each other over time, albeit sometimes at a distance, and who had been drawn together through love on the part of one of them at least.

Nevertheless, the Greeks seem to have compared same-sex couplings with heterosexual couplings from a very early date. Many classicists remain wary of seeing anything sexual in the relationship between Achilles and Patroclus, but few deny that Homer is highlighting a parallel with a heterosexual couple when he compares Achilles on strike to the hero Meleager on strike and renames Meleager's wife Cleopatra, which is simply an inversion of Patroclus's name. More subtly, Achilles' care for the dead Patroclus is paralleled by Andromache's concern for the brutalized corpse of Hector, her spouse.

More generally, Xenophon talks of Boeotian men associating "once they have been yoked together" (*syzygenetes*), a normal word for "marriage," and Sappho refers to other women as "yoke-mates." The homo-amatory women of Alcman's *Partheneion* carrying the mysterious *pharos* ("cloak"/"plow"?) for the goddess "at the dawn" are implicitly yoke-mated. Thucydides himself seems to provide evidence for an Athenian same-sex association when he says not merely that Aristogiton "was Harmodius's *erastēs*" but also "took him to spouse." Plato talks of his eternal same-sex couple who consummate their relationship as "men who have exchanged the greatest pledges."[25] Aeschines remembers someone labeling Hegesander as "Leodamas's wife" in a public meeting and Timarchus as Hegesander's. The very abducting of the Cretan Boy connected the ceremony with mythical (and ritual) abductions of brides such as Hippodamia by Pelops, and the myth of Laius's abduction of Pelops's son Chrysippus not only alludes implicitly to that previous marital abduction, but was explicitly said to have outraged Hera in her role as goddess of marriage, which is why she sent a plague on Thebes in the form of the man-eating she-monster known as the Sphinx.[26]

3. HOMOSEX Finally, it seems clear that the local varieties of Greek Homosexuality might also include local varieties of Greek Homosex, not just a preferred or fashionable way for males to sexually pleasure themselves, but a strongly patterned and distinctive mode of sex with a structural and symbolic significance, associated with all the other traditional love-ways "laid down by the lawgiver": archaeologicable sex. We can

identify at least three modes of Homosex. All of them, as it happens, involve face-to-face encounters.

Thanks to Cicero, we know that the Spartans were associated with their own peculiar mode of "sex-in-cloak," perhaps that which is elsewhere referred to as *kusolakōn*. It seems to be illustrated only once on a fragment of a cup made in Athens that seems to show Zephyr penetrating the cloak of Spartan Hyacinthus (Fig. 25). The position of the couple—in midair!—is clearly fantastic, but one could infer that the halfdozen or so Athenian images of Zephyrus and Hyacinthus interlocked indicate that Spartan sex was consummated horizontally. The punch bowl in the British Museum seems to insist upon another distinctive variety, which we might call "cock sitting" or "chair sex" (Fig. 33). This latter clearly has a very definite and rather serious ritual context, linked to the gymnasium (shown on the other side of the vase) and the crowns worn by the Striplings, but we have no idea what the ritual is or in what city it was performed. My best guess, for various reasons, is that the vase illustrates the very notorious Homosex of the city of Elis, which organized the Olympic Games, but I would not insist upon it.

The most famous of these sexual *schēmata* is the position shown on a number of archaic Athenian vases, a standing position that the Athenians seem to have called *diamērion*, "through the thighs," which Kenneth Dover Latinized as "intercrural," and which others have labeled "frottage," or, for some reason, "Princeton First-Year" or "the Princeton rub."[27] It appears out of the blue around 550 BC, and there may be as many as twenty-five such scenes from the period of the next thirty or so years, most often in association with dancing "supernumeraries," the gymnasium, and/or crowns. This is not a huge number in relation to the thousands of vases that survive and the far more numerous scenes of gift giving and importuning, yet it does represent a clear-cut statistical blip, more notable because it was a scene painted by a *range* of artists on a *range* of fabrics. In other words it never became merely a stock scene mass-manufactured. There was something going on out there that each painter had to reimagine for himself.

After *c.*520 BC such scenes decrease rapidly in number to just a handful, especially if one discounts the few fanciful images of Zephyr interlocking with Hyacinthus. On the few red-figure scenes of *diamērion* from *c.*500 onward there is evidence for anxiety, as if it was no longer something to look at or to be seen; on one such vase a youth or slave in the foreground actually looks away (Fig. 49).[28] Instead of Men and beefy Striplings surrounded by jolly supernumeraries, *diamērion* is now shown in scenes of entrapment of Boys, as on the Peithinos Cup (Fig. 45).[29] The Gotha Cup, a heavily restored vase set in a gymnasium with gym-kit swinging in the background, shows a Stripling having enclosed a Boy with his staff, bending to kiss him (Fig. 47). On the wall behind is a hare in a cage and a dog barking at it. Trapped hare, trapped Boy: We are bound to identify the two.[30]

Dover suggested that intercrural was a position insisted upon by the *erōmenos* to avoid the humiliation of buggery, but sources (written a century or more after the scenes began their steep decline) refer generally to *charizesthai* or *charisasthai*—"graciously favoring" or "putting out"—for good or bad reasons, not to "standing up" or "bending over." What does seem clear is that in its heyday on the vases in the sixth century BC, *diamērion* was a positively symbolic act associated with the formal and traditional and supposedly very ancient Homosexuality of the gymnasium, with the formulaic gifts of gamecocks given to Striplings, and with the festival where crowns could be awarded. We may find it hard to

53. A recently discovered example of a typical scene of Athenian Homosex from the three decades when scenes of intercrural were most popular (*c.*550–520; *c.*25 examples). A bearded man has intercrural (*diamērion*) sex with a beefy, crown-sporting *neaniskos,* while "dancing supernumeraries" (beardless *neaniskoi*) look on, probably indicating a specific festive occasion, rather than general nonspecific "festivity." Skyphos Cup first published in 1995 and attributed to the Amasis Painter (*c.*540).

believe that such a sex act was ever performed in front of witnesses, dancing or not dancing, but *to show an act as carried out in public* ought at least to indicate its public recognition, which will have served inevitably to create a bond between the participants. Just such a bond is indicated by Aeschylus when he makes Achilles allude to the "holy honor of thighs" to signify his relationship with Patroclus, as if it were a kind of pledge that Patroclus might seem to have betrayed by returning to battle and getting himself killed.[31]

54. Three-footed *pyxis* (box). One foot shows a bride unveiling to a bridegroom, another shows two women sharing a single *pharos* ("cloak"), in this context a symbol of female same-sex pair bonding. Most effort was devoted to the third scene, which shows courting and intercrural sex between long-haired and short-haired beardless ephebes, framed by two supernumeraries, one dancing. The shape itself is strongly associated with wedding scenes, and the vase seems to provide remarkable testament to a sense of comparability between male-homosexual, female-homosexual and heterosexual erotic alliances, a century and a half before Plato had Aristophanes make the comparison explicit in the *Symposium,* but more than a century and a half after Homer implicitly compared Patroclus to Meleager's wife, Cleopatra. Perhaps most significant is the way it links the archetypical Athenian Homosex Act to a heterosexual wedding, i.e., to a formal, publicly acknowledged troth plighting. Attic, said to have been found in Athens, unattributed (second third of sixth century).

Two other vases link *diamērion* with troth plighting. One is a red-figure vase found in the Athenian agora, from the time when such scenes had grown extremely rare (Fig. 58). Fragmentary, like many of the most interesting artifacts, it seems to have shown a gymnasium scene on the outside, since there are traces of javelins and a lion-footed stool. The interior showed a scene of *diamērion* frottage, but with no onlookers, i.e., in private. Although the heads of the couple, and therefore their respective ages, are lost, the owner scratched the word *philotēsion*, "love pledge," alongside them. The term is associated with the practice of pledging from a "loving cup," and heterosexual marriage alliances also featured the drinking of pledges between the bride's father and his new son-in-law.[32] The idea had been nicely captured by jovial Anacreon, who had arrived in Athens a couple of decades earlier and may, just possibly, still have been alive: "Pledge to me instead, dear friend, a toast of your slender thighs."[33] The odd metaphor may be more graphic than it appears, if we remember the custom of tossing the dregs from one's cup at a target in honor of a beloved Boy, the *kottabos* toast. On a wine cooler (*psykter*) in the Hermitage in St. Petersburg Euphronios painted a *hetaira* called Smikra playing the game while saying in Dorian dialect: "I toss for you, Leagros."[34]

Just as striking is a tripod box, found in Athens but now in Oxford, Mississippi (Fig. 54). The shape itself was associated with weddings.[35] One foot has two women joined by a *pharos*, in this case very definitely a cloak, as if making a visual pun on the *pharos* (plow?) in Alcman's *Partheneion*.[36] A second foot has an image of a cloaked woman and a man. The third foot has two pairs of youths engaged in *diamērion* surrounded by excited onlookers. The gesture of the woman in the heterosexual scene has been read as an image of a bride at the critical moment of her unveiling. The tripod, therefore, seems to show three kinds of wedding, with the same-sex frottage apparently functioning as a symbol of male same-sex connection, just as the shared cloak indicates female same-sex bonding and the marriage a heterosexual bond.[37] It could almost be an illustration of the images of the three types of human sexual pairing that Aristophanes describes in Plato's *Symposium*.

What is interesting about Greek Homosexualities is that they combine several different elements of a continuous narrative of "ordinary" homosexuality, what the Greeks might call "unmarshaled [*ataktos*] Aphrodite"[38]: falling in love and pursuing someone, having sex, becoming a couple in a relationship. But the narrative is broken down into a series of discrete elements, each element rigidly formulaic, with a life and structure of its own. The river of a homosexual narrative is transformed into a canal with locks, the slippery slope from fancying someone to seducing them to wedded bliss terraced into distinctive steps. Just as the sources create a composite of local love-ways from archaeologicable facts, so those love-ways break up the narrative of an "ordinary" homosexual affair, monumentalize and archaeologify its constituent parts as discrete practices, and then reconstitute it as a Greek Homosexuality. Falling in love with Leagros becomes writing "Beautiful is Leagros" on a vase. Seducing Leagros becomes offering him a gift of a gamecock. Getting Leagros into bed becomes frottage, standing up, quite possibly with an audience at a festival. Establishing a relationship with a Cretan boy meant abducting him, making gifts of a costume, a cup and an ox, followed by a great public feast.

It is almost as if Greek cultures were deliberately and strenuously localizing something universal, conventionalizing something natural, depersonalizing and socializing something intensely personal, complicating something simple.

AGE

A popular image of Greek Homosexuality imagines a society that not merely tolerated but positively encouraged "intergenerational sex," in which mature men abused "young boys" many years younger. This is mistaken. But age is a central structural feature of Greek Homosexuality, as it is of Greek culture *tout court*.

We have enough information about three Greek communities, fourth-century Athens, Sparta and "Crete," to be quite certain that they belonged to the group of societies anthropologists have labeled "age-class societies." New citizens were put in annual age-sets, or "years," and accorded a particular grade status. Each set would advance a level, or "go up a year" on the formation of a new age-set, at every New Year. After clocking up a defined number of levels (i.e., "years") the members of the set would achieve a grade promotion—from Boys to Striplings,

Striplings to Young Men, Young Men to Seniors, etc.—which would entail a change in rights and responsibilities, the right to go and fight abroad, or the right to become a councilor, a magistrate, a general, a juryman, etc. Although we have less explicit evidence for other cities and for Athens before c.400 BC, there is no evidence that such age-class organization was considered unusual or even something to be remarked upon; indeed so unremarkable was it that we almost passed it by. There is certainly no evidence for the revolutionary introduction of an age-class system in Athens after 400 BC, and we would have expected at least one of our many sources for the period to have said something about such a big change. On the other hand, there is plenty of positive evidence, albeit of a more general and circumstantial sort, to indicate both that Athens had long been an age-class society and that other Greek cities were too.[39]

There is evidence for a wide variety of different age-class structures and age-class terms in Greece, different calendars, different New Years, which makes translations between them difficult. One important difference is between the forty-year cycles known from Sparta and Crete, in which boys became citizens at Twenty when they had achieved something that could be called a "beard," and forty-two-year cycles such as that of Athens, where boys became citizens at Eighteen, when they first hit puberty and spent two years as "Off-of-a-beard" *ageneioi,* Striplings (*meirakia*), or Cadets (*neaniskoi*); for in antiquity puberty seems to have arrived about four years later than it does now and classical Greek males—this is a crucial point—did not shave.

It is unlikely that Athens was the only city to award citizenship at Eighteen, and there are signs, from lists of the age-groups who competed in athletic competitions, that Corinth, Argos and Boeotia may also have acknowledged a (two-year-long) age-grade intermediate between Boys and Men. Elsewhere, however, the idea of a citizen without a proper beard may have been found strange. One complication is that the term *pais* could refer to any male under Twenty—hence Lucian can say that Apollo was shown as "an eternal *pais.*" But *pais* could also be used to refer to the formal age-class of Boys, *en paisi, ek paidōn,* not yet assigned the age of Eighteen.

From what we can tell from Athens, measures were taken there to prevent over-Eighteens who were not members of the family from engaging in unchaperoned intimacy with under-Eighteens, most conspicuously through the institution of *paidagōgoi* who escorted the wealthier Boys around. Admiring, acclaiming and following Boys seems to have been permissible, however, a paradox the Athenians themselves noticed—indeed it was this same paradox that led Pausanias in the *Symposium* to describe Athenian *erōs* as "complicated" and "not easy to grasp." At Eighteen the ephebes of the gymnasium had a spectacular coming-out when they ran a naked torch race, probably a relay race, from the altar of Eros in the Academy to the altar on the Acropolis, a distance of nearly two miles (Fig. 4). Crowds gathered at the entrance to the city in the Ceramicus to slap the slower runners. From now on they were no longer so well guarded, although Socrates is still very circumspect about talking unchaperoned to the Stripling Charmides. Men of Forty or above were supposed to pose no threat, and could sponsor Boys' choruses, while mature men who continued to fight over Striplings, albeit outside the context of traditional Athenian Homosexuality, might apologize in court for not acting their age.

The age-class system exaggerated differences between age-groups, which leads at least one classical author, Antiphon, to talk of age-grades as rivalrous "races" or "species": "the race [*genos*] of Young Men [*neoi*]." The riddle of the Sphinx focuses precisely on this human peculiarity, a species that is in fact three different species at different times: Boy, Man, Elder. Most references to and images of Greek Homosexuality assume admiring love *between* grades, normally Men and Striplings, and Striplings and Boys, so intergrade *erōs* may well have involved something partially heteroerotic: a "love for the other." In fact Plato is probably referring to Greek Homosexuality when he adduces a "mixed" *erōs* that combines "love for the other" with "love for the like."[40]

Age-class rivalries and conflicts are a prominent feature not just of Antiphon's late fifth-century rhetorical exercises known as the *Tetralogies,* but of many of Aristophanes' comedies of the 420s and 410s BC, notably *Acharnians, Wasps, Clouds* and *Birds.* Elsewhere we hear of age-class civil wars. Plato in *Laws* alludes very vaguely to such age-grade "stasis" in Miletus, Boeotia and Thurii, and Polybius has left an account of such a conflict in Hellenistic Crete.[41] One might well follow those students of age-class societies who have seen in formalized intergrade loves and best friendships a way of balancing interclass conflict and bridging the age-class divisions, or as modes of "social reproduction."

Love between grades need apply only to the period of courting and making friends. In the course of time both the Cadet Hippothales and his *erōmenos* Lysis will have been in the grade of Young Men at the same time, their age-sets separated by just a few years. So a Stripling could be *erastēs* of another Stripling, but one perhaps in the year below, as Ctesippus is *erastēs* of Clinias in Plato's *Euthydemus*. It does seem that it would have been difficult for those in the same year, however, to have a recognizable relationship of Greek Love; they were already intimates, already affined. That would not stop classmates from falling in love with each other, as Critobulus seems to have fallen in love with Clinias, his "more advanced" classmate, but it would make it difficult for Critobulus to be Clinias's *erastēs,* and, as Xenophon tells the story, so it was.[42]

Outside Athens, there seems to be a general assumption that *erastai* would be young warriors and that *erōmenoi* in a relationship would be at least the equivalent of Striplings. Elean and Boeotian boyfriends slept together and fought together in battle; there cannot have been much of an age-gap between them. Prince Archidamus was in his Twenties when he established his relationship with Cleonymus, who was Eighteen. But Boys in Sparta and Crete lived communal lives and were not segregated from admirers, with only the cloaks they had to wear winter and summer for protection. This intimacy between under-Eighteens and their adult admirers was probably rather scandalous for an Athenian and may be one reason why Xenophon (like Plutarch) is so concerned to infer that the lawgiver made them "no-touching" relationships and so quick to emphasize that Cleonymus was "out of Boys." The relationships were also supposed to last some years, so that a Spartan *erastēs* would do the shopping for his *erōmenos* when he was in his Twenties.

In the aristocratic and dynastic societies of the north, age-patterning is less obvious and regular. Other priorities dictated with whom one would find it advantageous to forge a relationship. Plato seems to think it notable that the Thessalian dynast Meno "still" had *erastai,* as if he was of an age when one would not normally expect to have pursuers. But those *erastai* included a very useful one in the form of Aristippus, dynast of Larissa, and Xenophon makes much of the fact that Meno took as his *erōmenos* Tharypas when he had a beard, but this bearded *erōmenos* was quite possibly or even quite probably the exiled Molossian king. Macedonians seemed unorthodox in the amatory and, according to Theopompus, sexual roles they played. The Royal Boys, all Striplings, had conspiratorial relationships with each other. The crowned Boys about to have chair sex on the vase by the Dinos Painter in the British Museum are clearly the same age too, wherever they come from.

CLASS AND TOPOGRAPHY

Accounts of Spartan and Cretan Homosexuality state that *erastai* had to be men of a certain status or class. There is less emphasis on the status of their *erōmenoi,* who were selected more on account of their physical excellence. There is a chance therefore that the relationships consisted of members of some elite group selecting *erōmenoi* from a more general group. It may be significant that one source refers to the Spartan *erōmenos* as "Laconian," "from the territory of Sparta," as opposed to his "Spartiate" *erastēs,* i.e., "a citizen of Sparta."[43] The Cretan ceremony also involved the transfer of substantial wealth from the *philētōr* and the "friends" to the abductee, while the Theban practice in which *erastai* gave their *erōmenoi* a panoply of weapons on coming-of-age may have been more than a symbolic gesture. One consequence would have been to allow boys who could not afford hoplite equipment to join the army.

But the key to the elitist character of Greek Homosexuality is its long, profound and ubiquitous association with the gymnasium. Indeed the Athenian Stranger in Plato's *Laws* thinks the whole phenomenon can be blamed on those cities, especially Crete and Sparta, which are most attached to gymnasia.[44] This connection can be demonstrated in numerous ways, from the gym-settings of scenes on Athenian vases to the oil-scraping strigils buried with the bodies of the Sacred Band. Greek Homosexuality is, to all intents and purposes, identical with the "Homosexuality of the training ground," which means this was probably the place where Greek Homosexuality largely took place: the paying court and admiring, as in *Charmides,* the "mingling" permitted during the festival of Hermes in *Lysis,* the sacrifices to Eros in the Academy, the gift giving shown on Athenian vases, the exchange of pledges, as in Thebes—for the tomb of Iolaus was attached to a gymnasium. The gymnasium might even be associated with, if not the site for, Greek Homosex. The inscriptions from Thera recording who *oiphed* and who *oiphed* whom were found near the gymnasium. The images of *diamērion* on archaic Athenian vases are often set in the gymnasium. The Striplings about to engage in chair sex on the vase in the British Museum probably won their crowns in the gymnasium depicted on the other side.

Inevitably therefore Greek Homosexuality was associated with the groups who attended the training grounds. In Athens those shown training on vases seem to belong very definitely to the elite—Boys like Leagros, for instance. These *kaloi* formed something like a *jeunesse dorée*. The Boys and Striplings who attend the late fifth-century gymnasia described by Plato are no less distinguished. Perhaps this gymnasium elite was composed simply of the rich, those who could afford the spare time and the fees. But Lysis also clearly belonged to a family with a distinguished mythological and athletic history, probably a *genos,* a family with a lock-hold on a priesthood. Charmides is no less distinguished, and if either Ctesippus or Hippothales is nouveau riche their horsey, knightly, names disguise the fact. More explicitly and specifically Pausanias in the *Symposium* seems to indicate that Athenian *erōs* was peculiar in the fact that Athenians admired the "noblest and best [*tōn gennaiotatōn kai aristōn*] even if they are uglier than the rest," perhaps drawing a contrast with the Cretans and Spartans, with their interest in sheer physical excellence.[45] On the other hand, while Spartan law insisted that a Spartan *erastēs* had to be, in Xenophon's words, "the necessary sort" (*hoion dei*), in Athens, since the laws of Solon in the early sixth century, the only group forbidden to "be in love" were slaves. In fact those who admire seem to come from a rather more socially diverse group than the admired: comic poets, Aeschines the orator, the vase painters.[46] If the full technicolor version of Athenian Homosexuality was open only to the gymnasium elite, yet there was room for participation by the masses at a distance.

This is the true paradox of Athenian Homosexuality, a radical democracy that "erotically" worshipped a tiny elite whose members— the oligarchic revolutionary Charmides, for instance—might be hostile to its democratic values and even attempt to overthrow it. There seems no doubt at all that Athenian Love had a deeply elitist or even aristocratic coloring, but there are very few signs of popular antipathy to the phenomenon and plenty of indications that the Athenian *erōs* that flourished only in the exclusive world of the gymnasium was thought to belong to Athens as a whole. Eros had a central part to play in the civic rituals of Athens, in the torch race during the Panathenaea, or looking out from the Parthenon frieze, or embodied in the statues of Harmodius and Aristogiton of the glamorous *genos* of the *Gephyraioi*, "who killed the tyrant and made Athens free," the same-sex, thoroughly aristocratic couple who became a symbolic bulwark of the democracy. It is almost as if the elite were seen to be performing a service for the city, keepers of Eros's flame, and keeping the democracy Greek through the practices of Greek Love. Timarchus's defense team certainly thought that a general making a speech extolling the love of the training grounds was a vote winner in the 340s, and Aeschines clearly has to prove that he is by no means *erōs*'s enemy, an uneducated man.

"A HOLY ACT IN A HOLY PLACE"[47]

Perhaps one of the most controversial claims to have been made about Greek Homosexuality is that there was something sacred about it. Students of religion have tended in recent years to play down the sexier aspects of Greek cult such as sacred prostitution, while students of homosexuality have been skeptical of claims that the whole phenomenon was merely "ritualistic," a case of men reluctantly doing their religious duty. In fact most often religion has been invoked in discussions of transitory and transitional homosexual rituals of initiation into adulthood, rituals that have proven quite hard to track down. But the claim that there was a religious aspect to Greek Homosexuality has a long history, associated with the name of Erich Bethe and his article on "Dorian Pederasty," published one hundred years ago in 1907, which turned the previous opposition between the sexual and the noble aspects of Greek Love upside down. Bethe was especially impressed by the recently discovered *oiph*-inscriptions on the rocks on the sacred promontory of Thera, and particularly by the one in which Crimon invokes the name of Delphinian Apollo. He compared it to the oaths of the Theban couple at the tomb of Iolaus: "wedding before divine witnesses."[48]

But that there were religious aspects to Greek Homosexuality is only to be expected. It would be strange if there were not. Gymnasia, after all, were also shrines with altars. The Academy was sacred to Athena and included altars to a range of other gods as well as Eros. The gymnasium of Cynosarges was sacred to Heracles and included altars to Iolaus, his boyfriend, Alcmene, his mother, and Hebe, his wife. "Mingling" between Boys and Striplings took place under the gaze of Hermes, at whose festival alone it was sanctioned. So the question is not whether or not Greek Homosexuality intersected with religion, but how.

As Bethe pointed out, gods and heroes would certainly be invoked in oaths. Any kind of wedding (= "troth plighting") would have involved metaphysical guarantors, whether between a Theban same-sex couple or Philip V of Macedon and Hannibal of Carthage. What is interesting is evidence for connections between the powers involved in same-sex-loving myths and rituals and those powers who specialized in guaranteeing oaths of any sort. It was not just troth-plighting lovers who swore (one assumes) "by Iolaus" as they stood by his tomb. Swearing "by Iolaus" was a typical Theban oath, any Theban, anywhere, anytime. Likewise, Megarians would swear "by Diocles." Other sources note that Diocles was an *erastēs* who sacrificed himself for his beloved and that a strange ritual Boy-kissing contest was performed in spring around his tomb.[49] It is not that same-sex lovers were merely invoking the ordinary oath-guaranteeing heroes of the polis, but that same-sex loving was believed to involve what Plato calls "the greatest pledges." Iolaus seemed a perfect oath hero because he had been so devotedly bonded to Heracles. Diocles' loyalty to his *erōmenos* extended to death. The myth of Dionysus at Lerna, moreover, revealed a homosexual pledge so unbreakable that it was fulfilled even after death, by sitting on a dildo on Prosymnus's tomb. We don't hear of any oaths sworn during the Cretan abduction ceremony, but the great sacrificial feast in honor of Zeus will have served to bind the couple in a sacrificial commensality, rather like the mass in Catholic marriages.

A rather less positive aspect of Love is revealed by the cult of the demon Anteros, worshipped with Eros and Aphrodite at the foot of the cliff below the Erechtheum, since he is referred to as an avenging spirit who drove the disdainful beloved Timagoras to his death. It is hard to think he received many sacrifices from happy and successful lovers. This cult of Eros was probably the oldest in Athens. It is associated with a distinctive image, found on a vase of the mid sixth century, of a man with a pair of cocks in the crooks of his arms, an image that might show the

55. A distinctive image of a man "carrying two cocks of extremely fine pedigree in the crooks of his arms," connected to the cult of Eros-Anteros below the acropolis (Suda sv "Meletos," Mu 497). The image described by Suda was that of "a seasonably beautiful boy" plummeting headlong; this figure probably represents his spurned *erastēs,* Meletus, in the form of the demon, Anteros, Love's "Avenger." The bearded *erastai* may be offering him gifts for assistance in seductions. What look like labels are nothing more than dots. Water jar (*hydria*) by the Ready Painter, whose market, according to J. Boardman, was "perhaps elderly customers with slender means" (*c.*530).

demon himself approached with appeasing lovers' gifts.[50] The other cult of Eros in the Academy was believed to be later, established by the tyrant Pisistratus's beloved Charmus, for Pausanias the tour guide explains that Charmus's inscription did not say he was "the first" to make a dedication to Eros but "the first Athenian"; the cult of Eros-Anteros had been set up by resident foreigners.[51]

There are some vaguer connections between cult acts and Homosexualities. The Sacred Band of Thebes was indeed "Sacred." Achilles in Aeschylus's *Myrmidons* refers to "the holy honor of thighs." The chair sex on the Dinos Painter's vase in the British Museum must certainly be part of some ritual, and may even be taking place in a temple, but to which god the gymnasium was sacred, which god was honored in the presumed festival, we do not know. Aristophanes seems to be targeting a similar combination of homosexual sex and religiousness in the opening scene of *Thesmophoriazusae.* Perhaps he was just satirizing the poet Agathon's highfalutin but meretricious style, or the devotion paid to him by Pausanias his partner, or perhaps he is presenting the most vivid and extensive account of a homosexual ritual, but in a satirical vein. Theocritus refers to the technical term for a Spartan *erastēs*—*eispnēlas*—as an "Amyclaean" term as if it was associated with the sanctuary of Hyacinthus in particular. Knowing that Hyacinthus was placed in heaven, probably as the constellation Orion, knowing that Orion was generated from gods scattering droplets of white sperm on an ox hide, that, according to the Derveni Papyrus, the "whitest and brightest" of the *aither,* i.e., the starry firmament, was the ejaculate of the phallus of heaven, that "Heavenly" Aphrodite Ourania of the starry sky was born from the genitals of Ouranos, that Spartan men had sex with boys in cloaks, a practice that will have left its own peculiar constellations, that Zephyr was shown performing precisely this peculiar act on a cloaked Hyacinthus in midair (Fig. 25), we are forced to draw the extraordinary but necessary conclusion that the bizarre sex act could be linked to the epiphany of a starry Hyacinthus "led up to heaven" manifested above the horizon on the "night of gladness" that followed the day of mourning. Certainly it would have been impossible for an Athenian Stripling who had lit his torch at Eros's altar in Athena's Academy and run with it to the altar in the city, who had then imitated the war dance and "gorgon glare" of the goddess Athena in the competition called "pyrrhic," not to remember the myth of how the first Athenian, Erichthonius, the constellation Auriga, came to be born from the ejaculate of Hephaestus onto the goddess, when he wiped a certain something from his thigh. The Athenian *erōmenos* was inevitably reenacting a mythical foundational act of Athena. The Spartan *eispnēlas* was mimicking Zephyrus. As for the Cretans, according to Plato they thought they were reenacting Ganymede's abduction; "since they believed their laws were from Zeus, they added this story accusing Zeus, so that they might enjoy this pleasure too, following, forsooth [*dē*], the god's example."[52]

Bethe was not going too far when he called the *Liebesakt* "a holy act in a holy place."

Most extraordinary of all perhaps is a mysterious but rather explicit tripod box first published in 1985. It was commissioned from the Amasis Painter, one of the most esteemed of all vase painters. One leg showed the devoted twins Castor and Pollux leaving their father. One showed Heracles fighting Cycnus and Ares and contained a metrical ac-

56AB. Two legs of a superb tripod *pyxis* (box) dedicated to the goddess
Aphaea in her sanctuary on Aegina. One leg shows Heracles and (white-
footed) Athena fighting Cycnus and his father, Ares. The inscription along
the right-hand side seems to refer to some secret about the "beautifulness"
of a boy that is known only to the author and Sun. This is probably
connected to the scene on another leg which shows a "contemporary" (non-
mythological) scene of *diamērion* with the *erastēs* reaching around (uniquely?)
to masturbate his partner, watched by an onlooker with a hunting spear and
a slightly tipping oil bottle. The fourth figure with a hunting dog offers a
hare to a (lost) boy (5), who was framed by an acclamation of someone's
beautifulness (. . . *kalo*) and the artist's signature (. . . [*epoie*]*sen:* ". . . made
it"). Then there are the legs of another courting couple and between them
the inscription . . . [*apro*]*phasistos* ["Not]hing loath," and finally another
onlooker. The third leg of the tripod depicts the Dioscuri taking leave of
their father, Tyndareus. The Amasis Painter (*c*.540).

clamation along its right edge in Athenian dialect: "The Sun-god knows and I alone know likewise that the boy is beautiful."[53] The relevance of this enigmatic statement becomes more obvious on the fragments of the third leg. It seems to have shown three same-sex pairs, the first pair locked together intercrurally, the intercruralist reaching around to masturbate his partner at the same time. The boy wears a red ribbon around his wrist. Next to them a man with a dog holds out a live hare as a love gift. There is another couple whose lower legs alone survive. The three couples are flanked by two onlookers, one holding an oil bottle. There are "beautiful" acclamations, and one of the participants is labeled [apro]phasistos, "nothing loath." The owner dedicated the box to the goddess Aphaea on the island of Aegina, in the years around c. 530 BC. At one time, presumably, the box contained some kind of deposit.

GREEK HOMOSEXUALITIES VERSUS HOMOSEXUALITY

The "unmarshaled" kind of homosexuality exists in the shadow of Greek Love, its casual, informal, less "ethnographic" cousin. Such ordinary loves and lusts and passionately loyal relationships must always have existed off the radar, many of them as passionate and uncalculating as the archaeologicable and thoroughly marshaled kind—between Spartans who were not Spartiates, for instance, or Cretans of the wrong sort, between Athenian classmates such as Clinias and Critobulus, or relationships of the vase painters between themselves, or those "utter Striplings," perhaps, who pleasured other Striplings on the slopes of Lycabettus. But such loves become much more noticeable when the objects of love and desire are handsome slaves, when "the beautifuls" are not the sons of the elite in the gymnasium, but prostitutes and cithara-boys. It may first have become visible at the courts of tyrants. It seems quite likely that some of those mentioned in Anacreon's sixth-century songs about the court of Polycrates tyrant of Samos, long-haired Smerdies the Thracian and shawm-playing Bathyllus were more like toyboys, decorative embellishments, rather than erōmenoi in the traditional manner. But they explode into our sources in the fourth century BC, a change that can be seen most obviously by comparing Aristophanes—who would seem almost oblivious of the possibility of male sex slaves—with the Roman comedian Plautus, who translated and adapted the work of

Aristophanes' lost fourth-century successors and whose plays are full of them. Now soldiers seem to have taken their boys on expeditions, as their comrades took their girls. The elite group of Macedonians called *hetairoi* took two or three male prostitutes around with them, according to Theopompus's famous invective.[54] And someone or other thought that Alexander might be thought to have been pleased to be made a present of such a kind.

This may in fact be one of the oddest and most revolutionary developments in the history of Greek Love, the way that the exalted traditional practices of the elite Greek Homosexuality of the training grounds seem to have created a tolerance for homosexuality *tout court*, even for squalid relationships with purchased boys. For commoditized as it was, the homosex market nevertheless looked up to the traditional version and approximated its rules and roles. Simon used the language of *erōs*, if not of *erastēs* and *erōmenos*, when talking of Theodotus whom he claimed expensively to have hired under contract, and even his opponent who denies *erōs* nevertheless hints at the traditional discourse of *charis* when he talks of "offering benefactions" in order to make the boy "his intimate friend." Epicrates positively vaunted his mind-befuddling *erōs* for the son of Midas, whom he had recently bought, though he had intended at first merely to pay for his freedom, he claims. The consumers of the homosex market were as much obsessed with the "blooming" years of handsome Striplings as were the admirers of the elite young men of the gymnasium. And a cithara-boy may not have been very classy, but he looked classy with a cithara in his hands and even sounded classy as he sang the lyric poets' highfalutin songs. How could it be coarse and "uneducated" to admire a boy who could sing Timotheus, Simonides, Bacchylides and Pindar?

But homosexuality did not get a free ride on the embroidered coattails of Greek Love. The revolutionary development was neither uncontroversial nor did it pass unremarked. There was fierce resistance to such attempts at assimilation. At some point the Spartans seem to have legislated (somehow or other) that it was illegal for one of the beautifuls to choose a wealthy *erastēs* over a "poor man of good quality [of better social class]," imposing a fine on the handsome boy for such manifest meretriciousness.[55] In Athens the rise of visible homosexual lust seems to have triggered a great debate that has left its traces in the most famous texts on Greek Homosexuality, notably in the works of

Plato and Aeschines, creating in response an artificial antithesis between uncalculating love and calculating lust, between *charis* and *porneia,* the beautiful bodies of the *kaloi* and the commoditized bodies of whores. Such explicit polarization makes "unmarshaled Aphrodite" as much of an artificial construction as organized Eros. It becomes Greek Love's other, its diametrically opposed vulgar twin, what Greek Love is not.

But all the talk of how different they are only provokes a game of spot the difference. Commoditized *erōs* introduces explicitness into the ineffable exchanges of grace. It puts an impertinent question on the table: "What is really going on here?"—a question for the lover: "What really attracts you to that handsome, wellborn and athletic Stripling?"—a question for the beloved: "What is your real motive in letting that rich and powerful politician get you into bed?" Was there in fact a difference between Misgolas's relationships with slaves and the relationship he had had with a citizen like Timarchus in his youth? For finally all the homosexual lust made visible by the marketplace exposed to the public gaze the fact that certain men, such as Misgolas, seemed unusually, "demonically," devoted to "this thing," but nevertheless immune to the charms of courtesans, or men such as the "extreme *paiderastai,*" the "savage beastly" trio of Cedonides, Autoclides and Thersander, or a womanish, seductive *kinaidos* like Demosthenes, a predator on vulnerable young men. Already in the early fourth century Plato could put a speech into the mouth of Aristophanes in which he claimed that all humanity was divided into those attracted to their own or to the opposite sex. Alongside the very various archaeologicable practices of Greek Homosexuality, the homosex market had catalyzed the materialization of a brand-new archaeologicable fact; a new kind of person type previously not quite so noticeable, the homosexual, was coming out. But if this was indeed the first time this had happened in the historical record, it would certainly not be the last.

II
WHAT WAS IT FOR?

One must always be careful of coming up with an overly functional explanation for a peculiar cultural phenomenon, as if a society has to devise some mechanism to get itself out of a mess it has got itself into. In the case of Greek H/homosexuality especially, a phenomenon found in so many different kinds of society, manifested in so many different forms, over so long a period, any argument from necessity as to its causes seems a priori improbable. What single factor could account for the loves between Lesbian women and the Macedonian Royal Boys, for Homosexuality in wife-swapping Sparta and in wife-secluding Athens, in Solon's coin-free world and Aeschines' polis of courtesans and rent-boys? One can, on the other hand, more modestly and more positively, explore the kinds of "work" an institution does within a culture, and how it meshes with and plays off against other features of a civilization. So my question may be misleading. By "What was it for?" I mean "What did it do?" Any such exploration must bear in mind several distinctive and characteristic elements of Greek Love: the noisy besotted-ness, the gaze of admiration, the gracious exchanges, the bonding of males to other males, and the sex. And it might be useful in this instance to look separately at two overlapping spheres of the life of the culture: war and the polis.

WAR

Outside Athens talk about Greek Homosexuality tends to focus on its military uses, notably its role in selection, mixing, *menos,* competition, self-sacrifice, solidarity and a sense of shame.[56]

No ancient source actually gives an account of *erōs* being used in recruitment. It is simply a (rather compelling) conclusion drawn by putting two and two together. On the one hand, there are the Armies of Lovers, battalions of (three hundred) champions composed of *erastai* and *erōmenoi,* who fight together and "sleep together," known from both Elis and, more famously, Thebes.[57] On the other, there is the elaborate ritual described by Ephorus for pairing a Cretan *philētōr* with his "Famed" *parastatheis,* "Stood Alongside." Since it was shameful for a beauty *not* to be chosen to be one of the Famed, Ephorus must also be describing the method of recruitment into the ranks of "the most beautiful," who were involved in the sacrifice to Eros before Cretan battles, as recorded by Sosicrates.[58] So, while it is surely safe to assume that a Theban champion would choose his "favorite" with the greatest care, knowing his life might depend on it, knowing he would soon be relying on his boyfriend to cover his back, and while it is therefore possible that the less exalted members of the army, and the population in general, whose lives would also ultimately depend on that selection, would trust him to make the right choice, nevertheless Ephorus's account of the involvement of the "friends" in the selection of a Cretan Famed and of a ceremonial tug-of-war at a place announced three days before, which would allow crowds to gather and doubtless make their opinions about the selection known, entitles us to suppose a rather less risky method of *erōtikos* recruitment, in which a final decision on a warrior's avowedly "personal" choice as to who should join the ranks of the bulwark of Boeotia was not left to him alone.

That leaves hanging the question of what exactly different Greeks at different times meant by *kalos*. Ephorus insists the Cretan *erōmenoi* were not just "beautifully behaved" or "beautiful personalities" but "beautiful to look at" (*kaloi tēn idean*), although he also insists, somewhat contradictorily, that it was not necessarily extreme beauty but extreme "manliness and decorum" that made a boy a love object (*erasmion*).[59] In Sparta, meanwhile, we learn that it was necessary to choose *erōmenoi* who were "beautifully formed," *kalōs pephukotes*.[60] In general it is probably safe to assume that by "beauty" the Greeks were talking of more than a pretty face. They had in mind the physical beauty of an athletic naked male body, something not irrelevant to fighting fitness, a body that might at least impress the enemy with its physical splendor.

I am tiptoeing toward a horribly banal conclusion. When success in battle—the push and shove of the hoplite battle—depended so much on sheer physical fitness, there was a considerable overlap between looking good and being a useful member of the team. When one bears in mind that "beautiful" meant "beautiful with his clothes off"—"If Charmides were willing to strip, you would forget about his face"—then Greeks who selected "beautiful warriors" were not being as frivolous as it might seem.[61] When placed in the battle line, the *erōs*-inspiring body of a beautiful beloved might inspire a more efficacious terror in the opposing side:

Isidas was exceptionally handsome and exceptionally big, in that lovely season of life when men pass out of the ranks of Boys and into the ranks of Men, blossoming most pleasantly. Naked, wearing neither armor nor clothing, covered in nothing but oil, he took a spear in one hand and in the other a sword, and rushed out of his house. He pushed into the midst of the mass of fighting men and threw himself at the enemy, striking anyone who came in his way and laying them low. He did not receive a single wound, either because a god was guarding him on account of his heroics, or because he appeared to the enemy bigger and mightier than a human being. The ephors crowned him for his exploits and imposed a fine of one thousand drachmas for having had the audacity to risk his life in battle without wearing armor.[62]

When Plutarch describes the creation of the Sacred Band he cites the views of a Theban called Pammenes, who contrasts an army made of lovers with an army based on inherited divisions of clan and tribe.[63] One of the most significant features of the Cretan abduction ceremony is the fact that families, tribes and phratries, which are so important in other areas, play no role. Instead there are only personal ties: The bond itself is made through sheer *erōs,* through the mediation of "friends." In fact Ephorus assumes that the *erastēs* would choose someone from outside his own Men's House, since the tug-of-war ends with a welcoming embrace there, rather than a boy's coming home. The election of a Cretan boy to the honored ranks of "front-row dancer" (*proorchestēr*)—which in Thessaly meant the same as "front-row fighter" (*promachos*)[64]—could not be left to those he was related to and so was passed to those from rival groups, just as the Greeks at Troy eavesdropped on the Trojans in order to decide who was the best of the Achaeans. The elite groups chosen through such a process would be a cross section of the community, above divisions, each member tied to someone from another group. This is why the Sacred Band alone was "the Band from the City," the only one of Thebes's many battalions that represented Thebes itself. The apparent frivolousness of recruiting an elite group of champions or beautifuls through an exaggeratedly capricious *erōs* is precisely what recommended it. The image of an intense subjectivity, however carefully moderated in practice by the community, was being put into action in order to bypass the inevitable favoritism of kin, House and clan, in order to create a group of the objectively most splendid, rather than the best-connected. The personal was being deployed to dissolve the political in the service of the polis as a whole.

Naturally in those cities such as Elis and Thebes where couples fought together and slept together, the ties of *erōtikē philia* would aid cohesion, although Plutarch interestingly emphasizes competition between the two, as if boyfriends would seek to outperform each other, like the horses in a chariot team.[65] "Erotik" links between soldiers in any Greek army might serve to intensify a general feeling of loyalty to one's comrades by transforming it into a more vivid and personal devotion to one comrade in particular. The sources, however, emphasize three more explicit aspects of love that make it efficacious in war. The warriors feel ashamed *to be seen* by their beloveds doing anything unmanly.[66] One imagines this must be an imaginary gaze, an image in the warrior's own head of himself being observed by his beloved, or the image of cowardly flight presented by the discovery of a wound in his back when his beloved attends to his corpse. But in those armies where *erastai* and *erōmenoi* did not fight together one may imagine a literal gaze across the battlefield from one group to another, from the Cretan battalion of Beauties to the place where the men whose love had put them there were fighting. It is the cavalry of Chalcis in particular who seem to need the encouragement of a beloved's eyes in the view of Cleomachus of Thessaly. Secondly there is the motif of disregarding personal interests that Pericles invokes when he calls on her soldiers to be *erastai* of Athens, a motif best expressed in the stories of men who sacrifice themselves on behalf of their beloveds, men such as Diocles of Megara, or Achilles going off to avenge Patroclus or Antilochus, knowing that by so doing he goes toward certain death. This seems to be the same exaggeratedly romantic *erōs* of the most altruistic *charis* translated onto the field of war, that *erōs* which is as far away as possible from any expectation of return, the pure objective *erōs* that inspired poets in the days before they started writing for pay. The love-besotted warrior who hurls himself into battle thinking nothing of himself is an analogue of the love-besotted *erastēs* who makes no calculation of the gifts he has given, or Meletus who jumps off a cliff because Timagoras told him to.

Finally, more positively, Love's arrows have a transformative effect on warriors, as in the Theban epigram: "Direct the arrow of Eros at these here bachelors, that, bold in the love of youths, they may defend their fatherland; for the dart fires boldness and of all the gods Eros is supreme at exalting the frontline champions."[67] Phaedrus in the *Symposium* says, more simply, that Eros "blows in the breath of *menos*" the "manly fighting spirit" that Archilochus in the seventh century BC identified with sperm.[68] Those bizarre acts of Greek Homosex that involve face-to-face intercourse with an *erōmenos,* who is usually inert, and the exosomatic ejaculation that resulted, must, inevitably I am afraid, be read as graphic little spectacles of the warrior being filled with a *menos* that is provoked by *erōs* for the *erōmenos* and that is produced under his gaze. Perhaps Plato was alluding to a similar idea when he noted that the greatest opposition to his measures to discourage homosex in Magnesia would come from "someone of exuberant virility and young and full of sperm."[69] We can imagine a range of thoughts therefore crossing the minds of Spartans and Cretans as they performed the sacrifice to Eros before beginning a battle or setting off for war, but above all they were asking the god to make them as fierce as Achilles fighting Memnon over Antilochus's corpse, to fill them with uncalculating berserker spirit—not a selfish reckless breaking of ranks, which might expose their backs to a shameful wound, but one that incorporated a bond with other warriors and with the polis, a sense of fierce self-sacrificing homosocial solidarity through the mediation of a special boy from another group.

WITHIN THE POLIS

Back home, the same-sex bonds of warriors might look rather different, more secretive and conspiratorial, invisible ties that helped to forge new factions that cut across the "natural" groupings based on family, parish and clan, bonds that rose above old political divisions in order to create new kinds. This already seems to be a feature of the relationship of Achilles of Thessaly and Patroclus of Opuntian Locris within the Greek camp: "Alive no longer, no longer will we, sitting apart from our dear comrades, counsel each other with counsels . . ."[70] Around a century later same-sex *erōs* had become a tool of partisan solidarity in the context of civil war.

The songs of Alcaeus of Lesbian Mytilene were notorious for their factionalism. Indeed one author called them "Party Politicals" (*Stasiōtika*); others said that if you unversified his verses you would end up with speeches, albeit extraordinary ones.[71] Civil strife leading to coups, exiles, tyranny, seems to have been a conspicuous feature of the politics of many archaic cities, and Alcaeus and his brothers were leading figures in the factionalism that broke out in Mytilene: "Alcaeus was so acrimonious that he expelled many men from the city by the harshness of his poetry."[72] But there was also a lot of off-duty, even self-consciously decadent content, about drinking and abandoning shields, as we have seen, and also what Cicero calls "lustful" loving of Striplings, among whom were one Meno and one Lycus. A tiny fragment found on a papyrus and first published in 1963 reveals that the beautiful Boys were involved in the faction fighting too, as if *erōs* was being deployed to en-roll new members and to bind them each to each other. Love and Hate, Praise and Vituperation are two sides of the same coin: Loyalty or Else.[73] One scholar wittily juxtaposes the mixture of the minatory and the amatory in a conversation between the mafia boss John Gotti and his associates taped by the FBI: "You know Frankie, I don't like you—I love you. I don't like Sammy—I love him. I love you guys. I don't fabricate no part of it."[74]

A similar conspiratorial vein is found half a century later in Theognis.[75] Many of Theognis's elegies look like words of advice to his *erōmenos* Cyrnus, a perfect example of an educational relationship, but the relationship is not so much that of a teacher instructing a pupil on how to behave properly, as that of an intimate passing on secrets about what people are really like: So-called friends will stab you in the back; no one, not even a brother, will stand by your side in difficulties; those "men of quality" are really savages in disguise. These are things Theognis claims he learned from previous men and that he is now passing on, a kind of social reproduction of mistrustfulness and spite.[76] For there is a powerfully paranoid atmosphere, and for all the complaints about other people's inauthenticity, in truth the two are themselves only to themselves. So while Theognis chastises Cyrnus for "pulling the wool over my eyes," anyone else is fair game: "Out of your mouth seem everyone's friend, but don't get mixed up in any earnest venture, not any, not with anyone";[77] "Take on the disposition of the wily octopus that makes itself look like whichever rock it attaches itself to."[78] He wants, in other words, to monopolize Cyrnus's authenticity in a treach-erous environment, to be his sole companion when push comes to shove—"A man you can trust is worth his weight in gold and silver,

Cyrnus, at times of grievous factionalism"[79]—and ultimately to die by his side: "Here we are. We have reached that place of evil, Cyrnus, despite all our prayers. Would that our allotted death would take us both together."[80]

Sometimes one faction would effect a more permanent change of power and establish a tyranny. The altar of Eros set up in the gymnasium of the Academy by Charmus, *erōmenos* of the Athenian tyrant Pisistratus and/or the *erastēs* of one of his sons, was originally just another relic of elite archaic infighting.[81] The relationship had probably been established during the years of exile and uncertainty and the altar set up to celebrate the final success. But, once in power, the tyrant was faced with the prospect of creating and maintaining a coalition of the not unwilling from the surly remnants of those he had defeated in war, and *erōs* remained a most useful tool for winning over new adherents. One way of looking at the story of Harmodius and Aristogiton, both members of the old family of Gephyraioi, is as an attempt on the part of Hipparchus,

57. The familiar agora statues of love-paired Harmodius and Aristogiton come to life, having put their clothes back on (cf. Fig. 52). This is how a vase painter reimagines the birth of "democracy," i.e., the assassination of "the tyrant Hipparchus" (514), around the start (472) of the first new age-set-cycle (= 42 years) after the event. Stamnos by the Copenhagen Painter "of distinctive and unpleasant profile (broad-mouthed, hunch-shouldered)," according to J. Boardman (*c.*475).

the brother of the tyrant Hippias, Pisistratus's son and successor, to seduce Harmodius from his clan allegiance and to win a new recruit for the regime.[82] That, certainly, is how it would have looked to contemporary observers, had Harmodius said "Yes." The tyrants however had overreached themselves in this instance and the Tyrant-Killers plotted to kill them, though they succeeded in killing only one of them in fact.

In the politics of the democracy that succeeded the tyranny, Love played no less of a role. Very often, to all intents and purposes, *erōmenos-erastēs* look like "client-patron" relationships under another name; a beloved who put out for the wrong reasons might be accused of "flattery" (*kolakeia*), according to Pausanias in the *Symposium,* while a handsome beloved like Timarchus could be called his boyfriend's "freeloading" *asymbolos, parasitos,* or his *sykophantēs,* his "maliciously litigious" agent. At the end of the fifth century, the anxious, newly restored democracy passed a law banning "the convening of a comrade-type thing [*hetairikon*]," a *hetaireia* such as those that offered assistance in lawsuits or that engaged in outrageous frat pranks like clipping the beard of poor Hermes.[83] But whatever was meant by *hetairikon* or *hetaireia,* one could hardly prevent a one-to-one relationship of besotted devotion between a man such as Hegesander and Timarchus who so "very buddy-lovingly" (*philetairōs*) conspired, allegedly, to defraud the state.

What allowed Political Eros to remain so useful for so long in so many cities under so many different regimes? Four things above all: the inherited glamour of an ancient, culturally central, all-Greek tradition, the intense ideology of self-sacrificing loyalty transported from the battlefield to the city, the capacity to generate new connections where none had previously existed, the interest-obscuring power of lots of purple smoke. Eros handed the regent Pausanias an utterly trusted secretary to carry treacherous messages to Persia attempting to secure a position for himself as king of All Greece. Eros allowed Alexander to maneuver Hephaestion, his much-to-be-mourned, personally loyal Patroclus, into a position as his Second over the heads of the old guard, and then to establish a new relationship with Bagoas, the beloved and influential eunuch of Darius, his predecessor on the Persian throne. Eros excused the inexcusable acquittal of Sphodrias, thanks to the besottedness of Prince Archidamus for Sphodrias's son, and Xenophon seems to have thought his long sentimental digression, with its reference to Cleonymus's tears, would somehow mitigate his readers' sense of outrage at "what seemed to many the most unjust judgment ever known in Lacedaemon" (*Hell.* 5.4, 24).

It is almost as if the very outrageousness of favors performed for favorites somehow guaranteed the authenticity of the uncalculating *erōs* that inspired them. The proper response to an accusation of special treatment was: "Yes indeed, and I would have done much more for him if I could, so hopelessly in love was I with him." So mindlessly besotted was Dymnus, who conspired to assassinate Alexander the Great, that he offered his boyfriend, a rent-boy, the Persian throne, supposedly. Even now we remain somewhat under Eros's spell when we think of "the great romance" of Antony and Cleopatra, forgetting that the queen had already arranged to have some members of her entourage kitted out as Cupids long before her famous meeting with Antony at Tarsus. This was the ancient spectacle of Greek Love having one last spectacular fling. Cleopatra was casting a pall of purple smoke around a very dangerous and very geopolitical alliance. That does not mean that Cleopatra was not in love with Antony, or he in love with her, or that Archidamus was unaffected by Cleonymus's tears, or that Xenophon invented the whole thing in the first place. Theatrics do not have to be mere pretenses, and rhetoric need not tell lies. In a world obsessed with tangible archaeologicable facts, performance of such facts, acting them out, meant making them real, the distinction between socially significant action and sincerity of feeling mattered much less than it does to us. Hephaestion, his Grand Vizier, was Alexander's very significant other and his death was a terrible loss. That does not mean that Alexander's scandalously extravagant Achillean mourning of Hephaestion was simply a straightforward reaction to the news of a lover's death. Alexander could be both sincerely grieving for Hephaestion, communicating that grief in a noisy and visible way, and also proving postmortem a point about their relationship.

So we must somehow be awake to the usefulness of useless uncalculating *erōs* in the calculations of politicians (useful precisely because of the long ideological construction of *erōs* as uncalculating and structurally "above suspicion"), but we must also be alive to a culture that understood the theater of *erōs* much better than we can possibly do today, and was able to distinguish between sincerity and pretense, forcing politicians to act out, at least, an extravagant commitment. The invocation of a bounds-breaking love offered cover for the formation of relationships of cooperation that were necessary to keep the polis going, to enable the consolidation of a group of semiprofessional politicians in a democracy that went out of its way to promote amateurism, or to allow Alexander to pick his own loyal and efficient prime minister, whose political and familial connections might otherwise, in the status-conscious world of the Macedonian aristocracy, have ruled him out. It was, if you like, a way of formally putting certain aspects of a political relationship in parenthesis, "personal," "off the record," thereby making them possible in the first place.

That public function by no means exhausts the kinds of work that Eros might be called upon to do in Greek culture. He also played a role in the *imaginaire*. Eros made sense of the Thessalian practice of making offerings to Patroclus "to please" Achilles, of the fact that Heracles and Iolaus could share an altar. Eros in the myth of Ganymede helped to construct a sense of a great gulf between mortals and immortals that might nevertheless be bridged through ambrosial sacrifice. And Eros could be used to form the very basis of the philosophy of *erōtikos* Socrates and Plato, by constructing a powerful sense of the philosophical soul besottedly in love with knowledge and the distant memory of the beauties of the outer reaches of heaven, a "wisdom-loving" *philosophos* love that could never be finally consummated in doctrine, a knowledge that could only emerge from the gracious exchanges of *logos*.

This is where we come closest to an "all about" answer to the problem of Greek Love. It was a bridge between the culture's structurally given gaps, between age-classes, between men who were not related, between endogamous "in-marrying" families with their weddings of cousins to cousins and uncles to nieces, between the human and the divine. It was a mechanism for reaching across a distance without suspicion of devious intent. And it thereby helped to build a sense of a unified political society out of divided groups, a pan-Athenian Eros of the Academy, a pan-Theban Sacred Band "of the polis," and finally, in images of Thessalian Achilles fighting foreign Memnon over the beloved body of Antilochus of Pylos, a pan-Hellenic Eros, a sense of Team

Greece itself in opposition to the Barbarians. One solution to the knotty problem of Greek Love, in other words, is that it tied lots of otherwise disassociated people together.

III
WHERE DID IT COME FROM?

The questions "What was it?" and "What was it for?" inevitably affect any investigation into where Greek Love originated. There are two main schools of thought on this: one, the rigorously Rankean positivist and empirical school of Meier, Dover, Halperin et al., results in a terribly "late" date for the origins of the phenomenon, meaning not long before *c*.600 BC; the other, much more diverse, but that we might call the "genealogical" school, results in a terribly early date among the Dorians *c*.1050 BC, the Indo-Europeans *c*.4000 BC (?) or even earlier.

EROTIC PHENOMENA

Ever since Richard Bentley's famous seventeenth-century *Dissertation,* often considered the very *fons et origo* of Classics as a modern discipline (i.e., of "scientific philology"), Greek Love has been identified with homosexual lust, with what Bentley himself called a "flagitious love of boys."[84] This was "the thing," *die Sache,* that Meier wanted dispassionately to examine and explain in his seminal article on "Päderastie," published in 1837. And it was this that provoked John Addington Symonds's "problem in Greek ethics." After the sexual liberation of the sixties, Kenneth Dover actually defined *erōs* as essentially and necessarily sexual, a one-sided *desire to penetrate,* with all nonsexual uses of the word being viewed as "metaphorical." He was followed in this by Foucault and his adherents, resulting in the sodomania that has characterized academic writing on Greek Love ever since. Having positively identified the essence of "the thing" in "impure" and "flagitious" same-sex (boy-) loving, the empirical method could identify the first traces of "the thing" in the materials, which meant, since explicit pre-600 BC homosexual images were—and remain—lacking, a quest for traces of flagitiousness and impurity in pre-600 BC texts.

The earliest texts (*c.*700 BC or earlier?), it was soon agreed, produced next to no traces, no *certain* traces, of such libidinousness. Although it was true, noted Meier, that one could detect in Homer, as almost everywhere "among warlike primitive peoples" (*bei kriegerischen Naturvölkern*), the "institution of brothers-in-arms" (*Waffenbrüderschaft*), such as that which existed between Achilles and Patroclus, and that was transformed by later writers into "a love-relationship" (*Liebesverhältnis*), nevertheless "nowhere in Homer or Hesiod is there any definite [*bestimmte*] indication of the relationship with which we are here concerned."[85] This "erotic premise" drove a coach-and-horses through what classical Greeks considered the unified field of Greek Love, by separating off as not pertinent the heroically devoted same-sex relationship of brother-like "dear companions" described by Homer and Hesiod, as if it was a completely different thing: "heroes and their pals."[86] The classical Greeks were making a big mistake in presuming that what they got up to had anything whatsoever to do with what Achilles got up to with Patroclus. The unity of the field and therefore the antiquity of Greek Love was an illusion: "Man-love was a product of the modern period . . . quite foreign to Greek prehistory."[87]

The earliest references to a more obviously amorous same-sex love, to loving boys or being attractive to boys, are found in the mid-seventh-century Elegies of Mimnermus of Ionian Smyrna (Izmir): "Though previously most beautiful of men, when his season is gone, boys neither rate him nor love him, not even his sons."[88] Meanwhile Alcman, unbeknownst to Meier, was composing his songs for Spartan girls, flirting and admiring each other as they carried the *pharos* plowlike for the goddess at the dawn. A generation later, another Ionian, Solon the great lawgiver of Athens, born by *c.*625 BC, wrote his famously scandalous elegy.[89] It is a brief quote and unplaced, but there is not much doubting its affinity with classical Greek Homosexuality: "so long as one makes love to a boy [*paidophilein*], with urge for thighs and sweet-tasting mouth."[90] Around the same time, Sappho was writing about the charming yoke-mated ladies of Lesbos and Alcaeus was composing his extraordinary lyrics combining political bitterness with lust for Lycus, lyrics now lost, but which Cicero, nearly six hundred years later, found very definitely apropos.

There is certainly a change in tone between those Greek writers considered earliest and their successors, normally reckoned to have been writing fifty or sixty years later. But they differ also in style and content. And if there really was a mid-seventh-century Homosexual Revolution—by which is meant not the invention of homosexuality but the invention of Greek Homosexuality, the arrival of homosexuality into the publicized "light of day," *Tageslicht,* its archaeologification in images and texts—it happened very fast, and very fast became both highly varied and quite ubiquitous.[91] Some indeed have come up with powerful arguments that would downdate Homer and Hesiod so that they are (elder) contemporaries of Alcman and Mimnermus.[92] Either way, Greek Love is supposed to have exploded all over the far-flung Greek world in the space of a generation, not just coming out into the light of day, but quickly domesticated and calcified in rites and institutions, and not just among males in the gymnasium but even among their sisters. Lesbian women would have learned to make syzygies with each other. In distant Sparta girls will have learned to flirt with one another, abnormally and unnaturally, and without giggling, as they solemnly carried the *pharos* through the last hours of the night. The Boys of Thera on the island of Santorini will have learned to *oiph* with each other near the sanctuary and to record their *oiphing* in the rocks. The Athenians will have grown anxious enough to pass laws forbidding slaves from *erōtikos* acts of pursuing free Boys, and will have developed a peculiar Homosexual practice involving "urge for thighs."

Sparse as they are, the earliest definite references to a decidedly amorous Greek Love reveal that the "abnormality and unnaturalness" had already been thoroughly normalized and naturalized, already, indeed, institutionalized in peculiar local varieties that look for all the world like the products of long-term local development. The theory of the seventh-century revolution, Greek homo-amorousness arising out of nowhere, may be rigorously respectful of (the absence of) proofs, but it also defies common sense. And the "erotic premise" itself is doubtful. If same-sex attachment looks different in sober Homer and Hesiod from how it appears in the more flirtatiously "homoerotik" lyrics of Alcman and Mimnermus, there were nevertheless plenty of resonances in the earlier poets for later writers to pick up on. We have looked at a few: the intense relationship between Achilles and Patroclus; the fantasy about the two of them being the last two standing and destroying Troy's battlements solitarily arm in arm; Achilles' sacrificing of his own future to avenge the Opuntian Locrian, and, after avenging him, discovered by his mother off his food and sleepless as he misses Patroclus's "manliness and *menos*," reaching in vain to embrace his dismal ghost and agreeing to arrange for the reburial of his corpse, sooner rather than later, with his own in the golden urn given to his mother on her wedding day by Dionysus; Homer's sly comparison of Patroclus with Meleager's wife "Cleopatra"; the allusions to a future and more Greekly orthodox relationship with younger handsome Antilochus and the association of all three, plus an Ajax, in the afterlife on the Isles of the Blessed; the admiration for the beauty of males evident throughout both Homeric epics, not least in the story of Ganymede taken up to heaven because of his beauty; the image of Hermes offering salvation to Odysseus in the classical form of a gracious Stripling just getting his beard; the unusual sleeping arrangements imposed on Odysseus's son Telemachus and Antilochus's brother Pisistratus as they tour the Peloponnese; Hesiod's vaunting of a primordial fourth-born Eros; his anxiety that his brother might contract a brotherlike relationship with a man to whom he is not related.

Almost every element of later Greek Loving is to be found in the earliest hexameter epics. Men admire the beauty of men and there is admiration too for the particular beauty of Striplings just beginning to grow a beard.[93] Men are passionately devoted to each other. Male couples are compared with heterosexually married couples. Men sleep with each other, die for each other. The only things missing are first-person expressions of amorous intent and third-person narratives of homosexual sex, neither of which might be suited to epic hexameters. Doubtless Greek Homosexuality altered and was modified as Greece itself altered and was modified after 700 BC, but the theory of its seventh-century invention is, inasmuch as it might be meaningful, a nonstarter. I am by no means the first to observe that the kind of Greek Homosexuality that first theatrically manifests itself in the seventh century unfolds in so many peculiarly different ways that it must have had *much* deeper roots.[94]

GENEALOGIES

Finding those roots has been the objective of "the genealogists." Bethe noted the similarities between Dorian pederasties, and concluded that his sacred Homosex Act must have had its origins in the Dorian migration or even before the dispersal of the various Dorian groups from their homeland in the tiny region of Doris, north of Delphi.[95] The Dorian migration was associated in Greek myth with the "Return of the Sons of Heracles" from the north, who (re)conquered the southern Peloponnese after the Trojan War and deposed old "Achaean" (i.e., "Mycenaean") rulers. The myth had long been incorporated into modern reconstructions of Greek prehistory and received dramatic confirmation when the Mycenaean Greek of the Linear B tablets (c.1400–1200 BC) was deciphered. The dialect, there revealed for the first time, was close to the language of the Arcadians of the Peloponnese's mountainous interior, who had even, it emerged, preserved some Mycenaean month-names, but not at all like Doric. Doric-speakers must have supplanted the Mycenaeans, although recent scholarship has tended to see the Dorians as opportunists rather than destroyers, arriving in Greece c.150–300 years after the destruction of the Mycenaean palaces c.1200 BC, and bringing, so Bethe believed, their quasi-magical and sacred acts of "boy-love" with them.[96]

The other main genealogical argument has taken a much broader array of data from many different places and a much longer perspective. In 1980 Jan Bremmer noted that Greek Homosexuality revealed parallels with practices ascribed to the Celts, to tribes such as the Heruli and Taifali and to nineteenth-century AD Albanians, all of them speaking Indo-European languages, which pointed to an originally Indo-European institution. Bremmer strongly emphasized the pederastic element, and inferred that anal insemination was a ritual for the initiation of boys into adulthood. Since similar practices of (usually oral) insemination in order to "grow" boys had been described among the remotest communities of Papua New Guinea, he concluded that pederasty belonged "to the oldest historical strata of the initiatory ritual," a ritual that he seems to have thought was once universal, at least in Eurasia.[97]

Robert Koehl, on the other hand, zoomed in on Crete, aligning the abduction ritual described by Ephorus with the myth of Ganymede's abduction and the myth that the Cretans got their laws from Zeus via his son Minos. He thought he could detect evidence for pederastic initiation on the famous Chieftain Cup that dated to the years around 1500 BC before the Minoans had been conquered by the (Mycenaean) Greeks.[98] In support he adduced the seventh-century BC bronze cut-out reliefs from the mountain shrine of Kato Syme Viannou that showed beardless youths alongside bearded men. Kato Syme in southern-eastern Crete was the site of a Hellenistic sanctuary of Hermes and Aphrodite, who figure in the Greek *imaginaire* as the perfectly wedded heterosexual couple, an idea powerfully embodied in their son Hermaphroditos, who blends the two sexes in one body and who was honored as the originator of "marriage bonds" in a beautiful (to look at) and poetic inscription discovered in the 1990s at his most important, now submerged, cult site in Bodrum (Halicarnassus).[99] What is so extraordinary about Cretan Kato Syme, however, is that it seems (uniquely?) to have been in continual use since its foundation by the Minoans *c.* 1700 BC.[100] Whatever the origins of Greek Homosexuality as a whole, the particular Cretan variety, Koehl concluded, seemed to have deep local roots in initiation rites in pre-Greek Minoan Crete.

Bernard Sergent eventually attempted to reconcile the pre-Greek evidence with the Indo-Europeans who had long formed his main area of expertise. In *Homosexuality in Greek Myth* he concluded that such "gay myths" represented the long-lost and much-sought-after Indo-European level of Greek mythology, and noted the element of instruction and initiation in such tales. Two years later, he noted that some of the heroes involved in homosexual myths, e.g., Hya*cinthus* and Nar*cissus,* had "pre-Greek" names, which, he argued, had come from Anatolia and therefore established a link with the oldest Indo-Europeans to split off from the main group, the Hittites of eastern Turkey, who were so terribly ancient that they alone were still using Saussure's long-lost Aryan laryngeals: $h_1 h_2 h_3$. Sergent could therefore reaffirm that homosexuality was not merely Indo-European but an early development among the Indo-Europeans: "Initiatory pederasty was one of the most ancient, one of the most archaic, institutions of the indo-european world."[101]

INITIATION AND INSEMINATION

It might help to have a closer look at the ethnographic evidence on initiatory pederasty that has so impressed so many students of Greek Homosexuality from Erich Bethe to Daniel Ogden, and that even persuaded

Kenneth Dover to agree that he should have given initiation "a better run for its money."[102] What used to be called "ritualized homosexuality," but some prefer to call "boy-inseminating" or "ritualized adult-male/ adolescent-male sexual behavior," seems to be (or, in most cases, thanks to the intervention of missionaries, seems to *have been*) practiced among a substantial minority of the tribes of Papua New Guinea, especially in the southern lowlands where there is good evidence for the practices among almost two-fifths of the population in the area.[103] These behaviors have been described as "one of the most complex and intricate sexual systems in culture that has ever evolved."[104] There are wide variations between tribes, much ignorance still about what actually happens (used to happen), and a certain amount of debate about characterizing and interpreting the rituals.

The Sambia, one of the most intensively studied groups, believe sperm is both strength and strengthening, and boys had to receive sperm, usually by drinking it, in order to grow—to that extent, "homosexual" fellation was compulsory. Adults or young teenagers were prepared to sacrifice some of their sperm for the good of the community and liked to spread their manhood around the tribe, so to speak. Elsewhere, fathers-in-law inseminated prospective sons-in-law to make them strong enough to father grandchildren. Among some groups insemination was effected anally rather than orally.

Among the Sambia these practices were kept secret from the women (supposedly) and children and their revelation at the first initiation was sometimes a great shock; it took boys a while to get over their shame and humiliation and fear of drinking urine or of damage to the neck. The ultimate object of this flow of "milk" was to "grow" the boys, in particular to make them strong enough to be able to have sex with women successfully and produce their own sperm and children. Among the Sambia, semen is discussed by boys as if by "wine connoisseurs" (a revealing use of metaphor on the ethnographer's part), and boys might prefer certain bachelors for the amount and taste of their semen.[105] Bachelors likewise might show preference for certain boys depending on their willingness to fellate and the degree of sexual aggression shown by the boys. Sperm, for the Sambia, is loaded with cosmological significance. The secret of it is closely guarded and very important for articulating the age structure and gender structure of the tribe, its revelation to each new group of initiates takes place in a very tense ritualized context, but fellatio is still a sexual transaction, and there is evidence for flirting, pining, and for the development of erotic fantasy around this cosmological act.[106] Ritual behavior doesn't just mean "going through the motions." Ejaculation is never *just* a ritual.

Insemination might go on for several months or for as much as fifteen years, sometimes viewed as a mere boost for growth, elsewhere as the essential fuel for development. Among the Sambia a few boys were initiated into penis sucking as early as seven and changed roles from being inseminated to inseminating when they reached the age of about fourteen, or on the appearance of facial hair. Some groups believed the appearance of beards in adolescents demonstrated the efficacy of the practice and wondered how Westerners managed without it. At this point the adolescents were believed strong enough to donate sperm to the next age-group but not yet to women; boys were thought to be less draining than women. Even so, after ejaculation a secret white sap was sometimes consumed to replenish vital forces. The practice of inseminating boys often stopped after marriage or after the production of two children, which was the sign that full adulthood had been reached. Some adults continued the practice sporadically and surreptitiously after they were supposed to have given it up.[107]

As the first rumors of such practices began to emerge from the region, Bethe used them as an analogue for what he had deduced about Dorian practices. In Crete and Sparta at least, he argued, homosexual behavior may have been in fact a transference of manly spirit (*pneuma*) and heroism (*heldenthum*) or virtue (*aretē*) by means of injections of sperm through the bottom, the purpose being to turn boys into strong warriors.[108] At first, classicists were not prepared for such a gross analysis of Greek Love and didn't take kindly to Bethe's "holy" or to his comparisons between noble Greeks and primitive savages.[109] In the 1980s, however, when detailed accounts of Papuan rituals and beliefs were published, Bethe's theory of heroism-injecting sodomy enjoyed something of a renaissance among classicists for whom cross-cultural comparisons were now de rigueur. This is what they mean by "pederastic initiation."

But the anthropology of Papua New Guinea has moved on. Bruce Knauft, in particular, has argued that to separate sperm rituals between males from all the other body-substance rituals (once) prevalent in the region—involving brain tissue, vaginal juices, nosebleeds, combined intercourse fluids, cadaver fluids, etc., ingested or smeared or otherwise deployed—begs a lot of questions. Rituals involving heterosexual copulation—ritualized wife-exchange, ritual adultery, great festival orgies, etc.—could be said to be more characteristic of the region. Semen is only one out of a wide range of substances human beings are capable of producing, drinking is only one way of using these substances, and younger members of the same sex are not the only groups on whom these substances can be used. Collectively the people of southern Papua New Guinea make use of a very broad palette, deploying several different body products in several different ways on various occasions to achieve many different things. The drinking of sperm has a very specific context here, and Jan Bremmer's suggestion that it is merely a surviving remnant of some once ubiquitous primitive initiation ritual ignores that fact.[110]

There are important insights to be gained from comparisons with the people of Papua New Guinea. They may help to clarify, for instance, the distinction between Homosexuality and homosexuality. Knauft went to study a remote tribe of homicidal banana farmers called the Gebusi, "first effectively contacted in 1962." They are described as unhierarchical, status-unconscious, "friendly and self-effacing" but with personal violence accounting for 32.7 percent of all adult deaths. They too make use of semen exchange, believing semen to be a powerful life force. Adolescents are recipients, without being formally initiated into the practice, until the age of seventeen or twenty-five, at which point they go through ceremonies of adulthood and become "donors" until marriage at twenty or twenty-five. Then they are supposed to stop. But the ethnographer notes that "the strongest homosexual relationship in our village—also having the most heightened displays of public homoeroticism—was an unsanctioned reciprocal relationship between newly initiated age-mates. The partners, one of whom was in his mid-20s, claimed that their sexual attraction was so strong that they had no immediate desire to 'claim a woman,' that is, to get married."[111]

There are also interesting parallels with the Greeks in Papuan ideas about the contrast between male and female sexuality, the care that needs to be taken with a man's precious ejaculate and the threat posed by women to men's vital forces. Among the Sambia and Gebusi, women were considered latently ravenous but were believed to be kept under some control through social constraints. The women of their fictions and fantasies, however, especially supernatural female spirits, rather like nymphomaniac Greek nymphs, were rather more forward. Among the Sambia, strange sounds were heard in the forest in the weeks before the initiation into the secret of "the flutes." The boys were told the eerie sounds were produced by ancient female spirits of the village coming to get them. During the ceremony itself the female spirits were introduced. Bachelors entered with their faces covered, playing flutes and waddling like ducks. The boys are informed that these are old woman spirits, full of lust for them, a bad thing; it is the prelude to the fellatio, which is a good thing, and the selfsame bachelors, now without their masks, will be the donors of the fortifying liquid.[112] In fact, anthropologists in Papua New Guinea have been able to array the different tribes on a line running from extreme anxiety over ejaculation and as a consequence an extreme stinginess as regards sperm at one end of the scale, to extreme seminal extravagance at the other, with the Sambia positioned halfway, only moderately parsimonious. Greek men may have operated an even looser sperm economy in fact. Having sex with women, they were rather like tourists in a foreign bazaar, happy to spend some money, but terrified of being ripped off.

But too often in their rush to see similarities between Greeks and the Papuan tribes, scholars ignore the awkward details and the differences; indeed in many respects Greek Homosexuality seems not only quite different from Papuan Homosexuality but its very reverse. Greek Homosex, for instance, is characterized by its apparent avoidance of insemination. Two of the practices we hear about, *diamērion* and Spartan cloak sex, involved exosomatic ejaculation. The chair sex shown on the Dinos Painter's vase in the British Museum would seem to show an imminent act of penetration, but it happens between two age-identical Striplings. And, according to the sources, it was Men who were supposed to be inspired by their *erōmenoi,* transformed by them into better warriors, not the other way around. The Athenians went to great lengths to protect Boys even from talking to Men to whom they were not related, to the extent of employing slaves whose job it was to chaperon them, and forbidding Striplings to mix or chat with under-Eighteens in the gymnasium. It was only when Boys showed signs of fuzz on the face, when they had become citizens, officially Eighteen, that they were released from the protection of the *paidagōgoi*. It was Striplings already on their way to growing full beards who were the celebrated objects of Love. The Greek idea of physical maturity was of a natural body clock that was aligned with the calendar and ultimately with the phases of the moon and the cycle of the stars, a given fact, a characteristic feature of the mortal condition, what separated men from gods, not something that had to be engineered. The rites involved one-to-one pair bonding. One such rite, the Cretan abduction, cannot have involved more than a small minority of boys, and seems to have taken place at no particular festival but at a time chosen by the suitor at a place chosen by the "friends." In this it was quite different from the mass-marriages to underage girls that in Crete and probably in classical Sparta marked the transition from "off-marriage Cadets" to adults at Twenty. And it did not, finally, result in a change of age-grade status for the Famed, since Ephorus talks of them receiving a costume from the *philētōr,* and then adds that they *continued to wear* a distinctive costume, *even after* they had been initiated into the ranks of Men at some later date, presumably at a New Year festival. And how, finally, did the women of Sappho's Lesbos fit into this Greek Homosexuality centered on sperm?

Above all, classicists have ignored the difference between the two kinds of data that are being compared: on the one hand fiercely guarded secrets prized from reluctant informants by anthropologists and published around the world, on the other, the noisy and unmissable practices of Greek Love. The Sambia ritual is not meant to be common knowledge; any boy who reveals it to the women is threatened with death (of course the Sambia women knew all about it, but pretended not to, thereby colluding in their sons' subsequent trauma). This secrecy surrounding homosexual relations is crucial. It gives fellatio its effectiveness in initiation. For the boys are not only initiated into the practice, they are initiated into the knowledge of it.[113]

One of the most characteristic features of what we call Greek Homosexuality, on the other hand, so obvious it is often overlooked, is its spectacular, even monumental nature—it generates statues, literature, painting, graffiti, declarations. Any understanding of the phenomenon must take account of its archaeologicability, the fact that there is a construct there to be studied in the first place. From this perspective, Greece and Papua New Guinea are at opposite ends of the spectrum. "While male sexual activity in early adulthood is preeminently homosexual, its primary ideology and verbal fantasy remains *heterosexual:* the ultimate sexual prize is always said to be a beautiful young woman."[114] Without the careful work of Western ethnographers making the practices archae-ologicable by monumentalizing them in books, there would be no Sam-bia homosexuality for scholars to study in two and a half thousand years' time, thanks to rigorous concealment. Talking to the resident an-thropologist, one Kambo casually mentions singing the songs of his sex-ual partners. But this is not Theognis writing songs in honor of Cyrnus to be broadcast around the Mediterranean. Kambo is singing to himself alone in the forest, unheard.[115]

PAIRS, YOKES AND CHARIOTS

The only thing that seems to unite these various, mostly quite academi-cally respectable, theories on the origins of Greek Homosexuality is that they fundamentally contradict each other: "It's extremely late," "It's ex-tremely ancient," "It's very local," "It's an import from outside." One group of theories, overly tied to explicit evidence for amorousness, pro-duces conclusions that are as formally irrefutable as they are—once one considers the practical possibilities of diffusion, ritualization and the growth overnight of local variations—impossible to believe. Another group of theories seems to have taken leave of methodology com-pletely, deciding that a myth must be pre-Greek because it involves a hero with a pre-Greek name, or that a ritual must be prehistoric because it involves age-differentiated males and there is evidence for age-differentiation in Minoan Crete inferred from haircuts on Bronze Age vases, or that Greek Homosexuality was like Papuan practices of insem-inating prepubescent children to make them into men, even if it in-volved neither insemination nor prepubescent children. A general reader might conclude that all theories are equally possible and that coming up with a new theory is a mug's game. Certainly, seeking the sources of Greek Homosexuality needs to be a delicate operation, neces-sarily speculative, not something to be carved in stone.

There are, to begin with, a couple of important principles. We should be concerned as much as possible with the Greek Homosexuality we know to have actually existed, not a postulated mock-up of a prehistoric Greek Homosexuality that had ceased to exist by the historical period. Second, we should be economical with our accounts of the origins of such an extraordinary phenomenon and wary of having it invented over and over again: the sodomitical variety, the passionate asexual same-sex loving of heroes buried in one tomb, a Cretan variety, a variety for women.

This last example draws attention to one other thing that unites all previous theories of origin: a preoccupation with male homosexual sex. The Homosexuality that actually existed in ancient Greece might exist between women, and might not involve sex. Nor was a difference in age a necessity, as can be seen on the Dinos Painter's vase or among the Macedonian Royal Boys. In Thessaly and Macedonia, especially, age-patterning seems much less rigid. Whatever Meno was up to with elder Tharypas, he was not inseminating him in order to help him grow a beard. Even the softer versions of initiation theories that emphasize the pedagogical aspects seem built on sand. The gods do not in fact, *pace* Sergent, seem to be teaching their mortal *erōmenoi* any useful skills, any more than Achilles teaches Patroclus or Patroclus Achilles; when Xenophon and Pausanias invoke the improving aspects of Spartan and Athenian Homosexuality respectively, they are in apologetic mode. If Pausanias concludes that a boy should put out only in order to acquire a virtue, it is because he is only too aware that boys might well put out for money and political power.

From all this it becomes obvious that the stable universal core of Greek Homosexuality is simply the pairing of two members of the same sex: Leodamas and "his wife Hegesander," Harmodius and Aristogiton, the *Phaedrus*'s same-sex couples who walk hand in hand in the anteroom of reincarnation or who consummate having exchanged "the greatest pledges," Theban couples at Iolaus's tomb, the Cretan *philētōr* and his Famed *parastatheis*, Sappho and her *syndygoi* "yoke-mates," the cloak-sharing women of the Pharos Painter, the *pharos*-bearing women of Alcman's Maidensong, Crimon and "his brother," the son of Bathycles, *oiphing* high on the caldera of Santorini, while calling on Apollo Delphinios as witness, Achilles and Patroclus in their golden urn, Alexander and Hephaestion, Orestes and Pylades, *eispnēlas* and *aïtas* . . . These pairs are not a peculiar way to construct collective

58. Cup fragment found in the agora of Athens. The outside
depicts a gymnasium scene. This interior seems to show intercrural sex.
After it was fired, someone, presumably the owner, scratched the
word "[*phil*]*otesion*," "love pledge" (*c.*500).

Sambia-style homosexual rites of passage into manhood. These pairs
are what Greek Love is.

Different communities may well have had very different ways of
courting and coming together. In Thebes and Elis there might be hardly
any courting as such if we believe Pausanias, while in Athens it sometimes seems to be the main focus of energy, so much so that many scholars have confused the courting of *paides* by *erastai* with Athenian
Homosexuality *tout court*. In Crete the get-together might be fixed up by
the "friends" without, quite possibly, the future Famed one's knowledge. But at some point there was of necessity an initiation, not into
adulthood necessarily, but into a same-sex pair. It is the institution of
the same-sex syzygy that the women of Aeolian Lesbos share with the
men of Aeolian Thebes. It is the syzygy that provides the bedrock of
Greek Homosexualities.

What characterizes such yoke mating is, to begin with, simply the
very weddedness, i.e., their troth plighting, their exchange of oaths.
This automatically makes them comparable to heterosexual married
couples, who are also commonly described as syzygies. The sixth-
century Athenian tripod box in Oxford, Mississippi, underlines the
point by putting a heterosexual wedded couple alongside female pairs
cloaked in one *pharos* and male pairs engaged in the "love pledge," the
philotēsion, the *sebas mēriōn,* the "holy honor of thighs." Centuries earlier, Homer had already drawn an analogy between Achilles' Patroclus
and Meleager's wife. And if it is true that the sanctuary at Kato Syme
was associated in the seventh century with homosexual couples, and in

the Hellenistic period with Hermes and Aphrodite, the divine model of perfect marital unity, then the one unbroken thread that runs from the less to the more recent levels at this singularly ancient shrine is couple-dom itself.

More specifically, male couples are frequently imagined as chariot pairs, one the "reins-holding" Driver, one the "standing-by" Chariot Fighter: Patroclus drives younger Achilles, Iolaus drives older Heracles. One can see straightforward reflections of the institutionalization of the model of the chariot pair in the fifth-century Boeotian battalion of three hundred "Drivers" (*hēniochoi*) and "Chariot-Fighters" (*parabatai*) even though both are fighting on foot. The Thebans who swore oaths at Io-laus's tomb can scarcely have avoided viewing the chariot pair of Hera-cles and Iolaus, who appear as early as the eighth century, as models for their hoplitic relationships. Hans van Wees has noted that the relation-ship between the poet Theognis and Cyrnus in sixth-century BC Megara was also presented in one fine couplet as analogous with a Homeric char-iot pair: "Shining from the far-bright vantage point, the silent courier, Cyrnus, wakes up sobbing war. So be it, bridle the swift-heeled horses. I think they'll meet the foemen face-to-face." Cyrnus performs the role of horse-bridling "squire" just like Patroclus in the *Iliad,* though we are not talking of chariots here, but horse-transported hoplites.[116]

The chariot pair are not just imaginary figures. In the distant past there really were such comrades-in-arms. Two-man chariots appear among the matchstick mourners on Geometric vases of the early first millennium BC. Among them we can occasionally discern the famous Siamese chariot-driving twins of Elis, known as the Molione or Twain [Sons] of Actor, Actorione, who are mentioned in the epics and appear, pretty unmistakably, in eighth-century art. They allow us to conclude that the idealized image of an intimately bonded same-sex chariot pair, the very image that Aristophanes deploys in his story of the invention of love in Plato's *Symposium,* was already fully realized, flourishing in the very earliest recognizable images. Arguments as to whether such blended bodies represent the Actorione in particular, or "inseparable twins or sworn brothers," seem beside the point.[117]

Twin brothers or Siamese twins, they are, according to the epic scheme, the most perfect expression of the relationships of strict sol-idarity that exist between the driver and the master of the chariot.

Pistotatos, the most faithful, this is the epithet of [the charioteer] Automedon. From *hetairos* to *hetairos,* from companion to companion, *pistis* is the rule: an institution, it denotes contractual relationships, sanctified—as in the relationship between Theseus and Pirithous— by *horkia,* oaths, accompanied by libations of undiluted wine, or sacrifices both bloody and chthonic.[118]

Here then in the eighth century is one definite *ante quem* for the idealized image of a male syzygy: the pledge-wedded male chariot pair in the hexameters of the *Iliad* and/or in the welded bodies of the Twain of Actor. Perhaps then the idea of bonding was transferred from the chariot pair to the yoked draft animals, just as Cleobis and Biton yoked themselves together in order to pull the oxcart of Hera's priestess and died quietly and happily when they arrived there, just as the women of seventh-century Sparta and Lesbos took the yoke pair as a model when forming their own one-to-ones.

But same-sex chariot pairs also appear on Mycenaean pottery of the second millennium BC. From the administrative documents in Linear B discovered at Greek-conquered Cnossus, we can safely assume they were an actuality rather than a pictorial fantasy. The documents reveal that Mycenaean chariots were indeed manned by two men, and that chariot men were an elite and privileged group. They also seem to have been administered by the central authority and were provided for and equipped by the palace, which is normally assumed to have been headed by a king.[119] There is a good chance, therefore, that the idea of a special group of paired warriors who enjoyed an exceptional relationship with a supralocal central authority goes back to the Bronze Age. Recent finds from Thebes show that it was the center of an important Mycenaean state or province, probably one as great as or greater than the better-known sites of Mycenae, Pylos and Cnossus.[120] It would be not at all surprising to discover that Mycenaean Thebes, like Mycenaean Cnossus, had a palace battalion of elite chariot pairs who might, therefore, seem to be the direct ancestors of the elite groups of champions of the classical period, the three hundred "Drivers" and "Chariot-Fighters" who fought at Delium many centuries later in the fifth century BC and the Sacred Band "of the City" in the fourth, although it would be hard, if not impossible, to join up the dots between them.

Do chariot pairs necessarily mean same-sex pair bonding between elite troops? Xenophon seems to think so. According to him, chariot pairs like those found in the *Iliad* could still be found in the classical period, for instance in the Theran colony of Cyrene. The chariot pairs he knew of in Persia were different, however, from "the Trojan" kind. He imagines reasons why the old pairs were got rid of in the sixth century by his hero Cyrus the Great:

> It seemed to him that since the best men were on the chariots, the mightiest—one might reasonably expect—element of the force played the part of mere javelin-tossing skirmishers and made no substantial contribution to the business of winning through. For three hundred chariots means three hundred fighters, but twelve hundred horses. And their drivers, not unreasonably, were the men in whom they had most faith, the very best. That means another three hundred men who do no damage to the enemy whatsoever.[121]

It is hard not to view the same-sex paired Cretan *Parastathentes* as equivalents of the paired-up *Parabatai* of Boeotia. Certainly the sacrifice to Eros before battle, led by the battalion of Beauties, a sacrifice that the Cretans shared with the Spartans, is singular enough to infer a single common origin, which might be found among the southern Dorians in the early first millennium. That does not mean the Dorians brought it with them, however. It may have been a Mycenaean practice they picked up when they arrived in the Peloponnese, just as they seem to have picked up and passed on the Mycenaean cult they found in Hyacinthian Amyclae, as witnessed not just by the spread of Hyacinthian month-names across the Dorian Aegean, but also by the name of a sanctuary called "Amyklaion" in Crete.[122]

So, to summarize, the *idea* of a personally devoted chariot pair was probably flourishing in the early first millennium, and there were already sacrifices to Eros by men in all-male groups, i.e., war bands, armies. Myths located such devoted pairs in the heroic period that the Greeks associated with the "Achaeans" (Mycenaeans) of the second millennium BC. The Mycenaeans did indeed have chariot pairs. One may therefore postulate a Mycenaean same-sex pairing closely tied to the palace that was adopted by the later invaders once the palaces had been destroyed. The Mycenaean polities with their kings look nothing like age-class societies (which are said by anthropologists to be structurally hostile to the institution of dynastic monarchies), while in Athens *c.*1050 BC there is evidence for a sudden reorganization of cemeteries according to age and gender, a kind of (re)tribalization or what I have called a "demological" revolution.[123] The marriage of age-class structure with same-sex pair bonds produced the classic age-patterned Greek Homosexualities of the *poleis*. In dynastic Thessaly and farther north, age-classes were less important and age-patterning in same-sex relationships less pronounced.

The problem with this theory, however, is that it flies in the face of both ancient and modern assumptions that Greek Homosexuality originated among the invaders, especially the Dorians; and there are reasons for those assumptions. The general consensus is that the Greeks arrived in Greece not long after *c.*2000 BC. By *c.*1500 BC they had begun to split into different dialect groups. "East Greek" was the ancestor of the Arcadian, Cypriot, Attic and Ionic dialects. The Linear B texts show that Mycenaean Greek belonged to this group also. It seems fair to assume, therefore, that these were the Greeks who lived within the sphere of Mycenaean civilization that began to crystallize around 1550 and reached its climax in the Palace Period that lasted just two hundred and fifty years: *c.*1450–1200. "West Greek" was the ancestor not just of Doric but of the dialects of Delphi, Elis, Phocis, etc. They must have been culturally separated for some time from their East Greek cousins, outside the Mycenaean world, probably in the northwest toward Albania. The third main group, the Aeolic dialect, which probably originated in Thessaly on the northern border of the Mycenaean civilization, can be considered a kind of mixture of the two, with West Greek predominating.[124]

Rough-and-ready though arguments from cultural or linguistic genealogy may be, the overwhelming impression is that same-sex pairing, the image of the pair, myths about pairs, cults of the pair, the practices of pairing, the specialized terminology for each partner in a pair, were much more deeply embedded among those with origins on the margins of or outside the Mycenaean world—the Therans, Cretans, Spartans, Thessalians, Lesbians, Boeotians, Eleans—than among those we now believe to have come from inside it. There is also the rather striking fact that in Dorian Sparta and Aeolian Thessaly they had a similar strange technical term for an *erōmenos: Aïtas, Aitēs.* The obvious conclusion is that same-sex pairing was already flourishing among the West Greek and proto-Aeolian groups in the middle of the second millennium BC. One East Greek group, the Ionians of Chalcis, actually had a legend of their being "converted" to Homosexuality by a Thessalian. So the East Greeks living within the Mycenaean sphere may have rejected the practice, or it may have been confined to the palace's privileged chariot pairs, and been lost when the palaces were destroyed, or they may have known nothing of it in the first place. The association of same-sex couples with the "Achaean" world may have been a development of Thessalian epic in particular, marrying the political and military institutions of East Greek Mycenaean civilization with the practices of same-sex coupling of the West Greeks.

If we try to go beyond the West Greeks of the second millennium we find ourselves in the world of Aryan Indo-European comparisons. The Greeks are normally considered to have taken good care of their Aryan linguistic inheritance but to have been careless of their cultural inheritance. More specifically only three of their gods, Zeus, Dawn (*Eōs*) and Sun (*Hēlios*), seem to have Indo-European origins, and of those only Zeus himself retained any importance in their religion. Outside Harvard University, students of Greece have tended to be extremely skeptical about those who try to trace Indo-European origins for anything apart from some meters and a couple of epic phrases. There is one important exception, however, the divine Spartan twins called Dioscuri, the "youths of Zeus," who seem to have an awful lot in common with the Asvins, the divine horse twins of Vedic mythology; few would dispute a common Indo-European origin for both. In Greek mythology they form another chariot pair of exceptional brotherly love and devotion, if not quite as close as the Twain of Actor. The Dioscuri therefore allow us to trace a genealogy of the Greek same-sex chariot pair via the Spartans, the Dorians and the West Greeks all the way back to the Aryans.

What of the practices of same-sex pairing? Here there is one very striking possibility. In the Vedic hymns, the Asvin twins are strongly associated with the goddess Usas, Dawn. They are said to appear just before her, and she springs to life when they yoke their chariot.[125]

Alcman's song for the homoamatory maidens who carry the *pharos*/plow, like an ox team, toward the Greek Usas, i.e., Eos (*Aōtis, Orthria*), in the last hours of the night was linked by Bruno Gentili to Sappho's same-sex yoke-mates.[126] Since this is almost the only cult practice in Greece in honor of the Indo-European Dawn goddess, it has a not unreasonable chance of being a remnant of an Indo-European ritual act.

In fact it is not initiatory pederasty so much as same-sex wedding—one-to-one troth plighting—that seems so strikingly prominent among Indo-European groups, at least those who came to settle in Europe. Since the pioneering work of John Boswell on *Same-Sex Unions* and the varied responses to them of ancient and medieval historians, the rather extensive material on these made-brothers or "federated brothers" is now much better known.[127] The Celts certainly seem to have practiced a rather intense form of male bonding. The Romans emphasized the extraordinarily committed and self-sacrificing friendships found among Celtic warriors, the *devotio* (vowing oneself to another) of men called *soldurii* who could not leave the battlefield alive if the man to whose friendship they had dedicated themselves had been killed.[128] The most elaborate description of a Celtic ritual of same-sex wedding comes centuries later in the AD 1180s, when Gerald of Wales described an Irish practice: "First they exchange covenants of comradeship [or "cofatherhood," *compaternitas*]. Then they take it in turns to carry each other around the church three times. Next, they go inside, relics of saints are placed at the altar, all kinds of solemn obligations are given out, and then finally with a mass and priestly prayers they are indissolubly bonded as if by a betrothal [*desponsatio*]."[129]

In fact such "wed brothers," "troth i-plighted," seem to have been rather common in medieval Europe. They feature in chronicles, ballads, and even in accounts that show knights were remunerated as a pair. Edward II seems to have made just such a love-brother contract with the Gascon Piers Gaveston: The minute Edward set eyes on him (probably in 1297), says the Cottonian chronicle, "he bombarded [?] him with love [*amorem*] to the extent that he entered into a covenant of brotherhood [*fraternitatis fedus*] with him. He chose with steadfast determination to tie him to him indissolubly with a chain of loving devotion [*dileccionis vinculum*]."[130] We know of a couple of pairs of knights, one Spanish pair, one English, who marked their union with the heraldic device called "impalement," the blending of the arms of one with the arms of the other, a practice normally used to designate a heterosexual marriage alliance. Some have suggested that same-sex wedding was originally a Nordic practice imported by Scandinavians, but it was also found from an early date among more southerly German tribes, such as the Franks, while the emperor Diocletian, who came from Dalmatia on the eastern side of the Adriatic, is known to have entered into a relationship of brotherhood with his fellow emperor Maximianus (*frater adscitus*).[131]

The Celts were also renowned for engaging in homosexual sex. The sexual act was probably an important part of the male bonding. There seems to be a hint at this in Aristotle's observation that the Celts are among those peoples who have "publicly honored intercourse with males [*tēn pros tous arrhenas sunousian*]."[132] And when the third-century AD author known as Pseudo-Bardasanes referred to Celtic men marrying each other (*gamountai*) he clearly inferred shameless acts too.[133] The sources on the mysterious Taifali, probably a Germanic tribe, are even more explicit about the link between the "marriage," *foedus,* and the "unspeakable sex," *nefandi concubitus.*[134]

Amazing though it may appear, in my view the institution of male bonding noticed by Aristotle among the Celts in the fourth century BC, by Gerald among the Irish in the AD 1180s, and by various writers—Diodorus, Posidonius, Caesar, Valerius Maximus, Pseudo-Bardasanes—in between, sometimes emphasizing the devotion, sometimes the sex, sometimes both, is not on each occasion a report of something newly invented, but a single thing. Same-sex wedding was an institution of Celtic culture, one that had doubtless undergone many developments, but one that was deeply embedded. Since such similar practices of both one-to-one same-sex troth plighting and same-sex sex are ascribed to the Greeks, as well as some other Indo-Europeans, there is indeed a strong case to be made that it reflects a common inheritance, not an institution of pederastic insemination and initiation into adulthood, but rather of homosexual pair bonding, associated, perhaps, with the divine twins. With that proviso, I conclude that Bernard Sergent was probably right: The origins of Greek Homosexuality may well be discovered among the Aryans.

That was by no means the conclusion I anticipated I would come up with when I first began to examine the Greek knot, but then unraveling the various strands that Greek Love ties together has taken me to many places I never thought I would visit and produced many surprises along the way. I have learned an awful lot I didn't know before, despite nearly thirty years of study, and some of what I have learned I did not even know I was ignorant of. The world I was familiar with when I embarked on writing this book has been transformed, by the end, into something odder and richer. Every time a new window of clarity opened up an area of antique obscurity, something that had once seemed unremarkable began to seem rather more strange. The Greeks were always extraordinary but now they seem more extraordinary. For me at least they have changed and, changed, they make a little more sense.

NOTES

INTRODUCTION

1 Nepos, *Alcibiades* 2.2: "*ineunte adulescentia amatus est a multis more Graecorum,*" Cic., *Tusc.* 5.58: "*haberet etiam more Graeciae quosdam adulescentis amore coniunctos,*" cf. ibid. 4.70 etc.

2 Symonds, *A Problem in Greek Ethics,* p. v. Symonds partly resolved his "problem" by identifying two separate forms of Greek Love in the post-Homeric world, a spiritual and a sensual version, cf. section XIII, pp. 30–31.

3 Arr., *An.* 2.3,1 and 3,6–4,1, cf. M. A. Littauer, J. H. Crouwel, "New Light on Priam's Wagon?," *JHS* 108 (1988), 194–96.

PART I: THE GREEKS HAD WORDS FOR IT
1: EROS IN LOVE

1 Dover, *Greek Homosexuality,* p. 50, X., *Lac.* 2.13, Plu., *Pelopidas* 18.2, [D.] 61.30, Hallett, "Beloved Cleïs."

2 Cf. C. Calame, *L'Éros dans la Grèce antique* (Paris, 1996), pp. 42–46.

3 X., *Mem.* 2.6,28.

4 Weiss, "Erotica," esp. 34. Hard though it is to believe, looking at it, *pothos* is closely linked not only to Greek *thessesthai* "seek" (Hsch. s.v.), but to Welsh *gweddio* "pray."

5 Himeros putting a sandal on Dionysus, Ruvo, Museo Jatta, 36818 1093 (*BA* 215689), Himeros pouring from a *phialē* over Ariadne's bowed head, Tübingen, Eberhard-Karls-Univ., Arch. Inst., 5439 (*BA* 213727); cf. also the "Pronomos Vase" with Himeros pulling on one of Dionysus's female companions, Naples Mus. Arch. 81673 H3240 (*BA* 217500), and the one with the three beefy Erotes led by Himeros, with Odysseus and the Sirens on the reverse, one of whom is labeled Himeropa, BM E440 (*BA* 202628). H. A. Shapiro, "Eros in Love: Pederasty and Pornography in Greece," in A. Richlin (ed.), *Pornography and Representation in Greece and Rome* (New York, 1992) [53–72], 70, thinks such beefy Erotes are a specialty of *c.*480–450, and in general, A. Hermary, *LIMC* s.v. "Himeros, Himeroi."

6 We must be careful; Plato is playing on words, *himeros>hiemenos*—"rushing,"

Cra. 419e–420a, E., *Medea* 56, Hdt. 1.30,2; cf. Calame, *Poetics,* pp. 188–89, and, on taking Plato's etymologies seriously, David Sedley, *Plato's Cratylus* (Cambridge, 2003), pp. 25–50.

7 Solon fr. 25.

8 *Phdr.* 255bc, cf. the vase in Tübingen with Himeros drenching Ariadne, Eberhard-Karls-Univ., Arch. Inst., 5439 (*BA* 213727).

9 So Hermary, Cassimatis, Vollkommer, *LIMC* "Eros," 933–42, esp. 934–35, cf. esp. [Lucian] *Amores* 11: "he would have preferred to have had Eros of Thespiae instead of Aphrodite of Cnidus." Down to *c.*450 BC, he appears above all around boys. In that respect, he embodies the fantasy of the beautiful youth, who is the object of most attention in Greek Love. On the Spartan Cup in the Louvre (Fig. 2), he alternates with female Sirens; one could argue that he represents a distinct type of love, the love of a male for a male in particular, and the Sirens Vase in the British Museum (among others) seems to reveal a similar opposition between masculine Erotes and feminine Sirens, BM E440 (*BA* 202628). Pipili, *Laconian Iconography,* pp. 71–76, thinks the Spartan "Erotes" or little winds may be symbols of *eudaimonia,* prosperity, but that does not really account for the Sirens. However, since Eros is only supposed to appear at a woman's wedding, so long as she is decent, appearing spontaneously and vanishingly only at the moment when she unveils and gazes are exchanged with the bridegroom, there was not much room for him to spread his wings in approved heterosexual encounters. So Eros's homosexual coloring may well be a mirage; he was always going to be a male because the noun is masculine, and of course a god of love should be beautiful and young, and it was above all in relations between males that he was so much onstage or in the spotlight, where the gap between Love and Sexual Satisfaction was widest, i.e., there is nothing *essentially* or *definitionally* male homosexual about Eros, it is just that Love (in general) is more of an active player in relations between males. For a god of homosexual relations cf. the Chinese Hu Tianbao, Michael Szonyi, "The Cult of Hu Tianbao and the Eighteenth-Century Discourse of Homosexuality," *Late Imperial China* 19 (1998), 1–25.

10 Paus. 1.43,6. Pirenne-Delforge, *L'Aphrodite,* pp. 89–91, wonders whether Pausanias can actually have been to Megara, but I suspect Pausanias is alluding to the poses of the statues when he wonders if you can really distinguish their fields of action. Scopas did other Aphrodites, and his Aphrodite and Pothos on Samothrace were honored with very holy rites, Pliny, *Nat. Hist.* 36.25; cf. also Lattimore, "Skopas and the Pothos."

11 Berlin, F2633, *BA* 215722; cf. the cup by Makron, Berlin F2291, *BA* 204685.

12 *Iliad* 13.636–39, cf. Calame, *Poetics of Eros,* p. 22, Ludwig, *Eros and Polis,* pp. 124–31, esp. 126: "[The difficulty] is to show any passages in which *erōs* conclusively means 'sexual desire.' "

13 Weiss, "Erotica," 39, 41, "divided for myself."

14 Louvre E667, Pipili, *Laconian Iconography* #194, fig. 103, cf. 214 fig. 108 (BM B1).

15 *LIMC,* "Eros" # 842b, "au début du VIe s. av. J.-C." The figure of "wild Eros

playing (like the boy he is) coming down over the flower-tips" may also find his first mention in a seventh-century poem from Sparta, Alcman fr. 58.

16 *Smp.* 177ad.

17 On the race see especially Scanlon, *Eros,* pp. 255–59; there were a number of these torch-relay races starting from the Academy, and there is some debate about which altar(s) marked the finishing line; cf. Parker, *Polytheism,* 472, 183 with n.

18 We should note also the strange artificial wall (still visible) of undressed stone at Aphrodite's rock-sanctuary at Daphne in Attica, and the three rocks representing the Graces, who also belong to the retinue of Aphrodite, at Orchomenus, Paus. 1.37,7 (cf. Musti and Beschi ad loc.) 9.38,1. It is clear from Pausanias's comments on the latter that he thought marble statues were closer to the nature of these unhewn rocks than, say, bronze or ivory statues.

19 Hurwit, *Acropolis,* p. 41, figs. 3.18, 34–35, Pirenne-Delforge, *L'Aphrodite,* pp. 72–73.

20 The task of getting a dog from a foreign country immediately recalls the equally unfortunate relationship of the Cretan Euxynthetus tasked with getting a dog from Praisos (Strabo 10.4,12 = Thphr. fr. 560) as Sergent noticed (*Homosexuality in Greek Myth,* p. 176), cf. Conon, *Narr.* 16 with Brown ad 3–4, for further examples of cruel beloveds and impossible tasks; even Heracles' Labors were said to be due to a demanding boyfriend: Eurystheus. Closer to home, the leap off a cliff with birds attached recalls Strabo's story of Athenian Cephalus's hopeless love for Pterelas and the associated scapegoat ritual in which a criminal was thrown off the White Rock of Leucas covered in feathers and birds (10.2,9).

21 Suda (mu 497) s.v. "Melētos" = Aelian fr. 69 Hercher, Paus. 1.30,1. Pausanias's version is highly compressed (though there seem to be some linguistic echoes of Suda). Timagoras is the *erastēs* and a resident alien (metic), the beloved Athenian youth is called Meles (*melēma* = "darling"); the only task Meles sets his poor *erastēs* is to "take a flying leap," which Timagoras duly does (for Meletos/Melitides, a proverbial Athenian fool; cf. Gomme-Sandbach ad Men., *Aspis* 269, Dover ad *Frogs* 991, perhaps especially one who is his own worst enemy in affairs of the heart). It seems possible that Anteros was at first simply a topographical designation, "Eros Opposite [the Eros in the Academy]," especially if, as some believe, this altar was the finish line for one of the torch races that began in the Academy. Of course, following Plato's lead, the name was open to all kinds of commentary and interpretation. Metics were involved in one torch-race festival, the Hephaisteia, Parker, *Polytheism,* pp. 170–71, 471–72; heroes connected to same-sex *erōs* were often said to be foreign to the city in which they were celebrated and/or honored, Diocles (pp. 197–98), Cleomachus (p. 354).

22 Scanlon, *Eros,* pp. 258–59; the people of Parium on the Hellespont were as devoted to Eros as the Thespians, Paus. 9.27,1.

23 Sosicrates, *FGrHist* 461 F7 ap Ath. 13.561ef.

24 Scanlon, *Eros,* pp. 266–69, for Leuctra on the gulf of Messenia, Paus. 3.26,5
    with Musti and Torelli ad loc, Shipley, *IAPC,* 557–58.

25 Pausanias seems to me a bit vaguer on the matter than many have realized,
    9.27,1. Pirenne-Delforge *L'Aphrodite,* pp. 289–93, 297, provides a partial anti-
    dote to Schachter's undue skepticism about the antiquity of Eros in Thespiae
    (*Cults of Boiotia* 1, 216–19), which has unduly influenced Hansen, in his turn,
    bizarrely to exclude Thespiae's most important deity from his list of the city's
    archaic and classical cults (*IACP,* 458) because there is no unequivocal attesta-
    tion (i.e., an inscription) before the fourth century. This kind of thing is what
    gives positivism a bad name. The cult of Eros in Thespiae is no Eisteddfod.

26 Pellizer, "Reflections" makes the same connection.

27 Gibbon, *Decline and Fall* c. 53, "Revival of Greek Learning" [III, p. 418].

28 Conon, *Narr.* 24; cf. Brown ad loc. It would be tidiest if Narcissus was believed
    to have done himself in with his admirer's own sword, but it is clear also that
    he left no corpse—no hero's "tomb"—which fits Ovid's description of Nar-
    cissus vanishing away like wax rather better. The problem with Photius is that
    he sometimes paraphrases at length, even using the same words, and at other
    times is "wretchedly concise" (Gibbon, op. cit. c. 36 n. 112 [II, p. 400]) and it is
    hard to know which mode he is in at any particular time.

29 Paus. 9.31,6 thought the Narcissus myth completely idiotic—no one could be
    so foolish as to fall in love with his own reflection—revealing thereby how se-
    riously he took all the other myths; as for the flowers, he cites literary refer-
    ences to narcissuses that predate the Thespian, thus disproving the myth of
    metamorphosis. Wheler on narcissuses: ". . . we passed by another little Vil-
    lage called Tadza, where are some marks of Antiquity; and by it a curious lit-
    tle Fountain, which I guess to be that which was so celebrated in old times for
    the Fable of *Narcissus:* and if so, the Town should have been called Donacon or
    Hedonacon as some read it. I saw no *Narcissus* then growing, it being yet too
    early in the Year. But another time I saw abundance in the next Plain, and sev-
    eral other places adjacent"—*A Journey Into Greece,* p. 471; cf. Hansen, *IAPC,*
    434, and Schachter again, *Cults of Boiotia* 2, p. 154 n. 2, in uncharacteristically
    lyrical mode—"[Helikon] can be an eerie place; or, it can be a delightful
    one"—and on the cult of Narcissus, 181–82 with n. 3: "no evidence for a cult
    in historical times . . . late . . . romanticized . . . appealed to the imagina-
    tion . . . all that there is to say."

30 Ovid, *Met.* 3.400–405. The paucity of explicit references to Narcissus until late
    is striking. It may be that there was something rude and/or secret about the
    myth or the ritual practices associated with it. Primordial Eros played an im-
    portant role in Orphic "mystery" religions, and below Narcissus's spring in the
    vale of the Muses (the original "Museum") was a statue of Orpheus with a per-
    sonification of Mystery, while pious Pausanias (9.27,2) seems reluctant to say
    all he knows—"I shall say no more about this." The Eretrian (i.e., foreign-
    born) Narcissus, who had some kind of memorial (*mnēma*) on the eastern ex-

tremity of Boeotia in Oropos, was called "Silent One" (Sigelos), because men passed him in silence, Strabo 9.2.10.

31 Gutzwiller, "Gender and Inscribed Epigram," provides the most up-to-date bibliography.

32 Plu., *Mor.* 748e–771e, esp. 749b.

33 Cic., *Verr.* 4.4.

34 Paus. 1.20,1.

35 Dio Cassius 59.29,2.

36 Paus. 9.27,3.

37 *IG* 7.1828, cf. Page, *Further Greek Epigrams* "Hadrian" 5, pp. 565–66, E. Bowie, "Hadrian and Greek poetry" in E. Ostenfeld (ed.), *Greek Romans and Roman Greeks* (Aarhus, 2002), 172–97, P. Goukowsky, "Sur un épigramme de Thespies" in J. Dion (ed.), *L'épigramme de l'Antiquité au XVIIe siècle ou du ciseau à la pointe* (Nancy, 2002), 217–46.

38 Though C. Vout might demur: "Antinous, Archaeology and History," *JRS* 95 (2005), 80–96.

39 Ovid, *Met.* 3.441.

40 So Robert, "Documents d'Asie Mineure," 441 n. 29, but also, of course, in this case, that of *Archer* Eros, son of Aphrodite.

41 Hesiod, *Theogony,* 120–22, cf. Schachter, *Cults of Boiotia* 1, 217 n. 1.

42 Schachter, *Cults of Boiotia* 1, 217, 218. The notoriously disputatious Thespians would not have responded well to such condescension.

43 Or the Sun to the Rhodians or Olympian Zeus to the Eleans, Ath. 13.561e; coinage: Hansen, *IACP,* 458.

44 Vernant, "One, Two, Three: Eros" is excellent on the connection between Narcissus, *Symposium* and Hesiod's primordial Eros, but Pausanias 9.27,2 is better at counting. Eros is not a "third" member of a trio, neat though that might be in theory. Plato has Phaedrus make the same mistake in *Smp.* 178b, quoting Hesiod, but inaccurately, missing out a line. One should by no means assume this was not deliberate on Plato's part. Phaedrus is not necessarily the cleverest of his symposiasts.

45 This may be what lies behind the myths that the primordial Eros was son of Night or of a primordial "Diana," i.e., the Moon.

46 Nonnus, *Dion.* 10.215–16 and 48.582–83. Perhaps Nonnus explains how Oscar Wilde got here before me: "Truth in art is not any correspondence between the essential idea and the accidental existence; it is not the resemblance of shape to shadow, or of the form mirrored in the crystal to the form itself; it is no echo coming from a hollow hill, any more than it is a silver well of water in the valley that shows the moon to the moon and Narcissus to Narcissus." *De Profundis.* Perhaps indeed the primordial Eros is the semicircular *base* on which the statues of Praxiteles, Aphrodite, Phryne etc. seem to have stood, a distinctive feature of Thespian architecture, apparently, as of its coins: Gutzwiller, "Gender and Inscribed Epigram," 387 n. 14.

47 "Infelix, quod non alter et alter eras," *Fasti* 5.226. Both the name Narcissus and that of his father, according to the "Euboean" tradition, Amarynthus, are pre-Greek words. Both the place Amarynthus and the heights of Helicon above Thespiae (the river "Lamos") were known, it seems, to the bureaucrats of Mycenaean Thebes, C. Piteros, J-P. Olivier, and J. L. Melena, "Les inscriptions en linéaire B des nodules de Thèbes (1982): la fouille, les documents, les possibilités d'interprétation," *BCH* 114 (1990) [103–84], 153–54.

48 Many have pointed out the connection between Hesiod's primordial Eros and the speech of Aristophanes in *Symposium,* a dialogue to which Hadrian too alludes with his "chaste Eros" breathing *charis* from "Heavenly Aphrodite," the speech that describes the origin of love as the slicing in half of four-legged humans, each half destined thereafter to seek out its other, Brisson, *Sexual Ambivalence,* pp. 72–114. One should also note that the starting point for Aristophanes' myth making is the Homeric myth of the terrible twins, the nine-year-olds Otus and Ephialtes, who are, of course, like Narcissus, one single person, an ephebe, eighteen years old, divided in half. What is not always noticed is that they are connected to the same site as Narcissus and primordial Eros; they were said to have been the first to offer cult to the Muses on Helicon and to have built Ascra, Hesiod's hometown, Paus. 9.29,1.

49 X., *Mem.* 2.6 esp. 28–33, Calame, *Poetics,* pp. 23–27.

50 Servius ad *Aen.* 4.520, R. V. Merrill, "Eros and Anteros," *Speculum,* 19 (1944), 265–84; curse, *per antherōtas:* a Latin curse in Greek letters from second century AD Hadrumentum (*Sousse*), Audollent, *Defixionum tabellae* 270,2 [*IGRR* 1.949.2].

51 Themistius, *Or.* 24. At the warm springs of Gadara in Syria, there were two adjacent springs smaller than the others and more beautiful. When the mystical neo-Platonist philosopher Iamblichus came here around AD 300 he asked the locals what the pools had been called in ancient times; one was Eros, he was told, the other Anteros. Then he spoke a few holy words standing on the edge of the pool and out popped Eros, a beautiful boy with white skin and golden hair, soaking wet. He did the same at the second pool and out popped Anteros, very similar but with dark hair flowing down, already drying in the sun. They clung to Iamblichus as if he were their natural father. After a while he put them back, Eunapius, *Lives of the Philosophers* 459. This is an allusion to the *Phaedrus*'s "spring" of Himeros, which drenches the one inspired by Eros, while merely wetting the beloved, creating in him an Anteros.

52 Cic., *De Nat Deorum,* 3.23.

53 *Smp.* 192b.

54 Thuc. 2.43,1.

55 *Suppliants* 1088.

56 *Peace* 191: *erastēs pragmatōn,* cf. Boyle, *Dr. Bentley's Dissertations,* pp. 65–66.

57 Paus. 9.26,5; cf. Schachter, *Cults of Boiotia* 3, pp. 152–53; I am not entirely sure on what grounds he thinks the *erastēs* Menestratus is also an ephebe.

58 Aelian, *N.A.* 4.1; for other such stories, see Ogden, "Homosexuality and warfare," 107–68.

59 *Phdr.* 237b.

60 *Lysis* 210e.

61 Aeschin. 1.139.

62 *An.* 2.6,28. Or indeed entered into a formal relationship with him that put his bearded friend in the role of *aïtas,* e.g., by giving him some armor decorated with his own symbol.

63 Dover, "Greek Homosexuality and Initiation," pp. 123–24.

64 *Iō erastēs eichen auton* 6.54,2.

65 *Hipparchus* 229cd.

66 *Phdr.* 279b, Suda s.v. (Pi 858). If Athenaeus is quoting the *ipsissima verba* of Ariston, the term *paidika* may already have needed explaining in the third century BC, Ariston fr. 17 Wehrli ap. Ath. 13.564e.

67 *Iliad* 18.80–2, Theog. 1315–16, 1367–68, cf. Calame, *Poetics* p. 28, X., *Smp.* 8.3.

68 Plato, *Lysis* 211e, Aeschin. 1.110, And., *On the Mysteries* 110 with MacDowell ad loc. Semonides 7.49, Ar., *Ecc.* 912.

69 *Matt.* 26.50.

70 Anthony T. Edwards, *Hesiod's Ascra* (Berkeley, 2004), p. 93. Hesiod uses both *hetairos* and *hetaros;* it is possible there is a difference in nuance, that you have one *hetairos,* "your partner," but can be *hetaros,* "associate," of many.

71 *Amare*—*amo, amas, amat*—the Latin equivalent of *eran,* has a direct object.

72 "A Syntactician," 92–93, cf. David Blank, "Analogy, Anomaly and Apollonius Dyscolus," in S. Everson (ed.), *Language* (Cambridge, 1994) [149–65], 161–62.

73 2.418–19.

74 Calame, *Poetics,* p. 22.

75 Plato, *Cra.* 420b; cf. Calame, *Poetics,* p. 21.

76 Herbert Weir Smyth, *A Greek Grammar for Colleges* (Cambridge, MA, 1920), #1349–50, cf. Raphael Kühner, rev. Bernhard Gerth, *Ausführliche Grammatik der griechischen Sprache* (Hanover and Leipzig, 1904), "Syntaxe des Einfachen Satzes," # 416 n. 9: "Die Begriffe a) der hastigen Bewegung, des Zielens und Strebens nach etwas, b) des Verlangens und Sehnens nach etwas." Note that "to be in an amatory condition as regards someone" *erōtikōs echein, erōtikōs diakeisthai,* also takes genitive, for English, cf. Gildersleeve, "A Syntactician," 93.

77 *Hiero* 1.30, so since anything and everything is "ready to hand" for dictators, they cannot properly experience the delights of love.

78 Vernant, "One, Two, Three: Eros."

79 *Eumenides* 851–52.

80 See, e.g., Lysias 3, Hyp., *Ath.*

81 Isaeus 10.25.

82 Sosicrates, *FGrHist* 461 F7 ap Ath. 13.561e.

83 *Smp.* 192b.

84 X., *Mem.* 3.11, 9–10, *Cyr.* 6.1,32; cf. Calame, *Poetics,* pp. 39–43, Meier, "Päderastie," 153 n. 44, Vattuone, *Il Mostro e Il Sapiente,* pp. 197–223.

85 X., *Mem.* 3.11,10.

86 Solon fr. 25.

87 Schofield, *Stoic Idea of the City,* pp. 28–31, Cic., *Tusc.* 4.70.

88 Konstan, *Friendship* manages to exclude relationships based on *erōs* from his book, arguing that although *philia, philein* and *philos* (adjectival "dear") can be used of sexual amorous relationships, *philos* as a substantive noun does indeed mean something equivalent to our "friend" (p. 9), despite what everyone had concluded, and even that there is a "sharp distinction between amorous and amicable ties" (p. 6), but Plato uses "becoming friends" to gloss *erōtikōs charizesthai,* "amorous favoring," in *Smp.* 183c, and the "friends" of the courtesan Theodote, or the sexual friends of Critobulus (X., *Mem.* 3.11,4 and 15; 2.6,28–33) are all perfectly "amorous" or, better, "amatory." Elsewhere Konstan concedes that the sharply distinct entities do indeed "bleed into each other," "Friends and Lovers," 11, but even there he does not seem to take fully into account the fact that the relationship between his prime example of "friends" as opposed to "lovers" is described as an *erōs* by his source, Lucian, *Toxaris* 7.

89 See Faraone, *Ancient Greek Love Magic,* passim, though his premises are flawed.

90 *Phdr.* 241d, using Rowe's edition.

91 *Smp.* 181be, 182c. Plu., *Pelopidas* 18.2.

92 *Topics* 146a, *Prior Analytics* 68ab, cf. Price, *Love and Friendship,* appx 4., esp. pp. 238–39.

93 *Lac.* 12.

94 *Cyr.* 4.1.10, demonstrating, in contradiction to Apollonius Dyscolus, that you can choose with whom to fall in love. For the impossibility of asexual *erōs* for a woman, or a Boy under Eighteen, see Plato, *Smp.* 181b.

95 It seems that the claim that *erōs* for boys was nonsexual had become a cliché by the time of Plutarch albeit a claim few believed, cf. *Amatorius* (*Mor.*) 752a: "This Love denies pleasure . . . but when night falls and all is quiet . . ."

96 "I shall use the terms 'Greek Love,' understanding thereby a passionate and enthusiastic attachment subsisting between man and youth, recognized by society and protected by opinion, which, though it was not free from sensuality, did not degenerate into mere licentiousness." Symonds, *A Problem in Greek Ethics,* p. 19. Of course it depends what you mean by "sensuality" and "licentiousness."

97 Plu., *Mor.* 759e, C. Calame, "Eros inventore e organizzatore della società greca antica" in Calame (ed.), *L'amore in Grecia* (Rome/Bari, 1988) [IX–XL], XXXV.

98 *An.* 2.6,28.

2: Grace, Sex and Favors

1 The starting point for discussions about this central idea is MacLachlan, *Age of Grace.* For its less exalted uses in Athenian politics and society, where it implies either "due return" or "due return plus," see Paul Millett, *Lending and Borrow-*

ing in Ancient Athens (Cambridge, 1991), pp. 123–26. As to the word's origins, Chantraine, *Dictionnaire* s.v. *"charis"* thinks it *has to be* derived from the verb *chairō*: "enjoy," that it is very old and must be linked to a root recoverable in Armenian (and no other Indo-European language), which gives *jirk* "gift, grace" and *jri* "for free"; as to any core or original meaning, he adduces, without sanctioning, Beneviste's "pleasing, agreeableness [*agreement*], favor." Future philologists may be able to improve upon this.

2 Luke 1.28.

3 MacLachlan, *Age of Grace,* p. 149.

4 See the articles in Gill, Postlethwaite and Seaford, *Reciprocity in Ancient Greece* (Oxford, 1998), by Parker, "Pleasing Thighs," esp. 108–109, and Jan-Maarten Bremer, "Giving and Thanksgiving in Greek Religion," 127–37.

5 Wheler, *A Journey into Greece,* p. 469.

6 Or "on top of him," 9.38,1, MacLachlan, *The Age of Grace,* pp. 41–55, cf. Schachter, *Cults of Boiotia* 1, pp. 140–44. Pausanias wonders how the Graces went from rocks to clothed to naked, a central passage for any understanding of *types*.

7 The *OED* s.v. "graceless" 1b does not quite get this point.

8 Empedocles fr. B116 ap. Plu., *Mor.* 745D.

9 Arist., *Nicomachean Ethics* 1332b.

10 *Rhet.* 2.7.1385ab.

11 ll.105–12, 955–56.

12 Preisendanz and Henrichs, *Papyri Graecae Magicae* 12.270–80, translation after M. Smith.

13 Pindar, *Ol.* 6.76, MacLachlan, *Age of Grace,* pp. 87–123, the longest of her chapters.

14 Pindar fr. 123.13–15, Anacreon 395.3, *Od.* 10.279–80, Sappho fr. 138, cf. Aelian, *VH* 12.41: Protogenes spent seven years on his painting of the founding hero Ialysus. Apelles was at a loss for words. Then he looked more closely; "The work lacks *charis*," he said. The film *Zoolander* perfectly satirizes the ineffableness of this precisely imprecise quality in a person, providing one of few Hollywood jokes that might have had Socrates rolling in the aisles.

15 *Theog.* 1319–22. From the "pederastic coda" (ll. 1231–1389), an anthology of seventh–fifth-century Elegies.

16 *Cheia de graça* is the second line of the Portuguese "Ave Maria" translating *gratia plena,* which in turn translates Luke's *charitōmenē.*

17 The original lyrics are those of Vinicius de Moraes; cf. Brown, "Chopin came from Ipanema" with Gimbel's response, *TLS* Letters August 15, 2003.

18 Pindar, *Ol.* 10.93–94.

19 Brown, op. cit.

20 Plato, *Smp.* 181b.

21 *Theog,* 1263–66. A classical Greek would certainly smile at the irony, surmising that "bare-faced cheek" (literally "utter shamelessness") is exactly what the

poet would like from his beneficiary, but I doubt the poet intended such irony. A sense of shame is precisely the quality that would prevent someone receiving gifts they had no intention of ever paying back. Grace is itself *aidoia* (full of a sense of shame), Pindar, *Ol.* 6.76, MacLachlan, *Age of Grace*, pp. 109–10.

22 Theog. 1367–68.

23 Stobaeus 10.38.

24 Robert, Documents d'Asie Mineure, 441, n. 29.

25 *IG* XIV 2424.

26 Ar., *Knights* 517.

27 Ant. Lib. 41.6–7.

28 *Phdr.* 256a.

29 Pindar fr. 127, the last two lines are: "Do not, my heart, pursue action (*praxis*), older than the number of years."

30 *Cyr.* 5.1,18.

31 6.1,31–32.

32 *Mem.* 3.11,10.

33 183c, 184c.

34 *Mor.* 751cd. The shock of "forced favor" may be deliberate, an oxymoron or at least heavily sarcastic. Currently we lack the context. It might turn up.

35 *Rhet.* 2.7.1385ab.

36 Archilochus fr. 327.

37 Petronius chs 85–87.

38 Cf. *Courtesans and Fishcakes*, p. 177: barking up the wrong tree.

39 Suda s.v. "Euathlous Deka" (Epsilon 3367), cf. Ar., *Ach.* 705, 710, fr. 424 K-A, D. Rosenbloom, "From *Ponēros* to *Pharmakos*," *Class Ant* 21 (2002) [283–346], 295 n. 48.

40 *Ach.* 713–18.

41 Ar. fr. 424 K-A, *Thesm.* 200–201, *Frogs* 238, *Knights* 719–21; cf. esp. Hunter ad Eubulus 107 K on the arsehole Callistratus.

42 *Clouds* 1089–1094.

43 Milne and von Bothmer, "*Katapugōn, Katapugaina*," 221: "not as crass as *katapugōn*."

44 Suda (Iota 759), s.v. "*iunx*."

45 Hunter, *Theocritus and the Archaeology of Greek Poetry*, pp. 78–79. Such a characterization of Sotades is just asking to be knocked down; until then let's enjoy it.

46 One is referred to as *mousikos*, a performer, another was accused of raping a woman, Dominic Montserrat, *Sex and Society in Graeco-Roman Egypt* (London, 1996), p. 117; cf. Sandy, "*Scaenica Petroniana*," 340 n. 25.

47 Pollux 6.126–27, Suda (Kappa 1635) s.v. "*kinaidos*" (Epsilon 1834) s.v. *exōlēs* (Gamma 494) s.v. "*gunandros*" (Alpha 885) s.v. "*akinaidos*."

48 A composite of various physiognomists each adding to the others' descriptions, translation after Tamsyn Barton, *Power and Knowledge* (Ann Arbor, 2002), p. 117, and Gleason, "Semiotics of Gender," 395.

49 D.L. 7.173.

50 Tamsyn Barton, *Ancient Astrology* (London, 1994), pp. 163–64.

51 *Praep. Evang.* 6.10,27, cf. Shaw, "Ritual brotherhood," 335.

52 Gleason, "Semiotics of Gender," p. 397.

53 Notably Robert Dyer at the Suda website (December 16, 2001): "He treated him comically as a gay . . ." *hōs kinaidos* s.v. "Kubele" (Kappa 2586).

54 Plato, *Gorgias* 493a–494e.

55 A loose, but not that loose, translation. The meter is Sotadean. For something similar also in Sotadean meter, cf. the fragments of *Iolaus,* with P. J. Parsons's comments *POxy* 3010 = 42 (1974) [34–41], p. 34.

56 Cc 21 and 23–24.

57 Plu., *Mor.* 126a and 705e.

58 Formerly, Munich Coll. P. Arndt, M. Rostovtzeff, *Social and Economic History of the Hellenistic World* (Oxford 1941), I, pp. 176–77, pl. xxv.

59 Suda (Mu 1360) s.v. "*moichos.*"

60 Phylarchus, *FGrHist* 81 F 45 ap. Ath. 12.521b.

61 A similar process is believed to have produced the word for "companion," *hetairos,* from the archaic *hetaros* via *hetaira,* Chantraine *Dictionnaire* s.v. "*hetairos.*" He compares *chimaros/chimaira,* "goat." *Kinados,* which also appears in names as Kinadēs and Kinadōn, may carry some of the same connotations as *kinaidos,* cf. esp. Theocritus 5.25, where Lakon addresses Comatas (who recently buggered him) as "*kinados.*" Of course copyists sometimes confused the two words; cf. J. D. Morgan "Marikas," *CQ* 36 (1986), 529–31.

62 Chantraine, *Dictionnaire* s.v. "*kinaidos*" cites *Etymologicum Gudianum* 322,13 "*para to kineisthai tēn aidō ē para to kineisthai ta aidoia,*" but notes the problem that the iota in *kineō* is long, whereas in *kinaidos* it is short. That does not seem to have prevented the ancient etymologist, however, and it wouldn't be the first time in the history of the language that a vowel was shortened before a diphthong; cf., e.g., *Kuthereia* from *Kuthērē.*

63 Rostovtzeff, "Two Homeric Bowls," 90, cf. Ulrich Sinn, *Die Homerischen Becher* (Berlin, 1979) nos. 64–67, pp. 117–20, M. Rostovtzeff, *Social and Economic History of the Hellenistic World* (Oxford, 1941) vol. I, pp. 176–77, Sandy, "*Scaenica Petroniana,*" 340.

64 Suda (Alpha 885) s.v. "*akinaidos*": *ho mē kinōn ta aidoia.*

65 Ar., *Birds* 137–42.

66 Aeschin. 1.131 with Fisher ad loc.

67 1.171.

68 3.162.

69 Fisher ad Aeschines 1.131 makes the same connection between the sexual insults and the charge of seducing boys. Demosthenes may also have been alleged to have been "impure with his mouth," like Petronius's *cinaedus.* If *moichoi* and *kinaidoi* are already viewed as similar types, the one seducing women, the other boys, it might assist in explaining Pausanias's argument that boy-seducers

should be treated in exactly the same painful way as adulterers, Plato, *Smp.* 182a.

70 Bain, "Six Greek Verbs," 67 n. 120, M. Lombardo, "Il graffito," *La Parola del Passato* 40 (1985), 294–307, Milne and von Bothmer, "*Katapugōn, Katapugaina,*" 215–24.

71 776, 137.

72 Ar. fr. 128 K-A.

73 Milne and von Bothmer, "*Katapugōn, Katapugaina,*" 217.

74 The most comprehensive collection of graffiti is Lombardo, op. cit.

75 Lang, *Graffiti and Dipinti,* pp. 11–15, C19, C22, C26, with Milne and von Bothmer "*Katapugōn, Katapugaina,*" 220 no. 6. The graffiti concerning Alcaeus and Sosias come from a well deposit in the agora, with rubbish from some kind of state-sponsored dining room possibly that of the archons and their secretaries. They have been carefully analyzed by Steiner, "Private and Public," who concludes they come from a mock ostracism *c.*460 BC, cf. especially 360: ". . . the *repetition* of names, possibly at one event, suggests repartee that might include incremental 'one-upmanship': 'Alkaios is *kalos!*' 'No! Alkaios is *katapugon!*' 'Who says so?' 'The writer!' "

76 Stefan Brenne, "Ostraka and the process of Ostrakophoria," in W. D. E. Coulson, O. Palagia, T. L. Shear, Jr., H. A. Shapiro, F. J. Frost (eds.), *The Archaeology of Athens and Attica under the Democracy* (Oxford, 1994) [13–24], pp. 13–15.

77 Brenne, *ibid.,* p. 14: "It accuses Themistocles of lewdness or more concretely of being presumably the passive partner in practicing anal homosexuality."

78 Idomeneus of Lampsacus, *FGrHist* 338 F4, ap. Ath. 13.576c, 12 533d.

79 *LSJ* s.v. "*katakardios.*"

80 639–40.

81 D.L. 6.34.

82 Pollux 2.184, 6.126.

83 Timaeus, *FGrHist* 566 fr.124b.

84 Dover, "Eros and Nomos," 33–34.

85 The Beroea gymnasium inscription, *SEG* 27.261, 1.29. For some reason this is normally translated "if he is a pederast," cf. Austin, *Hellenistic World,* #118 l. 29, or as a ban on "homosexuals"—perhaps just wishful thinking on the part of sports historians, cf. Scanlon, *Eros,* pp. 214, 407 n. 54.

86 It is possible he occupied some post other than governor. For Timarchus's career, see Fisher (ed.), *Aeschines: Against Timarchos,* pp. 20–24 and 244–47. For the trial: pp. 1–8.

3: Age-Classes, Love-Rules and Corrupting the Young

1 Antiphon, *Tetralogies* 2.1, 1; 2.2,3–7.

2 Aeschin. 1.11.

3 Lysias 3.4.

4 1.139.

5 *SEG* 27.261 B ll. 13–15.

6 For more on age-classes, see Davidson, "Revolutions in Human Time."

7 W. K. C. Guthrie's translation of Plato, *Protagoras* 315d (Harmondsworth, 1956), p. 46; Dover, *Greek Homosexuality,* p. 84, Barry Strauss, *Fathers and Sons* (London, 1993), p. 94; Todd, *Lysias,* p. 42 n. 2, Anthony J. Podlecki, *Perikles and his Circle* (London, 1998), p. 35, Hammond, *Macedonian State,* p. 56; Heckel, *Marshals,* p. 242.

8 Plato, *Lysis* 207bc.

9 Thuc. 5.43,2.

10 Plato *Smp.* 181ce.

11 Étienne Bernand, *Inscriptions métriques de l'Égypte gréco-romaine* (Paris, 1969), #79: *neon te kai artigeneion eonta.*

12 Lucian, *On Sacrifices* 11.

13 Cf., e.g., Tim G. Parkin, *Old Age in the Roman World: A Cultural and Social History* (Baltimore, 2003), pp. 31–35.

14 Hannah, *Greek and Roman Calendars,* presents the most accessible and up-to-date introduction to what can be an extremely complicated and disputatious field.

15 2.2,1.

16 Cf. E. Poste, "Age Eponumoi at Athens," *CR* 10 (1896), 4–6.

17 Philochorus, *FGrHist* 328 F 121.

18 Aeschin. 2.168, Etym. Magn. 369,15, cf. Suda s.v. *"Strateia en tois epōnymois"* = Sigma 1165. Ch. Habicht, "Neue Inschriften aus dem Kerameikos," *AM* 76 (1961) [127–48], 145–46 suggests the year-heroes are identical to the "heroes of the *lēxeis.*" Historians tend to accept that Eighteen was always the age of citizenship and, if they think about it, also accept there were age-sets (or "age-classes"), but some have suggested to me in discussion that the year-heroes, certainly in place by 366 BC (M. Christ, "Conscription of Hoplites in Classical Athens," *CQ* 51 (2001) [398–422], esp. 416), were a fourth-century invention, which means that there wouldn't have been even one cycle on whitened boards before the bronze tablets were substituted. That forty-two heroes could be selected at so late a date and their cults reorganized without us knowing about it seems highly unlikely however, and it is inconsistent to accept *Ath. Pol.'s* information about the process of coming-of-age as dating back to the origins of the democracy while rejecting the year-heroes. They must be more ancient, probably much more ancient.

19 1.49. Greek counting is difficult. I cannot guarantee that "in the sixtieth year" means fifty-nine, while "having the forty-fifth year" means forty-five.

20 Ar., *Wasps* 578, cf. Todd, *Shape of Athenian Law,* p. 180 n. 23.

21 The thirteenth-century *Sachsenspiegel, Landrecht* I, art. 42,1.

22 Cf. S. Simonse, "Age, conflict and power in the 'monyomiji' age systems" in E. Kurimoto and S. Simonse (eds), *Conflict, Age and Power in North East Africa: Age Systems in Transition* (Oxford, 1998) [51–78], p. 65.

23 X., *Mem.* 1.2,35.

24 Arr., *An.* 4.13,1.

25 *Lyc.* 17.3, Kennell, *Gymnasium of Virtue,* p. 36.

26 237b.

27 181ce.

28 Dio Cassius 48.34,3.

29 Herbert Moller, "The Accelerated Development of Youth: Beard Growth as a Biological Marker," *Comparative Studies in History and Society* 29 (1987), 748–62; Steve Jones, *Y: The Descent of Men* (London, 2002), pp. 72–73. It is hard to be more precise at the moment about where the Greeks and Romans should be placed on a puberty graph of premodern populations. Other evidence about nutrition levels, e.g., calculations of average height from measurements of skeletons, indicates that the people of Pompeii, say, may have been slightly better nourished than, say, the early twentieth-century inhabitants of the Bay of Naples: Peter Garnsey, *Food and Society in Classical Antiquity* (Cambridge, 1999), p. 58. The staples of the ancient Mediterranean diet, wheat and barley, are more nutritious grains than, say, rice and maize and the fact that meat was almost always consumed at big communal sacrifices must have meant that protein was more evenly shared out. But judging from height, there seems to have been significant variation in nutrition levels, and therefore, probably, in age at puberty, from place to place. For what it's worth, classical Athenian citizens were probably better fed than most, because they were "more religious," i.e., they had bigger and more frequent sacrifices. Beards are also of course *ethnically* marked. There is a great "Barbigerous Crescent" that runs from northwest Europe to western Asia, from hairy Scotsmen to hairy Bengalis via hairy Arabs, which has produced some of the most spectacular facial growths in the world, probably thanks to intense sexual selection on the part of females at a crucial point in history, a genetic inheritance that Western anthropologists have not always been hesitant about exploiting when they travel to barbatulous parts of the world, discovering that their status as a man increases in inverse proportion to the number of times they shave.

30 Arist., *H. A.* 581a and 582a says puberty hits *after* fourteen, or in the third "week" of life, and the beard appears at twenty-one, at the start of the fourth. He cannot be saying that pubic hair appears "at fourteen" and a beard seven years later, unless he is being unusually unobservant or Procrustean.

31 Lucian, *On Sacrifices* 11.

32 Ferrari, *Figures of Speech,* pp. 132–38.

33 Athens Nat. Mus. 10426, for the ephebic grade-hero Neanias; cf. Despoina Tsiafaki, *LIMC* Suppl. s.v. "Neanias I/II."

34 Boston 95.28, *BA* #205036, cf. Davidson, "Revolutions," 56–57 and 65–67.

35 Arist., *H.A.* 7.581a, quoting the Pythagorean Alcmaeon of Croton (fifth century).

36 Ferrari, *Figures of Speech,* p. 124, Plato, *Prot.* 315d, *Charm.* 498b.

37 X., *Hell.* 5.4,25.

38 1.39.

39 Suda s.v. "Ibycus" (Iota 80).

40 *Tusc.* 4.71.

41 *De Re Publica* 4.4.

42 *Or.* 20.8. I am not quite sure where Maximus, a reader of Plato, who condemned the licensed *pleasure* of the Cretans has got the idea that it is shameful for a *neaniskos* to touch the boy.

43 Plato, *Charm.* 155a.

44 *Lysis* 203ab, 206d. Socrates is *gerōn anēr,* 223b.

45 Herbert Musurillo, *Acts of the Pagan Martyrs* (Oxford, 1954), VII *Acta Maximi,* ll. 49–59. Interesting to note here that the distinction between *erastēs* and *erōmenos* seems to have been lost (perhaps in translation from Latin); "they were *erastai*" seems to mean "they were lovers," 1.62.

46 The Pisander-scholium ad E. *Phoenissae* 1760 [*FGrHist* 16 F 10].

47 Unfortunately Hupperts' massive University of Amsterdam thesis *Eros Dikaios* (2000) was published only in Holland (and in Dutch), with postscripts summarizing his conclusions in English: ". . . a lot of vase paintings show youths, of equal age, involved in a seduction scene, or even grown-up men courting each other. Particularly red-figure vase paintings [from *c.*520 BC onward] show youths of the same age in a courting scene (one-third of all courtship scenes bear upon this category of lovers)" (I, p. 383). I am not convinced by all his examples, printed in a separate volume of plates, but there are plenty that are cogent enough, cf. id. "Greek Love."

48 Theopompus fr. 30: "*Par' emoi ta lian meirakia charizetai tois hēlikiōtais.*"

49 Does it mean "young Striplings" like saying someone was "very much a boy" or "those too typically Striplings," i.e., "flirtatious," "coquettish," as we might say someone was "too much of a teenager"? What it probably cannot mean, however, is "those who have *too long* been youths"—"in other words men who have shaved their beards to continue looking young even after reaching a mature age," as Hubbard renders it, *Homosexuality in Greece and Rome,* p. 114 with footnote.

50 Cf. Davidson, "Revolutions in Human Time," p. 50 n. 95.

51 *Smp.* 4.23–26.

52 *Mem.* 1.3, 8–13, cf. Davidson loc. ct.

53 X., *Smp.* 4.21–22.

54 Aeschin. 1.42.

55 Plato, *Phdr.* 227cd.

56 Plato, *Charm.* 154c.

57 X., *An.* 2.6,28, *Smp.* 4.28, Lysias 14.25.

58 Ar., *Frogs* 1096 with Dover ad loc. On torch races, Scanlon, *Eros,* pp. 255–59, Parker, *Polytheism,* p. 472.

59 Vlastos, *Socrates,* p. 246 n. 36.

60 180a.

61 Arist., *Pol.* 1311a 1332b.

62 Polybius 4.53.3–55.6, with Walbank, *Commentary* ad loc, *IC* IV, 162–63, F. Halbherr, "Cretan Expedition III. Epigraphical Researches in Gortyna," *AJA* 1.3 (1897) [159–238], 191–98 (nos. 19–20). Plato seems to allude to other classical age-class conflicts in his brief allusion to the involvement in civil wars of "the boys of Miletus, Boeotia and Thurii" in *Laws* 636b.

63 *IC* I ix 1, Austin, *Hellenistic World,* no. 91.

64 3.3,2 and .4,2.

65 Ar., *Ach.* 716.

66 The most straightforward recent discussion is Kato, "The *Apology.*"

67 Parker, *Athenian Religion,* p. 199.

68 Plato, *Apology* 24bc, X., *Mem.* 1.1.1, Parker, ibid., pp. 199, 201.

69 Parker, ibid., p. 201: "The official charge ran 'Socrates does wrong by not acknowledging the gods the city acknowledges, and introducing other new powers' "; Todd, *Shape of Athenian Law,* p. 309 with n. 23: "the indictment in what was a *graphē asebeias* [indictment for impiety] specifically mentioned 'corrupting the young' (that is his activity as a teacher) as one example of his impiety.—[n.] . . . The charge of corrupting, in other words, is seen not as a consequence of his impiety, but as one of two manifestations of it"; D. Cohen, *Law Violence and Community* (Cambridge, 1995), pp. 189–90 and 192: "There was no objection to including a charge of 'corrupting the young' in a prosecution for impiety despite the fact that the statute on impiety in no way suggested that such behavior fell within its scope."

70 Aeschin. 1.7–8.

71 Aeschin. 1.173, 170.

72 1.43. Dover thinks the accusers "were bluffing," *Greek Homosexuality,* p. 34, on no good grounds. Aeschines certainly doesn't seem to think his audience will see it that way, which is the only point.

73 Satyrus ap. Ath. 13.584a.

74 X., *Smp.* 4.53.

75 Suda s.v. "*Prodikos*" (= Pi 2365). Execution through being forced to drink hemlock was an innovation of the later fifth century associated especially with the oligarchic regime of Critias and the Thirty, cf. Danielle Allen, *The World of Prometheus* (Princeton, 2000), pp. 232–37.

76 *Apology* 24bc, *Euthyphro* 2c, 3a.

77 *Mem* 1.1.1 but cf. X., *Apol* 10.

78 *Mem* 1.2,2.

79 X., *Apol.* 19–20.

80 *Apol.* 21.

81 *Mem* 1.2,9 and 12.

82 *Mem* 1.2,48.

83 *Mem.* 1.2,64. What other contrast might Xenophon be drawing between the

two parts of the indictment, between what Meletus "had written in the *graphē*"—*egegrapto*—and what "he actually accused him of"—*ēitiato*? What other purpose does it serve to put the emphatic particle *dē*—"in actual fact"— mid-sentence?

84 Lysias 7 and 16.18.

85 *Mem.* 1.2,31 and 34.

86 J. H. Driberg, "The 'Best Friend' among the Didinga," *Man* 35 (1935), #110, 101–102.

87 Graham, *Performing Dreams*, pp. 176–77, citing A. Lopes da Silva, *Nomes e Amigos* (São Paolo, 1986).

88 Aeschin. 1.111 with Fisher ad 68.

89 Maybury-Lewis, *Akwe-Shavante Society*, pp. 138–42.

90 Hdt. 7. 208–9,1.

PART II: SODOMANIA
4: SEXING UP THE GREEKS

1 Dover (ed.), Plato, *Symposium*, p. 3.

2 Dover, "Eros and Nomos," 33; "Classical Greek Attitudes," 67; Foucault, *Use of Pleasure*, pp. 209, 223, 269 n. 21.

3 Dover rev. of E. Cantarella, *Bisexuality in the Ancient World*, CR 44 (1994), 140.

4 Burkert, *Structure and History*, p. 29, Gregory Nagy, *Pindar's Homer* (rev. edn. Baltimore, 1994), p. 130, Bremmer, "An Enigmatic Indo-European Rite," 287, Halperin, *One Hundred Years*, p. 58. It isn't entirely clear to me if these authors think Ephorus is telling them his esteemed Cretans raped boys or if they just know that's what happened, even if Ephorus was trying to hide the fact from them.

5 Burkert, *Homo Necans*, p. 58.

6 Arist., *Politics* 1311b on Hellanocrates of Larissa.

7 Foucault, *History of Sexuality*, I, *Introduction*, pp. 7–8, 59.

8 Ludwig, *Eros and Polis*, p. 147. Ludwig carefully goes over almost every reference to *erōs*-words, in exemplary fashion, showing how *erōs* is not essentially sexual, but even he falls for it at the last fence and all his careful work is of no avail.

9 Monoson, "Citizen as Erastes," 255, 257, 259, 260.

10 Neer, *Style and Politics*, p. 249 n. 103.

11 Bentley, *A dissertation*, XIII, p. 53, cf. Bray, *Homosexuality in Renaissance England*, ch. 4, esp. pp. 91–92.

12 DeJean, "Sex and Philology," 148.

13 "*Man hat der Historie das Amt, die Vergangenheit zu richten, die Mitwelt zum Nutzen zukünftiger Jahre zu belehren, beigemessen: so hoher Ämter unterwindet sich gegenwärtiger Versuch nicht: er will bloß zeigen, wie es eigentlich gewesen.*" Leopold von

Ranke, *Geschichten der romanischen und germanischen Völker von 1494 bis 1514,*
[1824] (2nd edn, Leipzig, 1874), p. vii. On Ranke, see R. J. Evans, *In Defence of
History* (London, 1997), pp. 16–23. Commentators have perhaps placed too
much weight on the word *eigentlich* in this famous final phrase, which, in context, requires no corresponding English word to convey the sense. Most often
it is translated ". . . show as it *actually* ["*truly*" or "*really*"] happened [or was],"
as if Ranke is laying claim to the last word, a final inflexible truth on the subject. Scholars of German philosophy, on the other hand, prefer ". . . show as it
essentially was," as if Ranke was laying claim to some kernel of historical
essence or "inner being." This too seems to underplay Ranke's rhetoric of
nonchalance here, perhaps, then, ". . . as it was in its bare essentials" is better
or "as it, essentially, was." The basic idea seems to be that of a historian simply
presenting what he finds to the public, without making any claims as to its importance, its relevance or its finality: There you go, an attempt at a piece of
history presented *au naturel,* unencumbered by any exemplary moral or didac-
tic positioning. Such a posture begs many questions, of course, and Ranke's
rhetoric should not be taken at face value. False modesty became a staple of
nineteenth-century scholarship, despite Mommsen's rebuke: "We are not
modest by any means and do not wish it to be thought of us," Acton, "German
Schools of History," 30. Note also the beauty of Ranke's prose.

14 By "boys" Meier meant *meirakia,* which he thought were boys fifteen and over,
about three years too young, chronologically speaking. Of course, the classicists did not need Ranke to teach them about objectivity. Already in 1816, Wel-
cker had written *Sappho Freed from Prevailing Prejudice;* for the whole
background, see DeJean's important article on "Sex and Philology."

15 Meier, "Päderastie," 149 col. 2: "Wir wollen Wahrheit und nichts als Wahrheit."

16 Ibid., 153 col. 1.

17 J. F. Killeen responded in a short article published in *The Classical Quarterly.*
After a review of the opinions of Körte, Beare and Quadlbauer on the subject
of the comedy phallus he notes that it would have been difficult for an ancient
costumier to stitch a large stuffed leather phallus onto a costume in such a
way that it didn't dangle somewhat. Aristophanes' innovation, according to
this theory, was to put on stage a comic actor who was not *membrosior aequo*
"more than equally bemembered," Killeen, "The Comic Costume," 52–54,
citing *Carmina Priapea* 1.5, but cf. Taplin, *Comic Angels,* p. 102: "There must be
well over 300 phalluses on the vases to date, and of these either one or none is
erect . . ." The "dangle" may be a red herring. The word *katheimenon,* which
Dover translates "hanging down," means more properly "let drop," or "un-
furled," used of a ship's mast being taken down, of a cascading beard or of hair
being loosened.

18 E.g., Sommerstein ad 539: "i.e., circumcised." The "chopped-off" is from Horace, *Sat.* 1.9.70.

19 *Marginal Comment,* pp. 20–21, cf. p. 31 on his detestation of the Nazis: "If they

had declared infant circumcision illegal, brushing aside 'religious reasons' as a contradiction in terms, I would have thought them truly civilized. But they persecuted people whose parents had adhered to the Jewish religion, and it seemed to me irrational to the point of insanity to hurt any individual for somebody else's choices," and p. 1, "What interests me most when I contemplate my own life is the interaction of the personal and the professional."

20 Taplin's suggestion in "Phallology, *phlyakes,*" retracted in *Comic Angels,* p. 103.

21 Few reviewers missed the note, which Bernard Knox, "The Socratic Method," saw as "a new standard of liveliness in the exegesis of classical Greek texts"; cf. Charles Segal, *AJP* 92 (1971), 101, Colin Austin, *CR* 20 (1970), 19; Dover, typically, was unrepentant, *Greek Homosexuality,* p. 125 n. 1.

22 Henderson, *Maculate Muse,* p. 145 n. 194, a book that is not otherwise prudish in the discovery of sexual innuendo, with the review of Hugh Lloyd-Jones, *Class Phil* 71 (1976), 358.

23 MacDowell ad *Wasps* 592, *Clouds* 1083–98, Henderson, *Maculate Muse,* p. 210, Suda s.v. "*Euathlous deka.*"

24 S. Goldhill, *Class Phil* 90 (1995), p. 86, Foucault, "Des caresses d'hommes considérées comme un art," *Dits et Écrits* IV # 314, 316.

25 *Marginal Comment,* p. 114.

26 Knox, "The Socratic Method."

27 *AJP* 101 (1980), 123.

28 Cf. Kilmer, *Greek Erotica,* p. 15, Dover, "Classical Greek Attitudes," 66, *Greek Homosexuality,* p. 100 n. 81, caption to C19.

29 Ar., *Knights,* 638–42, Thornton, *Eros,* p. 111.

30 Dover, *Greek Homosexuality,* p. 91.

31 Ar., *Knights* 424, 484, cf. Dover, *Greek Homosexuality,* p. 98, plate B634 [= Berlin 1798].

32 Aulus Gellius, *Noctes Atticae* 18.3,1.

33 *Marginal Comment,* p. 111; in fact, judging from his own publications, this realization seems to have come rather later and to have dawned more gradually than Dover remembers: Davidson, "Dover, Foucault," 7–8.

34 Dover, *Greek Homosexuality,* pp. 33, 100, 104.

35 J. Boardman, *JHS* 100 (1980), 245.

36 Desmond Morris, *The Human Zoo* (London, 1969), p. 114.

37 *Greek Homosexuality,* p. 36 n. 18.

38 It may be that it is the mere "obscenity" of the word "fuck" that allowed it to substitute for damn, "Damn you!" simply as another forbidden word "violently" invading discourse in "extreme" and "aggressive" situations, and it was only as a consequence of its place in discourse that its referent, i.e., sex, came to be seen as itself a violent and aggressive act.

39 Parker, *Miasma,* pp. 99–100 with refs. at n. 101, cf. Veyne, "Famille et l'amour," 53.

40 *Marginal Comment,* p. 113, *Greek Homosexuality,* pp. 16, 43.

5: Sex Versus Homosexuality

1 Interviewed by Rick Fulton, *Daily Record,* July 16, 2004.

2 Wilde, *The Complete Letters,* pp. 656–57 with editors' notes, Halperin, *One Hundred Years,* pp. 34–35, 45, 49, 51–53, rev. by Dover, *CR* 41 (1991), 161–62.

3 *Greek Homosexuality,* pp. 59, 91.

4 *Marginal Comment,* pp. 122–24, 17–19.

5 Dover, *Marginal Comment,* p. 114, Dover ad *Symposium,* p. 5.

6 Devereux, "Greek Pseudo-Homosexuality," esp. 69, 70, 72, "The Nature of Sappho's Seizure," esp. 22, 25, 30, Dover, *Marginal Comment,* p. 123.

7 Dover ad *Smp.* 184a, 192a.

8 Ephorus, *FGrHist* 70 F 149, Strabo 10.4,21.

9 Boswell, *Marriage of Likeness,* pp. 88–91. Link, *Kreta,* pp. 24–28, gets there with little problem and may actually be playing *erōs* down too much in favor of socioeconomic significance. Gehrke, on the other hand, still has to inch his way past the imaginary sodomy of the ceremony and all the humiliation it would have entailed had it taken place, "Gewalt and Gesetz," 33: "*Am Anfang steht . . . die nackte Gewalt . . . Anderseits kann aber die homosexuelle Verbindung die Solidarität in der Gruppe fördern . . .*"

10 Cartledge, "Politics of Spartan Pederasty," 17–36, esp. 30.

11 West, *Homosexuality,* pp. 177–78, 180; see also ch. 11, "Prevention."

12 Aldrich, *Seduction,* ch. 6, esp. pp. 166, 177–78, 183. For Housman's gondolier, pp. 85–86. Accounts of sex and sexuality in early modern Britain often look very similar to what people found in the Mediterranean in the last couple of centuries, probably because the oppression was constructed in a similar fashion.

6: Language as a Mirror of the World

1 Boas, "Alternating Sounds," 50–53.

2 Sapir, *Language,* p. 23.

3 Sapir, "Language and Environment," 226–29, 238–39, "The Status of Linguistics," 209–10.

4 Whorf, *Language, Thought and Reality,* pp. 21, 57–58, 85, 252.

5 Martin, " 'Eskimo words for snow.' " There was never any "hoax," just a series of misunderstandings of how Inuit languages work, by accumulating suffixes supercalifragilistically. The actual number of words for snow is therefore "incalculable." "Hopi time" however, may well be a hoax, at least Whorf seems deliberately to have ignored data that was in his own field-notes; cf. Brown, *Human Universals,* pp. 27–31.

6 Foucault, *Dits et Écrits,* IV, p. 286.

7 Sapir, "Sound Patterns," 48–51. It was these patterns rather than the actual sounds that were the proper object of study: "Phonetic phenomena are not

physical phenomena per se and expert phoneticians are confusing the way they study and record sounds with the proper "linguistic structure."

8 "Sapir's earlier analyses of language, which described the unconscious patterning of sound and grammatical concepts, informed the work of Ruth Benedict," Christina Toren, "Culture and Personality," in Barnard and Spencer. Boas perhaps revealed best the linguistics-influenced structuralism of this approach to culture, in the introduction to Benedict's *Patterns of Culture,* X: "It is not historical except in so far as the general configuration, as long as it lasts, limits the directions of change that remain subject to it. In comparison to changes of content of culture the configuration has often remarkable permanency."

9 Benedict, "Configurations," 26, *Patterns of Culture,* p. 186.

10 *Patterns of Culture,* pp. 188–89, 191.

11 Mead, "The Training of the Cultural Anthropologist," 344–45.

12 Mead, "More Comprehensive Field Methods" 12, 14–15.

13 For a recent account cf. Mageo, "Male transvestism," although she doesn't examine the redundancy of "playfulness" critically. Cf. 449–50: "Samoans never did, and in some measure still do not, categorize sexual practices as heterosexual and homosexual. Boys are known to play homosexual games, but no one considers such behavior significant. In the 1920s, casual homosexual relations between girls were likewise ignored (Mead 1961 [1928]: 147). A boy who goes to bars in Apia or Pago Pago and finds no willing girl may let a transvestite take him home, but he is not thought 'queer' as a result. However, the fact that Samoans are spared the discontents of Western categorizations of sexuality does not mean that their sexuality escapes regulation by society." And 454–55: "Although personal levels of sexual activity vary, it seems unlikely that *fa'afafine* are only newly homosexual . . . the public denial of transvestite homosexuality by citizens concerned with Samoa's public image, and even by *fa'afafine* themselves, might once have been credible. Indeed in 1981, when I first came to Samoa, one old man took pains to deny *fa'afafine* were homosexual. No one has issued similar denials to me in recent years."

14 Not that I have anything against French-speaking intellectuals.

15 The following is indebted to Glick, "Types Distinct from Our Own." The story of the formation of the Boasians' cultural determinism, its consequences for feminism, civil rights and gay rights, and its background in the fight against biological racial theory has been told since the 1960s, but it was new to me.

16 *Worcester Daily Telegram,* May 3, 1891, quoted by Baker, "Franz Boas."

17 The sentence concerned the useful role played by Jews in the ancient world at the time of the death of Julius Caesar. "*Auch in der alten Welt war das Judentum ein wirksames Ferment des Kosmopolitismus und der nationalen Dekomposition,*" *Römische Geschichte* III, 507. Mommsen referred briefly to the misuse of his phrases by anti-Semites in *Auch ein Wort über unser Judentum,* but just told people to go and read his actual words, he wouldn't be changing them, cf. Malitz,

"Mommsen, Caesar und die Juden" for the background and an assessment of Mommsen's theory.

18 Mead, *Sex and Temperament,* p. 280 but cf. "A reply to a review."

19 I am going on the information in my 1968 copy that also noted on the blurb that "For the lay reader it affords a way to understanding of the non-European peoples with whom Great Britain as an administrative Power is vitally concerned."

20 In England anti-German propaganda was linked to homosexuality for some reason. Lord Alfred Douglas, with all the zeal of a convert, wrote a satirical pamphlet that informed wartime Britain: "Two foes thou hast, one there one here, one far one ultimately near, two filthy fogs blot out thy light: the German, and the Sodomite." The pamphlet ran into four editions and sold thousands of copies, but, although he had had the pleasure of seeing several of his enemies and old acquaintances ruined, in jail or, at the very least, visited by the police, Bosie wasn't satisfied. A better chance came in the Billing trial of 1918. Noel Pemberton Billing, an MP, had alleged that for over two decades German agents had been doing energetic research in England "spreading such debauchery and such lasciviousness as only German minds can conceive and only German bodies execute." The result of this study program was a Black Book kept in the Black Cabinet of a certain German Prince containing the names of 47,000 British perverts, a Fifth Column of vice. In a follow-up article headlined "The Cult of the Clitoris" Billing suggested the police would make a good start in winkling out the 47,000 if they seized the list of those who had applied to see the actress and dancer Maud Allan in a private performance of Wilde's *Salome.* Allan and her producer sued and the case was tried at the Old Bailey; thanks in part to Bosie, Allan lost; cf. Hoare, *Oscar Wilde's Last Stand.*

21 Glick, "Types distinct from Our Own," esp. 556, Benedict, *Patterns of Culture,* pp. 5–6.

22 Dover's ancient Greece looks very like Samoa in fact, with lots of homosexual behavior, and just one or two confirmed homosexuals: Plato taking on the role that Mead had given to Sasi.

23 Gay activist Chris Woods in 1991: "OutRage! is all about challenging the concept that your sexuality is defined by the gender of the person you sleep with. It's not. Homosexuality is a social construct that came out of such things as homophobic legislation and Freudian psychoanalysis," as reported by Simon Garfield, "The Age of Consent," *The Independent on Sunday,* November 10, 1991, (Review), 3ff.

24 Gay activist Peter Tatchell in Mark Simpson (ed.), *Anti-Gay* (London, 1996), esp. p. 36. The title of the essay has to be a little ironic, but not the argument and not the title of the book.

25 Lynn Barber, "Two for the show," *The Independent* (Review), October 13, 1991. The preliminaries: "What really gets them going is my casual remark that their work is 'obviously homoerotic.' Gilbert yelps, 'Not at all, it's not so clear,' and

George agonizes, 'How can you say that? What do you mean?' I mean all the muscular, bare-chested young men who feature in their canvases; the total absence of women and children; the prevalence of phallic symbols. The young men are not blatantly eroticized, as in Mapplethorpe, but they are sex objects nonetheless. 'But they are just boys we find in the street,' wail Gilbert and George, 'they are not gays. You can't sex a person on the street, anyway.' Gilbert: 'In the eighteenth century, every man was bisexual . . .' "

26 Sapir starts out gently: "An age-old blindness tends to be corrected by opened eyes that are too confident and undiscriminating . . ." before moving in for the kill: "Certain recent attempts, in part brilliant and stimulating, to impose upon the actual psychologies of actual people . . . a generalized psychology based upon the real or supposed psychological implications of cultural forms, show clearly what confusions in our thinking are likely to result when social science turns psychiatric . . . We then learn that whole societies are paranoid or hysterical or obsessive!" "The Contribution of Psychiatry," 865–66.

27 De Saussure, *Mémoire.*

28 Macey, *The Lives of Michel Foucault,* p. 354.

29 *Introduction,* p. 43, cf. Halperin, *One Hundred Years,* p. 155 n. 2.

30 Macey, ibid., p. 354.

31 Actes du Congrès Internationale, November 1–3, 1973.

32 "La Révolution des homosexuels," *Le Nouvel Observateur,* January 10, 1972, 34.

33 Veyne, "Témoignage hétérosexuelle," 17–18, see also 17–24; cf. Eribon, *Foucault et ses contemporains,* pp. 270–76, Macey, *The Lives of Michel Foucault,* pp. 362–64.

34 Paul Veyne, "Foucault Revolutionizes History," in Arnold I. Davidson (ed.), *Foucault and His Interlocutors* (Chicago, 1997), 146–82, Peter Garnsey, "The Generosity of Veyne," *JRS,* lxxxi (1991), 164–66, Eribon, *Michel Foucault,* pp. 322–33; Foucault, *Introduction,* pp. 43, 105, cf. Veyne "Famille et l'amour," 52: "Il ne reflète pas la logique profonde d'une lutte éternelle entre la répression et le désir."

35 Veyne, "Homosexuality in Ancient Rome," pp. 29 and 34.

36 "Entretien avec M. Foucault" in Foucault, *Dits et Écrits,* IV, #311, 286–87; "Des caresses d'hommes considérées comme un art," ibid. #314, 316–17.

37 Foucault, *Use of Pleasure,* pp. 269 n. 21, 215, 219, 221, 85–86; cf. Poster, "Foucault and the Tyranny of Greece," 213.

38 Rabinow, *Foucault Reader,* pp. 340, 345.

39 *Foucault Reader,* p. 346, Foucault, *Dits et Écrits* IV, 388 and 614 with the editors' notes at pp. 383 and 609, cf. Eribon: "C'est dégoûtant," *Foucault et ses contemporains,* 285.

40 Macey, *Lives of Michel Foucault,* p. 4; Miller, *The Passion of Michel Foucault,* p. 39.

41 Ibid., p. 7.

42 Ibid., p. 369.

43 Miller, op. cit., pp. 364–66, 368–69, 370–71.

44 Roy Harris, "A Warning to Students," *TLS* January 30, 2004: "In this letter Saussure fulminates against Jews as these 'swarms of parasites' (*essaims de parasites*) who have colonized Paris since 1830. Whenever this letter was written (perhaps during Saussure's period in Paris, 1880–91), it obviously springs from a deeply ingrained racism."

PART III: GREEK LOVE AND GREEK RELIGIONS
7: GANYMEDE RISING

1 A. O. Prickard, "The 'Mundus Jovialis' of Simon Marius," *The Observatory* 39 (1916), 380.

2 Saslow, *Ganymede in the Renaissance;* Leonard Barkan, *Transuming Passion: Ganymede and the Erotics of Humanism* (Stanford, 1991), Jane Davidson Reid, *Oxford Guide to Classical Mythology in the Arts,* 1300–1990s (Oxford, 1993), s.v. "Ganymede."

3 Thanks to some confusion with the rather different hemispherical dog-cap or *pilus* worn by manumitted slaves and used by Brutus and Cassius on their coins as a symbol of the liberty they brought to Rome by killing Julius Caesar.

4 X., *Smp.* 8.30

5 Pliny, *Natural History* 34.79, writing of Leochares, a sculptor working from the 360s until perhaps the 320s, cf. the Christian fundamentalist Tatian—"Destroy these memorials of iniquity!"—in his *Oratio ad Graecos* 34.3 (Whittaker): "And for what reason do you honor the hermaphrodite Ganymede by Leochares, as if you possessed something admirable?" Almost nothing survives of famous Leochares' works, although to him have been ascribed the original of the Apollo Belvedere, most highly esteemed of all ancient sculptures until the eighteenth century, and the Amazon frieze from Mausolus's mausoleum in the British Museum, J. Boardman, *Greek Sculpture: The Late Classical Period* (London, 1995), p. 55, A. F. Stewart, "Leochares," *OCD;* more cautious is R. Neudecker, "Leochares," *Brill's New Pauly.*

6 Cf. M. Beard and J. Henderson, "The Emperor's New Body," in M. Wyke (ed.), *Parchments of Gender* (Oxford, 1998), 191–219.

7 Antonio Averlino, see John Onians, *Bearers of Meaning* (Princeton, 1988), pp. 158–70, and for the complicated political situation, Evelyn Welch, *Art and Society in Italy 1350–1500* (Oxford, 1997), pp. 243–45.

8 Cf. Jacques Thuillier, "La mythologie à l'âge 'baroque,' " in Stella Georgoudi and Jean-Pierre Vernant (eds), *Mythes grecs au figuré* (Paris, 1996), 167–87.

9 M. Russell, "The iconography of Rembrandt's *Rape of Ganymede,*" *Simiolus* 9 (1977), 5–18.

10 Ath. 3.602e = Sophocles fr. 345 Radt lit. "with his thighs putting a fire under Zeus's tyranny"; probably the point is something to do with love triumphing over even the mighty.

11 Free translations of *A.P.* 12.68 (Meleager), 67 (Anon.), 65 (Meleager).

12 Virg., *Aen.* 1.28, cf. Saslow, *Ganymede in the Renaissance,* fig. 3.18.

13 *Iliad,* 20.234–35. A later epic says it was a golden vine, *Little Iliad* fr. 6 (West).

14 *Homeric Hymn to Aphrodite,* 5.202–26.

15 Ibyc. T 1, cf. T 11 (Phld. *Mus.*): Ibycus corrupted *neoi,* i.e., singing his songs corrupted them?

16 Ibyc. fr. 289 cf. 282B iv. Apollonius refers to Ganymede's abduction in very respectful terms. Zeus was "smitten with desire for his beauty and set him to dwell in heaven as hearthmate of the deathless ones," ll. 115–17. We don't know what it was in Apollonius that set the commentator on Ibycus's trail; if it was simply the notion of Zeus's love and agency, it is interesting that such a by now well-established part of the tradition was still remembered as an innovation, although hardly startling, given Homer's authority. For Ibycus's life see D. A. Campbell, *Greek Lyric* III (Cambridge, MA, 1991), pp. 6–9; Hutchinson, *Greek Lyric Poetry,* pp. 228–35.

17 Theognis, 1345–48, from "the pederastic coda" (*c.*650–400 BC?). E. *Orestes* 1389–92. *Orestes,* a brilliant play, but highly inventive and very nasty, is often viewed as a reflection of Euripides' bitterness as he arranged to leave Athens at the end of a less-than-brilliant career, or a comment on the imminent destruction of his motherland as the war with Sparta drew to a close. The author riffed on myth quite freely without any regard to tradition—"the story isn't found anywhere else," says the ancient introduction—and puts figures from heroic myth in a very nasty light—"Everyone is awful," he continues, "except Pylades." "Insane" is William Arrowsmith's response to that assessment: "the bitterness is unrelieved, the quality of nightmare pervasive," D. Grene and R. Lattimore (eds.), *The Complete Greek Tragedies: Euripides IV* (Chicago, 1958), 108. *Eunetēs* in its feminine form usually refers to Hera; the implication would be that Ganymede is not only Zeus's "sex-partner," but his "bride." J. Diggle, editor of the 1994 Oxford text, prints "*otototoi/ialemōn ialemōn;/Dardania tlamōn,/ Ganumēdeos hipposuna, Dios euneta,*" but suspects some corruption.

18 The classic account of Ganymede in Greek art remains Sichtermann, *Ganymed,* cf. id. "Zeus und Ganymed in frühklassischer Zeit," *Antike Kunst* 2 (1959), 10–15, "Ganymedes," *LIMC,* with bib., Kaempf-Dimitriadou, *Liebe der Götter,* esp. 7–12, 59–60, 76–9, K. W. Arafat, *Classical Zeus* (Oxford, 1990), pp. 64–76.

19 *LIMC* "Ganymedes" #57, "third quarter of sixth cent.," Athens, Acropolis 1.1629, *BA* 32419. Heracles' elevation to heaven, a popular subject in the sixth century, provides the background for the god's loves and makes Ganymede look less of an anomaly.

20 Oakley, "An Athenian Red-Figured Workshop," 198–200, suggests a survival rate of 0.2 percent is "much more likely" than the alternative of 1 percent.

21 But perhaps when Hermes pursues a boy he is acting as Zeus's proxy, and Poseidon could be said to have abducted Pelops for Zeus.

22 Kaempf-Dimitriadou thinks Ganymede has dropped his cock in shock: "*Zeus*

erreicht den Knaben, der unbekümmert mit seinem Hahn spielt, und fasst ihn an der Schulter. Ganymed erschrickt, seine Finger losen sich und lassen den Vogel fallen," Liebe der Götter, p. 8.

23 But cf. K. W. Arafat, *Classical Zeus* (Oxford, 1990), p. 68 = cat. 3.21. Koch-Harnack gently chides Sichtermann for playing down the erotic implications, *Knabenliebe,* pp. 228–29 n. 532: "*Bei den päderastischen Götterdarstellungen ging es wohl weniger um das, was geschenkt wurde, als um die Kenntlichmachung der Beziehung z.B. durch den Hahn als erotisches Attribut.*" A hen for a *hetaera:* Lissarrague, *Greek Vases,* pp. 50–51, Paris Louvre A479, *BA* 310509. Very interesting is a late archaic vase (Campanian?), *LIMC* "Ganymedes" #73: Zeus hails Ganymede who gestures down toward a cockerel between them, the writing of his name completing the gesture; from behind, Hera is about to crown him; Hebe (?) is behind her. This dignified scene is perhaps an antidote to the "triviality" Arafat sometimes detects in such scenes; the cockerel is no symbol of "daily life" here, I think. Of course it could be both symbolic and a gift, a symbol *is* an exchange of thing with the thing symbolized; in other words you might well give someone something of themselves.

24 E. P. Blegen, "News Items from Athens," *AJA* 46 (1942), 477–82.

25 Is "Ganymede" in fact Pelops? Sichtermann, *Ganymed,* has a sensible discussion, pp. 28–31, allowing a nod in Pelops's direction, but concluding that the spirit of the work is Ganymedean, with bib. p. 79, #81.

26 Pliny, *Nat. Hist.* 34. 79, *LIMC* "Ganymedes" # 200, and the swans, 84–91, one of them has "Ganymede" written on; the earliest given date for the first in the series is 360 BC.

27 Aeschin. 1.7–8, cf. Cohen, *Law, Sexuality and Society,* p. 222: "These provisions protect young boys from molestation at school and at the gymnasium, and provide that if any boy is hired out for homosexual activities by his father or guardian, both the father and the client are liable to the statutory penalties. Acting as a procurer for a free boy seems punishable by death, and Aeschines also discusses the law of *hubris,* which prohibits the rape or violent misuse of both children and adults (as well as, perhaps, seduction in the case of children)."

28 U. von Wilamowitz, *Die Ilias und Homer* (Berlin, 1916), p. 83.

29 As has long been recognized, the author of the story of Moses and the Golden Calf in *Exodus* 32, esp. 20, projects back into time a burning issue of later politics, 1 *Kings* 12.26, *Hosea* 8.5, 13.2.

30 Smith, "Aineiadai," opposes the old consensus that Homer was hired by "sons of Aeneas," but while doing so collects all the evidence for it. Of course, having read Homer, later princelings would try to attach themselves to what the poet claimed would be the only surviving branch of the royal house of Troy, often through the local toponymous hero Ascanius, not linked to Aeneas in the *Iliad,* but later thought to be his son. Some of the later myths about the descendants of Aeneas in the Troad do seem to have a life of their own, beyond what Homer says.

31 Strabo 13.1,32.

32 Heracles and Ganymede have some odd connection; certainly Ganymede's elevation is connected to the apotheosis of Heracles, since Heracles creates a job vacancy by marrying his predecessor Hebe "Youthful bloom," to mark his immortalization.

33 *Iliad* 5.628–51, 20.221–29: Aeneas tells another story of how Erichthonius, son of Dardanus the founder of Troy, had three thousand mares impregnated by Boreas, the north wind, to produce twelve magical colts.

34 2 *Kings* 2.11 and 16–18, West, *East Face of Helicon,* pp. 477–78.

35 Walter Burkert, *The Orientalizing Revolution* (Cambridge, MA, 1992), p. 122.

36 *Homeric Hymn* [5] *To Aphrodite* 75–160.

37 She is already up to no good on the "Cypselus Chest" and the Amyclae throne (lost works of sixth century?).

38 For lamentation = heroes, Seaford, *Reciprocity and Ritual,* pp. 139–41, cf. Lucian *On Slander,* c. 17: tears for Hephaestion indicate heroic rather than divine status.

39 Nymphis, *FGrHist* 432 F5 ap Ath. 14.619f–620a.

40 For Hylas, Bormos and all the other nymph tales, see Larson's excellent discussion, *Greek Nymphs,* esp. pp. 66–70.

41 Mnaseas, a third-century geographer with Euhemerist (rationalizing) tendencies, said Ganymede was snatched by Pelops's father, Tantalus, died while out hunting and was buried on Mount Olympus in Mysia, by the (*kata ton*) temple of Olympian Zeus. Dosiadas (*FGrHist* 458 F5) and Echemenes (*FGrHist* 259 F1) say the culprit was Minos. Others added other rationalizing unhappy endings: Ganymede throws himself off a cliff after Minos decided to have sex with him and Minos pretends to his father that it was a cloud and a gust of wind; Ganymede fell asleep out hunting and was ripped apart by wild beasts [i.e., no traces were left]; he was struck by lightning; see Jacoby *FGrHist* ad loc. A fuller version of the tale is preserved in Suda, Mu 1092, s.v. "Minos": "This man ruled the seas and sailed to all sorts of foreign [places] and commanded many [men]. Arriving in Asia and hearing of the great fame, in Phrygia, of Tros the king of Troy and of his sons, he went to the city of Dardanos where Tros lived. Tros had three sons: Ilos, Assarakos, and Ganymede, [the last] of whom had a great name for beauty. So Minos stayed as a guest with Tros, both giving and receiving presents, and he ordered Tros to summon his sons, so that he might see them and give them presents too. But Tros said that they had gone on a hunt. [So] Minos too wanted to hunt with them. At first [Tros] sent one of his attendants into the place where the boys were hunting, around the Granikos river; but Minos, having sent out his ships a little beforehand to the river, came later to the sons and saw Ganymede and fell in love with him. And having given out orders to the Cretans and snatched the boy, he [put] him in the ship and sailed away. The place was called Harpagia. Minos took the boy and went to Crete. The boy to ease his pain killed himself with a sword, and Minos buried him in the temple. Hence, of course, it is said that Ganymede serves with Zeus," Jennifer Benedict (trans.) at Suda Online

(stoa.org.), D. Whitehead (ed.). The southern side of the Sea of Marmara is full of swamps and lakes; Hylas disappeared a little farther up the coast from here. For Harpagion, see Alexandru Avram, *IACP,* 979.

42 Many scholars, however, think Dawn means death, just as children who died might be said to have been "taken by the nymphs," especially if they fell into a well. Funerals were often carried out at night so as not to pollute the day, so Dawn brought an end to the burning of the pyre and allowed the soul to depart. One ancient rationalist is quite explicit about this meaning of Dawn's abductions: "There was an ancient custom that the bodies of those on their deathbed, once they had stopped living, should not be taken for their burials at night, nor when the noontide heat spreads over the earth, but in deep dawn when the rays of the rising sun were still fireless. When a young man well-born and beautiful should die, they euphemistically describe the dawn funeral procession as the snatching by Day not of a dead man, but through *erōs* for the one who is snatched. Following Homer they say this," E. Vermeule, *Aspects of Death* (Berkeley, 1979), p. 163; Artemidorus is unequivocal: in a dream "to have sexual intercourse with a god or a goddess . . . signifies death for a sick man" 1.80, but Kaempf-Dimitriadou thinks this death theme is being overemphasized, *Liebe der Götter,* p. 17; I agree.

43 Homer, *Iliad* 6.345.

44 Nagy, *Greek Mythology and Poetics,* pp. 242–46.

45 Larson, *Greek Nymphs,* Borgeaud, *Cult of Pan,* pp. 104–109; W. R. Connor, "Seized by the Nymphs: Nympholepsy and symbolic expression in classical Greece," *Class Ant* 7 (1988), 155–89.

46 Arist., *Eudemian Ethics* 1214a.

47 *LIMC* "Ganymedes" #52, *BA* 205140 by Douris, but note that the exterior has courting scenes.

48 Larson, *Greek Nymphs,* pp. 193–98, esp. 194–95.

49 For Aeneas and Rome see Gantz, pp. 713–17 and Christopher P. Jones, *Kinship Diplomacy in the Ancient World* (Cambridge, MA, 1999), pp. 82–88.

50 Dia was also greatly venerated in nearby Sicyon, Strabo 8.6,24. Hebe also had an important cult center in the Attic village of Aixone, alongside Heracles and his mother Alcmena, Whitehead, *Demes of Attica,* p. 207 n. 186. For Phlius, which had relocated, see S. Alcock, "Urban Survey and the Polis of Phlius," *Hesperia* 60 (1991), 421–63, and for a possible identification of the temple of Ganymeda, Henry S. Washington, "Excavations at Phlius in 1892," *AJA* 27 (1923), 444, cf. 441 fig. 3. Cook, "Wife of Zeus?," *CR* 20 (1906), 367, esp. n. 1, notes that Ganymeda should really have been Ganymedeia, which may be more evidence, *contra* Cook, for her antiquity.

51 2.13,3, with Musti and Torelli ad loc.

52 Paus. 7.24,4.

53 West found this reading far too awkward and printed ". . . *gan hos* . . . ," "Dictaean Hymn," 151–52, cf. Perlman, "*Invocatio* and *imprecatio,*" Sporn,

Heiligtümer und Kulte, p. 47—"Gott des *ganos*"—Vikela, *Weihreliefs,* p. 124, and on the underworld character of Zeus Pankrates, pp. 57–80, esp. 79. The *kouros* has been linked to the Minoan ivory statuette found nearby, MacGillivray, Driessen and Sackett, *Palaikastro Kouros,* (= Orion, suggest MacGillivary/Sackett, ibid., pp. 168–69, largely on the basis of its fists-to-the-chest posture— does the hymn mark the reappearance of Orion coming from the Underworld then?), but see Lapatin's caveats about the identification of the Minoan figurine, *AJA* 106 (2002), 326–28.

54 Ath. 13.601f, from "the Chalcidians." Myrtles are a favorite plant in ritual processions, often associated with Aphrodite, even marriage.

55 *Archaeological Reports* (1969), 10, *LIMC* "Ganymedes" #201, citing P. G. Themelis, *Archaiologika analekta ex Athenon* 2 (1969), 163–65, Meiggs and Lewis 51.61–62, Trümpy, *Untersuchungen,* pp. 41, 46–69. The same nexus is found at Olympia: eagle snatching snake, Olympus, Zeus, Ganymede. For "Zeus Lightning," F. Mosino, "Graffito vascolare greco da Reggio Calabria," *Xenia Antiqua* 4 (1995), 23–24.

56 L. Loukopoulou and A. Laitar, *IACP,* 913.

57 It is noticeable that it is at tyrants' courts that comparisons of mortal with heroic beauty, mortal loves and immortal loves first seem to appear, with Ibycus at the court of Polycrates of Samos.

58 One might also note the rise of the cult of Herms, a homely personal cult, at the same time. For this discovery see esp. Kaempf-Dimitriadou, *Liebe der Götter,* pp. 43–47, esp. p. 44: "*Es war ein ungehörtes Wagnis attischer Kunst und attischen Geistes, die Götter aus der Ruhe ihres archaischen Wesens in die Bewegung des Lebens zu reissen*" and most esp. p. 46: Kaempf-Dimitriadou argues from the coincidence of the astonishing rise of loves of gods in art with one of the greatest cultural and political upheavals in the history of Athens that the events of the late sixth century, especially the freedom from tyranny and the opening up of politics, produced a new consciousness of the divine and with it of the human. A bit later the contrast with the Persians, both militarily and culturally (*Geist*), put the stamp on it. At the same time the apparent intervention of the gods in human affairs during these dramatic years, most relevantly the help of princess-snatching Boreas in blowing away the Persians, brought to attention the possibility of the gods' power to intervene in human affairs and to affect outcomes dramatically. Loves of gods were a prime site for appreciating and representing this new closeness between the divine and the human spheres, as never before and never thereafter.

The main problem is that the earliest and most popular subject, Dawn, fits least well. I would play up the importance of the age of tyrants (both their presumptions to divine comparison, and their encouragement of new pieties outside the traditional cults controlled by the "aristocrats," some of whom were now in exile) and play down the parallels with everyday affairs—love of a patriarch like Zeus for a young teenager like Ganymede is hardly a model of

Greek Homosexuality, Dawn is hardly a typical Athenian lady (Osborne, "Desiring Women," esp. p. 72, although, to be sure, all women have a randy Dawn inside them)—though, on the other hand, points of comparison/contrast between the human and the divine *are* emphasized in images of erotic pursuit, if only by juxtaposition. Also I would play up the concentration on Eros as the greatest boundary-crossing force between human and divine spheres and/or on the distance between heaven and earth as the greatest *challenge* to demonstrate his power to close gaps. And how precisely do you distinguish between the contrast-across-a-distance between human and divine in the earlier period and the contrast-at-close-quarters *c.*500? Is there any more immediate and direct connection between a god and a mortal than that between Sappho and Aphrodite way back in *c.*600 BC, or the Spartan girls of a generation earlier, apparently so worried about their men choosing goddesses, Dawn (?), and nymphs instead of them, Alcman 1.16–20?

59 Burkert, *Greek Religion,* pp. 246–50 has an excellent discussion of the whole problem of naughty gods, "most vulnerable were the unbridled love-affairs," p. 246.

60 Aelian, *V.H.* 6.1, Hdt. 5.77, 6.100, Thuc. 1.114, Plu. *Per.* 23. The Athenian colonists of Chalcis were dispatched to help fight the Persians in 490 but fled; whether or not they came back has been much disputed. For Sigeum, Strabo 13.1,38 (599). The Athenians were adjudicated Sigeum at the end of the seventh century, it was lost, then reconquered by the tyrant Pisistratus; see Simon Hornblower, *OCD* s.v. "*Sigeum.*" It is interesting that the tribe assigned to the pot painters under the democratic revolution had as hero-mascot Acamas, son of Theseus, whose myths made him a kind of Athenian imitator/inheritor of Aeneas and his sons in the Troad, a territory-claiming myth that could have been invented at any time from 600–500 BC, cf. Dionysius of Chalcis, ap. schol. E. *Andromache* 10, Smith "Aineiadai," 36 n. 32, 54–55. Acamas rescues elderly Aethra, his grandmother, from Troy in a way highly reminiscent of Aeneas rescuing Anchises.

61 Lysis in Plato's *Lysis* and Autolycus, an all-in wrestling champion, who loves his daddy, in Xenophon's *Symposium* are good examples. And the Ganymedes of Apollonius Rhod and Lucian sound and behave like six-year-olds. One might contrast an early modern coeval, say, England's prematurely adult Edward VI.

62 Ath. 10. 424e, Sappho fr. 203; *neoi* normally (sc. *andres* "young *men*") equals "Twenty-somethings," but it could just mean "young." In general see Bremmer, "Adolescents," 135–48. When the Odyssey shows us Menelaus back home in Sparta with his lovely Helen, the guests are served wine by his bastard son, Megapenthes, who is betrothed but not married, it seems, 4.10–12, 15.120–23. Pindar, *Ol.* 1 may have been thinking of a similar role when he had Poseidon fall in love with Pelops, the host's young son, at a dinner party, cf. Philostratus, *Imagines* 1.17. With images of nudity, you can never say if it's symbolic or real-

istic, but perhaps where others in the scene are dressed and the boy is nude, the chances are increased slightly. The Romans especially loved to think of their slave-attendants as their own little Ganymedes.

63 Boardman, *Early Greek Vase Painting,* fig. 506, Athens *Nat. Arch. Mus.* 10426.

64 See Ekroth, *Sacrificial Rituals,* esp. pp. 330–34.

65 Sissa and Detienne, *Daily Life,* pp. 79–80.

66 Those who object that Ganymede is "wine pourer" not "nectar pourer" to the gods were anticipated by Arist., *Poetics* 25 1461a, who ascribes the usage either to "custom" or metaphor.

67 Although as Gantz, p. 82, points out, if Hebe actively guaranteed the gods' youthfulness no one says so and "no one ever attempts to strike at the gods by abducting her." It is what she serves that is important and other divinities can serve it.

68 One must point out here the strange opposition between Ganymede, whose mother, according to Hellanicus [*FGrHist* 4 F138, Apollod. 3.140], was Callirrhoe, "Beautiful flow" daughter of the river Scamander, and the sons of Callirrhoe, daughter of the river Achelous, who, at their mother's request, aged prematurely so they could avenge their father, Gantz, pp. 526–27. Rivers often play a role as "*kourotrophoi,*" youth nurturers.

69 Sissa and Detienne, *Daily Life,* pp. 44–47.

70 For ambrosia and nectar as "perfumed" see Cynthia W. Shelmerdine, "Shining and Fragrant Cloth in Homeric Epic," in Jane. B. Carter and Sarah P. Morris (eds), *The Ages of Homer* (Austin, 1995), pp. 99–107; she also notes continuities with the Mycenaean period. Linear B tablets reveal an entire industry of scented oils (for the gods).

71 Ath. 3.602e = Sophocles fr. 345 Radt. The idea that Sophocles meant nothing more than that Ganymede's sexy thighs get Zeus all hot under the collar will appeal only to those who have not read any Sophocles. Parker's article on sacrificial exchange between mortals and immortals "Pleasing Thighs" never really investigates the resonances of its titular joke, p. 106 "(which has nothing to do with private fantasy)." Of course a youth's thighs certainly were the object of sexual fantasy as the thighs of a hundred cows were the object of divine fantasy, a coincidence that is most interesting.

72 Although the name is always written Doris (a woman's name), even by a painter who takes care to distinguish "ou" from "o" (cf. Neer, *Style and Politics,* p. 233 n. 14), he or she is invariably transliterated as "Douris" in modern scholarship, and reluctantly I follow the practice.

73 In fact it almost certainly came from a tomb in Italy, where most Greek vases have come from. Malibu 84.AE.569, *BA* 16200.

74 It is a shame Kaempf-Dimitriadou did not have access to this vase when she wrote her book. It fits her thesis and yet wants to refine it somewhat profoundly.

75 Paus. 7.24,4 with Moggi and Osanna ad loc. Theocritus 12.27–37.

76 Plu., *Solon* 8, D. 19.255 cf. Solon fr. 10 ap. D.L. 1.49, "A little time will show the townsfolk my mania, it will show, when the truth (*aletheiē*) comes into the center (*meson*)," G. Tedeschi, "Solone e lo spazio della communicazione elegiaca," *QUCC* 10 (1982), 33–46, esp. 44, cf., less urgently, R. Flacelière, "Le bonnet de Solon," *REA* 49 (1947), 235–47, on other skullcaps, Josephus, *Jewish Antiquities* 3.157, Appian, *Bell. Civ.* 1.8,74, Paus. 4.27,2 cf. 3.24,5. The twin hats of Castor and Pollux, more than mere hemispheres, are shown on the lintels of merchant houses on Delos. Suda glosses *pilidion* as *kamelaukion,* originally, a hemispherical crown worn by Byzantine emperors, now the tall brimless black hat of Orthodox priests. Dicaeopolis's *pilidion* (Ar., *Ach.* 437) must in context function like Solon's. People who were sick in general seem to have sported head swaddlings too. The crucial parallel for Ganymede is the headgear of the winning-side seer known as "L" on the front (east) pediment of Zeus's Olympian temple, and the two old men with skullcaps on *BA* 205036, Boston 95.28, which probably shows the revelation of the site of the Pytheion (Daphne) to the Cephalids, between Attica and Eleusis. Polygnotus gave old Nestor a *pilos* in his *Sack of Troy,* Paus. 10.25,11. The significance of the general use of the yarmulke by Jews, from first century BC?, is probably to be found in the notion that the Jews were a "nation of priests." Irwin, *Solon,* pp. 113–46, has a different take, linking the *pilidion* to travel in general and Odysseus in particular. The questions are: (1) Are references to the *pilidion* necessarily allusions to Solon's famous ruse? (2) Is *pilidion* a technical term consistently used for a very specific type of headgear, or does it just mean "little felt hat"? (3) How would a Greek label a skullcap?

8: NOONDAY PHAEDRUS. CEPHALUS AT DAWN

1 One of Plato's innovations was to give Socratic dialogues realism, avoiding obvious anachronisms and locating the dialogue in a specific place, above all in a particular moment in his characters' lives or in history, even at a particular time of year, Kahn, *Plato and the Socratic Dialogue,* pp. 34–35, but decoding Plato's "datifications" (date flags) is sometimes difficult. From antiquity to Martha Nussbaum, scholars have wanted Phaedrus to be young and sexy. Unfortunately this is impossible. Even Rowe, who goes for an early (way too early) dramatic date in his edition of *Phaedrus,* p. 11, acknowledges that Phaedrus is "at the end of his thirties." For Phaedrus is an adult in *Protagoras,* a dialogue multiply datified to *c.*430 BC, when Isocrates would be *circa* five years of age. Since Isocrates is "still a young man" (*neos* = "under-Thirty") in *Phaedrus* 278e, Phaedrus (fifteen years, minimum, his senior) can be "still a young man" no longer. Moreover, Plato's datifications are not supposed to be obscure to his contemporary audience who would almost certainly have placed the *Phaedrus* in the last decade of the fifth century: Lysias is in town (he arrived 412/411, D.H., *Lys.* 1) and is already being denounced as a *speechwriter* (*Phdr.* 257c); all

Lysias's speech writings are *c.*403–380; Isocrates on the other hand (first writings from 390s) is already a promising writer, 278e–279a. Few contemporaries would have inferred from this a dramatic date long before 400, therefore; the modern consensus, "before 415," is far too early. This consensus derives from the fact, not mentioned by Plato, but known from inscriptions, that Phaedrus escaped into exile in 415. Most of the exiles did not return until 404, which leaves the *Phaedrus* only a little time slot before the death of Lysias's brother Polemarchus (d. 404–403), who is mentioned as still living (257b). Hypothetical responses of Euripides (d. 406) and Sophocles (d. 406/405) are mentioned, 268c–269a, but so are those of Pericles (d. 429), so it does not mean Plato meant to date *Phaedrus* to before the tragedians' deaths, *pace* Dover, *Lysias,* pp. 32–33, cf. Todd, *Lysias,* p. 4. There is some room for flexibility. Dover (p. 32) lists three men, Alcibiades, Adeimantus, Axiochus, exiled at the same time as Phaedrus who were back in Athens several years earlier than 404, plus, perhaps, Eryximachus, Todd, *Lysias* p. 379. But most likely, Plato is describing a very precise moment in the summer of 404; Athens has been defeated, there is peace, the exiles have returned, the walls are (about to come?) tumbling down; Phaedrus is *c.*45 minimum, probably rather older, but younger than Socrates, who is *c.*66, *Phdr* 236d. Moreover, Lysias—who in 404 is either *c.*55, according to later ancient sources, or *c.*40, according to modern revisions, is Phaedrus's "favorite," *paidika* 236b, 279b. Ath. 11.505f has Plato accused of fabrication. "That Phaedrus was contemporary with Socrates (*kata Sōkratēn einai*) is impossible, never mind that he was his *erōmenos.*" Probably Athenaeus's source is thinking of a more famous Phaedrus, Phaedrus of Sphettos, contemporary of Plato but not of Socrates.

2 227abd, 230cd.

3 Nussbaum, *Fragility,* pp. 207–13, ignores the realities; Phaedrus's patronymic, Pythocles, "Pythian-Famed," is not a "significant fiction," p. 207, but the real name of real Phaedrus's real father. Plato may well, like Aristophanes, select his characters for their names and patronymics, as here, I would argue, he plays games with Lysias as "son of Cephalus," but I cannot see any great significance in Pythocles.

4 Cf. Todd, *Lysias,* pp. 378–81.

5 Lysias 19.15.

6 The spring (*nama*) is mentioned at 278b, cf. Strabo 9.1.24. Some have suggested they are close to the rock carving of Pan, just south of the church of Ayia Photeini in the southeast corner of the enclosure of the temple of Olympian Zeus, but they must be much farther toward Hymettus, if the crossing to Agra is "below."

7 The area of the river Ilissus, now buried under tarmac, was full of shrines, strung out along its banks, like a giant elongated sanctuary.

8 For Agra or Agrae, site of temples of Demeter and Artemis, see Paus. 1.19,6, probably the deme of Agryle.

9 Ibycus fr. 310.

10 For cicadas, cf. Helen King, "Tithonos and the Tettix," in Falkner, Thomas M. and de Luce, Judith (eds), *Old Age in Greek and Latin Literature* (Albany, 1989), pp. 68–89.

11 For students of Plato who usually treat him as a world unto himself, the evolution of his doctrine of the soul is an important part of his trajectory and useful for putting his dialogues in sequence. The approach taken here is quite different; how that affects the narrative of his intellectual development has not been my concern.

12 Gibson ad Ovid *AA* 3, pp. 356–59, provides a bibliography, p. 360—"vast"— cf. E. Simantoni-Bournia, *LIMC* "Kephalos," Kearns, *Heroes of Attica*, p. 177 (Kephalos) and p. 195 (Prokris), Gantz, pp. 36, 182, 238–39, 245–57, cf. J. Davidson, "Antoninus Liberalis and the Story of Prokris," *Mnemosyne* 50 (1997), 165–84.

13 Pherecydes, *FGrHist* 3 F 34.

14 Ovid, *Met.* 7.690–865.

15 In Apollodorus's version, Procris, true to form, had wanted Minos for herself, and cured him with the same root Odysseus used to counter the witchcraft of Circe (*moly*). She fled from Crete to avoid Pasiphaë, Minos's wife, Circe's sister and daughter of the Sun.

16 Ant. Lib. 41.6–7.

17 It would be tempting to imagine that this Aura is another Hellenistic or Ovidian invention, but Aura is one of the most colorful characters in Greek mythology and a bit of a lesbian. Her story is told as the climax to Nonnus, *Dionysiaca* 48. A very boyish virgin huntress, daughter of the Titan Lelantos, and resident in the highlands of Phrygia, west of Gordium, Aura takes an opportunity while swimming with Artemis to fondle the goddess's melony breasts and compares them with her own round little apple, "male breasts," and teases the Virgin for being so voluptuous. As punishment it is arranged for her to be raped. Dionysus makes a fountain of wine come from the ground and surrounds it with flowers, hyacinths, narcissuses etc., very similar to Ovid's description of Kaisariani, where Cephalus seems to have an affair with Aura, ll. 574–78. Aura, thirsty in the heat, drinks and falls unconscious, Dionysus has his wicked way. Aura wakes up and starts taking vengeance on any man she can find in the mountains, especially those who represent mortals who have slept with goddesses. Hunters get it too, when Aura remembers that Cephalus slept with Dawn, forgetting apparently that he too was a rape victim. Aura gives birth to twins (quickly and easily, 851, 854) feeds one of them to a big cat and when the big cat won't eat, eats it herself, having bashed it around a bit. Dionysus makes sure the other child, Iacchos, is well looked after. Athena nurses it herself with the same breast she once gave to Erechtheus. Finally he is entrusted to the "Bacchants of Eleusis," 948–78. Aura meanwhile had drowned herself and was turned into a spring next to the mighty river Sangarius, 931.

The myth links Aura to this spring, to the mountain Dindyma (twins) where she gave birth, to a "loving-cup hill of Aphrodite" where sexual partners (*akoitai*) steal girls' virginity and run away (756–59: some marital or premarital sex ritual apparently), and to the festivals of Eleusis, shrine of Demeter and Persephone, and the Lenaea. Aura's chthonic character, typical of wind spirits, oddly, seems to be confirmed long before Nonnus. Fourth-century vases from southern Italy often have a woman's head on the neck, sometimes with wings attached. One of these with a *polos* hat, looking for all the world like Persephone, is inscribed with the name Aura. It is quite likely the "nymphs" decorating the magnificent "Nereid" tomb from Xanthos in the British Museum (*c.*380 BC) are also Anatolian *Aurai*, A. D. Trendall, *Red Figure Vases of South Italy and Sicily* (London, 1989), pp. 92–93, and fig. 6, J. Six "Aurae," *JHS* 13 (1892/3), 131–36 with further references and suggestions.

18 Strabo 10.2,9.

19 Suda (Mu 497) s.v. "*Melētos*" = Aelian fr. 69 Hercher, Paus. 1.30,1.

20 Sources in *LIMC* s.v. "*Kephalos*," Kearns, *Heroes of Attica,* p. 177.

21 BM E466 (*BA* 5967), Griffiths, "What Leaf-fringed legend . . . ?" 65–66 pl. IIIa, Kaempf-Dimitriadou *Liebe der Götter,* pp. 19–20.

22 Davidson, "Revolutions in Human Time," 65–67.

23 For the Greeks, people with the same name were akin: "Socrates is called the same name as me, and for us naming provides kinship (*oikeiotēs*). And we should always be enthusiastic in getting to know our relatives . . ." Plato, *Politicus* 258a. From the "Persuasive" painter Peithinos onward, the Greeks often played games with names, real or invented.

24 For the shrine, see above all Pirenne-Delforge, *L'Aphrodite,* pp. 74–75.

25 Hamilton, *Greek Saints,* pp. 151ff.

26 *Ars Amatoria* 3.725.

27 Probably a satyric drama, *POxy.* 2436 (col. ii 2–8). Text and tune in West, *Ancient Greek Music,* pp. 281, 310–11. Only the end of Hermes' name is readable— *mou,* but few alternatives fit. Borthwick, "Oxyrhynchus Musical Monody," first suggested the connection with the spring at Cylloupera, but didn't adduce the Hermes connection.

28 Attributed to Eretria Painter, second half of fifth century, Kansas City, Nelson-Atkins Museum of Art, 31.80, *BA* 216944.

29 Ar. fr. 283 K-A, *Arch. Reports* 50 (2004), 8.

30 Cf. Peter Green for instance in his Penguin translation of Ovid's *Erotic Poems* (Harmondsworth, 1982), p. 401.

31 9.1,24, ". . . the Ilissus, which flows . . . (1) from the parts above (or beyond) Agra and the Lyceum and (2) from the fountain hymned by Plato in Phaedrus."

32 Burkert, *Greek Religion,* op. cit., pp. 142, 321–29.

33 In general see Borgeaud, *Cult of Pan,* pp. 104–107. Socrates is not equally in favor of all types of holy madness and carefully distinguishes between sane prophecy and inspired prophecy and different types of possession, human

sickness or seizure by different Muses, Nymphs, Apollo, Love. How these different possessions authorize different kinds of speech and which ones are negatively or positively valued, and how Plato's presentation here squares with his presentation of divine madnesses elsewhere, is not my concern here.

34 Kahn, *Plato and the Socratic Dialogue,* pp. 1–35, cf. p. 4: "Socratic *erōs* . . . is the theme most fully represented in the surviving material."

35 Dillon, "Ganymede as the Logos," for Philo in general id. *The Middle Platonists* (rev. with new afterword London, 1996), pp. 139–83. Philo's big thing was to read the ancient Jewish scriptures, in Greek translation, through the prism of Platonic philosophy, cf. ibid., p. 140: ". . . steeped in Plato. His particular favorites are the *Timaeus* and the *Phaedrus* . . ." Philo saw Plato as a student of Pythagoras, student of Moses, resulting in a Judaism that looks remarkably like "Stoicized Platonism," an influence in its turn on Christian Platonists like Clement and Origen, ibid., pp. 143–34. For Philo "The Logos, the divine reason-principle, is the active element of God's creative thought, and is often spoken of as the 'place' of the Ideas. Through the influence of the Logos, the Ideas become seminal reason-principles (*logoi spermatikoi*) . . . more often it is the Logos itself in the singular that is referred to as *spermatikos* (e.g., *Leg, All.* III 150; *Heres* 119) . . ." ibid., p. 159, i.e., communication is insemination.

36 Burkert, *Greek Religion,* pp. 321–22.

9: PELOPS AND HYACINTHUS AT NEW YEAR

1 Unlike the Celts, Romans, and Indians, it is generally agreed that the Greeks, preserving so much of their Indo-European linguistic inheritance, seem to have been a bit careless with their mythical legacies. But even Georges Dumézil, doyen of Indo-European structural mythology (and Foucault's fondest mentor), wasn't impressed by the notion of Indo-European pederasty. In the preface to Sergent's book he undermines his disciple before readers have had a chance to read him, by asking somewhat mysteriously, "Were the forms sufficiently *typical* or 'improbable' that one may legitimately speak of a common heritage? . . . That remains to be proven . . . it all goes back to the freeing of forelegs and the proliferation of neurons." Sergent, *Homosexuality in Greek Myth,* p. ix.

2 Gunnel Ekroth has come up with a subtler analysis allowing for the variety of different combinations of god, hero and deceased along the continuum from god to dead, from "all-god" via "all-hero" to "all-deceased," and the different types of offering that can be made to them, see esp. *Sacrificial Rituals,* 330–34; heroes who are supposed to be dead most often receive godlike sacrifices. From there the following table is taken. "Offer up" corresponds to *thusia,* divine sacrifice, contrasted with "offer down," *enagizein,* esp. holocaust (all burned, no distribution among worshippers) or pourings, *choai,* into the ground.

Immortality	Offer Up	God/God		
Immortality	Offer Up	God/Hero		
Immortality	Offer Up	Hero/Hero	Offer Down	Mortality
		Hero/Deceased	Offer Down	Mortality
		Deceased/Deceased	Offer Down	Mortality

3 For recent references, see Scanlon, *Eros,* pp. 32–34, Carla Antonaccio, "The Archaeology of Ancestors," in Carol Dougherty and Leslie Kurke (eds), *Cultural Poetics in Archaic Greece* (Cambridge, 1993) [46–70], pp. 62 and 69 n. 68.

4 Burkert, *Homo Necans,* pp. 93–103.

5 Pindar, *Ol.* 1.8–13.

6 Pindar, *Ol.* 1.25–52.

7 Pelops uses the metaphor of "sitting in darkness boiling an anonymous old age to no purpose" (83), significant language in the context of the myth that he was cooked for the gods as a child.

8 Pindar, *Ol.* 1.71–87.

9 Here we see most immediately how the pretensions of monarchic leaders make a context for talk of *amours des dieux,* and the crossing of the boundary between mortal and immortal.

10 Bacchylides also chose to focus on a myth of mortality, the story of Meleager, immortal until his mother put the log that preserved his youth on the fire. I imagine Hiero got the point.

11 The wings appear on the ivory-and-gold covered cedar "Chest of Cypselus," probably early sixth century, contemporary of the François Vase, which is no less as amazing in fact as the Chest of Cypselus sounds, Paus. 5.17,7 with Maddoli and Saladino ad loc., pp. 293–94.

12 Apollod., *Epitome* 2.3.

13 Parker, *Polytheism,* pp. 254–55.

14 Gantz, pp. 285–88.

15 E., *Hippolytus* 1247–48.

16 Theony Condos, *Star Myths* (Grand Rapids, 1997), is a useful translation with commentary of [Eratosthenes] *Katasterismoi* and Hyginus *De Astronomia* II, reorganized by constellation, see "Auriga." For Hippolytus as Auriga, Paus 2.32,1.

17 No archaeo-astronomer, I owe this information and much of what I say about stars to Robert Hannah, who agrees with some of what I say, sometimes enthusiastically, but not all and not always.

18 Sophocles, *Electra* 508–12, E., *Orestes* 988–96.

19 Paus. 6.20,7 with Madoli-Nafissi-Saladino ad loc.

20 *LIMC* "Chrysippos I" ##1–7, "Laios" #1.

21 The myth/drama may provide a self-conscious opposition to Elis's notoriously straightforward homosexual transactions *dia chariton*.

22 Or a later variation inspired by it. Euripides' *Chrysippus* was performed with his *Oenomaus* and the *Phoenician Women,* a play about Thebes. On the problem

of Euripides' *Chrysippus* see D. Mastronade, *Euripides: Phoenissae* (Cambridge 1994), pp. 31–38.

23 "Un jeune homme, imberbe," Odette Touchefeu-Meynier, *LIMC* "Laios," 186.

24 Euripides fr. 840 Nauck ap. Clement, *Stromata* 2.15, on the nature of sin, not knowing what is right or wrong, or knowing full well, and still not being able to do anything about it. A more literal translation: "None of what you say (*noutheteis*) has escaped my attention, but being of such opinion (*gnōmēn d'echonta m'*) I am, nevertheless, compelled by [my] Nature (*hē phusis biazetai*)."

25 Euripides fr. 841 Nauck.

26 Schachter, *Cults of Boiotia* I, pp. 242–50, esp. 242 n. 2 citing the Pisander-scholium ad E. *Phoenissae* 1760 *FGrHist* 16 F10. "Hera (Plataia)": this is the famous Hera of Rameau's comic opera *Platée,* Hera of the extraordinary festival called "Daidala" whose epithets are "Gamelia," "Gamostolos," "Kithaironia," "Nympheuomene," "Teleia."

27 If Atreus and Thyestes are asked to murder Chrysippus they must be reasonably mature, and if they need to murder him because of Chrysippus's seniority he must be maturer than they are in this version, Gantz, pp. 489–90.

28 Cf. Easterling's comments on the three surviving scenes of Electra's visit to her murdered father's tomb, "Form and Performance," pp. 168–69.

29 This explains why bluebells, named after another beautiful youth, Moon-loved Endymion, were surnamed *non scripta,* "unwritten."

30 1465–74.

31 D. 23.74, cf. Rhodes, ad *Ath. Pol.* 57.3, pp. 644–45, Boegehold, *Lawcourts,* pp. 135–39; in Draco's law, it seems it was only if the victim is an opponent in competition that the killer was absolved. A fragment of [Hesiod] *Catalogue of Women* of *c.*580 has been reconstructed as follows: ". . . fair-tressed Diomede. [She bore Hyacinthus], excellent and strong, [. . .] whom once [unshorn Phoebus] himself [killed unintentionally with a pitiless] discus." Fr. 120.5–8 (Most). So much can be restored from so little because the *Catalogue* was used as a source by (Pseudo-)Apollodorus, 3.10,3, which means that there is a reasonable chance that Apollodorus's reference to the love of Apollo "they say he was *erōmenos* of Apollo whom Apollo killed unintentionally with a discus he had thrown" was also mentioned in the *Catalogue,* although restorers have resisted this temptation. It is rare for gods to kill accidentally. On the other hand, there are many examples of "contests" or sporting rivalries between gods and humans that result in the punishment of the presumptuous mortals. The idea of a fatal yet "friendly" discus contest between Apollo and Hyacinthus seems a bit odd. Why did "strong" Hyacinthus issue such a foolish challenge? Apollo's sister Artemis killed Orion for challenging her at the discus [= the Pleiades?], Apollod. 1.4,5; Perseus of neighboring Argos "when in his prime of coming of age" (*hēlikiai . . . akmazōn*) kills his wicked grandfather King Acrisius with a discus that hits him on the foot, *accidentally* (Apollod. 2.4,4), during a "demonstration" of the new sport (Paus. 2.16,2).

32 Martial 14.173, Karl Lehmann, "A Roman Poet Visits a Museum," *Hesperia* 14

(1945), 259–69, esp. 262–63, reconstructs the layout of the temple's art collection at the end of the first century AD.

33 Polybius 5.191–92.

34 For the Hyacinthia, see Calame, *Choruses of Young Women,* pp. 175–85. Trümpy, *Untersuchungen,* pp. 131–32, 136, 138–39, thinks the Spartan month Hyakinthios corresponds to Athenian Hecatombaeon, July/August: complicated but cogent. For paean as healing-song, see especially Proclus, *Chrestomathia* 320a, "sung for delivery from plague and illnesses," but cf. Rutherford, *Pindar's Paeans,* pp. 101–108, with L. Käppel, *BMCR* 2002.10.38: "Perhaps R.'s new description has one advantage: It avoids naming any "purposes"—as I did by putting the appeal or thanksgiving for health, prosperity, or well-being in general into the functional center of the paean."

35 Hdt. 8.140–9.7. The Persians had marched into Athens in 480 to find the city evacuated. They destroyed it, such as it was, and withdrew for the winter to the fertile plains of Thessaly. From there they flattered the Athenians with tempting opportunities. If only they would sign up to join Xerxes' empire, they could have a dominant position in Greece. The Spartans were well aware of the profitable terms the Athenians had been offered and knew that if the Athenians went over to Persia with their huge fleet, the odds would tilt to the Persians' decisive advantage; Apollo speaking from his oracle at Delphi had predicted as much. If the Hyacinthia was an excuse, then, it was designed to be an excuse the Athenians might actually take seriously; the Spartans did not want the Athenians to lose faith.

36 X., *Hell.* 4.5, 11–18.

37 Polycrates, *FGrHist* 588 F1 = Ath. 4.139df.

38 X., *Agesilaus* 8.7.

39 *FGrHist* 588 F1 = Ath. 4.139d, cf. Brelich, *Paides,* pp. 143–44, Bruit, "The meal at the Hyakinthia."

40 Cf. Polybius 5.19,3, Musti and Torelli ad Paus. 3.18 ll. 56ff, Habicht, *Pausanias,* p. 161 and n. 82.

41 The quote is from Andrew Stewart, *Contra,* Faustoferri, *Il trono* p. 181: "le immagini non fossero casuali e meramente 'decorative,' " cf. n. 2. Faustoferri provides a detailed commentary on each scene, a thorough survey of earlier scholarship and her own analysis of its scheme, summarized in figs. 32–33. That the scenes are not purely random seems clear, if only because so many are found nowhere else, cf. ibid., p. 181 n. 1, but I am not sure Faustoferri's complex but comprehensive solutions, heavily dependent on appeal to "rites of passage," are more realistic. For detailed commentary, Musti and Torelli ad loc. (Paus. 3.18 ll.56 ff); Pipili, *Laconian Iconography,* pp. 81–82 summarizes the most obvious characteristics of the scheme.

42 Zeus gets Taÿgete and fathers Lacedaemon, Lacedaemon marries Sparta, daughter of the river Eurotas, and fathers Amyclas, Amyclas marries the Lapith Diomede and fathers Hyacinthus. Poseidon gets Alcyone and fathers Hyrieus, Gantz, pp. 212–18.

43 Athens's national hero, Faustoferri, *Il trono,* pp. 96–99, esp. on the Minotaur's Bronze Age style trussing up, 98–99, n. 16.

44 This particular part of the scheme with Castor and Pollux abducting the daughters of Leucippus (good links to Dionysus and Hyacinthus's mysterious nocturnal fests of women), with Dionysus and two apotheoses, is a "hot point" on the throne, see esp. Faustoferri, pp. 201–205, 227–35.

45 Pausanias was from a sister-city, Magnesia-at-Mount-Sipylus.

46 3.18,10–16.

47 An altar-tomb-throne ought to mean a sacrificed king, like Priam, Hélène Cassimatis ". . . autel-trône? . . ." in Christiansen and Melander, *Ancient Greek and Related Pottery,* pp. 117–29.

48 Gantz, pp. 473–78. Semele was a popular goddess/heroine and not just in Thebes.

49 Dorian Cnidus had a cult of Artemis "Raising Hyacinthus" Hiacinthotrophos. Ino is another mortal who becomes "the White Goddess" Leucothea, often identified with Phoenician Astarte.

50 Paus. 3.19,3–5. How Pausanias knew who was who is open to question; elsewhere we find Pausanias contradicting what his guides say, once he has read the labels (2.9,8; 1.2,4) and there are very obscure characters in his description—Anaxias? a good Spartan kingly name? Mnasinous?—of whom he seems to know their names only. At any rate, we can probably discount the possibility that Pausanias simply looked at the images and deduced. Most interesting is Callisthenes, *FGrHist* 124 F 13, ap. Ath. 10.452ab—who mentions the throne had a figure of "Famine" (*Limos*). Is this one of the figures passed over by Pausanias or is it a "nickname" for the figure of Hera imprisoned on a throne? Faustoferri, *Il trono,* pp. 168–71, cf. 42–44. Phylarchus, *FGrHist* 81 F 32b cf. Parthenius, *Amat. Narr.* 15, says Hyacinthus's sister was Daphne, the laurel, another of Apollo's amatory victims, which gives added poignancy to Apollo teaching the tale (of Hyacinthus, probably) to the laurels that flourish by the Eurotas at Amyclae in Virgil's Sixth *Eclogue* ll. 82–86, cf. Knox, "In Pursuit of Daphne," who notes Daphne's Spartan connections and the parallel with Gallus, objects, correctly, to any dirgelike element in Apollo's song, but errs, I think, in identifying Daphne as the subject of Apollo's song: the myth of Daphne is one myth the laurels of the Eurotas would not need to be taught. John Webster, *Duchess of Malfi,* Act III, Scene 2 puts his finger on what Hyacinthus's sister(s) unmarried Polyboea and Daphne had in common: "Daphne, for her peevish flight,/Became a fruitless bay-tree."

51 The famous *Hyacinthus* then on display in the temple of Augustus, as old in the time of Pausanias as a Leonardo da Vinci is for us today. Nicias was a notoriously painstaking and dedicated artist of the early Hellenistic period; he had to ask his attendant whether or not he had had breakfast and refused to let go of his commissions, having become overly attached to them, Plu., *Mor.* 1093de.

52 Hall, *Ethnic Identity,* p. 39 n. 53. Willetts, *Cretan Cults,* pp. 222–23: Hyacinthus

is a Minoan fossil, "an annually dying and reborn god of vegetation"; hence at the Spartan Hyacinthia "the compromise between the Olympian and the Minoan youthful god was ritually honored." Faustoferri complains about all the attention Hyacinthus gets, *Il trono*, p. 37, with recent examples at n. 125.

53 The archaeological evidence is neatly summarized by Brelich, *Paides*, pp. 177–78.

54 Trümpy, *Untersuchungen*, p. 126: "*Mit den Hyakinthia und den Karneia können wir jedenfalls den dorischen Stamm von derjenigen Zeitperiode an als Einheit greifen, die zwischen der 'dorischen Wanderung' und der weitern dorischen Ausbreitung nach Südosten liegt,*" cf. 131 and n. 572. On Crete, Hyacinthus was probably known at Malla and Lato (month-names), Gortyn (an "Amyklaion"), Tylissos and/or Cnossus probably (a reference to the Wacinthia, apparently a politically central New Year cult, in a treaty with Argos [Meiggs and Lewis 42, B 1.17]), Sporn, *Heiligtümer und Kulte*, esp. pp. 341, n. 2528, 147, n. 992.

55 In the same way Spartans honored Poseidon under his *indigenous* name as Pohoidan (cf. Arcadian Posoidanos) rather than in their own dialect as Poteidan, Buck, *Greek Dialects*, p. 38.

56 Burkert, *Greek Religion*, p. 34.

57 *Iliad*, 5.401, 899.

58 Cf. Sergent, *Homosexuality in Greek Myth*, p. 88.

59 *Helen* 1465–74.

60 Nonnus, *Dionysiaca* 19.104.

61 The rhythm is the same as that used in Spartan marching songs. For the conquest and/or absorption of "Achaean" Amyclae, in the seventh century supposedly, see Arist. fr. 532 (Rose), Paus. 3.2,6, Cartledge, *Sparta and Lakonia*, pp. 79–81 and 106–108.

62 On supposed links between the Hyacinthia and the Panathenaea, see Mikalson "Erechtheus and the Panathenaia," *AJP*97 (1976), 141–53.

63 The hill has not so far been identified, but Robert Hannah has calculated that when viewed from the Acropolis, the Hyades seem to set alongside Auriga behind the mountain of Aigaleos (which divides Athens from Eleusis) on either side of the Sacred Way, a most significant fact when one takes into account the myth of the war between Eleusis and Athens in which Erechtheus-Auriga and his daughters the Hyades died. This would seem to me a good place to start looking for the "tombs of the Hyacinthidai."

64 E., *Erechtheus* fr. 370.

65 Brûlé, "Hyakinthies et Panathénées," Mikalson, "Erechtheus and the Panathenaia."

66 Gantz, p. 94. Swan-Boy clearly wearing a yarmulke is *LIMC*, "Hyakinthos" #10 cf. #41; on #12 he is carrying a plate or sacrificial *phialē*. Images so far discovered conform fairly well to a pattern: (1) Boy riding swan, (2) Stripling embraced by winged Stripling. It is unproven that Boy and Stripling are the same mythical personage. That Swan-Boy appears infrequently but over a long period implies a stable source for the images in a cult image or cult tale. In the

foundation myth of some Milesian Boys' contests, Smicrus (Little), father of Apollo's beloved Branchus, is a native of Apollo's sanctuary at Delphi. At age Thirteen he is taken on a journey, but is left behind at Miletus. He meets another Boy, a goatherd, and is adopted by the Boy's father Eritharses, who loved him like a son. One day, when the two Boys were pasturing goats, they came upon a beautiful swan. They put a dress on it. Then they fought over who should take it to the father/stepfather. When they took the dress off the swan, they found a woman, Leucothea, the "White Goddess," who told them to tell the Milesians to honor her with a Boys' contest, cf. J. Fontenrose, *Didyma* (Berkeley, 1988), pp. 106–107. It seems most significant, therefore, that Swan-Boy appears on the early classical electrum (silver amalgamated with gold) two-drachma pieces of Cyzicus on the Propontis, at around the time Swan-Boy appears on Athenian Vases—Cyzicene staters were familiar in Athens; Cyzicus is a colony of Miletus and Didyma was probably directly involved in Miletus's colonizing movement. But Cyzicus has no connections, so far as I know, with Amyclae. There was also a cult of Leukos, "the white god," at Miletus, a figure quite possibly identified with Achilles. For the coins and the vases, see Laurence and François Villard, *LIMC* "Hyakinthos" #31, cf. ##8, 10, 12.

67 Kaempf-Dimitriadou, *Liebe der Götter,* p. 14, says of Swan-Boy: "a link with the god is doubtless indicated, but a real love-relationship is not expressed" (although she is prepared, on the other hand, to see plenty of amorous Zephyrs); the Villards beg to differ: "*l'amour d'Apollon pour le beau* pais *s'inscrit fort bien,*" *LIMC* "Hyakinthos," p. 550. "Erotikism" does seem to be implied in images of Swan-Boy—*kalos*-inscriptions, for instance; it is the original identification (dating back many decades) of Swan-Boy as Hyacinthus that should remain in doubt.

68 Burkert, *Greek Religion,* p. 175, Parker, *Athenian Religion,* pp. 293, 156 n. 14.

69 Ovid, *Fasti* 5.222.

70 [Bacchylides] *A.P.* 6.53, Eudemus dedicates a shrine to him on his land.

71 Lucretius, *De Rerum Natura* 1.11; Pliny *Nat. Hist.* 16.93; Vitruvius 6.7,1; Lactantius *Inst* 1.8, 7–8; Aug., *Civ. Dei* 21.5.

72 Paus. 1.37,2, cf. Parker, *Athenian Religion,* p. 318.

73 *Homeric Hymn* 6.3–5.

74 Alcaeus fr. 327, Nonnus, *Dionysiaca* 6.43 31.110–12, 47.341–42.

75 A typical "Middle-Comedy" plot would have involved mythological characters transported into the hodiernal world; much depends on whether there should be an "or" in Anaxilas's title as handed down.

76 Paus. 3.20,4, Festus 181, Rutherford, *Pindar's Paeans,* p. 46 n. 46, Pipili, *Laconian Iconography,* pp. 20–22, 40–42, 64–65, 71–74, 76.

77 Ovid, *Met.* 10.174–75, Macrobius, *Sat.* 1.17,11, Cartledge, *Sparta and Lakonia,* pp. 26–27.

78 Ovid, *Fasti* 5.531–33.

79 Strabo 9.2,12.

80 Cols 13–14, Janko, "The Derveni Papyrus," 24.

PART IV: MEN OF WAR
10: ACHILLES AND HERACLES

1 19.282–300.

2 19.301–302.

3 Clarke, "Achilles and Patroclus in Love," provides by far the best scholarly summary of the arguments and debates. His conclusions seem unexceptionable. Note especially 393 and 395: "Are they lovers? Some physical expression of their feelings for one another seems virtually certain on the evidence of Achilles' behavior after Patroclus dies. But no sexual relationship is conclusively proved; and those whom the idea offends are free to reject it. The essential question, however, is not whether the heroes engage in sodomy, but whether they are in love . . . The sexual question is anyway irrelevant. It is clear from the language, precedents and dramatic development of the *Iliad* that Achilles and Patroclus are not Homeric 'friends,' but are lovers from their hearts. Patroclus lives his life only in the life of Achilles; and is in turn the only human being more important to Achilles than himself, than his own life, his own ego and honor." Cf. 394: "The fact is that Achilles has no wife. He has Patroclus, whom he loves as other men love their wives; for only Patroclus can move him as Cleopatra moved Meleager in exactly similar circumstances." Published the same year as Dover's sodomaniacal *Greek Homosexuality*, Clarke shows how different the study of Greek love might have been over the following decades and the opportunity that was lost.

4 Clarke, "Achilles and Patroclus," 384.

5 Homer is here "zooming" into the present, implying that there is a monument somewhere in this world where Achilles and Patroclus lie together. Aelian says that by the time of Alexander there was a separate tomb where Patroclus was buried; it is here, he says, that Alexander's beloved Hephaestion placed his wreath, *V.H.* 12.7.

6 23.69–101. I think there can be no doubt that Homer is playing with an erotic image here, all the dual forms and the wrapping up in each other, even, finally, an impulse to join in an embrace, to share together the delights of . . . mourning.

7 *Iliad* 23.135–51.

8 Archilochus fr. 196a.52, cf. Solon fr. 9.1.

9 Clarke, "Achilles and Patroclus," 385.

10 24.128–31.

11 Clarke, "Achilles and Patroclus," 386–88.

12 Daniel Ogden is quite right to talk of "a bogus philological claim" on the part

of those who avoid translating "*even* with a woman," "Homosexuality and Warfare in Ancient Greece," 124 and n. 157; cf. Fisher ad Aeschines 1.142.

13　Nagy notes that *therapōn* derives from the Hittite word for ritual substitute, *tarpan(alli)-*, borrowed by Greek in the second millennium BC and meaning an *alter ego* upon whom the impurities of this entity may be transferred, *Best of the Achaeans,* pp. 292–95. The notion of *therapōn* as "representative," "substitute" or "student" seems guaranteed in this period by usages such as "servants of Ares" = "warriors," and "servant of the Muses" = "poet." But this information doesn't really add very much to the fact that in Greek culture, demonstrated on countless different occasions over a long period, plagiarism really is the sincerest form of flattery, with fawning allegiance configured as mimicking. *Lakonize* means both "imitate Spartans" and "be a political ally of Sparta," *medize* means both "go over to the Persians" and "wear Persian clothes," etc. Patroclus reveals himself as Achilles' *therapōn* by dressing up as him and imitating him; he is an "Achillesizer," as Hephaestion is later an "Alexanderizer."

14　See especially Fisher ad Aeschines 1.141.

15　Aeschylus frr. 135–37 Radt.

16　Ath. 13.602e.

17　180a.

18　178d–179b.

19　179bd.

20　179e–180b.

21　Ford, "Reading Homer from the Rostrum."

22　1.141–42.

23　This is the same contrast between what is *erōtikos* and *hubris* that Aristotle uses in his discussion of Hellanocrates of Larissa, *Pol.* 1311b. There, as here, it seems to be a contrast between sincere noble feelings of love and "abusive" relationships, not between sexual and asexual relationships, cf. Dover, "Eros and Nomos."

24　There is early, if fragmentary, evidence for Patroclus and Achilles being first cousins (which by no means excludes an amatory relationship), but Homer prefers to make Patroclus's grandfather one Actor, who appears to have been second husband of Achilles' great-grandmother Aegina, even though this would put Patroclus in a previous generation—the same as that of old Peleus, Gantz, p. 222.

25　1.143.

26　1.145.

27　1.146.

28　1.147–49.

29　Berlin F 2278, *BA* 200108. I am not qualified to assess more recent alternative attributions to, e.g., early Euthymides. I do suspect, however, that it makes a pair with another equally huge and exceptional cup, the Peithinos Cup, which has similar pleated chiffon shoulder-sleeves and spotted lion seat-coverings and the conception of Achilles as its centerpiece and which was discovered at Vulci around the same time. "Peithinos" is another great master who may be someone better known in disguise, though certainly not the same as the "Sosias Painter."

30 Gantz, p. 579; Achilles' intimate relationship with the doctor-god Asclepius at Brasiae is also relevant, Paus. 3.24,5.

31 For Ram-bearing Hermes at Tanagra, cf. Schachter, *Cults of Boiotia* II, pp. 44–50. On the cult image he normally carries the ram around his shoulders, but here he has not yet reached that point.

32 Eva Stehle, "Help Me to Sing, Muse, of Plataea," *Arethusa* 29 (1996), 205–22.

33 No one knows how Athenian vases, sometimes with very personal inscriptions, found their way to Tuscany in such large numbers. Perhaps the best bet is that they were created for a particular occasion, then transported to the Etruscans as secondhand goods, cf. esp. M. Robertson, "Adopting an Approach I," pp. 6–8 on Exekias's Dinos (*BA* 310402, Villa Giulia M446), found at Cervetri but inscribed after firing "at the request of the purchaser Epainetos" (*CAVI*); "Epainetos came to Exekias' shop and said 'I'll take this one, but I want your signature, and also this other inscription' and gave him a copy in the Siyonian alphabet." Robertson, p. 8, cf. Mus. Naz. Etrusc. Villa Giulia 47231, *BA* 301710, a Panathenaic victory amphora inscribed with the chariot-race winner's (?) name: "Euphiletos kalos." But some were definitely made for the Etruscans: Spivey, "Greek vases in Etruria."

34 Slatkin, *Power of Thetis,* pp. 30–31, 40–41, index s.v. "Eos" and *passim* thinks Achilles' mother, Thetis, is a kind of equivalent for Dawn.

35 Paus. 6.23,3.

36 It isn't impossible that Cronus had to yield the festival at Olympia, which looks much more like a midmonth, midsummer Cronia than a festival of Olympian Zeus, more typically celebrated in spring.

37 Helen was often believed to have become Achilles' partner in the afterlife, although other heroines were given the same role: Medea, Iphigeneia, cf. Paus. 3.24,10 with Musti and Torelli ad loc.

38 Philostratus, *Heroikos* 54.2–57.17, esp. 56.

39 Hedreen, "Cult of Achilles." For more recent finds, Michail J. Tresiter and Yuri G. Vinogradov, "Archaeology on the Northern Coast of the Black Sea," *AJA* 97 (1993), 533–54. Achilles was called "Ruler of the Black Sea," Pontarches. (I wonder if this has anything to do with the story that the great Zeus of Olympia had "Pantarkes kalos," said to be Pheidias's *erōmenos,* inscribed on his finger.)

40 Vanessa B. Gorman, *Miletos, the Ornament of Ionia* (Ann Arbor, 2001), pp. 175–76.

41 J. Hind, "The Portland Vase," *JHS* 115 (1995), 153–55, cf. S. Woodford, *Images of Myths in Classical Antiquity* (Cambridge, 2003), pp. 229–35.

42 Philostratus, *Heroikos* 53.8–13. Achilles was often associated with the sprint, note the *dromos* (running-track) at Olbia and the mourning for Achilles that

opened the Olympic Games, which originally comprised just one event, the *stadion* (200m dash). For the custom of nude sprints in honor of Achilles at Troy, Plu., *Alex.* 15.7–8.

43 Paus. 10.31,2, Ogden, *Crooked Kings,* pp. 10 and 99.

44 Paus. 3.19,11–13.

45 Paus. 5.7,8.

46 13.95, 19.569, 23.587, 604, 785–93.

47 15.579–91.

48 E. V. Rieu's unimprovable Penguin translation.

49 23.555–6.

50 23.796.

51 Probably the Ethiopians were originally from the land that meets the sun, far west or far east. Later they were located in the far south.

52 Paris, Louvre, G 115 (*BA* 205119).

53 Gantz, pp. 622–25.

54 Paus. 5.19,1 and 5.17,7 with Maddoli and Saladino ad loc., pp. 293–94, for dating. It seems quite likely that a Memnon vs. Achilles is to be reconstructed on the metopes of the very early temple of Artemis in Corfu *c.* 580 BC.

55 Bumke, *Statuarische Gruppen,* pp. 95–96 n. 543. A black stone with Memnon's name is notable.

56 Bumke, *Statuarische Gruppen,* pp. 179–84.

57 Paus. 5.22,3.

58 White-skinned figures in Greek art are usually women or effeminates it would seem, and men are dark, i.e., tanned, and hard from a life of nudity in the gymnasium. Achilles' mother Thetis may also be color-coded as goddess of the deep, dark sea.

59 On this point, and the monument, see Malkin, *Returns of Odysseus,* pp. 26–27 and ch. 4, esp. pp. 138–39.

60 Thuc. 1.26. At least Corinth and her allies marched overland to Apollonia and used it as their base and Thucydides mentions no unwillingness on Apollonia's part.

61 Clarke, "Achilles and Patroclus," 383. The point is not whether Homer gives any indications of hanky-panky but (1) why Telemachus cannot sleep alone and (2) why Homer draws such conspicuous attention to the parallel between Telemachus and Pisistratus sleeping together and husbands and wives sleeping together. Just as Plato "datifies" his dialogues by flagging up particular time-indications in his text, so Homer is here "pairifying" Telemachus and Pisistratus, by flagging up particular relationship indications in his narrative: two-horse chariot pair, shared proto-sympotic sleeping couch, etc. In other words, he is making Pisistratus and Telemachus "an item."

62 4.187–88.

63 24.15–19.

64 24.73–84.

65 "Homer and the Neoanalytiker," cf. Ken Dowden, "Homer's sense of text," *JHS* 116 (1996) [47–61], 58 n. 62: "Page's sarcasm recoils on itself"; J. Burgess, "Beyond Neo-Analysis: Problems with the Vengeance Theory," *AJP* 118 (1997), 1–19, is still taking issue with it.

66 Transl. from Burgess, *Tradition of the Trojan War*, pp. 178–79. Burgess has a useful translation of the late summaries in Appendix A, and lists of early images. The schematic date-graph of images from Cook, Appendix B, makes clear how much more popular extra-Homeric myths were at an earlier date in art, though the sample size is tiny. There seems no doubt to me, looking at the evidence, of the general principle that at his première Homer was not telling the famous "Tale of Troy" that contemporaries might have been expecting nor even the "tale of the wrath of Achilles," but newish stuff (or more obscure traditions) that drew on more famous myths. I think he was a much more creative artist as regards content as well as presentation, in other words. I doubt that anything like the *Iliad* was to be heard before Homer ("like" being used in the meaningful sense).

67 Pindar, *Isthmian* 8.37.

68 Pindar, *Nemean* 3.43–52.

69 Nagy, *Best of the Achaeans*, pp. 325–26.

70 On Troilus in art and poetry and the addition of Briseida/Cressida and sex, Gantz, pp. 597–602.

71 Gantz, p. 627: ". . . little doubt that Achilleus was wounded in the foot at an early point in the tradition." The arrow goes into Achilles' ankle (*talos*), which later—cf. French *talon*, Italian *tallone*—becomes "heel."

72 Jane Lightfoot, "Greek Literature after the Classical Period," in Oliver Taplin (ed.), *Literature in the Greek and Roman Worlds: A New Perspective* (Oxford, 2000) [217–56], p. 226.

73 Lycophron, *Alexandra* 307–13.

74 Schol. ad. Lycophron 307, Servius ad *Aeneid* 1.474.

75 D'Agostino and Cerchiai, *Il mare, la morte, l'amore*, pp. 91–128, esp. pp. 107–114, figs. 48–49, 61–62.

76 Gantz, pp. 601–602.

77 Maria Pipili, *LIMC* s.v. "*Iolaos*"; for Iolaus as helper against the Lernaean Hydra, Gantz, pp. 384–86; for his rejuvenation (or, indeed, resurrection), pp. 464–65.

78 Ar., *Ach*. 867, Plato Comicus 202 K-A.

79 Pindar, *Pythian* 9.81–82.

80 The play makes Athenian Creusa mother of all Greeks, with a god, Apollo, the father of the branch from which the Athenians and their fellow Ionians are descended, a mortal the father of the rest.

81 Euripides, *Ion* 190–202.

82 Too old, you can't help thinking, to have a grandmother still living, for Alcmene also features.

83 E., *Heraclidae* 727–39.

84 E., *Heraclidae* 849–63. According to other versions, he came back from the dead. Eurystheus is spared by the Athenians but handed over to Alcmene, who decides to have him killed. Eurystheus promises his body, buried at the pass that gives access to the plain of Athens, will protect them when they too are attacked by Heracles' descendants, i.e., the Dorian Spartans during the Peloponnesian War, an allusion to a local hero-cult. Iolaus is represented with a beard as often as without one in Athens and is by no means an exemplary ephebe, therefore.

85 Plu., *Pel.* 18.5

86 Plu., *Mor.* 492c.

87 D.S. 4.24, 1–6.

88 Polybius 7.9.

89 Philostratus, *Life of Apollonius* 5.5.

90 C. Bonnet, *Melqart: cultes et mythes de l'Héraclès tyrien en Méditerranée* (Leuven, 1988), p. 252, pp. 179–80 and index s.v. "*Iolaos,*" "Hydre de Lerne," Walbank ad Polybius 7.9,2.

91 Bonnet, *Melqart* index s.v. "Hydre de Lerne."

92 Clement, *Exhortation to the Heathen (Protrepticus)* 34, with Heraclitus fr. 15. The Lenaea (*lēnē,* "maenad") is an old festival of Dionysus on the 12th of "Marriage month," Gamelion, Jan/Feb. associated (in Mykonos) with a "song on behalf of fruit (*karpos*) [or 'harvest']" and in Athens, in the classical period, with a little drama festival. There it was presided over by the official called "King," and a priest of Eleusis, who stands during the drama contest with a torch and says, "Call on the god," and the audience shouts back, "Son of Semele, Iacchos, *Ploutodotēs* (Giver of Wealth)," schol. *Frogs* 482, *Ath. Pol.* 57.1 (with Rhodes's notes ad loc. for bib.).

93 Pseudo-Clement, *Homily* 5.23. If at Lerna Pluto (or perhaps, as at the Lenaea, Ploutodotes) is Dionysus, it would explain why Clement cited Heraclitus here on the identity of Dionysus and Hades.

94 For Lerna, G. Casadio, *Storia del culto di Dioniso in Argolide* (Rome, 1994) with J. Hall's rev. *JHS* 117 (1997), 224–25, and on the rites and the links between Demeter and Dionysus at Lerna, Piérart, "La mort de Dionysos," who, oddly, refuses to see any connection between Dionysus shown the Underworld by Prosymnus and Demeter Prosymna, although he is right to distinguish Demeter's Lernaia from the things done at night by the lake, as Casadio does not. Wilson, "Politics of Dance," 174–75, 188 n. 53, cites the research of Barbara Kowalzig on dithyramb at Lerna and notes dedications to "Bacchus and Prosymnaia" by initiates into the cult of Demeter.

95 Casadio, "Préhistoire de l'initiation," 212: "L'initiant était soumis à un rite de pénétration anale."

96 *IG* 13 253.6, 9. Icarion sounds as if it is simply "the shrine of Icarius." For the myth, Apollod. 3.191, Hyg., *Fab* 130, *Astr.* 2.4, Nonnus, *Dion.* 47.34–264, Paus.

1.2,5, Burkert, *Homo Necans,* p. 223 n. 37, cf. Eratosthenes, *Erigone* frr. 22–26 (Powell).

97 Dioscorides *A.P.* 7.410–11.

98 Wilson, Khoregia, pp. 12–16, Seaford, *Reciprocity and Ritual,* pp. 275–56.

99 Paus. 1.2,5, Whitehead, *Demes of Attica,* pp. 215–18.

100 For references and the latest on the myth and Eratosthenes, see Luppe, "Die Ikarios-Sage."

101 Perhaps the damage was done (at the start of the growing season apparently) by the early summer-appearing star called "Aix" (Capella, brightest star of Auriga), "The Goat," who destroyed the tender shoots. On a famous image illustrating a sacrifice, a butchered goat is hung up on the vine. The star Capella had a propitiatory Goat statue in Phlius, Paus. 2.13,4, Cerchiai, "Il programma figurativo," esp. 131; perhaps one ought to be more pedantic about the exact species and sex of the goats in question; *aix* can be male in early literature and it can refer to a "wild goat" or ibex.

102 Schol. Lucian, *Deorum Concilium* 5. The text is printed as an appendix to Lowe, "Thesmophoria and Haloa"; the author's main concern is with techniques of explaining myth; he concludes a Hellenistic exegete is the least unlikely author.

103 Parker, *Polytheism,* pp. 290–97.

104 *BA* 305526 from Paris *Cab. des Med.* Torches are very often carried by stars, by Phosphoros etc. I don't know why Lissarrague doesn't see the light, here, *Greek Vases,* p. 200: *phōs* = "mortal" of Zeus. The Diosphos Painter paints weird subjects and doesn't seem to have been terribly literate, often just putting letters on his vases that don't actually mean anything, but here he seems to have had help. A young male springing out of Zeus's loins cannot but be Dionysus.

105 Plato, *Timaeus* 91bd. For the Underworld Pankrates, associated with Palaemon, Heracles, Pluto (and Zeus) in his shrine at Ilissus, Vikela, *Weihreliefs,* pp. 57–80.

11: Crete and Sparta

1 Plato, *Laws* 1.636cd. Henri van Effenterre, among others, thought Plato had firsthand knowledge of Crete, *La Crète et le Monde grec de Platon à Polybe* (Paris, 1948), pp. 35–36, 40–44; P. A. Brunt is doubtful, *Studies in Greek History and Thought* (Oxford, 1993), pp. 269–72, in which case Plato knew nothing of the abduction ceremony; his ascription to the Cretans of the myth of Ganymede's abduction was based merely on the fact that Cretans were famous for homosexual practices and believed their laws came from Zeus. But an archaeological cultural artifact like the abduction ritual is just the kind of thing that would attract the attention of ancient ethnographers. Aristotle says it was not the Dorian colonizers but the indigenous population they dominated who preserved Minos's laws, *Pol.* 1371b, although he also says the Dorian newcomers adopted the preexisting constitution, revealing a slight inconsistency.

2 Fornara, *Nature of History,* pp. 42–45, on the subject of lost historians in general, cf. Pearson: " 'Writing books about books that don't exist' sounds like a suitable occupation for Wonderland, and it deserves an explanation that would satisfy Alice. 'How can you understand the books that exist,' they might have told her, 'unless you read the non-existent books first?' 'Yes, I know,' Alice might reply, 'but there are so many lost Greek historians.' There are indeed," *Greek Historians of the West,* p. vii.

3 Ephorus, *FGrHist* 70 F 149, Strabo 10.4,21.

4 F. Lasserre in the Budé edition of Strabo vol. 6 (Paris, 1971) marks a gap in the text at this point, corresponding to an unreadable section about thirty letters long in the palimpsest manuscript, which may have explained exactly who these mysterious "friends" are. In his translation (followed by Schnapp, *Le Chasseur et la cité,* p. 130 and Schmitt Pantel, *La cité au banquet,* p. 78), Lasserre assumes it is the *abductor's* friends, but Link, *Kreta,* pp. 24–25 and Vattuone, "Eros Cretese," 18 n. 18 think the friends are friends of the boy, since their role is to protect his interests more than those of the abductor. The most recent editor, Stefan Radt, cannot see Lasserre's thirty-letter gap at all (personal communication) and no other manuscript records it; if Ephorus did explain who the "friends" were, in other words, it is probably Strabo himself and not some later copyist of Strabo who left something out. The concluding sacrifice seems to induct the abductor/lover, *philētōr,* into the community of the friends, *philoi;* for the Greeks "lover" and "friend" were by no means mutually exclusive categories.

5 By referring to the *lover's andreion*—a place in space, evidently, rather than a group of people, and not an otiose way of describing a unique City *Andreion*— Ephorus contradicts the common view that each city had only one; cf. idem F 149 ap. Strabo 10.4.20: "The younger boys [i.e., younger than the ephebic *agelaoi* "herdsmen"] from the same mess [*syssition*] fight against each other and against other messes [*syssitia*]." The problem is that Dosiadas *FGrHist* 458 F 2 (Ath. 4.143ad) says there are two buildings for messes throughout Crete, one for dining, one for putting up guests, and a majority of scholars, under the influence, I suspect, of modern ethnography (Willetts, *Aristocratic Society,* pp. 19–20, Schmitt Pantel, *La cité au banquet,* p. 76 n. 73) have read this as implying that all male citizens ate together in one building, drawing conclusions about the exclusivity, in terms of numbers (tiny) and symbolic impact (highly visible) of Cretan elites, cf. S. Hodkinson *OCD3* s.v. "*syssitia,*" Willetts, *Aristocratic Society,* p. 26, Schmitt Pantel, op. cit., p. 76: "You and I (reader and author) arrive in an archaic Greek village. We see a building constructed in a prominent place at the heart of the village, someone says it is the *syssition.* Some groups of men accompanied by some youths make their way toward it and go inside, while the rest of the inhabitants stay outside: children, women and the vast majority of men who, slaves or foreigners, have no right to cross the threshold."

   To resolve the apparent discrepancy, Link, *Kreta,* pp. 9–21, esp. p. 20 and nn.

10, 36 and 45, must distinguish two meanings for *andreia,* envisaging a competitive display by (1) *men's clubs*—i.e., rival *tables*—within (2) the city's single *men's club.* Dosiadas, however, is less than explicit and often unclear (he uses the word "table," pace Link, p. 20, to mean both a single "table" within a men's club and more generally "fare") and it seems rather reckless to draw such elaborate conclusions from the fragment, especially when Ephorus seems to contradict them straightforwardly. Not only are "glass walls"—lots of "commensal" societies "dining with" *sys—sition* each other but not "with" other commensal societies in the same room—unprecedented in the annals of Greek commensality, but we would certainly expect these immense (hundreds of members, surely) communal buildings to be noticed and this extraordinary difference from Spartan practice, with its many well-attested men's clubs, to be highlighted by our sources more explicitly, since the nature of the *andreion* was central to the debate over the priority of Cretan institutions. Plutarch, *Mor.* 714b, seems to equate the separate Spartan men's clubs with the Cretan clubs, *each* (contra Link, p. 21) forming a kind of aristocratic assembly (*synhedrion*). On the issue of single or multiple Men's Houses, cf. Gehrke, "Gewalt und Gesetz," 38 n. 65.

6 The text is "*en te gar tois chorois kai tois dromois echousi tas entimotatas chōras*"; Lasserre translates "*On leur réserve les places les plus en vue sur les sièges publics et dans les stades . . .*" ["the most conspicuous places on the public benches and in the stadiums"]. But the first part must mean "they have the positions of most esteem in dancing choruses . . ." The problem is *dromois.* The most straightforward translation is ". . . positions in runs," but how could any but the winning position be a "position of greatest honor" in, say, a foot race? There are really only two possibilities: (1) Certain positions on the starting line have greater honor; (2) These are not races at all, but some kind of ritual running display, perhaps connected to cults of Hermes Dromios (or Apollo Dromaios?) and/or a probable "festival of running," Dromeia (inferred from the name of a month at Priansos (? = *Himalios,* cf. Hesychius s.v., i.e., around harvest time in early summer?), Willetts, *Cretan Cults,* pp. 264–65, 109, 289. In the Spartan midsummer festival, Carneia, runners were selected to chase another, garlanded with fillets, down a *dromos.* According to Maybury-Lewis, the races of the Shavante of Brazil had to be run with great vigor and oomph, but nobody was all that worried about fairness and winning. Running might go on for ages, until someone decided there had been enough. It was not considered a good race if it was not reasonably close and might need to be run again, *Akwe-Shavante Society,* pp. 245–47, 251–52.

7 Ephorus, *FGrHist* 70 F 149 [= Strabo 10.4, 21]. Vattuone, "Eros Cretese," esp. 22 n. 26, suggests Strabo is giving only the "main points" he found in Ephorus, but that he is accurate, even preserving some of Ephorus's terminology.

8 Schnapp, *Le Chasseur et la cité,* pp. 126–33, has a survey of earlier treatments. Vattuone, "Eros Cretese," has a more detailed and polemical discussion, arguing against use of the passage to *explain away* the erotic elements.

9 Boswell, *Marriage of Likeness,* pp. 88–96. Boswell's interpretation is better than most, and is in line with more recent treatments, such as Schnapp, *Le Chasseur et la cité,* p. 132 and Link, *Kreta,* pp. 24–28, which emphasize bonding between individuals and their families, rather than ritual initiation.

10 Strabo 10.4,17.

11 On precociously early Cretan laws—impossible to separate, surely, from myths about Minos going up into the mountain to receive commandments—and the position of Cretan scribes, closer in role to the elite scribes of the Mycenaean world and the Near East, rather than to the stonecutters of democratic Athens, see Osborne, *Greece in the Making,* pp. 185–90; Schmitt Pantel, *La cité au banquet,* pp. 71–73; Thomas, *Literacy and Orality,* pp. 65–72; Whitely, "Literacy and Law-making." For the bizarre absence of archaeological evidence for habitation during the efflorescence of lawmaking cf. Morris, "Archaeology and archaic Greek history," 68: "If we take the evidence at face value, then Crete suffered a rapid population decline . . . On the other hand, if the silence is more a product of fluctuations in archaeological visibility than of demographic factors, then the sixth and fifth centuries were an extraordinary episode in which the Cretans turned their backs on the outside world every bit as thoroughly as did Tokugawa Japan between 1639 and 1854. Either way, the early sixth century was decisively important in Cretan history . . ."

12 Willetts, *Aristocratic Society,* c. iv, pp. 37–45, Link, *Kreta,* p. 29.

13 Buck, *Greek Dialects,* no. 117 col ii, 2–45.

14 *IC* I.IX.I.A.11. Herdsman, *"agelatēs"* = "ephebe" acc. to Hesychius, fifth century AD collector of rare words.

15 Hesychius s.v. *"apagelos: ho mēdepō sunagelazomenos pais. ho mechri etōn heptakaideka. Crētes"* and s.v. *"apageloi: skotioi."* Schmitt Pantel, *La cité au banquet,* p. 76, is perhaps misleading when she talks of the members of the "herd" as *"jeunes garçons,"* "young boys," when they were ephebes, Striplings, Eighteen and Nineteen.

16 Some would like to make this a dormitory for the "herds" of bachelors, or some other age-group, since we learn that Cretans "for the most part sleep together," Arist. fr. 611,15 (Rose), Willetts, *Aristocratic Society,* pp. 18–19.

17 Dosiadas, *FGrHist* 458 F2, with Jacoby ad loc. There are clearly some problems with the text here, or Dosiadas is simply an unclear writer. Link, *Kreta,* pp. 12–21, thinks, plausibly, that there were two elements to the meal, a basic sustenance guaranteed by the state, supplemented by individual contributions of a tenth to each particular table-club, so that those with wealthy members might dine more luxuriously; at Sparta there were two separate meals, a basic equal universal ration followed by a second course made up of individual gifts to the club.

18 Link, *Kreta,* p. 19 n. 37 explains why a woman has this role.

19 Ath. 4.143af [= Dosiadas, *FGrHist* 458 F2, Pyrgion, *FGrHist* 467 F1], Ephorus, *FGrHist* 70 F 149.

20 "Frequent" (*phoitan* ap. Strabo 10.4,16) would most naturally imply "go frequently," a word used of Athenians going to school every day, for instance. If Ephorus wanted to say the troops formed their own community he could have been more explicit. Perhaps Strabo has omitted the clarification.

21 It seems to me this "selection" is the equivalent of the Athenian selection of people who seem Eighteen, i.e., it doesn't matter what the ephebic age-classes imply about your maturity: if you don't look Twenty, if you don't have a decent beard, you cannot be allowed to enter the *proper* forty-year-long age-class system (*hēlikia*) and you will be "kept down" a year. Inauguration into the age-class at Twenty may represent a profound structural difference from other (e.g., Athenian) age-class systems and may help to explain why the beardless *kouros* (a new citizen at Eighteen) is so much less in evidence west of Corinth.

22 The official in charge of each Men's House is called the *paidonomos* ("boy-herder," "governor of the boys"), Ephorus, *FGrHist* 70 F 149 [= Strabo 10.4,20]. One possible implication is that the "troops" or "herds," *agelai,* are still in the Men's House.

23 As almost all scholars assume, cf. Willetts, *Aristocratic Society,* pp. 120–22. Inscriptions seem to connect "stripping-off" with graduation into the ranks of Runners, and at Phaistos the stripping off festival was linked to "marriage," i.e., lying down next to a girl. *IC* II xxiii.20 (third to second century, Willetts, p. 122 n. 1) is an epitaph for one Adrastus: "Out of the herd and into the Underworld [*ex agelas . . . eis Acheronta*]." No wedding song for your mother, but a dirge.

24 Buck, *Greek Dialects* 117, col. 12.34, cf. Hesychius "*to kata nomon mignusthai,*" Chantraine, *Dictionnaire,* s.v. *opuiō.* Lupi, *L'ordine delle generazioni,* p. 91 n. 91, thinks the girl was married at twelve and not taken to her husband's house until twenty or a little younger, which would give their young husbands some eight years of "semi-marriage" (like Cephalus and Procris!). Ovid, incidentally, says the boy/girl Iphis at Phaistos starts getting ready for what seems to be a sexual marriage, at thirteen, Ovid, *Met.* 9.666–797.

25 There seems no alternative to this interpretation of the evidence. In particular it is hard to see how the references in Dosiadas and Pyrgion to the "younger men" who receive half what their fathers get could refer to members of herds, fed at public expense. These authors in fact make no mention of ephebes or herds (perhaps because they didn't figure in the Men's Houses that concern them) but to men, "younger men" and "youngest."

26 Cf. Willetts, *Aristocratic Society,* p. 12.

27 Ephorus, *FGrHist* 70 F 149 [ap. Strabo 10.4,16], Dosiadas, *FGrHist* 458 F2. In Sparta you had to be voted into a mess using ballots made of squashed barley dumplings (*mazai*). You ran the danger of losing both membership and, thereby, citizenship if you failed to pay subs. Crete was seen as superior inasmuch as all citizens qualified automatically, thanks to the status of their fathers, joining the same club, perhaps.

28 Probably it means "having participated ten times at the annual Running Festival," a very Greek way of reckoning age, cf. Willetts, *Aristocratic Society,* pp. 13 n. 2 and 122–23.

29 *IC* I.ix.1.ll 99–100: *tous toka egduomenous* (Dreros); *IC* I.xix.1.ll 17–18: *tan agelan tan toka esduomenan* (Malla) cf. Willetts, *Aristocratic Society,* pp. 119–23.

30 Ovid, *Met.* (transl. Mary M. Innes) 9.666–797.

31 Ant. Lib. 17, cf. Willetts, *Aristocratic Society,* pp. 120–22, *Cretan Cults,* pp. 175–56.

32 Dover, "Greek Homosexuality and Initiation," cf. his review of Percy, *Pederasty and Pedagogy, Gnomon* 71.5 (1999), 472. Conceding the validity of Dover's criticisms, Schnapp, *Le Chasseur et la cité,* p. 548 n. 31, nevertheless tries to salvage "*une dimension initiatique.*" Of course it is initiatory; it's a wedding.

33 Link, *Kreta,* 25–27 cf. Hodkinson *OCD*3 s.v. "*syssitia*"—recruitment of (rich) boys for your mess—Vattuone, "Eros Cretese," p. 25—"*il ratto è il vertice dell' aghele,*" a graduation *summa cum laude* from the troops—cf. id. "*Paidika.* Considerazioni inattuali su un libro recente," *Rivista Storica dell'Antichità* 29 (1999), 283–307, 288—Vattuone is rightly suspicious of the motives of scholars who *explain away* homosexuality with initiation but then proceeds to impose coming-of-age on a document which makes no mention of any such thing— Sergent, *Homosexuality in Greek Myth,* p. 36—the gifts make the boy "a warrior, a banqueter, a sacrificer." By means of this "chosen one," his contemporaries are enabled to make the transition to adulthood and marriage—Schmitt Pantel, *La cité au banquet,* pp. 80–81—the "young boys" of the herd (!) initiated into public sacrifice—Willetts, *Aristocratic Society,* p. 14; "it is clear, from the gifts . . . that he had now entered upon the first stages of manhood," Bremmer, "An Enigmatic Indo-European Rite," 286—drinking age.

34 Max. Tyr *Or.* 20.8.

35 Aelian, *N.A.* 4.1. Vattuone, "Eros Cretese," 14–15, 25, notes there was probably a great deal of homoeros in Crete that never involved an abduction ceremony; it was too costly and disruptive. Aelian's boy does seem to have had a socially recognized role, laying out the lover's corpse, etc. Aelian claims to have given the names of the couple in some (lost?) book. Comparison with similar tales from elsewhere may indicate the story was linked to a heroic tomb in the center of a Cretan city.

36 Nepos, *Preface 4,* "*Laudi in Creta* [or *Graecia*] *ducitur adulescentulis quam plurimos habuisse amatores.*"

37 For the idea of the "friends" as an *eranos,* Ephorus ap. Strabo 10.4,21: *hôste suneranizein tous philous.* Greeks thought an *eranos* was a grouping based on *erôs,* cf. Weiss, "Erotica," Parker, *Athenian Religion,* p. 337: a dedication by *eranistai* to, of course, a Zeus Philios, and another in which all the political (demotic) identifications of the members of the love-club have been omitted.

38 Inasmuch as the "club" is a medium of citizenship, it corresponds to the (pseudo-)genealogical Athenian phratry or "clan," cf. Willetts, *Aristocratic Society,* p. 67. In Cyrene, *hetaireiai* may be subdivisions of a phratry; the new

colonists will be assigned to a tribe, a phratry and to nine *Hetaireiai,* Meiggs and Lewis #5 ll.15–16, Graham, "The Authenticity of the *horkion,*" 108–109.

39 Cf. Buck, *Greek Dialects* 117, col. iv, 33–35 (a serf "residing in the country" [*epi korai*], i.e., not "the bush!"), cf. Willetts, *Aristocratic Society,* p. 49 n. 4. There may be an escape route in Heraclides' epitome of the Aristotelian *Constitution:* "The Cretans seem to have been the first to employ passionate intercourses directed at males (*tais de pros tous arrhenas erōtikais homiliais heoikasi prōton kechrēsthai*), and this is not ugly (*aischron*) among them. When they achieve mastery (*hotan de kratēsōsin*), they lead (him) off to a mountain or their lands and there they feast sixty days (*apagousi eis oros ē tous heautōn chōrous*). For more is not permitted. And the Philētōr gives raiment and other gifts and an ox. All the Cretans spend their time sitting on thrones etc. . . ." Arist. fr. 611.15 (Rose). There is no mention of being able to go where you like, and to go to the mountains or your *own lands* you would not need permission. This seems to contradict Ephorus straightforwardly, but of course there are many different Cretan cities.

40 *Or.* 20.8. I am not quite sure where a reader of Plato (who in *Laws* condemned the licensed *pleasure* of the Cretans) has got the idea that it is shameful for a *neaniskos* to touch the boy unless, like a Spartan boy, he had to be kept wrapped up in a cloak and it was taboo to be seen to touch his flesh?

41 Timaeus, *FGrHist* 566 F 144.

42 *Laws* 636bd, 835e–842a.

43 Arist., *Pol.* 1272a, Sextus, *Outlines of Pyrrhonism* 3.199 cf. *AP* 12.247.

44 *FGrHist* 70 F 147 [= Strabo 10.4,8], Dosiadas, *FGrHist* 458 F5, Echemenes, *FGrHist* 459 F1 [= Ath. 13. 601e]—Minoan religion made great use of mountain caves and peak sanctuaries, continued through the seventh century, Preziosi and Hitchcock, *Aegean Art and Architecture,* pp. 86–87, 145–48, Burkert, *Greek Religion,* pp. 24–28.

45 *Kartei* (forcibly) *oipēi* . . . Although they clearly refer to sex, the verbs *oiphein* and *opuiein,* which seem to have a Dorian character, are difficult to translate precisely. *Oiphein/oipein* is something you can do to someone—"x *screwed* y," or with several people—"x, y and z *got off together*"—or alone—"x *got off.*" Possibly *oipein* was contrasted with *opuiein* to refer to nonmarital or violent "spunking," something like "fornication"; see G. P. Edwards, "Meaning and Aspect in the Verb *OPUIŌ,*" *Minos* 20–22 (1987), 173–81, cf. *LSJ* s.v.v. with *Suppl.,* Bain, "Six Greek verbs," 72–74, Chantraine, *Dictionnaire* s.v.v. *oiphō* and *opuiō,* "*épouser, prendre comme femme legitime,*" the etymology of which Chantraine lists as "obscure," making no connection with *oiphein* and doubtful about any Indo-European links, marginally preferring an indigenous Mediterranean root of which a derivative might be found in Etruscan *puia,* "*épouse.*"

46 Buck, *Greek Dialects* 117 col ii, 2–10. There follow penalties for the "forced mastering" of a domestic slavewoman (a different verb for sex with those with least rights, apparently) unless she has already been "mastered" in which case

the fine is reduced from 2 *staters* to one *obol,* the price of the cheapest prostitute, although if the rape takes place at night the fine is increased to two *obols;* and measures for "attempted sex with a free woman under the guardianship of a relative."

47 Harrison, *Law of Athens,* i, p. 34, ii, pp. 74–82, Todd, *Shape of Athenian Law,* pp. 276–79; one important difference is that a *dikē* can be brought only by the offended party, a *graphē* by "anyone who wishes." For Solon's use of the word *benein* to refer to violent sex, Bain, "Six Greek verbs," 57–58, although perhaps it just refers to sex with ejaculation.

48 Buck, *Greek Dialects* 117, ll. 21–24, but we should remember that the laws concern only legal suits for rape; it is entirely possible that, as in Athens, if you caught a man on top of your wife or daughter you would kill him first, making sure you had witnesses and then apply for impunity, without necessarily asking the woman whether or not she had been forced or persuaded.

49 Doubtless there were times when consent was anticipated and the friends turned a blind eye. Vattuone, "Eros Cretese," 21, who assumes an (unmentioned) sexual rape during the abduction, seems to be arguing that the boy's speech makes the rape unhappen: ". . . *la negazione di un gesto consente di stabilire la sua inesistenza* . . ."

50 *Kosmiotēs* refers to qualities of "orderly arrangement" (cf. *cosmos*), particularly with regard to outward appearance (cf. *cosmetics*). It means something like "smart," "not tarty" or "with not a hair out of place"; we are told Athenian women could be fined the enormous sum of 1,000 drachmas for appearing in public *akosmousai,* i.e., "dressed inappropriately," Hyperides F 14 (Blass).

51 Hermonax, author of a Hellenistic (?) collection of *Cretan Dialect Words,* ap. Ath. 11.502b, cf. *Der Kleine Pauly* s.v. "Glossographie." Our knowledge of the meaning of the cup is dependent on the information that it is similar to a *Therikleios* (Ath. 470e–472e) about which the sources say a great deal. The *therikleian* seems to have been valuable, old-fashioned-looking (said to be used by Heracles—hence by Alexander? in his fatal draft from a "Heraclean cup"— and dedicated by Achilles' son Neoptolemus on the Athenian Acropolis), with two stubby handles, indicating, like almost all Greek cups, passage between drinkers, sometimes wooden and gilded, perhaps embossed (with wild animals" (*theria*) skins! 471b), deep (an ancient *kylix* is any "cup," not necessarily the shallow *kylix* of modern usage, *pace* Schmitt Pantel, *La cité au banquet,* p. 79), often described as wreathed, used especially for toasts, pledges and as a cup of friendship (*philotēsion*). When Timaeus, *FGrHist* 566 F33, alleges that his father's political enemy received a *therikleian* cup from the tyrant Nicodemus of Centuripae, he is probably inferring not just bribery but a treacherous pledged relationship with him; see Jacoby ad loc. cf. D.S. 16.82,4.

52 Arist. fr. 611.15 (Rose), cf. Dover, "Greek Homosexuality and Initiation," p. 117.

53 Cf. Davidson, *Courtesans and Fishcakes,* pp. 61–68.

54 Some have noticed that Gortyn's laws insist that a man wishing to adopt another man as heir must also sacrifice a victim and use it, along with a quantity of wine, to feast his club. The abducted boy, therefore, is being adopted, kind of, by his lover. The coincidence, however, is underwhelming. Willetts, *Aristocratic Society*, pp. 63–68, Schmitt Pantel, *La cité au banquet*, p. 81, Link, *Kreta*, pp. 26–27.

55 Burkert, *Greek Religion*, p. 130.

56 Used probably not to fight but to ferry their riders to the battlefield, cf. Willetts, *Aristocratic Society*, p. 155 n. 2.

57 Sosicrates, *FGrHist* 461 F 7 ap. Ath. 13.561ef. "Front lines" could also just mean "battle lines."

58 Lucian, *On Dance* 14.

59 For Xenophon and Sparta, Cartledge, *Agesilaos*, pp. 55–73.

60 Sahlins, *Apologies to Thucydides* has some interesting thoughts, as usual, on this oppositioning, which he sees as not merely a question of propaganda but of real "schismogenesis."

61 That there were differences over time is not unlikely, but the supposed discrepancies are found within sources of the same epoch, indeed in the same author; in fact the problems are often more apparent than real.

62 *Lexeis* Hdt. s.v. "*eirēn*," on this see esp. Lupi, *L'ordine delle generazioni*, pp. 29–31, with texts nn. 11–12; very similar terms are found on late inscriptions, with the addition of the prefix *pan-* indicating a collectivity.

63 "*eikosi etē gegonōs*," *Lyc.* 17.2; if we see *rhobidas*, not found in inscriptions, not as a name for a particular annual level, but as a general term for all those below the first junior-grade, as *eirēn* is not just Twenty but Twenty-plus, then there are five age-levels of boys, corresponding to the pentads of adult age-levels, "ten . . . ," "fifteen . . . ," "forty from *hēbē*."

64 Xenophon talks of those "exiting Boys on coming-of-age-as-Striplings (*eis to meirakiousthai*)," a group he refers to not as *meirakia/neaniskoi* but "boylets," *paidiskoi;* he infers a sequence, *paides, paidiskoi, hēbōntes,* "in bloom," a term that almost certainly refers to adult age-classes of Twenty-plus; hence Agesilaus noted that Sphodrias had served Sparta well, as *pais, paidiskos* and *hēbōn Lac.* 3.1,5; 4.1, *Hell.* 5.4,32. Plutarch likewise refers to two years between Boys and *eirenes* and contrasts "littler" (cf. *mikizomenos*, from *mikkos = mikros*) and "robust" boys *hadroi,* which has a better claim to be the Spartan term for these two senior boy-grades (*pais* and *mel(l)eirēn*) than Xenophon's *paidiskoi,* since an inscription (*IG* V.1.278) refers to *Atropanpais,* probably for **hadropanpais,* Chantraine, *Dictionnaire* s.v. *atropanpais.* For a full examination of the texts and modern debate about them, see Lupi, *L'ordine delle generazioni*, pp. 27–46 with a nice table at p. 42.

65 Plu. *Cimon* 16.5.

66 Chantraine, *Dictionnaire* s.v. *boua.* This implies a *sumboua* is a "member of a sworn band," which looks very odd. Presumably a letter has dropped out of the

messy manuscript, and we should read either "*sumbou[t]ai*" or "*sunōmot[i]ai*," "bands of co-sworns."

67 *Lac.* 2.2,11,5.

68 Maybury-Lewis, *Akwe-Shavante Society*, pp. 111–12.

69 *Lyc.* 16.5. I have found no reference to "selection" or formal age-assessment at Twenty in the Spartan system, but I find it hard to believe that annual promotion through grades was automatic from Seven (or even from birth) with no (re-)adjustment to take account of physiological development, which is so prominent in nomenclature (*mikizomenos, *hadropanpais*).

70 *Lyc.* 17.2.

71 Thus, more or less, Hodkinson, "Social order," 109–10 n.14.

72 X., *Lac.* 2.4, Plu., *Lyc.* 16.6.

73 Plato, *Laws* 633C Sosibius, *FGrHist* 595 F 5, Ath. 15.678 bc.

74 *Lyc.* 21.2. Judging by its derivative *lēma,* "*volonté, résolution,* courage" or even "arrogance," the verb *lō* seems to have a sense of challenge, not "if you like," or "if you wish," but "if you are man enough," Chantraine, *Dictionnaire* s.v.

75 Lévy, *Sparte,* pp. 190–203 for texts and recent bibliography on the Ephors, esp. 192–93 for their observation of stars and supervision of body-signs, i.e., mustaches. They inspected the naked bodies of the Young Men, *neoi,* in each third of the moon, Agatharcides, *FGrHist* 86 F10, ap. Ath. 12.550cd. Selection for and supervision of the age-classes may have been a primary function of these "Inspectors."

76 X., *Hell.* 6.4,16; *Lac.* 2.4; Plu., *Lyc* 15.1.

77 Polemon ap. Ath. 4.139e.

78 Trümpy, *Untersuchungen* suggests interposing the month Herasios between the month of Hyacinthus/Apollo (= Athenian Hecatombaeon [month i]) and Karneios (= Boedromion [month iii]), pp. 128–32, 135–40, esp. 140 n. 605.

79 Paus. 3.14,6. The "running hare" *lagōs dromaios* would be an entirely appropriate name for the quarry, although Burkert, *Greek Religion,* pp. 234–36, thinks the ribbon-festooned man represented a ram.

80 Cf. Lévy, *Sparte,* pp. 84–89.

81 *Lac.* 1.6.

82 [Plu.] *Mor.* 228a Hermippus ap. Ath 13.555bc.

83 Plu., *Lyc.* 15, X., *Lac.* 1,6, Lupi, *L'ordine delle generazioni,* pp. 65–95, esp. 90.

84 X., *Lac.* 1.5.

85 *Lyc.* 15.

86 Graham, *Performing Dreams,* pp. 66–67, 70.

87 Maybury-Lewis, *Akwe-Shavante Society,* p. 85.

88 "Kayapo Indians of the Brazilian Rain Forest."

89 *Lyc.* 15.

90 X., *Lac.* 1.7–9.

91 Cartledge, *Spartan Reflections,* p. 97: "In short, I have no doubt that the evidence of Xenophon and Plutarch is sufficient to establish the important conclusion that pederasty in Sparta was institutionalized and compulsory."

92 Theocritus 12.13.

93 For the possible meanings, see Dover, "Greek Homosexuality and Initiation" and Ogden, "Homosexuality and Warfare," pp. 144–47.

94 [Plu.], *Mor.* 237bc, Aelian, *V.H.* 3.10.

95 For these well-attested *Leuktrides* see Schachter, *Cults of Boiotia,* II, p. 122.

96 [Plu.], *Mor.* 773f–774a.

97 Plu., *Lyc.* 25.1. I wonder if this means that no Spartan under Thirty would go to the marketplace or only the elite of the elite.

98 Cf. N. Fisher, "Gymnasia and the Democratic Values of Leisure," in Cartledge, Millett and von Reden, *Kosmos,* 84–104.

99 X., *Lac.* 2.12, Max. Tyr., *Or.* 20, Aelian, *V.H.* 3.12, cf. Plato, *Laws* 836b et seqq.

100 *Lac.* 2.12.

101 *Lac.* 2.13.

102 Plu., *Lyc.* 17.1.

103 *Lac.* 2.13–14.

104 *Smp.* 8.35.

105 Paus. 3.20, 10–11 with Musti and Torelli ad loc. Penelope, just married to Odysseus, was being taken from her home in Sparta to Ithaca. Her father wanted them to set up home in Sparta and followed after them begging Penelope to stay. She didn't answer but veiled her face out of a sense of shame. Her father set up the statue. Such a myth would have enormous resonance in Sparta, where a husband would spend nights under his father-in-law's roof for years before taking her away (?) to his own house. For Odysseus, the husband, to move to his wife's home—*uxorilocal*—was not normal practice in the historical period, although it features in many myths: Helen, Hippodamia, Clytaemnestra, Jocasta are local princesses whose royal husbands are from elsewhere.

106 Aelian, *V.H.* 3.12.

107 Cic., *De Re Publica* 4.4: "*Mitto [aput] Eleos et Thebanos, apud quos in amore ingenuorum libido etiam permissam habet et solutam licentiam: Lacedaemonii ipsi, cum omnia concedunt in amore iuvenum praeter stuprum, tenui sane muro dissaepiunt id quod excipiunt; conplexus enim concubitusque permittunt palliis interiectis.*"

108 The contrast between Spartiate and Laconian may well be significant, i.e., the Stripling need not be a Spartiate.

109 Or "what is more seen by admirers." *Erastai* is in the dative but the reference surely is to the sun as all-seeing, not all seen.

110 *Or.* 20.8.

111 X., *Mem.* 1.2,30.

112 The sources do generally refer to Spartan boys as Striplings when they are talking of hot-blooded *erōs,* and the archetypical Spartan *erōmenos* Hyacinthus is a Stripling when Athenians show him with Zephyrus, but nothing precludes the possibility that the boys might, in this case, be younger. They are not as well protected from intimacy as Athenian Boys.

113 So far as I can tell, tree-ring measures, lake-sediment sifters, ice-core readers

and glass-chemists are still arguing over the date of the explosion, which was sometime between *c.* 1600 and *c.* 1350 BC.

114 The bibliography on the inscriptions alternates between two extremes, (1) holy and reverential sexual acts or (2) ordinary boastful or malign graffiti of the kind you might find in a public lavatory (Dover); cf. Edward Brongersma, "The Thera Inscriptions Ritual or Slander?," *Journal of Homosexuality* 20 (1990), 31–40, who comes down firmly and convincingly on the side of reverence. The difficulty with dating derives from the fact that Theran script is "primitive" anyway, i.e., conservative.

115 On Thera's colonization and its cultural and political links to Sparta and Crete, see Malkin, *Myth and Territory,* pp. 67–114.

116 *IG* XII.3. 540–45.

117 Ancient dictionaries say *oiphos* was a word for "penis" and we find *oipholēs,* "lewd fellow," but also *oipholis,* "lewd woman," cf. *LSJ s.v.v.* with *Suppl.,* David Bain, "Six Greek verbs," 72–74, Chantraine, *Dictionnaire* s.v. *oiphō,* which he sees as a derivative of a proto-Indo-European root with derivatives in Sanskrit and Russian, probably connected to Spartan Oibalos, Hyacinthus's father or relative.

118 *IG* XII.3. 536–69.

119 Fritz Graf, "Apollon Delphinios," *Museum Helveticum* 36 (1979) [2–22], 13, a god of ephebes, and political, communal institutions? cf. 22: ". . . *eine Gottheit, die mit der Ephebie einerseits, mit den zentralen Institutionen gewisser Poleis anderseits verbunden ist, und beide Teilbereiche ergänzen sich sinnvoll durch die Annahme, es seien die Funktionen historischer Zeit Transformationen und Weiterentwicklungen aus der uralten Einrichtung von Männerhaus und Initiation.*" But Graf doesn't always define what he means by "initiation" or, indeed "ephebe," in terms of widely differing age-class systems, and he does not always make full allowances for the impact of "popular etymologies"; Sparta's "Delphidios" cannot so lightly be set aside.

120 Bethe, "Dorische Knabenliebe," 450.

121 Nos. 536, 730.

122 Suda s.v. = Alpha 641.

123 Cartledge, "Politics of Spartan Pederasty."

124 Thuc. 1.131.

125 Thuc. 1.95.

126 Thuc. 1.132, 5.

127 Thuc. 1.133.

128 Thuc. 1.134.

129 Ogden, *Necromancy,* pp. 39–41, does not trust the name Argilios and argues that something strange is going on in this story, which involves the necromantic shrine at Taenarum. Something strange certainly is going on, for Pausanias was said to have visited another necromantic shrine in Heraclea to get rid of the ghost of a woman who was haunting him, and his own ghost eventually needed

laying to rest, while others seem to have thought Argillios was the man's personal name, not his ethnic. See, in general, Hornblower ad Thuc. 1.128–135.1.

130 Cartledge, *Agesilaos,* p. 113.

131 Ibid., p. 21.

132 Plu., *Lys.* 22.3. It does sound from Plutarch's description that this was a one-to-one relationship, i.e., not "one of Agesilaus's many *erastai.*"

133 Cartledge, *Agesilaos,* p. 29.

134 Ibid., pp. 20–22, 28–29, 77–115.

135 X., *Hell.* 5.4.24.

136 5.4, 20–33. Cartledge, *Agesilaos,* pp. 136–68.

137 *Hellenica Oxyrhynchia* 21.4, X., *Hell.* 3.4,10, 4.1,26–28, *Agesilaus* 5.4–7.

138 X., *Hell.* 4.1,39, Cartledge, *Agesilaos,* pp. 192–93. Pharnabazus got his brother and his uncle to carry out the task. They set fire to the house where Alcibiades was staying with his mistress Timandra in a village, and killed him as he came out. Others said he had a girl with him of a distinguished family and it was her brothers who set fire to the house. On balance I would go for Pharnabazus, Plu., *Alc.* 39.

139 X., *Hell.* 4.1, 15–40.

12: THE SECRETS OF ELIS, THE SACRED BAND AND ALEXANDER: REGIONAL VARIATIONS

1 *BA* 215288, British Museum F65. Beazley's remarks, as reported by Martin Robertson, are in the *CAVI* entry.

2 We should not infer that territories without artifacts are unpopulated, necessarily. The Cretans inscribed numerous laws in the late sixth, early fifth centuries at a time when archaeologists might infer there was nobody on the island. The Gaulish invasion of Turkey—the Galatians—left lots of traces in histories and sculptures—Dying Gauls, etc.—and in dialectical contributions, but archaeological evidence for the invasion remains minimal. Likewise the native Britons suddenly vanished during the invasion of the Angles, Saxons and Jutes, but that they remained in place is documented from surveys of genes and the survival of Celtic languages. Cultures sometimes just seem to go through very tidy phases, "paper-plate" phases.

3 He misremembers the speech, mixing it up with the speech of Pausanias, *erastēs* of Agathon, in fact ascribing it to him instead of to Phaedrus.

4 Plato, *Smp.* 182ab, X., *Lac.* 2.12—*dia charitōn tēi hōrai chrōntai*—*Smp.* 8.34–35, Cic., *De Re Publica* 4.4 "*mitto* [aput] *Eleos et Thebanos, apud quos in amore ingenuorum libido etiam permissam habet et solutam licentiam . . .*" Maximus of Tyre, *Or.* 20.8.

5 X., *Hell.* 7.4,13. They may have been recent inventions but I think it more likely they are traditional. Generally, see Detienne's brilliant little piece of deduction: "Remarques sur le char."

6 *Phdr.* 256c.

7 For Testimonia and the surviving fragments of Phaedo, Giannantoni, vol. I, III A, pp. 487–93, with a detailed discussion of modern attempts to make sense of the biography, IV "Nota 11," pp. 115–19.

8 X., *Lac.* 2.12. The "yoking" probably had something to do with the ritual of same-sex pledging at Iolaus's tomb, Plu., *Pel.* 18.4 [= Arist. fr. 97 Rose].

9 X., *Smp.* 8.32–35.

10 *Mark* 10.9.

11 Plu., *Pel.* 18–19, for the whole text with excellent commentary see Ogden, "Homosexuality and Warfare," pp. 111–13. Leitao, "Legend of the Sacred Band," in dismissing each source, many of them impeccable and primary (Plato, Xenophon), also usefully collects them.

12 Plu., *Mor.* 761b.

13 D.S. 12.70,1. On the meaning of these terms in Homeric context, see J. N. O'Sullivan, "*hēniochoi kai parabatai*" *Philologus* 144 (2000), 383–85, cf. Ogden, "Homosexuality and Warfare," pp. 114–15.

14 *A.P.* 13.22 ll. 4–8. It is normally assumed the Band was not re-formed after Chaeronea, but Boeotian pairing of men, modeled on the relationship of Iolaus and Heracles, probably predates and postdates the famous Sacred Band.

15 [Plu], *Mor.* 227cd.

16 Frank Harris, *My Life and Loves* (New York, 1963), II, p. 279.

17 On the identification of the lion with the polyandrion of the Thebans, Paus. 9.40,10, Strabo 9.2,37, Pritchett, "Observations on Chaironeia," 115.

18 Arthur Stoddard Cooley, "The Macedonian Tomb and the Battlefield at Chaironeia," in *Records of the Past* 3.5 (May 1904) [131–43], 131–32 and 143 is not concerned with the Sacred Band but gives the information about Androutsos and quotes letters from Soteriades. The lion in Homer represents *menos,* Bruno Snell, *The Discovery of the Mind* (New York, 1982), p. 202, and is often used in funerary monuments, on which see Pritchett, op. cit.

19 Hesychius s.v., Ath. 13.601e.

20 Plu., *Mor.* 760e–761b.

21 *BA* 215288, London British Museum F65, with *CAVI* entry.

22 Aeschines talks of the *anthrōpos,* the "person," not of the "woman," "man" or "boy." Considering the circumstances—"the male prostitute Timarchus"— this is striking. Because of that, Aeschines is no evidence that "cubicles for homosexual prostitution" were visible from the law court in Athens, though he would be good supporting evidence if it could be proven from other sources, cf. Fisher ad loc., who suggests male prostitutes sat in the very marketplace of Athens or in the Ceramicus, citing my own *Courtesans and Fishcakes,* not without out reason. Crucial also is the opening phrase "See those" or "See these" with a little emphatic suffix "i" on the second word, *toutousi.* This has three main meanings: (i) "these here," implying Aeschines could point to the cubicles from where he was speaking; (ii) "those well-known and familiar," i.e., "con-

jure up before your eyes a picture of those persons you are all familiar with who sit in cubicles"; or (iii) "those infamous . . . ," full of contempt.

23 1.74.

24 *SEG* 27.261, P. L. Gauthier; M. B. Hatzopoulos, *La Loi Gymnasiarchique de Beroia* (Athens, 1993), B 57–58.

25 Ath. 13.565f.

26 Marie-Louise Säflund, *The East Pediment of the Temple of Zeus at Olympia* (Gothenburg, 1970), pp. 99–102.

27 Paus. 6.23,8. The legend of the spying raid doesn't seem to make sense. Pausanias fudges it. It is called the Street of Silence because of the agreement to keep quiet in order that they could listen to what was happening *on the other side* of the wall, and then this street is *where they entered* the city quietly listening and taking note.

28 Ar., *Thesm.* 26–62.

29 Paus. 5.18,6.

30 5.4, 1–4. And Phaedo, of course, was said to sit in a cubicle because he was "captured by the spear point" (*aichmalōtos*), a normal word for prisoner of war.

31 Roland Hampe, *LIMC,* "Aktorione."

32 1.78. This flies in the teeth of the claims of the penetration people that sex in ancient Greece is "nonrelational," e.g., Halperin, *One Hundred Years,* p. 30: "Not only is sex in classical Athens not intrinsically relational or collaborative in character; it is, further, a deeply polarizing experience . . . ," a statement that applies only to his own "fuck-you" culture, not to the ancient Mediterranean.

33 Theocritus 12.14.

34 Philostratus, *Heroikos* 53.12.

35 Weiss, "Erotica," 61. I don't necessarily agree with this interpretation of the name of the Thessalians, though I don't doubt the link of the name with longing.

36 This kind of deep "dialect-kinship" is perhaps best illustrated by the fact that Hesiod's father from Cyme in Aeolis, the Aeolian territory in Turkey opposite Lesbos, emigrated to Askra, a village on Helicon in Boeotia, miles away and apparently in the middle of nowhere, but within the Aeolic group: *Works and Days* 635–40.

37 For the most up-to-date survey of the organization of Thessaly see Jean-Claude Decourt, Thomas Heine Nielsen and Bruno Helly, "Thessalia and Adjacent Regions," *IACP,* 676–731.

38 It has been suggested that the use of this title in this grand sense is a fourth-century invention, B. Helly, *L'État thessalien, Aleuas le Roux, les tétrades et les tagoi* (Lyons, 1995).

39 Ar., *Pol.* 1331a.

40 D. 23.199.

41 Thuc. 2.22.

42 For the historical background, Morrison, "Meno of Pharsalus"; for Meno's city of origin, 75 n.1, Mark Munn, *The School of Athens* (Berkeley, 2003), p. 282. For Meno's career, Nails, *People of Plato,* pp. 50 and 204–205.

43 Plato, *Meno* 70b, 76bc, 78d, 80cd.

44 *An.* 2.6,28.

45 Thuc. 2.80,6.

46 E., *Andr.* 1231–72, cf. Paus. 1.11,1, W. Allan, *The* Andromache *and the Spread of Attic Tragedy* (Oxford, 2003), pp. 153–54, Malkin, *Returns of Odysseus,* pp. 142–43.

47 S. Hornblower, *The Greek World* (London, 1991), p. 199.

48 Malkin, *Returns of Odysseus,* p. 139; certainly the inclusion of an opposition between Helenus, from whom Molossians also claimed descent, and Odysseus seems especially pointed on the part of Apollonia.

49 Plu., *Pyrrhus* 1.6, Heckel, *Marshals,* p. 193 n. 113.

50 He actually lived with Pammenes, Plu., *Pel.* 26.4–5, cf. Libanius, *Progymnasmata* 9.3, but Dio Chrysostom 49.5 says Philip was *erōmenos* of Pelopidas.

51 Theopompus, *FGrHist* 115 F225b, cf. Michael Attyah Flower, *Theopompus of Chios: History and Rhetoric in the Fourth Century BC* (Oxford, 1994), p. 107: "Evidence of various kinds suggests that Theopompus's description is accurate in its essentials," vs. Gordon S. Shrimpton, ". . . it is quite possible that the attraction of the punning possibilities has influenced the author's decision to include or emphasize, even invent, descriptions of sexual mores for the Macedonian court." He cites an ancient critic: "We avoid antithesis and homonyms in our sentences because they are bombastic and lack forcefulness. They are more frigid than forceful. Theopompus provides an example of this when he attacks the 'Friends of Philip.' He destroys the forcefulness with the antithesis"—man killers, man whores, *androphonoi, andropornoi*—". . . when the reader must apply himself to too much style, rather than to bad style, he loses contact with all feeling." Shrimpton thinks Theopompus also took a swipe at the whorishness of Philip's Theban-style infantry, *Theopompus the Historian* (Kingston/Montreal, 1991), pp. 119, 128 and T44.

52 D.S. 16.93,3–94.

53 For the background, Morrison, "Meno of Pharsalus," 70.

54 Diodorus, who seems well informed about Macedonian scandal, says it was a hunting accident, which would be highly significant, since it was normally *neaniskoi* who accompanied the king. Others say Crateuas (or Crataeas, or Crateros) had designs on the throne, a theory not inconsistent with the tradition that he was promised the king's daughter's hand, but ruled for only a few days before he was himself assassinated. Thucydides, who may also have been a guest of Archelaus after his banishment from Athens, provides (2.100,2, with Hornblower ad loc.) what seems a glowing (apologetic?) obituary of this notorious king, making no mention of the manner of death or the motivation. It has often seemed odd that Greek homosexuality so rarely makes it into Thucy-

dides; here is a nice example of its being excised. Plato, *Gorgias* 471; Arist., *Pol.* 1311b, D.S. 14,37,5; Aelian, *V.H.* 8.9; Plu., *Mor.* 768f; Plato, *Alcibiades II* 141ce; Hammond, *History of Macedonia,* II, pp. 167–68; M. B. Hatzopoulos, *Cultes et rites de passage en Macedonie* (Athens, 1994), pp. 96–97, underestimates the politics involved.

55 Heckel, *Marshals,* pp. 284–85 distinguishes the Philip and Iolaus who are bodyguards of Alexander IV in *IG* ii 561 (*SEG* 31.80) from Philip and Iolaus, sons of Antipater and wine pourers to Alexander III the Great, pp. 293–94, arguing that any "temptation to identify [the two Philip + Iolauses] . . . must be resisted," ibid., p. 285. I am less resistant. Certainly there is no reason to think that as "wine pourers" Philip and Iolaus, the sons of Antipater, need to have been Royal Boys, i.e., Striplings. It would be perfectly appropriate to perform this role, like Ganymede, as underage Boys.

56 [Plu.], *Mor.* 849f, D.S. 19.11,8.

57 Heckel, *Marshals,* p. 38. On the Royal Boys and their relationship to the "Bodyguards," apparently a group of seven slightly older men, possibly graduates from the Royal Boys, see Heckel, ibid., pp. 237–53.

58 Arr., *An.* 4.13,1, describes them as boys who had reached the age of *meirakia, emeirakieuonto.* This terminology and their duties certainly imply boys of an older age-group than Hammond's fourteen- to eighteen-year-olds, Hammond, *Macedonian State,* p. 56. Since they accompanied the king hunting it seems very likely they are the beardless young men depicted in the hunting scenes on walls and floors of Pella and the Royal Tombs at Vergina, and on the Alexander Sarcophagus. If the institution was already formed under Archelaus, Crataeas must have been a member in order to hunt with the king and he was old enough to be thinking of both marriage and throne, apparently.

59 Heckel, *Marshals,* p. 238.

60 Q.C. 8.6,7.

61 On the identity of individual Royal Boys, Heckel, *Marshals,* pp. 289–95; on the frequency of such conspiracies, see E. Carney, "Regicide in Macedonia," *Parola del Passato* 210 (1983), 260–72.

62 Plu., *Alex.* 48.3, in Yardley's unimprovable translation; Waldemar Heckel and J. C. Yardley, *Alexander the Great* (Oxford, 2004), p. 228.

63 On the plot, Arr., *An.* 3.26, Plu., *Alex.* 48–49, D.S. 17.79, Q.C. 6.7–11, Badian, "Death of Parmenio," 324–38, Heckel, *Marshals,* pp. 23–33.

64 Q.C. 6.7,2.

65 *"Amatoris et scorti iurgio interponi aures meas credidi infelix,"* Q.C. 6.10,16.

66 Q.C. 6.7,30.

67 Heckel, *Marshals,* p. 23.

68 Badian, "Death of Parmenio," 326 n. 8.

69 "Eunuchs"—Greek for "bed-keepers"—were terribly important in Persia, confidants of the king, agents of court and empire and famed, above all, for

their personal loyalty. Eunuchs are such a trope of Western orientalist discourse that orientalists are very sensitive about the subject. Briant is so impressed by their status and influence in the Persian court that he cannot believe they were all castrati, though he concedes there were certainly some (low-ranking) palace servants who were. He suggests there was an official designation equivalent to the Hebrew term *saris,* which derived from an Assyrian court official, *ša rēši,* whose title may have meant "to whom the king's head was of concern," a term the Greeks and later Babylonians misunderstood. *Saris* is used in the Hebrew Bible to refer to Near-Eastern officials, such as Egyptian Potiphar, who in the Greek translation is simply "*dynastes.*" Unfortunately *ˀsa rēši* too is often translated "eunuch" by Assyriologists and contrasted with *ˀsa ziqni,* "the bearded"—which may explain why Potiphar's wife wanted Joseph to be her lover (but not why Potiphar had a wife in the first place), and the arguments against the presence of large numbers of eunuchs in the courts of both Assyria and Persia often seem to come down to squeamishness: there are simply too many of them to stomach. In Persia "eunuchs" are often called Bagoas. Just before Alexander, a "eunuch" Bagoas was Grand Vizier, plotter and kingmaker. He is one of the best candidates for "eunuch" as an official court rank. The same must, then, apply also to Alexander's boyfriend Bagoas, although he seems young for such rank. At any rate Alexander didn't just fancy someone who happened to have had his testicles removed, he entered, supposedly, into an "erotik" relationship with someone who was part of an institution that assumed intense personal devotion to the monarch, another clear case of political *erōs,* Briant, *L'Empire Perse,* pp. 279–88, Amélie Kuhrt, *The Ancient Near East: c.3000–330 BC* (London, 1995), II, p. 530.

70 Ath. 13.603ac, 10.434f–435a, Plu., *Alex.* 67, *Mor.* 717f, cf. 65f., *Alex.* 22.1–3.

71 Q.C. 8.11, 9–10: *amici corpus procubuit exanimis.*

72 Plu., *Alex.* 22.

73 Theodorus of Tarentum was a Pythagorean philosopher, it would appear, Iamblichus, *Vit. Pyth.* 265, and Hagnon of Teos was a notorious wastrel.

74 Plu., *Alex.* 47.9–12.

75 Arr., *An.* 7.14, Lucian, *On Slander,* ch. 17. Lucian's testimony has no authority of its own, but it is confirmed by Diodorus (17.115,6) who has Hephaestion honored with sacrifices as *proedros,* which is probably a scribal error for *paredros* and has been emended by editors accordingly.

76 *FGrHist* 126.

77 D.S. 17.115, 18.4,2ff., A. B. Bosworth, *Conquest and Empire* (Cambridge, 1988), pp. 164, 167–68 is a little inconsistent, insisting on the authenticity of the elaborate funeral plans, supposing Babylonian hostility and suggesting the edifice may never have been "formally begun." The structure would obviously have taken time to complete, but it was unlikely the work was not started before Alexander's arrival in Babylon the spring following Hephaestion's death in late summer or autumn of the previous year, or during his few months there. Such

set-piece descriptions were a popular genre. Ephippus's pamphlet is once called *On the Funeral of Alexander and Hephaestion,* but fragments talk only of drinking parties. *The Last Days of A. and H.* is probably the most appropriate title, cf. Jacoby ad Ephippus, *FGrHist* 126, who thinks the pyre description is from Clitarchus.

78 Brunt, *Arrian II,* appendix 24.4, A. B. Bosworth, "Hephaestion," *OCD3.*

79 For the most judicious assessment of Hephaestion, see Heckel, *Marshals,* pp. 65–90, who nevertheless underplays the relationship and Hephaestion's importance. The Achilles-Patroclus comparison must have long predated Alexander's death, and as "head" bodyguard, whatever that means, and leader of the inquisition of conspirators, Hephaestion already had a most significant role, close to the king, and well on the way to his ultimate position of Grand Vizier. Indeed it is precisely his role as a complement to the king (the dependent role that has led historians to view him as unimportant or undistinguished) that makes Hephaestion so unique, Alexander's other half. His "promotion" after the death of Philotas might not have seemed like a promotion, more like a detour from his place at Alexander's side, putting an Alexanderman in charge of a potentially rebellious group whose leader had just been executed.

80 The relationship between the inner Seven and outer core of bodyguards, "Royal Shield-bearers," *hupaspistai basilikoi,* is complicated, cf. Heckel, *Marshals,* pp. 244–53, who makes Philip's two lovers, Pausaniases I and II, Shield-bearers, pp. 297–98.

81 Heckel, *Marshals,* p. 258.

82 Heckel, *Marshals,* p. 67. We should not dismiss Choerilus of Iasos as a poetaster, necessarily. The story that Alexander rejected his sycophancy is part of a long (and flattering) tradition of Alexander rejecting flattery and of a general movement starting in the first century BC to reject a quarter of a century of the purple literature, both poetic and prosaic, of the age of Alexander and his successors; a neoclassical movement, in other words, sometimes called neo-Atticism or the Second Sophistic. Doubtless lush, such literature was not necessarily bad, though doubtless it would not have been to our taste either; Marco Fantuzzi, *Brill's New Pauly,* s.v. "Choerilus 3 from Iasus" has some wise comments.

83 There are some great stories about Protesilaus, his widow and her devotion to him beyond the grave.

84 Strabo 13.1,27.

85 Plu., *Alex.* 15.7–8, Arr., *An.* 1.12,1, D.S. 17.17,2, Justinus 11.5,12. Brunt has a sensible and succinct account in his edition of *Arrian I,* pp. 464–65.

86 Arr., *An.* 1.12,5.

87 2.12, 3–8.

88 Q.C. 6.10,31.

89 Heckel, *Marshals,* p. 83 n. 118, citing E. D. Carney's dissertation, *Alexander the Great and the Macedonian Aristocracy,* p. 221.

90 Heckel, *Marshals,* pp. 71–74.

91 Heckel, *Marshals,* p. 85.

13: SYZYGIES

1 Perhaps the tomb of this "homoerotik" hero, Diocles of Corinth, resident alien in Thebes, has nothing to do with the tomb of the "homoerotik" hero Diocles of Athens resident alien in Megara, who died defending his *erōmenos;* but it is a bit of a coincidence and it would be surprising if no one noticed the similarities. Diocles' mythic mother may have been supposed to put him off women altogether; he certainly seems to have resented it up until his death.

2 *Pol.* 1274ab. Philolaus, "People-lover," is described as a Bacchiad (a narrow oligarchy of 200) from Corinth, which means his code was probably dated to before the expulsion of the Bacchiads, i.e., the early seventh century at the latest, in conformity with Diocles' Olympic victory in 728. Philolaus must be one of the lawgivers to whom Plutarch ascribes the invention of Theban Homosexuality. Aristotle puts him alongside Solon, Draco, and Lycurgus, as if he was *the* lawgiver of Thebes.

3 E., *Iphigeneia Among the Taurians,* esp. ll. 498, 72, 608.

4 Xenophon, who knew Spartans well, implies that they really did talk like that, *An.* 6.6,34, *Hell.* 4.4,10.

5 Simonides fr. 510 with references, a popular tale, the point of which was to demonstrate the power of memory, for the building caused such destruction that the victims were unrecognizable, but Simonides was able to remember who had been sitting where. Quintilian, *Inst.* 11.2,11–16, thought the whole Dioscuri business *fabulosum:* "The poet himself mentions this affair nowhere, and he was the least likely to keep quiet about a matter which brought him such glory."

6 Burkert, *Greek Religion,* p. 213, Robert Parker, "Dioscuri," *OCD3.* Pipili, *Laconian Iconography,* p. 36, thinks the structure most resembles a sacrificial table. A late source says the same word *dokana* was used at Sparta for tombs.

7 While Zethus carries a stone as big as a mountain to build a Cyclopean wall around seven-gated Thebes, Amphion simply strums his seven-stringed lyre and a stone twice as large follows in its footsteps and falls harmoniously into position, Apollonius Rhod. 1, 740–41.

8 Apollod. 3.10,1, Paus. 9.17,4–6.

9 Hdt. 1.31, cf. for the rituals at the Heraion; cf. Richard Seaford, "The Eleventh Ode of Bacchylides," *JHS* 108 (1988) [118–36], 122–23, and Charles C. Chiasson, "Myth, Ritual, and Authorial Control in Herodotus' Story of Cleobis and Biton (*Hist.* 1.31)," *AJP* 126 (2005), 41–64.

10 Paus. 2.20,2. The statues in Delphi might possibly be Dioscuri, "Wanakes," however, and were found near the Athenian Treasure House; G. Vatin, "Monuments Votifs de Delphes. V: Les couroi d'Argos," *BCH* 106 (1982), 509–25; cf.

C. Morgan's review, *CR* 43 (1993), 458; D. Sansone, "Cleobis and Biton in Delphi," *Nikephoros,* 4 (1991), 121–32. For further references, *SEG* 41 (1991) #132, 45 (1995) #493, 46 (1996) #564. I am not entirely sure it makes much difference. Both Cleobis and Biton and the Dioscuri are same-sex yoke pairs.

PART V: EROS OFF DUTY
14: Sappho, Samos and the Tomb of the Diver: Lyrics of Greek Love

1 On the tomb, M. Napoli, *La Tomba del Tuffatore* (Bari, 1970), on the diver as a star, F.-H. Massa-Pairault, "La Transmission des idées entre grande Grèce et Étrurie," in G. Pugliese Carratelli (ed.), *Magna Grecia, Etruschi, Fenici. Atti del XXXIII Convegno di Studi sulla Magna Grecia* (Taranto, 1996) [377–421], 389–92, for up-to-date bibliography, R. Ross Holloway, "The Tomb of the Diver," *AJA* 110 (2006), 365–88, playing down esoteric eschatology.

2 For Olynthus, see Cahill, *Household,* pp. 180–93 and index s.v. *andron,* Nevett, *House and Society,* pp. 70–73, and index s.v. *andron.*

3 Lissarrague, *The Aesthetics of the Greek Banquet,* ch. 7.

4 Murray, *OCD3* s.v. "sympotic poetry" claims "most or all Archaic monodic lyric poetry, and at least some choral lyric, and much of elegiac and iambic poetry." The bibliography on the sympotic in poetry is big and growing, Murray, *Sympotica* pp. 332–35, with the contributions to that volume from Bowie, "*Miles Ludens?,*" adding military exhortation in elegy to the symposium, and Rösler, "*Mnemosyne,*" adding the poetry of memory and "history," cf. also Stehle, *Performance and Gender,* pp. 213–61, with a brief review of literature, p. 215, n. 11. Rösler, loc. cit. p. 230, reminds us of a stricter definition: "that particular area of melic, elegiac, and iambic poetry which often makes direct and explicit reference to the sympotic situation."

5 The big question being when is a symposium not a symposium? For although there is a big difference between a drinking party for close comrades in a private house, where the group is defined *only* through made ties of love and friendship, and a public banquet for fellow tribesmen, demesmen, clansmen, citizens, where the group is defined by given ties, there was a whole range of intermediate groups, who might gather together for feasting and drinking, cf. Schmitt Pantel, "Sacrificial Meal and *Symposion,*" Fisher, "Symposiasts," 356–71. Few Greek gatherings finished without some consumption of alcohol and performance of music; even the *Hermaia,* a gymnasium festival for Boys, Striplings and chaperons, has a bar, Plato, *Lysis* 223ab.

6 Callinus fr. 1, cf. Bowie, "*Miles Ludens?,*" p. 223.

7 Of Tlepolemus, Polybius 6.21,12. "*Akroamata*" is used by Polybius, as by Plu., *Quaest. Conv.* 7.8, cf. *Luc.* 40.1, to refer to sympotic entertainment cf. Pol. 4.20,10, Plu., *Ant.* 24.2 with Pelling ad loc.

8 Thomas, "The place of the poet," and esp. p. 121, with notes.

9 Theog. 237–43.

10 On elegy see E. Bowie, *Brill's New Pauly* s.v. "Elegy." For the break in the second line of the couplet, see Landels, *Music in Ancient Greece and Rome,* pp. 115–16; otherwise it will have sounded abrupt and "broken."

11 Paus. 10.7,4–6, Plu., *Solon* 21.4. *Elegos* always seems to mean "lament" in the fifth century, Dunbar ad *Birds* 217, and already perhaps by the early sixth century.

12 The lyre and *barbitos* were sometimes played horizontally, like proto-guitars, but not the cithara, West, *Ancient Greek Music,* p. 65.

13 Landels, *Music in Ancient Greece and Rome,* pp. 60–61, cf. 74 on *magadis.*

14 *Iliad* 3.54, 9.186.

15 Plato, *Laws* 809e, cf. 812d, not allowing time for virtuoso stuff, *Lysis* 209b, Ar., *Frogs,* 1284–97. In general see West, *Ancient Greek Music* ch. 3, esp. p. 69, and for aristocratic lyre, pp. 25–26, Plu., *Alc.* 2.5: Alcibiades despises the shawm and praises the lyre because it does not destroy the face and leaves it "fitting for a free man." MacDowell ad Ar., *Wasps* 959: "Learning to play the lyre was part of the traditional education of an Athenian gentleman. It is a symbol of artistic and intellectual activity; the opposite is digging . . ." citing also *Knights* 987–96, *Clouds* 964, cf. fr. 232, Plu., *Themistocles* 2.3: Themistocles was of low birth . . . "So, later, in the midst of the pastimes called liberal and sophisticated he was mocked by those who supposed themselves educated and was compelled to defend himself in vulgar fashion. He said he didn't know how to tune a lyre or attempt the plucking little harp, but he did know how to make a paltry inglorious city into a great and glorious one." Players tried to play quickly, Plato, *Charm.* 159c.

16 Aeschin. 1.168 with Fisher's notes ad loc., cf. Aelian, *V.H.* 3.32. Alexander had apparently been bossy, making *antikrouseis* (probably = "mild rebukes") to another boy, but Aeschines says Demosthenes had made innuendos ("casting shameful suspicions") about little Alexander and then had had the cheek to accuse Aeschines of cozying up to Philip, Alexander's father, when he rebuked him. Alexander would have his revenge on Demosthenes, when he grew up.

17 Anacreon, *Eleg* 2. frr. 396, 356.

18 Fr. 428. What exactly Alcaeus left behind, the "arms and armor" has been mangled by the scribe. When the Greeks dedicated trophies they often identified their enemies by ethnic (*Attikoi*) rather than political (*Athēnaioi*) names, as if they were fighting against "nations" rather than "cities." Even in the fifth century Athenians inscribed "of the Lesbians" on their captured booty, though it was only certain cities of Lesbos, notably Mytilene, they had been fighting against.

19 Plu., *Mor.* 858ab, Hdt. 5.94–95, Strabo 13.1,38.

20 Fr. 133.

21 Fr. 38a.

22 Antiphanes' *Sappho* ap. Ath. 10.450e–451b.

23 Cf. Williamson, *Sappho's Immortal Daughters,* pp. 34–49, which attempts an arresting version of Hamlet's soliloquy were Shakespeare ever to suffer Sappho's fate.

24 Winkler, *Constraints of Desire,* p. 177, thinks Sappho is contrasting what men love with what she as a woman loves—"men are in love with masculinity"—but the point surely is to compare Menelaus's love for Helen with Sappho's for Anactoria.

25 Campbell, *Golden Lyre,* p. 11, cf. Jenkyns, *Three Classical Poets,* pp. 9–10, 23–34. For Lasus of Hermione's s-less songs, see D'Angour, "How the dithyramb got its shape," esp. 334–39, who argues it was simply an extreme example of a general attempt to avoid hissing, although he acknowledges, n. 50, that Lasus loved other kinds of word games too.

26 A. Meillet, *Aperçu d'une histoire de la langue grecque* (first edn 1913: Paris, 2004), esp. p. 146. Few doubt that the *distinctive* features of the Aeolic hendecasyllable (i.e. the *c.* eleven syllables, the 5 + 6 or 4 + 7 syllable division of the line, and the rigid dum di dum—*aphrodi-; lissomai; -aisi damn-* . . . *-ōs diōx-; alla dō-; -ōs philē*–pattern of syllables nos. 8–10) that most resonate with the Vedic pattern demonstrate a common origin thousands of years BC. Here cultural history comes closest to genetic genealogy.

27 Fr. 2, cf. fr. 17 a summons of Hera, T 47, Burgess, *Epideictic Literature,* pp. 174–80, Jenkyns, *Three Classical Poets,* pp. 7–42, esp. p. 38.

28 Strabo 13.2,3, *POxy* 1800 fr. 1, Max. Tyr., *Or.* 18.7, schol. Lucian, *Imagines* 18, Ovid, *Heroides* 15.31–36; this last is full of details drawn from Sappho's own poems; there must be a possibility Sappho had described herself as small, dark and ugly in her own songs, cf. the newly restored fr. 58, first published by Martin West, *TLS* 24 June 2005: "Study not least the lyre, you girls, of all the lovely things the violet-breasted Muses have given, song-loving, tortoise-shelled, clear. Me, my once-soft skin's been oldened, white the once-black hair. And my spirit's gotten heavy for my knees to carry, that once were light as lambs in dances. I moan on about it, but what can I do? Not aging is not for us humans. Indeed once Tithonus, they told me, was carried by love-struck rose-armed Dawn, away to the world's extremities, beautiful and young; still, gray oldness got him nevertheless, him a goddess's husband." My own translation, but it gets the gist, if too jerkily.

29 For lesbian syzygies see especially Gentili, "Ways of love."

30 Anacreon fr. 358, cf. Marcovich, "Anacreon, 358 PMG" and for more recent discussion of this much-discussed poem, Patricia A. Rosenmeyer, "Girls at Play," *AJP* 125 (2004) [163–78], 166–68.

31 The Spartan practice of allowing under-Eighteens to mix with men stood out as exceptional and, if anything, the Greeks of the eastern Aegean had a reputation for being more refined, polite and protective of the chasteness of both women and boys than mainland Greeks, though, of course, one could always look and stare and fall in love from a distance with under-Eighteens. Ibyc.

282C fr 1 col i.11 refers to a *paidiskos* but this may refer to the age-class of Eighteen and Nineteen, as in Sparta (X., *Hell.* 5.4,32, *Lac* 3.1 and 5). Anacreon (346, *POxy* 2321) talks of a boy kept under control by a woman at home who escapes and sets the hearts of citizens aflutter.

32 Alcaeus 352, 347, 338.

33 Horace, *Odes* 2.13, 21–32, Quintilian, *Inst.* 10.1.63, Cic. *Tusc.* 4.71 ". . . *quae de iuuenum amore scribit Alcaeus!*," i.e., despite the fact that he was a man of bravery and distinction, Horace, *Odes* 1.32 (cf. schol. Pindar, *Isthmians* 2.1b), Alcaeus fr. 368, not quoted by name, but very probably by him, considering the language and meter.

34 Suda s.v. "Ibycus," Cic., *Tusc.* 4.71, Ar., *Thesm* 159–65, schol. Pindar, *Isthmians* 2.1b.

35 Jenkyns, *Three Classical Poets*, pp. 32–38 has a detailed analysis comparing Ibycus with Sappho. The wind is the North Wind, and the point of the simile is surely that the storms of winter have ceased in the lovely garden allowing fruit trees and vine to grow, but have not ceased in Ibycus. The Cretan quince is in fact "Cydonian," i.e., from modern Chanea in western Crete. In *c.*524 by chance some Samian exiles, unsuccessful in their attempt to overthrow Polycrates, settled there. Let's imagine that one or two of them, when they landed, had visions of Ibycus's tranquil quinces before their eyes, Her. 3.44,1.

36 Sappho frr. 211, 199.

37 Ibyc. 289, 282 cf. 282B v fr.12; for the tyrants and poets, see Shipley, *History of Samos,* pp. 70–80.

38 Suda s.v. Ibycus (= T 1); for Corinth, *A.P.* 7.745 (= T 5); for the theater, Plu., *Mor.* 509e–510a. The story is similar to that told of Arion and the dolphin, which also involved pirates, animals and confession in Corinth, and may be linked to dithyrambic performances in the city.

39 The judgment is Sir Maurice Bowra's, *Greek Lyric Poetry,* p. 268.

40 fr. 372, T12.

41 Duris of Samos, *FGrHist* 76 F 60, quoting Asius, a local epic poet of uncertain date.

42 Cicadas were linked in the first place with desiccated Tithonus, immortality, and autochthony, cf. Ogden, *Necromancy,* pp. 38–39, esp. n. 30.

43 Ormerod, *Piracy,* pp. 98–105, Shipley, *History of Samos,* p. 71. We might compare Telestagoras of the "pirate clan" who received gifts from the people of Naxos at around this time and was highly esteemed. The story is very odd. Fishmongers refuse to give some youths a large fish, saying they would rather give it to Telestagoras for free. The youths get drunk and attack the good man and his daughters. This leads to a popular uprising in his defense, Arist. fr. 510 (Rose). For archaic piracy as a way of life, cf. the early Athenian law on associations *epi leian oichomenoi,* "for plundering expeditions," P. de Souza, *Piracy in the Graeco-Roman World* (Cambridge, 1999), p. 23, Ormerod, pp. 67–68.

44 Strabo 14.1,16.

45 Arist., *Pol.* 1313b, Shipley, *History of Samos,* pp. 74–80.

46 This does not mean, I think, that he was in the "carpet-hire" business, Shipley, *History of Samos,* pp. 81–82.

47 Ath. 13.602d, Scanlon, *Eros,* pp. 267–69.

48 Hdt. 1.51, 3.41, 123,1; 3.125, Paus. 3.12,10; 8.14,8; 9.41,1; 10.38,6 Osborne, *Archaic and Classical Greek Art,* p. 79; Spivey, *Understanding Greek Sculpture,* pp. 72–74. For Polycrates' Lydian-style paradise, cf. Briant, *L'Empire Perse,* pp. 94–95.

49 Strabo 14.1,6.

50 Polycrates dedicated a statuette around 570, when he should have been at least eighteen, Shipley, *History of Samos,* pp. 74–75, *IG* 4.565.

51 Ath. 12.540e.

52 Aelian, *V.H.* 9.4.

53 *POxy* 2322 fr. 1 (fr. 347) seems to be about the same thing: ". . . and the long hair which was providing shade for your soft neck; and now look! you are bald, while your hair has fallen into dismal hands a mass of strands spooling down on black dust, ambushed by cutting iron, poor wretched thing. And I am worn away with anguish; for what is one to do, when one is disappointed even in one's ambitions for Thrace?"

54 Apuleius, *Flor.* 15.51,54 [= T 5] cf. Ath. 10.429b.

55 Hdt. 3.121–24.

56 Frontisi-Ducroux and Lissarrague, "From Ambiguity to Ambivalence."

15: WORDS AND PICTURES: THE ATHENIAN SYSTEM

1 These are both real cult titles of Aphrodite but Pausanias's interpretation is wrong. Heavenly Aphrodite is often associated with the starry Astarte of the Near East. Pandemos probably emphasizes her role as protector of the city, Pirenne-Delforge, *L'Aphrodite,* p. 432, index s.vv. "Aphrodite *Ourania,*" "Aphrodite *Pandemos.*"

2 Plato, *Smp.* 181d.

3 182a.

4 The reference is not to "philosophy" but to debate in general, especially the kind of discussion encouraged in "civic" societies, notably the Athenian democracy, cf. Thuc. 2.40. The distinction between sophistry and "philosophy" is not originally a distinction between a sophistic (clever-clever) and a higher form of "philosophical" inquiry, but between the professional cleverness of specialists, the "sophists" and "rhetoricians," and the down-to-earth wisdom or "good sense" of wise poets, statesmen and counselors.

5 182c.

6 183de.

7 184a, a common notion, Sophocles, *Oedipus Tyrannus* 614, cf. 1213; E., *Hippolytus* 1051–52, cf. Pindar, *Ol.* 10.53–55, fr. 159.

8 In fact ancient authors find it more difficult than Pausanias to distinguish between "paying court," *therapeuein,* and "flattery," *kolakeia,* Thuc. 3.12,1.9.

9 It is difficult to differentiate between the "service" performed by an admirer

and by the admired. *Hupēretein* seems to have its origins in a metaphor of rowing. Often it is service to a superior, "serving the gods," etc. Sometimes it is the equivalent of *leitourgia*, a rich man's "service" to the community.

10 183b, Ar., *Ecc.* 190. Aphrodite also seems to have made a speech extolling the power of love as greater than an oath in a speech in Aeschylus's *Danaids* defending a bride who had fallen in love with her husband and therefore broke her oath to kill him; it would not be at all surprising if it was an etiological myth. There must be more to Pausanias's insistent statement than a general perception that Athenians do not take seriously oaths made in the heat of sexual passion.

11 The laws refer to Athens in the 340s.

12 *Neaniskoi*/ephebes were under the overall charge of the official called *kosmētēs*, *Ath. Pol.* 42.2 with Rhodes ad loc., pp. 504–505.

13 In this speech, unfortunately, the actual quotes from the laws, as opposed to Aeschines' paraphrases, are almost certainly not original but laws from a different time and place, or just guessed from the text, cf. Fisher, *Aeschines: Against Timarchos,* p. 68, but this is what it says if you're interested: "LAWS The school-teachers will not open the schools before dawn, and will close them before sunset. No one who is beyond the age-class (*hēlikia*) of boys will be allowed to enter when the boys are inside with the exception of the teacher's son, brother or daughter's husband; if anyone does enter in contravention of these laws, the penalty will be death. The officials in charge of the gymnasium will allow no one in an age-class (*en hēlikiai* a "proper" one? a military one? 20+?) to participate alongside the boys in the festival of Hermes under any pretext. Any official who does allow it and does not keep them out will be liable to prosecution under the law that protects free boys from ruin (*phthora*). The sponsors of choruses designated by the people must be over forty years of age."

14 Tough to translate succinctly—"outrageous conduct, indicating disregard for one's, including one's own, personhood," e.g., rape, suicide, insult, laying a hand on someone, treating someone like a (sex) object. Fisher's treatise on *Hybris* usefully collects the evidence, but reading that evidence, its conclusions, e.g., p. 147 "intentional insult," cannot stand, as others, e.g., Cairns, "Hybris, Dishonor . . ." have noted, cf. MacDowell, "Hybris in Athens."

15 Again not original, but this is what it says: "(16.) If any man of Athens commits an act of *hubris* against a Boy of free status, let the Boy's legal guardian accuse him before the Thesmothetai [an ancient board of magistrates called "archons"] and demand redress. If the jurors vote against him and he is condemned to death, let him be put in the hands of the Eleven and die that day. If the vote goes against him and he is condemned to pay a fine, let him pay within eleven days from the time of the trial, if not let him remain incarcerated until the fine is paid. Let the same charges apply to those who abuse the bodies of slaves."

16 139. Some have thought Aeschines is borrowing from Pausanias's speech in Plato's *Symposium,* cf. Fisher ad loc.

17 X., *Lac* 2.12.

18 Berlin, Antikensammlung, F2279, *BA* 200977.

19 *Pais* only occurs on this side, in that part of the decoration where there are under-Eighteens, just as the feminine only occurs alongside women. On this vase, therefore, *pais* specifies an age-group of under-Eighteens. This may not always be apparent from reading the scholarly literature on the subject, or viewing earlier drawings, cf. Lissarrague, "Femmes au figuré," p. 233 fig. 50— *"les inscriptions alternent—ho pais kalos, kalé—masculin et feminin. L'image réunit deux modalités différentes du rapport amoureux, le désir et la jouissance, en les répartissant entre femmes et adolescents, de manière dissymétrique, toujours du point de vue de l'homme adulte."*—also mistaken is Stewart, *Art, Desire and the Body,* p. 157: "On both sides [Peithinos] exclaims 'The boy is beautiful, yes indeed!' " For more accuracy, see A. Greifenhagen's description in the *Corpus Vasorum Antiquorum* (Germany 21, Berlin Antiquarium 2), cf. *CAVI.* Note especially that each *kale* is written as if it emanates from the image of the woman like a perfume (a charm or a spell), going against the grain of a left-to-right reading, whereas the comments attached to the males seem to come from the painter/reader, as if in dialogue with each other. I doubt that *kalē* has the same connotations of nobility and goodness as *kalos.* I think here especially it just means "beautiful" to look at. Sorry, ladies.

20 One other fragment (Basel, H. Cahn, HC52, *BA* 200976), showing a tondo with a satyr and a mixing bowl, was signed with the name Peithinos and a couple more unsigned vases are tentatively ascribed to the same painter, a very meager trawl for such a great artist. The cup seems to have something to do with the Sosias Cup, which is so similar in size and shape and pelts and fabrics, and which is equally hard to assign to an artist, though certainly a different one. Stewart, *Art, Desire and the Body,* p. 157, suggests the painter was christened Peithinos and simply followed his *calling,* "his personal credo," but the name is unique in Attica and it is a bit of a coincidence that the one complete vase of the one Athenian called "Seductive" depicts seduction; surely it's a nom de plume. Or perhaps it was indeed a kind of "signature vase." Onesimus too has but one signed vase in existence so far, *BA* 203218 Louvre G105, and the name "Onesimus" = "Profitos" may also be of significance, although, unlike Peithinos, it is a common name. Crucially, Onesimus and his circle are the biggest fans of Athenodotus, who is acclaimed on the Peithinos Cup.

21 *BA* 203265, Boston (MA), Museum of Fine Arts, 01.8021 ". . . the suffixes *-doros* and *-dotos* indicate, at least potentially, true gifts . . . they present the child as granted in response to prayer and offerings . . . ," Parker, "Theophoric names," p. 60, with a strong emphasis on "potentially" and "present."

22 Almost all Athenodotus acclamations are by "Onesimus" and the "Proto-Panaetian Group" = early Onesimus? Athens 1666, *BA* 350911 shows a youth at

an altar with wine jug and cup, on the rim of which is an address (?) to the painter Douris, O DORI, possibly (ascr. Beazley, tentatively) by Douris himself. "Onesimus" admired others over the years. Panaitios received eighteen acclamations, Lykos has nine, Erothemis three, and one each for Aristarchus, Leagros, and two girls, Loda (found in Corsica) and Chironeia (a scooping cup, *kyathos,* not Onesimus (?), but made for Etruscan market (?), cf. de la Genière, "Quelques réflexions," p. 418).

23 Oakley, "An Athenian Red-Figured Workshop," 198–200, favoring 0.2 percent rather than the alternative of 1 percent. The 1 percent is derived from statistics comparing estimates for the total production of vases commissioned for victors at the Panathenaea with surviving Panathenaic vases. It is likely that these vases were looked after with greater care, but also that they were distributed in areas (Athens and the Aegean) from which few vases survive. Basically, vases increased their chances of survival enormously by making it to Etruria, whose graveyards preserve the most and best Attic vases; if one particular Etruscan city, Vulci, had been erased, our database would be catastrophically diminished. Survival rates of different types of vase from different workshops must vary enormously depending on where they ended up, from much less than 0.25 percent to even more than 1 percent, I would guess.

24 Perhaps because she had kneed him in the testicles, as we can see on a clay tablet of *c.*450 Scanlon, *Eros,* pp. 185–98, and esp. fig. 7-6.

25 Stewart, *Art Desire and the Body,* p. 157. Stewart seems to think the forward courtesans are modest ladies because they are heavily draped, and there are no money bags or other signs of mercenary sex, but there is a big difference between a courtesan or *hetaira* and a common prostitute, see Davidson, *Courtesans and Fishcakes,* chs 3–4, and elaborate drapery is one of the main distinguishing features of a courtesan in the classical period at least. True, putting your head down is a sign of shame, but in contrast to the youths the ladies are positively brazen, and heads uncovered as well, the hussies. A viewer would immediately identify fancy women approaching *neaniskoi* as *hetairai,* rather than demure little fourteen-year-old virgin brides. There is a lot of ill-informed debate about which women on vases are courtesans or common prostitutes and which wives, cf. Sian Lewis, *The Athenian Woman* (London, 2002), passim, but in this case I really don't see any room for reasonable doubt.

26 Vases unmatched in size and shape might be matched in decorative elements, though often the parallels might be quite naïve, e.g., a vase, otherwise a singleton, might be matched with the other vases because it has a "woman with wings," although the winged woman may be messenger Iris on one vase and on another rapist Dawn. For Greece, cf. Burn, on the Sotades tomb, "Honeypots," 101: "Six of the nine are clearly pairs . . ." with n. 39: "On the remarkably common incidence of surviving pairs of vases, see A. Lezzi-Hafter, 'Mänaden und Götterliebe in Malibu,' in *Greek Vases in the J. Paul Getty Museum* (1983), 85–114, esp. 110–14, with bibliography. No triplets are mentioned." For

Etruria the best way to see the pattern in the deposits is to wander around the collections of the Villa Giulia in Rome, where, in 2002 at least, the cabinets were arranged by grave, cf. Williams, "The Brygos Tomb Reassembled," and see now, Bagnasco Gianni (ed.), *Cerveteri* (Milan, 2002), with her article, "Singoli casi," 607–608 for further bibliography. In a handful of Etruscan tombs (a much larger sample than known Greek tombs), a pattern of three and its multiples was observed. All of which makes me wonder: were the Getty Ganymede Cup (Malibu 1984.AE.569, *BA* 16200) and the Ganymede in the Met. (Shelby White & Leon Levy Collection, *BA* 43265) possibly from the same tomb?

27 Berlin F 2278, *BA* 200108.

28 Such lion skins and leopard skins may have been common. At least one of those at Ephesus was of a young lion, Bammer, "Sanctuaries in the Artemision," p. 40. Alexander and others said to have worn lion skins probably really did.

29 Kilmer, *Greek Erotica,* p. 95, who thinks the scenes of copulation belong to a quite different world from the laws and the texts and indicate a laissez-faire attitude.

30 Pliny, *Nat. Hist.* 28.50–52, David Sansone, *Greek Athletics and the Genesis of Sport* (Berkeley, 1988), pp. 123–24.

31 *BA* 13607, Françoise Frontisi-Ducroux, "Eros, Desire and the Gaze," in Kampen, *Sexuality in Ancient Art,* pp. 81–100, pp. 90, cf. 92, fig. 39, p. 98 n. 63.

32 *BA* 301082 Boston 13.105. One might also note the distinction between oil flasks in shape and design. Were flasks which held sacred oil marked in some way?

33 1.138.

34 *Smp.* 181be, with Dover ad 181d1.

35 182a, 182d.

36 Neer, *Style and Politics,* p. 101.

37 So Neer, ibid.

38 Wilson, Khoregia, p. 255: "*khoregia* [sponsorship of choruses of Boy bands] provided . . . the prime context for an adoring public gaze," and see index s.v. "Glaukon."

39 *BA* 204034, Oxford, Ashmolean Museum, 1967.304.

40 *Phaedrus* 255b.

41 *Birds* 137–42.

16: THE FOURTH CENTURY: POLITICS AND THE PROFESSIONALS

1 Foucault, *Dits et Écrits* IV, pp. 286–87.

2 Plato, *Smp.* 182a.

3 Lysias 3.5, *pace* Carey, *Lysias,* p. 87. Quite possibly the choice of verb contradicts a statement of Simon, "We were both in love with Theodotus."

4 Todd, *Lysias,* p. 42.

5 24–26. The speaker claims the contract is a fiction, but it seems plausible to me, because Simon was obviously embarrassed by it (26), and claimed the money had been paid back to him already by the speaker.

6 6–10.

7 10–14,19.

8 31.

9 Aeschin. 3.162.

10 Lysias 3.33. It should be noted that although the possibility of a slave's tortured testimony is frequently referred to—"if you have nothing to hide, offer your slaves up for torture"—in practice it seems to have been very rare.

11 Aeschin. 1.15–17.

12 3.5, 44, 39.

13 3.40, 43.

14 29.

15 Hyp., *Ath.*, 2, 21. For background on the speech, see Whitehead ad loc.

16 23–24.

17 Hyp., *Ath.* 21; Lysias 3.

18 1.158, with Fisher ad loc.

19 1.165, with Fisher ad loc.

20 On the highly developed market in skills and training, cf. Davidson, "Making a Spectacle of Her(self)," 38–40, 42–44.

21 Alexis 3 K–A, Antiphanes 27 K–A, Timocles 32 K–A.

22 4.53–54.

23 For all that follows, I have made much use of Fisher, *Aeschines: Against Timarchos,* the first proper commentary on this long-famous speech. Almost every reference to the text would be usefully accompanied by "and see Fisher ad loc."

24 On the date and the legal basis for the prosecution, Fisher, pp. 5–8.

25 22–23. Aeschines creates a powerful sense of steady progressions, his own speech carefully following in the footsteps of the Lawgiver's progressive thinking—"first he turned his attention to . . . next he considered"—conjuring up the image of going through a marble document, a single long inscription listing the basic laws, very similar to the Athenian's exposition in (Aeschines's teacher?) Plato's *Laws,* written around the same time. The Lawgiver himself is seen to follow the natural lifecycle of an Athenian from birth to death—"first laws on Boys . . . then Striplings . . . then the rest of the grades . . ."—and then the sequence of events at an Assembly from purificatory sacrifice to invitations to speak, at which point the natural order of age-classes is reversed: Fifty-pluses first. This apparently irrelevant archaeologifying of what every Athenian who has ever attended an Assembly ought already to know not only makes it easier for his audience to follow this terribly long discourse, to know where they are up to, but it creates its own sense of orderliness per se, which stands in contrast to Timarchus's disorderly progress, not a New-Critical text

turning in upon itself to talk about its own composition, but a text that embodies in its orderly structure the orderliness that is its moral and political theme. That may sound clever-clever, but I also think it was what clever-clever Aeschines was in fact doing.

26 Aeschines himself was sculpted like this, because he imitated the old-time orators and/or because of this passage in this speech, which would be a nice example of an image "archaeologizing" from a passage in a text.

27 28. Elsewhere, 3.2–4, complaining about the "disorderliness" (*akosmia*) of orators, Aeschines is much more insistent about the existence of Solonian legislation "On the orderliness of orators." Possibly he has taken an authentic piece of Solonian-looking legislation on the "orderliness" of events at an Assembly and mixed it up with other "constitutional" legislation. The idea of "orderliness" (*kosmos*) could well be an authentic term of archaic legislation, which was later defined more precisely. For contrasting views, cf. Fisher, pp. 5–6 and ad 22, Hansen, *The Athenian Assembly,* pp. 71–72, reviewed by J. Ober, "The Nature of Athenian Democracy," *Class Phil* 84 (1989) [322–34], 325 n. 7.

28 It would be nice to know how old this particular clause was, at what point in the history of Athens lawgivers became worried about the possibility of rentboys elbowing their way onto the speaker's platform, and how old the distinction it makes between a man being a common prostitute and a male courtesan. It may have been introduced as part of the general restoration of the democracy on a more formal and orderly basis after the political disorder of the end of the Peloponnesian War, so Carey, *Aeschines,* p. 19 n. 2, a consequence perhaps of all the talk of politicians as whores in Aristophanes' *Knights* and elsewhere.

29 D. 19.233, cf. Aeschin. 1.41, 75, 126.

30 Cf. Fisher ad 41, pp. 170–74, and 162 ad 31.

31 "*epitēdeion pros to pragma ho prōeireito ekeinos men prattein, houtos de paschein.*" "Do/have done to," *prattein/paschein* is a common formula found, e.g., in Aeschines' allusion to Demosthenes' relationship with Aristion 3.162 and Philip's curse at Chaeronea over the bodies of the Sacred Band, Plu., *Pelopidas* 18,7, a formula perhaps directly relevant to a man such as Timarchus who was of the pro-Theban anti-Macedonian party. If Aeschines wishes to imply Misgolas was the lustful active and Timarchus the mercenary passive partner, he by no means exonerates Misgolas as a macho sexual penetrator. Quite the contrary: "blameless but for this" (41).

32 42.

33 Davidson, "Revolutions in Human Time," pp. 42–43.

34 Parker, *Polytheism,* pp. 317–21.

35 43. This view is quite different from that of Fisher ad loc., who, like other scholars, does not credit the existence of laws "against corruption of the youth," despite Plato's own contemporary and probably eyewitness evidence in *Apology.*

36 51.

37 Harpocration s.v. "*Autoclides*" [= Suda Alpha 4498].

38 41.

39 Antiphanes 27 K–A.

40 *An.* 2.6,28.

41 Plato, *Smp.* 189–193.

42 53.

43 54. For Pittalacus's status as *anthrōpos dēmosios oiketēs tēs poleōs* "a public person, servant of the city," see Fisher ad loc., pp. 189–91. Athens owned numerous "public servants" often given important jobs of responsibility in the city, policing weights and measures, executioners, etc. Pittalacus must have been a former slave who had grown rich through his business, not that uncommon a phenomenon. For quail tapping, Fisher, ad 59, p. 196, and for the context of gambling and an attempt to work out what was really going on, id. "The Perils of Pittalakos: Settings of Cock Fighting and Dicing in Classical Athens" in S. Bell and G. Davies (eds.), *Games and Festivals in the Ancient World, BAR* International Series 1220 (2004), 65–78. He notes, 71–76, that the temple of Athena Skiras called "Skiron," center of the Skirophoria (cf. Parker, *Polytheism,* p. 480) celebrated in the last month of the year ("Skirophorion"), was associated with gambling, and that therefore another temple of Athena Skiras in Phalerum may have been too. Since the Phalerum shrine was associated with the clan called "Salaminians," and since Hegesander was very probably a member of the clan, the dispute may have been a kind of "turf war," Pittalacus, an ex-employee(?) encroaching on the shrine's business and punished by having all his gambling equipment destroyed. Perhaps Pittalacus had even been the state's gambling officer, watching out for loaded dice, etc. If the idea of the clan of Salaminians being involved with ritual gaming seems incredible, one might add that Salaminian Ajax had long been depicted playing the first board game with Achilles, while waiting at Aulis (probably) for the heat of the dog days to be replaced by an Etesian wind, to fill the Greek fleet's sails, and that already in the first half of the sixth century one such board-game scene was assimilated to cockfighting and indeed surrounded by Striplings buggering each other, etc., *BA* 300833: a Salaminian, gaming and homosexual fornication all on one vase!

44 Cf. Fisher ad 56, pp. 193–95 ad 107, pp. 244–45 ad 109–10, pp. 247–49 and p. 21.

45 71.

46 55.

47 One could argue that the Parthenon is not so much a temple as a bank; those columned neoclassical temple facades in modern capital cities where central bankers decide interest rates are not as inappropriate as they look.

48 Hansen, *The Athenian Democracy,* pp. 232–33.

49 107 and Fisher ad 110.

50 110–11. *Gunē,* like French *femme,* can mean woman or wife, but the phrase "Leodamas's woman" must surely imply the latter.

51 Fisher ad 68, X., *Lac.* 2.12.

52 69–70.

53 64.

54 1.171—2,3.162.

55 132. So, as late as this, Eros retains his links to the gymnastic elite. In fact the link is still there in the Roman period, in Plutarch and Petronius and the Greek novels.

56 102, 155–57 with Fisher, p. 20.

57 Jírí Frel, "Griechischer Eros," *Listy Filologické* 86 (1963) [60–64], 61–62 counted only nine homosexual scenes for *c.*500–475, partly by dating the CHC *skyphoi* to the previous quarter-century, which is probably too early, Shapiro, "Courtship Scenes," 133–43.

58 Demophantus's decree, Andocides 1.96–98.

59 Plu., *Mor.* 806f–807e.

60 Plu., *Per. 7,* Nicias 5. 1–2 cf. Connor, *New Politicians,* pp. 121–22, 127–78.

61 Cf. Connor ibid., pp. 91–94.

62 Ar., *Knights* 876–80. "Buggered" translates *binoumenoi*—"males who are humped." The archaeologicable fact must be some kind of recent successful indictment against Gryttus for prostitution, pimping or sexual abuse, but Gryttus (Grypus?) is otherwise unknown.

63 425–28.

64 The *allas,* "black pudding," is used as a metaphor for a big lustful penis already in Hipponax 84.17 (West), but cf. Ralph M. Rosen, "Hipponax, Boupalos, and the Conventions of the Psogos."

65 Lysistrata ("Army-Dissolving") clearly has something to do with a real-world contemporary, Lysimache ("Battle-Dissolving"), for sixty-four years the priestess of Athena Polias on the Acropolis in the "Erechtheum" and one of the most publicly prominent women in Athens, cf. D. M. Lewis, "Who Was Lysistrata?," *ABSA* 50 (1955), 1–12, Joan Connelly, *Portrait of a Priestess* (Princeton, 2007), pp. 62–64. But it is also likely that other women in the family were actually called Lysistrate, as we know they were some decades later. Presumably we have missed some archaeologicable incident concerning a Lysimache or Lysistrate (or even a feminized Lysistratos), brought to Aristophanes' attention not long before 411 when *Lysistrata* was staged, or perhaps the plot was just an outrageous play on Lysimache's name.

66 110–14.

67 Cf. Sommerstein ad *Ecclesiazusae* 112–13: "It is a standing joke in comedy that all the most successful politicians were once male prostitutes." However they are not all charged with being paid for sex, necessarily, nor is it necessarily something that had happened only in their pasts.

68 192a.

69 256bc.

70 183a, 184b.

71 These few words on *Laws* do not do justice to a work the subtlety, irony, play-fulness and complexity of which have only recently come to be appreciated. The best introductions are Laks, "The *Laws*" and R. F. Stalley, *Introduction to Plato's Laws* (Oxford, 1983). I do not agree 100 percent with Nussbaum's account of what Plato has to say about homosexuality in *Laws*, and—a technical, but not irrelevant issue—find myself almost always preferring Burnet's old conservative and much scorned *Oxford Classical Text* to the "new improved" (and overly adventurous) Budé which she, and, e.g., Christopher Bobonich, unaccountably prefer, but her conclusions nevertheless seem quite right to me 90 percent of the time and she has certainly got the gist of what Plato was saying and places it in the context of Plato's other writings on the subject very nicely, "Platonic Love," Appendix 3, "Homosexuality in *Laws*," 1623–40.

72 835c, 836bc.

73 838b: *mēdamōs hosia, theomisē de kai aischrōn aischista.*

74 837e cf. 842a.

CONCLUSION: A MAP OF GREEK LOVE

1 *OED* s.v. "nodal," 14.

2 Meier, "Päderastie," 156 col ii. Meier finished (187 col ii–188) with an account of "factors": *Momente*. First and foremost was the exclusion of women from the lives of men and from political life; the apparent contradiction that pederasty was least prominent in Ionia, where women seemed most secluded, was put down to political inhibition. For, second, pederasty was related to political associations and dining societies, which were suppressed in those places. Third, following Plato in *Laws* and Ennius, was the nude homo-socializing of the gymnasium. Fourth, following Xenophon, the communal living of the Dorians, which led to an absence of paternal guidance in the domestic sphere, so that pederasty had to fill the educational gap. Fifth, following Pausanias's "right reasons for putting out," was the fact that boys, especially in Athens, had no alternative but to turn to an older expert in order to acquire a deeper practical or philosophical knowledge and since payments were, with a few exceptions, not considered appropriate, the teaching was offered in the context of a reciprocal relationship; pederasty fulfilled some of the functions of "high school."

3 Meier, "Päderastie," 156 col i, has a useful description of what needs to be explained, i.e., a pan-Hellenic unhidden and enacted thing, which must be more than simply "the product of a singular abnormality and unnaturalness" (*das Erzeugnis einer singulairen Abnormität und Unnatur*).

4 836bc.

5 *Od.* 19.172–77.

6 D.S. 12.70,1.

7 Heraclides' epitome of [Aristotle]'s *Constitutions*, Arist. fr. 611.15 (Rose).

8 *Pelopidas* 19.1.
9 636d.
10 634d–635a, 836b.
11 *Wasps* 1025, *Peace* 762–63. The ancient commentators tell us that Eupolis had boasted of vaunting himself in front of the boys in his play about the boy *Autolycus,* fr. 65, cf. K–A ad loc. for problems with that information— Aristophanes' joke precedes both Eupolis's two *Autolycus* comedies—and suggestions as to how to get around them.
12 *Smp.* 8.35.
13 Paus. 3.20, 10–11 with Musti and Torelli ad loc.
14 *Lac.* 2.12.
15 1.139.
16 *Lac.* 2.13–14.
17 *Smp.* 8.35.
18 Cic., *De Re Publica* 4.4. Since the passage is so little known—the crucial part often omitted in older translations—and so important, it might be appropriate also to cite the revised translation of James E. G. Zetzel: "I will set aside the people of Elis and of Thebes, where the amatory passions of free men are given complete license. Even the Spartans, in permitting everything except penetration in amatory relationships with young men, use a very slender barrier to prohibit this one exception: they allow them to embrace and to sleep together provided that they are separated by a cloak." *Cicero: On the Commonwealth and On the Laws* (Cambridge, 1999).
19 Plato, *Lysis* 205ab, Pindar, *Isthmian* 2.1–12.
20 *Preface* 4, *Alcibades* 2.2.
21 We have still not got to the bottom of these acclamations, I think. Some clearly make comments broadcasting the beauty or "decency" of a boy, the *kaloses* that surround Athenodotus, for instance, as he modestly ties up his penis with a "dog leash," *BA* 203265, Boston, Museum of Fine Arts, 01.8021. But other acclamations, those of the Achilles Painter, were destined for graves. Apart from those inscribed by quarrymen in Thasos (v. infra), acclamations were inscribed by bullet makers—one with *kalos* (reference lost!) cf. *Olynthus* X 422, 2180: *Archies hōraios*—and tile-makers, cf. D. M. Robinson, "Inscriptions from Olynthus, 1934," *TAPA* 65 (1934) [103–37], 134–35. I suspect acclamations also had an efficacious function, for the success of the boy, pot or bullet.
22 A. Coulié, "Nouvelles inscriptions érotiques de Thasos," *BCH* 122 (1998), 445–53, makes the same comparison with the Ceramicus (452).
23 Plato, *Phdr.* 279b, Suda s.v. (Pi 858).
24 Wilson, Khoregia, p. 255.
25 Thuc. 6.54, with Hornblower ad loc.; Plato, *Phdr.* 256d.
26 Bethe, "Dorische Knabenliebe," 447: "*in Kreta die Verbindung von Mann und Knaben in der Form des Brautraubes vor sich ging.*"
27 That does not mean it was necessarily a position exclusive to Athens. Analyz-

ing the vase images properly would need a book in itself. I have been able to make use of the catalogue of homosexual scenes on Greek vases, compiled by the late Keith DeVries of the University of Pennsylvania, as an improvement on Beazley, "Some Attic Vases," 198–223. DeVries's catalogue is now published in Andrew Lear and Eva Cantarella, *Images of Greek Pederasty* (London, 2007).

28 *BA* 13607, Françoise Frontisi-Ducroux, "Eros, Desire and the Gaze," in Kampen, *Sexuality in Ancient Art* [81–100], p. 90, cf. p. 92, fig. 39, p. 98 n. 63.

29 Knud Friis Johansen, "Attic Motives on Clazomenian Sarcophagi," in *From the Collections of the Ny Carlsberg Glyptotek* iii (1942) [123–43], 131. Beazley, "Some Attic Vases," 219–21, already made the connection between the entrapped boys on the Peithinos Cup and the Gotha Cup.

30 *BA* 200100, Gotha, Schlossmuseum, 48, cf. *BA* 7242, Kusnacht, Hirschmann Collection, G64, Schnapp, "Eros the Hunter," p. 85, fig. 118.

31 Aeschylus, *Myrmidones*. Fr. 135 (Radt).

32 *BA* 43790, Athens, Agora Museum, P7690, Kilmer, *Greek Erotica,* p. 18 and pl. R1123. On *philotēsia,* Olson, ad Ar. *Ach.* 983.

33 Fr. 407.

34 *BA* 200078, Hermitage 644. "Smikra" must surely be a transgendered rendering of Euphronios's fellow worker, Smikros, who is thereby revealed to have had an accent.

35 On early *pyxides,* their contents and uses, S. Schmidt, *Rhetorische Bilder auf attischen Vasen* (Berlin, 2005), pp. 88–93, 107–14 (a reference I owe to Barbara Borg). This particular example, and not only this, shows that *pyxides* might be structurally linked to marriages long before the classical period; Schmidt's theory may need modifying.

36 In fact instead of a visual pun, might *pharos* never have meant "plow" at all? The ancient commentator who suggested it (one Sosiphanes, according to a papyrus commentary on the poem, a Tragedian?) may simply have misunderstood a reference to yoke-mating in Alcman's song and could not understand how a cloak and a yoke went together unless the "cloak" was a plow, but cf. Bowra, *Greek Lyric Poetry,* p. 55. Koch-Harnack has already noted the *erōtik* symbolism, the "*Homoemotionalität,*" in such scenes of "cloak-women" by the Pharos Painter and others, *Erotische Symbole,* esp. pp. 119, 138–43.

37 *BA* 7285, University of Mississippi 1977.3.72.

38 Plato, *Laws* 840e.

39 Davidson, "Revolutions in Human Time."

40 *Laws* 837ae. One way in which culture could affect homosexuality, therefore, would be through cultural constructions of difference.

41 Plato, *Laws* 636b. Polybius 4.53.3–55.6, with Walbank ad loc., *IC* IV 162–63, F. Halbherr, "Cretan Expedition III. Epigraphical Researches in Gortyna," *AJA* 1.3 (1897) [159–238], 191–98 (nos. 19–20).

42 *Smp.* 4.23–26.

43 Maximus of Tyre, *Or.* 20.8.

44 *Laws* 636bc.

45 *Smp.* 182d.

46 X., *Lac.* 2.13.

47 Bethe, "Dorische Knabenliebe," 459: ". . . *der Liebesakt selbst als eine heilige Handlung am heilgen Orte* . . ."

48 Bethe ibid., 450: ". . . *Eheschliessung vor göttlichen Zeugen* . . ."

49 Theocritus 12.29 with Gow ad loc., Ar., *Ach.* 774. For the oath at the tomb of Iolaus, Plu., *Pelopidas* 18.4 [= Arist. fr. 97 Rose], cf. Hunter, *Theocritus and the Archaeology of Greek Poetry,* p. 191, who adduces the possible parallel in the kissing contest at the tomb of Diocles in Megara.

50 *BA* 301002, Louvre F43.

51 Paus. 1.30,1.

52 636bd.

53 *BA* 14701, *SEG* 35 (1985), 252, Martha Ohly-Dumm, "Tripod-Pyxis from the Sanctuary of Aphaia in Aegina," in D. von Bothmer, *The Amasis Painter and His World* (London, 1985), Appendix 4, 236–38. Ohly-Dumm, reading *autos* rather than *autōs,* preferred, less convincingly, to see the lines as an incomplete quote: ". . . the Sun-god knows and I alone; the beautiful boy he [the Sun] himself has . . ."

54 *FGrHist* 115 F225b.

55 Aelian, *V.H.* 3.10.

56 In general see Ogden, "Homosexuality and Warfare."

57 X., *Smp.* 8.34.

58 Sosicrates, *FGrHist* 461 F 7 ap. Ath. 13.561ef.

59 Ephorus, *FGrHist* 70 F 149 ap. Strabo 10.4,21.

60 Aelian, *V. H.* 3.10.

61 Plato, *Charm.* 154cd.

62 Plu., *Agesilaus* 34.7–8.

63 Plu., *Pelopidas* 18.2.

64 Lucian, *On Dance* 14.

65 Plu., *Pel.* 19.5, referring to the fourth-century reform that made the band fight as a single unit. Perhaps, as a patriotic Boeotian, he was just coming up with a more worthy explanation—rivalry—for the practice of sleeping together and fighting together, that Xenophon thought was so shocking. On the other hand Athenian black-figure vase painters often juxtapose courting scenes with cockfights, as if analogous. Sometimes it is clear the rivalrous cocks refer to *erastai* competing over an *erōmenos,* but sometimes the cockfight and the rivalry are between the bearded *erastēs* and the Stripling *erōmenos, BA* 2506, Boston, Museum of Fine Arts, 63.4, Koch-Harnack, *Knabenliebe,* pp. 104–105. This must be how the fight between winged Eros and Anteros was viewed, especially when we take into account the pair of gamecocks carried by Timagoras in the crooks of his arms in the sanctuary of Eros-Anteros below the Erechtheum.

66 Cf. Plato, *Smp.* 178d–179a.

67 *A.P.* 13.22 ll.4–8.

68 Plato, *Smp.* 179b, Archilochus 196a.52. It now seems clear that Solon was using *menos* in the same sense, when he talked of snow and hail as "cloud-spunk," fr. 9.1.

69 *Laws* 839bd.

70 Homer, *Iliad* 23.77–78.

71 Strabo 13.2,3.

72 Alcaeus TT 20 and 23. For a charming example of Alcaeus's "stylistic dissonance," his mingling of high and low tone, see fr. 129 ll. 9–21: "Come hear our prayers . . . but let their avenging Fury go after the son of Hyrrhas . . . the fat bastard . . . ," see Kurke, "Crisis and Decorum," attempting a Bourdieu-esque analysis and seeing the abuse not so much as reckless factionalism but as an attempt to create a healed community of Lesbian listeners through the verbal driving out of scapegoat Pittacus. For an imaginative archaeologizing of archaic Mytilene see Nigel Spencer, "Exchange and Stasis in Archaic Mytilene," in Brock and Hodkinson (eds.), *Alternatives,* 68–81, although he may be exaggerating the peculiarity of Mytilene's factionalism, and neglecting the degree to which the city's reputation came from ancient archaeologizing from the artifacts produced by her famous poets. For a summary of what is known, and up-to-date bibliography, M. H. Hansen, N. Spencer and H. Williams, "Lesbos," *IACP,* 1018–32.

73 T 9 = *POxy* 2506 b 24–25, Vetta "Poesia pederotica," 18: "*Il frammento dei rr. 24–25 . . . ci apre ad un quadro di contestualità di epainos e psogos che avevamo testimoniato solo in quel codice della stretta interferenza del legame erotico coll'allineamento eterico . . .*"

74 Van Wees, "Megara's Mafiosi," 53, with reference to Theognis.

75 There have been a number of somewhat disputatious attempts to sort out the "Theognis" mess, which can be divided up into the "mishmash" theory of Nagy, who as a good Harvard post-Parryian sees almost all early poetry as a collective enterprise in which questions of "authorship" just get in the way, and the "mishmashed" theory articulated in most detail by West, that sees discrete corpora composed by specific poetic personalities (often quite jealous of their authorship), being stripped of their identities in the Hellenistic period and frog-marched into useful anthologies, cf. G. Nagy, "Theognis and Megara. A poet's vision of his city," in G. Nagy, and T. J. Figueira (eds.), *Theognis of Megara: Poetry and the Polis* (Baltimore, 1985), 22–81. Martin West, *OCD3* "Theognis," divides the collection as follows:

  1. 1–18: addresses to gods, gathered at the beginning.
  2. 19–254: nearly all Cyrnus-poems, serious in tone, with the first and last excerpts chosen as prologue and epilogue.
  3. 255–1022: a much more heterogeneous and disorderly collection, with a few Cyrnus-blocks here and there.

4. 1023–1220: similar in character, but with a high proportion of couplets duplicated elsewhere. (1221–30: added by [modern] editors from other sources.) 5. 1231–1389: amatory poems mostly addressed to boys. This section survives only in the tenth-century MS A (where it is designated "book 2") and was unknown until Bekker's edition of 1815.

cf. West, *Studies in Greek Elegy and Iambus,* esp. pp. 40–60 on the later collations, with E. L. Bowie, "The Theognidea: A Step Toward a Collection of Fragments?" in G. W. Most (ed.), *Collecting fragments—Fragmente sammeln* (Göttingen, 1997), 53–66. For an attempt to sift out an authentic Theognis and place him in history, perhaps a little too precisely, West, op. cit., pp. 65–70; West offers a somewhat modified and slightly more cautious summary in *OCD*[3] s.v. "Theognis." For a useful survey of arguments about the authentic core and its dating that he puts at c.600–560 BC, cf. Lane Fox, "Theognis." Van Wees, "Megara's Mafiosi" suggests, p. 52 n. 2, there is no reason to reject the traditional date of 540s. H. Friis Johansen thinks a date before *c.*550 is ruled out on linguistic grounds, "A poem by Theognis (Thgn. 19–38), Part II," *Classica et Mediaevalia* 44 (1993), 5–29. My general impression is that scholars have underplayed Plato's evidence for a *Sicilian* "Theognis," and overplayed the importance of geographical or temporal proximity to places and events "Theognis" mentions. When he refers to a city suffering disaster, we need not look for occasions when the city was actually destroyed; he may merely be alluding to a well-known song about a city's afflictions, i.e., archaeologizing.

76 27–28.

77 254 and 63–64.

78 215–16, not a "Cyrnus-poem," but well within the main "Cyrnus-block."

79 77–78.

80 819–20.

81 Plu., *Solon* 1.8 says Pisistratus dedicated a statue (*agalma*) of Eros. It is quite possible Plutarch is confusing Pisistratus with Charmus, who dedicated the altar. Or possibly the statue (*agalma*) was dedicated alongside the altar. For a probable image of the altar and (possibly) of Eros getting onto his platform, *BA* 210126, Munich Antikensammlungen 2669, Shapiro, *Art and Cult,* p. 124 and pl. 56. On Charmus's dedication, Ath. 13.609d, Paus. 1.30,1 with Musti and Beschi ad loc., Scanlon, *Eros,* pp. 255–56.

82 Thuc. 6.54. There is a good account of the affair and its implications for the politics of Eros in Ferrari, *Figures of Speech,* pp. 155–58. On the "glamorous" Gephyraioi Parker, *Athenian Religion,* pp. 288–89.

83 Hyp. 3.8 with Whitehead ad loc.: "convening a (political) association."

84 Bentley, *A Dissertation,* p. 53 on the meaning of *erastēs.* Boyle's response, citing evidence that *erastēs* need not refer to flagitiousness, has been ignored, Boyle, *Dr. Bentley's Dissertations,* pp. 65–66.

85 Meier, "Päderastie," 156 col ii: ". . . *aber nirgends bei Homer oder Hesiod bestimmte Andeutung des Verhältnisses, mit dem wir uns hier beschäftigen.*"

86 Halperin, *One Hundred Years,* pp. 75–87.

87 Meier, "Päderastie," 156 col ii.

88 Mimnermus fr. 3, more literally: "not even though he be their father." There is a nice if odd-sounding oscillation in this remarkable couplet, from Greek Love to filial love and back to Greek Love, from boys in general to one's sons in particular, reconstructing an inherited *philia* (which ought to be an assumption of all close blood relationships) as if it were a made *philia* provoked by boundary crossing *erōtikos* attraction to a father's beauty, cf. fr. 1.9, Alexander of Aetolia fr. 5.4–5 (Powell) ap. Ath. 15.699b.

89 Rhodes ad *Ath. Pol.* 17.2.

90 Solon fr. 25.

91 Meier, "Päderastie," 156 col. i.

92 M. L. West, "The Date of the *Iliad*," *Museum Helveticum* 52 (1995), 203–19.

93 Ewen Bowie first drew my attention to this, some years ago, with regard to Hermes' epiphany to Odysseus on Circe's island.

94 Bethe, "Dorische Knabenliebe," 447: "*Es geht die Sitte also in sehr hohes Alter hinauf . . .*" Cf. also his quote from C. O. Müller, *Die Dorier* II2 (Breslau, 1844), p. 289: "*eine solche das ganze Leben durchdringende Sitte tiefer wurzeln muss, als auf einem einzelnen Institut, einer einzelnen Ueberlegung.*"

95 Bethe, "Dorische Knabenliebe," 447: "*Auf die Zeit vor der dorischen Einwanderung oder doch vor der Zerstreuung der Dorer zurückgehen.*"

96 Birgitta Eder, "Doric migration" in *Brill's New Pauly,* provides a nice summary.

97 Bremmer, "An Enigmatic Indo-European Rite," 290.

98 Robert B. Koehl, "The Chieftain Cup and a Minoan Rite of Passage," *JHS* 106 (1986), 99–110.

99 Signe Isager and Poul Pedersen (eds.), *The Salmakis Inscription and Hellenistic Halikarnassos* (Odense, 2004).

100 Pirenne-Delforge, *L'Aphrodite,* pp. 457–58, Brice L. Erickson, "Aphrati and Kato Syme: Pottery, Continuity, and Cult in Late Archaic and Classical Crete," *Hesperia* 71 (2002), 41–90.

101 *Homosexualité et initiation chez les peoples indo-européens* (Paris, 1996), pp. 549–50 [This volume combines both earlier books with a "Postface"].

102 Bethe, "Dorische Knabenliebe," 463–64, 474, although to talk of his work as "based on" ethnography or even inspired by it is going too far, cf. p. 464 n. 57: "Ich konnte diesen Aufsatz nicht einsehen," he remarks of J. Holmes, "Initiation Ceremonies of the Papuan Gulf," *Journal of the Anthropological Institute* 32 (1902), Ogden, "Homosexuality and Warfare," 107–68, K. J. Dover, review of H. Patzer, *Die griechische Knabenliebe* (Wiesbaden, 1982), *JHS* 104 (1984) [239–40], 240.

103 Herdt, *Ritualized Homosexuality,* p. xiv, Knauft, *South Coast New Guinea Cultures,* p. 51.

104 Herdt, ibid., p. xxxii.

105 Herdt, *Sambia Sexual Culture,* p. 75 and n. 11.

106 Ibid., pp. 49, 108–109.

107 Herdt, *Sambia Sexual Culture,* esp. pp. 167–85; for a brief survey of Sambia insemination rituals, id. "Semen Transactions in Sambia Culture," in id. *Ritualized Homosexuality,* pp. 167–210; for a survey of evidence for such practices from all over Melanesia as of 1982, ibid., pp. 9–48.

108 Bethe, "Dorische Knabenliebe," 459.

109 Percy, *Pederasty and Pedagogy,* pp. 32–33, Halperin, *One Hundred Years,* p. 56 and 171 n. 14.

110 Moreover, body-substance rituals are only one part of the cultural system. Knauft identifies four "themes" that can be emphasized in one zone and played down elsewhere: "i) a cosmological cycle of growth and fertility that included the taking and incorporation of life-force, especially through head-hunting, ii) the creation, exchange, and transmission of life-force in ritual heterosexual and (sometimes) homosexual activity, iii) the coalescence of spiritual force in sacred costumes, carvings, trophies, or relics and iv) the enactment of cosmological growth cycles through elaborate spirit-cult performances," p. 173. Knauft's attempt tentatively to sketch how a single group of beliefs might be elaborated over many centuries in different ways by different groups in different (social, ecological, historical) circumstances, leading to radically different results—one group developing theatrically, another murderously, another sexily—is, for an ancient historian, quite remarkable, like watching some kind of cultural Big Bang in slow motion. *South Coast New Guinea Cultures,* pp. 172–209, esp. 206–209, and passim.

111 Knauft, "Text and Social Practice," 268.

112 Herdt, *Sambia Sexual Culture,* pp. 96, 103, Knauft, "Text and Social Practice," 272. One often feels that these lustful nymphs that lustful men (in both ancient Greece and Papua New Guinea) are so fond of representing are not so much misogynistic images, i.e., reflections of sincere contempt for women's inability to control their lusts, as alter egos—that by projecting insatiable lust onto women they are trying very hard and very obviously to eject lust from the field of men, insisting it's not manly to behave like that, because they fear it probably is.

113 Secrecy, of course, helps in the construction of semen as both hidden and precious, like a secret hoard of gold. The implication being that if the women knew the true value of the substance it would be threatened still more.

114 Knauft, "Text and Social Practice," 268. He notes that homosexuality is not only absent from the narratives of sexual "longing," told by men to an audience of men, but the plot of the narratives denies even the possibility of this regular practice, "the epitome of male false-consciousness." "The only sexual outlet for the proprietous but sexually frustrated male hero is, ostensibly, the beautiful young woman," 269.

115 Herdt, *Sambia Sexual Culture,* p. 109.

116 Van Wees, "Megara's Mafiosi," 53 n. 3.

117 K. W. Arafat, "Moliones," *OCD3*.

118 Detienne, "Remarques sur le char," 426.

119 Detienne, "Remarques sur le char," 421–22.

120 C. Piteros, J-P. Olivier and J. L. Melena, "Les inscriptions en linéaire B des nodules de Thèbes (1982): La fouille, les documents, les possibilités d'interprétation," *BCH* 114 (1990), 103–83, Vassilis Aravantinos, "Mycenaean Texts and Contexts at Thebes: The Discovery of New Linear B Archives on the Kadmeia," in *Floreant Studia Mycenaea* [Acts of X. International Mycenaean Studies Colloquium in Salzburg, May 1–5, 1995] (Vienna, 1999), vol. I, 45–78, id. "Le scoperte archeologiche ed epigrafiche micenee a Tebe," in Paola Angeli Bernardini ed, *Presenza e Funzione della città di Tebe nella Cultura Greca* [= *Atti del Convegno Internazionale* (Urbino 7–9 luglio 1997)] (Pisa/Rome, 2000), 27–59.

121 X., *Cyr.* 6.1,28.

122 *IC* IV 72.III.7–8.

123 Davidson, "Revolutions in Human Time," 30–31.

124 J. L. Garcia Ramon, "Greek Dialects," *Brill's New Pauly*.

125 10.39,12.

126 Gentili, "Ways of love," 72–104.

127 Boswell, *Marriage of Likeness;* Bray, "Friendship, the Family and Liturgy," Bray, *The Friend;* Brown, "Introduction," Brown, "Ritual Brotherhood"; Rapp, "Ritual Brotherhood in Byzantium"; Shaw, "Ritual Brotherhood."

128 King, "Male homosocial readership," n. 52, citing Val. Max. 2.6.11: "*Celtiberi etiam nefas esse ducebant proelio superesse, cum is occidisset, pro cuius salute spiritum deuouerant,*" Caesar, *Gallic Wars* 3.22.1 on the *soldurii*: "*Omnibus in uita commodis una cum iis fruantur quorum se amicitiae dediderint,*" cf. Plu., *Sertorius* 14 and Servius ad Virgil, *Georgics* 4.218.

129 Bray, "Friendship, the Family and Liturgy."

130 *Quem filius regis intuens, in eum tantum protinus amorem iniecit [?] quod cum eo fraternitatis fedus iniit, et pre ceteris mortalibus indissolubile dileccionis vinculum secum elegit et firm[i]ter disposuit innodare.*

131 Shaw, "Ritual Brotherhood," 339–40 with n. 43.

132 *Politics* 2.1269b.

133 Eusebius, *Praeparatio Evangelica* 6.10,27, Shaw, "Ritual Brotherhood," 335–36.

134 Amm. Marc. 31.9,5: "*Taifalorum gentem turpem obscenae vitae flagitiis ita accepimus mersam, ut apud eos nefandi concubitus foedere copulentur maribus puberes, aetatis viriditatem in eorum pollutis usibus consumpturi.*"

ABBREVIATIONS

AJA	*American Journal of Archaeology*
AJP	*American Journal of Philology*
AM	*Mitteilungen des Deutschen Archäologischen Instituts, Athenische Abteilung*
BA	*Beazley Archive*
BAR	*British Archaeological Reports*
BCH	*Bulletin de correspondance hellénique*
BICS	*Bulletin of the Institute of Classical Studies*
CAVI	H. Immerwahr et al., *Corpus of Attic Vase Inscriptions* (at *Beazley Archive*)
Class Ant	*Classical Antiquity*
Class Phil	*Classical Philology*
CQ	*Classical Quarterly*
CR	*Classical Review*
FGrHist	Felix Jacoby et al. (eds), *Die Fragmente der griechischen Historiker* (Berlin/Leiden, 1923–)
Gantz	Gantz, Timothy, *Early Greek Myth* (Baltimore, 1996)
HSCP	*Harvard Studies in Classical Philology*
IACP	Hansen, Mogens Herman and Nielsen, Thomas Heine (eds), *An Inventory of Archaic and Classical Poleis* (Oxford, 2004)
IC	*Inscriptiones Creticae*
IG	*Inscriptiones Graecae*
JHS	*Journal of Hellenic Studies*
K–A	Kassel, Rudolf and Austin, Colin (eds), *Poetae Comici Graeci* (Berlin, 1983–)
LIMC	*Lexicon Iconographicum Mythologiae Classicae* (Zurich, 1981–1999)
LSJ	*A Greek-English Lexicon,* compiled by Henry George Liddell and Robert Scott, revised by Sir Henry Stuart Jones (9th edn, Oxford, 1940)
OCD	Hornblower, Simon and Spawforth, Antony (eds), *The Oxford Classical Dictionary* (3rd edn Oxford, 1996)
POxy	*The Oxyrhynchus Papyri*
PCPhS	*Proceedings of the Cambridge Philological Society*

QUCC	*Quaderni Urbinati di Cultura classica*
REA	*Revue des études anciennes*
SEG	*Supplementum Epigraphicum Graecum*
TAPA	*Transactions of the American Philological Association*
ZPE	*Zeitschrift für Papyrologie und Epigraphik*

PRIMARY SOURCES AND ABBREVIATIONS
OF AUTHORS AND WORKS

Fragments and Testimonia (T) of poets are from D. A. Campbell (ed.), *Greek Lyric,* 5 vols. (Cambridge, MA, 1982–1993); D. E. Gerber, *Greek Elegiac Poetry* (Cambridge, MA, 1999); id. *Greek Iambic Poetry* (Cambridge, MA, 1999).

Abbreviations of authors and works are standard (cf. *LSJ, OCD*) with square brackets used to mark a falsely ascribed work—[D.] = "Pseudo-Demosthenes." Some less obvious ones:

Aelian, *N.A., V.H.* = *De Natura Animalium, Varia Historia* ("Historical Miscellany")
And. = Andocides
Ant. Lib. = Antoninus Liberalis
A.P. = *Anthologia Palatina* ("The Greek Anthology")
Ar. = Aristophanes
    Ecc. = *Ecclesiazusae* ("Assemblywomen," "Parliament of Women")
    Thesm. = *Thesmophoriazusae* ("Women at the Thesmophoria," "The Poet and the Women")
Arist., *H.A.* = Aristotle, *Historia Animalium*
Ath. Pol. = [Arist.] *Athēnaiōn Politeia* ("Constitution of the Athenians")
Ath. = Athenaeus
D. = Demosthenes
D.H. = Dionysius of Halicarnassus
D.L. = Diogenes Laertius
D.S. = Diodorus Siculus
E. = Euripides
Hdt. = Herodotus
Hyp. = Hyperides
Max. Tyr. = Maximus of Tyre
Plato, *Cra. Phdr. Smp.* = *Cratylus, Phaedrus, Symposium*
Plu. = Plutarch
    Alex. = *Life of Alexander*
    Lyc. = *Life of Lycurgus*

Mor. = *Moralia* ("Moral Essays," i.e., all works other than *Lives*)

Pel. = *Life of Pelopidas*

Q.C. = Quintus Curtius Rufus

Theog. = Theognis (and [Theognis])

Thphr. = Theophrastus

X. = Xenophon

An. = *Anabasis* ("The Persian Expedition")

Cyr. = *Cyropaedia* ("Education of Cyrus")

Hell. = *Hellenica* ("Greek History," "A History of My Times")

Lac. = *Respublica Lacedaemoniorum* ("Constitution of the Spartans")

Mem. = *Memorabilia* ("Memoirs of Socrates")

Smp. = *Symposium*

SELECTED BIBLIOGRAPHY

Acton, Lord. "German Schools of History," *The English Historical Review* 1 (1886), 7–42

Aldrich, Robert. *The Seduction of the Mediterranean* (London, 1993)

Audollent, A. *Defixionum tabellae* (Paris, 1904)

Austin, M. M. *The Hellenistic World from Alexander to the Roman Conquest* (Cambridge, 1981)

Badian, E. "The Death of Parmenio," *TAPA* 91 (1960), 324–38

Bain, David. "Six Greek Verbs of Sexual Congress," *CQ* 41 (1991), 51–77

Baker, Lee D. "Franz Boas Out of the Ivory Tower," *Anthropological Theory* 4 (2004), 29–51

Bammer, A. "Sanctuaries in the Artemision of Ephesus," in R. Hägg (ed.), *Ancient Greek Cult Practice from the Archaeological Evidence* (Stockholm, 1998), 27–47

Barnard, Alan and Spencer, Jonathan (eds.). *Encyclopedia of Social and Cultural Anthropology* (London, 1996)

Beazley, J. D. "Some Attic Vases in the Cyprus Museum," *Proceedings of the British Academy* 33 (1947), 195–242

Benedict, Ruth. "Configurations of Culture in North America," *American Anthropologist,* 34 (1932), 1–27

Benedict, Ruth. *Patterns of Culture* (London, 1935 [tenth impression, 1968])

Bentley, Richard. *A Dissertation Upon the Epistles of Phalaris* (London, 1697)

Bethe, E. "Die Dorische Knabenliebe," *Rheinisches Museum für Philologie* 62 (1907), 438–75

Boardman, J. *Early Greek Vase Painting* (London, 1998)

Boas, Franz. "On Alternating Sounds," *American Anthropologist* 2 (1889), 47–54

Boegehold, Alan *et al.* *The Lawcourts at Athens* [= *The Athenian Agora* XXVIII] (Princeton, 1995)

Borgeaud, Philippe. *The Cult of Pan in Ancient Greece* (Chicago, 1988)

Borthwick, E. K. "The Oxyrhynchus Musical Monody and Some Ancient Fertility Superstitions," *AJP* 84 (1963), 225–43

Boswell, John. *The Marriage of Likeness: Same-Sex Unions in Pre-Modern Europe* (London, 1995)

Bowie, E. L. "*Miles Ludens*? The problem of martial exhortation in early Greek lyric," in Murray (ed.), *Sympotica* (1990), 221–29

Bowra, Maurice. *Greek Lyric Poetry from Alcman to Simonides* (Oxford, 1936)

Boyle, Charles. *Dr. Bentley's Dissertations on the Epistles of Phalaris, and the Fables of Æsop, Examin'd* (London, 1698)

Bray, Alan. *Homosexuality in Renaissance England* (London, 1982)

Bray, Alan. "Friendship, the Family and Liturgy: A Rite for Blessing Friendship in Traditional Christianity," *Theology and Sexuality* 13 (Sept. 2000), 15–33

Bray, Alan. *The Friend* (Chicago, 2003)

Brelich, Angelo. *Paides e Parthenoi* (Rome, 1969)

Bremmer, J. N. "An Enigmatic Indo-European Rite: Paederasty," *Arethusa* 13 (1980), 279–98

Bremmer, J. N. (ed.) *Interpretations of Greek Mythology* (London, 1988)

Bremmer, J. N. "Adolescents, *Symposion,* and Pederasty," in Murray (ed.), *Sympotica* (1990), 135–48

Briant, Pierre. *Histoire de L'Empire Perse* (Paris, 1996)

Brisson, Luc. *Sexual Ambivalence: Androgyny and Hermaphroditism in Graeco-Roman Antiquity* (Berkeley, 2002)

Brock, Roger, and Hodkinson, Stephen. *Alternatives to Athens* (Oxford, 2000)

Brown, D. E. *Human Universals* (New York, 1991)

Brown, Elizabeth A. R. "Introduction," *Traditio* 52 (1997), 261–83

Brown, Elizabeth A. R. "Ritual Brotherhood in Western Medieval Europe," *Traditio* 52 (1997), 357–81

Brown, Malcolm Kenneth. *The Narratives of Konon* (Munich, 2002)

Brown, Stephen. "Chopin came from Ipanema," *TLS,* June 20, 2003

Bruit, L. "The meal at the Hyakinthia," in Murray (ed.), *Sympotica* (1990), 162–74

Brûlé, Pierre. "Fêtes grecques: periodicité et initiation. Hyakinthies et Panathénées," in Moreau (ed.), *L'initiation* (1992), 19–38

Brunt, P. A. *Arrian: History of Alexander and Indica* (Cambridge MA, 1976–83)

Buck, Carl Darling. *The Greek Dialects* (Chicago, 1955)

Bumke, Helga. *Statuarische Gruppen in der frühen griechischen Kunst.* [= *Jahrbuch des Deutschen Archäologischen Instituts,* 32] (Berlin, 2004)

Burgess, Jonathan S. *The Tradition of the Trojan War in Homer and the Epic Cycle* (Baltimore, 2001)

Burgess, Theodore C. *Epideictic Literature* (Diss. Chicago, 1902)

Burkert, Walter. *Structure and History in Greek Mythology and Ritual* (Berkeley, 1979)

Burkert, Walter. *Homo Necans* (Berkeley, 1983)

Burkert, Walter. *Greek Religion* (Oxford, 1985)

Burn, L. "Honey-pots: three white-ground cups by the Sotades Painter," *Antike Kunst* 28 (1985), 93–105

Cahill, N. D. *Household and City Organization at Olynthus* (New Haven, 2002)

Cairns, Douglas L. "*Hybris,* Dishonor, and Thinking Big," *JHS* 116 (1996), 1–32

Calame, C. *Choruses of Young Women in Ancient Greece* (Lanham, 1997)

Calame, C. *The Poetics of Eros in Ancient Greece* (Princeton, 1999)

Campbell, D. A. *The Golden Lyre: The Themes of the Greek Lyric Poets* (London, 1983)

Carey, C. *Lysias: Selected Speeches* (Cambridge, 1989)

Carey, C. *Aeschines* (Austin, 2000)

Cartledge, P. *Sparta and Lakonia* (London, 1979)

Cartledge, Paul. "The Politics of Spartan Pederasty," *PCPhS* 27 (1981), 17–36 [reprinted in *Spartan Reflections,* pp. 91–105]

Cartledge, P. *Agesilaos and the Crisis of Sparta* (London, 1987)

Cartledge, P. *Spartan Reflections* (London, 2001)

Cartledge, P. and Spawforth, A. *Hellenistic and Roman Sparta* (London, 1989)

Cartledge, P., Millett, P. and von Reden, S. (eds.). *Kosmos: Essays in Order, Conflict and Community in Classical Athens* (Cambridge, 1998)

Casadio, G. "Préhistoire de l'initiation dionysiaque," in Moreau (ed.), *L'initiation* (1992), 209–13

Cerchiai, L. "Il programma figurativo dell' hydria Ricci" in d'Agostino and Cerchiai, *Il mare, la morte, l'amore,* 129–43

Chantraine, Pierre. *Dictionnaire étymologique de la langue grecque: Histoire des mots,* new edn. with suppl. (Paris, 1999)

Christiansen, J. and Melander, T. (eds.). *Proceedings of the 3rd Symposium on Ancient Greek and Related Pottery* (Copenhagen, 1988)

Clarke, W. M. "Achilles and Patroclus in Love," *Hermes* 106 (1978), 381–96

Cohen, D. *Law, Sexuality and Society: The Enforcement of Morals in Classical Athens* (Cambridge, 1991)

Connor, W. R. *The New Politicians of Fifth-Century Athens* (Princeton, 1971)

Connor, W. R. "Seized by the Nymphs: Nympholepsy and Symbolic Expression in Classical Greece," *Class Ant* 7 (1988), 155–89

Cook, A. B. "Who Was the Wife of Zeus?," *CR* 20 (1906), 365–78

D'Agostino, Bruno and Cerchiai, Luca. *Il mare, la morte, l'amore* (Rome, 1999)

D'Angour, A. "How the dithyramb got its shape," *CQ* 47 (1997), 231–51

Davidson, James. *Courtesans and Fishcakes: The Consuming Passions of Classical Athens* (London, 1997)

Davidson, James. "Dover, Foucault and Greek Homosexuality. Penetration and the Truth of Sex," *Past & Present* 170 (2001), 3–51

Davidson, James. "Making a Spectacle of Her(self): The Greek Courtesan and the Art of the Present," in Martha Feldman and Bonnie Gordon (eds.), *The Courtesan's Arts: Cross-Cultural Perspectives* (Oxford, 2006), 29–51

Davidson, James. "Revolutions in Human Time," in Simon Goldhill and Robin Osborne (eds.), *Rethinking Revolutions Through Ancient Greece* (Cambridge, 2006), 29–67

De La Genière, J. "Quelques réflexions sur les clients de la céramique attique," in M.-C. Villanueva-Puig, F. Lissarrague, P. Rouillard and A. Rouveret (eds.), *Céramique et peinture grecques: Modes d'emploi* (Paris, 1999), 411–23

De Pogey-Castries, L.-R. *Histoire de l'amour grec dans l'antiquité* (Paris, 1930)

De Saussure, Ferdinand. *Mémoire sur le système primitif des voyelles dans les langues indo-européennes* (Leipzig, 1879)

DeJean, Joan. "Sex and Philology. Sappho and the Rise of German Nationalism," *Representations* 27 (1989), 148–71

Detienne, Marcel. "Remarques sur le char en Grèce," in Jean-Pierre Vernant (ed.), *Problèmes de la guerre en Grèce ancienne* (Paris, 1968; rev. edn. 1999), 421–28

Devereux, George. "Greek Pseudo-Homosexuality and 'the Greek Miracle,'" *Symbolae Osloenses* 42 (1967), 69–92

Devereux, George. "The Nature of Sappho's Seizure in fr. 31 LP as Evidence of Her Inversion," *CQ* 20 (1970), 17–31

Dillon, John. "Ganymede as the Logos—Traces of a forgotten allegorization in Philo," *CQ* 31 (1981), 183–85

Dover, K. J. "Eros and Nomos (Plato, *Symposium* 182A–185C)," *BICS* 11 (1964), 31–42

Dover, K. J. *Aristophanes: Clouds* (Oxford, 1968)

Dover, K. J. *Lysias and the* Corpus Lysiacum (Berkeley, 1968)

Dover, K. J. "Classical Greek Attitudes to Sexual Behavior," *Arethusa* 6 (1973), 59–73

Dover, K. J. *Greek Homosexuality* (London, 1978)

Dover, K. J. (ed.). *Plato: Symposium* (Cambridge, 1980)

Dover, K. J. "Greek Homosexuality and Initiation," in *The Greeks and Their Legacy: Collected Papers* II (Oxford, 1988), 115–34

Dover, K. J. *Aristophanes: Frogs* (Oxford, 1993)

Dover, K. J. *Marginal Comment* (London, 1994)

Dunbar, Nan. *Aristophanes: Birds* (Oxford, 1995)

Easterling, Pat. "Form and Performance," in Pat Easterling (ed.), *The Cambridge Companion to Greek Tragedy* (Cambridge, 1997), 151–77

Ekroth, Gunnel. *The Sacrificial Rituals of Greek Hero-cults in the Archaic to the Early Hellenistic Periods* [= *Kernos* Suppl. 12] (Liège, 2002)

Eribon, Didier. *Michel Foucault* (London, 1992)

Eribon, Didier. *Foucault et ses contemporains* (Paris, 1994)

Faraone, C. *Ancient Greek Love Magic* (Cambridge, MA, 1999)

Faustoferri, Amalia. *Il trono di Amyklai e Sparta: Bathykles al servizio del potere* (Napoli, 1996)

Ferrari, Gloria. *Figures of Speech: Men and Maidens in Ancient Greece* (Chicago, 2002)

Fisher, N. R. E. *Hybris: A Study in the Values of Honor and Shame in Ancient Greece* (Warminster, 1992)

Fisher, N. R. E. "Symposiasts, Fish-eaters and Flatterers: Social Mobility and Moral Concerns," in D. Harvey and J. Wilkins (eds), *The Rivals of Aristophanes: Studies in Athenian Old Comedy* (London, 2000), 355–96

Fisher, N. R. E. *Aeschines: Against Timarchos* (Oxford, 2001)

Fisher, N. R. E. and van Wees, Hans (eds.). *Archaic Greece. New Approaches and New Evidence* (London, 1998)

Ford, Andrew. "Reading Homer from the Rostrum: Poetry and Law in Aeschines, *In Timarchus,*" in S. Goldhill and R. Osborne (eds.), *Performance Culture and Athenian Democracy* (Cambridge, 1999), 281–313

Fornara, Charles W. *The Nature of History in Ancient Greece and Rome* (Berkeley, 1983)

Foucault, Michel. *The History of Sexuality: Volume I: An Introduction* (New York, 1978)

Foucault, Michel. *The Use of Pleasure* (New York, 1985)

Foucault, Michel. *Dits et Écrits 1954–1988,* 4 vols. (Paris, 1994)

Frontisi-Ducroux, F. and Lissarrague, F. "From Ambiguity to Ambivalence: A Dionysiac Excursion Through the 'Anakreontic' Vases," in Halperin, Winkler, Zeitlin (eds.), *Before Sexuality* (1990), 211–56

Gantz, Timothy. *Early Greek Myth* (Baltimore, 1996)

Garbini, Giovanni. "The Question of the Alphabet," in Sabatino Moscati (ed.), *The Phoenicians* (London, 2001), 101–19

Garland, Robert. *The Greek Way of Death* (Ithaca, NY, 1985)

Gehrke, Hans-Joachim. "Gewalt und Gesetz: Die Soziale und Politische Ordnung Kretas in der Archaischen und Klassischen Zeit," *Klio* 79 (1997), 23–68

Gentili, Bruno. "The Ways of Love in the Poetry of *Thiasos* and Symposium," in id., *Poetry and its Public* (Baltimore, 1988), 72–104

Giannantoni, G. *Socratis et Socraticorum Reliquiae* (Rome, 1990)

Gibbon, Edward. *The History of the Decline and Fall of the Roman Empire* (Harmondsworth, 1994)

Gibson, Roy. *Ovid: Ars Amatoria Book 3 (Cambridge, 2003)*

Gildersleeve, Basil L. *"A Syntactician among the Psychologists,"* The Journal of Philosophy, Psychology and Scientific Methods 2.4 (1905), 92–97

Gill, C., Postlethwaite, N. and Seaford, R. (eds). *Reciprocity in Ancient Greece* (Oxford, 1998)

Gleason, Maud. "Semiotics of Gender," in Halperin, Winkler, Zeitlin (eds.), *Before Sexuality* (1990), 389–415

Glick, Leonard. "Types Distinct from Our Own," *American Anthropologist* 84 (1982), 545–65

Goldhill, S. and Osborne, R. (eds.). *Performance Culture and Athenian Democracy* (Cambridge, 1999)

Gomme, A. W. and Sandbach, F. H. *Menander: A Commentary* (Oxford, 1973)

Gow, A. S. F. *Theocritus* (Cambridge, 1952)

Graf, Fritz. "Apollon Delphinios," *Museum Helveticum* 36 (1979), 2–22

Graham, A. J. "The Authenticity of the *horkion tōn oikistērōn* of Cyrene," *JHS* 80 (1960), 94–111

Graham, Laura. *Performing Dreams: Discourses of Immortality Among the Xavante of Central Brazil* (Austin, 1995)

Griffiths, Alan. " 'What Leaf-fringed Legend . . . ?' A Cup by the Sotades Painter in London," *JHS* 106 (1986), 58–70

Gutzwiller, K. "Gender and Inscribed Epigram: Herennia Procula and the Thespian Eros," *TAPA* 134 (2004), 383–418

Habicht, Christian. *Pausanias' Guide to Ancient Greece* (Berkeley, 1985)

Halbherr, F. "Cretan Expedition III: Epigraphical Researches in Gortyna," *AJA* 1.3 (1897), 159–238

Hall, Jonathan M. *Ethnic Identity in Greek Antiquity* (Cambridge, 1997)

Hallett, J. P. "Beloved Cleïs," *QUCC* 10 (1982), 21–31

Halperin, D. M. *One Hundred Years of Homosexuality* (London, 1990)

Halperin, D. M., Winkler, J. J. and Zeitlin, F. I. (eds.). *Before Sexuality: The Construction of Erotic Experience in the Ancient Greek World* (Princeton, 1990)

Hamilton, Mary. *Greek Saints and their Festivals* (London, 1910)

Hammond, N. G. L. *History of Macedonia,* II (Oxford, 1979)

Hammond, N. G. L. *The Macedonian State* (Oxford, 1989)

Hannah, Robert. *Greek and Roman Calendars: Constructions of Time in the Classical World* (London, 2005)

Hansen, M. H. *The Athenian Assembly in the Age of Demosthenes* (Oxford, 1987)

Hansen, M. H. *The Athenian Democracy* (Oxford, 1991)

Hansen, M. H. and Nielsen, T. H. (eds.). *An Inventory of Archaic and Classical Poleis* (Oxford, 2004)

Harrison, A. R. W. *The Law of Athens* (Oxford, 1968–71)

Heckel, Waldemar. *The Marshals of Alexander's Empire* (London, 1992)

Hedreen, Guy. "The Cult of Achilles in the Euxine," *Hesperia* 60 (1991), 313–30

Henderson, J. *The Maculate Muse: Obscene Language in Attic Comedy* (Oxford, 1991)

Herdt, G. H. (ed.) *Ritualized Homosexuality in Melanesia* (rev. edn. Berkeley, 1993)

Herdt, G. H. *Sambia Sexual Culture* (Chicago, 1999)

Herman, G. *Ritualized Friendship and the Greek City* (Cambridge, 1987)

Hoare, Philip. *Oscar Wilde's Last Stand: Decadence, Conspiracy and the First World War* (London, 1997)

Hodkinson, S. "Social order and the conflict of values in classical Sparta," in M. Whitby (ed.), *Sparta* (Edinburgh, 2002), 104–30

Hornblower, Simon. *The Greek World* (London, 1991)

Hornblower, Simon. *A Commentary on Thucydides* (Oxford, 1992–)

Hornblower, Simon and Spawforth, Antony (eds.). *The Oxford Classical Dictionary* (3rd edn. Oxford, 1996)

Hubbard, Thomas. *Homosexuality in Greece and Rome* (Berkeley, 2003)

Hunter, Richard L. *Eubulus: The Fragments* (Cambridge, 1983)

Hunter, Richard L. *Theocritus and the Archaeology of Greek Poetry* (Cambridge, 1996)

Hupperts, Charles. "Greek Love: Homosexuality or Paederasty? Greek Love in Black Figure Vase-Painting," in Christiansen and Melander (eds.) (1988), 255–68

Hurwit, J. *The Athenian Acropolis: History, Mythology, and Archaeology from the Neolithic Era to the Present* (Cambridge, 1999)

Hutchinson, G. O. *Greek Lyric Poetry* (Oxford, 2001)

Irwin, Elizabeth. *Solon and Early Greek Poetry* (Cambridge, 2005)

Isager, Signe and Pedersen, Poul (eds.). *The Salmakis Inscription and Hellenistic Halikarnassos* (Odense, 2004)

Janko, Richard. "The Derveni Papyrus," *Class Phil* 96 (2001), 1–32

Jenkyns, Richard. *Three Classical Poets: Sappho, Catullus and Juvenal* (London, 1982)

Johansen, Knud Friis. "Attic Motives on Clazomenian Sarcophagi," in *From the Collections of the Ny Carlsberg Glyptotek* III (1942), 123–43

Kaempf-Dimitriadou, Sophia. *Die Liebe der Götter in der attischen Kunst des 5. Jahrhunderts v. Chr.* [= *Antike Kunst* Suppl. 11] (Bern, 1979)

Kahn, C. *Plato and the Socratic Dialogue* (Cambridge, 1996)

Kampen, N. B. (ed.). *Sexuality in Ancient Art* (Cambridge, 1996)

Kassel, Rudolf and Austin, Colin (eds.). *Poetae Comici Graeci* (Berlin, 1983–)

Kato, Shinro. "The *Apology:* The Beginning of Plato's Own Philosophy," *CQ* 41 (1991) 356–64

Kearns, Emily. *The Heroes of Attica* [= *BICS* Suppl. 57] (1989)

Kennell, N. *The Gymnasium of Virtue* (Chapel Hill, 1995)

Killeen, J. F. "The Comic Costume Controversy," *CQ* 21 (1971), 51–54

Kilmer, Martin F. *Greek Erotica on Attic Red-Figure Vases* (London, 1993)

King, Richard J. "Male homosocial readership and the dedication of Ovid's *Fasti,*" *Arethusa* 37 (2004), 197–223

Knauft, Bruce. "Text and Social Practice: Narrative 'Longing' and Bisexuality Among the Gebusi of New Guinea," *Ethos* 14 (1986), 252–81

Knauft, Bruce. *South Coast New Guinea Cultures: History, Comparison, Dialectic* (Cambridge, 1993)

Knox, Bernard. "The Socratic Method," *New York Review of Books,* January 25, 1979

Knox, P. E. "In Pursuit of Daphne," *TAPA* 120 (1990), 183–203

Koch-Harnack, Gundel. *Knabenliebe und Tiergeschenke: Ihre Bedeutung im päderastischen Erziehungssystem Athens* (Berlin, 1983)

Koch-Harnack, Gundel. *Erotische Symbole: Lotosblüte und gemeinsamer Mantel auf antiken Vasen* (Berlin, 1989)

Konstan, David. "Friends and Lovers in Ancient Greece," *Syllecta Classica* 4 (1993), 1–12

Konstan, David. *Friendship in the Classical World* (Cambridge, 1997)

Kurke, Leslie. "Crisis and Decorum in Sixth-Century Lesbos," *QUCC* 47 (1994), 67–92

Laks, André. "The *Laws,*" in C. Rowe and M. Schofield (with S. Harrison and M. Lane) (eds.), *The Cambridge History of Greek and Roman Political Thought* (Cambridge, 2000), 258–92

Landels, J. G. *Music in Ancient Greece and Rome* (London, 1999)

Lane Fox, Robin. "Theognis: An Alternative to Democracy," in Brock and Hodkinson (eds.), *Alternatives to Athens* (2000), 35–51

Lang, Mabel. *Graffiti and Dipinti* [= *The Athenian Agora* XXI] (Princeton, 1976)

Larson, Jennifer. *Greek Nymphs* (Oxford, 2001)

Lattimore, Steven. "Skopas and the Pothos," *AJA* 91 (1987), 411–20

Lear, Andrew and Cantarella, Eva. *Images of Pederasty* (London, 2007)

Leitao, David. "The Legend of the Sacred Band," in Martha Nussbaum and Julia Sihvola (eds.), *The Sleep of Reason* (Chicago, 2002), 143–69

Lévy, Edmond. *Sparte: Histoire politique et sociale jusqu'à la conquête romaine* (Paris, 2003)

Lewis, D. M. "Who Was Lysistrata?" *Annual of the British School at Athens* 50 (1955), 1–12

Link, Stefan. *Das griechische Kreta: Untersuchungen zu seiner staatlichen und gesellschaftlichen Entwicklung vom 6.* bis zum *4. Jahrhundert v. Chr.* (Stuttgart, 1994)

Lissarrague, François. *L'Autre Guerrier. Archers, peltastes, cavaliers dans l'imagerie attique* (Paris/Rome, 1990)

Lissarrague, François. *The Aesthetics of the Greek Banquet: Images of Wine and Ritual* (Princeton, 1991)

Lissarrague, François. "Femmes au figuré," in Pauline Schmitt Pantel (ed.), *Histoire des femmes en Occident. 1.* L'Antiquité (Paris, 1991), 159–251

Lissarrague, François. *Greek Vases: The Athenians and their Images* (New York, 2001)

Lowe, N. J. "Thesmophoria and Haloa: Myth, Physics, and Mysteries," in Sue Blundell and Margaret Williamson (eds.), *The Sacred and the Feminine in Ancient Greece* (London, 1998), 149–73

Ludwig, Paul W. *Eros and Polis: Desire and Community in Greek Political Theory* (Cambridge, 2002)

Lupi, Marcello. *L'ordine delle generazioni: Classi di età e costumi matrimoniali nell'antica Sparta* (Bari, 2000)

Luppe, Wolfgang. "Die Ikarios-Sage im Mythographus Homericus," *ZPE* 112 (1996), 29–33

MacDowell, D. M. *Aristophanes: Wasps* (Oxford, 1971)

MacDowell, D. M. "Hybris in Athens," *Greece and Rome* 23 (1976), 14–31

MacDowell, D. M. *Andokides: On the Mysteries* (Oxford, 1989)

Macey, David. *The Lives of Michel Foucault* (New York, 1993)

MacGillivray, J. A., Driessen, J. M. and Sackett, L. H. (eds.). *The Palaikastro Kouros* [= *BSA* Studies 6] (London, 2000)

MacLachlan, B. *Age of Grace: Charis in Early Greek Poetry* (Princeton, 1993)

Maddoli, Gianfranco and Saladino, Vincenzo. *Pausania, Guida della Grecia, Libro V. L'Elide e Olimpia* (Milan, 1995)

Maddoli, Gianfranco, Nafissi, Massimo and Saladino, Vincenzo. *Pausania, Guida della Grecia, Libro VI: L'Elide e Olimpia* (Milan, 1999)

Mageo, Jeannette M. "Male Transvestism and Cultural Change in Samoa," *American Ethnologist* 19 (1992), 443–59

Malitz, J. "Mommsen, Caesar und die Juden," in Hubert Cancik, Hermann Lichtenberger and Peter Schäfer (eds.), *Geschichte—Tradition—Reflexion* (Tübingen, 1996), 371–87

Malkin, Irad. *Myth and Territory in the Spartan Mediterranean* (Cambridge, 1994)

Malkin, Irad. *The Returns of Odysseus: Colonization and Ethnicity* (Berkeley, 1998)

Marcovich M. "Anacreon, 358 PMG," *AJP* 104 (1983), 372–83

Martin, Laura. " 'Eskimo Words for Snow': A Case Study in the Genesis and Decay of an Anthropological Example," *American Anthropologist* 88 (1986), 418–23

Maybury-Lewis, David. *Akwe-Shavante Society* (Oxford, 1967; rev. edn. 1974)

Mead, Margaret. *Coming of Age in Samoa* (New York, 1928)

Mead, Margaret. "More Comprehensive Field Methods," *American Anthropologist* 35 (1933), 1–15

Mead, Margaret. *Sex and Temperament in Three Primitive Societies* (New York, 1935)

Mead, Margaret. "A Reply to a Review of 'Sex and Temperament in Three Primitive Societies,'" *American Anthropologist* 39 (1937), 558–61

Mead, Margaret. "The Training of the Cultural Anthropologist," *American Anthropologist* 54 (1952), 343–46

Meier, M.-H.-E. "Päderastie," in J. S. Ersch and J. G. Gruber (eds.), *Allgemeine Encyclopädie der Wissenschaften und Künste,* Section 3, Bd 9 (Leipzig, 1837), 149–88

Meiggs, R. and Lewis, D. *A Selection of Greek Historical Inscriptions to the End of the Fifth Century BC* (rev. edn. Oxford, 1988)

Mikalson, J. "Erechtheus and the Panathenaia," *AJP* 97 (1976), 141–53

Miller, James E. *The Passion of Michel Foucault* (New York, 1993)

Milne, M. J. and D. von Bothmer. "*Katapugōn, Katapugaina?,*" *Hesperia* 22 (1953), 215–24

Moggi, M. and Osanna, M. *Pausania, Guida della Grecia, Libro VII: L'Acaia* (Milan, 2000)

Mommsen, T. *Römische Geschichte* (Leipzig, 1854–56)

Mommsen, T. *Auch ein Wort über unser Judentum* (Berlin, 1880)

Monoson, S. "Citizen as Erastes: Erotic Imagery and the Idea of Reciprocity in the Periclean Funeral Oration," *Political Theory* 22 (1994), 253–76

Moreau, A. (ed.). *L'initiation* (Montpellier, 1992)

Morgan, Charles H. "Pheidias and Olympia," *Hesperia* 21 (1952), 295–339

Morris, Ian. "Archaeology and Archaic Greek History," in Fisher and van Wees (eds.), *Archaic Greece* (1998), 1–91

Morrison J. S. "Meno of Pharsalus, Polycrates, and Ismenias," *CQ* 36 (1942), 57–78

Murray, Oswyn (ed.). *Sympotica: A Symposium on the* Symposion (Oxford, 1990)

Musti, D. and Beschi, L. *Pausania, Guida della Grecia, Libro I. L'Attica* (Milan, 1982)

Musti, D. and Torelli, M. *Pausania, Guida della Grecia, Libro II. La Corinzia e L'Argolide* (Milan, 1986)

Musti, D. and Torelli, M. *Pausania, Guida della Grecia, Libro III. La Laconia* (Milan, 1991)

Nagy, G. *Greek Mythology and Poetics* (rev. edn. Baltimore, 1992)

Nagy, G. *The Best of the Achaeans* (rev. edn. Baltimore, 1999)

Nails, Debra. *The People of Plato: A Prosopography of Plato and Other Socratics* (Indianapolis, 2002)

Neer, Richard. *Style and Politics in Athenian Vase-Painting: The Craft of Democracy, ca.530–460 BCE* (Cambridge, 2002)

Nevett, Lisa C. *House and Society in the Ancient Greek World* (Cambridge, 1999)

Nussbaum, Martha C. *The Fragility of Goodness* (Cambridge, 1986)

Nussbaum, Martha C. "Platonic Love and Colorado Law," *Virginia Law Review* 80.7 (1994), 1515–1651

Nussbaum, Martha C. and Sihvola, Julia (eds.). *The Sleep of Reason* (Chicago, 2002)

Oakley, John H. "An Athenian Red-Figured Workshop from the Time of the Peloponnesian War," in *Les ateliers de potiers dans le monde grec aux époques géométrique, archaïque et classique* [= *BCH* Supplément XXIII] (Paris 1992), 195–203

Ogden, Daniel. "Homosexuality and Warfare in Ancient Greece," in A. B. Lloyd (ed.), *Battle in Antiquity* (London, 1996), 107–68

Ogden, Daniel. *The Crooked Kings of Ancient Greece* (London, 1997)

Ogden, Daniel. *Greek and Roman Necromancy* (Princeton, 2001)

Olson, Douglas S. *Aristophanes: Acharnians* (Oxford, 2002)

Ormerod, H. A. *Piracy in the Ancient World* (Liverpool, 1924)

Osborne, R. G. *Greece in the Making* (London, 1996)

Osborne, R. G. "Desiring Women on Athenian Pottery," in Kampen (ed.), *Sexuality in Ancient Art* (1996), 65–80

Osborne, R. G. *Archaic and Classical Greek Art* (Oxford, 1998)

Page, D. L. "Homer and the Neoanalytiker," *CR* 13 (1963), 21–24

Page, D. L. *Further Greek Epigrams* (Cambridge, 1981)

Parker, R. *Miasma* (Oxford, 1983)

Parker, R. *Athenian Religion: A History* (Oxford, 1996)

Parker, R. "Pleasing Thighs: Reciprocity in Greek Religion," in Gill, Postlethwaite and Seaford (eds.), *Reciprocity* (1998), 105–25

Parker, R. "Theophoric Names and the History of Greek Religion," in S. Hornblower and E. Matthews (eds.), *Greek Personal Names and their Value as Evidence* (Oxford, 2000), 53–79

Parker, R. *Polytheism and Society at Athens* (Oxford, 2005)

Pearson, L. *The Greek Historians of the West: Timaeus and His Predecessors* [*Philological Monographs of the American Philological Association* 35] (Atlanta, 1987)

Pelling, C. B. R. *Plutarch: Life of Antony* (Cambridge, 1988)

Pellizer, Ezio. "Reflections, Echoes and Amorous Reciprocity: On Reading the Narcissus Story," in Bremmer (ed.), *Interpretations* (1988), 107–120

Percy, William Armstrong III. *Pederasty and Pedagogy in Archaic Greece* (Urbana, 1996)

Perlman, P. J. "*Invocatio* and *imprecation*. The Hymn to the Greatest Kouros from Palaikastro and the Oath in Ancient Crete," *JHS* 115 (1995), 161–67

Piérart, M. "La mort de Dionysos a Argos," in R. Hägg (ed.), *The Role of Religion in the Early Greek Polis* (Stockholm, 1996), 141–51

Pipili, M. *Laconian Iconography of the Sixth Century* BC (Oxford, 1987)

Pirenne-Delforge, Vinciane. *L'Aphrodite grecque* [= *Kernos* Supplement 4] (Liège, 1994)

Poster, Mark. "Foucault and the Tyranny of Greece," in David Couzens Hoy (ed.), *Foucault: A Critical Reader* (Oxford, 1986), 205–220

Powell, A. "Athens' Pretty Face," in A. Powell (ed.), *The Greek World* (1995), 245–70

Powell, A. (ed.), *The Greek World* (London, 1995)

Preisendanz, K. and Henrichs A. (eds.), *Papyri Graecae Magicae* (Stuttgart, 1973–74)

Preziosi, Donald and Hitchcock, Louise A. *Aegean Art and Architecture* (Oxford, 1999)

Price, A. W. *Love and Friendship in Plato and Aristotle* (Oxford, 1989)

Pritchett, W. K. "Observations on Chaironeia," *AJA* 62 (1958), 307–311

Rabinow, Paul (ed.). *The Foucault Reader* (New York, 1984)

Rapp, Claudia. "Ritual Brotherhood in Byzantium," *Traditio* 52 (1997), 285–326

Rasmussen, T. and Spivey, N. (eds.). *Looking at Greek Vases* (Cambridge, 1991)

Rhodes, P. J. *A Commentary on the Aristotelian* Athenaion Politeia (Oxford, 1993)

Robert, L. "Documents d'Asie Mineure," *BCH* 102 (1978), 395–543

Robertson, M. "Adopting an approach I," in Rasmussen and Spivey (eds.), *Looking at Greek Vases* (1991), 1–12

Rosen, Ralph M. "Hipponax, Boupalos, and the Conventions of the Psogos," *TAPA* 118 (1988), 29–41

Rösler, W. "*Mnemosyne* in the Symposion," in Murray (ed.), *Sympotica* (1990), 230–37

Rostovtzeff, M. "Two Homeric Bowls in the Louvre," *AJA* 41 (1937), 86–96

Rowe, C. J. *Phaedrus* (Warminster, 1986)

Rutherford, Ian. *Pindar's Paeans* (Oxford, 2001)

Sahlins, Marshall. *Apologies to Thucydides: Understanding History as Culture and Vice Versa* (Chicago, 2004)

Sandy, Gerald. "*Scaenica Petroniana*," *TAPA* 104 (1974), 329–46

Sapir, Edward. "Language and Environment," *American Anthropologist* 14 (1912), 226–42

Sapir, Edward. *Language: An Introduction to the Study of Speech* (New York, 1921)

Sapir, Edward. "Sound Patterns in Language," *Language* 1 (1925), 37–51

Sapir, Edward. "The Status of Linguistics as a Science," *Language* 5 (1928), 207–214

Sapir, Edward. "The Contribution of Psychiatry to an Understanding of Behavior in Society," *The American Journal of Sociology* 42 (1937), 862–70

Saslow, James M. *Ganymede in the Renaissance: Homosexuality in Art and Society* (New Haven, 1986)

Scanlon, Thomas F. *Eros and Greek Athletics* (New York, 2002)

Schachter, Albert. *Cults of Boeotia* [= *BICS Suppl.* 38] (London, 1981–94)

Schmitt Pantel, P. "Sacrificial Meal and *Symposion*" in Murray (ed.), *Sympotica* (1990), 4–36

Schmitt Pantel, P. *La cité au banquet: Histoire des repas publics dans les cités grecques* (Rome/Paris, 1992)

Schnapp, Alain. "Eros the Hunter," in C. Bérard *et al.* (eds.), *City of Images* (Princeton, 1989), 71–87

Schnapp, Alain. *Le Chasseur et la cité: Chasse et érotique dans la Grèce ancienne* (Paris, 1997)

Schofield, M. *The Stoic Idea of the City* (Cambridge, 1991)

Seaford, Richard. *Reciprocity and Ritual: Homer and Tragedy in the Developing City-State* (Oxford, 1994)

Sergent, Bernard. *Homosexuality in Greek Myth* (London, 1986)

Sergent, Bernard. *Homosexualité et initiation chez les peoples indo-européens* (Paris, 1996)

Shapiro, H. A. "Courtship Scenes in Attic Vase-painting," *AJA* 85 (1981), 133–43

Shapiro, H. A. *Art and Cult under the Tyrants in Athens* (Mainz, 1989)

Shaw, Brent D. "Ritual Brotherhood in Roman and Post-Roman Societies," *Traditio* 52 (1997), 327–55

Shipley, G. *A History of Samos 800–188 BC* (Oxford, 1987)

Sichtermann, Hellmut. *Ganymed: Mythos und Gestalt in der antiken Kunst* (Berlin, 1953)

Siewert, P. "The Ephebic oath in fifth-century Athens," *JHS* 97 (1977), 102–111

Sinn, Ulrich. *Die Homerischen Becher* (Berlin, 1979)

Sissa, G. and Detienne, M. *The Daily Life of the Greek Gods* (Stanford, 2000)

Slatkin, Laura M. *The Power of Thetis: Allusion and Interpretation in the* Iliad (Berkeley, 1992)

Smith, Peter M. "Aineiadai as Patrons of *Iliad* XX and the Homeric *Hymn to Aphrodite,*" *HSCP* 85 (1981), 17–58

Sommerstein, Alan H. *The Comedies of Aristophanes,* 12 vols. (Warminster, 1980–2002)

Spivey, N. "Greek vases in Etruria," in Rasmussen and Spivey (eds.), *Looking at Greek Vases* (1991), 131–50

Spivey, N. *Understanding Greek Sculpture: Ancient Meanings, Modern Readings* (London, 1996)

Sporn, Katja. *Heiligtümer und Kulte Kretas in klassischer und hellenisticher Zeit* (Heidelberg, 2002)

Stehle, Eva. *Performance and Gender in Ancient Greece: Non-dramatic Poetry in its Setting* (Princeton, 1997)

Steiner, Ann. "Private and Public," *Class Ant* 21 (2002), 347–80

Stewart, Andrew. *Art, Desire and the Body in Ancient Greece* (Cambridge, 1997)

Symonds, J. A. *A Problem in Greek Ethics* (London, 1901)

Taplin, O. "Phallology, *phlyakes* Iconography and Aristophanes," *PCPhS* 33 (1987), 92–104

Taplin, O. *Comic Angels: And Other Approaches to Greek Drama Through Vase-Paintings* (Oxford, 1993)

Thomas, R. *Literacy and Orality in Ancient Greece* (Cambridge, 1992)

Thomas, R. "The Place of the Poet in Archaic Society," in A. Powell (ed.), *The Greek World* (London, 1995), 104–129

Thornton, B. *Eros: The Myth of Ancient Greek Sexuality* (Boulder, 1997)

Tod, M. N. *Greek Historical Inscriptions* II (Oxford, 1948)

Todd, S. C. *The Shape of Athenian Law* (Oxford, 1993)

Todd, S. C. *Lysias* (Austin, 2000)

Trümpy, C. *Untersuchungen zu den altgriechischen Monatsnamen und Monatsfolgen* (Heidelberg, 1997)

Van Wees, Hans. "Megara's Mafiosi," in Brock and Hodkinson (eds.), *Alternatives to Athens* (2000), 52–67

Vattuone, R. "Eros Cretese (Ad Ephor. *FGrHist* 70 F 149)," *Rivista Storica dell'Antichità* 28 (1998), 7–50

Vattuone, R. *Il Mostro e Il Sapiente: Studi sull'erotica greca* (Bologna, 2004)

Vernant, Jean-Pierre. "One, Two, Three: Eros," in Halperin, Winkler, Zeitlin (eds.), *Before Sexuality* (1990), 465–78

Vetta, Massimo. "Il *P. Oxy* 2506 fr. 77 e la poesia pederotica di Alceo," *QUCC* 39 (1982), 7–20

Veyne, Paul. "La famille et l'amour sous le haut-empire romain," *Annales ESC* 33 (1978), 35–63

Veyne, Paul. "Témoignage hétérosexuelle d'un historien sur l'homosexualité," in "Arcadie" (ed.), *Actes du Congrès International: Le Regard des autres* (Paris, 1979), 17–24

Veyne, Paul. "Homosexuality in Ancient Rome," in Philippe Ariès and André Béjin (eds.), *Western Sexuality: Practice and Precept in Past and Present Times* (Oxford, 1985), 26–35

Veyne, Paul. *Did the Greeks Believe in Their Myths?* (Chicago, 1988)

Vikela, Evgenia. *Die Weihreliefs aus dem Athener Pankrates-Heiligtum am Ilissos* [= *AM* Suppl. 16] (Berlin, 1994)

Vlastos, Gregory. *Socrates, Ironist and Moral Philosopher* (Cambridge, 1991)

Walbank, F. W. *A Historical Commentary on Polybius,* 3 vols. (Oxford, 1957–79)

Weiss, Michael. "Erotica: On the Prehistory of Greek Desire," *HSCP* 98 (1998), 31–61

West, D. J. *Homosexuality* (rev. edn. Harmondsworth, 1960)

West, M. L. "The Dictaean Hymn to the Kouros," *JHS* 85 (1965), 149–59

West, M. L. *Studies in Greek Elegy and Iambus* (Berlin, 1974)

West, M. L. *Ancient Greek Music* (Oxford, 1992)

West, M. L. *The East Face of Helicon: West Asiatic Elements in Greek Poetry and Myth* (Oxford, 1997)

Wheler, George. *A Journey into Greece by George Wheler, Esq., in Company of Dr. Spon of Lyons in Six Books . . .: With Variety of Sculptures* (London, 1682)

Whitehead, D. *The Demes of Attica* (Princeton, 1986)

Whitehead, D. *Hypereides* (Oxford, 2000)

Whitely, James. "Literacy and Law-making: The Case of Archaic Crete," in Fisher and van Wees (eds.), *Archaic Greece* (1998), 311–31

Whorf, Benjamin. *Language, Thought and Reality* (Cambridge, MA, 1956)

Wilde, Oscar. *The Complete Letters* (London, 2000)

Willetts, R. F. *Aristocratic Society in Ancient Crete* (London, 1955)

Willetts, R. F. *Cretan Cults and Festivals* (London, 1962)

Williams, Dyfri. "The Brygos Tomb Reassembled and Nineteenth-century Commerce in Capuan Antiquities," *AJA* 96 (1992), 617–36

Williamson, Margaret. *Sappho's Immortal Daughters* (Cambridge, MA, 1995)

Wilson, Peter J. *The Athenian Institution of the* Khoregia (Cambridge, 2000)

Wilson, Peter J. "The Politics of Dance: Dithyrambic Contest and Social Order in Greece," in D. Phillips and D. Pritchard (eds.), *Sport and Festival in the Ancient Greek World* (London, 2003), 165–98

Winkler, J. J. *Constraints of Desire* (New York, 1990)

INDEX

Virgil, 210, 212, 217, 234, 349, 684*n*
Vitruvius, 304
Volk, 174–77, 179
Vulci, *xv,* 328, 532, 538, 689*n,* 720*n*

wars, warriors, xxxiii, 29, 84, 115, 138
  age-class, 105–13, 660*n*
  age-set and, 113–14
  Greek-Barbarian dualism and, 339,
    341–42
  Greek Homosexuality and, 613–17,
    729*n*
  see also Army of Lovers; Crete, battalion
    of beauties in; Peloponnesian War;
    Sparta, Athens's war with; Trojan
    War; *specific warriors*
Wasps (Aristophanes), 107, 601
Watteau, Jean Antoine, 53
Wedgwood, Josiah, 331, 332
West, D. J., 160, 163, 182, 672*n*
West, Martin, 228–29
Westphal, Carl, 190
"What We Demand of Modern Jewry"
    (Stoecker), 175
Wheler, Sir George, 13, 39, 648*n*
white-black opposition, 340–41, 349–50,
    690*n*
White Island (Leuke), *xv,* 330–34, 344, 357
  Achilles on, xxxiii, 319, 330–33, 338, 340,
    365, 448
White Rock of Leucas, *xvi,* 258–60, 489,
    647*n*
whores, *see* brothels; prostitutes,
    prostitution
Whorf, Benjamin, 166–67, 169, 173, 179,
    664*n*
wide-arsedness, as windbag speech, 57–59,
    70, 135
Wieland, Christoph Martin, 218
wife swapping, in Sparta, 396, 403
Wilamowitz, Ulrich von, 370
Wilde, Oscar, 149, 171, 191, 649*n,* 666*n*
Will to Know, The (*La Volonté de savoir*)
    (Foucault), 190
Winckelmann, Johannes J., 214
winds, 303, 399, 724*n*
  see also Boreas; Zephyrus
wine, 174, 361–62, 678*n*

pouring of, 218, 219, 239, 240, 457, 674*n,*
    675*n*
  Tomb of the Dead and, *486, 487*
Wolf, Hugo, 215
women, 193, 195, 329, 726*n*
  anal penetration of, 137, 141–42
  in Aristophanes, 66, 575–76, 725*n*
  bonding of, 507
  charis and, 46, 47, 52
  color of, 690*n*
  conjugal (yoke-pairs), 504–5
  development of talent of, 503–4
  Men's Houses and, 374
  musical instruments played by, 492, 518
  Sambia, 629, 631–32, 633
  seduction of, xxxi, 63, 67, 373, 520, 548,
    551, 655*n*
  White Island and, 331, 365
"Women in Parliament" (Aristophanes),
    575–76
Woods, Chris, 666*n*
Word About Our Jewry, A (Treitschke), 176
Works and Days (Hesiod), 24
World War II, 178, 179, 202, 224

Xenophon, xxx, 27, 36, 449–54, 528, 602,
    620–21
  age-grade and, 90, 97
  on Boeotian same-sex unions, 569, 594
  on changes in homosexuality, 554
  on chasteness, 4, 34
  on Critobulus, 101
  on Dorians, 726*n*
  Education of Cyrus of, 50–51
  on Elis, 402, 403, 405, 429, 430, 441, 528
  on Ganymede, 209, 213, *214,* 218, 384
  Greek Homosexuality and, 554
  on Hyacinthia, 291
  on Meno III, xxxiv, 23, 103, 449–51, 454,
    566, 602–3
  on *paidikos erōs,* 34–35
  protection of boys and, 99
  on Socrates, 51, 101, 267
  Socrates's trial and, 110, 111, 660*n*–61*n*
  on Sparta, 34, 90, 97, 119–20, 385, 388–94,
    396, 397, 401, 402–5, 408, 409, 410, 415,
    421–25, 431, 464, 585, 587–88, 589,
    604, 635, 701*n,* 702*n*

ABOUT THE AUTHOR

JAMES DAVIDSON is a classical scholar and history professor at the University of Warwick in England. He is the author of *Courtesans and Fishcakes: The Consuming Passions of Classical Athens* and is a regular contributor to the *London Review of Books* among other journals. He lives in London.

ABOUT THE TYPE

This book was set in Bembo, a typeface based on an old-style Roman face that was used for Cardinal Bembo's tract *De Aetna* in 1495. Bembo was cut by Francisco Griffo in the early sixteenth century. The Lanston Monotype Company of Philadelphia brought the well-proportioned letterforms of Bembo to the United States in the 1930s.